Springer Texts in Business and Economics

Springer Texts in Business and Economics (STBE) delivers high-quality instructional content for undergraduates and graduates in all areas of Business/Management Science and Economics. The series is comprised of self-contained books with a broad and comprehensive coverage that are suitable for class as well as for individual self-study. All texts are authored by established experts in their fields and offer a solid methodological background, often accompanied by problems and exercises.

Klaus Neusser

Time Series Econometrics

Second Edition

Springer

Klaus Neusser
Department of Economics
University of Bern
Bern, Switzerland

ISSN 2192-4333 ISSN 2192-4341 (electronic)
Springer Texts in Business and Economics
ISBN 978-3-031-88837-3 ISBN 978-3-031-88838-0 (eBook)
https://doi.org/10.1007/978-3-031-88838-0

This Springer imprint is published by the registered company Springer Nature Switzerland AG
The registered company address is: Gewerbestrasse 11, 6330 Cham, Switzerland

Preface to the Second Edition

Since the first edition, I received a number of comments and suggestions from students and colleagues alike. These reactions encouraged me and the publisher to tackle a second edition. Besides fixing bugs and typos, this new edition includes in particular additional exercises, an enlarged section on the identification of vector autoregressive (VAR) models and a section on Bayesian vector autoregressions (BVAR) models. Nevertheless, it goes without saying that all remaining glitches, errors, and shortcomings go solely to my expense.

Bern, Switzerland
September, 2024

Klaus Neusser

Preface to the First Edition

Over the past decades time series analysis has experienced a proliferous increase of applications in economics, especially in macroeconomics and finance. Today these tools have become indispensable to any empirically working economist. Whereas in the beginning the transfer of knowledge essentially flowed from the natural sciences, especially statistics and engineering, to economics, over the years theoretical and applied techniques specifically designed for the nature of economic time series and models have been developed. Thereby, the estimation and identification of structural vectorautoregressive models, the analysis of integrated and cointegrated time series, and models of volatility have been extremely fruitful and far-reaching areas of research. With the award of the Nobel prices to Clive W. J. GRANGER and Robert F. ENGLE III in 2003 and to Thomas J. SARGENT and Christopher A. SIMS in 2011, the field has reached a certain degree of maturity. Thus, the idea suggests itself to assemble the vast amount of material scattered over many papers into a comprehensive textbook.

The book is self-contained and addresses economics students who have already some prerequisite knowledge in econometrics. It is thus suited for advanced bachelor, master, or beginning PhD students, but also for applied researchers. The book tries to bring them in a position to be able to follow the rapidly growing research literature and to implement these techniques on their own. Although the book is trying to be rigorous in terms of concepts, definitions and statements of theorems, not all proofs are carried out. This is especially true for the more technically and lengthy proofs for which the reader is referred to the pertinent literature.

The book covers approximately a two-semester course in time series analysis and is divided in two parts. The first part treats univariate time series, in particular autoregressive moving-average processes. Most of the topics are standard and can form the basis for a one-semester introductory time series course. This part also contains a chapter on integrated processes and on models of volatility. The latter topics could be included in a more advanced course. The second part is devoted to multivariate time series analysis and in particular to vector autoregressive processes. It can be thought independently of the first part. The identification, modeling, and estimation of these processes form the core of the second part. A special chapter treats the estimation, testing, and interpretation of cointegrated systems. The book also contains a chapter with an introduction to state space models and the Kalman filter. Whereas the books is almost exclusively concerned with linear systems, the last chapter gives a perspective on some more recent developments in the context of nonlinear models. I have included exercises and worked out examples to deepen the teaching and learning content. Finally, I have produced five appendices which summarize important topics such as complex numbers, linear difference equations, and stochastic convergence.

As time series analysis has become a tremendously growing field with an active research in many directions, it goes without saying that not all topics received the attention they deserved and that there are areas not covered at all. This is especially true for the recent advances made in nonlinear time series analysis and in the application of Bayesian techniques. These two topics alone would justify an extra book.

The data manipulations and computations have been performed using the software packages EVIEWS and MATLAB.[1] Of course, there are other excellent packages available. The data for the examples and additional information can be downloaded from my home page www.neusser.ch To maximize the learning success it is advised to replicate the examples and to perform similar exercises with alternative data. Interesting macroeconomic time series can, for example, be downloaded from the following home pages:

GERMANY: www.bundesbank.de
SWITZERLAND www.snb.ch
UNITED KINGDOM: www.ons.gov.uk
UNITED STATES fred.stlouisfed.org

The book grew out of lectures which I had the occasion to give over the years in Bern and other universities. Thus, it is a concern to thank the many students, in particular to Philip Letsch, who had to work through the manuscript and who called my attention to obscurities and typos. I also want to thank my colleagues and teaching assistants Andreas Bachmann, Gregor Bäurle, Fabrice Collard, Sarah Fischer, Stephan Leist, Senada Nukic, Kurt Schmidheiny, Martin Wagner and Reto Tanner for reading the manuscript or part of it and for making many valuable criticism and comments. Special thanks go to my former colleague and coauthor Robert Kunst who meticulously read and commented the manuscript. It goes without saying that all errors and shortcomings go to my expense.

Bern, Switzerland Klaus Neusser
Eggenburg, Austria
February, 2016

[1] EVIEWS is a product of IHS Global Inc. MATLAB is a matrix-oriented software developed by MathWorks which is ideally suited for econometric and time series applications.

Contents

Notation and Symbols

$\mathbb{Z}$	integer numbers
$\mathbb{R}$	real numbers
$\mathbb{C}$	complex numbers
$\mathbb{R}^n$	set of n-dimensional vectors
$\imath$	imaginary unit
$\mathbf{P}$	probability
$\sim$	is distributed as
$\mathbb{E}$	expectation operator
$\mathbb{V}$	variance operator
cov(X, Y)	covariance beween random variables X and Y
corr(X, Y)	correlation coefficient beween random variables X and Y
$\xrightarrow{\text{d}}$	convergence in distribution
$\xrightarrow{\text{m.s.}}$	convergence in mean square
$\xrightarrow{\text{p}}$	convergence in probability
$\Longrightarrow$	weak convergence
n	dimension of stochastic process, respectively state space
$\{X_t\}$	stochastic process
X_t	time indexed random variable
x_t	realization of random variable X_t
γ_X, γ	covariance function of process $\{X_t\}$, covariance function
ACF, ρ_X, ρ	correlation function of process $\{X_t\}$, correlation function
ω, Ω	long-run variance
PACF, α_X, α	partial autocorrelation function of process $\{X_t\}$
WN(0, σ^2)	white noise process with mean zero and variance σ^2
WN(0, Σ)	multivariate white noise process with mean zero and covariance matrix Σ
IID(0, σ^2)	identically and independently distributed random variables with mean zero and variance σ^2
IID N(0, σ^2)	identically and independently normally distributed random variables with mean zero and variance σ^2
L	lag operator
Δ	difference operator, $\Delta = 1 - \mathrm{L}$
ARMA(p,q)	autoregressive moving-average process of order (p, q)

ARIMA(p,d,q)	autoregressive integrated moving-average process of order (p, d, q)
VAR(p)	vector autoregressive process of order p
I(d)	integrated process of order d
p	order of autoregressive polynomial
q	order of moving-average polynomial
d	order of integration
Φ(L)	autoregressive polynomial
Θ(L)	moving-average polynomial
Ψ(L)	causal representation, MA(∞) polynomial
$\Psi(1)$	persistence
$\mathbb{P}_T X_{T+h}$	linear least-squares predictor of X_{T+h} given information from period 1 up to period T
$\widetilde{\mathbb{P}}_T X_{T+h}$	linear least-squares predictor of X_{T+h} using the infinite remote past up to period T
$f(\lambda)$	spectral density
$F(\lambda)$	spectral distribution function
I_T	periodogram
$\Psi(\mathrm{e}^{-\imath\lambda})$	transfer function of filter Ψ
r	number of linearly independent cointegration vectors
α	$n \times r$ loading matrix
β	$n \times r$ matrix of linearly independent cointegration vectors
VaR	value at risk
tr	trace of a matrix
det	determinant of a matrix
$\Vert\,\Vert$	norm of a matrix
$\otimes$	Kronecker product
$\odot$	Hadamard product
vec(A)	stakes the columns of A into a vector
vech(A)	stakes the lower triangular part of a symmetric matrix A into a vector
GL(n)	general linear group of $n \times n$ matrices
$\mathcal{O}(n)$	group of orthogonal $n \times n$ matrices
sgn	sign function

List of Figures

List of Tables

List of Definitions

List of Theorems

Part I

Univariate Time Series Analysis

Introduction and Basic Theoretical Concepts 1

Time series analysis is an integral part of every empirical investigation, which aims at describing and modeling the evolution over time of some variable or set of variables in a statistically coherent way. In economics, time series analysis is thus very much intermingled with macroeconomics and finance, which are concerned with the analysis and construction of dynamic models. In principle, one can approach the subject from two complementary perspectives. The first one focuses on *descriptive statistics*. It characterizes the empirical properties and regularities using basic statistical concepts like mean, variance, and covariance. These statistics can be directly estimated from the data using standard statistical tools. Thus, they summarize the *external* (observable) or outside characteristics of a time series. The second perspective tries to capture the *internal data-generating mechanism*. The proper mechanism is usually unknown in economics as the models developed in economic theory are mostly of a qualitative nature and are usually not specific enough to single out a particular mechanism.[1] Thus, one has to consider some larger class of models. By far the most widely used class is the class of autoregressive moving-average (ARMA) models, which relies on linear stochastic difference equations with constant coefficients. Typically, these coefficients have to be estimated from the observed data. Of course, one wants to know how the two perspectives are related, which leads to the important problem of *identifying* a model from the data.

The observed regularities summarized in the form of descriptive statistics or as a specific model are, of course, of principal interest to economics. They can be used to test or corroborate certain theories or to uncover new features. One of the main

[1] One prominent exception is the random-walk hypothesis of real private consumption first derived and analyzed by Hall (1978). This hypothesis states that the current level of private consumption should just depend on private consumption one period ago and on no other variable, in particular not on disposable income. The random-walk property of asset prices is another very much discussed hypothesis. See Campbell et al. (1997) for a general exposition and Samuelson (1965) for a first rigorous derivation from market efficiency.

K. Neusser, *Time Series Econometrics*, Springer Texts in Business and Economics,
https://doi.org/10.1007/978-3-031-88838-0_1

assumptions underlying time series analysis is that the regularities observed in the sample period are not specific to that period, but can be extrapolated into the future. This leads to the issue of forecasting, which is another major application of time series analysis.

Although its roots lie in the natural sciences and in engineering, time series analysis, since the early contributions by Frisch (1933) and Slutzky (1937), has become an indispensable tool in empirical economics. Early applications mostly consisted in making the knowledge and methods acquired there available to economics. However, with the progression of econometrics as a separate scientific field, more and more techniques that are specific to the characteristics of economic data have been developed: the analysis of univariate and multivariate integrated, respectively cointegrated time series (Chaps. 7 and 16), the identification of vector autoregressive (VAR) models (Chap. 15), or the analysis of asset price volatility in financial markets (Chap. 8), to mention just a few. Each of these topics alone would justify the treatment of time series analysis in economics as a separate subfield.

1.1 Some Examples

Before immersing in the formal analysis, it is instructive to examine some prototypical economic time series by plotting them against time. This simple graphical inspection already reveals some of the issues encountered in this book. One of the most popular time series is the real gross domestic product per capita (chained 2017 dollars). Figure 1.1 plots the data for the US economy from 1947 first quarter to 2024 second quarter on a logarithmic scale. The figure also highlights some major events that have impinged on this time series. Several observations are in order:

(i) The data at hand cover just a part of the time series. There are data available before 1947 and there will be data available after 2024. As there is no natural starting nor end point, we think of a time series as extending back into the infinite past and into the infinite future.

(ii) The time series is treated as a realization of some random mechanism. This implies that we observe in principle only one realization. If we could turn time back and let run history again, we would obtain a second realization. This is, of course, impossible, in a nonexperimental research field such as macroeconomics. Thus, typically, we are faced with just one realization on which to base our analysis. However, sound statistical analysis needs many realizations. This implies that we have to make some assumption regarding the constancy of the regularities, respectively the random mechanism over time. This leads to the concept of stationarity that will be introduced more rigorously in the next section.

(iii) Even a cursory look at the plot reveals that the mean of US real GDP is not constant, but is upward *trending*. As we will see, this feature is typical of many

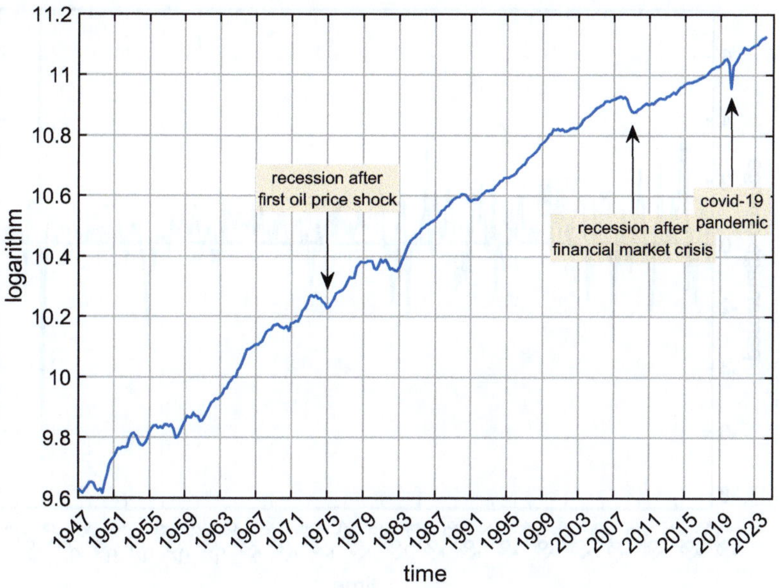

Fig. 1.1 US real gross domestic product (GDP) per capita logged (chained 2017 dollars; quarterly; seasonally adjusted annual rate)

economic time series.[2] The investigation into the nature of the trend and the statistical consequences thereof have been the subject of intense research over the last couple of decades.

(iv) A simple way to overcome this problem is to take *first differences*. As the data have been logged, this amounts to taking quarterly growth rates (percentage changes from one quarter to the next).[3] The corresponding plot is given in Fig. 1.2, which shows no trend anymore. Note also the reduced volatility in the second half of the time period, disregarding the Corona-19 pandemic episode, compared to the first one. This feature has been studied under the label "great moderation." See Neusser (2012) and the literature cited therein.

Another feature often encountered in economic time series is *seasonality*. This issue arises, e.g., in the case of quarterly real GDP, due to particular regularities within a year: the first quarter being the quarter with the lowest values, the second and fourth quarters being with the highest values, and the third quarter being in between. These movements are caused by climatical and/or holiday seasonal variations within the year and are usually viewed to be of minor economic

[2] See Footnote 1 for some theories analyzing nonstationary behavior.

[3] This is obtained by using the approximation $\ln(1+\epsilon) \approx \epsilon$ for small ϵ, where ϵ denotes the growth rate of GDP.

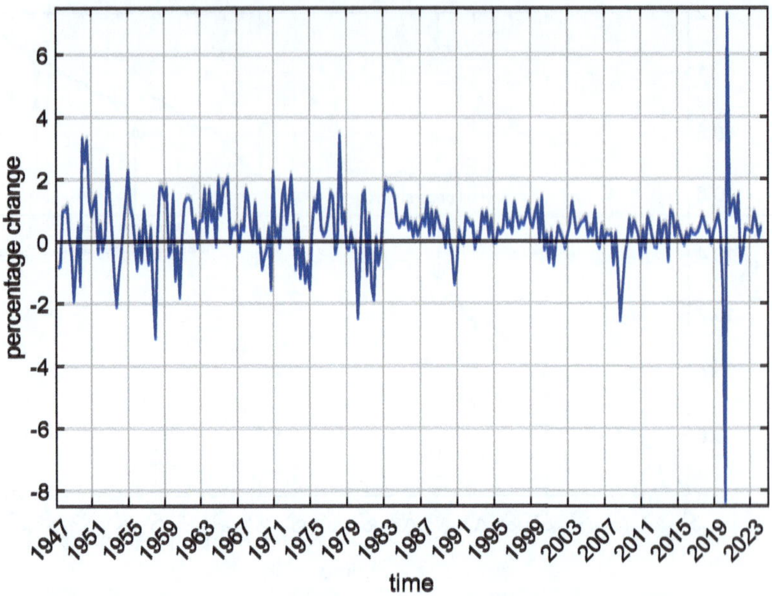

Fig. 1.2 Quarterly growth rate of US real gross domestic product (GDP) per capita

importance. Moreover, these seasonal variations, because of their sizes, hide the more important business cycle movements. It is therefore customary to work with time series that have been adjusted for seasonality beforehand.[4] Figure 1.3 shows the unadjusted and the adjusted real gross domestic product for Switzerland.[5] It shows how seasonally adjustment smoothes the time series and evens out the seasonal regularities. These issues will be dealt with in more detail in Sect. 6.5.3.

Other highly relevant economic time series are interest rates. Figure 1.4 plots the 3-month interbank rate and the 10-year government bond yield for the euro area. Over the period considered, these two variables also seem to trend. However, the nature of this trend must be different from the one encountered in GDP data because of the theoretically binding zero lower bound, despite the fact that this bound has been crossed in recent years. Although the relative level of the two series may change over time, they move more or less together. This *comovement* is in particular true with respect to the medium and long term. Section 16.1 provides a theoretical discussion of the relation between short- and long-run interest rates.

Finally, we take stock market indices as a final introductory example of time series typically encountered in economics. In Fig. 1.5, the Swiss Market Index (SMI) is plotted as an example. The first panel displays the raw data on a logarithmic scale. One can clearly discern the different crises: the burst of the dot-com bubble in

[4] The data are usually not only seasonally, but also calendar adjusted.

[5] Some countries, like the United States, just release seasonally adjusted national account data.

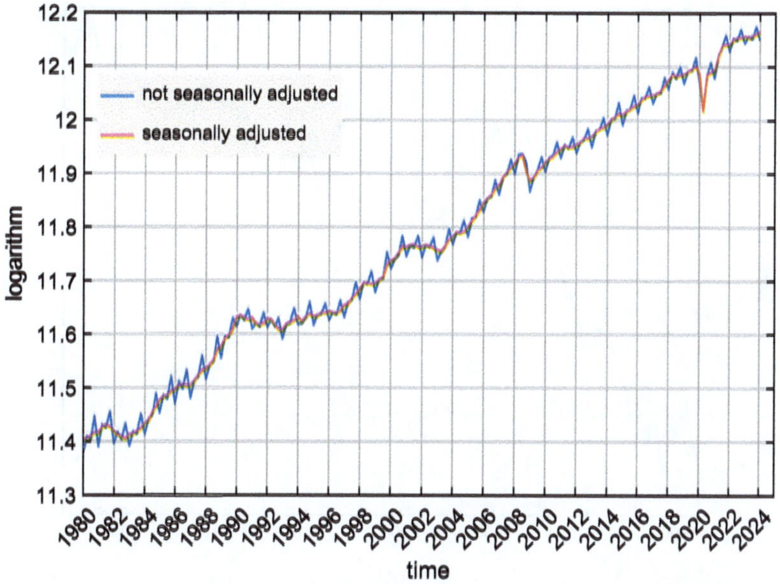

Fig. 1.3 Comparison of unadjusted and seasonally adjusted Swiss real GDP (chained 2015 Swiss Francs)

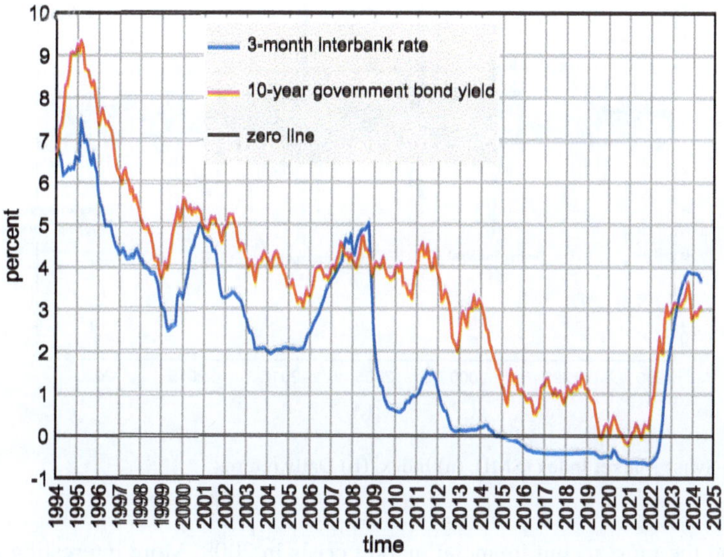

Fig. 1.4 Three-month interbank rate and 10-year government bond yield at monthly frequency

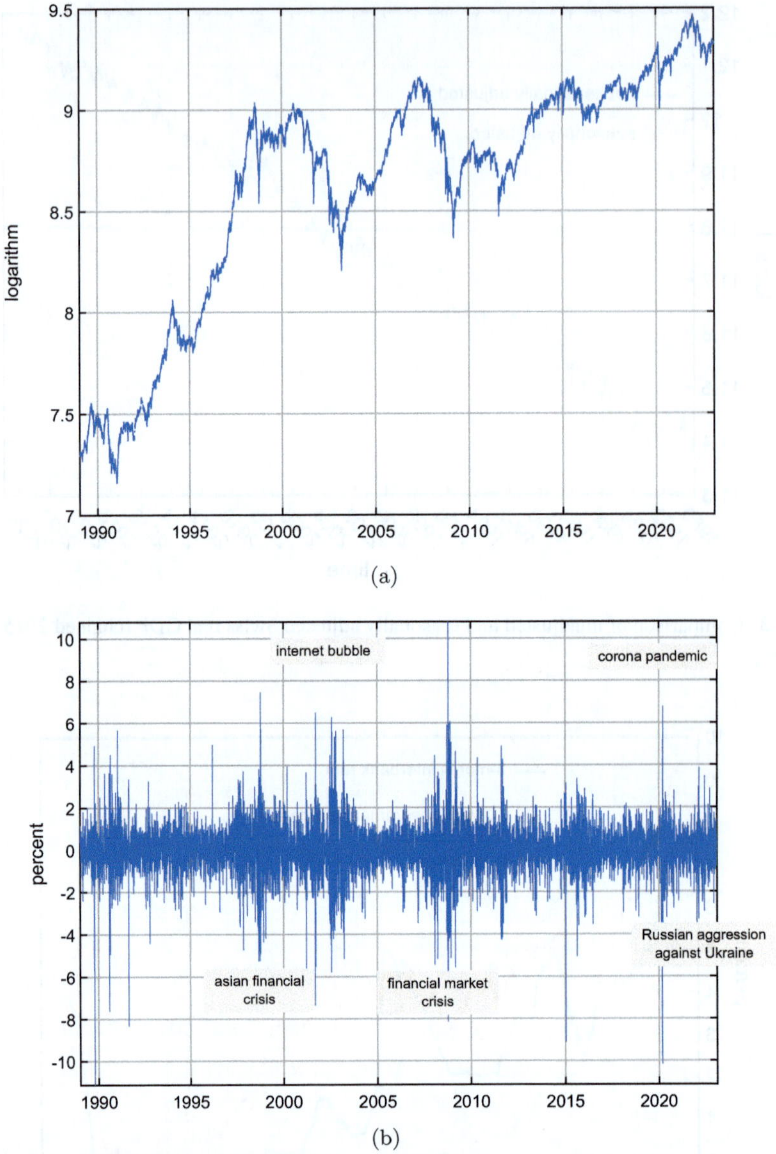

Fig. 1.5 Swiss Market Index (SMI). (**a**) Index. (**b**) Daily returns

2001 and the most recent financial market crisis in 2008. More interesting than the index itself is the return on the index plotted in the second panel. Whereas the mean seems to stay relatively constant over time, the volatility is not: in periods of crises, volatility is much higher. This *clustering of volatility* is a typical feature of financial market data and will be the subject of Chap. 8.

1.2 Stochastic Processes

The previous section provided an intuitive approach to the subject. A rigorous analysis, however, necessitates more precise definitions and concepts. For this purpose, we introduce the concept of a stochastic process. Thereby, the observation at some time t is treated as the realization of the random variable X_t. In time series analysis, we are, however, in general not interested in a particular point in time, but rather in a whole sequence. This leads to the following definition.

Definition 1.1 (Stochastic process) A stochastic process $\{X_t\}$, $t \in \mathcal{T}$, is a family of random variables defined on some given probability space.

Here $\mathcal{T}$ denotes an ordered index set, which is typically identified with time. In the time series literature, one encounters the following index sets:

$$\text{discrete time: } \mathcal{T} = \{1, 2, \ldots\} = \mathbb{N}$$

$$\text{discrete time: } \mathcal{T} = \{\ldots, -2, -1, 0, 1, 2, \ldots\} = \mathbb{Z}$$

$$\text{continuous time: } \mathcal{T} = [0, \infty) = \mathbb{R}^+, \mathcal{T} = (-\infty, \infty) = \mathbb{R}, \text{ or } \mathcal{T} = [0, 1].$$

Remark 1.1 Given that $\mathcal{T}$ is identified with time and thus has a direction, a characteristic of time series analysis is the distinction between past, present, and future. This is not possible when the index set is related to space.

For technical reasons, which will become clear later, we will work mostly with $\mathcal{T} = \mathbb{Z}$, the set of integers. This choice reflects the notion that the evolution of economies over time, usually, has no natural starting point nor a foreseeable endpoint. Although models in continuous time are well established especially in the theoretical finance literature, we will disregard them because observations are always of a discrete nature and because models in continuous time require a substantially higher mathematical level.

Remark 1.2 The random variables $\{X_t\}$ take values in a so-called *state space*. In the first part of this treatise, we take as the state space the space of real numbers $\mathbb{R}$ and thus consider only univariate time series. In part II, we extend the state space to $\mathbb{R}^n$ and study multivariate time series. Theoretically, it is possible to consider other state spaces as well (e.g., $\{0, 1\}$, the integers, or the complex numbers), but his will not be pursued here.

Definition 1.2 (Realization) The function $t \to x_t$ that assigns to each point in time t the realization of the random variable X_t, x_t, is called a realization or a trajectory of the stochastic process and is denoted by $\{x_t\}$.

The realization or trajectory (observations or data) of the underlying stochastic process is then called *time series*. A trajectory (event) therefore represents one observation of the stochastic process. Whereas in standard statistics a sample consists of several, typically, independent draws from the same distribution, a sample in time series analysis is just a single trajectory. Thus, we are confronted with a situation where there is in principle just one observation. We cannot turn back the clock and get additional trajectories. The situation is even worse as we typically observe only the realizations in a particular time window. For example, we might have data on US real GDP from the first quarter in 1947 up to the second quarter in 2024. But it is clear that the United States existed before 1947 and will continue to exist after 2024, so that there are in principle observations before 1947 and after 2024. To overcome this problem, we assume that the observed part of the trajectory is typical for the time series as a whole. This idea is related to the concept of *stationarity* that we will introduce more formally below. In addition, we want to require that the observations cover in principle all possible outcomes. This leads to the concept of *ergodicity*. We avoid a formal definition of ergodicity as this would require a sizeable amount of theoretical probabilistic background material that goes beyond the scope this treatise.[6]

An important goal of time series analysis is to build a model given the realization (data) at hand. This amounts to specify the *joint distribution* of some set of X_t's with corresponding realization $\{x_t\}$.

Definition 1.3 (Model) A time series model or a model for the observations (data) $\{x_t\}$ is a specification of the joint distribution of $\{X_t\}$ for which $\{x_t\}$ is a realization.

The Kolmogorov existence theorem ensures that the specification of all *finite-dimensional marginal* distributions is sufficient to characterize the stochastic process as a whole (see Billingsley (1986), Brockwell and Davis (1991), or Kallenberg (2002)).

In most circumstances, it is too involved to specify the complete distribution. Instead, only the first two moments are considered. These moments are given by the means $\mathbb{E}X_t$, the variances $\mathbb{V}X_t$, $t \in \mathbb{Z}$, and the covariances $\text{cov}(X_t, X_s) = \mathbb{E}(X_t - \mathbb{E}X_t)(X_s - \mathbb{E}X_s) = \mathbb{E}(X_t X_s) - \mathbb{E}X_t \mathbb{E}X_s$, respectively the correlations $\text{corr}(X_t, X_s) = \text{cov}(X_t, X_s)/(\sqrt{\mathbb{V}X_t}\sqrt{\mathbb{V}X_s})$, $t, s \in \mathbb{Z}$. If the random variables are jointly normally distributed, the specification of the first two moments is sufficient to characterize the whole distribution.

[6] In the theoretical probability theory, ergodicity is an important concept that asks the question under which conditions the time average of a property is equal to the corresponding ensemble average, i.e., the average over the entire state space. In particular, ergodicity ensures that the arithmetic averages over time converge to their theoretical counterparts. In Chap. 4, we allude to this principle in the estimation of the mean and the autocovariance function of a time series.

1.3 Stationarity

An important insight in time series analysis is that the realizations in different periods are related with each other. The value of GDP in some year obviously depends, through saving and investment decisions, on the values from previous years. This temporal dependence can be represented either by an explicit model or, in a descriptive way, by covariances, respectively correlations. Because the realization of X_t in some period t may depend, in principle, on all past realizations $X_{t-1}, X_{t-2}, \ldots$, we do not have to specify just a finite number of covariances, but infinitely many of them. This leads to the concept of the *covariance function*. The covariance function is not only a tool for summarizing the statistical properties of a time series but is also instrumental in the derivation of forecasts (see Chap. 3), the estimation of ARMA models, the most important class of models (see Chap. 5), and the Wold representation (see Sect. 3.2 in Chap. 3). It is therefore of utmost importance to get a thorough understanding of the meaning and properties of the covariance function.

Definition 1.4 (Autocovariance function) Let $\{X_t\}$ be a stochastic process with $\mathbb{V}X_t < \infty$ for all $t \in \mathbb{Z}$. The function that assigns to any two time periods t and s, $t, s \in \mathbb{Z}$, the covariance between X_t and X_s is called the *autocovariance function* of $\{X_t\}$. The autocovariance function is denoted by $\gamma_X(t, s)$, respectively $\gamma(t, s)$ for short. Formally, this function is given by

$$\gamma_X(t, s) = \operatorname{cov}(X_t, X_s) = \mathbb{E}\left[(X_t - \mathbb{E}X_t)(X_s - \mathbb{E}X_s)\right] = \mathbb{E}X_tX_s - \mathbb{E}X_t\mathbb{E}X_s.$$

Remark 1.3 The term *auto* emphasizes that the covariances are computed with respect to the same variable at different points in time. Alternatively, one may use the term *covariance function* for short.

Definition 1.5 (Stationarity) A stochastic process $\{X_t\}$, $t \in \mathbb{Z}$, is called *stationary* if and only if for all integers r, s, and t the following properties hold:

(i) $\mathbb{E}X_t = \mu$ constant.
(ii) $\mathbb{V}X_t < \infty$.
(iii) $\gamma_X(t, s) = \gamma_X(t + r, s + r)$.

Remark 1.4 Processes with these properties are often called weakly stationary, wide-sense stationary, covariance stationary, or second-order stationary. As we will mostly not deal with other forms of stationarity, we simply speak of stationary processes, for short.

Remark 1.5 For $t = s$, we have $\gamma_X(t, s) = \gamma_X(t, t) = \mathbb{V}X_t$. Thus, if $\{X_t\}$ is stationary, $\gamma_X(t, t) = \mathbb{V}X_t =$ constant. $\mathbb{V}X_t$ is known as the (unconditional) variance of X_t.

Remark 1.6 If $\{X_t\}$ is stationary, setting $r = -s$ leads to

$$\gamma_X(t, s) = \gamma_X(t - s, 0).$$

Thus, $\gamma_X(t, s)$ does not depend on the points in time t and s, but only on the number of periods t and s are apart from each other, i.e., on $t - s$. For stationary processes, one can therefore view the autocovariance function as a function of just one argument only. We denote the autocovariance function in this case by $\gamma_X(h)$, $h \in \mathbb{Z}$. Because the covariance is symmetric in t and s, i.e., $\gamma_X(t, s) = \gamma_X(s, t)$,

$$\gamma_X(h) = \gamma_X(-h) \qquad \text{for all integers } h.$$

It is thus sufficient to look at the autocovariance function for positive integers only, i.e., for $h = 0, 1, 2, \ldots$. In this case, we refer to h as the *order* or *lag* of the autocovariance. For $h = 0$, we get the (unconditional) variance of X_t, i.e., $\gamma_X(0) = \mathbb{V}X_t$.

In practice, it is often more convenient to work with correlations instead of autocovariances. The *autocorrelation function* (ACF) of a stationary process, denoted by $\rho_X(h)$, is defined as:

$$\rho_X(h) = \frac{\gamma_X(h)}{\gamma_X(0)} = \operatorname{corr}(X_{t+h}, X_t) \quad \text{for all integers } h$$

where h is again referred to as the order or lag. Note that this definition is equivalent to the ordinary correlation coefficients $\rho(h) = \frac{\operatorname{cov}(X_t, X_{t-h})}{\sqrt{\mathbb{V}X_t}\sqrt{\mathbb{V}X_{t-h}}}$, because stationarity implies that $\mathbb{V}X_t = \mathbb{V}X_{t-h}$ so that $\sqrt{\mathbb{V}X_t}\sqrt{\mathbb{V}X_{t-h}} = \mathbb{V}X_t = \gamma_X(0)$.

Most of the time, it is sufficient to rely on the first two moments only. However, there are situations where it is necessary to analyze the whole distribution. This leads to the concept of *strict stationarity*.

Definition 1.6 (Strict stationarity) A stochastic process $\{X_t\}$, $t \in \mathbb{Z}$, is called *strictly stationary* if the joint distributions of $\left(X_{t_1}, \ldots, X_{t_n}\right)$ and $\left(X_{t_1+h}, \ldots, X_{t_n+h}\right)$ are the same for all $h \in \mathbb{Z}$ and all $(t_1, \ldots, t_n) \in \mathcal{T}^n$, $n = 1, 2, \ldots$

Note that this definition does not require the existence of the first two moments. In Chap. 8, we will encounter stochastic process with infinite variance.

Remark 1.7 If $\{X_t\}$ is strictly stationary, setting $n = 1$, X_t has the same distribution for all t. Setting $n = 2$, X_{t+h}, and X_t have a joint distribution independent of t. This implies that the covariance, if it exists, depends only on h. Thus, every strictly stationary process with $\mathbb{V}X_t < \infty$ is also stationary.[7]

[7] An example of a process that is strictly stationary, but not stationary, is given by the IGARCH process (see Sect. 8.2). This process is strictly stationary with infinite variance.

The converse is, however, not true as shown by the following example:

$$X_t \sim \begin{cases} \text{exponential distribution with density } f(x) = e^{-x}, & t \text{ uneven;} \\ N(1, 1), & t \text{ even;} \end{cases}$$

with all X_t's mutually independent. In this example, we have the following:

- $\mathbb{E}X_t = 1$.
- $\gamma_X(0) = 1$ and $\gamma_X(h) = 0$ for $h \neq 0$.

Thus, $\{X_t\}$ is stationary, but not strictly stationary, because the distribution changes depending on whether t is even or uneven.

Definition 1.7 (Gaussian process) A stochastic process $\{X_t\}$ is called a *Gaussian process* if all finite-dimensional distributions of $\{X_t\}$ are jointly Gaussian (multivariate normal).

Remark 1.8 A Gaussian process is strictly stationary. For all $n, h, t_1, \ldots, t_n$, $\left(X_{t_1}, \ldots, X_{t_n}\right)$ and $\left(X_{t_1+h}, \ldots, X_{t_n+h}\right)$ have the same mean and the same covariance matrix.

At this point, we will not delve further into the relation between stationarity, strict stationarity, and Gaussian processes.

1.4 Construction of Stochastic Processes

One important notion in time series analysis is to build up more complicated process from simple ones. The simplest building block is a process with no autocorrelation called a *white noise* process, which is introduced below. Taking moving averages from this process or using it in a recursion gives rise to more sophisticated process with more elaborated autocovariance functions. Slutzky (1937) first introduced the idea that moving averages of simple processes can generate time series whose motion resembles business cycle fluctuations.

1.4.1 White Noise

The simplest building block is a process with zero autocorrelation, called *white noise* process.

Definition 1.8 (White noise) A stationary process $\{Z_t\}$, $t \in \mathbb{Z}$, is called a *white noise* process if

- $\mathbb{E}Z_t = 0$
- $\gamma_Z(h) = \begin{cases} \sigma^2 & h = 0; \\ 0 & h \neq 0. \end{cases}$

We denote this by $Z_t \sim \text{WN}(0, \sigma^2)$.

The white noise process is stationary and by definition temporally uncorrelated, i.e., the ACF always equals zero, except for $h = 0$, where it is equal to one. As the ACF possesses no structure, it is impossible to draw inferences from past observations to its future development, at least in a least square setting with linear forecasting functions (see Chap. 3). For this reason, one can say that a white noise process has no memory.

If $\{Z_t\}$ is not only temporally uncorrelated but also independently and identically distributed with $\sigma^2 < \infty$, we write $Z_t \sim \text{IID}(0, \sigma^2)$. If in addition Z_t is normally distributed, we write $Z_t \sim \text{IID N}(0, \sigma^2)$. An $\text{IID}(0, \sigma^2)$ process is always a white noise process. The converse is, however, not true as will be shown in Chap. 8.

1.4.2 Construction of Stochastic Processes: Some Examples

We will now illustrate how complex stationary processes can be constructed as functions of white noise processes. Table 1.1 reports in column 2 six consecutive observations of a white noise process $\{Z_t\}$. Figure 1.6a plots hundred consecutive observations of the same white noise process. We can now construct a new process $\{X_t^{(\text{MA})}\}$ by taking moving averages over adjacent periods. More specifically, we take $X_t^{(\text{MA})} = Z_t + 0.9Z_{t-1}$, $t = 2, 3, \ldots$. Thus, the realization of $\{X_t^{(\text{MA})}\}$ in period 2 is $\{x_2^{(\text{MA})}\} = -0.6387 = -0.8718 + 0.9 \times 0.2590$.[8] The realization in period 3 is $\{x_3^{(\text{MA})}\} = -1.5726 = -0.7879 + 0.9 \times -0.8718$ and so on. The resulting realizations of $\{X_t^{(\text{MA})}\}$ for $t = 2, \ldots, 6$ are reported in the third column of Table 1.1, and the plot is shown in Fig. 1.6b. One can see that the averaging makes the series smoother. In Sect. 1.4.3, we will provide a more detailed analysis of such moving-average processes.

Another construction device is a recursion: $X_t^{(AR)} = \phi X_{t-1}^{(AR)} + Z_t$, $t = 2, 3, \ldots$, with starting value $X_1^{(AR)} = Z_1$. Such a process is called autoregressive because it refers to its own past. Taking $\phi = 0.9$, the realization of $\{X_t^{(AR)}\}$ in period 2 is $\{x_2^{(AR)}\} = -0.6387 = 0.9 \times 0.2590 - 0.8718$, in period 3 $\{x_3^{(AR)}\} = -1.3627 = 0.9 \times -0.6387 - 0.7879$, and so on. Again the resulting realizations of $\{X_t^{(\text{AR})}\}$ for $t = 2, \ldots, 6$ are reported in the fourth column of Table 1.1, and the plot is shown

[8] The following calculations are rounded to four digits.

Table 1.1 Construction of stochastic processes from a white noise process

Time	White noise	Moving average	Autoregressive	Random walk
1	0.2590	0.2590	0.2590	0.2590
2	−0.8718	−0.6387	−0.6387	−0.6128
3	−0.7879	−1.5726	−1.3627	−1.4007
4	−0.3443	−1.0535	−1.5708	−1.7451
5	0.6476	0.3377	−0.7661	−1.0974
6	2.0541	2.6370	1.3646	0.9567
⋮	⋮	⋮	⋮	⋮

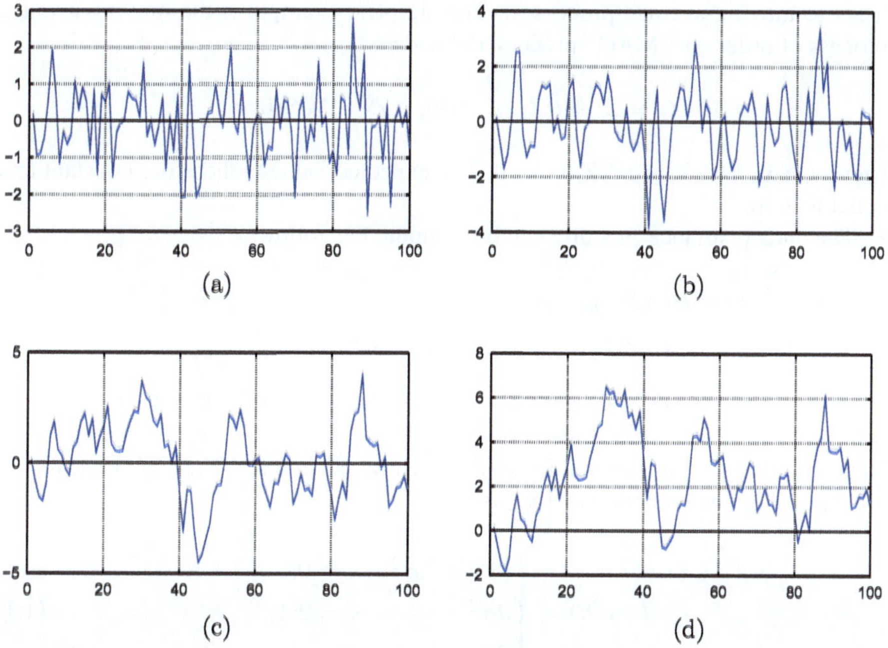

Fig. 1.6 Realizations of processes constructed from a given white noise process. (**a**) White noise. (**b**) Moving average with $\theta = 0.9$. (**c**) Autoregressive with $\phi = 0.9$. (**d**) Random walk

in Fig. 1.6c. One can see how the series becomes more persistent. In Sect. 2.2.2, we will provide a more detailed analysis of autoregressive processes.

Finally, we construct a new process by taking cumulative sums: $X_t^{(RW)} = \sum_{\tau=1}^{t} Z_\tau$. This process can also be obtained from the recursion above by taking $\phi = 1$ so that $X_t^{(RW)} = X_{t-1}^{(RW)} + Z_t$. It is called a random walk. Thus, the realization of $\{X_t^{(RW)}\}$ for period 2 is $\{x_2^{(RW)}\} = -0.6128 = 0.2590 - 0.8718$, for period 3 $\{x_3^{(RW)}\} = -1.4007 = -0.6128 - 0.7879$, and so on. Again the resulting realizations of $\{X_t^{(\mathrm{RW})}\}$ for $t = 2, \ldots, 6$ are reported in the last column of Table 1.1, and the plot is shown in Fig. 1.6d. One can see how the series drifts away from its mean of zero more persistently than all the other three processes considered. In Sect. 1.4.4, we will provide a more detailed analysis of random walk processes and show that they are not stationary.

1.4.3 Moving Average Process of Order One

As illustrated previously, white noise process can be used as a building block to construct more complex processes with a more involved autocorrelation structure. The simplest procedure is to take moving averages over consecutive periods.[9] This leads to moving-average processes:. The simplest example is the moving-average process of order one, MA(1) process, defined as

$$X_t = Z_t + \theta Z_{t-1} \quad \text{with} \quad Z_t \sim \mathrm{WN}(0, \sigma^2).$$

Clearly, $\mathbb{E}X_t = \mathbb{E}Z_t + \theta \mathbb{E}Z_{t-1} = 0$. The expected value is therefore constant and equal to zero.

The autocovariance function can be computed as follows:

$$\begin{aligned}
\gamma_X(t+h, t) &= \mathrm{cov}(X_{t+h}, X_t) \\
&= \mathrm{cov}(Z_{t+h} + \theta Z_{t+h-1}, Z_t + \theta Z_{t-1}) \\
&= \mathbb{E}Z_{t+h}Z_t + \theta \mathbb{E}Z_{t+h}Z_{t-1} + \theta \mathbb{E}Z_{t+h-1}Z_t + \theta^2 \mathbb{E}Z_{t+h-1}Z_{t-1}.
\end{aligned}$$

Recalling that $\{Z_t\}$ is white noise so that $\mathbb{E}Z_t^2 = \sigma^2$ and $\mathbb{E}Z_t Z_{t+h} = 0$ for $h \neq 0$, the autocovariance function of $\{X_t\}$ is

$$\gamma_X(h) = \begin{cases} (1+\theta^2)\sigma^2 & h = 0; \\ \theta\sigma^2 & h = \pm 1; \\ 0 & \text{otherwise.} \end{cases} \tag{1.1}$$

Thus, $\{X_t\}$ is stationary irrespective of the value of θ. The autocorrelation function is

$$\rho_X(h) = \begin{cases} 1 & h = 0; \\ \frac{\theta}{1+\theta^2} & h = \pm 1; \\ 0 & \text{otherwise.} \end{cases}$$

[9] This procedure is an example of a linear time-invariant filter. Section 6.4 provides a formal introduction to such filters.

Note that $0 \leq |\rho_X(1)| \leq \frac{1}{2}$. As the correlation between X_t and X_s is zero when t and s are more than one period apart, we call a moving-average process a process with finite or short memory or a process with finite-range dependence.

Remark 1.9 To motivate the name moving average, define the MA(1) process more generally as

$$X_t = \theta_0 Z_t + \theta_1 Z_{t-1} \quad \text{with} \quad Z_t \sim \text{WN}(0, \sigma^2) \text{ and } \theta_0, \theta_1 \neq 0.$$

Thus, X_t is a weighted average of Z_t and Z_{t-1}. If $\theta_0 = \theta_1 = 1/2$, X_t is the arithmetic average of Z_t and Z_{t-1}. This process is, however, observationally equivalent to the process

$$X_t = \tilde{Z}_t + \tilde{\theta} \tilde{Z}_{t-1} \quad \text{with} \quad \tilde{Z}_t \sim \text{WN}(0, \tilde{\sigma}^2)$$

where $\tilde{\theta} = \theta_1/\theta_0$ and $\tilde{\sigma}^2 = \theta_0^2 \sigma^2$. Both processes generate the same first two moments and are therefore observationally indistinguishable from each other, with regard to the first two moments. Thus, we can set $\theta_0 = 1$ without loss of generality.

1.4.4 Random Walk

Given a white noise process $Z_t \sim \text{WN}(0, \sigma^2)$, define a new process $\{X_t\}$, $t = 0, 1, 2, \ldots$, as a cumulative sum of the Z_t's:

$$X_t = Z_1 + Z_2 + \ldots + Z_t = \sum_{j=1}^{t} Z_j \tag{1.2}$$

and $X_0 = 0$. Such processes are called *random walks*. They may alternatively be defined through the recursion:

$$X_t = X_{t-1} + Z_t, \qquad t > 0 \text{ and } X_0 = 0.$$

If in each time period a constant δ is added such that

$$X_t = \delta + X_{t-1} + Z_t,$$

the process $\{X_t\}$ is called a *random walk with drift*. Note that, in contrast to $\{Z_t\}$, $\{X_t\}$ is only defined for $t \geq 0$. It may, however, be extended to a process with $t \in \mathbb{Z}$ by defining $X_t = X_0 - Z_0 - Z_1 - \cdots - Z_{t+1}$ for $t < 0$.

Although the random walk has a constant mean, i.e., $\mathbb{E}X_t = \mathbb{E}X_0$, provided $\mathbb{E}X_0$ is finite, it is nonetheless a nonstationary process.

Proposition 1.1 *The random walk $\{X_t\}$ as defined in Eq.* (1.2) *is nonstationary.*

Proof The variance of $X_{t+1} - X_1$ equals $\mathbb{V}(X_{t+1} - X_1) = \mathbb{V}\left(\sum_{j=2}^{t+1} Z_j\right) = \sum_{j=2}^{t+1} \mathbb{V}Z_j = t\sigma^2$. Assume for the moment that $\{X_t\}$ is stationary; then the triangular inequality implies for $t > 0$:

$$0 < \sqrt{t\sigma^2} = \text{std}(X_{t+1} - X_1) \leq \text{std}(X_{t+1}) + \text{std}(X_1) = 2\,\text{std}(X_1)$$

where "std" denotes the standard deviation. As the left-hand side of the inequality converges to infinity for t going to infinity, the right-hand side also must go to infinity. This means that the variance of X_1 must be infinite. This, however, contradicts the assumption of stationarity. Thus, $\{X_t\}$ cannot be stationary. □

A similar argument applies to the process $X_t = -X_{t-1} + Z_t$, $Z_t \sim \text{WN}(0, \sigma^2)$, which is also nonstationary.

The random walk represents by far the most widely used nonstationary process in economics. It has proven to be an important ingredient in many economic time series. Typical nonstationary time series, which are driven by random walks, are stock market prices, exchange rates, or the gross domestic product (GDP). Usually, it is necessary to apply some transformation (filter) first to achieve stationarity. In the example above, one has to replace $\{X_t\}$ by its first difference $\{\Delta X_t\} = \{X_t - X_{t-1}\} = \{Z_t\}$, which is stationary by construction. Time series that become stationary after differencing are called integrated processes and are the subject of a more in-depth analysis in Chap. 7. Besides ordinary differencing, other transformations are encountered: seasonal differencing, inclusion of a time trend, seasonal dummies, moving averages, etc. Some of them will be discussed as we go along.

1.4.5 Changing Expected Value

Starting from a stationary process $\{Y_t\}$, it is easy to construct a nonstationary process: $\{X_t\}$:

$$X_t = \begin{cases} Y_t, & t < t_c; \\ Y_t + c, & t \geq t_c \text{ und } c \neq 0 \end{cases}$$

where t_c is some specific point in time. $\{X_t\}$ is clearly not stationary because the expected value is not constant. In econometrics, we refer to such a situation as a *structural change*, which can be accommodated in this example by introducing a so-called dummy variable. Structural changes may also affect the variance of process as in the discussion on the "great moderation" (See Neusser (2012) and the literature cited therein). Chapter 18 discusses more elaborate models of structural change.

1.5 Properties of Autocovariance Functions

1.5.1 Characterization

The autocovariance function represents the directly accessible external properties of the time series. It is therefore important to understand its mathematical properties and how they are related to its inner structure. We will deepen this connection between the autocovariance function and a particular class of models in Chap. 2. The estimation of the autocovariance function will be treated in Chap. 4. For the moment, we will just analyze the case of the MA(1) model as a prototypical example.

Theorem 1.1 *The autocovariance function of a stationary process $\{X_t\}$ is characterized by the following properties:*

(i) $\gamma_X(0) \geq 0$.
(ii) $0 \leq |\gamma_X(h)| \leq \gamma_X(0)$.
(iii) $\gamma_X(h) = \gamma_X(-h)$.
(iv) $\sum_{i,j=1}^{n} a_i \gamma_X(t_i - t_j) a_j \geq 0$ *for all n and all vectors $(a_1, \ldots, a_n)'$ and $(t_1, \ldots, t_n)$. This property is called* nonnegative definiteness.

Proof The first property is obvious as variances are always nonnegative. The second property follows from the Cauchy-Bunyakovsky-Schwarz inequality (see Theorem C.1) applied to X_t and X_{t+h}, which yields $0 \leq |\gamma_X(h)| \leq \gamma_X(0)$. The third property follows immediately from the definition of the covariance. Define $a = (a_1, \ldots, a_n)'$ and $X = \left(X_{t_1}, \ldots, X_{t_n}\right)'$; then the last property follows from the fact that variances are always nonnegative: $0 \leq \mathbb{V}\left(a'X\right) = a'\mathbb{V}(X)a = \sum_{i,j=1}^{n} a_i \gamma_X(t_i - t_j) a_j$. □

The same properties hold for the correlation function ρ_X, except that $\rho_X(0) = 1$.

Theorem 1.2 *The autocorrelation function of a stationary stochastic process $\{X_t\}$ is characterized by the following properties:*

(i) $\rho_X(0) = 1$.
(ii) $0 \leq |\rho_X(h)| \leq 1$.
(iii) $\rho_X(h) = \rho_X(-h)$.
(iv) $\sum_{i,j=1}^{n} a_i \rho_X(t_i - t_j) a_j \geq 0$ *for all n and all vectors $(a_1, \ldots, a_n)'$ and $(t_1, \ldots, t_n)$.*

Proof The proof follows immediately from the properties of the autocovariance function. □

It can be shown that for any given function with the above properties, there exists a stationary (Gaussian) process (Gaussian process) that has this function as its autocovariance function, respectively autocorrelation function.

1.5.2 Autocovariance Function of MA(1) Processes

The autocovariance function describes the external observable characteristics of a time series that can be estimated from the data. Usually, we want to understand the internal mechanism that generates the data at hand. For this, we need a model. Hence, it is important to understand the relation between the autocovariance function and a certain class of models. In this section, by analyzing the MA(1) model, we will show that this relationship is not one-to-one. Thus, we are confronted with a fundamental *identification problem*.

To make the point, consider the following given autocovariance function:

$$\gamma(h) = \begin{cases} \gamma_0, \ h = 0; \\ \gamma_1, \ h = \pm 1; \\ 0, \quad |h| > 1. \end{cases}$$

The problem consists of determining the parameters of the MA(1) model, θ and σ^2, from the values of the autocovariance function. For this purpose, we equate $\gamma_0 = (1+\theta^2)\sigma^2$ and $\gamma_1 = \theta\sigma^2$ (see Eq. (1.1)). This leads to an equation system in the two unknowns θ und σ^2. This system can be simplified by dividing the second equation by the first one to obtain $\gamma_1/\gamma_0 = \theta/(1+\theta^2)$. Because $\gamma_1/\gamma_0 = \rho(1) = \rho_1$, one arrives at a quadratic equation in θ:

$$\rho_1\theta^2 - \theta + \rho_1 = 0.$$

The solutions of this equation are

$$\theta = \frac{1}{2\rho_1}\left(1 \pm \sqrt{1 - 4\rho_1^2}\right).$$

The solutions are real if and only if the discriminant $1 - 4\rho_1^2$ is nonnegative. This is the case if and only if $\rho_1^2 \le 1/4$, respectively $|\rho_1| \le 1/2$. Note that the product of the two roots equals one. This implies that the roots are inverses of each other. The identification problem thus takes the following form:

$\|\rho_1\| < 1/2$:	there exists two observationally equivalent MA(1) processes.
$\rho_1 = \pm 1/2$:	there exists exactly one MA(1) process with $\theta = \pm 1$.
$\|\rho_1\| > 1/2$:	there exists no MA(1) process with this autocovariance function.

The relation between the first-order autocorrelation coefficient, $\rho_1 = \rho(1)$, and the parameter θ of the MA(1) process is represented in Fig. 1.7. As can be seen, there exists for each $\rho(1)$ with $|\rho(1)| < \frac{1}{2}$ two solutions. The two solutions are inverses of each other. Hence, one solution is absolutely smaller than one, whereas the other is bigger than one. In Sect. 2.3, we will argue in favor of the solution smaller than one. For $\rho(1) = \pm 1/2$, there exists exactly one solution, $\theta = \pm 1$. For $|\rho(1)| > 1/2$, there is no real solution. For $|\rho_1| > 1/2$, $\rho(h)$ actually

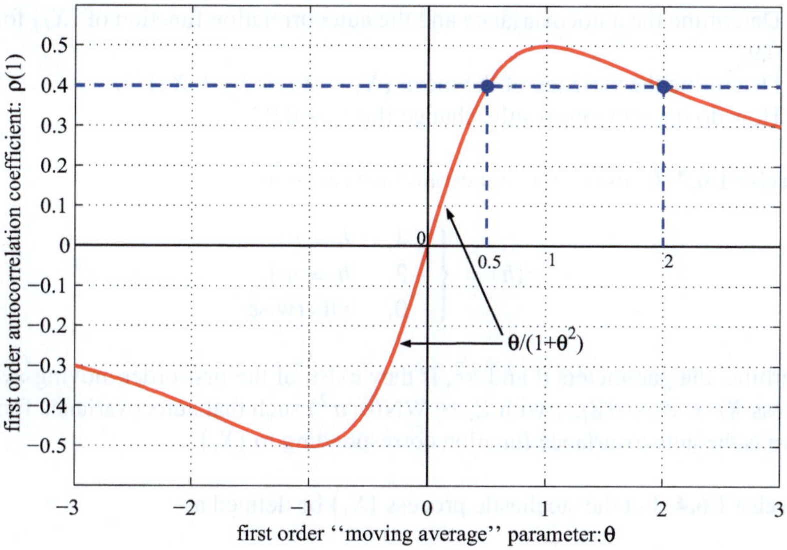

Fig. 1.7 Relation between the autocorrelation coefficient of order one, $\rho(1)$, and the parameter θ of a MA(1) process

does not represent a genuine autocorrelation function as the fourth condition in Theorem 1.1, respectively Theorem 1.2 is violated. Taking $\rho_1 = \frac{1}{2}$ and setting $a = (1, -1, 1, -1, \ldots, 1, -1)'$, one gets

$$\sum_{i,j=1}^{n} a_i \rho(i-j) a_j = n - 2(n-1)\rho_1 < 0, \quad \text{if } n > \frac{2\rho_1}{2\rho_1 - 1}.$$

For $\rho_1 < -\frac{1}{2}$, one sets $a = (1, 1, \ldots, 1)'$. Hence, the fourth property is violated.

1.6 Exercises

Exercise 1.6.1 Let the process $\{X_t\}$ be generated by a two-sided moving-average process:

$$X_t = 0.5 Z_{t+1} + 0.5 Z_{t-1} \qquad \text{with} \quad Z_t \sim \mathrm{WN}(0, \sigma^2).$$

Determine the autocovariance and the autocorrelation function of $\{X_t\}$.

Exercise 1.6.2 Let $\{X_t\}$ be the MA(1) process:

$$X_t = Z_t + \theta Z_{t-2} \qquad \text{with} \quad Z_t \sim \mathrm{WN}(0, \sigma^2).$$

(i) Determine the autocovariance and the autocorrelation function of $\{X_t\}$ for $\theta = 0.9$.
(ii) Determine the variance of the mean $(X_1 + X_2 + X_3 + X_4)/4$.
(iii) How do the previous results change if $\theta = -0.9$?

Exercise 1.6.3 Consider the autocovariance function

$$\gamma(h) = \begin{cases} 4, & h = 0; \\ -2, & h = \pm 1; \\ 0, & \text{otherwise.} \end{cases}$$

Determine the parameters θ and σ^2, if they exist, of the first-order moving-average process $X_t = Z_t + \theta Z_{t-1}$ with $Z_t \sim \mathrm{WN}(0, \sigma^2)$ such that autocovariance function above is the autocovariance function corresponding to $\{X_t\}$.

Exercise 1.6.4 Let the stochastic process $\{X_t\}$ be defined as

$$\begin{cases} Z_t, & \text{if } t \text{ is even;} \\ (Z_{t-1}^2 - 1)/\sqrt{2}, & \text{if } t \text{ is uneven,} \end{cases}$$

where $\{Z_t\} \sim \mathrm{IID\,N}(0, 1)$. Show that $X_t \sim \mathrm{WN}(0, 1)$, but not $\mathrm{IID}(0, 1)$.

Exercise 1.6.5 Which of the following processes is stationary?

(i) $X_t = Z_t + \theta Z_{t-1}$.
(ii) $X_t = Z_t Z_{t-1}$.
(iii) $X_t = a + \theta Z_0$.
(iv) $X_t = Z_0 \sin(at)$.

In all cases, we assume that $\{Z_t\} \sim \mathrm{IID\,N}(0, \sigma^2)$. θ and a are arbitrary parameters.

2 Autoregressive Moving-Average Processes

A basic idea in time series analysis is to construct more complex processes from simple ones. In the previous chapter, we showed, e.g., how the averaging of a white noise process leads to a process with first-order autocorrelation. In this chapter, we generalize this idea and consider processes that are solutions of linear stochastic difference equations. These so-called ARMA processes constitute the most widely used class of models in applied time series analysis.

Definition 2.1 (ARMA models) A stochastic process $\{X_t\}$, $t \in \mathbb{Z}$, is called an autoregressive moving-average process (ARMA process) of order (p, q), denoted by ARMA(p, q) process, if the process satisfies a linear stochastic difference equation of the following form:

$$X_t - \phi_1 X_{t-1} = \ldots - \phi_p X_{t-p} = Z_t + \theta_1 Z_{t-1} + \ldots + \theta_q Z_{t-q} \tag{2.1}$$

with $Z_t \sim \text{WN}(0, \sigma^2)$ and $\phi_p \theta_q \neq 0$ where p and q are nonnegative numbers. $\{X_t\}$ is called an ARMA(p, q) process with expected value μ if $\{X_t - \mu\}$ is an ARMA(p, q) process.

Remark 2.1 Many classic textbooks, e.g., Brockwell and Davis (1996) or Hannan and Deistler (1988), analyze only stationary ARMA processes. In this monograph, we abstain from this restriction as we cover nonstationary processes as well. See in particular Chaps. 7 and 16.

Remark 2.2 Despite the symmetric treatment of $\{X_t\}$ and $\{Z_t\}$ in Eq. (2.1), there is an important difference between the two processes. The realizations of $\{X_t\}$ are observable, whereas those of $\{Z_t\}$ are not.

The importance of ARMA processes is due to the fact that every stationary process can be approximated arbitrarily well by a stationary ARMA process. In

K. Neusser, *Time Series Econometrics*, Springer Texts in Business and Economics,
https://doi.org/10.1007/978-3-031-88838-0_2

particular, it can be shown that for any given autocovariance function γ with the property $\lim_{h\to\infty}\gamma(h) = 0$ and any positive integer k, there exists a stationary autoregressive moving-average process (ARMA process) $\{X_t\}$ such that $\gamma_X(h) = \gamma(h)$, $h = 0, 1, \ldots, k$.

For an ARMA process with expected value μ, one often adds a constant c to the right-hand side of the difference equation:

$$X_t - \phi_1 X_{t-1} - \ldots - \phi_p X_{t-p} = c + Z_t + \theta_1 Z_{t-1} + \ldots + \theta_q Z_{t-q}.$$

Assuming stationarity, the expected value of X_t is then $\mu = \frac{c}{1-\phi_1-\ldots-\phi_p}$. The expected value is therefore only well-defined if $\phi_1 + \ldots + \phi_p \neq 1$. The case $\phi_1 + \ldots + \phi_p = 1$ is, however, of special interest as it leads to the concept of integrated processes that are covered in Chap. 7 (see also Remark 2.2).

2.1 The Lag Operator

In times series analysis, it is customary to rewrite the above difference equation more compactly in terms of the *lag operator* L. This not only leads, however, to a compact notation but also will pave the way to analyze the inner structure of ARMA processes. The lag or back-shift operator L applied to the stochastic process $\{X_t\}$ moves the time index one period back:

$$\mathrm{L}\{X_t\} = \{X_{t-1}\}.$$

For ease of notation, we drop the curly brackets and write $\mathrm{L}X_t = X_{t-1}$. The lag operator is a linear operator with the following calculation rules:

(i) L applied to the process $\{X_t = c\}$ where c is an arbitrary constant gives:

$$\mathrm{L}c = c.$$

(ii) Applying L h times:

$$\underbrace{\mathrm{L}\ldots\mathrm{L}}_{h \text{ times}} X_t = \mathrm{L}^h X_t = X_{t-h}.$$

(iii) The inverse of the lag operator is the lead or forward operator. This operator shifts the time index one period into the future.[1] We can write L^{-1}:

$$\mathrm{L}^{-1} X_t = X_{t+1}.$$

[1] One technical advantage of using the double-infinite index set $\mathbb{Z}$ is that the lag operators form a group.

(iv) For any integers h and k, we have:

$$\mathrm{L}^h \mathrm{L}^h X_t = \mathrm{L}^{h+k} X_t = X_{t-h-k}.$$

(v) As $\mathrm{L}^{-1}\mathrm{L}X_t = X_t$, we have that

$$\mathrm{L}^0 = \mathbf{1}.$$

(vi) For any real numbers a and b, any integers h and h, and arbitrary stochastic processes $\{X_t\}$ and $\{Y_t\}$, we have

$$\left(a\mathrm{L}^h + b\mathrm{L}^k\right)(X_t + Y_t) = aX_{t-h} + bX_{t-k} + aY_{t-h} + bY_{t-k}.$$

In this way, it is possible to define *lag polynomials*: $A(\mathrm{L}) = a_0 + a_1\mathrm{L} + a_2\mathrm{L}^2 + \ldots + a_p\mathrm{L}^p$ where $a_0, a_1, \ldots, a_p$ are arbitrary fixed real numbers. For these polynomials, the usual calculation rules apply. Let, for example, $A(\mathrm{L}) = 1 - 0.5\mathrm{L}$ and $B(\mathrm{L}) = 1 + 4\mathrm{L}^2$; then $C(\mathrm{L}) = A(\mathrm{L})B(\mathrm{L}) = 1 - 0.5\mathrm{L} + 4\mathrm{L}^2 - 2\mathrm{L}^3$.

In the case of the stochastic difference equation, we write the autoregressive and moving-average polynomial as

$$\Phi(\mathrm{L}) = 1 - \phi_1\mathrm{L} - \ldots - \phi_p\mathrm{L}^p,$$

$$\Theta(\mathrm{L}) = 1 + \theta_1\mathrm{L} + \ldots + \theta_q\mathrm{L}^q.$$

The stochastic difference equation defining the ARMA process can then be written compactly as

$$\Phi(\mathrm{L})X_t = \Theta(\mathrm{L})Z_t.$$

Thus, the use of lag polynomials provides a compact notation for ARMA processes. Moreover and most importantly, $\Phi(z)$ and $\Theta(z)$, viewed as polynomials in the complex number z, reveal much of the inherent structural properties of ARMA processes (see Sect. 2.3).

2.2 Two Important Special Cases

Before we discuss the general theory of ARMA processes, we will analyze some important special cases first:

$p = 0$: moving-average process of order q, MA(q) process
$q = 0$ **and** $p = 1$: autoregressive process of order one, AR(1) process

2.2.1 Moving-Average Processes of Order q

The moving-average process of order q, MA(q) process, is defined by the following stochastic difference equation:

$$X_t = \Theta(\mathrm{L})Z_t = \theta_0 Z_t + \theta_1 Z_{t-1} + \ldots + \theta_q Z_{t-q} \qquad \text{with} \quad \theta_0 = 1 \text{ and } \theta_q \neq 0$$

and $Z_t \sim \mathrm{WN}(0, \sigma^2)$. Obviously,

$$\mathbb{E}X_t = \mathbb{E}Z_t + \theta_1 \mathbb{E}Z_{t-1} + \ldots + \theta_q \mathbb{E}Z_{t-q} = 0,$$

because $Z_t \sim \mathrm{WN}(0, \sigma^2)$. As can be easily verified, using the properties of $\{Z_t\}$, the autocovariance function of MA(q) processes is

$$\gamma_X(h) = \mathrm{cov}(X_{t+h}, X_t) = \begin{cases} \sigma^2 \sum_{i=0}^{q-|h|} \theta_i \theta_{i+|h|}, & |h| \leq q; \\ 0, & |h| > q. \end{cases}$$

This implies the following autocorrelation function:

$$\rho_X(h) = \mathrm{corr}(X_{t+h}, X_t) = \begin{cases} \frac{1}{\sum_{i=0}^{q} \theta_i^2} \sum_{i=0}^{q-|h|} \theta_i \theta_{i+|h|}, & |h| \leq q; \\ 0, & |h| > q. \end{cases}$$

Every MA(q) process is therefore stationary, irrespective of its parameters $\theta_1, \ldots, \theta_q$. Because the correlation between X_t and X_s is equal to zero if the two time points t and s are more than q periods apart, such processes are sometimes called processes with *short memory* or processes with *short-range dependence.*

Figure 2.1 plots a realization of an MA(1) process and its theoretical and estimated autocorrelation function.

2.2.2 First-Order Autoregressive Process

The autoregressive process of order one, AR(1) process, is defined by the following stochastic difference equation:

$$X_t = \phi X_{t-1} + Z_t, \qquad Z_t \sim \mathrm{WN}(0, \sigma^2) \text{ and } \phi \neq 0.$$

The above stochastic difference equation has in general several solutions. Given a sequence $\{Z_t\}$ and an arbitrary distribution for X_0, it determines all random variables X_t, $t \in \mathbb{Z} \setminus \{0\}$, by applying the above recursion. The solutions are, however, not necessarily stationary. As we will demonstrate, depending on the value of ϕ, there may exist no or exactly one stationary solution. In Sect. 1.4.4, we already showed there exists no stationary solution if $\phi = 1$.

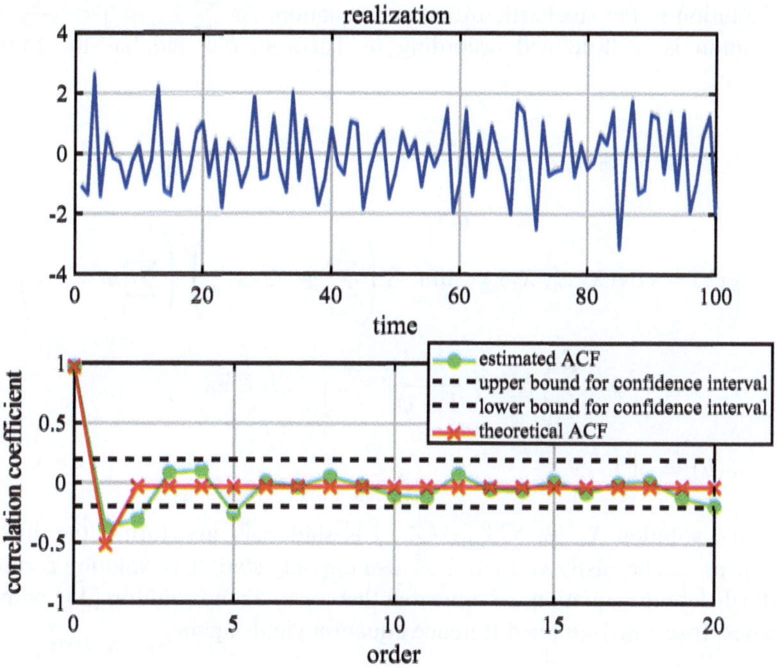

Fig. 2.1 Realization and theoretical and estimated ACF of the MA(1) process: $X_t = Z_t - 0.8Z_{t-1}$ with $Z_t \sim \text{IID N}(0, 1)$

Consider first the case $|\phi| < 1$. Inserting into the difference equation k times leads to

$$\begin{aligned} X_t &= \phi X_{t-1} + Z_t = \phi^2 X_{t-2} + \phi Z_{t-1} + Z_t \\ &= \ldots \\ &= Z_t + \phi Z_{t-1} + \phi^2 Z_{t-2} + \ldots + \phi^k Z_{t-k} + \phi^{k+1} X_{t-k-1}. \end{aligned}$$

If $\{X_t\}$ is a stationary solution, $\mathbb{V}X_{t-k-1}$ remains constant independently of k. Thus,

$$\mathbb{V}\left(X_t - \sum_{j=0}^{k} \phi^j Z_{t-j}\right) = \phi^{2k+2}\mathbb{V}X_{t-k-1} \to 0 \text{ for } k \to \infty.$$

This shows that $\sum_{j=0}^{k} \phi^j Z_{t-j}$ converges in the mean square sense, and thus also in probability, to X_t for $k \to \infty$ (see Theorem C.8 in Appendix C). This suggests to take

$$X_t = Z_t + \phi Z_{t-1} + \phi^2 Z_{t-2} + \ldots = \sum_{j=0}^{\infty} \phi^j Z_{t-j} \tag{2.2}$$

as the solution to the stochastic difference equation. As $\sum_{j=0}^{\infty} |\phi^j| = \frac{1}{1-\phi} < \infty$, this solution is well-defined according to Theorem 6.4 and has the following properties:

$$\mathbb{E}X_t = \sum_{j=0}^{\infty} \phi^j \mathbb{E}Z_{t-j} = 0,$$

$$\gamma_X(h) = \operatorname{cov}(X_{t+h}, X_t) = \lim_{k\to\infty} \mathbb{E}\left(\sum_{j=0}^{k} \phi^j Z_{t+h-j}\right)\left(\sum_{j=0}^{k} \phi^j Z_{t-j}\right)$$

$$= \sigma^2 \phi^{|h|} \sum_{j=0}^{\infty} \phi^{2j} = \frac{\phi^{|h|}}{1-\phi^2}\sigma^2, \qquad h \in \mathbb{Z},$$

$$\rho_X(h) = \phi^{|h|}.$$

Hence, the solution $X_t = \sum_{j=0}^{\infty} \phi^j Z_{t-j}$ is stationary and fulfills the difference equation, as can be easily verified. It is also the only stationary solution compatible with the difference equation. Assume that there is a second solution $\{\widetilde{X}_t\}$ with these properties. Inserting into the difference equation yields again

$$\mathbb{V}\left(\widetilde{X}_t - \sum_{j=0}^{k} \phi^j Z_{t-j}\right) = \phi^{2k+2}\mathbb{V}\widetilde{X}_{t-k-1}.$$

This variance converges to zero for k going to infinity because $|\phi| < 1$ and because $\{\widetilde{X}_t\}$ is stationary. The two processes $\{\widetilde{X}_t\}$ and $\{X_t\}$ with $X_t = \sum_{j=0}^{\infty} \phi^j Z_{t-j}$ are therefore identical in the mean square sense and thus with probability one. Figure 2.2 shows a realization of an AR(1) process with $|\phi| < 1$ and its theoretical and estimated autocorrelation function.

In the case $|\phi| > 1$, the solution (2.2) does not converge. It is, however, possible to iterate the difference equation forward in time to obtain

$$X_t = \phi^{-1}X_{t+1} - \phi^{-1}Z_{t+1}$$
$$= \phi^{-k-1}X_{t+k+1} - \phi^{-1}Z_{t+1} - \phi^{-2}Z_{t+2} - \ldots - \phi^{-k-1}Z_{t+k+1}.$$

This suggests to take

$$X_t = -\sum_{j=1}^{\infty} \phi^{-j} Z_{t+j}$$

as the solution. Similar arguments as before show that this is indeed the only stationary solution. This solution is, however, viewed to be inadequate because X_t

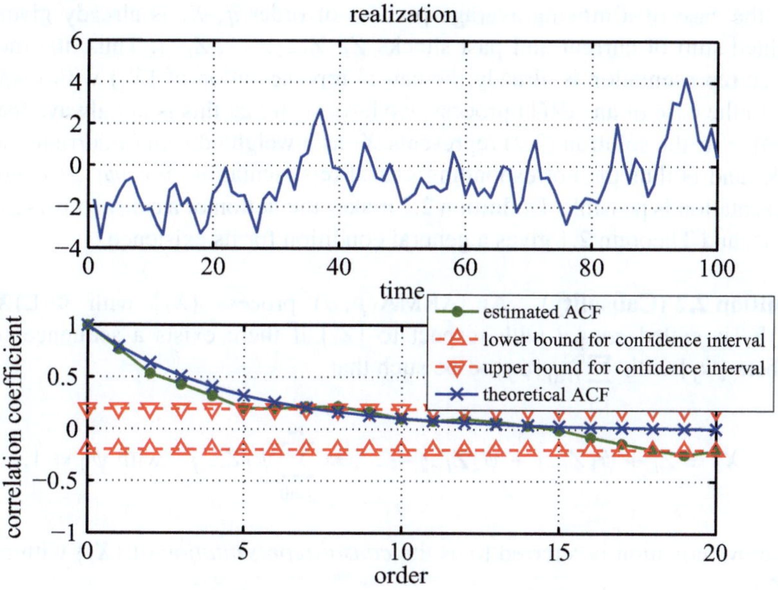

Fig. 2.2 Realization and theoretical and estimated ACF of the AR(1) process: $X_t = 0.8X_{t-1} + Z_t$ with $Z_t \sim \text{IID N}(0, 1)$

depends on future shocks Z_{t+j}, $j = 1, 2, \ldots$ Note, however, that there exists an AR(1) process with $|\phi| < 1$, which is observationally equivalent, in the sense that it generates the same autocorrelation function, but with a new shock or forcing process $\{\widetilde{Z}_t\}$ (see Sect. 2.3).

In the case $|\phi| = 1$, there exists no stationary solution (see Sect. 1.4.4). Processes with this property are called random walks, unit root processes, or integrated processes. They play an important role in economics and are treated separately in Chap. 7.

2.3 Causality and Invertibility

If we interpret $\{X_t\}$ as the state or output variable and $\{Z_t\}$ as the input variable, impulse, or shock, we can ask whether it is possible to represent today's state X_t as the outcome of current and past shocks $Z_t, Z_{t-1}, Z_{t-2}, \ldots$. In this case, we can view X_t as being *caused* by past shocks and call this a *causal representation*. Thus, current shocks Z_t will not only influence current X_t but will also propagate over time and affect also future X_t's. This notion of causality rests on the assumption that the past can cause the future but that the future cannot cause the past. See Sect. 14.5 for an elaboration of the concept of causality and its generalization to the multivariate context.

In the case of a moving-average process of order q, X_t is already given as a weighted sum of current and past shocks $Z_t, Z_{t-1}, \ldots, Z_{t-q}$. Thus, the moving-average representation is already the causal representation of $\{X_t\}$ with respect to $\{Z_t\}$. In the case of an AR(1) process, we have seen that this is not always feasible. For $|\phi| < 1$, the solution (2.2) represents X_t as a weighted sum of current and past shocks and is thus the corresponding causal representation. For $|\phi| > 1$, no such representation is possible. Definition 2.2 makes the notion of a causal representation precise, and Theorem 2.1 gives a general condition for its existence.

Definition 2.2 (Causality) An ARMA(p, q) process $\{X_t\}$ with $\Phi(\mathrm{L})X_t = \Theta(\mathrm{L})Z_t$ is called *causal* with respect to $\{Z_t\}$ if there exists a sequence of real numbers $\{\psi_j\}$ with $\sum_{j=0}^{\infty} |\psi_j| < \infty$ such that

$$X_t = Z_t + \psi_1 Z_{t-1} + \psi_2 Z_{t-2} + \ldots = \sum_{j=0}^{\infty} \psi_j Z_{t-j} \quad \text{with } \psi_0 = 1.$$

The above equation is referred to as the *causal representation* of $\{X_t\}$ with respect to $\{Z_t\}$.

Hence, if $Z_t \sim \mathrm{WN}(0, \sigma^2)$, the existence of a causal representation implies that the process is stationary. This even holds when $\{Z_t\}$ is stationary (see Sect. 6.4).

The coefficients $\{\psi_j\}$ are of great importance because they determine how an impulse or a shock in period t propagates to affect current and future X_{t+j}, $j = 0, 1, 2 \ldots$. In particular, consider an impulse e_{t_0} at time t_0, i.e., a time series that is equal to zero except for the time t_0 where it takes on the value e_{t_0}. If $e_{t_0} = 1$, it is called a unit impulse. Alternatively, e_{t_0} is sometimes taken to be equal to σ, the standard deviation of Z_t. Then, $\{\psi_{t-t_0} e_{t_0}\}$ traces out the time history of this impulse for $t = t_0 + j$, $j = 0, 1, 2, \ldots$. Seen as a function of $j \in \mathbb{Z}^+$, the coefficients ψ_j are called the *impulse response function*. It is customary to plot the impulse response function $\{psi_j\}$ against j, $j = 0, 1, 2, \ldots$.

Note that the notion of causality is not an attribute of $\{X_t\}$ alone, but is defined in relation to another process $\{Z_t\}$. It is therefore possible that a stationary process is causal with respect to one process, but not with respect to another process. In order to make this point more concrete, consider again the AR(1) process defined by the equation $X_t = \phi X_{t-1} + Z_t$ with $|\phi| > 1$. As we have seen, the unique stationary solution is given by $X_t = -\sum_{j=1}^{\infty} \phi^{-j} Z_{t+j}$, which is clearly not causal with respect to $\{Z_t\}$. Consider now the process

$$\tilde{Z}_t = X_t - \frac{1}{\phi} X_{t-1} = \phi^{-2} Z_t + (\phi^{-2} - 1) \sum_{j=1}^{\infty} \phi^{-j} Z_{t+j}.$$

This new process is white noise with variance $\tilde{\sigma}^2 = (1 - \phi^{-2} + \phi^{-4})\sigma^2$.[2] It is straightforward to verify that $\{X_t\}$ fulfills the difference equation:

$$X_t = \frac{1}{\phi} X_{t-1} + \tilde{Z}_t.$$

Because $\frac{1}{|\phi|} < 1$, $\{X_t\}$ is causal with respect to $\{\tilde{Z}_t\}$. This remark shows that there is no loss of generality involved if we concentrate on causal ARMA processes.

Theorem 2.1 (Causality of ARMA process) *Let $\{X_t\}$ be an ARMA(p, q) process with $\Phi(\mathrm{L})X_t = \Theta(\mathrm{L})Z_t$, and assume that the polynomials $\Phi(z)$ and $\Theta(z)$ have no common roots. $\{X_t\}$ is causal with respect to $\{Z_t\}$ if and only if $\Phi(z) \neq 0$ for $|z| \leq 1$, i.e., all roots of the equation $\Phi(z) = 0$ are outside the unit circle. The coefficients $\{\psi_j\}$ are then uniquely determined by*

$$\Psi(z) = \sum_{j=0}^{\infty} \psi_j z^j = \frac{\Theta(z)}{\Phi(z)}.$$

Proof Given that $\Phi(z)$ is a finite-order polynomial with $\Phi(z) \neq 0$ for $|z| \leq 1$, there exits an $\epsilon > 0$ such that $\Phi(z) \neq 0$ for $|z| \leq 1 + \epsilon$. This implies that $1/\Phi(z)$ is an analytic function on the disc with radius $1 + \epsilon$ and therefore possesses a power series expansion:

$$\frac{1}{\Phi(z)} = \sum_{j=0}^{\infty} \xi_j z^j = \Xi(z), \qquad \text{for } |z| < 1 + \epsilon.$$

This implies that $\xi_j (1 + \epsilon/2)^j$ converges to zero for j to infinity. Thus, there exists a positive and finite constant C such that

$$|\xi_j| < C(1 + \epsilon/2)^{-j}, \qquad \text{for all } j = 0, 1, 2, \ldots$$

This in turn implies that $\sum_{j=0}^{\infty} |\xi_j| < \infty$ and that $\Xi(z)\Phi(z) = 1$ for $|z| \leq 1$. Applying $\Xi(\mathrm{L})$ on both sides of $\Phi(\mathrm{L})X_t = \Theta(\mathrm{L})Z_t$ gives

$$X_t = \Xi(\mathrm{L})\Phi(\mathrm{L})X_t = \Xi(\mathrm{L})\Theta(\mathrm{L})Z_t.$$

Theorem 6.4 implies that the right-hand side is well-defined. Thus, $\Psi(\mathrm{L}) = \Xi(\mathrm{L})\Theta(\mathrm{L})$ is the sought polynomial. Its coefficients are determined by the relation $\Psi(z) = \Theta(z)/\Phi(z)$.

[2] The reader is invited to verify this in Exercise 2.5.5.

Assume that there exists a causal representation $X_t = \sum_{j=0}^{\infty} \psi_j Z_{t-j}$ with $\sum_{j=0}^{\infty} |\psi_j| < \infty$. Therefore,

$$\Theta(\mathrm{L})Z_t = \Phi(\mathrm{L})X_t = \Phi(\mathrm{L})\Psi(\mathrm{L})Z_t.$$

Define $\eta(z) = \Phi(z)\Psi(z) = \sum_{j=0}^{\infty} \eta_j z^j$, $|z| \leq 1$. Multiplying the above equation by Z_{t-k} and taking expectations shows that $\eta_k = \theta_k$, $k = 0, 1, 2, \ldots, q$, and that $\eta_k = 0$ for $k > q$. Hence, $\Theta(z) = \eta(z) = \Phi(z)\Psi(z)$ for $|z| \leq 1$. As $\Theta(z)$ and $\Phi(z)$ have no common roots and because $|\Psi(z)| < \infty$ for $|z| \leq 1$, $\Phi(z)$ cannot be equal to zero for $|z| \leq 1$. □

Remark 2.1 If the AR and the MA polynomial have common roots, there are two possibilities:

- No common root lies on the unit circle. In this situation, there may exist a unique stationary solution that can be obtained by canceling the common factors of the polynomials.
- If at least one common root lies on the unit circle, then more than one stationary solution may exist (see the last example below).

Some Examples
We illustrate the above theorem and remark by analyzing some exemplary ARMA processes $\Phi(\mathrm{L})X_t = \Theta(\mathrm{L})Z_t$ with $Z_t \sim \mathrm{WN}(0, \sigma^2)$.

$\Phi(\mathrm{L}) = 1 - 0.05\mathrm{L} - 0.6\mathrm{L}^2$ **and** $\Theta(\mathrm{L}) = 1$: The roots of the polynomial $\Phi(z)$ are $z_1 = -4/3$ and $z_2 = 5/4$. Because both roots are absolutely larger than one, there exists a causal representation with respect to $\{Z_t\}$.

$\Phi(\mathrm{L}) = 1 + 2\mathrm{L} + 5/4\mathrm{L}^2$ **and** $\Theta(\mathrm{L}) = 1$: The roots are conjugate complex and equal to $z_1 = -4/5 + 2/5\imath$ and $z_2 = -4/5 - 2/5\imath$. The modulus or absolute value of z_1 and z_2 equals $|z_1| = |z_2| = \sqrt{20/25}$. This number is smaller than one. Therefore, a stationary solution exists, but this solution is not causal with respect to $\{Z_t\}$.

$\Phi(\mathrm{L}) = 1 - 0.05\mathrm{L} - 0.6\mathrm{L}^2$ **and** $\Theta(\mathrm{L}) = 1 + 0.75\mathrm{L}$: $\Phi(z)$ and $\Theta(z)$ have the common root $z = -4/3 \neq 1$. Thus, one can cancel both $\Phi(\mathrm{L})$ and $\Theta(\mathrm{L})$ by $1 + \frac{3}{4}\mathrm{L}$ to obtain the polynomials $\tilde{\Phi}(\mathrm{L}) = 1 - 0.8\mathrm{L}$ and $\tilde{\Theta}(\mathrm{L}) = 1$. Because the root of $\tilde{\Phi}(z)$ equals 5/4, which is greater than one, there exists a unique stationary and causal representation with respect to $\{Z_t\}$.

$\Phi(\mathrm{L}) = 1 + 1.2\mathrm{L} - 1.6\mathrm{L}^2$ **and** $\Theta(\mathrm{L}) = 1 + 2\mathrm{L}$: The roots of $\Phi(z)$ are $z_1 = 5/4$ and $z_2 = -0.5$. Thus, one root is outside the unit circle, whereas one is inside. This would suggest that there is no causal solution. However, the root $-0.5 \neq 1$ is shared by $\Phi(z)$ and $\Theta(z)$ and can therefore be canceled to obtain $\tilde{\Phi}(\mathrm{L}) = 1 - 0.8\mathrm{L}$ and $\tilde{\Theta}(\mathrm{L}) = 1$. Because the root of $\tilde{\Phi}(z)$ equals $5/4 > 1$, there exists a unique stationary and causal solution with respect to $\{Z_t\}$.

$\Phi(L) = 1 + L$ and $\Theta(L) = 1 + L$: $\Phi(z)$ and $\Theta(z)$ have the common root -1, which lies on the unit circle. Based on the argument in the previous example, one is tempted to cancel both polynomials by $1+L$ to obtain the trivial stationary and causal solution $\{X_t\} = \{Z_t\}$. This is, however, not the only stationary solution. Additional solutions are given by $\{Y_t\} = \{Z_t + A(-1)^t\}$ where A is an arbitrary random variable with expected value zero and finite variance σ_A^2, independent of both $\{X_t\}$ and $\{Z_t\}$. The process $\{Y_t\}$ has an expected value zero and an autocovariance function $\gamma_Y(h)$, which is equal to

$$\gamma_Y(h) = \begin{cases} \sigma^2 + \sigma_A^2, & h = 0; \\ (-1)^h \sigma_A^2, & h = \pm 1, \pm 2, \ldots \end{cases}$$

Thus, this new process is therefore stationary and fulfills the difference equation.

Remark 2.2 If the AR and the MA polynomial in the stochastic difference equation $\Phi(L)X_t = \Theta(L)Z_t$ have no common roots, but $\Phi(z) = 0$ for some z on the unit circle, there exists no stationary solution. Models with this property are said to have a unit root and are treated in Chap. 7.

As stated in the previous theorem, the coefficients $\{\psi_j\}$ of the causal representation are uniquely determined by the relation $\Psi(z)\Phi(z) = \Theta(z)$. If $\{X_t\}$ is a MA process, $\Phi(z) = 1$ and the coefficients $\{\psi_j\}$ just correspond to the coefficients of the MA polynomial, i.e., $\psi_j = \theta_j$ for $0 \le j \le q$ and $\psi_j = 0$ for $j > q$. Hence, no additional computations are necessary. In the general case, there are two ways to find the coefficients $\{\psi_j\}$. The first one uses polynomial division or partial fractions, and the second one uses the method of undetermined coefficients. This book relies on the second method because it is more intuitive and provides some additional insights. For this purpose, write out the defining relation $\Psi(z)\Phi(z) = \Theta(z)$:

$$\left(\psi_0 + \psi_1 z + \psi_2 z^2 + \ldots\right)\left(1 - \phi_1 z - \phi_2 z^2 - \cdots - \phi_p z^p\right)$$
$$= 1 + \theta_1 z + \theta_2 z^2 + \cdots + \theta_q z^q$$

Multiplying out the left-hand side one leads to

$$\begin{aligned} &\psi_0 - \psi_0\phi_1 z - \psi_0\phi_2 z^2 - \psi_0\phi_3 z^3 - \cdots - \psi_0\phi_p z^p \\ &\qquad \psi_1 z - \psi_1\phi_1 z^2 - \psi_1\phi_2 z^3 - \cdots - \psi_1\phi_p z^{p+1} \\ &\qquad\qquad + \psi_2 \; z^2 - \psi_2\phi_1 z^3 - \cdots - \psi_2\phi_p z^{p+2} \\ &\qquad\qquad \ldots \\ &= 1 + \theta_1 z + \theta_2 z^2 + \theta_3 z^3 + \cdots + \theta_q z^q. \end{aligned}$$

Equating the coefficients of the powers of z, z^j, $j = 0, 1, 2, \ldots$, one obtains

$$\begin{aligned} z^0 : \quad & \psi_0 = 1, \\ z^1 : \quad & \psi_1 = \theta_1 + \phi_1 \psi_0 = \theta_1 + \phi_1, \\ z^2 : \quad & \psi_2 = \theta_2 + \phi_2 \psi_0 + \phi_1 \psi_1 = \theta_2 + \phi_2 + \phi_1 \theta_1 + \phi_1^2, \\ & \ldots \end{aligned}$$

This shows that the unknown coefficients $\{\psi_j\}$ can be computed recursively. This is convenient when it comes to numerical computations, but in some cases, one wants an analytical solution. Such a solution can be obtained by observing that, for $j \geq \max\{p, q+1\}$, the recursion leads to a constant coefficient linear homogeneous difference equation of order p:

$$\psi_j = \sum_{k=1}^{p} \phi_k \psi_{j-k} = \phi_1 \psi_{j-1} + \phi_2 \psi_{j-2} + \ldots + \phi_p \psi_{j-p}, \quad j \geq \max\{p, q+1\}.$$

The solution of such an equation is of the following form (see Eq. (B.1) in Appendix B):

$$\psi_j = c_1 z_1^{-j} + \ldots + c_p z_p^{-j}, \qquad j \geq \max\{p, q+1\} - p, \tag{2.3}$$

where $z_1, \ldots, z_p$ denote the roots of $\Phi(z) = 1 - \phi_1 z - \ldots - \phi_p z^p = 0$.[3] Note that the roots are exactly those that have been computed to assess the existence of a causal representation. The coefficients $c_1, \ldots, c_p$ can be obtained using the p boundary conditions obtained from $\psi_j = \sum_{0<k\leq j} \phi_k \psi_{j-k} = \theta_j$, $\max\{p, q+1\} - p \leq j < \max\{p, q+1\}$. Finally, the values for ψ_j, $0 \leq j < \max\{p, q+1\} - p$, must be computed from the first $\max\{p, q+1\} - p$ iterations (see the example in Sect. 2.4).

As mentioned previously, the coefficients $\{\psi_j\}$ are of great importance as they quantify the effect of a shock to Z_{t-j} on X_t, respectively of Z_t on X_{t+j}. In macroeconomics, they are sometimes called *dynamic multipliers* of a transitory or temporary shock. Assuming that the underlying ARMA process is stationary and causal with respect to $\{Z_t\}$, the infinite sum $\sum_{j=0}^{\infty} |\psi_j|$ converges. This implies that the effect ψ_j converges to zero as $j \to \infty$. Thus, the effect of a shock dies out eventually:[4]

---

[3] In the case of multiple roots, one has to modify the formula according to Eq. (B.2).

[4] The use of the partial derivative sign actually represents an abuse of notation. It is inspired by an alternative definition of the impulse responses: $\psi_j = \frac{\partial \tilde{\mathbb{P}}_t X_{t+j}}{\partial x_t}$ where $\tilde{\mathbb{P}}_t$ denotes the optimal (in the mean squared error sense) linear predictor of X_{t+j} given a realization back to infinite remote past $\{x_t, x_{t-1}, x_{t-2}, \ldots\}$ (see Sect. 3.1.3). Thus, ψ_j represents the sensitivity of the forecast of X_{t+j} with respect to the observation x_t. The equivalence of alternative definitions in the linear and especially nonlinear context is discussed in Potter (2000).

$$\frac{\partial X_{t+j}}{\partial Z_t} = \psi_j \to 0 \text{ for } j \to \infty.$$

As can be seen from Eq. (2.3), the coefficients $\{\psi_j\}$ even converge to zero exponentially fast because each term $c_i z_i^{-j}$, $i = 1, \ldots, p$, converges to zero exponentially fast as the roots z_i are greater than one in absolute value.

The effect of a *permanent shock* in period t on X_{t+j} is defined as the cumulative effect of a transitory shock. Thus, the effect of a permanent shock to X_{t+j} is given by $\sum_{i=0}^{j} \psi_i$. Because $\sum_{i=0}^{j} \psi_i \leq \sum_{i=0}^{j} |\psi_i| \leq \sum_{i=0}^{\infty} |\psi_i| < \infty$, the cumulative effect remains finite under the assumption of stationarity and causality with respect to $\{Z_t\}$.

In time series analysis, we view the observations as realizations of $\{X_t\}$ and treat the realizations of $\{Z_t\}$ as unobserved. It is therefore of interest to know whether it is possible to recover the unobserved shocks from the observations on $\{X_t\}$. This idea leads to the concept of invertibility.

Definition 2.3 (Invertibility) An ARMA(p,q) process $\{X_t\}$ with $\Phi(\mathrm{L})X_t = \Theta(\mathrm{L})Z_t$ is called *invertible* with respect to $\{Z_t\}$ if and only if there exists a sequence $\{\pi_j\}$ with the property $\sum_{j=0}^{\infty} |\pi_j| < \infty$ such that

$$Z_t = \sum_{j=0}^{\infty} \pi_j X_{t-j}, \qquad \text{with } \pi_0 = 1.$$

Note that like causality, invertibility is not an attribute of $\{X_t\}$, but is defined only relative to another process $\{Z_t\}$. In the literature, one often refers to invertibility as the strict miniphase property.[5]

Theorem 2.2 (Invertibility of ARMA process) *Let $\{X_t\}$ be an ARMA(p,q) process with $\Phi(\mathrm{L})X_t = \Theta(\mathrm{L})Z_t$ such that the polynomials $\Phi(z)$ and $\Theta(z)$ have no roots in common. Then, $\{X_t\}$ is invertible with respect to $\{Z_t\}$ if and only if $\Theta(z) \neq 0$ for $|z| \leq 1$. The coefficients $\{\pi_j\}$ are then uniquely determined by the following relation:*

$$\Pi(z) = \sum_{j=0}^{\infty} \pi_j z^j = \frac{\Phi(z)}{\Theta(z)}.$$

Proof The proof is analogous to the proof of Theorem 2.1 with X_t and Z_t interchanged. □

[5] Without the qualification strict, the miniphase property allows for roots of $\Theta(z)$ on the unit circle. The terminology is, however, not uniform in the literature.

The discussion in Sect. 1.3 revealed that there are in general two MA(1) processes compatible with the same autocorrelation function $\rho(h)$ given by $\rho(0) = 1$, $\rho(1) = \rho$ with $|\rho| \leq \frac{1}{2}$, and $\rho(h) = 0$ for $h \geq 2$. However, only one of these solutions is invertible because the two solutions for θ are inverses of each other. As it is important to be able to recover Z_t from current and past X_t, one prefers the invertible solution. Wold's theorem in Sect. 3.2 further elucidates this issue.

Remark 2.3 If $\{X_t\}$ is a stationary solution to the stochastic difference equation $\Phi(\mathrm{L})X_t = \Theta(\mathrm{L})Z_t$ with $Z_t \sim \mathrm{WN}(0, \sigma^2)$ and if in addition $\Phi(z)\Theta(z) \neq 0$ for $|z| \leq 1$, then

$$X_t = \sum_{j=0}^{\infty} \psi_j Z_{t-j},$$

$$Z_t = \sum_{j=0}^{\infty} \pi_j X_{t-j},$$

where the coefficients $\{\psi_j\}$ and $\{\pi_j\}$ are determined for $|z| \leq 1$ by $\Psi(z) = \dfrac{\Theta(z)}{\Phi(z)}$ and $\Pi(z) = \dfrac{\Phi(z)}{\Theta(z)}$, respectively. In this case, $\{X_t\}$ is causal and invertible with respect to $\{Z_t\}$.

Remark 2.4 If $\{X_t\}$ is an ARMA process with $\Phi(\mathrm{L})X_t = \Theta(\mathrm{L})Z_t$ such that $\Phi(z) \neq 0$ for $|z| = 1$, then there exists polynomials $\tilde{\Phi}(z)$ and $\tilde{\Theta}(z)$ and a white noise process $\{\tilde{Z}_t\}$ such that $\{X_t\}$ fulfills the stochastic difference equation $\tilde{\Phi}(\mathrm{L})X_t = \tilde{\Theta}(\mathrm{L})\tilde{Z}_t$ and is causal with respect to $\{\tilde{Z}_t\}$. If in addition $\Theta(z) \neq 0$ for $|z| = 1$, then $\tilde{\Theta}(\mathrm{L})$ can be chosen such that $\{X_t\}$ is also invertible with respect to $\{\tilde{Z}_t\}$ (see the discussion of the AR(1) process after the definition of causality and Brockwell and Davis (1991, p. 88)).

2.4 Computation of the Autocovariance Function of Stationary ARMA Processes

Whereas the autocovariance function summarizes the external and directly observable properties of a time series, the coefficients of the ARMA process give information of its internal structure. Although there exists for each stationary ARMA process a corresponding autocovariance function, the converse is not true as we have seen in Sect. 1.3 where we showed that two MA(1) processes are compatible with the same autocovariance function. This brings up a fundamental identification problem. In order to shed some light on the relation between autocovariance function and ARMA models, it is necessary to be able to compute the autocovariance function for a given ARMA process. In the following, we will discuss two such procedures. Each procedure relies on the assumption that the ARMA process $\Phi(\mathrm{L})X_t = \Theta(\mathrm{L})Z_t$ with $Z_t \sim \mathrm{WN}(0, \sigma^2)$ is stationary and causal with respect to $\{Z_t\}$. Hence, there exists a representation of X_t as a weighted sum of current and past Z_t's: $X_t = \sum_{j=0}^{\infty} \psi_j Z_{t-j}$ with $\sum_{j=0}^{\infty} |\psi_j| < \infty$.

2.4.1 First Procedure

Starting from the causal representation of $\{X_t\}$, it is easy to calculate its autocovariance function given that $\{Z_t\}$ is white noise. The exact formula is proved in Theorem (6.5):

$$\gamma(h) = \sigma^2 \sum_{j=0}^{\infty} \psi_j \psi_{j+|h|},$$

where

$$\Psi(z) = \sum_{j=0}^{\infty} \psi_j z^j = \frac{\Theta(z)}{\Phi(z)} \qquad \text{for } |z| \leq 1.$$

The first step consists in determining the coefficients ψ_j by the method of undetermined coefficients. This leads to the following system of equations:

$$\psi_j - \sum_{0<k\leq j} \phi_k \psi_{j-k} = \theta_j, \qquad 0 \leq j < \max\{p, q+1\},$$

$$\psi_j - \sum_{0<k\leq p} \phi_k \psi_{j-k} = 0, \qquad j \geq \max\{p, q+1\}.$$

This equation system can be solved recursively (see Sect. 2.3):

$$\begin{aligned}
\psi_0 &= \theta_0 = 1, \\
\psi_1 &= \theta_1 + \psi_0 \phi_1 = \theta_1 + \phi_1, \\
\psi_2 &= \theta_2 + \psi_0 \phi_2 + \psi_1 \phi_1 = \theta_2 + \phi_2 + \phi_1 \theta_1 + \phi_1^2, \\
&\ldots
\end{aligned}$$

Alternatively, one may view the second part of the equation system as a linear homogeneous difference equation with constant coefficients (see Sect. 2.3). Its solution is given by Eq. (2.3). The first part of the equation system delivers the necessary initial conditions to determine the coefficients $c_1, c_2, \ldots, c_p$. Finally, one can insert the ψ's in the above formula for the autocovariance function.

A Numerical Example

Consider the ARMA(2,1) process with $\Phi(\mathrm{L}) = 1 - 1.3\mathrm{L} + 0.4\mathrm{L}^2$ and $\Theta(\mathrm{L}) = 1 + 0.4\mathrm{L}$. Writing out the defining equation for $\Psi(z)$, $\Psi(z)\Phi(z) = \Theta(z)$, gives

$$\begin{aligned} 1 + \psi_1 z + \psi_2 z^2 + \psi_3 z^3 + \ldots \\ - 1.3z - 1.3\psi_1 z^2 - 1.3\psi_2 z^3 - \ldots \\ + 0.4z^2 + 0.4\psi_1 z^3 + \ldots \\ \ldots \qquad = 1 + 0.4z. \end{aligned}$$

Equating the coefficients of the powers of z leads to the following equation system:

$$\begin{aligned} z^0 &: \quad \psi_0 = 1, \\ z &: \quad \psi_1 - 1.3 = 0.4, \\ z^2 &: \quad \psi_2 - 1.3\psi_1 + 0.4 = 0, \\ z^3 &: \quad \psi_3 - 1.3\psi_2 + 0.4\psi_1 = 0, \\ &\quad \ldots \\ &\quad \psi_j - 1.3\psi_{j-1} + 0.4\psi_{j-2} = 0, \quad \text{for } j \geq 2. \end{aligned}$$

The last equation represents a linear difference equation of order two. Its solution is given by

$$\psi_j = c_1 z_1^{-j} + c_2 z_2^{-j}, \qquad j \geq \max\{p, q+1\} - p = 0,$$

whereby z_1 and z_2 are the two distinct roots of the characteristic polynomial $\Phi(z) = 1 - 1.3z + 0.4z^2 = 0$ (see Eq. (2.3)) and where the coefficients c_1 and c_2 are determined from the initial conditions. The two roots are $\frac{1.3 \pm \sqrt{1.69 - 4 \times 0.4}}{2 \times 0.4} = 5/4 = 1.25$ and 2. The general solution to the homogeneous equation therefore is $\psi_j = c_1 0.8^j + c_2 0.5^j$. The constants c_1 and c_2 are determined by the equations:

$$\begin{aligned} j = 0: &\quad \psi_0 = 1 \quad = c_1 0.8^0 + c_2 0.5^0 = c_1 + c_2 \\ j = 1: &\quad \psi_1 = 1.7 = c_1 0.8^1 + c_2 0.5^1 = 0.8c_1 + 0.5c_2. \end{aligned}$$

Solving this equation system in the two unknowns c_1 and c_2 gives $c_1 = 4$ and $c_2 = -3$. Thus, the solution to the difference equation is given by

$$\psi_j = 4(0.8)^j - 3(0.5)^j.$$

Inserting this solution for ψ_j into the above formula for $\gamma(h)$ and using the formula for the geometric sum leads to

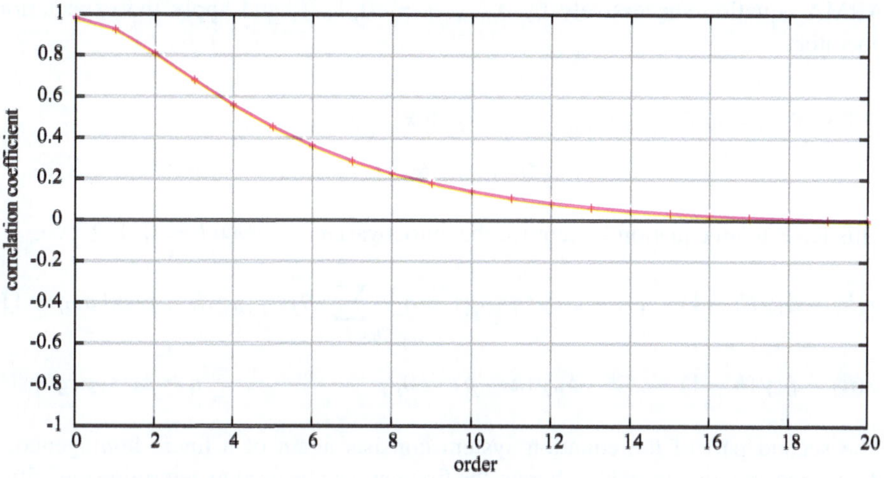

Fig. 2.3 Autocorrelation function of the ARMA(2,1) process: $(1 - 1.3\mathrm{L} + 0.4\mathrm{L}^2)X_t = (1 + 0.4\mathrm{L})Z_t$

$$\begin{aligned}
\gamma(h) &= \sigma^2 \sum_{j=0}^{\infty} \left(4 \times 0.8^j - 3 \times 0.5^j\right)\left(4 \times 0.8^{j+h} - 3 \times 0.5^{j+h}\right) \\
&= \sigma^2 \sum_{j=0}^{\infty} (16 \times 0.8^{2j+h} - 12 \times 0.5^j \times 0.8^{j+h} \\
&\qquad - 12 \times 0.8^j \times 0.5^{j+h} + 9 \times 0.5^{2j+h}) \\
&= 16\sigma^2 \frac{0.8^h}{1 - 0.64} - 12\sigma^2 \frac{0.8^h}{1 - 0.4} - 12\sigma^2 \frac{0.5^h}{1 - 0.4} + 9\sigma^2 \frac{0.5^h}{1 - 0.25} \\
&= \frac{220}{9}\sigma^2 (0.8)^h - 8\sigma^2 (0.5)^h.
\end{aligned}$$

Dividing $\gamma(h)$ by $\gamma(0)$ leads to the corresponding autocorrelation function displayed in Fig. 2.3:

$$\rho(h) = \frac{\gamma(h)}{\gamma(0)} = \frac{55}{37} \times 0.8^j - \frac{18}{37} \times 0.5^j.$$

2.4.2 Second Procedure

Instead of determining the ψ_j coefficients first, it is possible to compute the autocovariance function directly from the ARMA model. To see this, multiply the

ARMA equation successively by $X_{t-h}, h = 0, 1, \ldots$ and apply the expectation operator:

$$\begin{aligned}\mathbb{E}X_t X_{t-h} - \phi_1 \mathbb{E}X_{t-1}X_{t-h} - \cdots - \phi_p \mathbb{E}X_{t-p}X_{t-h} \\ = \mathbb{E}Z_t X_{t-h} + \theta_1 \mathbb{E}Z_{t-1}X_{t-h} + \cdots + \theta_q \mathbb{E}Z_{t-q}X_{t-h}.\end{aligned}$$

This leads to an equation system for the autocovariances $\gamma(h), h = 0, 1, 2, \ldots$:

$$\gamma(h) - \phi_1\gamma(h-1) - \ldots - \phi_p\gamma(h-p) = \sigma^2 \sum_{h \le j \le q} \theta_j \psi_{j-h}, \quad h < \max\{p, q+1\},$$

$$\gamma(h) - \phi_1\gamma(h-1) - \ldots - \phi_p\gamma(h-p) = 0, \qquad h \ge \max\{p, q+1\}.$$

The second part of the equation system consists again of a linear homogeneous difference equation in $\gamma(h)$, whereas the first part can be used to determine the initial conditions. Note that the initial conditions depend on $\psi_1, \ldots, \psi_q$, which have to be determined beforehand. The general solution of the difference equation is

$$\gamma(h) = c_1 z_1^{-h} + \ldots + c_p z_p^{-h} \tag{2.4}$$

where $z_1, \ldots, z_p$ are the distinct roots of the polynomial $\Phi(z) = 1 - \phi_1 z - \ldots - \phi_p z^p = 0$.[6] The constants $c_1, \ldots, c_p$ can be computed from the first p initial conditions after the $\psi_1, \ldots \psi_q$ have been calculated like in the first procedure. The form of the solution shows that the autocovariance and hence the autocorrelation function converge to zero exponentially fast.

A Numerical Example

We consider the same example as before. The second part of the above equation system delivers a difference equation for $\gamma(h)$: $\gamma(h) = \phi_1\gamma(h-1) + \phi_2\gamma(h-2) = 1.3\gamma(h-1) - 0.4\gamma(h-2), h \ge 2$. The general solution of this difference equation is (see Appendix B)

$$\gamma(h) = c_1(0.8)^h + c_2(0.5)^h, \qquad h \ge 2$$

where 0.8 and 0.5 are the inverses of the roots computed from the same polynomial $\Phi(z) = 1 - 1.3z - 0.4z^2 = 0$.

The first part of the system delivers the initial conditions that determine the constants c_1 and c_2:

$$\begin{aligned}\gamma(0) - 1.3\gamma(-1) + 0.4\gamma(-2) &= \sigma^2(1 + 0.4 \times 1.7) \\ \gamma(1) - 1.3\gamma(0) + 0.4\gamma(-1) &= \sigma^2 0.4\end{aligned}$$

[6] In case of multiple roots, the formula has to be adapted accordingly. See Eq. (B.2) in the Appendix.

where the numbers on the right-hand side are taken from the first procedure. Inserting the general solution in this equation system and bearing in mind that $\gamma(h) = \gamma(-h)$ leads to

$$0.216c_1 + 0.450c_2 = 1.68\sigma^2$$

$$-0.180c_1 - 0.600c_2 = 0.40\sigma^2$$

Solving this equation system in the unknowns c_1 and c_2 leads to $c_1 = (220/9)\sigma^2$ and $c_2 = -8\sigma^2$.

2.5 Exercises

Exercise 2.5.1 Consider the AR(1) process $X_t = 0.8X_{t-1} + Z_t$ with $Z_t \sim \text{WN}(0, \sigma^2)$. Compute the variance of $(X_1 + X_2 + X_3 + X_4)/4$.

Exercise 2.5.2 Check whether the following stochastic difference equations possess a stationary solution. If yes, is the solution causal and/or invertible with respect to $Z_t \sim \text{WN}(0, \sigma^2)$?

(i) $X_t = Z_t + 2Z_{t-1}$.
(ii) $X_t = 1.3X_{t-1} + Z_t$.
(iii) $X_t = 1.3X_{t-1} - 0.4X_{t-2} + Z_t$.
(iv) $X_t = 1.3X_{t-1} - 0.4X_{t-2} + Z_t - 0.3Z_{t-1}$.
(v) $X_t = 0.2X_{t-1} + 0.8X_{t-2} + Z_t$.
(vi) $X_t = 0.2X_{t-1} + 0.8X_{t-2} + Z_t - 1.5Z_{t-1} + 0.5Z_{t-2}$.

Exercise 2.5.3 Compute the causal representation of $\{X_t\}$ with respect to $Z_t \sim \text{WN}(0, \sigma^2)$ of the following ARMA processes:

(i) $X_t = 1.3X_{t-1} - 0.4X_{t-2} + Z_t$.
(ii) $X_t = 1.3X_{t-1} - 0.4X_{t-2} + Z_t - 0.2Z_{t-1}$.
(iii) $X_t = \phi X_{t-1} + Z_t + \theta Z_{t-1}$ with $|\phi| < 1$.

Exercise 2.5.4 Compute the autocovariance function of the following ARMA processes:

(i) $X_t = 0.5X_{t-1} + 0.36X_{t-2} + Z_t$.
(ii) $X_t = 0.5X_{t-1} + 0.36X_{t-2} + Z_t + 0.5Z_{t-1}$.

Assume $Z_t \sim \text{WN}(0, \sigma^2)$.

Exercise 2.5.5 Consider the first-order autoregressive process:

$$X_t = \phi X_{t-1} + Z_t, \quad \text{with } |\phi| > 1 \text{ and } Z_t \sim \text{WN}(0, \sigma^2).$$

(i) Compute the stationary solution. Is it causal with respect to $\{Z_t\}$?
(ii) Consider the alternative process $\{\widetilde{Z}_t\}$ defined as the stationary solution of the stochastic difference equation:

$$\widetilde{Z}_t = X_t - \frac{1}{\phi} X_{t-1} = \phi^{-2} Z_t + (\phi^{-2} - 1) \sum_{j=1}^{\infty} \phi^{-j} Z_{t+j}$$

(iii) Show that $\widetilde{Z}_t \sim \text{WN}(0, \widetilde{\sigma}^2)$ with $\widetilde{\sigma}^2 = (1 - \phi^{-2} + \phi^{-4})\sigma^2$.
(iv) Show that $\{X_t\}$ fulfills the stochastic difference equation:

$$X_t = \frac{1}{\phi} X_{t-1} + \widetilde{Z}_t$$

and that $\{X_t\}$ is causal with respect to $\{\widetilde{Z}_t\}$. Compute the causal representation. What is the autocovariance and the autocorrelation function?

Exercise 2.5.6 Show that for every stationary process $\{X_t\}$ satisfying

$$X_t = \sum_{j=-\infty}^{\infty} b_j Z_{t-j}, \qquad Z_t \sim \text{WN}(0, \sigma^2),$$

where $\sum_{j=-\infty}^{\infty} b_j^2 < \infty$, $\lim_{|h| \to \infty} \gamma(h) = 0$.

3 Forecasting Stationary Processes

An important application of time series analysis is forecasting. In the following, we will consider the problem of forecasting X_{T+h} with forecast horizon $h > 0$, given $\{X_T, \ldots, X_1\}$ where $\{X_t\}$ is a stationary stochastic process with known mean μ and known autocovariance function $\gamma(h)$.[1] We further assume that all deterministic components (trend, seasonality, etc.) with the exception of the constant have already been removed so that we can concentrate on the stochastic component. In practical applications, μ and γ are usually unknown and are replaced by their estimates. These estimates can be obtained directly from the data as explained in Sect. 4.2 or indirectly by first estimating an appropriate ARMA model (see Chap. 5) and then inferring the corresponding autocovariance function using one of the methods explained in Sect. 2.4. Thus, the forecasting problem is inherently linked to the problem of identifying an appropriate ARMA model from the data (see Deistler and Neusser 1994).

3.1 Linear Least-Squares Forecasts

We restrict our discussion to linear *forecast functions*, also called *linear predictors*, denoted as $\mathbb{P}_T X_{T+h}$. Given observations from period 1 up to period T, these predictors take the following form:

$$\mathbb{P}_T X_{T+h} \equiv a_0 + a_1 X_T + \ldots + a_T X_1 = a_0 + \sum_{i=1}^{T} a_i X_{T+1-i}$$

[1] The elegant theory presented in this chapter was originally developed by Kolmogorov (1939) and Wiener (1956).

K. Neusser, *Time Series Econometrics*, Springer Texts in Business and Economics,
https://doi.org/10.1007/978-3-031-88838-0_3

with unknown coefficients $a_0, a_1, a_2, \dots, a_T$. In principle, we should index these coefficients by T because they may change with every new observations. See the example of the MA(1) process in Sect. 3.1.2. In order not to overload the notation, we will omit this additional index.

In the Hilbert space of random variables with finite second moments, the optimal forecast in the mean squared error sense is given by the conditional expectation $\mathbb{E}(X_{T+h}|c, X_1, X_2, \dots, X_T)$. However, having practical applications in mind, we restrict ourself to linear predictors for the following reasons:[2]

(i) The determination of the conditional expectation is usually very difficult because all possible forecasting functions must in principle be considered, whereas linear predictors are easy to compute.
(ii) The coefficients of the optimal (in the sense of mean squared errors) linear forecasting function depend only on the first two moments of the time series, i.e., on $\mathbb{E}X_t$ and $\gamma(j)$, $j = 0, 1, \dots, h+T-1$.
(iii) In the case of Gaussian processes, the conditional expectation coincides with the linear predictor.
(iv) The optimal predictor is linear when the process is a causal and invertible ARMA process even when Z_t follows an arbitrary distribution with finite variance (see Rosenblatt 2000, chapter 5).
(v) Practical experience has shown that even nonlinear processes can be predicted accurately by linear predictors.

The coefficients $a_0, \dots, a_T$ of the forecasting function are determined such that the mean squared errors (MSE) are minimized. The use of mean squared errors as a criterion leads to a compact representation of the solution to the forecasting problem. It implies that positive and negative forecast errors are treated symmetrically so that under- and overestimation are viewed as equally bad.[3] Thus, we have to solve the following minimization problem:

$$\begin{aligned} S = S(a_0, \dots, a_T) &= \mathbb{E}(X_{T+h} - \mathbb{P}_T X_{T+h})^2 \\ &= \mathbb{E}(X_{T+h} - a_0 - a_1 X_T - \dots - a_T X_1)^2 \longrightarrow \min_{a_0, a_1, \dots, a_T} \end{aligned}$$

As S is a quadratic function, the coefficients, a_j, $j = 0, 1, \dots, T$, are uniquely determined by the so-called normal equations. These are obtained from the first-order conditions of the minimization problem, i.e., from $\frac{\partial S}{\partial a_j} = 0$, $j = 0, 1, \dots, T$:

[2] Elliott and Timmermann (2008) provide a general overview of forecasting procedures and their evaluations.

[3] In practice, this may not be always the case as some forecasters avoid to report negative predictions.

$$\frac{\partial S}{\partial a_0} = \mathbb{E}\left(X_{T+h} - a_0 - \sum_{i=1}^{T} a_i X_{T+1-i}\right) = 0, \tag{3.1}$$

$$\frac{\partial S}{\partial a_j} = \mathbb{E}\left[\left(X_{T+h} - a_0 - \sum_{i=1}^{T} a_i X_{T+1-i}\right) X_{T+1-j}\right] = 0, \quad j = 1, \ldots, T. \tag{3.2}$$

The first equation can be rewritten as $a_0 = \mu - \sum_{i=1}^{T} a_i \mu$ so that the forecasting function becomes

$$\mathbb{P}_T X_{T+h} = \mu + \sum_{i=1}^{T} a_i \left(X_{T+1-i} - \mu\right).$$

The expectation of the forecast error, $\mathbb{E}\left(X_{T+h} - \mathbb{P}_T X_{T+h}\right)$, is therefore equal to zero. Hence, forecasts are unbiased estimates: there is no systematic upward nor downward bias. Forecasts correspond on average to the "true" value.

Inserting in the second normal equation the expression for $\mathbb{P}_T X_{T+h}$ from above leads to

$$\mathbb{E}\left[\left(X_{T+h} - \mathbb{P}_T X_{T+h}\right) X_{T+1-j}\right] = 0, \qquad j = 1, 2, \ldots, T.$$

The forecast error is therefore uncorrelated with the available information represented by past observations. In this sense, it is not possible to improve the forecasts. Forecast errors $X_{T+h} - \mathbb{P}_T X_{T+h}$ are orthogonal to the information used in the forecast, i.e., to all variables $X_T, X_{T-1}, \ldots, X_1$. Geometrically speaking, the best linear forecast is obtained by finding the point (vector) in the linear subspace spanned by $\{X_T, X_{T-1}, \ldots, X_1\}$, which is closest to X_{T+h}. This point is found by projecting X_{T+h} on this linear subspace.[4] The Hilbert projection theorem implies that the linear predictor is uniquely determined by the normal equations.

We can rewrite the normal Eqs. (3.1) and (3.2) in matrix notation:

$$a_0 = \mu\left(1 - \sum_{i=1}^{T} a_i\right) \tag{3.3}$$

$$\begin{pmatrix} \gamma(0) & \gamma(1) & \ldots & \gamma(T-1) \\ \gamma(1) & \gamma(0) & \ldots & \gamma(T-2) \\ \vdots & \vdots & \ddots & \vdots \\ \gamma(T-1) & \gamma(T-2) & \ldots & \gamma(0) \end{pmatrix} \begin{pmatrix} a_1 \\ a_2 \\ \vdots \\ a_T \end{pmatrix} = \begin{pmatrix} \gamma(h) \\ \gamma(h+1) \\ \vdots \\ \gamma(h+T-1) \end{pmatrix}. \tag{3.4}$$

[4] Note the similarity of the forecast errors with the least-squares residuals of a linear regression.

Denoting by ι, α_T, and $\gamma_T(h)$ the vectors $(1, 1, \ldots, 1)'$, $(a_1, \ldots, a_T)'$, and $(\gamma(h), \ldots, \gamma(h + T - 1))'$ and by $\Gamma_T = [\gamma(i - j)]_{i,j=1,\ldots,T}$ the symmetric $T \times T$ covariance matrix of $(X_1, \ldots, X_T)'$, the normal equations can be written compactly as

$$a_0 = \mu \left(1 - \iota'\alpha_T\right) \tag{3.5}$$

$$\Gamma_T \alpha_T = \gamma_T(h). \tag{3.6}$$

Although the linear predictor is uniquely determined according to the projection theorem, this does not imply that the covariance matrix Γ_T is invertible for every $T > 0$. Assuming, however, that $\gamma(0) > 0$ and $\gamma(T) \to 0$ for $T \to \infty$ ensures that Γ_T is nonsingular for every $T > 0$. Under this assumption, the above equation system has a unique solution in $(a_0, a_1, \ldots, a_T) = (a_0, \alpha_T')$ (Brockwell and Davis 1996, proposition 5.1.1).

Dividing the second equation by $\gamma(0)$ leads to an equation in terms autocorrelations instead of autocovariances:

$$R_T \alpha_T = \rho_T(h), \tag{3.7}$$

where $R_T = \Gamma_T/\gamma(0)$ and $\rho_T(h) = (\rho(h), \ldots, \rho(h + T - 1))'$. The coefficients of the forecasting function α_T are obtained by inverting Γ_T, respectively R_T:

$$\alpha_T = \begin{pmatrix} a_1 \\ \vdots \\ a_T \end{pmatrix} = \Gamma_T^{-1} \gamma_T(h) = R_T^{-1} \rho_T(h).$$

The mean squared error or *variance of the forecast error* for the forecasting horizon h, $v_T(h)$, is given by

$$\begin{aligned} v_T(h) &= \mathbb{E}\left(X_{T+h} - \mathbb{P}_T X_{T+h}\right)^2 \\ &= \gamma(0) - 2\sum_{i=1}^{T} a_i \gamma(h + i - 1) + \sum_{i=1}^{T}\sum_{j=1}^{T} a_i \gamma(i - j) a_j \\ &= \gamma(0) - 2\alpha_T' \gamma_T(h) + \alpha_T' \Gamma_T \alpha_T = \gamma(0) - \alpha_T' \gamma_T(h), \end{aligned}$$

because $\Gamma_T \alpha_T = \gamma_T(h)$. Bracketing out $\gamma(0)$, one can write the mean squared forecast error as

$$v_T(h) = \gamma(0)\left(1 - \alpha_T' \rho_T(h)\right). \tag{3.8}$$

Because the coefficients of the forecast function have to be recomputed with the arrival of each new observation, it is necessary to have a fast and reliable algorithm at hand. These numerical problems have been solved by the development of appropriate computer algorithms, like the Durbin-Levinson algorithm or the innovation algorithm (see Brockwell and Davis 1991, Chapter 5).

3.1.1 Forecasting with an AR(p) Process

Consider first the case of an AR(1) process:

$$X_t = \phi X_{t=1} + Z_t \qquad \text{with } |\phi| < 1 \text{ and } Z_t \sim \mathrm{WN}(0, \sigma^2).$$

The equation system (3.7) becomes

$$\begin{pmatrix} 1 & \phi & \phi^2 & \ldots \phi^{T-1} \\ \phi & 1 & \phi & \ldots \phi^{T-2} \\ \phi^2 & \phi & 1 & \ldots \phi^{T-3} \\ \vdots & \vdots & \vdots & \ddots \quad \vdots \\ \phi^{T-1} & \phi^{T-2} & \phi^{T-3} & \ldots \quad 1 \end{pmatrix} \begin{pmatrix} a_1 \\ a_2 \\ a_3 \\ \vdots \\ a_T \end{pmatrix} = \begin{pmatrix} \phi^h \\ \phi^{h+1} \\ \phi^{h+2} \\ \vdots \\ \phi^{h+T-1} \end{pmatrix}.$$

The guess-and-verify method immediately leads to the solution:

$$\alpha_T = (a_1, a_2, a_3, \ldots, a_T)' = \left(\phi^h, 0, 0, \ldots, 0\right)'.$$

We therefore get the following predictor:

$$\mathbb{P}_T X_{T+h} = \phi^h X_T$$

The forecast therefore just depends on the last observation. All previous observations can be disregarded; they cannot improve the forecast further. To put it otherwise, all the useful information about X_{T+h} in the entire realization previous to X_T, i.e., in $\{X_T, X_{T-1}, \ldots, X_1\}$, is contained in X_T.

The variance of the prediction error is given by

$$v_T(h) = \frac{1 - \phi^{2h}}{1 - \phi^2}\sigma^2.$$

Thus, the variance of the forecast error $v_T(h)$ increases with h. For $h = 1$, the formula simplifies to σ^2 and for $h \to \infty$, $v_T(h) \to \frac{1}{1-\phi^2}\sigma^2$, which is nothing but the unconditional variance $\gamma(0)$.

The general case of an AR(p) process, $p > 1$, can be treated in the same way. The autocovariances follow a p-th order difference equation (see Sect. 2.4):

$$\gamma(j) = \phi_1\gamma(j-1) + \phi_2\gamma(j-2) + \ldots + \phi_p\gamma(j-p).$$

Applying again the guess-and-verify method for the case $h = 1$ and assuming that $T > p$, the solution is given by $\alpha_T = \left(\phi_1, \phi_2, \ldots, \phi_p, 0, \ldots, 0\right)'$. Thus, the one-step ahead predictor is

$$\mathbb{P}_T X_{T+1} = \phi_1 X_T + \phi_2 X_{T-1} + \ldots + \phi_p X_{T+1-p}, \qquad T > p. \tag{3.9}$$

The one-step ahead forecast of an AR(p) process therefore depends only on the last p observations.

The above predictor can also be obtained in a different way. View for this purpose $\mathbb{P}_T$ as an *operator* with the following meaning: take the linear least-squares forecast with respect to the information $\{X_T, \ldots, X_1\}$. Apply this operator to the defining stochastic difference equation of the AR(p) process forwarded one period:

$$\mathbb{P}_T X_{T+1} = \mathbb{P}_T\left(\phi_1 X_T\right) + \mathbb{P}_T\left(\phi_2 X_{T-1}\right) + \ldots + \mathbb{P}_T\left(\phi_p X_{T+1-p}\right) + \mathbb{P}_T\left(Z_{T+1}\right).$$

In period T, the observations of $X_T, X_{T-1}, \ldots, X_1$ are known so that $\mathbb{P}_T X_{T-j} = X_{T-j}$, $j = 0, 1, \ldots, T-1$. Because $\{Z_t\}$ is a white noise process and because $\{X_t\}$ is a causal function with respect to $\{Z_t\}$, Z_{T+1} is uncorrelated with $X_T, \ldots, X_1$. This reasoning leads to the same predictor as in Eq. (3.9).

The forecasting functions for $h > 1$ can be obtained recursively by successively applying the forecast operator. Take, for example, the case $h = 2$:

$$\begin{aligned}
\mathbb{P}_T X_{T+2} &= \mathbb{P}_T\left(\phi_1 X_{T+1}\right) + \mathbb{P}_T\left(\phi_2 X_T\right) + \ldots + \mathbb{P}_T\left(\phi_p X_{T+2-p}\right) + \mathbb{P}_T\left(Z_{T+2}\right) \\
&= \phi_1\left(\phi_1 X_T + \phi_2 X_{T-1} + \ldots + \phi_p X_{T+1-p}\right) \\
&\qquad + \phi_2 X_T + \ldots + \phi_p X_{T+2-p} \\
&= \left(\phi_1^2 + \phi_2\right) X_T + \left(\phi_1\phi_2 + \phi_3\right) X_{T-1} + \ldots + \left(\phi_1\phi_{p-1} + \phi_p\right) X_{T+2-p} \\
&\qquad + \phi_1\phi_p X_{T+1-p}.
\end{aligned}$$

In this way, forecasting functions for $h > 2$ can be obtained recursively.

Note that in the case of AR(p) processes, the coefficient of the forecast function remain constant as long as $T > p$. Thus, with each new observation, it is not necessary to recompute the equation system and solve it again. This will be different in the case of MA processes. In practice, the parameters of the AR model are usually unknown and have therefore been replaced by some estimate. Section 14.3 investigates how this substitution affects the results.

3.1.2 Forecasting with MA(q) Processes

The forecasting problem becomes more intricate in the case of MA(q) processes. To get a better understanding, we analyze the case of MA(1) processes first:

$$X_t = Z_t + \theta Z_{t-1} \qquad \text{with } |\theta| < 1 \text{ and } Z_t \sim \text{WN}(0, \sigma^2).$$

Taking a forecast horizon of one period, i.e., $h = 1$, the equation system (3.7) becomes

Table 3.1 Forecast function for a MA(1) process with $\theta = -0.9$ and $\sigma^2 = 1$

Time	Forecasting function $\alpha_T = (a_1, a_2, \ldots, a_T)'$	Forecast error variance
$T = 0$:		$v_0(1) = 1.8100$
$T = 1$:	$\alpha_1 = (-0.4972)'$	$v_1(1) = 1.3625$
$T = 2$:	$\alpha_2 = (-0.6606, -0.3285)'$	$v_2(1) = 1.2155$
$T = 3$:	$\alpha_3 = (-0.7404, -0.4891, -0.2432)'$	$v_3(1) = 1.1436$
$T = 4$:	$\alpha_4 = (-0.7870, -0.5827, -0.3849, -0.1914)'$	$v_4(1) = 1.1017$
$\vdots$	$\vdots$	$\vdots$
$T = \infty$:	$\alpha_\infty = (-0.9000, -0.8100, -0.7290, \ldots)'$	$v_\infty(1) = 1$

$$\begin{pmatrix} 1 & \frac{\theta}{1+\theta^2} & 0 & \ldots & 0 \\ \frac{\theta}{1+\theta^2} & 1 & \frac{\theta}{1+\theta^2} & \ldots & 0 \\ 0 & \frac{\theta}{1+\theta^2} & 1 & \ldots & 0 \\ \vdots & \vdots & \vdots & \ddots & \vdots \\ 0 & 0 & 0 & \ldots & 1 \end{pmatrix} \begin{pmatrix} a_1 \\ a_2 \\ a_3 \\ \vdots \\ a_T \end{pmatrix} = \begin{pmatrix} \frac{\theta}{1+\theta^2} \\ 0 \\ 0 \\ \vdots \\ 0 \end{pmatrix}. \tag{3.10}$$

Despite the fact that the equation system has a simple structure, the forecasting function will depend in general on all past observations of X_{T-j}, $0 \leq j \leq T$. We illustrate this point by a numerical example that will allow us to get a deeper understanding.

Suppose that we know the parameters of the MA(1) process to be $\theta = -0.9$ and $\sigma^2 = 1$. We start the forecasting exercise in period $T = 0$ and assume that, at this point in time, we have no observation at hand. The best forecast is therefore just the unconditional mean that in this example is zero. Thus, $\mathbb{P}_0 X_1 = 0$. The variance of the forecast error then is $\mathbb{V}(X_1 - \mathbb{P}_0 X_1) = v_0(1) = \sigma^2 + \theta^2\sigma^2 = 1.81$. This result is summarized in the first row of Table 3.1. In period 1, the realization of X_1 is observed. This information can be used and the forecasting function becomes $\mathbb{P}_1 X_2 = a_1 X_1$. The coefficient a_1 is found by solving the equation system (3.10) for $T = 1$. This gives $a_1 = \theta/(1+\theta^2) = -0.4972$. The corresponding variance of the forecast error according to Eq. (3.8) is $\mathbb{V}(X_2 - \mathbb{P}_1 X_2) = v_1(1) = \gamma(0)(1 - \alpha_1'\rho_1(1)) = 1.81(1 - 0.4972 \times 0.4972) = 1.3625$. This value is lower compared to the previous forecast because additional information, the observation of the realization of X_1, is taken into account. Row 2 in Table 3.1 summarizes these results.

In period 2, not only X_1 but also X_2 is observed, which allows us to base our forecast on both observations: $\mathbb{P}_2 X_3 = a_1 X_2 + a_2 X_1$. The coefficients can be found by solving the equation system (3.10) for $T = 2$. This amounts to solving the simultaneous equation system:

$$\begin{pmatrix} 1 & \frac{\theta}{1+\theta^2} \\ \frac{\theta}{1+\theta^2} & 1 \end{pmatrix} \begin{pmatrix} a_1 \\ a_2 \end{pmatrix} = \begin{pmatrix} \frac{\theta}{1+\theta^2} \\ 0 \end{pmatrix}.$$

Inserting $\theta = -0.9$, the solution is $\alpha_2 = (a_1, a_2)' = (-0.6606, -0.3285)'$. The corresponding variance of the forecast error becomes

$$\begin{aligned}\mathbb{V}(X_3 - \mathbb{P}_2 X_3) &= v_2(1) = \gamma(0)(1 - \alpha_2' \rho_2(1)) \\ &= \gamma(0)\left(1 - \begin{pmatrix} a_1 & a_2 \end{pmatrix}\begin{pmatrix} \frac{\theta}{1+\theta^2} \\ 0 \end{pmatrix}\right) \\ &= 1.81\left(1 - \begin{pmatrix} -0.6606 & -0.3285 \end{pmatrix}\begin{pmatrix} -0.4972 \\ 0 \end{pmatrix}\right) = 1.2155.\end{aligned}$$

These results are summarized in row 3 of Table 3.1.

In period 3, the realizations of X_1, X_2 and X_3 are known so that the forecast function becomes $\mathbb{P}_3 X_4 = a_1 X_3 + a_2 X_2 + a_3 X_1$. The coefficients can again be found by solving the equation system (3.10) for $T = 3$:

$$\begin{pmatrix} 1 & \frac{\theta}{1+\theta^2} & 0 \\ \frac{\theta}{1+\theta^2} & 1 & \frac{\theta}{1+\theta^2} \\ 0 & \frac{\theta}{1+\theta^2} & 1 \end{pmatrix}\begin{pmatrix} a_1 \\ a_2 \\ a_3 \end{pmatrix} = \begin{pmatrix} \frac{\theta}{1+\theta^2} \\ 0 \\ 0 \end{pmatrix}.$$

Inserting $\theta = -0.9$ and solving the equation system leads to the solution $\alpha_2 = (a_1, a_2, a_3)' = (-0.7404, -0.4891, -0.2432)'$. The corresponding variance of the forecast error becomes

$$\begin{aligned}\mathbb{V}(X_4 - \mathbb{P}_3 X_4) &= v_3(1) = \gamma(0)(1 - \alpha_3' \rho_3(1)) \\ &= \gamma(0)\left(1 - \begin{pmatrix} a_1 & a_2 & a_3 \end{pmatrix}\begin{pmatrix} \frac{\theta}{1+\theta^2} \\ 0 \\ 0 \end{pmatrix}\right) \\ &= 1.81\left(1 - \begin{pmatrix} -0.7404 & -0.4891 & -0.2432 \end{pmatrix}\begin{pmatrix} -0.4972 \\ 0 \\ 0 \end{pmatrix}\right) \\ &= 1.1436.\end{aligned}$$

These results are summarized in row 4 of Table 3.1. We can, of course, continue in this way and derive successively the forecast functions for $T = 4, 5, \ldots$.

From this exercise, we can make several observations:

- In contrast to the AR process, every new information is used. The forecast $\mathbb{P}_T X_{T+1}$ depends on all available information, in particular on $X_T, X_{T-1}, \ldots, X_1$.
- The coefficients of the forecast function are not constant. They change as more and more information comes in.

- The importance of the new information can be "measured" by the last coefficient of α_T. These coefficients are termed *partial autocorrelations* (see Definition 3.1) and are of particular relevance as will be explained in Sect. 3.3. In our example, they are -0.4972, -0.3285, -0.2432, and -0.1914.
- As more information becomes available, the variance of the forecast error (mean squared error) declines monotonically. It will converge to $\sigma^2 = 1$. The reason for this result can be explained as follows. Applying the forecasting operator to the defining MA(1) stochastic difference equation forwarded by one period gives $\mathbb{P}_T X_{T+1} = \mathbb{P}_T Z_{T+1} + \theta \mathbb{P}_T Z_T = \theta \mathbb{P}_T Z_T$ with forecast error $X_{T+1} - \mathbb{P}_T X_{T+1} = Z_{T+1}$. As more and more observations become available, it becomes better and better possible to recover the "true" value of the unobserved Z_T from the observations $X_T, X_{T-1}, \ldots, X_1$. As the process is invertible, in the limit, it is possible to recover the value of Z_T exactly (almost surely). The only uncertainty remaining is with respect to Z_{T+1}, which has a mean of zero and a variance of $\sigma^2 = 1$.

3.1.3 Forecasting from the Infinite Past

The forecasting function based on the *infinitely remote past* is of particular theoretical interest. Thus, we look at the problem of finding the optimal linear forecast of X_{T+1} given $X_T, X_{T-1}, \ldots, X_1, X_0, X_{-1}, \ldots$ taking the mean squared error again as the criterion function. The corresponding forecasting function (predictor) will be denoted by $\widetilde{\mathbb{P}}_T X_{T+h}$, $h > 0$.

Noting that the MA(1) process with $|\theta| < 1$ is invertible, we have

$$Z_t = X_t - \theta X_{t-1} + \theta^2 X_{t-2} - \ldots$$

We can therefore write X_{t+1} as

$$X_{t+1} = Z_{t+1} + \theta \underbrace{\left(X_t - \theta X_{t-1} + \theta^2 X_{t-2} - \ldots\right)}_{Z_t}$$

The predictor of X_{T+1} from the infinite past, $\widetilde{\mathbb{P}}_T$, is then given by

$$\widetilde{\mathbb{P}}_T X_{T+1} = \theta \left(X_T - \theta X_{T-1} + \theta^2 X_{T-2} - \ldots\right)$$

where the mean squared forecasting error is

$$v_\infty(1) = \mathbb{E}\left(X_{T+1} - \widetilde{\mathbb{P}}_T X_{T+1}\right)^2 = \sigma^2.$$

Applying this result to our example gives

$$\widetilde{\mathbb{P}}_T X_{T+1} = -0.9 X_T - 0.81 X_{T-1} - 0.729\theta^2 X_{T-2} - \ldots$$

with $v_\infty(1) = 1$. See last row in Table 3.1.

Example of an ARMA(1,1) Process
Consider next the case of a causal and invertible ARMA(1,1) process $\{X_t\}$:

$$X_t = \phi X_{t-1} + Z_t + \theta Z_{t-1},$$

where $|\phi| < 1$, $|\theta| < 1$ and $Z_t \sim \text{WN}(0, \sigma^2)$. Because $\{X_t\}$ is causal and invertible with respect to $\{Z_t\}$,

$$X_{T+1} = Z_{T+1} + (\phi + \theta) \sum_{j=0}^{\infty} \phi^j Z_{T-j},$$

$$Z_{T+1} = X_{T+1} - (\phi + \theta) \sum_{j=0}^{\infty} (-\theta)^j X_{T-j}.$$

Applying the forecast operator $\widetilde{\mathbb{P}}_T$ to the second equation and noting that $\widetilde{\mathbb{P}}_T Z_{T+1} = 0$, one obtains the following one-step ahead predictor:

$$\widetilde{\mathbb{P}}_T X_{T+1} = (\phi + \theta) \sum_{j=0}^{\infty} (-\theta)^j X_{T-j}.$$

Applying the forecast operator to the first equation, we obtain

$$\widetilde{\mathbb{P}}_T X_{T+1} = (\phi + \theta) \sum_{j=0}^{\infty} (\phi)^j Z_{T-j}.$$

This implies that the one-step ahead prediction error is equal to $X_{T+1} - \widetilde{\mathbb{P}}_T X_{T+1} = Z_{T+1}$ and that the mean squared forecasting error of the one-step ahead predictor given the infinite past is equal to $\mathbb{E} Z_{T+1}^2 = \sigma^2$.

3.2 Wold Decomposition Theorem

The predictors based on the infinite remote past allow a classification of stationary processes according to their forecasting behavior. One can consider two extreme cases: (linear) singular and regular processes. Whereas the former can be exactly forecasted based on the infinite remote past, i.e., $\widetilde{\mathbb{P}}_T X_{T+h} = X_{T+h}$ for all $h > 0$, for the latter,

$$\lim_{h \to \infty} \widetilde{\mathbb{P}}_T X_{T+h} = \mathbb{E} X_T = \mu.$$

Hence, for regular processes, knowledge of the infinite remote past provides no information, which would allow to improve the forecast beyond its unconditional mean.

The most important class of singular processes is the *harmonic processes*, which are characterized by finite or infinite sums of sine and cosine functions with stochastic amplitude.[5] A simple example of a harmonic process is

$$X_t = A\cos(\omega t) + B\sin(\omega t) \quad \text{with } \omega \in (0, \pi).$$

where A and B denote two uncorrelated random variables with mean zero and finite variance. One can check that X_t satisfies the deterministic difference equation:

$$X_t = (2\cos\omega)X_{t-1} - X_{t-2}.$$

Thus, X_t can be forecasted exactly from its past. In this example, the last two observations are sufficient.

The *Wold Decomposition theorem* is essential for the theoretical understanding of stationary stochastic processes. It shows that *any* stationary process can be represented as the sum of a singular and a regular process where the latter is given by a linear combination of current and past forecast errors.

Theorem 3.1 (Wold decomposition) *Every stationary stochastic process* $\{X_t\}$ *with mean zero and finite positive variance can be decomposed as*

$$X_t = Y_t + V_t$$

where $\{Y_t\}$ *and* $\{V_t\}$ *are regular and singular processes, respectively. The regular component* $\{Y_t\}$ *has a causal representation with respect to the process of forecast errors* $\{Z_t\} = \{X_t - \widetilde{\mathbb{P}}_{t-1}X_t\}$*:*

$$Y_t = \sum_{j=0}^{\infty} \psi_j Z_{t-j} = \Psi(\mathrm{L})Z_t, \tag{3.11}$$

such that:

(i) $Z_t = X_t - \widetilde{\mathbb{P}}_{t-1}X_t = \widetilde{\mathbb{P}}_t Z_t$
(ii) $\psi_0 = 1$ *and* $\sum_{j=0}^{\infty} \psi_j^2 < \infty$
(iii) $Z_t \sim \mathrm{WN}(0, \sigma^2)$ *with* $\sigma^2 = \mathbb{E}\left(X_{t+1} - \widetilde{\mathbb{P}}_t X_{t+1}\right)^2 > 0$
(iv) $\mathbb{E}(Z_t V_s) = 0$ *for all* $t, s \in \mathbb{Z}$

The sequences $\{\psi_j\}$, $\{Z_t\}$, *and* $\{V_t\}$ *are uniquely determined by* (3.11).

[5] More about harmonic processes can be found in Sect. 6.2.

Proof The proof, although insightful, requires some knowledge about Hilbert spaces, which is beyond the scope of this book. A rigorous proof can be found in Brockwell and Davis (1991, section 5.7) or Deistler and Scherrer (2022, chapter 2).
It is nevertheless instructive to give an intuition of the proof. Following the MA(1) example from the previous section, we start in period 0 and assume that no information is available. Thus, the best forecast $\mathbb{P}_0 X_1$ is zero, so that trivially

$$X_1 = X_1 - \mathbb{P}_0 X_1 = Z_1.$$

Starting with $X_1 = Z_1, X_2, X_3, \ldots$ can then be constructed recursively:

$$\begin{aligned}
X_2 &= X_2 - \mathbb{P}_1 X_2 + \mathbb{P}_1 X_2 = Z_2 + a_1^{(1)} X_1 = Z_2 + a_1^{(1)} Z_1 \\
X_3 &= X_3 - \mathbb{P}_2 X_3 + \mathbb{P}_2 X_3 = Z_3 + a_1^{(2)} X_2 + a_2^{(2)} X_1 \\
&= Z_3 + a_1^{(2)} Z_2 + \left(a_1^{(2)} a_1^{(1)} + a_2^{(2)}\right) Z_1 \\
X_4 &= X_4 - \mathbb{P}_3 X_4 + \mathbb{P}_3 X_4 = Z_4 + a_1^{(3)} X_3 + a_2^{(3)} X_2 + a_3^{(3)} X_1 \\
&= Z_4 + a_1^{(3)} Z_3 + \left(a_1^{(3)} a_1^{(2)} + a_2^{(3)}\right) Z_2 \\
&\quad + \left(a_1^{(3)} a_1^{(2)} a_1^{(1)} + a_1^{(3)} a_2^{(2)} + a_2^{(3)} a_1^{(1)} + a_3^{(3)}\right) Z_1 \\
&\ldots
\end{aligned}$$

where $a_j^{(t-1)}$, $j = 1, \ldots, t-1$, denote the coefficients of the forecast function for X_t based on $X_{t-1}, \ldots, X_1$. This shows how X_t unfolds into the sum of forecast errors. The stationarity of $\{X_t\}$ ensures that the coefficients of Z_j converge, as t goes to infinity, to ψ_j, which are independent of t. □

Every stationary stochastic process can thus be expressed as the sum of a moving average of infinite order and a singular process.[6] The weights of the infinite moving average are thereby normalized such that $\psi_0 = 1$. In addition, the coefficients ψ_j are square summable. This property is less strong than absolute summability that is required for a causal representation (see Definition 2.2). The process $\{Z_t\}$ is a white noise process with positive variance $\sigma^2 > 0$. The Z_t's are called *innovations* as they represent the one-period ahead forecast errors based on the infinite remote past, i.e., $Z_t = X_t - \widetilde{\mathbb{P}}_{t-1} X_t$. Z_t is the additional information revealed from the

[6] The Wold decomposition corresponds to the decomposition of the spectral distribution function of F into the sum of F_Z and F_V (see Sect. 6.2). Thus, the spectral distribution function F_Z has spectral density $f_Z(\lambda) = \frac{\sigma^2}{2\pi} |\Psi(e^{-\imath\lambda})|^2$.

t-th observation. Thus, the Wold decomposition theorem serves as a justification for using causal and invertible stationary ARMA processes as a modeling device.

The second part of Property (i) means that the innovation process $\{Z_t\}$ is *fundamental* with respect to $\{X_t\}$, i.e., that Z_t lies in the linear space spanned by $\{X_t, X_{t-1}, X_{t-2}, \ldots\}$ or that $Z_t = \widetilde{\mathbb{P}}_t Z_t$. This implies that $\Psi(\mathrm{L})$ must be invertible and that Z_t can be perfectly (almost surely) recovered from the observations of $X_t, X_{t-1}, \ldots$ Finally, Property (iv) says that the two components $\{Z_t\}$ and $\{V_t\}$ are uncorrelated with each other at all leads and lags. Thus, in essence, the Wold decomposition theorem states that every stationary stochastic process can be uniquely decomposed into a weighted sum of current and past forecast errors plus a deterministic process.

Although the Wold decomposition is very appealing from a theoretical perspective, it is not directly implementable in practice because it requires the estimation of infinitely many parameters $(\psi_1, \psi_2, \ldots)$. This is impossible with only a finite number of observations. It is therefore necessary to place some restrictions on $(\psi_1, \psi_2, \ldots)$. One possibility is to assume that $\{X_t\}$ is a causal stationary ARMA process and to recover the ψ_j's from the causal representation. This amounts to assume that $\Psi(\mathrm{L})$ is a rational polynomial:

$$\Psi(\mathrm{L}) = \frac{\Theta(\mathrm{L})}{\Phi(\mathrm{L})} = \frac{1 + \theta_1 \mathrm{L} + \theta_2 \mathrm{L}^2 + \ldots + \theta_q \mathrm{L}^q}{1 - \phi_1 \mathrm{L} - \phi_2 \mathrm{L}^2 - \ldots - \phi_p \mathrm{L}^p}.$$

Thus, the process is characterized by only a finite number, $p + q$, of parameters. Another possibility is to place restrictions on the smoothness of the spectrum (see Chap. 6).

The Wold decomposition theorem has several further implications summarized in the following remarks.

Remark 3.1 In the case of stationary ARMA processes, the singular part $\{V_t\}$ can be disregarded so that the process is represented only by a weighted sum of current and past innovations. Hence, ARMA processes are (linearly) *regular*, or *regular* for short. Moreover, it can be shown that every regular process $\{X_t\}$ can be approximated arbitrarily well by a stationary ARMA process $\{X_t^{(\mathrm{ARMA})}\}$, meaning that

$$\sup_{t \in \mathbb{Z}} \mathbb{E}\left(X_t - X_t^{(\mathrm{ARMA})}\right)^2$$

can be made arbitrarily small. The proof of these results can be found in Hannan and Deistler (1988, Chapter 1).

Remark 3.2 The process $\{Z_t\}$ is white noise, but not necessarily Gaussian. In particular, $\{Z_t\}$ need not be independently and identically distributed (IID). Thus, $\mathbb{E}(Z_{t+1}|X_t, X_{t-1}, \ldots)$ need not be equal to zero, although $\widetilde{P}_t Z_{t+1} = 0$. The reason is that $\widetilde{P}_t Z_{t+1}$ is only the best linear forecast function, whereas

$\mathbb{E}(Z_{t+1}|X_t, X_{t-1}, \ldots)$ is the best forecast function among all linear and nonlinear functions. Examples of processes that are white noise, but not IID, are GARCH processes discussed in Chap. 8.

Remark 3.3 The innovations $\{Z_t\}$ may not correspond to the "true" shocks of the underlying economic system. In this case, the shocks to the economic system cannot be recovered from the Wold decomposition. Thus, they are not fundamental with respect to $\{X_t\}$. Suppose, as a simplistic example, that $\{X_t\}$ is generated by a noninvertible MA(1) process:

$$X_t = U_t + \theta U_{t-1}, \qquad U_t \sim \mathrm{WN}(0, \sigma^2) \quad \text{and } |\theta| > 1.$$

This generates an impulse response function with respect to the true shocks of the system equal to $(1, \theta, 0, \ldots)$. The above mechanism can, however, not be the Wold decomposition because the non-invertibility implies that U_t cannot be recovered from the observation of $\{X_t\}$. As shown in the introduction, there is an observationally equivalent MA(1) process, i.e., a process that generates the same ACF. Based on the computation in Sect. 1.5, this MA(1) process is

$$X_t = Z_t + \tilde{\theta} Z_{t-1}, \qquad Z_t \sim \mathrm{WN}(0, \tilde{\sigma}^2),$$

with $\tilde{\theta} = \theta^{-1}$ and $\tilde{\sigma}^2 = \frac{1+\theta^2}{1+\theta^{-2}}\sigma^2$. This is already the Wold decomposition. The impulse response function for this process is $(1, \theta^{-1}, 0, \ldots)$, which is different from the original system. As $|\tilde{\theta}| = |\theta^{-1}| < 1$, the innovations $\{Z_t\}$ can be recovered from the observations as $Z_t = \sum_{j=0}^{\infty}(-\tilde{\theta})^j X_{t-j}$, but they do not correspond to the shocks of the system $\{U_t\}$. Hansen and Sargent (1991), Quah (1990), and Lippi and Reichlin (1993), among others, provide a deeper discussion of this issue and present additional more interesting economic examples.

3.3 The Partial Autocorrelation Function

Consider again the problem of forecasting X_{T+1} from observations $X_T, X_{T-1}, \ldots, X_2, X_1$. Denoting, as before, the best linear predictor by $\mathbb{P}_T X_{T+1} = a_1 X_T + a_2 X_{T-1} + a_{T-1} X_2 + a_T X_1$, we can express X_{T+1} as

$$X_{T+1} = \mathbb{P}_T X_{T+1} + Z_{T+1} = a_1 X_T + a_2 X_{T-1} + a_{T-1} X_2 + a_T X_1 + Z_{T+1}$$

where Z_{T+1} denotes the forecast error, which is uncorrelated with $X_T, \ldots, X_1$. We can then ask the question to what extent X_1 contributes to the forecast of X_{T+1} *controlling* for $X_T, X_{T-2}, \ldots, X_2$. If a_T is small or even zero, the contribution is small, respectively zero. Thus, a_T can be viewed as a measure of the importance of the additional information provided by X_1. It is referred to as the *partial autocorrelation*. In the case of an AR(p) process, the whole information useful for forecasting X_{T+1}, $T > p$, is incorporated in the last p observations so that $a_T = 0$. In the case of the MA process, all observations on $X_T, \ldots, X_1$ help in retrieving the unobserved $Z_T, Z_{T-1} \ldots, Z_{t-q+1}$. As Z_t is an infinite weighted sum of past X_t's, every new observation contributes to the recovering of the Z_t's. Thus, the partial autocorrelation a_T is in general not equal to zero. Setting T successively equal to 0, 1, 2, etc. we obtain a series of coefficients a_T known as the partial autocorrelation function (PACF).

We can, however, interpret the above equation as a regression equation. From the Frisch-Lovell-Waugh theorem (See Davidson and MacKinnon 1993), we can obtain a_T by a two-stage procedure. Project (regress) in a first stage X_{T+1} on $X_T, \ldots, X_2$ and take the residual. Similarly, project (regress) X_1 on $X_T, \ldots, X_2$ and take the residual. The coefficient a_T is then obtained by projecting (regressing) the first residual on the second. Stationarity implies that this is nothing but the correlation coefficient between the two residuals.

3.3.1 Definition

The above intuition suggests two equivalent definitions of the partial autocorrelation function (PACF).

Definition 3.1 (Partial autocorrelation I) The *partial autocorrelation function* (PACF) $\alpha(h)$, $h = 0, 1, 2, \ldots$, of a stationary process is defined as follows:

$$\alpha(0) = 1$$
$$\alpha(h) = a_h,$$

where a_h denotes the last element of the vector $\alpha_h = \Gamma_h^{-1}\gamma_h(1) = R_h^{-1}\rho_h(1)$ (see Sect. 3.1 and Eq. (3.7)).

Definition 3.2 (Partial autocorrelation II) The *partial autocorrelation function* (PACF) $\alpha(h)$, $h = 0, 1, 2, \ldots$, of a stationary process is defined as follows:

$$\alpha(0) = 1$$
$$\alpha(1) = \operatorname{corr}(X_2, X_1) = \rho(1)$$
$$\alpha(h) = \operatorname{corr}\left[X_{h+1} - \mathbb{P}(X_{h+1}|1, X_2, \ldots, X_h), X_1 - \mathbb{P}(X_1|1, X_2, \ldots, X_h)\right],$$

where $\mathbb{P}(X_{h+1}|1, X_2, \ldots, X_h)$ and $\mathbb{P}(X_1|1, X_2, \ldots, X_h)$ denote the best, in the sense mean squared forecast errors, linear forecasts of X_{h+1}, respectively X_1 given $\{1, X_2, \ldots, X_h\}$.

Remark 3.4 If $\{X_t\}$ has a mean of zero, then the constant in the projection operator can be omitted.

The first definition implies that the partial autocorrelations are determined from the coefficients of the forecasting function, which are themselves functions of the autocorrelation coefficients. It is therefore possible to express the partial autocorrelations as a function of the autocorrelations. More specifically, the partial autocorrelation function can be computed recursively from the autocorrelation function according to Durbin-Levinson algorithm (Durbin 1960):

$$\begin{aligned}
\alpha(0) &= 1 \\
\alpha(1) &= a_{11} = \rho(1) \\
\alpha(2) &= a_{22} = \frac{\rho(2) - \rho(1)^2}{1 - \rho(1)^2} \\
&\dots \\
\alpha(h) &= a_{hh} = \frac{\rho(h) - \sum_{j=1}^{h-1} a_{h-1,j}\rho_{h-j}}{1 - \sum_{j=1}^{h-1} a_{h-1,j}\rho_j},
\end{aligned} \tag{3.12}$$

where $a_{h,j} = a_{h-1,j} - a_{hh}a_{h-1,h-j}$ for $j = 1, 2, \dots, h-1$.

Autoregressive Processes

The idea of the PACF can be well illustrated in the case of an AR(1) process

$$X_t = \phi X_{t-1} + Z_t \qquad \text{with } 0 < |\phi| < 1 \text{ and } Z_t \sim \text{WN}(0, \sigma^2).$$

As shown in Chap. 2, X_t and X_{t-2} are correlated with each other despite the fact that there is no direct relationship between the two. The correlation is obtained "indirectly" because X_t is correlated with X_{t-1}, which is itself correlated with X_{t-2}. Because both correlations are equal to ϕ, the correlation between X_t and X_{t-2} is equal to $\rho(2) = \phi^2$. The ACF therefore accounts for all correlations, including the indirect ones. The partial autocorrelation on the other hand only accounts for the direct relationships. In the case of the AR(1) process, there is only an indirect relation between X_t and X_{t-h} for $h \geq 2$; thus, the PACF is zero.

Based on the results in Sect. 3.1 for the AR(1) process, the definition 3.1 of the PACF implies

$$\begin{aligned}
\alpha_1 &= \phi & &\Rightarrow \alpha(1) = \rho(1) = \phi, \\
\alpha_2 &= (\phi, 0)' & &\Rightarrow \alpha(2) = 0, \\
\alpha_3 &= (\phi, 0, 0)' & &\Rightarrow \alpha(3) = 0.
\end{aligned}$$

The partial autocorrelation function of an AR(1) process is therefore equal to zero for $h \geq 2$.

This logic can be easily generalized. The PACF of a causal AR(p) process is equal to zero for $h > p$, i.e., $\alpha(h) = 0$ for $h > p$. This property characterizes an AR(p) process as shown in the next section.

Moving-Average Processes

Consider next the case of an invertible MA process. For this process, we have

$$Z_t = \sum_{j=0}^{\infty} \pi_j X_{t-j} \qquad \Rightarrow \qquad X_t = -\sum_{j=1}^{\infty} \pi_j X_{t-j} + Z_t.$$

X_t is therefore "directly" correlated with each X_{t-h}, $h = 1, 2, \ldots$. Consequently, the PACF is never exactly equal to zero, but converges exponentially to zero. This convergence can be monotonic or oscillating.

Take the MA(1) process as an illustration:

$$X_t = Z_t + \theta Z_{t-1} \qquad \text{with } |\theta| < 1 \text{ and } Z_t \sim \mathrm{WN}(0, \sigma^2).$$

The computations in Sect. 3.1.2 showed that

$$\alpha_1 = \frac{\theta}{1+\theta^2} \qquad \Rightarrow \alpha(1) = \rho(1) = \frac{\theta}{1+\theta^2},$$

$$\alpha_2 = \left(\frac{\theta(1+\theta^2)}{1+\theta^2+\theta^4}, \frac{-\theta^2}{1+\theta^2+\theta^4}\right)' \qquad \Rightarrow \alpha(2) = \frac{-\theta^2}{1+\theta^2+\theta^4}.$$

Thus, we get for the MA(1) process

$$\alpha(h) = -\frac{(-\theta)^h}{1+\theta^2+\ldots+\theta^{2h}} = -\frac{(-\theta)^h(1-\theta^2)}{1-\theta^{2(h+1)}}$$

3.3.2 Interpretation of ACF and PACF

The ACF and the PACF are two important practical tools in determining the nature of the mechanism underlying a given stochastic process. In particular, they can be used to determine the orders of the underlying AR, respectively MA processes. The analysis of ACF and PACF to identify appropriate models is known as the Box-Jenkins methodology (Box and Jenkins 1976). Table 3.2 summarizes the properties of both tools for the case of a causal AR and an invertible MA process.

If $\{X_t\}$ is a causal and invertible ARMA(p,q) process, we have the following properties. As shown in Sect. 2.4, the ACF is characterized for $h > \max\{p, q+1\}$ by the homogeneous difference equation $\rho(h) = \phi_1\rho(h-1) + \ldots + \phi_p\rho(h-p)$. Causality implies that the roots of the characteristic equation are all inside the unit circle. The autocorrelation coefficients therefore decline exponentially to zero. Whether this convergence is monotonic or oscillating depends on the signs of the roots. The PACF starts to decline to zero for $h > p$. Thus, the coefficients of the PACF exhibit the same behavior as the autocorrelation coefficients of $\theta^{-1}(\mathrm{L})X_t$.

Table 3.2 Properties of the ACF and the PACF

Process	ACF	PACF
AR(p)	Declines exponentially (monotonically or oscillating) to zero	$\alpha(h) = 0$ for $h > p$
MA(q)	$\rho(h) = 0$ for $h > q$	Declines exponentially (monotonically or oscillating) to zero

3.4 Exponential Smoothing

Besides the method of least-squares forecasting, *exponential smoothing* is a valid and computationally cheap alternative. This method views X_t as a function of time:

$$X_t = f(t; \beta) + \varepsilon_t,$$

whereby $f(t; \beta)$ typically represents a polynomial in t with coefficients β. The above equation is similar to a regression model with error term ε_t. This error term is usually specified as a white noise process $\{\varepsilon_t\} \sim \text{WN}(0, \sigma^2)$.

Consider first the simplest case where X_t just moves randomly around a fixed mean β. This corresponds to the case where $f(t; \beta)$ is a polynomial of degree zero:

$$X_t = \beta + \varepsilon_t.$$

If β is known, then $\mathbb{P}_T X_{T+h}$, the forecast of X_{T+h} given the observations $X_T, \ldots, X_1$, clearly equals β. If, however, β is unknown, we can substitute β by $\overline{X}_T$, the average of the observations:

$$\widehat{\mathbb{P}}_T X_{T+h} = \hat{\beta} = \overline{X}_T = \frac{1}{T} \sum_{t=1}^{T} X_t,$$

where "^" means that the model parameter β has been replaced by its estimate. The one-period ahead forecast function can then be rewritten as follows:

$$\begin{aligned} \widehat{\mathbb{P}}_T X_{T+1} &= \frac{T-1}{T} \widehat{\mathbb{P}}_{T-1} X_T + \frac{1}{T} X_T \\ &= \widehat{\mathbb{P}}_{T-1} X_T + \frac{1}{T} \left(X_T - \widehat{\mathbb{P}}_{T-1} X_T \right). \end{aligned}$$

The first equation represents the forecast for $T + 1$ as a linear combination of the forecast of X_T given observations up to $T - 1$ and the last additional information, i.e., the last observation. The weight given to the last observation is equal to $1/T$ because we assumed that the mean remains constant and because the contribution of one observation to the mean is $1/T$. The second equation represents the forecast for

$T + 1$ as last period's forecast plus a correction term that is proportional to the last forecast error. One advantage of this second representation is that the computation of the new forecast, i.e., the forecast for $T + 1$, only depends on the forecast for T and the additional observation. In this way, the storage requirements are minimized.

In many applications, the mean does not remain constant, but is a slowly moving function of time. In this case, it is no longer meaningful to give each observation the same weight. Instead, it seems plausible to weigh the more recent observation higher than the older ones. A simple idea is to let the weights decline exponentially, which leads to the following forecast function:

$$\mathbb{P}_T X_{T+1} = \frac{1-\omega}{1-\omega^T} \sum_{t=0}^{T-1} \omega^t X_{T-t} \qquad \text{with } |\omega| < 1.$$

ω thereby acts like a discount factor that controls the rate at which agents forget information. $1 - \omega$ is often called the smoothing parameter. The value of ω should depend on the speed at which the mean changes. In case when the mean changes only slowly, ω should be large so that all observations are almost equally weighted; in case when the mean changes quickly, ω should be small so that only the most recent observations are taken into account. The normalizing constant $\frac{1-\omega}{1-\omega^T}$ ensures that the weights sum up to one. For large T, the term ω^T can be disregarded so that one obtains the following forecasting function based on *simple exponential smoothing*:

$$\begin{aligned}
\mathbb{P}_T X_{T+1} &= (1-\omega)\left[X_T + \omega X_{T-1} + \omega^2 X_{T-2} + \ldots\right] \\
&= (1-\omega) X_T + \omega\, \mathbb{P}_{T-1} X_T \\
&= \mathbb{P}_{T-1} X_T + (1-\omega)\left(X_T - \mathbb{P}_{T-1} X_T\right).
\end{aligned}$$

In the economics literature, this forecasting method is called *adaptive expectation*. Similar to the model with constant mean, the new forecast is a weighted average between the old forecast and the last (newest) observation, respectively between the previous forecast and a term proportional to the last forecast error.

One important advantage of adaptive forecasting methods is that they can be computed recursively. Starting with value S_0, the following values can be computed as follows:

$$\begin{aligned}
\mathbb{P}_0 X_1 &= S_0 \\
\mathbb{P}_1 X_2 &= \omega \mathbb{P}_0 X_1 + (1-\omega) X_1 \\
\mathbb{P}_2 X_3 &= \omega \mathbb{P}_1 X_2 + (1-\omega) X_2 \\
&\ldots \\
\mathbb{P}_T X_{T+1} &= \omega \mathbb{P}_{T-1} X_T + (1-\omega) X_T.
\end{aligned}$$

In doing so S_0 has still to be determined. Because

$$\mathbb{P}_T X_{T+1} = (1-\omega)\left[X_T + \omega X_{T-1} + \ldots + \omega^{T-1}, X_1\right] + \omega^T S_0,$$

the effect of the starting value declines exponentially with time. In practice, we can take $S_0 = X_1$ or $S_0 = \overline{X}_T$. The discount factor ω is usually set a priori to be a number between 0.7 and 0.95. It is, however, possible to determine ω optimally by choosing a value that minimizes the mean squared one-period forecast error:

$$\sum_{t=1}^{T} (X_t - \mathbb{P}_{t-1} X_t)^2 \longrightarrow \min_{|\omega|<1} .$$

From a theoretical perspective, one can ask the question for which class of models exponential smoothing represents the optimal procedure. Muth (1960) showed that this class of models is given by ARMA(1,1) models:

$$\Delta X_t = X_t - X_{t-1} = Z_t - \omega Z_{t-1}.$$

Note that the process generated by the above equation is no longer stationary. This has to be expected as the exponential smoothing assumes a nonconstant mean. Despite the fact that this class seems rather restrictive at first, practice has shown that it delivers reasonable forecasts, especially in situations when it becomes costly to identify and specify a particular model.[7] Additional results and more general exponential smoothing methods can be found in Abraham and Ledolter (1983) and Mertens and Rässler (2005).

3.5 Exercises

Exercise 3.5.1 Compute the linear least-squares forecasting function $\mathbb{P}_T X_{T+h}$, $T > 2$, and the mean squared error $v_T(h)$, $h = 1, 2, 3$, if $\{X_t\}$ is given by the AR(2) process:

$$X_t = 1.3X_{t-1} - 0.4X_{t-2} + Z_t \qquad \text{with} \quad Z_t \sim \text{WN}(0, 2).$$

To which values do $\mathbb{P}_T X_{T+h}$ and $v_T(h)$ converge for h going to infinity?

Exercise 3.5.2 Compute the linear least-squares forecasting function $\mathbb{P}_T(X_{T+1})$ and the mean squared error $v_T(1)$, $T = 0, 1, 2, 3$, if $\{X_t\}$ is given by the MA(1) process:

[7] This happens, for example, when many, perhaps thousands of, time series have to be forecasted in a real-time situation.

$$X_t = Z_t + 0.8Z_{t-1} \qquad \text{with} \quad Z_t \sim \text{WN}(0, 2).$$

To which values do $\mathbb{P}_T X_{T+h}$ and $v_T(h)$ converge for h going to infinity?

Exercise 3.5.3 Suppose that you observe $\{X_t\}$ for the two periods $t = 1$ and $t = 3$, but not for $t = 2$.

(i) Compute the linear least-squares forecast for X_2 if

$$X_t = \phi X_{t=1} + Z_t \qquad \text{with} \quad |\phi| < 1 \quad \text{and} \quad Z_t \sim \text{WN}(0, 4)$$

Compute the mean squared error for this forecast.

(ii) Alternatively, assume that $\{X_t\}$ is the MA(1) process

$$X_t = Z_t + \theta Z_{t-1} \qquad \text{with} \quad Z_t \sim \text{WN}(0, 4).$$

Compute the linear least-squares forecast for X_2 and its mean squared error.

Exercise 3.5.4 Assign the ACF and the PACF from Fig. 3.1 to the following processes:

$$\begin{aligned} X_t &= Z_t, \\ X_t &= 0.9X_{t-1} + Z_t, \\ X_t &= Z_t + 0.8Z_{t-1}, \\ X_t &= 0.9X_{t-1} + Z_t + 0.8Z_{t-1} \end{aligned}$$

with $Z_t \sim \text{WN}(0, \sigma^2)$.

Exercise 3.5.5 Consider the following ARMA(1,1) process:

$$X_t - \phi X_{t-1} = Z_t + \theta Z_{t-1}, \qquad |\phi| < 1 \text{ and } |\theta| < 1,$$

with $Z_t \sim \text{WN}(0, \sigma^2)$. Determine $\widetilde{\mathbb{P}}_{T+1}$, the one-step predictor from the infinite remote past, and the corresponding mean squared forecast error.

Exercise 3.5.6 Consider the following stochastic process:[8]

$$X_t = (-1)^t X_0, \qquad t \in \mathbb{N},$$

[8] This exercise is taken from Grimmett and Stirzaker (2001, section 9.2).

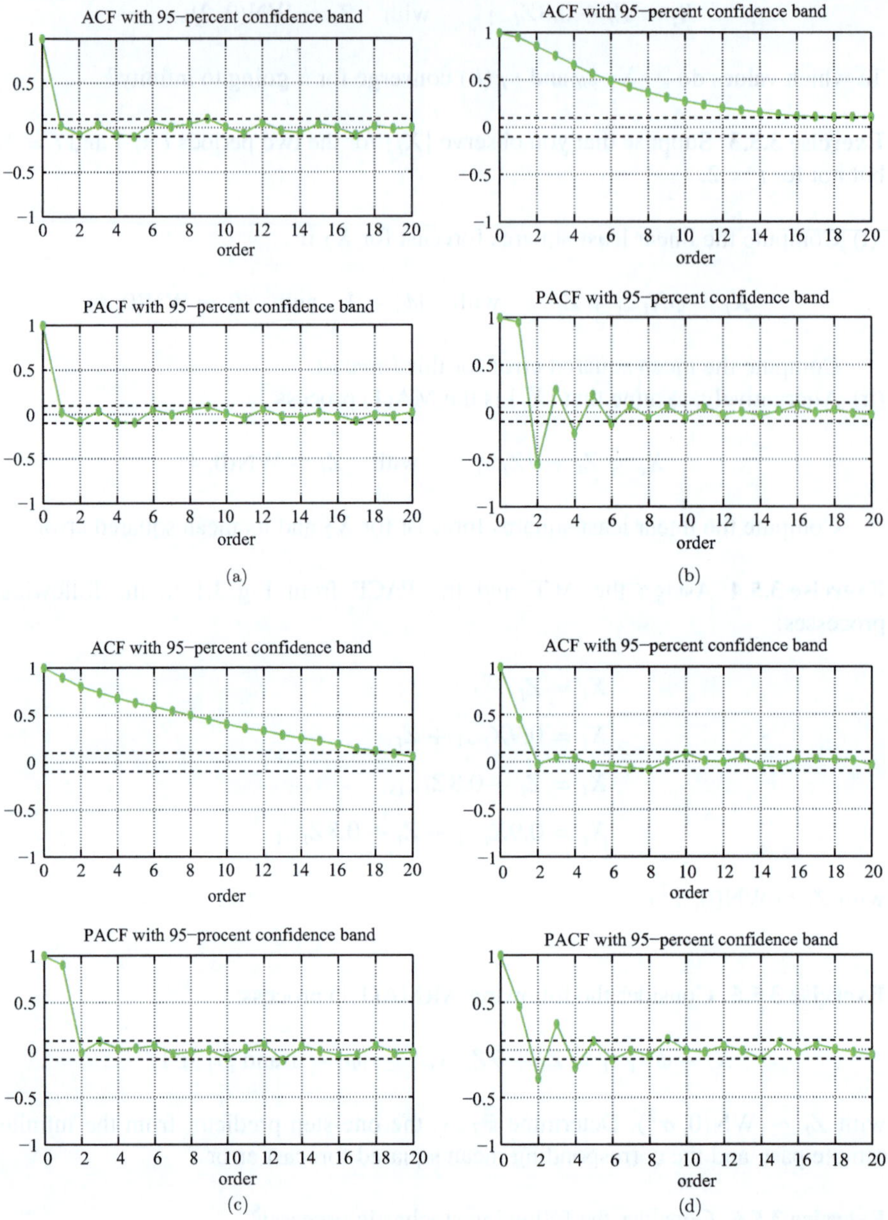

Fig. 3.1 Autocorrelation and partial autocorrelation functions. (**a**) Process 1. (**b**) Process 2. (**c**) Process 3. (**d**) Process 4

where the starting value X_0 obeys $\mathbf{P}[X_0 = -1] = \mathbf{P}[X_0 = 1] = \frac{1}{2}$.

(i) Show that $\{X_t\}$ is stationary with mean zero and autocovariance function $\gamma(h) = (-1)^h \mathbb{E}X_0^2$.

(ii) Find the best linear predictor for X_{T+h}, $h \geq 1$, given $X_T, X_{T-1}, \ldots, X_0$:

$$\mathbb{P}X_{T+h} = a_0 X_T + a_1 X_{T-1} + \cdots + a_T X_0.$$

Show that the solution is found by solving the equation system:

$$\sum_{i=0}^{T} a_i (-1)^{|i-j|} = (-1)^{h+j}, \qquad 0 \leq j \leq T.$$

(iii) Show that one solution of the above equation system is given by $a_0 = (-1)^h$ and $a_i = 0$, $i = 1, \ldots, T$.

(iv) Compute the mean squared forecast error of $\mathbb{P}X_{T+h}$.

Exercise 3.5.7 Let A and B be two uncorrelated, but not necessarily independent, random variables with mean zero and unit variance. Given $\omega \in (0, \pi]$, define the stochastic process $\{X_t\}$ by

$$X_t = A \cos \omega t + B \sin \omega t, \qquad t \in \mathbb{Z}.$$

(i) Compute $\mathbb{E}X_t$ and show that the autocovariance function is equal to $\gamma(r, s) = \cos(\omega(r - s))$, $r, s \in \mathbb{Z}$. Is $\{X_t\}$ stationary?

(ii) Set $\omega = \frac{\pi}{2}$ and show that $\{X_t\}$ is not strictly stationary.

(iii) Find a condition under which $\{X_t\}$ would be strictly stationary.

Estimation of the Expected Value and the Autocorrelation Function of a Stationary Stochastic Processes

4

In the previous chapters, we laid the theoretical foundations of the autocovariance function and, in particular, its relation to ARMA processes. We have seen how the autocovariance function, $\gamma(h)$, $h = 0, \pm 1, \pm 2, \ldots$, of a stationary stochastic process $\{X_t\}$ characterizes its dynamic properties, at least if we restrict ourselves to the first two moments. Thus, the estimation of the autocovariance function is interesting not only for its own sake but also for the specification and identification of appropriate ARMA models. It is therefore of utmost importance to have reliable (consistent and efficient) estimators for this entity at hand. Moreover, we may be interested in testing specific features for a given time series. This implies that we have to develop a corresponding testing theory. As the small sample distributions of the estimators are hard to establish analytically, we rely on asymptotic distributions instead.[1]

The estimators we consider are based on arithmetic averages and, hence, avoid the need to identify a particular model from the data. The approach is therefore termed *nonparametric* or *model-free*. However, it must be emphasized that more efficient estimators would be available if one is willing to assume a specific model for the underlying data-generating mechanism.

Throughout this chapter, we will assume that the stochastic process $\{X_t\}$ is stationary and observed for the time periods $t = 1, 2, \ldots, T$. We will refer to T as the sample size. As mentioned previously, the standard sampling theory is not appropriate in the times series context because the X_t's are not independent draws from some underlying distribution, but are systematically related to each other.

[1] Recently, bootstrap methods have also been introduced in the time series context.

K. Neusser, *Time Series Econometrics*, Springer Texts in Business and Economics,
https://doi.org/10.1007/978-3-031-88838-0_4

4.1 Estimation of the Expected Value

The arithmetic average constitutes a "natural" estimator of the expected value μ of a stochastic process. It is denoted by $\overline{X}_T$ and defined in the usual way as

$$\overline{X}_T = \frac{1}{T}(X_1 + X_2 + \ldots + X_T).$$

It is immediately clear from its definition that the arithmetic average is an unbiased estimator of the expected value μ:

$$\mathbb{E}\overline{X}_T = \frac{1}{T}(\mathbb{E}X_1 + \mathbb{E}X_2 + \ldots + \mathbb{E}X_T) = \mu.$$

Of greater interest are the asymptotic properties of the variance of the arithmetic mean $\mathbb{V}\overline{X}_T$, which are summarized in the following theorem:

Theorem 4.1 (Convergence of arithmetic average) *If $\{X_t\}$ is a stationary stochastic process with expected value μ and autocovariance function $\gamma(h)$, the variance of the arithmetic average $\mathbb{V}\overline{X}_T$ has the following asymptotic properties:*

$$\begin{aligned} \mathbb{V}\overline{X}_T = {} & \mathbb{E}\left(\overline{X}_T - \mu\right)^2 \to 0, && \text{if } \gamma(T) \to 0; \\ T\mathbb{V}\overline{X}_T = T\mathbb{E}\left(\overline{X}_T - \mu\right)^2 & \to \sum_{h=-\infty}^{\infty} \gamma(h), && \text{if } \sum_{h=-\infty}^{\infty} |\gamma(h)| < \infty, \end{aligned}$$

for T going to infinity.

Proof Immediate algebra establishes

$$\begin{aligned} 0 \le T\mathbb{V}\overline{X}_T &= \frac{1}{T}\sum_{i,j=1}^{T} \operatorname{cov}(X_i, X_j) = \sum_{|h|<T} \left(1 - \frac{|h|}{T}\right)\gamma(h) \\ &\le \sum_{|h|<T} |\gamma(h)| = 2\sum_{h=1}^{T} |\gamma(h)| + \gamma(0) \le \sum_{h=-\infty}^{\infty} |\gamma(h)|. \end{aligned}$$

The assumption $\gamma(h) \to 0$ for $h \to \infty$ implies that for any given $\varepsilon > 0$, we can find T_0 such that $|\gamma(h)| < \varepsilon/2$ for $h \ge T_0$. If $T > T_0$ and $T > 2T_0\,\gamma(0)/\varepsilon$,

$$\begin{aligned} 0 &\le \frac{1}{T}\sum_{h=1}^{T} |\gamma(h)| = \frac{1}{T}\sum_{h=1}^{T_0-1} |\gamma(h)| + \frac{1}{T}\sum_{h=T_0}^{T} |\gamma(h)| \\ &\le \frac{T_0\,\gamma(0)}{T} + \frac{1}{T}(T - T_0)\varepsilon/2 \le \frac{T_0\,\gamma(0)}{T} + \varepsilon/2 \le \frac{T_0\,\gamma(0)\varepsilon}{2T_0\,\gamma(0)} + \frac{\varepsilon}{2} = \varepsilon. \end{aligned}$$

Where we have used the property $0 \leq |\gamma(h)| \leq \gamma(0)$ of the covariance function (see Theorem 1.1). Therefore, $\mathbb{V}\overline{X}_T$ converges to zero for $T \to \infty$, which establishes the first claim. Moreover, we have

$$\lim_{T\to\infty} T\mathbb{V}\overline{X}_T = \lim_{T\to\infty} \sum_{|h|<T} \left(1 - \frac{|h|}{T}\right)\gamma(h) = \sum_{h=-\infty}^{\infty} \gamma(h) < \infty.$$

The infinite sum $\sum_{h=-\infty}^{\infty} \gamma(h)$ converges because it converges absolutely by assumption. □

This theorem establishes that the arithmetic average is not only an unbiased estimator of the mean but also a consistent one. In particular, the arithmetic average converges in the mean square sense, and therefore also in probability, to the true expected value (see Appendix C). This result can be interpreted as a reflection of the concept of ergodicity (see Sect. 1.2). The assumptions are relatively mild and are fulfilled for any stationary ARMA processes because for these processes, $\gamma(h)$ converges exponentially fast to zero (see Sect. 2.4.2, in particular Eq. (2.4)). Under little more restrictive assumptions, it is even possible to show that the arithmetic mean is asymptotically normally distributed.

The assumptions ensuring the asymptotic normality of the arithmetic average relate on the one hand to the existence of certain moments and on the other hand to the speed at which the dependence between two periods goes to zero as they get further apart. It would go too far to investigate the trade-off between these two assumptions in detail. We therefore rely on linear processes only. These are defined as follows.

Definition 4.1 (Linear process) $\{X_t\}$ is called a *linear process* with expected value μ if

$$X_t = \mu + \sum_{j=-\infty}^{\infty} \psi_j Z_{t-j}, \qquad Z_t \sim \text{IID}(0, \sigma_Z^2),$$

with $\sum_{j=-\infty}^{\infty} |\psi_j| < \infty$.

Note that Theorems 6.4 and 6.5 imply that linear processes are stationary with autocovariance function γ_X:

$$\gamma_X(h) = \sigma_Z^2 \sum_{j=-\infty}^{\infty} \psi_j \psi_{j+|h|}, \qquad h = 0, \pm 1, \pm 2, \ldots$$

The class of linear processes is quite large. They encompass in particular stationary ARMA processes with $Z_t \sim \text{IID}(0, \sigma_Z^2)$ because the ψ_j's converge exponentially fast to zero (see the discussion following Eq. (2.3)).

As pointed out in Theorem 4.1, the sum of all covariances plays an important role. This entity is known as the *long-run variance* and is denoted by ω_X.[2] When there is no risk of confusion, we omit the index and write just ω. In the case of linear processes, the long-run variance is given by

$$\omega_X = \sum_{h=-\infty}^{\infty} \gamma_X(h) = \gamma_X(0) + 2\sum_{h=1}^{\infty} \gamma_X(h) = \gamma(0)\left(1 + 2\sum_{h=1}^{\infty} \rho_X(h)\right) \tag{4.1}$$

$$= \sigma_Z^2 \sum_{h=-\infty}^{\infty} \sum_{j=-\infty}^{\infty} \psi_j \psi_{j+h} = \sigma_Z^2 \left(\sum_{j=-\infty}^{\infty} \psi_j\right)^2 = \sigma_Z^2\, \psi(1)^2 \tag{4.2}$$

Note that the assumption $\sum_{j=-\infty}^{\infty} |\psi_j| < \infty$ guarantees the convergence of the infinite sums. As the long-run variance takes into account the serial properties of the time series, it is also called heteroskedastic and autocorrelation consistent variance (HAC variance). If $\{X_t\}$ has some nontrivial correlation (i.e., $\rho_X(h) \neq 0$ for some $h \neq 0$.), the long-run variance ω_X is different from $\gamma_X(0)$. This implies among other things that the construction of the t-statistic for testing the simple hypothesis H$_0$: $\mu = \mu_0$ should use ω_X rather than $\gamma_X(0)$.

If $\{X_t\}$ is a AR(1) process with $X_t = \phi X_{t-1} + Z_t$, $Z_t \sim \mathrm{WN}(0, \sigma_Z^2)$, and $|\phi| < 1$, $\gamma_X(0) = \frac{\sigma_Z^2}{1-\phi^2}$ and $\rho_X(h) = \phi^{|h|}$. Thus, the long-run variance is given by $\omega_X = \gamma_X(0)(1+2\sum_{h=1}^{\infty} \phi^h) = \frac{\sigma_Z^2}{1-\phi^2} \times \frac{1+\phi}{1-\phi} = \frac{\sigma_Z^2}{(1-\phi)^2}$. From this example, it is clear that the long-run variance can be smaller or larger than $\gamma_X(0)$, depending on the sign of ϕ: for negative values of ϕ, $\gamma_X(0)$ overestimates the long-run variance; for positive values, it underestimates ω. More generally, we have for stationary ARMA processes with $\Phi(\mathrm{L})X_t = \Theta(\mathrm{L})Z_t$ and $Z_t \sim \mathrm{WN}(0, \sigma_Z^2)$

$$\omega_X = \sigma_Z^2 \Psi(1)^2 = \sigma_Z^2 \left(\frac{\Theta(1)}{\Phi(1)}\right)^2$$

where it is assumed that $\{X_t\}$ is causal with respect to $\{Z_t\}$. The estimation of the long-run variance is an intricate issue and will be dealt with in Sect. 4.4.

Theorem 4.2 (Asymptotic distribution of sample mean) *If $\{X_t\}$ is a linear process with mean μ such that $\sum_{j=-\infty}^{\infty} \psi_j \neq 0$, the arithmetic average $\overline{X}_T$ is asymptotically normal:*

$$\sqrt{T}(\overline{X}_T - \mu) \xrightarrow{\mathrm{d}} \mathrm{N}(0, \omega_X)\,.$$

Proof The proof uses the basic approximation theorem C.15 and the central limit theorem for m-dependent processes C.14. To this end, we define the approximate process

[2] The long-run variance equals 2π times the spectral density $f(\lambda)$ evaluated at $\lambda = 0$ (see Definition 6.1 of the spectral density in Sect. 6.1).

$$X_t^{(m)} = \mu + \sum_{j=-m}^{m} \psi_j Z_{t-j}.$$

Clearly, $\{X_t^{(m)}\}$ is a 2m-dependent process with long-run variance $V_m = \sum_{h=-m}^{m} \gamma(h) = \sigma_Z^2(\sum_{j=-m}^{m} \psi_j)^2$. The last assertion follows from Eq. (4.2) by setting $\psi_j = 0$ for $|j| > m$.

The arithmetic average of the approximating process is

$$\overline{X}_T^{(m)} = \frac{1}{T}\sum_{t=1}^{T} X_t^{(m)}.$$

The CLT for m-dependent processes C.14 then implies that for $T \to \infty$,

$$\sqrt{T}\left(\overline{X}_T^{(m)} - \mu\right) \xrightarrow{\text{d}} X^{(m)} = \text{N}(0, V_m).$$

As $m \to \infty$, $\sigma_Z^2(\sum_{j=-m}^{m} \psi_j)^2$ converges to $\sigma_Z^2(\sum_{j=-\infty}^{\infty} \psi_j)^2$ and thus

$$X^{(m)} \xrightarrow{\text{d}} X = \text{N}(0, V) = \text{N}\left(0, \sigma_Z^2\left(\sum_{j=-\infty}^{\infty} \psi_j\right)^2\right).$$

This assertion can be established by noting that the characteristic function of $X^{(m)}$ approaches the characteristic function of X so that by Theorem C.12, $X^{(m)} \xrightarrow{\text{d}} X$.

Finally, we show that the approximation error becomes negligible as T goes to infinity:

$$\sqrt{T}\left(\overline{X}_T - \mu\right) - \sqrt{T}\left(\overline{X}_T^{(m)} - \mu\right) = T^{-1/2}\sum_{t=1}^{T}(X_t - X_t^{(m)}) = T^{-1/2}\sum_{t=1}^{T} e_t^{(m)}$$

where the error $e_t^{(m)}$ is

$$e_t^{(m)} = \sum_{|j|>m} \psi_j Z_{t-j}.$$

Clearly, $\{e_t^{(m)}\}$ is a stationary process with autocovariance function γ_e such that $\sum_{h=-\infty}^{\infty} \gamma_e(h) = \sigma_Z^2\left(\sum_{|j|>m} \psi_j\right)^2 < \infty$. We can therefore invoke Theorem 4.1 to show that

$$\mathbb{V}\left(\sqrt{T}\left(\overline{X}_T - \mu\right) - \sqrt{T}\left(\overline{X}_T^{(m)} - \mu\right)\right) = T\mathbb{V}\left(\frac{1}{T}\sum_{t=1}^{T} e_t^{(m)}\right)$$

converges to $\sigma_Z^2\left(\sum_{|j|>m}\psi_j\right)^2$ as $T\to\infty$. This term converges to zero as $m\to\infty$. The approximation error $\sqrt{T}\left(\overline{X}_T-\mu\right)-\sqrt{T}\left(\overline{X}_T^{(m)}-\mu\right)$ therefore converges in mean square to zero and thus, using Chebyshev's inequality (see Theorem C.3 or C.7), also in probability. We have therefore established the third condition of Theorem C.15 as well. Thus, we can conclude that $\sqrt{T}\left(\overline{X}_T-\mu\right)\xrightarrow{\mathrm{d}}X$. □

Under a more restrictive summability condition, we can provide a less demanding proof.[3] This proof follows an idea of Phillips and Solo (1992) and is based on the Beveridge-Nelson decomposition (see Appendix D).[4]

Theorem 4.3 *For any linear process of the form*

$$X_t=\mu+\sum_{j=0}^{\infty}\psi_j Z_{t-j}$$

such that $\sum_{j=0}^{\infty}j^2|\psi_j|^2<\infty$, *the arithmetic average* $\overline{X}_T$ *is asymptotically normal:*

$$\sqrt{T}(\overline{X}_T-\mu)\xrightarrow{\mathrm{d}}\mathrm{N}(0,\omega_X)=\mathrm{N}(0,\sigma_Z^2\,\Psi(1)^2).$$

Proof The application of the Beveridge-Nelson decomposition (see Theorem D.1 in Appendix D) leads to

$$\begin{aligned}\overline{X}_T-\mu&=\frac{1}{T}\sum_{t=1}^{T}\Psi(\mathrm{L})Z_t=\frac{1}{T}\sum_{t=1}^{T}(\Psi(1)-(\mathrm{L}-1))\widetilde{\Psi}(\mathrm{L}))Z_t\\&=\Psi(1)\left(\frac{1}{T}\sum_{t=1}^{T}Z_t\right)+\frac{1}{T}\widetilde{\Psi}(\mathrm{L})(Z_0-Z_T)\\\sqrt{T}(\overline{X}_T-\mu)&=\Psi(1)\left(\sqrt{T}\,\frac{\sum_{t=1}^{T}Z_t}{T}\right)+\frac{1}{\sqrt{T}}\widetilde{\Psi}(\mathrm{L})Z_0-\frac{1}{\sqrt{T}}\widetilde{\Psi}(\mathrm{L})Z_T.\end{aligned}$$

The assumption $Z_t\sim\mathrm{IID}(0,\sigma_Z^2)$ allows to apply the Central Limit Theorem C.13 of Appendix C to the first term. Thus, $\sqrt{T}\,\frac{\sum_{t=1}^{T}Z_t}{T}$ is asymptotical normal with mean zero and variance σ_Z^2. Theorem D.1 also implies $|\Psi(1)|<\infty$. Therefore,

[3] Note that this more restrictive summability condition holds within the context of causal stationary ARMA processes.

[4] The Beveridge-Nelson decomposition is an indispensable tool for the understanding of integrated and cointegrated processes analyzed in Chaps. 7 and 16.

the term $\Psi(1)\sqrt{T}\frac{\sum_{t=1}^{T} Z_t}{T}$ is asymptotically normal with mean zero and variance $\sigma_Z^2\Psi(1)^2$. The variances of the second and third term are equal to $\frac{\sigma_Z^2}{T}\sum_{j=0}^{T}\widetilde{\psi}_j^2$. The summability condition then implies according to Theorem D.1 that $\sum_{j=0}^{T}\widetilde{\psi}_j^2$ converges for $T \to \infty$. Thus, the variances of the last two terms converge to zero implying that these terms converge also to zero in probability (see Theorem C.7) and thus also in distribution. We can then invoke Theorem C.10 to establish the theorem. □

Remark 4.1 If $\{X_t\}$ is a Gaussian process, then for any given fixed T, $\overline{X}_T$ is distributed as

$$\sqrt{T}\left(\overline{X}_T - \mu\right) \sim \mathrm{N}\left(0, \sum_{|h|<T}\left(1 - \frac{|h|}{T}\right)\gamma(h)\right).$$

4.2 Estimation of Autocovariance and Autocorrelation Functions

With two slight, asymptotically unimportant modifications, we estimate the autocovariance function, $\gamma(h)$, and the autocorrelation function, $\rho(h)$, of a stationary stochastic process by customary statistics:

$$\widehat{\gamma}(h) = \frac{1}{T}\sum_{t=1}^{T-h}\left(X_t - \overline{X}_T\right)\left(X_{t+h} - \overline{X}_T\right), \tag{4.3}$$

$$\widehat{\rho}(h) = \frac{\widehat{\gamma}(h)}{\widehat{\gamma}(0)}. \tag{4.4}$$

These estimators are biased because the $T - h$ summands are divided (normalized) by T rather than $T - h$. The normalization with $T - h$ delivers an unbiased estimate only if $\overline{X}_T$ is replaced by μ, which, however, is typically unknown in practice. The second modification concerns the use of the complete sample for the estimation of μ.[5] The main advantage of using the above estimators is that the implied estimator for the covariance matrix, $\widehat{\Gamma}_T$, respectively the autocorrelation matrix, $\widehat{R}_T$, of $(X_1, \ldots, X_T)'$,

[5] The standard statistical formula suggests to estimate the mean appearing in the first multiplicand from the sample $X_1, \ldots, X_{t-h}$, and the mean appearing in the second multiplicand from $X_{h+1}, \ldots, X_T$.

$$\widehat{\Gamma}_T = \begin{pmatrix} \widehat{\gamma}(0) & \widehat{\gamma}(1) & \ldots & \widehat{\gamma}(T-1) \\ \widehat{\gamma}(1) & \widehat{\gamma}(0) & \ldots & \widehat{\gamma}(T-2) \\ \vdots & \vdots & \ddots & \vdots \\ \widehat{\gamma}(T-1) & \widehat{\gamma}(T-2) & \ldots & \widehat{\gamma}(0) \end{pmatrix}$$

$$\widehat{R}_T = \frac{\widehat{\Gamma}_T}{\widehat{\gamma}(0)}$$

always delivers, independently of the realized observations, nonnegative definite and for $\widehat{\gamma}(0) > 0$ nonsingular matrices. The invertibility of $\widehat{\Gamma}_T$ ensures that the normal equations (3.5) used to compute linear predictors in empirical applications have a unique solution. Moreover, the resulting estimated autocovariance function will then always satisfy the characterization given in Theorem 1.1, in particular Property (iv).

According to Box and Jenkins (1976, p. 33), one can expect reasonable estimates for $\gamma(h)$ and $\rho(h)$ if the sample size is larger than 50 and if the order of the autocorrelation coefficient is smaller than $T/4$.

The theorem below establishes that under rather mild conditions, these estimators are consistent and asymptotically normally distributed.

Theorem 4.4 *Let $\{X_t\}$ be a linear stationary process:*

$$X_t = \mu + \sum_{j=-\infty}^{\infty} \psi_j Z_{t-j}$$

with $Z_t \sim \text{IID}(0, \sigma^2)$, $\sum_{j=-\infty}^{\infty} |\psi_j| < \infty$ and $\sum_{j=-\infty}^{\infty} j|\psi_j|^2 < \infty$. Then we have for $h = 1, 2, \ldots$

$$\begin{pmatrix} \widehat{\rho}(1) \\ \vdots \\ \widehat{\rho}(h) \end{pmatrix} \xrightarrow{\text{d}} \text{N}\left(\begin{pmatrix} \rho(1) \\ \vdots \\ \rho(h) \end{pmatrix}, \frac{W}{T} \right)$$

where the elements of $W = (w_{ij})_{i,j \in \{1,\ldots,h\}}$ are given by Bartlett's formula:

$$w_{ij} = \sum_{k=1}^{\infty} [\rho(k+i) + \rho(k-i) - 2\rho(i)\rho(k)][\rho(k+j) + \rho(k-j) - 2\rho(j)\rho(k)].$$

Proof Brockwell and Davis (1991, section 7.3) □

Brockwell and Davis (1991) offer a second version of the above theorem where $\sum_{j=-\infty}^{\infty} j|\psi_j|^2 < \infty$ is replaced by the assumption of finite fourth moments, i.e., by assuming $\mathbb{E}Z_t^4 < \infty$. As we rely mainly on ARMA processes, we do not pursue this distinction further because this class of process automatically fulfills the above assumptions as soon as $\{Z_t\}$ is identically and independently distributed (IID). A proof that relies on the Beveridge-Nelson polynomial decomposition (see Theorem D.1 in Appendix D) can be gathered from Phillips and Solo (1992).

Example ($\{X_t\} \sim \text{IID}(0, \sigma^2)$) The most important application of the above theorem relates to the case of a white noise process. For this process, $\rho(h)$ equals zero for $|h| > 0$ and $\rho(1) = 1$. The above theorem then implies that W equals the identity matrix I_h, i.e., that

$$w_{ij} = \begin{cases} 1, & \text{for } i = j; \\ 0, & \text{otherwise.} \end{cases}$$

The estimated autocorrelation coefficients converge to the true autocorrelation coefficient, in this case zero. The asymptotic distribution of $\sqrt{T}\widehat{\rho}(h)$ converges to the standard normal distribution. This implies that for large T, we can approximate the distribution of $\widehat{\rho}(h)$ by a normal distribution with mean zero and variance $1/T$. This allows the construction of a 95% confidence interval for the case that the true process is white noise. This confidence interval is therefore given by $\pm 1.96T^{-\frac{1}{2}}$. It can be used to verify if the observed process is indeed white noise.

Figure 4.1 plots the empirical autocorrelation function of a WN(0,1) process with a sample size of $T = 100$. The implied 95% confidence is therefore equal to ± 0.196. As each estimated autocorrelation coefficient falls within the confidence interval, we conclude that the observed times series may indeed represent a white noise process.

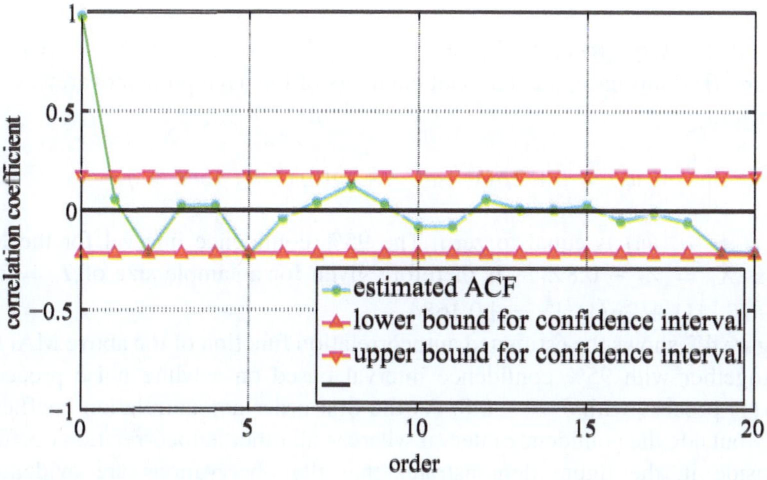

Fig. 4.1 Estimated autocorrelation function of a WN(0,1) process with 95% confidence interval for sample size $T = 100$

Instead of examining each correlation coefficient separately, we can test the joint hypothesis that all correlation coefficients up to order N are equal to zero, i.e., $\rho(1) = \rho(2) = \ldots = \rho(N) = 0$, $N = 1, 2, \ldots$. As each $\sqrt{T}\hat{\rho}(h)$ has asymptotically a standard normal distribution uncorrelated with $\sqrt{T}\hat{\rho}(k)$, $h \neq k$, the sum of the squared estimated autocorrelation coefficients is asymptotically χ^2 distributed with N degrees of freedom. This test statistic is called *Box-Pierce statistic*:

$$Q = T \sum_{h=1}^{N} \hat{\rho}^2(h) \quad \sim \chi^2_N.$$

A refinement of this test statistic is given by the *Ljung-Box statistic*:

$$Q' = T(T+2) \sum_{h=1}^{N} \frac{\hat{\rho}^2(h)}{T-h} \quad \sim \chi^2_N. \tag{4.5}$$

This test statistic is also asymptotically χ^2 distributed with the same degree of freedom N. This statistic accounts for the fact that the estimates for the autocorrelations for high orders h are based on a smaller number of observations and are thus less precise and more noisy and are therefore given less weight. The two test statistics are used in the usual way. The null hypothesis that all correlation coefficients are jointly equal to zero is rejected if Q, respectively Q', is larger than the critical value corresponding to the χ^2_N distribution. The number of summands N is usually taken to be rather large, for a sample size of 150 in the range between 15 and 20. The two tests are also referred to as *portmanteau tests*.

Example (MA(q) process: $X_t = Z_t + \theta_1 Z_{t-1} + \ldots + \theta_q Z_{t-q}$ with $Z_t \sim$ IID$(0, \sigma^2)$) In this case, the diagonal elements of the asymptotic covariance matrix are

$$w_{ii} = 1 + 2\rho(1)^2 + \ldots + 2\rho(q)^2 \qquad \text{for } i > q.$$

For $i, j > q$, w_{ij} is equal to zero. The 95% confidence interval for the MA(1) process $X_t = Z_t - 0.8Z_{t-1}$ is therefore given for a sample size of $T = 200$ by $\pm\, 1.96T^{-\frac{1}{2}}[1 + 2\rho(1)^2]^{\frac{1}{2}} = \pm 0.1684$.

Figure 4.2 shows the estimated autocorrelation function of the above MA(1) process together with 95% confidence interval based on a white noise process and a MA(1) process with $\theta = -0.8$. As the first-order autocorrelation coefficient is clearly outside the confidence interval whereas all other autocorrelation coefficients are inside it, the figure demonstrates that the observations are evidently the realization of the MA(1) process.

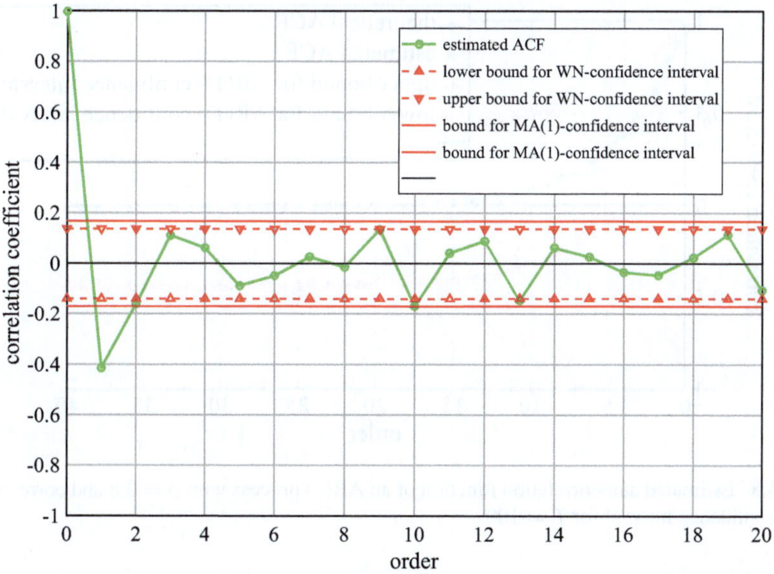

Fig. 4.2 Estimated autocorrelation function of a MA(1) process with $\theta = -0.8$ with corresponding 95% confidence interval for $T = 200$

Example (AR(1) process $X_t - \phi X_{t-1} = Z_t$ with $Z_t \sim \text{IID}(0, \sigma^2)$)
In this case, the diagonal elements of the asymptotic covariance matrix are

$$
\begin{aligned}
w_{ii} &= \sum_{k=1}^{i} \phi^{2i} \left(\phi^k - \phi^{-k}\right)^2 + \sum_{k=i+1}^{\infty} \phi^{2k} \left(\phi^i - \phi^{-i}\right)^2 \\
&= \frac{\left(1-\phi^{2i}\right)\left(1+\phi^2\right)}{1-\phi^2} - 2i\phi^{2i} \\
&\approx \frac{1+\phi^2}{1-\phi^2} \quad \text{for large } i.
\end{aligned}
$$

The formula for w_{ij} with $i \neq j$ are not shown. In any case, this formula is of relatively little importance because the partial autocorrelations are better suited for the identification of AR processes (see Sects. 3 and 3.3).

Figure 4.3 shows an estimated autocorrelation function of an AR(1) process. The autocorrelation coefficients decline exponentially, which is a characteristic for an AR(1) process.[6] Furthermore, the coefficients are outside the confidence interval up to order 8 for white noise processes.

[6] As a reminder: the theoretical autocorrelation coefficients are $\rho(h) = \phi^{|h|}$.

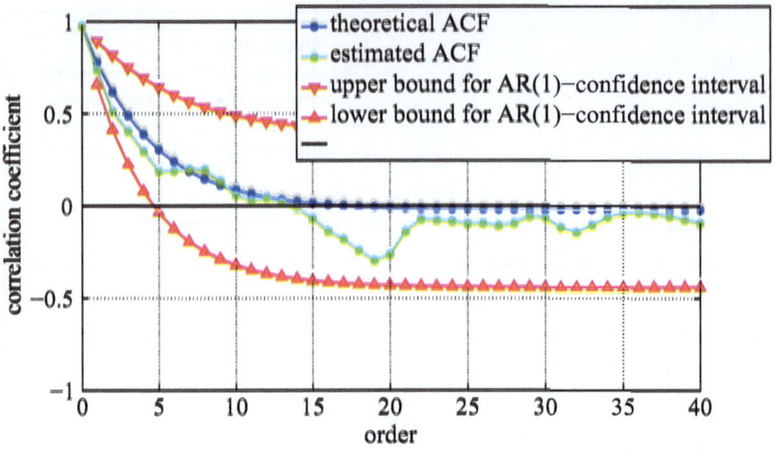

Fig. 4.3 Estimated autocorrelation function of an AR(1) process with $\phi = 0.8$ and corresponding 95% confidence interval for $T = 100$

4.3 Estimation of Partial Autocorrelation Functions

According to its definition (see Definition 3.1), the partial autocorrelation of order h, $\alpha(h)$, is equal to a_h, the last element of the vector $\alpha_h = \Gamma_h^{-1}\gamma_h(1) = R_h^{-1}\rho_h(1)$. Thus, α_h and consequently a_h can be estimated by $\hat{\alpha}_h = \widehat{\Gamma}_h^{-1}\hat{\gamma}_h(1) = \hat{R}_h^{-1}\hat{\rho}_h(1)$ (see also see formula (3.12)). As $\rho(h)$ can be consistently estimated and is asymptotically normally distributed (see Sect. 4.2), the *continuous mapping theorem* (see Appendix C) ensures that the above estimator for $\alpha(h)$ is also consistent and asymptotically normal. In particular, we have for an AR(p) process (Brockwell and Davis 1991)

$$\sqrt{T}\hat{\alpha}(h) \xrightarrow{\text{d}} \text{N}(0, 1) \quad \text{for } T \to \infty \text{ and } h > p.$$

This result allows to construct, as in the case of the autocorrelation coefficients, confidence intervals for the partial autocorrelation coefficients. The 95% confidence interval is given by $\pm \frac{1.96}{\sqrt{T}}$. The AR(p) process is characterized by the fact that the partial autocorrelation coefficients are zero for $h > p$. $\hat{\alpha}(h)$ should therefore be inside the confidence interval for $h > p$ and outside for $h \leq p$. Figure 4.4 confirms this for an AR(1) process with $\phi = 0.8$.

Figure 4.5 shows the estimated PACF for an MA(1) process with $\theta = 0.8$. In conformity with the theory, the partial autocorrelation coefficients converge to zero. They do so in an oscillating manner because θ is positive (see formula (3.12) in Sect. 3.3)

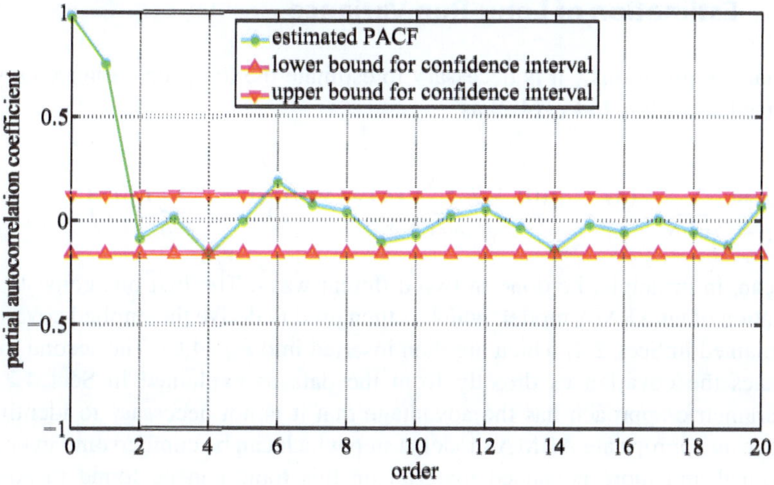

Fig. 4.4 Estimated PACF for an AR(1) process with $\phi = 0.8$ and corresponding 95% confidence interval for $T = 200$

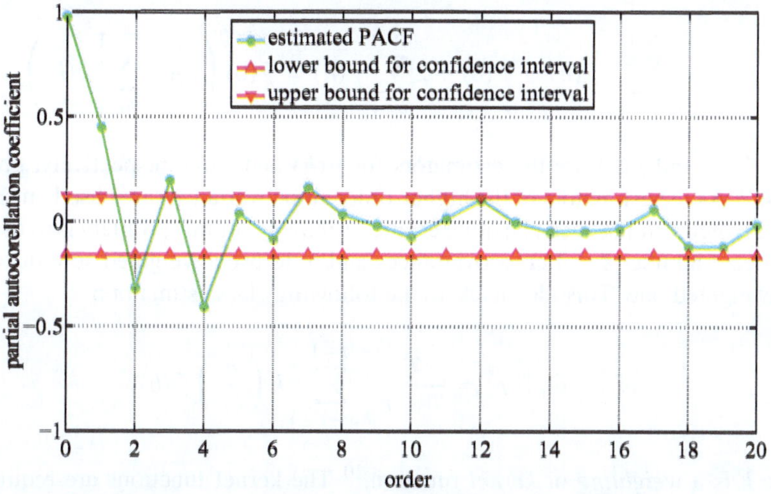

Fig. 4.5 Estimated PACF for a MA(1) process with $\theta = 0.8$ and corresponding 95% confidence interval for $T = 200$

4.4 Estimation of Long-Run Variance

For many applications,[7] it is necessary to estimate the long-run variance ω, which is defined according to Eq. (4.2) as[8]

$$\omega = \sum_{h=-\infty}^{\infty} \gamma(h) = \gamma(0) + 2\sum_{h=1}^{\infty} \gamma(h) = \gamma(0)\left(1 + 2\sum_{h=1}^{\infty} \rho(h)\right). \tag{4.6}$$

This can, in principle, be done in two different ways. The first one consists in the estimation of an ARMA model, which is then used to derive the implied covariances as explained in Sect. 2.4, which are then inserted into Eq. (4.6). The second method estimates the covariances directly from the data as explained in Sect. 4.2. This nonparametric approach has the advantage that it is not necessary to identify and estimate an appropriate ARMA model, a step which can be cumbersome in practice. Additional and more advanced material on this topic can be found in Andrews (1991), Andrews and Monahan (1992), Haan and Levin (1997), Jansson (2002), and Newey and West (1994), among others.[9]

If the sample size is T, only $T - 1$ covariances can be estimated. Thus, a first naive estimator of ω is given by $\hat{\omega}_T$ defined as

$$\hat{\omega}_T = \sum_{h=-T+1}^{T-1} \hat{\gamma}(h) = \hat{\gamma}(0) + 2\sum_{h=1}^{T-1} \hat{\gamma}(h) = \hat{\gamma}(0)\left(1 + 2\sum_{h=1}^{T-1} \hat{\rho}(h)\right),$$

where $\hat{\gamma}(h)$ and $\hat{\rho}(h)$ are the estimators for $\gamma(h)$ and $\rho(h)$, respectively, given in Sect. 4.2. As the estimators of the higher-order autocovariances are based on smaller samples, their estimates can be quite erratic. A remedy for this problem is to use only a restricted number ℓ_T of autocovariances and/or to use a weighted sum instead of an unweighted one. This idea leads to the following class estimators:

$$\hat{\omega}_T = \hat{\omega}_T(\ell_T) = \frac{T}{T-r} \sum_{h=-T+1}^{T-1} k\left(\frac{h}{\ell_T}\right) \hat{\gamma}(h),$$

where k is a *weighting* or *kernel* function.[10] The kernel functions are required to have the following properties:

[7] For example, when testing the null hypothesis H_0: $\mu = \mu_0$ in the case of serially correlated observations (see Sect. 4.1), or for the Phillips-Perron unit-root test introduced in Sect. 7.3.2.

[8] See Theorem 4.2 and the comments following it.

[9] Note the connection between the long-run variance and the spectral density at frequency zero: $\omega = 2\pi f(0)$ where f is the spectral density function (see Sect. 6.3).

[10] Kernel functions are also relevant for spectral estimators. See in particular Sect. 6.3.

Table 4.1 Some popular kernel functions

Name	$k(x) =$
Boxcar ("truncated")	1
Bartlett	$1 - \|x\|$
Daniell	$\frac{\sin(\pi x)}{\pi x}$
Tukey-Hanning	$(1 + \cos(\pi x))/2$
Quadratic spectral	$\frac{25}{12\pi^2 x^2}\left(\frac{\sin(6\pi x/5)}{6\pi x/5} - \cos(6\pi x/5)\right)$

The functions are, with the exception of the quadratic spectral function, only defined for $|x| \leq 1$. Outside this interval, they are set to zero

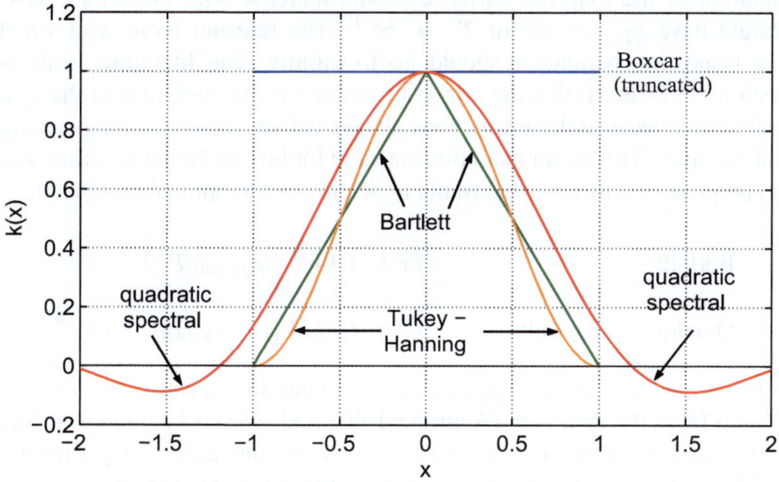

Fig. 4.6 Common kernel functions

(i) $k : \mathbb{R} \to [-1, 1]$ is, with the exception of a finite number of points, a continuous function. In particular, k is continuous at $x = 0$.
(ii) k is quadratically integrable, i.e., $\int_{\mathbb{R}} k(x)^2 dx < \infty$.
(iii) $k(0) = 1$.
(iv) $k(x) = k(-x)$ for all $x \in \mathbb{R}$, i.e., k is symmetric.

The basic idea of the kernel function is to give relatively little weight to the higher-order autocovariances and relatively more weight to the smaller-order ones. As $k(0)$ equals one, the variance $\hat{\gamma}(0)$ receives weight one by construction. The continuity assumption implies that also the covariances of smaller order, i.e., for h small, receive a weight close to one. Table 4.1 lists some of the most popular kernel functions.

Figure 4.6 shows a plot of these functions. The first three functions are nonzero only for $|x| < 1$. This implies that only the orders h for which $|h| \leq \ell_T$ are taken into account. ℓ_T is called the *lag truncation parameter* or the *bandwidth*. The quadratic spectral kernel function is an example of a kernel function that takes all covariances into account. Note that some weights are negative in this case as shown in Fig. 4.6.[11]

The estimator for the long-run variance is subject to the correction term $\frac{T}{T-r}$. This factor depends on the number of parameters estimated in a first step and is only relevant when the sample size is relatively small. In the case of the estimation of the mean, r would be equal to one and the correction term is negligible. If on the other hand $X_t, t = 1, \ldots, T$, are the residuals from multivariate regression, r designates the number of regressors. In many applications, the correction term is omitted.

The lag truncation parameter or bandwidth, ℓ_T, depends on the number of observations T. Intuitively, the number of autocovariances accounted for in the computation of the long-run variance should increase with the sample size, e.g., we should have $\ell_T \to \infty$ for $T \to \infty$.[12] The relevant issue is at which rate the lag truncation parameter should go to infinity. The literature made several suggestions.[13] In the following, we concentrate on the Bartlett and the quadratic spectral kernel because these functions always deliver a positive long-run variance in small samples. This is, for example, not valid for boxcar kernel function. Andrews (1991) proposes the following formula to determine the optimal bandwidth:

$$\text{Bartlett:} \qquad \ell_T = 1.1447 \left\lfloor \alpha_{\text{Bartlett}}\, T \right\rfloor^{\frac{1}{3}}$$

$$\text{Quadratic Spectral:} \qquad \ell_T = 1.3221 \left\lfloor \alpha_{\text{QuadraticSpectral}}\, T \right\rfloor^{\frac{1}{5}},$$

whereby α_{Bartlett} and $\alpha_{\text{QuadraticSpectral}}$ are constants that have to be determined in a first step from the data (see (Andrews 1991, 832–839), (Andrews and Monahan 1992, 958) and (Haan and Levin 1997)). $\lfloor x \rfloor$ denotes the largest integer less or equal to x. If the underlying process is approximated by an AR(1) model, we get

$$\alpha_{\text{Bartlett}} = \frac{4\hat{\rho}^2}{(1-\hat{\rho}^2)(1+\hat{\rho}^2)}$$

$$\alpha_{\text{QuadraticSpectral}} = \frac{4\hat{\rho}^2}{(1-\hat{\rho})^4},$$

where $\hat{\rho}$ is the first-order empirical autocorrelation coefficient.

[11] Phillips (2005) has proposed a nonparametric regression-based method that does not require a kernel function.

[12] This is true even when the underlying process is known to be a MA(q) process. Even in this case, it is advantageous to include also the autocovariances for $h > q$. The reason is twofold. First, only when $\ell_T \to \infty$ for $T \to \infty$, do we get a consistent estimator, i.e., $\hat{\omega}_T \to \omega_T$, respectively ω. Second, the restriction to $\hat{\gamma}(h), |h| \leq q$, does not necessarily lead to a positive value for the estimated long-run variance $\hat{\omega}_T$, even when the Bartlett kernel is used. See Ogaki (1992) for details.

[13] For an overview, see Haan and Levin (1997) and the literature cited at the beginning of this section.

In order to avoid the cumbersome determination of the α's, Newey and West (1994) suggest the following rules of thumb:

$$\text{Bartlett:} \qquad \ell_T = \beta_{\text{Bartlett}} \left\lfloor \frac{T}{100} \right\rfloor^{\frac{2}{9}} \tag{4.7}$$

$$\text{Quadratic Spectral:} \qquad \ell_T = \beta_{\text{QuadraticSpectral}} \left\lfloor \frac{T}{100} \right\rfloor^{\frac{2}{25}}. \tag{4.8}$$

It has been shown that values of 4 for β_{Bartlett} as well as for $\beta_{\text{QuadraticSpectral}}$ lead to acceptable results. A comparison of these formulas with the ones provided by Andrews shows that the latter imply larger values for ℓ_T when the sample sizes get larger. Both approaches lead to consistent estimates, i.e., $\hat{\omega}_T(\ell_T) - \omega_T \xrightarrow{p} 0$ for $T \to \infty$.

In practice, a combination of both parametric and nonparametric methods proved to deliver the best results. This combined method consists of five steps:

(i) The first step is called *prewhitening* and consists in the estimation of a simple ARMA model for the process $\{X_t\}$ to remove the most obvious serial correlations. The recorded residual process $\widehat{Z}_t$ should be close to a white noise process.[14] Usually, an AR(1) model is sufficient.[15]
(ii) Choose a kernel function and, if the method of Andrews has been chosen, the corresponding data-dependent constants, i.e., α_{Bartlett} or $\alpha_{\text{QuadraticSpectral}}$ for the Bartlett, respectively the quadratic spectral kernel function.
(iii) Compute the lag truncation parameter for the residuals using the corresponding formulas.
(iv) Estimate the long-run variance $\hat{\omega}_T^Z$ for the residuals $\widehat{Z}_t$.
(v) Recover the long-run variance $\hat{\omega}_T^Z$ for the original time series $\{X_t\}$.

If in the first step an AR(1) model, $X_t = \phi X_{t-1} + Z_t$, was used, the last step is given by

$$\hat{\omega}_T^X(\ell_T) = \frac{\hat{\omega}_T^Z(\ell_T)}{(1-\hat{\phi})^2},$$

where $\hat{\omega}_T^Z(\ell_T)$ and $\hat{\omega}_T^X(\ell_T)$ denote the estimated long-run variances of $\{X_t\}$ and $\{\hat{Z}_t\}$. In the general case, of an arbitrary ARMA model, $\Phi(\mathrm{L})X_t = \Theta(\mathrm{L})Z_t$, we get

$$\hat{\omega}_T^X(\ell_T) = \left(\frac{\Theta(1)}{\Phi(1)}\right)^2 \hat{\omega}_T^Z(\ell_T).$$

[14] This idea originally goes back to Press and Tukey (1956). See also Priestley (1981).

[15] If in this step an AR(1) model is used and if a first-order correlation $\hat{\phi}$ larger in absolute terms than 0.97 is obtained, Andrews and Monahan (1992, 457) suggest to replace $\hat{\phi}$ by -0.97, respectively 0.97. Instead of using an arbitrary fixed value, it turns out that a data-driven value is superior. Sul et al. (2005) suggest to replace 0.97 by $1 - 1/\sqrt{T}$ and -0.97 by $-1 + 1/\sqrt{T}$.

4.4.1 An Example

Suppose we want to test whether the yearly growth rate of Switzerland's real GDP in the last 42 years was higher than 1.4%. For this purpose, we compute the percentage change against the corresponding quarter of the last year over the period 1981:1 to 2023:1 (169 observations in total), i.e., we compute $X_t = 100(1 - \mathrm{L}^4)\log(\mathrm{BIP}_t)$. The arithmetic average of these growth rates is $\hat{\mu} = 1.7076$ with a variance of $\gamma(0) = 3.9501$. We test the null hypothesis that the growth rate is smaller than 1.4% against the alternative that it is greater than 1.4%. The corresponding value of the t-statistic is $(1.7076 - 1.4)/\sqrt{3.9501/169} = 2.0120$. Taking a 5% significance level, the critical value for this one-sided test is 1.661. Thus, the null hypothesis is clearly rejected.

The above computation is, however, not valid because the serial correlation of the time series was not taken into account. Indeed, the estimated autocorrelation function shown in Fig. 4.7 clearly shows that the growth rate is indeed subject to high positive and statistically significant autocorrelations.

The rule of thumb formula (4.7) for the lag truncation parameter for the Bartlett kernel function suggests $\ell_T = 4\left\lfloor\left(\frac{169}{100}\right)^{2/9}\right\rfloor = 4\lfloor 1.1295\rfloor = 4$. The weights in the computation of the long-run variance are therefore

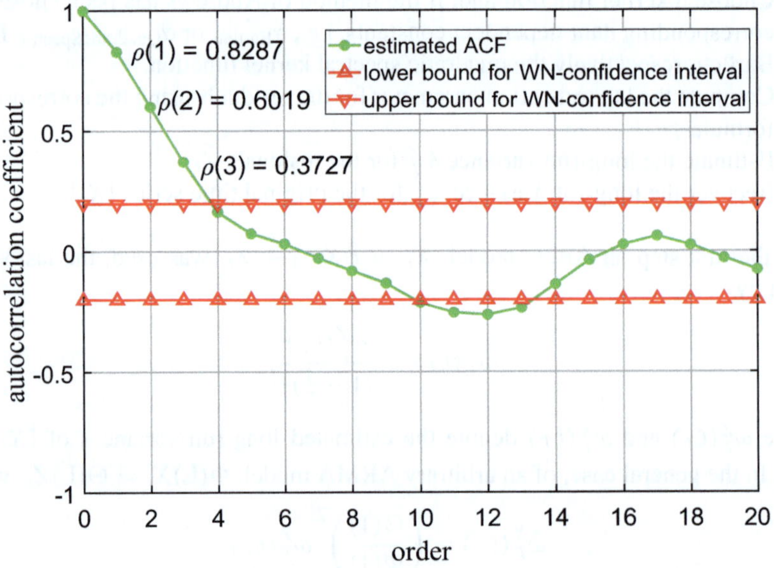

Fig. 4.7 Estimated autocorrelation function for Switzerland's real GDP growth (percentage change against corresponding last year's quarter)

$$k(h/\ell_T) = \begin{cases} 1, & h = 0; \\ 3/4, & h = \pm 1; \\ 2/4, & h = \pm 2; \\ 1/4, & h = \pm 3; \\ 0, & |h| \geq 4. \end{cases}$$

The corresponding estimate for the long-run variance is therefore given by

$$\hat{\omega}_T = 3.9501 \left(1 + 2\frac{3}{4}0.8287 + 2\frac{2}{4}0.6019 + 2\frac{1}{4}0.3727 \right) = 11.9739.$$

Using the long-run variance instead of the simple variance leads to a quite different value of the t-statistic: $(1.7076 - 1.4)/\sqrt{11.9739/169} = 1.1556$. The null hypothesis is thus not rejected at the 5% significance level when the serial correlation of the process is taken into account.

4.5 Exercises

Exercise 4.5.1 You regress 100 realizations of a stationary stochastic process $\{X_t\}$ against a constant c. The least-squares estimate of c equals $\hat{c} = 0.4$ with an estimated standard deviation of $\hat{\sigma}_c = 0.15$. In addition, you have estimated the autocorrelation function up to order $h = 5$ and obtained the following values:

$$\hat{\rho}(1) = -0.43, \ \hat{\rho}(2) = 0.13, \ \hat{\rho}(3) = -0.12, \ \hat{\rho}(4) = 0.18, \ \hat{\rho}(5) = -0.23.$$

(i) How do you interpret the estimated parameter value of 0.4?
(ii) Examine the autocorrelation function. Do you think that $\{X_t\}$ is white noise?
(iii) Why can the estimated standard deviation $\hat{\sigma}_c = 0.15$ be misleading?
(iv) Estimate the long-run variance using the Bartlett kernel.
(v) Test the null hypothesis that $\{X_t\}$ is a mean-zero process.

Exercise 4.5.2 Show that for any realizations $x_1, \ldots, x_T$ of a stochastic process,

$$\sum_{|h|<T} \hat{\gamma}(h) = 0,$$

if $\hat{\gamma}(h)$ is computed according to Eq. (4.3).

Exercise 4.5.3 Download the annual real GDP times series $\{X_t\}$ of a country of your choice. Then, compute the growth rate by taking logarithmic differences $\{\Delta \ln X_t\}$.

(i) Estimate the ACF and the PACF of $\{\Delta \ln X_t\}$.
(ii) Test the hypothesis that the series is white noise.
(iii) Given your estimates of ACF and PACF, guess which ARMA model is likely to have generated the data.
(iv) Estimate the long-run variance.

Exercise 4.5.4 You observe 169 realizations of a stationary time series $\{X_t\}$.

(i) The arithmetic mean of the observations is 0.21. The arithmetic mean is an estimator for which entity?
(ii) The estimated standard error is 0.132. Based on this information, can you decide whether the expected value $\mathbb{E}X_t$ is different from zero? What are conditions under which you can test reliably the hypothesis $\mathbf{H}_0 : \mathbb{E}X_t = 0$ against $\mathbf{H}_1 : \mathbb{E}X_t \neq 0$?
(iii) You have also estimated the autocorrelation function $\rho(h)$ for $h = 1, 2, \ldots, 6$ and obtained the following estimates:

$$\hat{\rho}(1) = -0.697 \qquad \hat{\rho}(2) = 0.331 \qquad \hat{\rho}(3) = -0.206$$
$$\hat{\rho}(4) = 0.138 \qquad \hat{\rho}(5) = -0.110 \qquad \hat{\rho}(6) = 0.059$$

(iv) Based on these estimates, do you think that $\{X_t\}$ is white noise? Justify your answer by an appropriate test.
(v) Based on these estimates, what would be a suitable ARMA model?
(vi) If you decided that the times series is not white noise, what are the implications of using the standard error for testing the hypothesis $\mathbf{H}_0 : \mathbb{E}X_t = 0$ against $\mathbf{H}_1 : \mathbb{E}X_t \neq 0$?
(vii) Using the Bartlett kernel with lag truncation parameter $\ell_T = 5$, estimate the long-run variance ω of $\{X_t\}$.
(viii) Carry out again the hypothesis test $\mathbf{H}_0 : \mathbb{E}X_t = 0$ against $\mathbf{H}_1 : \mathbb{E}X_t \neq 0$ using the estimated long-run variance.
(ix) If your conclusion in (viii) is different from the one in (ii), which one would you prefer?

Modeling Stationary ARMA Processes 5

The specification of stationary ARMA(p,q) processes and the estimation of its parameters for a given realization involve several intermingled steps. First, one must determine the orders p and q. Once the orders have been determined, one can estimate the parameters ϕ_j, $j = 0, 1, \ldots p$, θ_j, $j = 0, 1, \ldots, q$, with $\phi_p\theta_q \neq 0$, and σ^2. Finally, the estimated ARMA model has to pass several robustness checks to be accepted as a valid model. These checks may involve tests of parameter constancy, forecasting performance, or tests for the inclusion of additional exogenous variables. This is usually an iterative process in which several models are examined. It is rarely the case that one model imposes itself. All too often, one is confronted in the modeling process with several trade-offs, like simple versus complex models or data fit versus forecasting performance. Finding the right balance among the different dimensions therefore requires some judgment based on experience.

We start the analysis by assuming that the orders p and q of the stationary ARMA process are known and the problem just consists in estimating the corresponding parameters from a given realization. The number of observations or sample size is denoted by T. For simplicity, we assume in the theoretical exposition that the data are already mean adjusted. In practice, one has to include a constant term in the specification to account for a nonzero mean. We will introduce three estimation methods. The first one is a method of moments procedure where the theoretical moments are equated to the empirical ones. This procedure leads to the so-called Yule-Walker estimator. The second procedure interprets the stochastic difference equation as a regression model and estimates the parameters by ordinary least squares (OLS). These two methods are asymptotically equivalent and work well if the underlying model is a purely AR process involving no MA terms. If the model comprises MA terms, a maximum-likelihood (ML) approach must be pursued.

K. Neusser, *Time Series Econometrics*, Springer Texts in Business and Economics,
https://doi.org/10.1007/978-3-031-88838-0_5

5.1 The Yule-Walker Estimator

We investigate the parameter estimation in the context of a mean zero stationary purely autoregressive model of known order p:

$$\Phi(\mathrm{L})X_t = X_t - \phi_1 X_{t-1} - \cdots - \phi_p X_{t-p} = Z_t \qquad \text{with } Z_t \sim \mathrm{WN}(0, \sigma^2).$$

In addition, we assume that $\{X_t\}$ is causal with respect to $\{Z_t\}$, i.e., $\Phi(z) \neq 0$ for $|z| \leq 1$. Hence, there exists a sequence $\{\psi_j\}$ with $\sum_{j=0}^{\infty} |\psi_j| < \infty$ such that $X_t = \Psi(\mathrm{L})Z_t$.

Multiplying the difference equation successively by $X_{t-j}, j = 0, 1, \ldots, p$, and taking expectations, leads to an equation system in the parameters $\Phi = (\phi_1, \ldots, \phi_p)'$ and σ^2:

$$\begin{aligned}
\gamma(0) - \phi_1\gamma(1) - \ldots - \phi_p\gamma(p) &= \sigma^2 \\
\gamma(1) - \phi_1\gamma(0) - \ldots - \phi_p\gamma(p-1) &= 0 \\
&\ldots \\
\gamma(p) - \phi_1\gamma(p-1) - \ldots - \phi_p\gamma(0) &= 0
\end{aligned}$$

This equation system is known as the *Yule-Walker equations*. It can be written compactly in matrix algebra as

$$\gamma(0) - \Phi'\gamma_p(1) = \sigma^2,$$

$$\begin{pmatrix} \gamma(0) & \gamma(1) & \ldots & \gamma(p-1) \\ \gamma(1) & \gamma(0) & \ldots & \gamma(p-2) \\ \vdots & \vdots & \ddots & \vdots \\ \gamma(p-1) & \gamma(p-2) & \ldots & \gamma(0) \end{pmatrix} \begin{pmatrix} \phi_1 \\ \phi_2 \\ \vdots \\ \phi_p \end{pmatrix} = \begin{pmatrix} \gamma(1) \\ \gamma(2) \\ \vdots \\ \gamma(p) \end{pmatrix},$$

respectively

$$\begin{aligned}
\gamma(0) - \Phi'\gamma_p &= \sigma^2, \\
\Gamma_p \Phi &= \gamma_p,
\end{aligned}$$

where $\gamma_p = (\gamma(1), \ldots, \gamma(p))'$.

The *Yule-Walker estimator* is obtained by replacing the theoretical moments by the empirical ones and solving the resulting equation system for the unknown parameters:

$$\begin{aligned}
\widehat{\Phi}_{YW} &= \widehat{\Gamma}_p^{-1}\,\widehat{\gamma}_p = \widehat{R}_p^{-1}\,\widehat{\rho}_p \\
\widehat{\sigma}^2_{YW} &= \widehat{\gamma}(0) - \widehat{\Phi}'\,\widehat{\gamma}_p = \widehat{\gamma}(0)\left(1 - \widehat{\rho}_p{}'\,\widehat{R}_p^{-1}\,\widehat{\rho}_p\right)
\end{aligned}$$

where $\rho_p = (\rho(1), \ldots, \rho(p))'$. As long as $\widehat{\gamma}(0) > 0$, the matrix $\widehat{\Gamma}_p$ will always be non-singular (see Sect. 4.2). Hence, the Yule-Walker estimator is well-defined under this condition. Furthermore, the equation system is recursive: the estimate $\widehat{\Phi}_{YW}$ is obtained without knowledge of $\widehat{\sigma}^2_{YW}$ because the estimator $\widehat{R}_p^{-1}\widehat{\rho}_p$ involves only autocorrelations. The estimates $\widehat{\Gamma}_p$, $\widehat{R}_p$, $\widehat{\gamma}_p$, $\widehat{\rho}_p$, and $\widehat{\gamma}(0)$ are obtained according to the methods outlined in Sect. 4.2.

The construction of the Yule-Walker estimator implies that the first p values of the autocovariance, respectively the autocorrelation function, implied by the estimated model exactly correspond to their estimated counterparts. It can be shown that this moment estimator always delivers coefficients $\widehat{\Phi}_{YW}$, which imply that $\{X_t\}$ is causal with respect to $\{Z_t\}$. In addition, the following theorem establishes that the estimated coefficients are asymptotically normally distributed.

Theorem 5.1 (Asymptotic normality of Yule-Walker estimator) *Let $\{X_t\}$ be a stationary AR(p) process that is causal with respect to $\{Z_t\}$ whereby $\{Z_t\} \sim \mathrm{IID}(0, \sigma^2)$. Then, the Yule-Walker estimator is consistent, and $\widehat{\Phi}_{YW}$ is asymptotically normal with distribution given by*

$$\sqrt{T}\left(\widehat{\Phi}_{YW} - \Phi\right) \xrightarrow{d} \mathrm{N}\left(0, \sigma^2 \Gamma_p^{-1}\right).$$

In addition, we have that

$$\widehat{\sigma}^2_{YW} \xrightarrow{p} \sigma^2.$$

Proof See Brockwell and Davis (1991, 233–234). □

Noteworthy, the asymptotic covariance matrix of the Yule-Walker estimate is independent of σ^2.

Example (AR(1) process)
In the case of an AR(1) process, the Yule-Walker equation is $\widehat{\Gamma}_1 = \widehat{\gamma}(1) = \widehat{\gamma}(0)\phi$. The Yule-Walker estimator thus becomes

$$\widehat{\Phi}_{YW} = \widehat{\phi}_{YW} = \frac{\widehat{\gamma}(1)}{\widehat{\gamma}(0)} = \widehat{\rho}(1).$$

According to the above theorem, the asymptotic distribution is

$$\sqrt{T}\left(\widehat{\phi}_{YW} - \phi\right) \xrightarrow{\mathrm{d}} \mathrm{N}\left(0, \frac{\sigma^2}{\gamma(0)}\right) = \mathrm{N}\left(0, 1 - \phi^2\right).$$

This shows that the assumption of causality, i.e., $|\phi| < 1$, is crucial. Otherwise, no positive value for the variance would exist. Note that the asymptotic variance approaches 0 as $\phi \to 1$. In the case $\phi = 1$, the difference $(\widehat{\phi}_{YW} - \phi)$ has to be scaled by a rate greater than $\sqrt{T}$ to obtain a nondegenerate asymptotic distribution (see Sect. 7.2).

In practice, the order of the model is usually unknown. However, one can expect when estimating an AR(m) model, whereby the true order p is strictly smaller than m that the estimated "superfluous" coefficients $\hat{\phi}_{p+1}, \ldots, \hat{\phi}_m$ should be close to zero.[1] This is indeed the case as shown in Brockwell and Davis (1991, 241). In particular, under the assumptions of Theorem 5.1, it holds that

$$\sqrt{T}\,\hat{\phi}_m \xrightarrow{\ d\ } \mathrm{N}(0,1) \qquad \text{for } m > p. \tag{5.1}$$

This result justifies the following strategy to identify the order of an AR model. Estimate in a first step a highly parameterized model (overfitted model), i.e., a model with a large value of m, and test via a t-test whether ϕ_m is zero. If the hypothesis cannot be rejected, reduce the model order from m to $m-1$ and repeat the same procedure but with respect to ϕ_{m-1}. This is done until the hypothesis can no longer be rejected. Finally, one may test the joint hypothesis $\phi_{p+1} = \cdots = \phi_m = 0$ by an F-test. Although this successive testing procedure is not consistent when the significance level is kept constant, it nevertheless represents a practical and easy to implement strategy.

If the order of the initial model is too low (underfitted model) so that the true order is higher than m, one incurs an "omitted variable bias." The corresponding estimates are no longer consistent. Section 5.4 takes a closer look at the problem of determining the order of a model.

Example (MA(q) process)
The Yule-Walker estimator can, in principle, also be applied to MA(q) or stationary ARMA(p,q) processes with $q > 0$. However, the analysis of the simple MA(1) process in Sect. 1.5.2 showed that the relation between the autocorrelations and the model parameters is nonlinear and may have two, one, or no solution. Consider again the MA(1) process as an example. It is given by the stochastic difference equation $X_t = Z_t + \theta Z_{t-1}$ with $Z_t \sim \mathrm{IID}(0, \sigma^2)$. The Yule-Walker equations are then as follows:

$$\hat{\gamma}(0) = \hat{\sigma}^2(1 + \hat{\theta}^2)$$
$$\hat{\gamma}(1) = \hat{\sigma}^2\hat{\theta}$$

The above equation system has two solutions if $|\hat{\rho}(1)| = \left|\hat{\gamma}(1)/\hat{\gamma}(0)\right| < 1/2$; one solution if $|\hat{\rho}(1)| = \left|\hat{\gamma}(1)/\hat{\gamma}(0)\right| = 1/2$; and no real solution if $|\hat{\rho}(1)| = \left|\hat{\gamma}(1)/\hat{\gamma}(0)\right| > 1/2$. In the case of several solutions, we usually take the invertible one, which corresponds to $|\theta| < 1$. Invertibility is, however, a restriction that is hard

[1] Compare this with the partial autocorrelations analyzed in Sect. 3.3.

to implement in the case of higher-order MA processes. Moreover, it can be shown that the Yule-Walker estimator is no longer consistent in general (see Brockwell and Davis (1991, 246) for details). For these reasons, it is not advisable to use the Yule-Walker estimator in the case of MA processes, especially when there exists with the maximum-likelihood-estimator a consistent and efficient alternative.

5.2 The Ordinary Least-Squares (OLS) Estimator for AR Models

An alternative approach is to view the difference equation defining the AR process as a regression model with X_t as the dependent variable, $X_{t-1}, \ldots, X_{t-p}$ as the regressors, and Z_t as the error term:

$$X_t = \phi_1 X_{t-1} + \ldots + \phi_p X_{t-p} + Z_t, \qquad Z_t \sim \text{WN}(0, \sigma^2).$$

Given observation for $X_1, \ldots, X_T$, the regression model can be written compactly in matrix algebra as

$$\begin{pmatrix} X_{p+1} \\ X_{p+2} \\ \vdots \\ X_T \end{pmatrix} = \begin{pmatrix} X_p & X_{p-1} & \ldots & X_1 \\ X_{p+1} & X_p & \ldots & X_2 \\ \vdots & \vdots & \ddots & \vdots \\ X_{T-1} & X_{T-2} & \ldots & X_{T-p} \end{pmatrix} \begin{pmatrix} \phi_1 \\ \phi_2 \\ \vdots \\ \phi_p \end{pmatrix} + \begin{pmatrix} Z_{p+1} \\ Z_{p+2} \\ \vdots \\ Z_T \end{pmatrix},$$

or more compactly as

$$Y = \mathbf{X}\Phi + Z. \tag{5.2}$$

Note that the first p observations are lost and that the effective sample size is thus reduced to $T - p$. The least-squares estimator (OLS estimator) is obtained as the minimizer of the error sum of squares $S(\Phi)$:

$$\begin{aligned} S(\Phi) &= Z'Z = (Y - \mathbf{X}\Phi)'(Y - \mathbf{X}\Phi) \\ &= \sum_{t=p+1}^{T} (X_t - \phi_1 X_{t-1} - \ldots - \phi_p X_{t-p})^2 \\ &= \sum_{t=p+1}^{T} (X_t - \mathbb{P}_{t-1} X_t)^2 \longrightarrow \min_{\Phi}. \end{aligned} \tag{5.3}$$

Note that the optimization problem involves no constraints; in particular, causality is not imposed as a restriction. The solution of this minimization problem is given by the usual formula:

$$\widehat{\Phi}_{OLS} = (\mathbf{X}'\mathbf{X})^{-1} (\mathbf{X}'Y).$$

Although Eq. (5.2) resembles very much a classical ordinary regression model, there are some important differences. First, the usual orthogonality assumption between regressors and the error term is violated. The regressors X_{t-j}, $j = 1, \ldots, p$, are correlated with the error terms $Z_{t-j}, j = 1, 2, \ldots$. In addition, there is a dependency on the starting values $X_p, \ldots, X_1$. The assumption of causality, however, insures that these features do not play a role asymptotically. It can be shown that $(\mathbf{X}'\mathbf{X})/T$ converges in probability to $\widehat{\Gamma}_p$ and $(\mathbf{X}'Y)/T$ to $\widehat{\gamma}_p$. In addition, under quite general conditions, $T^{-1/2}\mathbf{X}'Z$ is asymptotically normally distributed with mean 0 and variance $\sigma^2\Gamma_p$ (see Sect. 13.1 for a proof of these assertions in the multivariate case). Then, by Slutzky's lemma C.10, $\sqrt{T}(\widehat{\Phi}_{OLS} - \Phi) = \left(\frac{\mathbf{X}'\mathbf{X}}{T}\right)^{-1}\left(\frac{\mathbf{X}'Z}{\sqrt{T}}\right)$ converges in distribution to $\mathrm{N}(0, \sigma^2\Gamma_p^{-1})$ Thus, the OLS estimator is asymptotically equivalent to the Yule-Walker estimator.

Theorem 5.2 (Asymptotic property of OLS estimator) *Under the same conditions as in Theorem 5.1, the OLS estimator* $\widehat{\Phi}_{OLS} = \left(\mathbf{X}'\mathbf{X}\right)^{-1}\left(\mathbf{X}'Y\right)$ *is asymptotically normally distributed:*

$$\sqrt{T}\left(\widehat{\Phi}_{OLS} - \Phi\right) \xrightarrow{d} \mathrm{N}\left(0, \sigma^2\Gamma_p^{-1}\right),$$

$$s_T^2 \xrightarrow{d} \sigma^2$$

where $s_T^2 = \widehat{Z}'\widehat{Z}/T$ *and* $\widehat{Z}_t$ *denotes the OLS residuals.*

Proof See Chap. 13 and in particular Sect. 13.1 for a proof in the multivariate case. Additional details may be gathered from Brockwell and Davis (1991, chapter 8).

□

Remark 5.1 In practice, the true value of $\sigma^2\Gamma_p^{-1}$ is unknown and approximated by $s_T^2(\mathbf{X}'\mathbf{X}/T)^{-1}$. Thus, for large T, $\widehat{\Phi}_{OLS}$ can be viewed as being normally distributed as $\mathrm{N}(\Phi, s_T^2(\mathbf{X}'\mathbf{X})^{-1})$. This result justifies the application of the usual t- and F-tests in practice.

Remark 5.2 Although, for large samples, the distribution of the t-statistic is approximatively standard normal and the F-statistic multiplied by the number of restrictions approaches a χ^2-distribution with degrees of freedom equal to the number of restrictions, one may still use in applied hypothesis testing the critical values of the t-statistic, respectively F-statistic, with the corresponding degrees of freedom.

Because the regressors X_{t-j}, $j = 1, \ldots, p$, are correlated with the error terms Z_{t-j}, $j = 1, 2, \ldots$, the Gauss-Markov theorem cannot be applied. This implies that the least-squares estimator is no longer unbiased in finite samples. It can be shown that the estimates of an AR(1) model are downward biased when the true value of

ϕ is between zero and one. MacKinnon and Smith (1998, figure 1) plots the bias as a function of the sample size and the true parameter (see also Fig. 7.1). As the bias function is almost linear in the range $-0.85 < \phi < 0.85$, an approximately unbiased estimator for the AR(1) model has been proposed by Marriott and Pope (1954), Kendall (1954), Orcutt and Winokur (1969), and MacKinnon and Smith (1998, for further details):

$$\widehat{\phi}_{OLS}^{\text{corrected}} = \frac{1}{T-3}(T\widehat{\phi}_{\text{OLS}} + 1).$$

Remark 5.3 The OLS estimator does in general not deliver coefficients $\widehat{\Phi}_{OLS}$ for which $\{X_t\}$ is causal with respect $\{Z_t\}$. In particular, in the case of an AR(1) model, it can happen that, in contrast to the Yule-Walker estimator, $|\widehat{\phi}_{OLS}|$ is larger than one despite the fact that the true parameter is absolutely smaller than one. Nevertheless, the least-squares estimator is to be preferred in practice because it delivers small-sample biases of the coefficients that are smaller than those of Yule-Walker estimator, especially for roots of $\Phi(z)$ close to the unit circle (Tjøstheim and Paulsen, 1983; Shaman and Stine, 1988; Reinsel, 1993).

5.3 Maximum-Likelihood Estimation of ARMA Models

While the estimation of the coefficients of an AR process by OLS is rather straightforward and leads to consistent and asymptotically efficient estimates, parameter estimation in the context of ARMA processes is more complex. The reason is that, in contrast to past X_t's, $Z_t, Z_{t-1}, \ldots, Z_{t-q}$ are not directly observable from the data. They must be inferred from the observations of X_t. The standard estimation method for the parameters of ARMA processes is *the method of maximum likelihood* (ML method).

We assume that the data-generating mechanism for $\{X_t\}$ is a stationary ARMA(p,q) process, which is causal and invertible with respect to $\{Z_t\}$:

$$X_t - \phi_1 X_{t-1} - \ldots - \phi_p X_{t-p} = Z_t + \theta_1 Z_{t-1} + \ldots + \theta_q Z_{t-q}$$

with $Z_t \sim \text{IID}(0, \sigma^2)$. We also assume that $\Phi(z)$ and $\Theta(z)$ have no roots in common. We stack the parameters of the model into a vector β and a scalar σ^2:

$$\beta = (\phi_1, \ldots, \phi_p, \theta_1, \ldots, \theta_q)' \quad \text{and} \quad \sigma^2 > 0.$$

The set of admissible parameters for β is denoted by $\mathcal{C} \subseteq \mathbb{R}^{p+q}$:

$$\mathcal{C} = \{\beta \in \mathbb{R}^{p+q} : \Phi(z)\Theta(z) \neq 0 \text{ for } |z| \leq 1, \phi_p\theta_q \neq 0,$$
$$\Phi(z) \text{ and } \Theta(z) \text{ have no roots in common.}\}$$

The *method of maximum-likelihood estimation* (ML method) is based on an assumption about the joint distribution of $\mathbf{X}_T = (X_1, \ldots, X_T)'$ given the parameters β and σ^2. This joint distribution function is called the likelihood function. The method of maximum-likelihood estimation then determines the parameters such that the probability of observing a given sample $\mathbf{x}_T = (x_1, \ldots, x_T)$ is maximized. This amounts to maximize the likelihood function with respect to $\beta \in C$ and $\sigma^2 > 0$.

By far the most important case is given by assuming that $\{X_t\}$ is a Gaussian process with mean zero and autocovariance function γ. This implies that $\mathbf{X}_T = (X_1, \ldots, X_T)'$ is distributed as a multivariate normal with mean zero and variance Γ_T.[2] The *Gaussian likelihood function* given the observations $\mathbf{x}_T$, denoted by $\mathrm{L}_T(\beta, \sigma^2|\mathbf{x}_T)$, is given in this case by

$$\begin{aligned}
\mathrm{L}_T(\beta, \sigma^2|\mathbf{x}_T) &= (2\pi)^{-T/2}(\det \Gamma_T)^{-1/2} \exp\left(-\frac{1}{2}\mathbf{x}_T'\Gamma_T^{-1}\mathbf{x}_T\right) \\
&= (2\pi\sigma^2)^{-T/2}(\det G_T)^{-1/2} \exp\left(-\frac{1}{2\sigma^2}\mathbf{x}_T' G_T^{-1}\mathbf{x}_T\right)
\end{aligned}$$

where $G_T = \sigma^{-2}\Gamma_T$. Note that, in contrast to Γ_T, G_T depends only on β and not on σ^2.[3] If one wants to point out the dependence of G_T from β, we write $G_T(\beta)$. The method of maximum likelihood then consists in the maximization of the above likelihood function with respect to β and σ^2 taking the data $\mathbf{x}_T$ as given.

The first-order condition of this maximization problem with respect to σ^2 is obtained by taking the logarithm of the likelihood function $\mathrm{L}_T(\beta, \sigma^2|\mathbf{x}_T)$, differentiating with respect σ^2 and setting the resulting expression equal to zero:

$$\frac{\partial \ln \mathrm{L}_T(\beta, \sigma^2|\mathbf{x}_T)}{\partial \sigma^2} = -\frac{T}{2}\frac{1}{\sigma^2} + \frac{\mathbf{X}_T' G_T^{-1}\mathbf{X}_T}{2\sigma^4} = 0.$$

Solving this equation with respect to σ^2 leads to $\sigma^2 = T^{-1}\mathbf{x}_T' G_T^{-1}\mathbf{x}_T$. Inserting this expression into the original likelihood function and taking the logarithm, one obtains the *concentrated log-likelihood function*:

$$\ln \mathrm{L}_T(\beta|\mathbf{x}_T) = -\ln(2\pi) - \frac{T}{2}\ln\left(T^{-1}\mathbf{x}_T' G_T(\beta)^{-1}\mathbf{x}_T\right) - \frac{1}{2}\ln\det G_T(\beta) - \frac{T}{2}.$$

This function is then maximized with respect to $\beta \in C$. This is, however, equivalent to minimizing the function

$$\ell_T(\beta|\mathbf{x}_T) = \ln\left(T^{-1}\mathbf{x}_T' G_T(\beta)^{-1}\mathbf{x}_T\right) + T^{-1}\ln\det G_T(\beta) \longrightarrow \min_{\beta \in C}. \tag{5.4}$$

---

[2] If the process does not have a mean of zero, the data have to be demeaned in a preliminary step or a constant has to be introduced in determining difference equation as an additional parameter.

[3] In Sect. 2.4, we showed how the autocovariance function γ and as a consequence Γ_T, respectively G_T, can be inferred from a given ARMA model, i.e., from a given β.

The value of β that minimizes the above function is called *maximum-likelihood estimator* of β. It will be denoted by $\hat{\beta}_{\text{ML}}$. The maximum-likelihood estimator for σ^2, $\hat{\sigma}^2_{\text{ML}}$, is then given by

$$\hat{\sigma}^2_{\text{ML}} = T^{-1}\mathbf{x}_T' G_T(\hat{\beta}_{\text{ML}})^{-1}\mathbf{x}_T.$$

The actual computation of $\det G_T(\beta)$ and $G_T(\beta)^{-1}$ is numerically involved, especially when T is large, and should be avoided in practice. It is therefore convenient to rewrite the likelihood function in a different, but equivalent, form:

$$\begin{aligned} \mathrm{L}_T(\beta, \sigma^2|\mathbf{x}_T) =& (2\pi\sigma^2)^{-T/2}(r_0 r_1 \ldots r_{T-1})^{-1/2} \\ & \exp\left(-\frac{1}{2\sigma^2}\sum_{t=1}^{T}\frac{(X_t - \mathbb{P}_{t-1}X_t)^2}{r_{t-1}}\right). \end{aligned}$$

Thus, $\mathbb{P}_{t-1}X_t$ denotes least-squares predictor of X_t given $X_{t-1}, \ldots, X_1$ and r_t is defined via $v_t = \mathbb{E}(X_t - \mathbb{P}_{t-1}X_t)^2 = \sigma^2 r_t$ where v_t is the mean squared forecast error as defined in Sect. 3.1. Several numerical algorithms have been developed to compute these forecast in a numerically efficient and stable way.[4]

$\mathbb{P}_{t-1}X_t$ and r_t do not depend on σ^2 so that the partial differentiation of the log-likelihood function $\ln \mathrm{L}(\beta, \sigma^2|\mathbf{x}_T)$ with respect to the parameters leads to the maximum-likelihood estimator. This estimator fulfills the following equations:

$$\hat{\sigma}^2_{\text{ML}} = \frac{1}{T} S(\hat{\beta}_{\text{ML}}),$$

where

$$S(\hat{\beta}_{\text{ML}}) = \sum_{t=1}^{T}\frac{(X_t - \mathbb{P}_{t-1}X_t)^2}{r_{t-1}}$$

and where $\hat{\beta}_{\text{ML}}$ denote the value of β that minimizes the function

$$\ell_T(\beta|\mathbf{x}_T) = \ln\left(\frac{1}{T}S(\beta)\right) + \frac{1}{T}\sum_{t=1}^{T}\ln r_{t-1}$$

subject to $\beta \in C$. This optimization problem does usually not possess an analytical solution so that it must be solved numerically. In practice, one chooses a starting value $\beta_0 \in C$ as an initial estimate for the iteration. In the following steps, this restriction is no longer imposed to enhance speed and reduce the complexity of the

[4] One such algorithm is the innovation algorithm. See Brockwell and Davis (1991, section 5.) for details.

optimization problem. This implies that one must check whether the so obtained final estimates are indeed elements in the admissible parameter space $\mathcal{C}$.

If instead of $\ell_T(\beta|\mathbf{x}_T)$, the function

$$S(\beta) = \sum_{t=1}^{T} \frac{(X_t - \mathbb{P}_{t-1}X_t)^2}{r_{t-1}}$$

is minimized subject to constraint $\beta \in \mathcal{C}$, we obtain the *least-squares estimator* of β denoted by $\hat{\beta}_{\text{LS}}$. The least-squares estimator of σ^2, $\hat{\sigma}^2_{\text{LS}}$, is then

$$\hat{\sigma}^2_{\text{LS}} = \frac{S(\hat{\beta}_{\text{LS}})}{T - p - q}.$$

The term $\frac{1}{T}\sum_{t=1}^{T} \ln r_{t-1}$ disappears asymptotically because, given the restriction $\beta \in \mathcal{C}$, the mean-squared forecast error v_T converges to σ^2 and thus r_T goes to one as T goes to infinity. This implies that for T going to infinity, the maximization of the likelihood function becomes equivalent to the minimization of the least-squares criterion. Thus, the maximum-likelihood estimator and the least-squares estimator share the same asymptotic normal distribution.

Note also that in the case of autoregressive models, r_t is constant and equal to one. In this case, the least-squares criterion $S(\beta)$ reduces to the criterion (5.3) discussed in the previous Sect. 5.2.

Theorem 5.3 (Asymptotic distribution of ML estimator) *If $\{X_t\}$ is an ARMA process with true parameters $\beta \in \mathcal{C}$ and $Z_t \sim \text{IID}(0, \sigma^2)$ with $\sigma^2 > 0$, the maximum-likelihood estimator and the least-squares estimator are consistent and share the same asymptotic normal distribution:*

$$\sqrt{T}\left(\hat{\beta}_{\text{ML}} - \beta\right) \xrightarrow{d} \text{N}(0, V(\beta)),$$

$$\sqrt{T}\left(\hat{\beta}_{\text{LS}} - \beta\right) \xrightarrow{d} \text{N}(0, V(\beta)).$$

The asymptotic covariance matrix $V(\beta)$ is thereby given by

$$V(\beta) = \begin{pmatrix} \mathbb{E}\mathbf{U}_t\mathbf{U}_t' & \mathbb{E}\mathbf{U}_t\mathbf{V}_t' \\ \mathbb{E}\mathbf{V}_t\mathbf{U}_t' & \mathbb{E}\mathbf{V}_t\mathbf{V}_t' \end{pmatrix}^{-1}$$

$$\mathbf{U}_t = \left(U_t, U_{t-1}, \ldots, U_{t-p+1}\right)'$$

$$\mathbf{V}_t = \left(V_t, V_{t-1}, \ldots, V_{t-q+1}\right)'$$

where $\{U_t\}$ and $\{V_t\}$ denote autoregressive processes defined as $\Phi(\text{L})U_t = W_t$ and $\Theta(\text{L})V_t = W_t$ with $W_t \sim \text{IID}(0, 1)$.

Proof See Brockwell and Davis (1991, Section 8.8). □

It can be shown that both estimators are also asymptotically efficient.[5] Note that the asymptotic covariance matrix $V(\beta)$ is independent of σ^2.

The use of the Gaussian likelihood function makes sense even when the underlying process is not Gaussian. First, the Gaussian likelihood can still be interpreted as a measure of fit of the ARMA model with respect to the data. Second, the asymptotic distribution is still Gaussian even when the process is not Gaussian as long as $Z_t \sim \text{IID}(0, \sigma^2)$. The Gaussian likelihood is then called the quasi-Gaussian likelihood. The use of the Gaussian likelihood under this circumstance is, however, in general no longer efficient.

Example (AR(p) process)
In this case, $\beta = (\phi_1, \ldots, \phi_p)$ and $V(\beta) = \left(\mathbb{E}U_t U_t'\right)^{-1} = \sigma^2 \Gamma_p^{-1}$. This is, however, the same asymptotic distribution as the Yule-Walker estimator. The Yule-Walker, the least-squares, and the maximum-likelihood estimator are therefore asymptotically equivalent in the case of an AR(p) process. The main difference lies in the treatment of the first p observations.

In particular, we have

$$\text{AR}(1): \qquad \widehat{\phi} \sim \text{N}\left(\phi, (1-\phi^2)/T\right),$$

$$\text{AR}(2): \qquad \begin{pmatrix} \widehat{\phi}_1 \\ \widehat{\phi}_2 \end{pmatrix} \sim \text{N}\left(\begin{pmatrix} \phi_1 \\ \phi_2 \end{pmatrix}, \frac{1}{T} \begin{pmatrix} 1-\phi_2^2 & -\phi_1(1+\phi_2) \\ -\phi_1(1+\phi_2) & 1-\phi_2^2 \end{pmatrix} \right).$$

Example (MA(q) process)
Similarly, one can compute the asymptotic distribution for an MA(q) process. In particular, we have

$$\text{MA}(1): \qquad \widehat{\theta} \sim \text{N}\left(\theta, (1-\theta^2)/T\right),$$

$$\text{MA}(2): \qquad \begin{pmatrix} \widehat{\theta}_1 \\ \widehat{\theta}_2 \end{pmatrix} \sim \text{N}\left(\begin{pmatrix} \theta_1 \\ \theta_2 \end{pmatrix}, \frac{1}{T} \begin{pmatrix} 1-\theta_2^2 & \theta_1(1-\theta_2) \\ \theta_1(1-\theta_2) & 1-\theta_2^2 \end{pmatrix} \right).$$

Example (ARMA(1,1) process)
For an ARMA(1,1) process, the asymptotic covariance matrix is given by

$$V(\phi, \theta) = \begin{pmatrix} \left(1-\phi^2\right)^{-1} & (1+\phi\theta)^{-1} \\ (1+\phi\theta)^{-1} & \left(1-\theta^2\right)^{-1} \end{pmatrix}^{-1}.$$

[5] See Brockwell and Davis (1991) and Fan and Yao (2003) for details.

Therefore, we have

$$\begin{pmatrix}\hat{\phi}\\ \hat{\theta}\end{pmatrix} \sim \mathrm{N}\left(\begin{pmatrix}\phi\\ \theta\end{pmatrix}, \frac{1}{T}\frac{1+\phi\theta}{(\phi+\theta)^2}\begin{pmatrix}(1-\phi^2)(1+\phi\theta) & -(1-\theta^2)(1-\phi^2)\\ -(1-\theta^2)(1-\phi^2) & (1-\theta^2)(1+\phi\theta)\end{pmatrix}\right).$$

5.4 Estimation of Orders p and q

Up to now, we have always assumed that the true orders of the ARMA(p,q) process are known. This is, however, seldom the case in practice. As economic theory does usually not provide an indication, it is all too often the case that the orders of the ARMA model must be identified from the data. Thereby, one can make two types of errors: p and q are too large in which case we speak of *overfitting*; p and/or q are too low in which case we speak of *underfitting*.

In the case of overfitting, the maximum-likelihood estimator is no longer consistent for the true parameters, but still consistent for the coefficients of the causal representation ψ_j, $j = 0, 1, 2, \ldots$, where $\psi(z) = \frac{\theta(z)}{\phi(z)}$. This can be illustrated by the following example. Suppose that $\{X_t\}$ is a white noise process, i.e., $X_t = Z_t \sim \mathrm{WN}(0, \sigma^2)$, but we fit an ARMA(1,1) model given by $X_t - \phi X_{t-1} = Z_t + \theta Z_{t-1}$. Then, the maximum-likelihood estimator does not converge to $\phi = \theta = 0$, but only to the line segment $\phi = -\theta$, $|\phi|, |\theta| < 1$. For values of ϕ and θ on this line segment, we have $\psi(z) = \theta(z)/\phi(z) = 1$. The maximum-likelihood estimator converges to the true values of ψ_j, i.e., to the values $\psi_0 = 1$ and $\psi_j = 0$ for $j > 0$. The situation is depicted in Fig. 5.1. There, it is shown that the estimator has a tendency to converge to the points $(-1, 1)$ and $(1, -1)$, depending on the starting values. This indeterminacy of the estimator manifests itself in a numerical problem in the optimization of the likelihood function. Generally, models with similar roots for the AR and MA polynomials close to the unit circle (with absolute values near one) are probably overparameterized. The problem can be overcome by reducing the orders of both the AR and MA polynomial.

This problem does not appear in purely autoregressive models. As explained in Sect. 5.1, the estimator for the redundant coefficients converges to zero with asymptotic distribution $\mathrm{N}(0, 1/T)$ (see the result in Eq. (5.1)). This is one reason why purely autoregressive models are often preferred. In addition, the estimator is easily implemented, and every stationary stochastic process can be arbitrarily well approximated by a stationary AR process. This approximation may, however, necessitate high-order models when the true process encompasses a MA component.

In the case of underfitting, the maximum-likelihood estimator converges to those values that are closest to the true parameters given the restricted parameter space. The estimates are, however, inconsistent due to the "omitted variable bias." It is therefore advisable to start the modeling exercise with models of higher order as the problem of overfitting is considered less severe.

For these reasons, the identification of the orders is an important step. One method that goes back to Box and Jenkins (1976) consists in the analysis of the autocorrelation function (ACF) and the partial autocorrelation function (PACF) (see

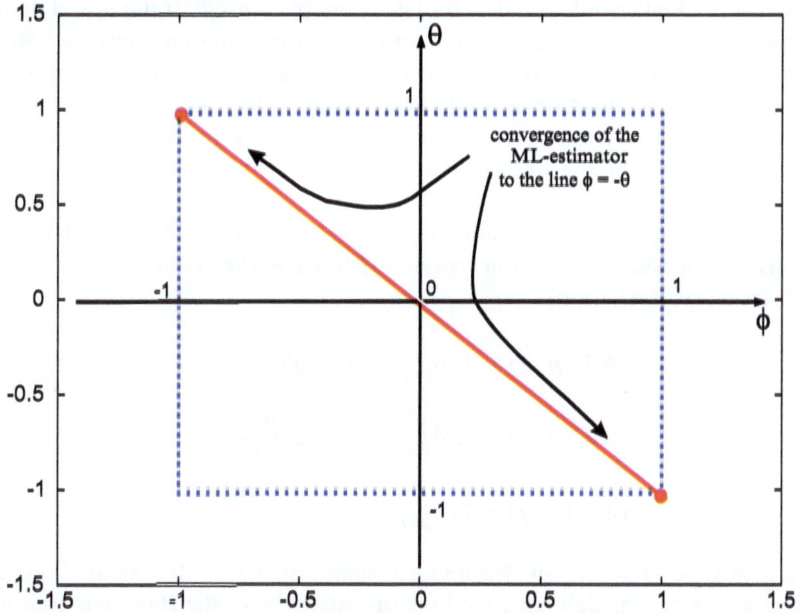

Fig. 5.1 Parameter space of a causal and invertible ARMA(1,1) process

Sect. 3.3). Although this method requires some experience, especially when the process is not a purely AR or MA process, the analysis of the ACF and PACF remains an important first step in every practical investigation of a time series.

An alternative method relies on automatic data-dependent order selection procedures. The objective is to minimize a so-called information criteria over different values of p and q. These criteria are based on the following consideration. Given a fixed number of observations, the successive increase of the orders p and q increases the fit of the model so that the residual variance $\hat{\sigma}^2_{p,q}$ steadily decreases. In order to compensate for this overfitting tendency, a penalty term is introduced. This penalty term depends on the number of free parameters and on the number of observations at hand.[6] The most important information criteria have the following additive form:

$$\ln \hat{\sigma}^2_{p,q} + (\text{\# free parameters}) \frac{C(T)}{T} = \ln \hat{\sigma}^2_{p,q} + (p+q)\frac{C(T)}{T} \longrightarrow \min_{p,q},$$

where $\ln \hat{\sigma}^2_{p,q}$ measures the goodness of fit of the ARMA(p,q) model. The second term, $(p+q)\frac{C(T)}{T}$, represents a penalty for using higher-order models. Thus, $C(T)$ represents a nondecreasing function of T that governs the trade-off between goodness of fit and complexity (dimension) of the model. Thus, the information

[6] See Brockwell and Davis (1991) and Stoica and Selén (2004) for details and a deeper appreciation of information criteria.

criteria choose higher-order models for larger sample sizes T. If the model includes a constant term or other exogenous variables, the criterion must be adjusted accordingly. However, this will introduce, for a given sample size, just a constant term in the objective function and will therefore not influence the choice of p and q. Alternatively, one may use $-2(\ell_T(\beta|\mathbf{x}_T)/T)$ as a measure of fit where $\ell_T(\beta|\mathbf{x}_T)$ denotes the corresponding log-likelihood function of the ARMA(p,q) model (see Eq. (5.4)).

The most common criteria are the Akaike information criterion (AIC), the Schwarz or Bayesian information criterion (BIC), and the Hannan-Quinn information criterion (HQ criterion):

$$\mathrm{AIC}(p,q) = \ln \hat{\sigma}^2_{p,q} + (p+q)\frac{2}{T}$$

$$\mathrm{BIC}(p,q) = \ln \hat{\sigma}^2_{p,q} + (p+q)\frac{\ln T}{T}$$

$$\mathrm{HQC}(p,q) = \ln \hat{\sigma}^2_{p,q} + (p+q)\frac{2\ln(\ln T)}{T}$$

Because AIC $<$ HQC $<$ BIC for a given sample size $T \geq 16$, Akaike's criterion delivers the largest models, i.e., the highest-order $p + q$; the Bayesian criterion is more restrictive and delivers therefore the smallest models, i.e., the lowest $p + q$. Although Akaike's criterion is not consistent with respect to the true parameters p and q and has a tendency to deliver overfitted models, it is still widely used in practice. This feature is sometimes desired as overfitting is seen as less damaging than underfitting.[7] Only the BIC and HQC deliver to consistent estimates of the orders p and q.

5.5 Modeling a Stochastic Process

In practice, the identification of a satisfactory ARMA model typically involves several steps.

Step 1: Transformations to achieve stationary time series
Economic time series are often of a nonstationary nature. It is therefore necessary to transform the time series in a first step to achieve stationarity. Popular time series that have typically a pronounced trend are (real) GDP, stock market indices, and interest rates, among many others. They should not be modeled in (log)-levels, but in (log)-differences. Taking first differences of a variable already in logs effectively amounts to working with growth rates. Sometimes first differences are not enough and further differences have to be taken. Price indices or monetary aggregates are typical examples where first differences may not be sufficient to achieve stationarity. Thus, instead of X_t, one works with the series $Y_t = (1-\mathrm{L})^d X_t$

[7] See, for example, Sect. 7.3 on the unit root tests.

with $d = 1, 2, \ldots$. A nonstationary process $\{X_t\}$ that needs to be differentiated d-times to obtain a stationary time series is called *integrated of order d*, $X_t \sim I(d)$.[8] If $Y_t = (1 - \mathrm{L})^d X_t$ is generated by a stationary ARMA(p,q) process, $\{X_t\}$ is said to be an ARIMA(p,d,q) process.

An alternative method to eliminate the trend is to regress the time series against a polynomial in t of degree s, i.e., against $(1, t, \ldots, t^s)$, and to proceed with the residuals. These residuals can then be modeled as a stationary ARMA(p,q) process. Chapter 7 discusses in detail which of the two detrending methods is to be preferred under which circumstances.

The data are also often subject to seasonal fluctuations. As with the trend, there are several alternative procedures available to remove seasonality from the data.[9] The first possibility is to pass the time series through a seasonal filter and work with the seasonally adjusted data. The construction of seasonal filters is discussed in Chap. 6. A second alternative is to include seasonal dummies in the ARMA model. A third alternative is to take seasonal differences. In the case of quarterly observations, this amounts to work with $Y_t = (1 - \mathrm{L}^4)X_t$. As $1 - \mathrm{L}^4 = (1 - \mathrm{L})(1 + \mathrm{L} + \mathrm{L}^2 + \mathrm{L}^3)$, this transformation involves a first difference and will therefore also account for the trend. Likewise, for monthly data, $Y_t = (1-\mathrm{L}^{12})X_t = (1 - \mathrm{L})(1 + \mathrm{L} + \mathrm{L}^2 + \cdots + \mathrm{L}^{11})X_t$.

Step 2: Finding the orders p and q
Having achieved stationarity, one has to find the appropriate orders p and q of the ARMA model. Thus, one can rely either on the analysis of the ACF and the PACF or on information criteria as outlined in Sect. 5.4.

Step 3: Estimating the corresponding ARMA/p,q) model
Having determined the orders p and q, one can estimate the corresponding ARMA(p,q) model using one of the methods proposed in the previous sections.

Step 4: Checking the plausibility of the obtained model
After having identified and estimated a particular model or a set of models, one has to inspect its or their adequacy. There are several dimensions along that the model(s) can be evaluated.

(i) Are the residuals white noise? This can be checked by investigating the ACF and by applying the Ljung-Box test (4.5). If they are not, this means that the model failed to capture all the dynamics inherent in the data.
(ii) Are the estimated parameters plausible?
(iii) Are the estimated parameters constant over time? Are there structural breaks? This can be investigated by looking at a plot of the residuals or by comparing parameter estimates across different subsamples. More systematic approaches

[8] An exact definition will be provided in Chap. 7. In this chapter, we will analyze the consequences of non-stationarity and discuss tests for specific forms of non-stationarity.

[9] Many statistical offices publish seasonally adjusted data only.

are discussed in Sect. 18.2 and Perron (2006). These involve the revolving estimation of parameters by allowing the break point to vary over the sample. Thus, different types of structural breaks can be distinguished.

(iv) Does the model deliver sensible forecasts? It is particularly useful to investigate the out-of-sample forecasting performance. If one has several candidate models, one can perform a horse race among them.

In case the model turns out to be unsatisfactory, one has to go back to steps 1 to 3.

5.6 Modeling Swiss Real GDP

This section illustrates the concepts and ideas just presented by working out a specific example. We take the seasonally unadjusted Swiss real GDP as an example. The data are plotted in Fig. 1.3. To take the seasonality into account, we transform the logged time series by taking first seasonal differences, i.e., $X_t = (1 - L^4) \ln \mathrm{GDP}_t$. Thus, the variable corresponds to the growth rate with respect to the quarter of the previous year. The data are plotted in Fig. 5.2. A cursory inspection of the plot reveals that this transformation eliminated the trend as well as the seasonality.

First, we analyze the ACF and the PACF. They are plotted together with corresponding confidence intervals in Fig. 5.3. The slowly monotonically declining ACF suggests an AR process. As only the first two orders of the PACF are significantly different from zero, it seems that an AR(2) model is appropriate. The least-squares estimates of the parameters are

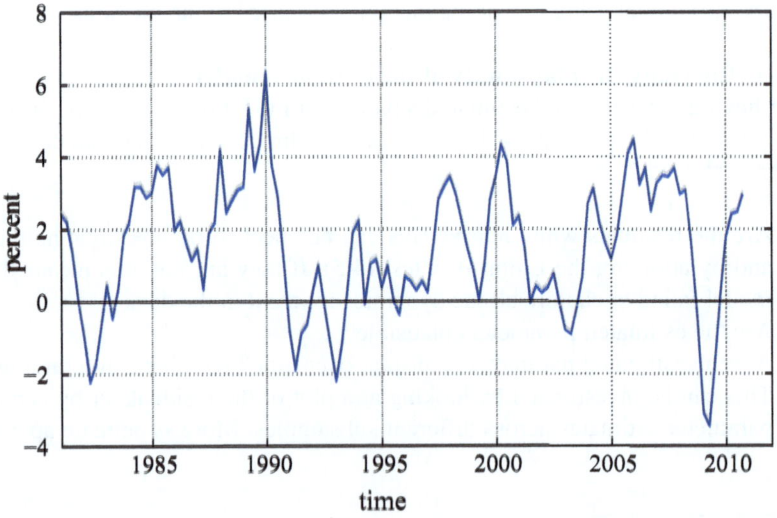

Fig. 5.2 Real GDP growth rates of Switzerland

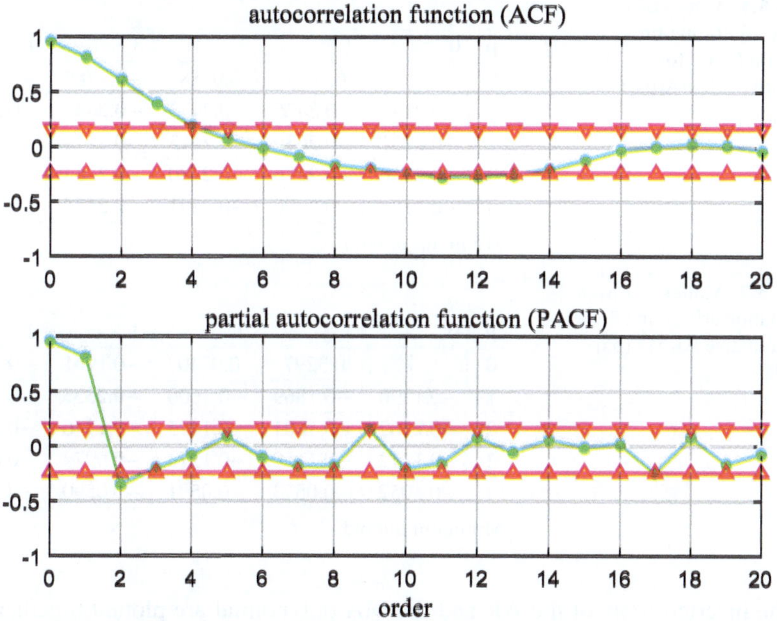

Fig. 5.3 Autocorrelation (ACF) and partial autocorrelation (PACF) function (PACF) of real GDP growth rates of Switzerland with 95% confidence interval

$$X_t - \underset{(0.103)}{1.134} X_{t=1} + \underset{(0.104)}{0.310} X_{t-2} = 0.218 + Z_t \qquad \text{with } \hat{\sigma}^2 = 0.728$$

The numbers in parenthesis are the estimated standard errors of the corresponding parameter above. The roots of the AR polynomial are 1.484 and 2.174. They are clearly outside the unit circle so that there exists a stationary and causal representation.

Next, we investigate the information criteria AIC and BIC to identify the orders of the ARMA(p,q) model. We examine all models with $0 \leq p, q \leq 4$. The AIC and the BIC values are reported in Tables 5.1 and 5.2. Both criteria reach a minimum at $(p, q) = (1, 3)$ (bold numbers) so that both criteria prefer an ARMA(1,3) model. The estimated parameters of this models are

$$X_t - \underset{(0.134)}{0.527} X_{t=1} = 0.6354 + Z_t + \underset{(0.1395)}{0.5106} Z_{t-1}$$

$$+ \underset{(0.1233)}{0.5611} Z_{t-2} + \underset{(0.1238)}{0.4635} Z_{t-3} \qquad \text{with } \hat{\sigma}^2 = 0.648.$$

The estimated standard errors of the estimated parameters are again reported in parenthesis below. The AR(2) model is not considerably worse than the ARMA(1,3) model; according to the BIC criterion, it is even the second best model.

Table 5.1 Values of Akaike's information criterium (AIC) for alternative ARMA(p,q) models

	q				
p	0	1	2	3	4
0		0.3021	0.0188	−0.2788	−0.3067
1	−0.2174	−0.2425	−0.2433	**−0.3446**	−0.2991
2	−0.2721	−0.2639	−0.2613	−0.3144	−0.2832
3	−0.2616	−0.2276	−0.2780	−0.2663	−0.2469
4	−0.2186	−0.1990	−0.2291	−0.2574	−0.2099

Minimum in bold

Table 5.2 Values of Bayes' information criterium (BIC) for alternative ARMA(p,q) models

	q				
p	0	1	2	3	4
0		0.3297	0.0740	−0.1961	−0.1963
1	−0.1896	−0.1869	−0.1600	**−0.2335**	−0.1603
2	−0.2162	−0.1801	−0.1495	−0.1746	−0.1154
3	−0.1772	−0.1150	−0.1373	−0.0974	−0.0499
4	−0.1052	−0.0573	−0.0591	−0.0590	0.0169

Minimum in bold

The inverted roots of the AR and the MA polynomial are plotted together with their corresponding 95% confidence regions in Fig. 5.4.[10] As the confidence regions are all inside the unit circle, also the ARMA(1,3) has a stationary and causal representation. Moreover, the estimated process is also invertible. In addition, the roots of the AR and the MA polynomial are distinct.

The autocorrelation functions of the residuals from the AR(2) and the ARMA(1,3) model are plotted in Fig. 5.5. They show no sign of significant autocorrelations so that both residual series are practically white noise. We can examine this hypothesis formally by the Ljung-Box test (see Sect. 4.2 Eq. (4.5)). Taking N $=$ 20, the values of the test statistics are $Q'_{\text{AR}(2)} = 33.80$ and $Q'_{\text{ARMA}(1,3)} = 21.70$, respectively. The 5% critical value according to the χ^2_{20} distribution is 31.41. Thus, the null hypothesis $\rho(1) = \ldots = \rho(20) = 0$ is rejected for the AR(2) model, but not for the ARMA(1,3) model. This implies that the AR(2) model does not capture the full dynamics of the data.

Although the AR(2) and the ARMA(1,3) models seem to be quite different at first glance, they deliver similar impulse response functions as can be gathered from Fig. 5.6. In both models, the impact of the initial shock is first built up to values higher than 1.1 in quarters one and two, respectively. Then, the effect monotonically declines to zero. After 10–12 quarters, the effect of the shock has practically dissipated.

As a final exercise, we use both models to forecast real GDP growth over the next nine quarters, i.e., for the period fourth quarter 2003 to fourth quarter 2005. As can be seen from Fig. 5.7, both models predict that the Swiss economy should move out

[10] The confidence regions are determined by the delta method (see Appendix E).

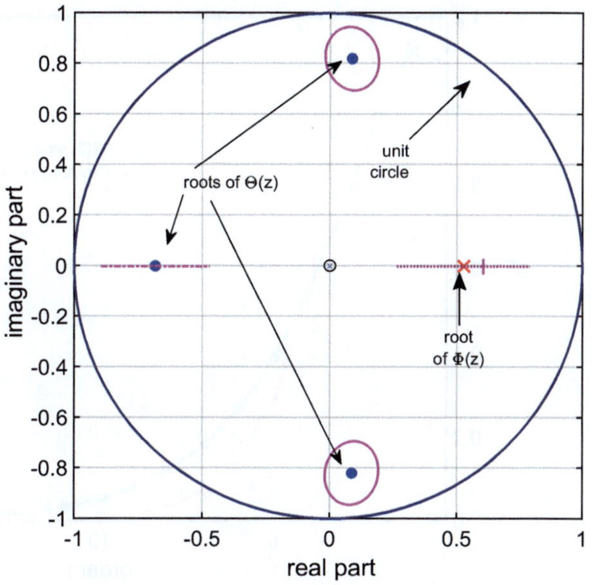

Fig. 5.4 Inverted roots of the AR and the MA polynomial of the ARMA(1,3) model together with the corresponding 95% confidence regions

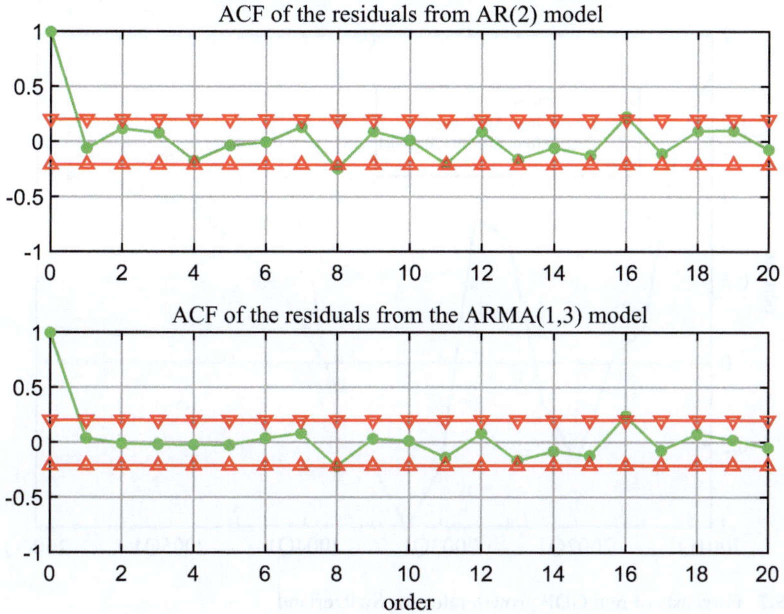

Fig. 5.5 Autocorrelation function (ACF) of the residuals from the AR(2) and the ARMA(1,3) models

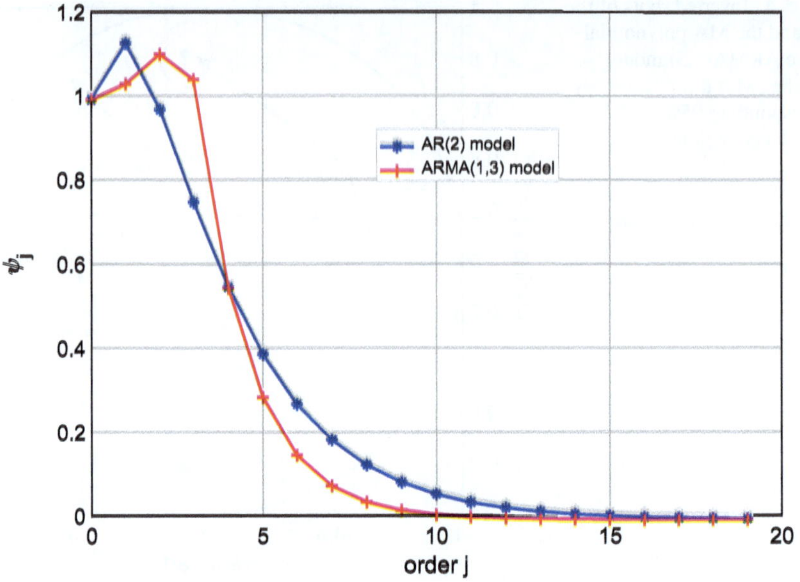

Fig. 5.6 Impulse responses of the AR(2) and the ARMA(1,3) models

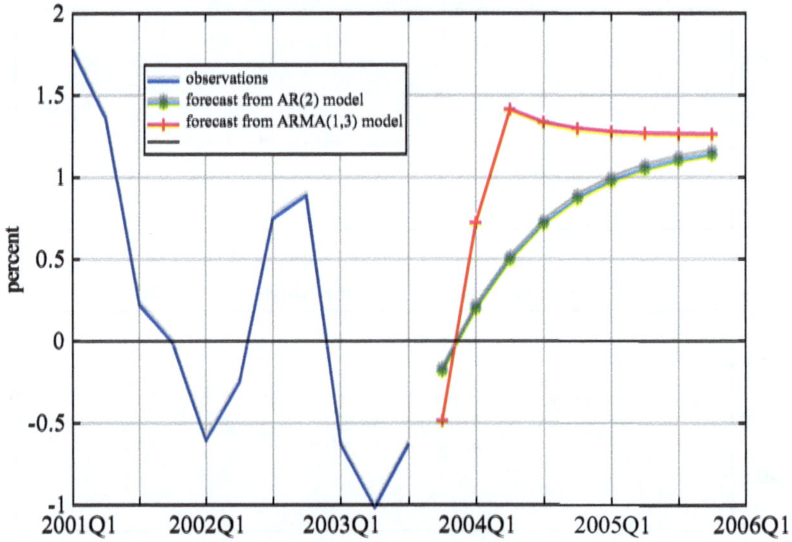

Fig. 5.7 Forecasts of real GDP growth rates for Switzerland

of recession in the coming quarters. However, the ARMA(1,3) model indicates that the recovery is taking place more quickly and the growth overshooting its long-run mean of 1.3% in about a year. The forecast of the AR(2) predicts a more steady approach to the long-run mean.

Spectral Analysis and Linear Filters

6

Up to now, we have viewed a stochastic process as a time-indexed sequence of random variables. The class of ARMA processes was seen as an adequate framework for the analysis of stationary time series. This approach is usually termed as time series analysis in the *time domain*. There is, however, an equivalent perspective that views a stochastic process as overlaid waves of different frequencies and amplitudes. This view is termed time series analysis in the *frequency domain*. The decomposition of a stochastic process into sinusoids of different frequencies is called the *spectral representation*. The estimation of the importance of the waves at particular frequencies is referred to as *spectral or spectrum estimation*. Priestley (1981) provides an excellent account of these methods. The use of frequency domain methods, in particular *spectrum estimation*, which originated in the natural sciences, was introduced to economics by Granger (1964).[1] Notably, he showed that most of the fluctuations in economic time series can be attributed to low-frequency cycles (Granger 1966).

Although both approaches are equivalent from a mathematical point of view, the analysis in the frequency domain is more convenient when it comes to the analysis and construction of *linear filters*. The application of a filter to a time series amounts to take some moving average of the time series. These moving averages may extend, at least in theory, into the infinite past, but also into the infinite future. A causal ARMA process $\{X_t\}$ may be regarded as filtered white noise process with filter weights given by ψ_j, $j = 0, 1, 2, \ldots$. In economics, filters are usually applied to remove cycles of a particular frequency, like seasonal cycles (e.g., Christmas sales in a store), or to highlight particular cycles, like business cycles.

From a mathematical point of view, the equivalence between time and frequency domain analyses rest on the theory of *Fourier series*. A rigorous representation of

[1] The use of spectral methods in the natural sciences can be traced many centuries back. The modern statistical approach builds on to the work of N. Wiener, G. U. Yule, J. W. Tukey, and many others. See the interesting survey by Robinson (1982).

K. Neusser, *Time Series Econometrics*, Springer Texts in Business and Economics,
https://doi.org/10.1007/978-3-031-88838-0_6

this theory is beyond the scope of this book. The interested reader may consult Brockwell and Davis (1991, chapter 4) or Deistler and Scherrer (2022, Chapter IV), among others. An introduction to the underlying mathematical theory can be found in standard analysis textbooks like Rudin (1987).

6.1 The Spectral Density

In the following, we assume that $\{X_t\}$ is a mean-zero (centered) stationary stochastic process with autocovariance function $\gamma(h)$, $h = 0, \pm 1, \pm 2, \ldots$. Mathematically, $\gamma(h)$ represents a double-infinite sequence that can be mapped into a real-valued function $f(\lambda)$, $\lambda \in \mathbb{R}$, by the Fourier transform. This function is called the *spectral density function* or *spectral density*. Conversely, we can retrieve from the spectral density each covariance $\gamma(h)$. Hence, there is a one-to-one relation between autocovariance functions and spectral densities: both objects summarize the same properties of the time series, but represent them differently. Clearly, this holds also for the autocorrelation function $\rho(h) = \gamma(h)/\gamma(0)$.

Definition 6.1 (Spectral density function) Let $\{X_t\}$ be a mean-zero stationary stochastic process with an absolutely summable autocovariance function $\gamma(h)$, i.e., $\sum_{h=-\infty}^{\infty} |\gamma(h)| < \infty$; then the function

$$f(\lambda) = \frac{1}{2\pi} \sum_{h=-\infty}^{\infty} \gamma(h) \mathrm{e}^{-\imath h\lambda}, \qquad -\infty < \lambda < \infty, \tag{6.1}$$

is called the *spectral density function* or *spectral density* of $\{X_t\}$. $\imath$ denotes the imaginary unit (see Appendix A).

The sine is an odd function, whereas the cosine and the autocovariance function are even functions.[2] This implies that the spectral density can be rewritten as

$$\begin{aligned} f(\lambda) &= \frac{1}{2\pi} \sum_{h=-\infty}^{\infty} \gamma(h)(\cos(h\lambda) - \imath \sin(h\lambda)) \\ &= \frac{1}{2\pi} \sum_{h=-\infty}^{\infty} \gamma(h) \cos(h\lambda) + 0 = \frac{1}{2\pi} \sum_{h=-\infty}^{\infty} \gamma(h) \cos(-h\lambda) \\ &= \frac{\gamma(0)}{2\pi} + \frac{1}{\pi} \sum_{h=1}^{\infty} \gamma(h) \cos(h\lambda). \end{aligned} \tag{6.2}$$

[2] A function f is called even if $f(-x) = f(x)$; the function is called odd if $f(-x) = -f(x)$. Note that $\sin(-\theta) = -\sin(\theta)$ and $\cos(-\theta) = \cos(\theta)$.

Because of the periodicity of the cosine function, i.e., because

$$f(\lambda + 2k\pi) = f(\lambda), \qquad \text{for all } k \in \mathbb{Z},$$

it is sufficient to consider the spectral density only in the interval $(-\pi, \pi]$. As the cosine is an even function, so is f. Thus, we restrict the analysis of the spectral density $f(\lambda)$ further to the domain $\lambda \in [0, \pi]$.

In practice, we often use the *period* or *oscillation length* instead of the radiant λ. They are related by the following formula:

$$\text{period length} = \frac{2\pi}{\lambda}. \tag{6.3}$$

If, for example, the data are quarterly observations, a value of 0.3 for λ corresponds to a period length of approximately 21 quarters.

Remark 6.1 We gather some properties of the spectral density function f:

- f is an even function so that $f(\lambda) = f(-\lambda)$.
- Because $f(0) = \frac{1}{2\pi}\sum_{h=-\infty}^{\infty} \gamma(h)$, the long-run variance ω of $\{X_t\}$ equals $2\pi f(0)$, i.e., $2\pi f(0) = \omega$ (see Sect. 4.4).
- $f(\lambda) \geq 0$ for all $\lambda \in (-\pi, \pi]$. The proof of this proposition can be found in Brockwell and Davis (1996, chapter 4). This property corresponds to the nonnegative definiteness of the autocovariance function (see Property 4 in Theorem 1.1 of Sect. 1.3).
- The single autocovariances are the Fourier coefficients of the spectral density f:

$$\gamma(h) = \int_{-\pi}^{\pi} e^{\imath h\lambda} f(\lambda)d\lambda = \int_{-\pi}^{\pi} \cos(h\lambda) f(\lambda)d\lambda. \tag{6.4}$$

  For $h = 0$, we therefore get $\gamma(0) = \int_{-\pi}^{\pi} f(\lambda)d\lambda$.

The last property allows us to compute the autocovariances from a given spectral density. It shows how time and frequency domain analyses are related to each other and how a property in one domain is reflected as a property in the other.

These properties of a nonnegative definite function can be used to characterize the spectral density of a stationary process $\{X_t\}$ with autocovariance function γ.

Theorem 6.1 (Properties of a spectral density) *A function f defined on $(-\pi, \pi]$ is the spectral density of a stationary process if and only if the following properties hold:*

- $f(\lambda) = f(-\lambda)$.
- $f(\lambda) \geq 0$.
- $\int_{-\pi}^{\pi} f(\lambda)d\lambda < \infty$.

Corollary 6.1 *An absolutely summable function γ is the autocovariance function of a stationary process if and only if*

$$f(\lambda) = \frac{1}{2\pi} \sum_{h=-\infty}^{\infty} \gamma(h) e^{-\imath h\lambda} \geq 0, \qquad \text{for all } \lambda \in (-\pi, \pi].$$

In this case, f is called the spectral density of γ.

The function $f(\lambda)/\gamma(0)$ can be considered as a density function of some probability distribution defined on $[-\pi, \pi]$ because $\frac{f(\lambda)}{\gamma(0)} \geq 0$ and

$$\int_{-\pi}^{\pi} \frac{f(\lambda)}{\gamma(0)} \mathrm{d}\lambda = 1.$$

The corresponding cumulative distribution function G is then defined as

$$G(\lambda) = \int_{-\pi}^{\lambda} \frac{f(\omega)}{\gamma(0)} \mathrm{d}\omega, \qquad -\pi \leq \lambda \leq \pi.$$

It satisfies $G(-\pi) = 0$, $G(\pi) = 1$, $1 - G(\lambda) = G(\lambda)$, and $G(0) = 1/2$. The autocorrelation function ρ is then given by

$$\rho(h) = \frac{\gamma(h)}{\gamma(0)} = \int_{-\pi}^{\pi} e^{\imath h\lambda} \mathrm{d}G(\lambda).$$

This integral is a so-called Riemann-Stieltjes integral.[3] If the distribution function G possesses a density function g, then $\rho(h) = \int_{-\pi}^{\pi} e^{\imath h\lambda} g(\lambda)\mathrm{d}\lambda$.

Some Examples
The following examples illustrate the concepts introduced above.

White noise: Let $\{X_t\}$ be a white noise process with $X_t \sim \mathrm{WN}(0, \sigma^2)$. For this process, all autocovariances, except $\gamma(0)$, are equal to zero. The spectral density therefore is equal to

$$f(\lambda) = \frac{1}{2\pi} \sum_{h=-\infty}^{\infty} \gamma(h) e^{-\imath h\lambda} = \frac{\gamma(0)}{2\pi} = \frac{\sigma^2}{2\pi}.$$

Thus, the spectral density is equal to a constant that is proportional to the variance. This means that no particular frequency dominates the spectral density. This justifies the name white noise for such processes.

[3] The Riemann-Stieltjes integral is a generalization of the Riemann integral. Let f and g be two bounded functions defined on the interval $[a, b]$; then the Riemann-Stieltjes integral $\int_a^b f(x)\mathrm{d}g(x)$ is defined as $\lim_{n\to\infty} \sum_{i=1}^{n} f(\xi_i)[g(x_i) - g(x_{i-1})]$ where $a = x_0 < x_1 < \cdots < x_{n-1} < x_n = b$ and $\xi_i \in [x_{i-1}, x_i]$. Typically, g is assumed to have bounded variation (i.e., $\lim_{n\to\infty} \sum_{i=1}^{n} |g(x_i) - g(x_{i-1})| < \infty$). For $g(x) = x$, we obtain the standard Riemann integral. If g is a step function with a countable number of steps x_i of height h_i, then $\int_a^b f(x)\mathrm{d}g(x) = \sum_i f(x_i)h_i$.

MA(1): Let $\{X_t\}$ be a MA(1) process with autocovariance function:

$$\gamma(h) = \begin{cases} 1, & h = 0; \\ \rho, & h = \pm 1; \\ 0, & \text{otherwise.} \end{cases}$$

The spectral density therefore is

$$f(\lambda) = \frac{1}{2\pi} \sum_{h=-\infty}^{\infty} \gamma(h) e^{-\imath h\lambda} = \frac{\rho e^{\imath\lambda} + 1 + \rho e^{-\imath\lambda}}{2\pi} = \frac{1 + 2\rho \cos\lambda}{2\pi}.$$

Thus, $f(\lambda) \geq 0$ if and only $|\rho| \leq 1/2$. According to Corollary 6.1, γ is the autocovariance function of a stationary stochastic process if and only if $|\rho| \leq 1/2$. This condition corresponds exactly to the condition derived in the time domain (see Sect. 1.3). The spectral density for $\rho = 0.4$ or equivalently $\theta = 0.5$, respectively for $\rho = -0.4$ or equivalently $\theta = -0.5$, and $\sigma^2 = 1$ is plotted in Fig. 6.1a. As the process is rather smooth when the first-order autocorrelation is positive, the spectral density is large in the neighborhood of zero and small in the neighborhood of π. For a negative autocorrelation, the picture is just reversed.

AR(1): The spectral density of an AR(1) process $X_t = \phi X_{t-1} + Z_t$ with $|\phi| < 1$ and $Z_t \sim \text{WN}(0, \sigma^2)$ is

$$\begin{aligned} f(\lambda) &= \frac{\gamma(0)}{2\pi} \left(1 + \sum_{h=1}^{\infty} \phi^h \left(e^{-\imath h\lambda} + e^{\imath h\lambda}\right)\right) \\ &= \frac{\sigma^2}{2\pi(1-\phi^2)} \left(1 + \frac{\phi e^{\imath\lambda}}{1-\phi e^{\imath\lambda}} + \frac{\phi e^{-\imath\lambda}}{1-\phi e^{-\imath\lambda}}\right) \\ &= \frac{\sigma^2}{2\pi} \times \frac{1}{1 - 2\phi\cos\lambda + \phi^2} \end{aligned}$$

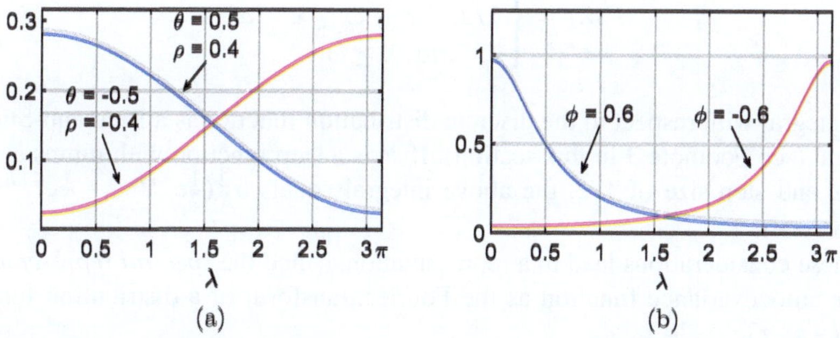

Fig. 6.1 Examples of spectral densities with $Z_t \sim \text{WN}(0, 1)$. **(a)** MA(1) process. **(b)** AR(1) process

The spectral density for $\phi = 0.6$ and $\phi = -0.6$ and $\sigma^2 = 1$ is plotted in Fig. 6.1b. As the process with $\phi = 0.6$ exhibits a relatively large positive autocorrelation so that it is rather smooth, the spectral density takes large values at low frequencies. In contrast, the process with $\phi = -0.6$ is rather volatile due to the negative first-order autocorrelation. Thus, high frequencies are more important than low frequencies as reflected in the corresponding figure.
Note that, as ϕ approaches one, the spectral density evaluated at zero tends to infinity, i.e., $\lim_{\lambda \downarrow 0} f(\lambda) = \infty$. This can be interpreted in the following way. As the process gets closer to a random walk, more and more weight is given to long-run fluctuations (cycles with very low frequency or very high periodicity) (Granger 1966).

6.2 Spectral Decomposition of a Time Series

Consider the simple harmonic process $\{X_t\}$ that just consists of a cosine and a sine wave with random amplitudes A and B:

$$X_t = A\cos(\omega t) + B\sin(\omega t), \tag{6.5}$$

where A and B are two uncorrelated random variables with $\mathbb{E}A = \mathbb{E}B = 0$ and $\mathbb{V}A = \mathbb{V}B = \sigma_X^2$. The autocovariance function of this process is $\gamma(h) = \sigma_X^2 \cos(\omega h)$. This autocovariance function cannot be represented as $\int_{-\pi}^{\pi} e^{\imath h\lambda} f(\lambda) d\lambda$. However, it can be regarded as the Fourier transform of a discrete distribution function F:

$$\gamma(h) = \sigma_X^2 \cos(\omega h) = \sigma_X^2 \int_{(-\pi,\pi]} e^{\imath h\lambda} dF(\lambda),$$

where

$$F(\lambda) = \begin{cases} 0, & \text{for } \lambda < -\omega; \\ 1/2, & \text{for } -\omega \le \lambda < \omega; \\ 1, & \text{for } \lambda \ge \omega. \end{cases} \tag{6.6}$$

The integral with respect to the discrete distribution function is a Riemann-Stieltjes integral (see Footnote 3 in this section). If F is a step function with jumps at $-\omega$ and ω and step size of 1/2, the above integral equals $\sigma_X^2(\frac{1}{2}e^{-\imath h\omega} + \frac{1}{2}e^{-\imath h\omega}) = \sigma_X^2 \cos(h\omega)$.

These considerations lead to a representation, called the *spectral representation*, of the autocovariance function as the Fourier transform of a distribution function over $(-\pi, \pi]$.

Theorem 6.2 (Spectral representation) *γ is the autocovariance function of a stationary process $\{X_t\}$ if and only if there exists a right-continuous, nondecreasing, bounded function F on $(-\pi, \pi]$ with the properties $F(-\pi) = 0$ and*

$$\gamma(h) = \int_{(-\pi,\pi]} e^{\imath h\lambda} dF(\lambda). \tag{6.7}$$

F is called the spectral distribution function of γ.

Remark 6.2 If the spectral distribution function F has a density f such that $F(\lambda) = \int_{-\pi}^{\lambda} f(\omega)d\omega$, then f is called the *spectral density* and the time series is said to have a continuous spectrum.

Remark 6.3 According to the Lebesgue-Radon-Nikodym theorem (see, e.g., Rudin 1987), the spectral distribution function F can be represented uniquely as the sum of a distribution function F_Y, which is absolutely continuous with respect to the Lebesgue measure and a discrete distribution function F_V. The distribution function F_Y corresponds to the regular part of the Wold decomposition (see Theorem 3.1 in Sect. 3.2) and has spectral density:

$$f_Y(\lambda) = \frac{\sigma^2}{2\pi} \left|\Psi(e^{-\imath\lambda})\right|^2 = \frac{\sigma^2}{2\pi} \left|\sum_{j=0}^{\infty} \psi_j e^{-\imath j\lambda}\right|^2.$$

The discrete distribution F_V corresponds to the singular part $\{V_t\}$.

The process (6.5) considers just a single frequency ω. We may, however, generalize this process by superposing several sinusoids. This leads to the class of *harmonic processes*:

$$X_t = \sum_{j=1}^{k} A_j \cos(\omega_j t) + B_j \sin(\omega_j t), \qquad 0 < \omega_1 < \cdots < \omega_k < \pi, \tag{6.8}$$

where $A_1, B_1, \ldots, A_k, B_k$ are random variables that are uncorrelated with each other and that have means $\mathbb{E}A_j = \mathbb{E}B_j = 0$ and variances $\mathbb{V}A_j = \mathbb{V}B_j = \sigma_j^2$, $j = 1, \ldots, k$. The autocovariance function of such a process is given by $\gamma(h) = \sum_{j=1}^{k} \sigma_j^2 \cos(\omega_j h)$. According to the spectral representation theorem, the corresponding distribution function F can be represented as a weighted sum of distribution functions like those in Eq. (6.6):

$$F(\lambda) = \sum_{j=1}^{k} \sigma_j^2 F_j(\lambda)$$

with

$$F_j(\lambda) = \begin{cases} 0, & \text{for } \lambda < -\omega_j; \\ 1/2, & \text{for } -\omega_j \leq \lambda < \omega_j; \\ 1, & \text{for } \lambda \geq \omega_j. \end{cases}$$

This generalization points to the following properties:

- Each of the k components $A_j \cos(\omega_j t) + B_j \sin(\omega_j t)$, $j = 1, \ldots, k$, is completely associated with a specific frequency ω_j.
- The k components are uncorrelated with each other.
- The variance of each component is σ_j^2. The contribution of each component to the variance of X_t given by $\sum_{j=1}^k \sigma_j^2$ therefore is σ_j^2.
- F is a nondecreasing step function with jumps at frequencies $\omega = \pm\omega_j$ and step sizes $\frac{1}{2}\sigma_j^2$.
- The corresponding probability distribution is discrete with values $\frac{1}{2}\sigma_j^2$ at the frequencies $\omega = \pm\omega_j$ and zero otherwise.

The interesting feature of harmonic processes as represented in Eq. (6.8) is that *every* stationary process can be represented as the superposition of uncorrelated sinusoids. However, in general, infinitely many (even uncountably many) of these processes have to be superimposed. The generalization of Eq. (6.8) then leads to the spectral representation of a stationary stochastic process:

$$X_t = \int_{(-\pi,\pi]} e^{\imath t\lambda} dZ(\lambda), \tag{6.9}$$

where $\{Z(\lambda)\}$ is a complex-valued stochastic process with uncorrelated increments defined on the interval $(-\pi, \pi]$. The above representation is known as the *spectral representation* of the process $\{X_t\}$.[4] Note the analogy to the spectral representation of the autocovariance function in Eq. (6.7).

For harmonic processes like those represented in Eq. (6.8), we have

$$dZ(\lambda) = \begin{cases} \frac{A_j + \imath B_j}{2}, & \text{for } \lambda = -\omega_j \text{ and } j = 1, 2, \ldots, k; \\ \frac{A_j - \imath B_j}{2}, & \text{for } \lambda = \omega_j \text{ and } j = 1, 2, \ldots, k; \\ 0, & \text{otherwise.} \end{cases}$$

In this case, the variance of dZ is given by

$$\mathbb{E} dZ(\lambda)\overline{dZ(\lambda)} = \begin{cases} \frac{\sigma_j^2}{2}, & \text{if } \lambda = \pm\omega_j; \\ 0, & \text{otherwise.} \end{cases}$$

[4] A mathematically precise statement is given in Brockwell and Davis (1991, chapter 4) where also the notion of stochastic integration is explained.

In general, we have

$$= \begin{cases} F(\lambda) - F(\lambda^-), & \text{discrete spectrum;} \\ f(\lambda)\mathrm{d}\lambda, & \text{continuous spectrum.} \end{cases}$$

Thus, a large jump of the spectrum at frequency λ is associated with a large sinusoidal component with frequency λ.[5]

6.3 Periodogram and Estimation of Spectral Densities

Although the spectral distribution function is uniquely determined, its estimation from a finite sample with realizations $\{x_1, x_2, \ldots, x_T\}$ is not easy. This has to do with the problem of estimating a function from a finite number of points. We will present a nonparametric and a parametric approach.

6.3.1 Nonparametric Estimation

A simple estimator of the spectral density, $\hat{f}_T(\lambda)$, can be obtained by replacing in the defining equation (6.1) the theoretical autocovariances $\gamma(h)$ by their estimates $\hat{\gamma}(h)$. As in the estimation of the long-run variance in Sect. 4.4, we consider a weighted instead of a simple sum:

$$\hat{f}_T(\lambda) = \frac{1}{2\pi} \sum_{|h| \leq \ell_T} k\left(\frac{h}{\ell_T}\right) \hat{\gamma}(h) e^{-\imath h\lambda}. \tag{6.10}$$

The weighting function k, also known as the *lag window*, is assumed to have exactly the same properties as the kernel function introduced in Sect. 4.4. This correspondence is not accidental. Indeed, the long-run variance defined in Eq. (4.2) is just 2π times the spectral density evaluated at $\lambda = 0$. Thus, one might choose a weighting function, kernel function, or lag window from Table 4.1, e.g., the Bartlett window, and use it to estimate the spectral density. The lag truncation parameter is chosen in such a way that $\ell_T \to \infty$ as $T \to \infty$. The rate of divergence should, however, be smaller than T so that $\frac{\ell_T}{T}$ approaches zero as T goes to infinity. As an estimator of the autocovariances, one uses the estimator given in Eq. (4.3) of Sect. 4.2.

The above estimator is called an *indirect spectral estimator* because it requires the estimation of the autocovariances in the first step. The *periodogram* provides an alternative *direct spectral estimator*. For this purpose, we represent the observations as linear combinations of sinusoids of specific frequencies. These so-called Fourier

[5] $F(\lambda^-)$ denotes the left-sided limit, i.e., $F(\lambda^-) = \lim_{\omega \uparrow \lambda} F(\omega)$.

frequencies are defined as $\omega_k = \frac{2\pi k}{T}$, $k = -\lfloor\frac{T-1}{2}\rfloor, \ldots, \lfloor\frac{T}{2}\rfloor$, where $\lfloor x \rfloor$ denotes the floor of x, i.e., the largest integer smaller or equal to x. With this notation, the observations x_t, $t = 1, \ldots, T$, can be represented as a sum of sinusoids:

$$x_t = \sum_{k=-\lfloor\frac{T-1}{2}\rfloor}^{\lfloor\frac{T}{2}\rfloor} a_k e^{\imath\omega_k t} = \sum_{k=-\lfloor\frac{T-1}{2}\rfloor}^{\lfloor\frac{T}{2}\rfloor} a_k(\cos(\omega_k t) + \imath \sin(\omega_k t)).$$

The coefficients $\{a_k\}$ are the *discrete Fourier-transform* of the observations $\{x_1, x_2, \ldots, x_T\}$. The periodogram I_T is then defined as follows.

Definition 6.2 (Periodogram) The periodogram corresponding to observations $\{x_1, x_2, \ldots, x_T\}$ is the function

$$I_T(\lambda) = \frac{1}{T}\left|\sum_{t=1}^{T} x_t e^{-\imath t\lambda}\right|^2 .$$

For each Fourier frequency ω_k, the periodogram $I_T(\omega_k)$ equals $|a_k|^2$. This implies that

$$\sum_{t=1}^{T} x_t^2 = \sum_{k=-\lfloor\frac{T-1}{2}\rfloor}^{\lfloor\frac{T}{2}\rfloor} |a_k|^2 = \sum_{k=-\lfloor\frac{T-1}{2}\rfloor}^{\lfloor\frac{T}{2}\rfloor} I_T(\omega_k).$$

The value of the periodogram evaluated at the Fourier frequency ω_k is therefore nothing but the contribution of the sinusoid with frequency ω_k to the variation of $\{x_t\}$ as measured by the sum of squares. In particular, we get for any Fourier frequency different from zero that

$$I_T(\omega_k) = \sum_{h=-T+1}^{T-1} \hat{\gamma}(h) e^{-\imath h\omega_k}.$$

Thus, the periodogram represents, disregarding the proportionality factor 2π, the sample analogue of the spectral density.

Unfortunately, it turns out that the periodogram is not a consistent estimator of the spectral density. In particular, the covariance between $I_T(\lambda_1)$ and $I_T(\lambda_2)$, $\lambda_1 \neq \lambda_2$, goes to zero for T going to infinity. The periodogram thus has a tendency to get very jagged for large T, leading to the detection of spurious sinusoids. A way out of this problem is to average the periodogram between neighboring frequencies. This makes sense because the variance is relatively constant within a small frequency band. The averaging (smoothing) of the periodogram over neighboring frequencies leads to the class of *discrete spectral average estimators*, which turn out to be consistent:

$$\hat{f}_T(\lambda) = \frac{1}{2\pi} \sum_{|h| \leq \ell_T} K_T(h) I_T\left(\tilde{\omega}_{T,\lambda} + \frac{2\pi h}{T}\right) \tag{6.11}$$

where $\tilde{\omega}_{T,\lambda}$ denotes the multiple of $\frac{2\pi}{T}$ closest to λ. ℓ_T is the bandwidth of the estimator, i.e., the number of ordinates over which the average is taken. ℓ_T satisfies the same properties as in the case of the indirect spectral estimator (6.10): $\ell_T \to \infty$ and $\ell_T/T \to 0$ for $T \to \infty$. Thus, as T goes to infinity, on the one hand, the average is taken over more and more values, but on the other hand, the frequency band over which the average is taken is getting smaller and smaller. The *spectral weighting function* K_T is a positive even function satisfying $\sum_{|h| \leq \ell_T} K_T(h) = 1$ and $\sum_{|h| \leq \ell_T} K_T^2(h) \to 0$ for $T \to \infty$. It can be shown that under these conditions, the discrete spectral average estimator is consistent. For details and the asymptotic distribution, the interested reader is referred to Brockwell and Davis (1991, Chapter 10).

A simple weighting function is given by $K_T(h) = (2\ell_T + 1)^{-1}$ for $|h| \leq \ell_T$ where $\ell_T = \sqrt{T}$. This function corresponds to the Daniell kernel function (see Sect. 4.4). It averages over $2\ell_T + 1$ values within a frequency band of approximate width $\frac{4\pi}{\sqrt{T}}$.

In practice, the sample size is fixed and the researcher faces a trade-off between variance and bias. On the one hand, a weighting function that averages over a wide frequency band produces a smooth spectral density, but has probably a large bias because the estimate of $f(\lambda)$ depends on frequencies that are rather far away from λ. On the other hand, a weighting function that averages only over a small frequency band produces a small bias, but probably a large variance. It is thus advisable in practice to work with alternative weighting functions and to choose the one that delivers a satisfying balance between bias and variance.

The following two examples illustrate the large variance of the periodogram. The first example consists of 200 observations from a simulated white noise process with unit variance, i.e., $X_t \sim \text{WN}(0, 1)$. Whereas the true spectrum is constant and equal to one, the raw periodogram, i.e., the periodogram without smoothing, plotted in Fig. 6.2 is quite erratic. However, it seems obvious that by taking averages over adjacent frequencies, it becomes smoother and more in line with the theoretical spectrum. The second example consists of 200 observations from an AR(2) process with $X_t = 0.9X_{t-1} - 0.7X_{t-2} + Z_t$ and $Z_t \sim \text{WN}(0, 1)$. Figure 6.3 demonstrates again the jaggedness of the raw periodogram. However, the erratic movements are distributed around the true spectrum that has a peak at $\lambda = 1$. Thus, by smoothing the periodogram, one gets closer to the true spectrum and may even detect the dominant cycle at $\lambda = 1$. From this example, it also becomes clear that by smoothing over a too large range, in the extreme over all frequencies, no cycle could be detected.

Figure 6.4 illustrates these considerations by estimating the spectral density of quarterly growth rates of real private residential investment for the US economy using alternative weighting functions. To obtain a better graphical resolution, we have plotted the estimates on a logarithmic scale. All three estimates show a peak

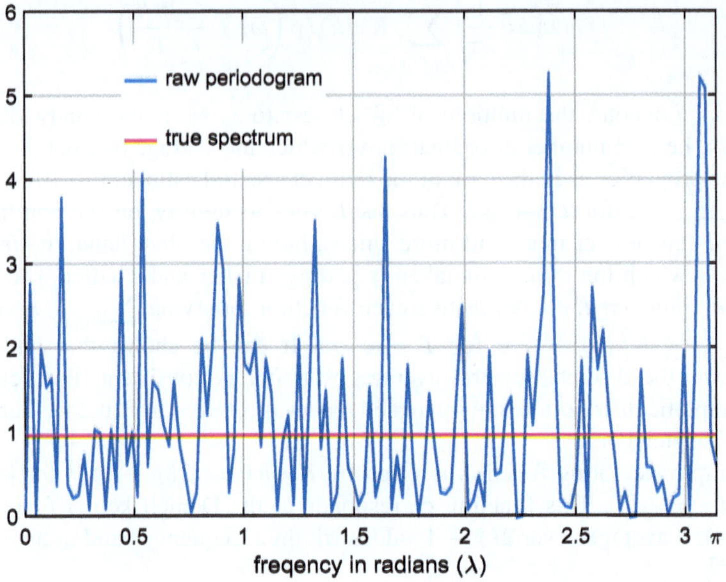

Fig. 6.2 Raw periodogram and true spectrum of a white noise process ($X_t \sim \text{WN}(0, 1)$)

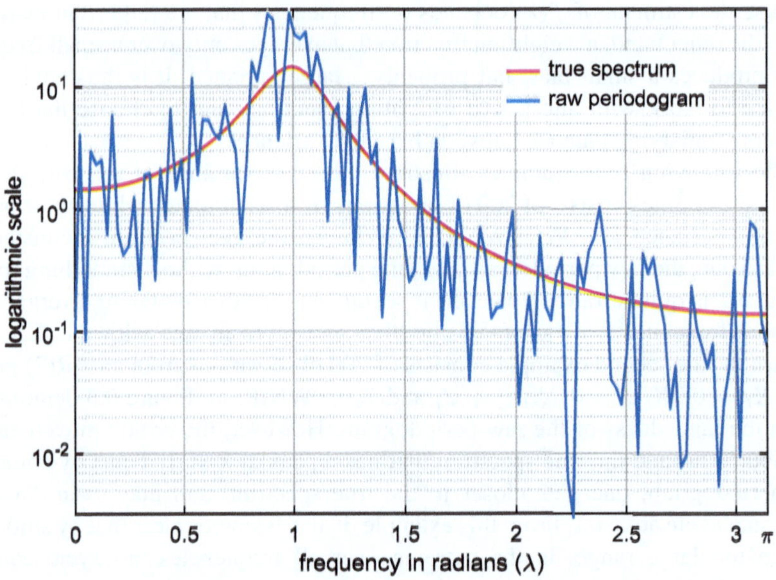

Fig. 6.3 Raw periodogram and true spectrum of an AR(2) process ($X_t = 0.9X_{t-1} - 0.7X_{t-2} + Z_t$, $Z_t \sim \text{WN}(0, 1)$)

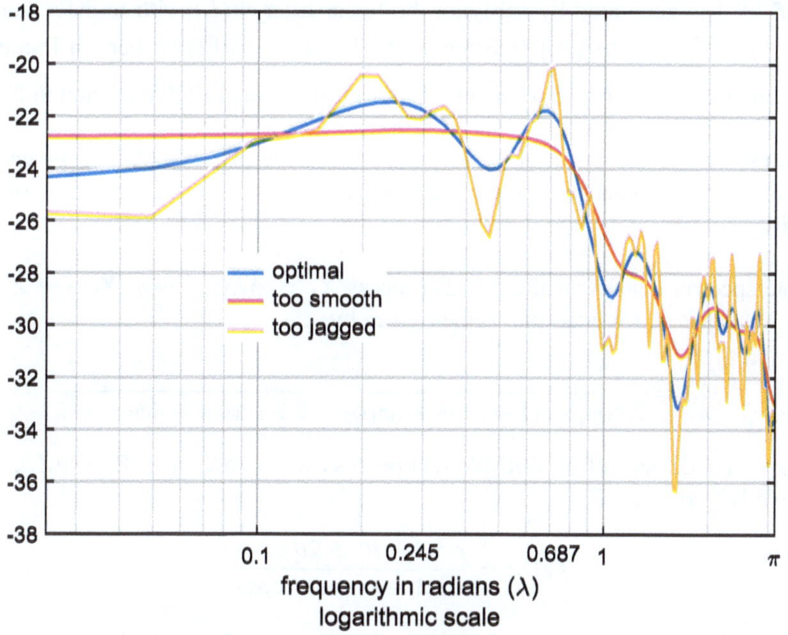

Fig. 6.4 Nonparametric direct estimates of a spectral density with alternative weighting functions

(local maximum) at the frequencies $\lambda = 0.245$ and $\lambda = 0.687$. This corresponds according to Eq. (6.3) approximately to cycles of length $2\pi/0.687 \approx 9$, respectively $2\pi/0.245 \approx 25$ quarters. The estimator with a comparably wide frequency band (red line) smoothes both maxima away. The estimator with a comparable small frequency band (brown line), on the contrary, is too jagged and reveals additional waves. Whether these waves are just artifacts of the weighting function or whether there really exist cycles of that periodicity remains open.

6.3.2 Parametric Estimation

An alternative to the nonparametric approaches just outlined consists in the estimation of an ARMA model and inferring the spectral density from it. This approach was essentially first proposed by Yule (1927).

Theorem 6.3 *Let $\{X_t\}$ be a stationary ARMA(p,q) process given by $\Phi(L)X_t = \Theta(L)Z_t$, which is causal with respect to $Z_t \sim WN(0, \sigma^2)$. Then, the spectral density f_X is given by*

$$f_X(\lambda) = \frac{\sigma^2}{2\pi} \frac{\left|\Theta(e^{-\imath\lambda})\right|^2}{\left|\Phi(e^{-\imath\lambda})\right|^2}, \qquad -\pi \leq \lambda \leq \pi. \tag{6.12}$$

Proof $\{X_t\}$ is generated by applying the linear filter $\Psi(L)$ with transfer function $\Psi(e^{-\imath\lambda}) = \frac{\Theta(e^{-\imath\lambda})}{\Phi(e^{-\imath\lambda})}$ to $\{Z_t\}$ (see Sect. 6.4). Equation (6.12) is then an immediate consequence of Theorem 6.6 because the spectral density of $\{Z_t\}$ is equal to $\frac{\sigma^2}{2\pi}$. □

Remark 6.4 As the spectral density of an ARMA process $\{X_t\}$ is given by a quotient of trigonometric functions, the process is said to have a *rational spectral density*.

The spectral density of the AR(2) process $X_t = \phi_1 X_{t-1} + \phi_2 X_{t-2} + Z_t$ with $Z_t \sim \text{WN}(0, \sigma^2)$, for example, is then given by

$$f_X(\lambda) = \frac{\sigma^2}{2\pi(\phi_1^2 + (1+\phi_2)^2 + (\phi_1\phi_2 - 2\phi_1)\cos\lambda - 4\phi_2\cos^2\lambda)}.$$

The spectral density of an ARMA(1,1) process $X_t = \phi X_{t-1} + Z_t + \theta Z_{t-1}$ with $Z_t \sim \text{WN}(0, \sigma^2)$ is

$$f_X(\lambda) = \frac{\sigma^2(1+\theta^2+2\theta\cos\lambda)}{2\pi(1+\phi^2-2\phi\cos\lambda)}.$$

An estimate of the spectral density is then obtained by replacing the unknown coefficients of the ARMA model by their corresponding estimates and by applying Eq. 6.12 to the estimated model. Figure 6.5 compares the nonparametric to the

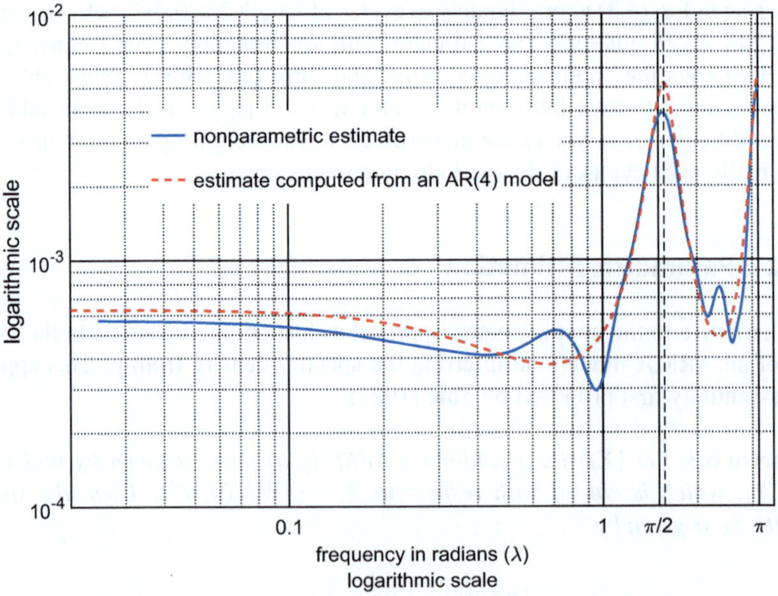

Fig. 6.5 Comparison of nonparametric and parametric estimates of the spectral density of the growth rate of investment in the construction sector

parametric method based on an AR(4) model using the same data as in Fig. 6.4. Both methods produce similar estimates. They clearly show waves of periodicity of half a year and a year, corresponding to frequencies $\frac{\pi}{2}$ and π. The nonparametric estimate is, however, more volatile in the frequency band [0.6, 1] and around 2.5.

6.4 Linear Time-Invariant Filters

Linear time-invariant filters are an indispensable tool in time series analysis. Their objective is to eliminate or amplify waves of a particular periodicity. For example, they may be used to purge a series from seasonal movements to get a seasonally adjusted time series that should bring out the cyclical movements more strongly. The spectral analysis provides just the right tools to construct and analyze the properties of such filters.

Definition 6.3 (Linear time-invariant filter) $\{Y_t\}$ is the output of the *linear time-invariant filter* (LTF) $\Psi = \{\psi_j\}$, $j \in \mathbb{Z}$ applied to the input $\{X_t\}$ if

$$Y_t = \Psi(L)X_t = \sum_{j=-\infty}^{\infty} \psi_j X_{t-j} \qquad \text{with} \sum_{j=-\infty}^{\infty} |\psi_j| < \infty.$$

The filter is called *causal* or *one-sided* if $\psi_j = 0$ for $j < 0$; otherwise, it is called two-sided.

Remark 6.5 Time invariance in this context means that the lagged process $\{Y_{t-s}\}$ is obtained for all $s \in \mathbb{Z}$ from $\{X_{t-s}\}$ by applying the same filter Ψ.

Remark 6.6 MA processes, causal AR processes, and causal ARMA processes can be viewed as filtered white noise processes.

It is important to recognize that the application of a filter systematically changes the autocorrelation properties of the original time series. This may be warranted in some cases, but may lead to the "discovery" of spurious regularities that just reflect the properties of the filter. See the example of the Kuznets filter below. The next two theorems show how the input series is related to the filtered one. The first theorem establishes conditions for the existence of the filtered series. The second theorem shows the relationship between the autocovariance functions of the two series when the input series is stationary.

Theorem 6.4 (Existence of filtered series) *Let* $\{X_t\}$ *be a stochastic process such that* $\sup_t \mathbb{E}|X_t| < \infty$ *and* Ψ *be a filter with the property* $\sum_j |\psi_j| < \infty$*; then the filtered process*

$$Y_t = \Psi(\mathrm{L})X_t = \sum_{j=-\infty}^{\infty} \psi_j X_{t-j}$$

exists with probability one. If in addition $\sup_t \mathbb{E}X_t^2 < \infty$, *the existence also holds in the mean square sense.*

Proof Based on the monotone convergence theorem, we have

$$\mathbb{E}\left|\sum_{j=-\infty}^{\infty} \psi_j X_{t-j}\right| \leq \mathbb{E}\left(\sum_{j=-\infty}^{\infty} |\psi_j||X_{t-j}|\right) = \lim_{n\to\infty} \mathbb{E}\left(\sum_{j=-n}^{n} |\psi_j||X_{t-j}|\right)$$
$$\leq \lim_{n\to\infty} \mathbb{E}\left(\sum_{j=-n}^{n} |\psi_j|\right) \sup \mathbb{E}|X_t| < \infty.$$

Due to Chebyshev's inequality (Theorem C.3), $|\Psi(L)X_t|$ is finite with probability one. Convergence in mean square is established via Cauchy's criterium:

$$\mathbb{E}\left(\sum_{m\leq|j|\leq n} \psi_j X_{t-j}\right)^2 = \sum_{m\leq|j|\leq n}\sum_{m\leq|k|\leq n} \psi_j\psi_k \mathbb{E}(X_{t-j}X_{t-k})$$
$$\leq \sup_t \mathbb{E}X_t^2 \left(\sum_{m\leq|j|\leq n} \psi_j\right)^2 \longrightarrow 0 \text{ for } m,n\to\infty.$$

It remains to show that both limits are identical. Denote by Y_t the limit in mean square; then by Fatou's lemma,

$$\mathbb{E}(Y_t - \Psi(\mathrm{L})X_t)^2 = \mathbb{E}\liminf_{n\to\infty}\left(Y_t - \sum_{j=-n}^{2} \psi_j X_{t-j}\right)^2$$
$$\leq \liminf_{n\to\infty}\mathbb{E}\left(Y_t - \sum_{j=-n}^{2} \psi_j X_{t-j}\right)^2 = 0.$$

Hence, the two limits are identical. □

Remark 6.1 The conditions $\sup_t \mathbb{E}|X_t| < \infty$, respectively $\sup_t \mathbb{E}X_t^2 < \infty$, are rather weak. In particular, they do not assume that $\mathbb{E}|X_t|$, respectively $\mathbb{E}X_t^2$, are constant, so that heterogeneity in the input process is allowed. However, if $\{X_t\}$ is stationary, the moment conditions for the supremum are fulfilled automatically because $\mathbb{E}|X_t| = (\mathbb{E}X_t^2)^{1/2} = \gamma_X(0)^{1/2} < \infty$.

Theorem 6.5 (Autocovariance function of filtered process) *Let $\{X_t\}$ be a mean-zero stationary process with autocovariance function γ_X. Then, the filtered process $\{Y_t\}$ defined as*

$$Y_t = \sum_{j=-\infty}^{\infty} \psi_j X_{t-j} = \Psi(\mathrm{L})X_t$$

with $\sum_{j=-\infty}^{\infty} |\psi_j| < \infty$ is also a mean-zero stationary process with autocovariance function γ_Y. Thus, the two autocovariance functions are related as follows:

$$\gamma_Y(h) = \sum_{j=-\infty}^{\infty} \sum_{k=-\infty}^{\infty} \psi_j \psi_k \gamma_X(h+k-j), \qquad h = 0, \pm 1, \pm 2, \ldots$$

Proof As outlined in the remark above, the stationarity of $\{X_t\}$ implies that conditions of Theorem 6.4 are fulfilled. Hence, $\{Y_t\}$ exists and is well-defined in the mean square sense.

The stationarity of $\{Y_t\}$ can be checked as follows:

$$\mathbb{E}Y_t = \lim_{m\to\infty} \sum_{j=-m}^{m} \psi_j \mathbb{E}X_{t-j} = 0,$$

$$\mathbb{E}Y_t Y_{t-h} = \lim_{m\to\infty} \mathbb{E}\left[\left(\sum_{j=-m}^{m} \psi_j X_{t-j}\right)\left(\sum_{k=-m}^{m} \psi_k X_{t-h-k}\right)\right]$$

$$= \sum_{j=-\infty}^{\infty} \sum_{k=-\infty}^{\infty} \psi_j \psi_k \gamma_X(h+k-j).$$

Thus, $\mathbb{E}Y_t$ and $\mathbb{E}Y_t Y_{t-h}$ are finite and independent of t. $\{Y_t\}$ is therefore stationary.

□

Corollary 6.2 *If $X_t \sim \mathrm{WN}(0, \sigma^2)$ and $Y_t = \sum_{j=0}^{\infty} \psi_j X_{t-j}$, $\sum_{j=0}^{\infty} |\psi_j| < \infty$, the above expression for $\gamma_Y(h)$ simplifies to*

$$\gamma_Y(h) = \sigma^2 \sum_{j=0}^{\infty} \psi_j \psi_{j+|h|}.$$

Theorem 6.6 *Under the conditions of Theorem 6.5, the spectral densities of $\{X_t\}$ and $\{Y_t\}$ are related as*

$$f_Y(\lambda) = \left|\Psi(e^{-\imath\lambda})\right|^2 f_X(\lambda) = \Psi(e^{\imath\lambda})\Psi(e^{-\imath\lambda}) f_X(\lambda)$$

where $\Psi(e^{-\imath\lambda}) = \sum_{j=-\infty}^{\infty} \psi_j e^{-\imath j\lambda}$. $\Psi(e^{-\imath\lambda})$ is called the transfer function *of the filter.*

To understand the effect of the filter Ψ, consider the simple harmonic process $X_t = 2\cos(\lambda t) = e^{\imath\lambda t} + e^{-\imath\lambda t}$. Passing $\{X_t\}$ through the filter Ψ leads to a transformed time series $\{Y_t\}$ defined as

$$Y_t = 2\left|\Psi(e^{-\imath\lambda})\right| \cos\left(\lambda\left(t - \frac{\theta(\lambda)}{\lambda}\right)\right)$$

where $\theta(\lambda) = \arg\Psi(e^{-\imath\lambda})$. The filter therefore amplifies or dampens some frequencies by the factor $g(\lambda) = \left|\Psi(e^{-\imath\lambda})\right|$ and delays X_t by $\frac{\theta(\lambda)}{\lambda}$ periods. Thus, we have a change in amplitude given by $g(\lambda)$ known as the *amplitude gain function* or *gain function* for short and a phase shift given by the *phase function* $\theta(\lambda)$. If the amplitude gain function is bigger than one, the corresponding frequency is amplified. On the other hand, if the value is smaller than one, the corresponding frequency is dampened.

Remark 6.2 If the filter is symmetric, i.e., if $\psi_j = \psi_{-j}$, $j = 1, 2, \ldots$,

$$\Psi(e^{-\imath\lambda}) = \psi_0 + 2\sum_{j=1}^{\infty} \psi_j \cos(j\lambda),$$

because $e^{\imath j\lambda} + e^{-\imath j\lambda} = 2\cos(j\lambda)$. Because $\Psi(e^{-\imath\lambda})$ is real valued in this case, symmetric filters produce no phase shift.

Examples of filters:

- First differences (changes with respect to previous period):

  $$\Psi(L) = \Delta = 1 - L.$$

  The transfer function of this filter is $(1 - e^{-\imath\lambda})$, which implies that the gain function is $2(1 - \cos\lambda)$. This function takes the value zero for $\lambda = 0$. Thus, the filter eliminates the trend that can be considered as a wave with an infinite periodicity.
- Change with respect to same quarter last year, assuming that the data are quarterly observations:

  $$\Psi(L) = 1 - L^4.$$

  The transfer function and the gain function are $1 - e^{-4\imath\lambda}$ and $2(1 - \cos(4\lambda))$, respectively. Thus, the filter eliminates all frequencies that are multiples of $\frac{\pi}{2}$ including the zero frequency. In particular, it eliminates the trend and waves with periodicity of four quarters.
- A famous example of a filter that led to wrong conclusions is the Kuznets filter (see Sargent 1987, 273–276). This filter is obtained from two transformations carried out in a row. The first transformation is supposed to eliminate cyclical movements by taking centered 5-year moving averages. The second one takes centered nonoverlapping first differences. Thus, the filter can be written as

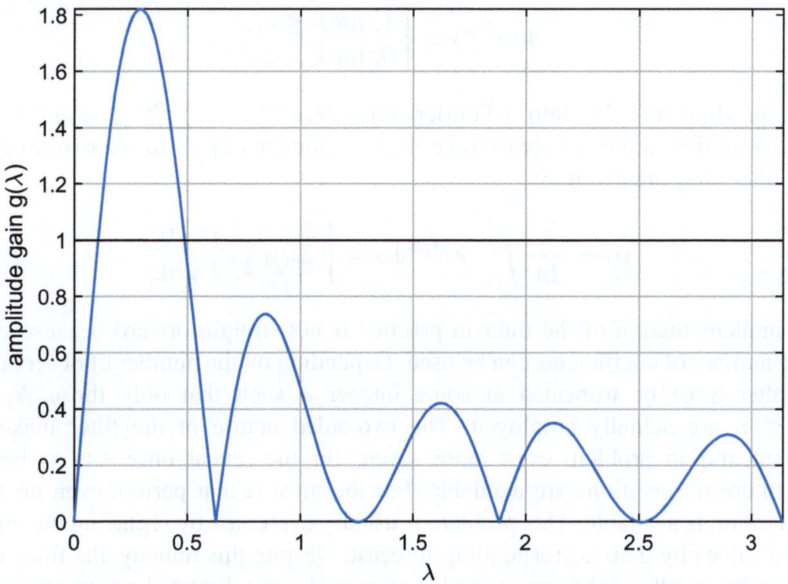

Fig. 6.6 Transfer function of the Kuznets filters

$$\Psi(\mathrm{L}) = \underbrace{\frac{1}{5}\left(\mathrm{L}^{-2} + \mathrm{L}^{-1} + 1 + \mathrm{L} + \mathrm{L}^{2}\right)}_{\text{first transformation}} \quad \underbrace{\left(\mathrm{L}^{-5} - \mathrm{L}^{5}\right)}_{\text{second transformation}} .$$

Figure 6.6 shows a plot of the amplitude gain function of the Kuznets filter. Thus, it can be seen that all frequencies are dampened, except those around $\lambda = 0.2886$. The value $\lambda = 0.2886$ corresponds to a wave with periodicity of approximately $2\pi/0.2886 \approx 21$ years. Thus, as first claimed by Howrey (1968), even a filtered white noise time series would exhibit a 21-year cycle. This demonstrates that cycles of this length, related by Kuznets (1930) to demographic processes and infrastructure investment swings, may just be an artifact produced by the filter and are not endorsed by the data.

6.5 Some Important Filters

6.5.1 Construction of Low- and High-Pass Filters

For some purposes, it is desirable to eliminate specific frequencies. Suppose, we want to purge a time series from all movements with frequencies above λ_c, but leave those below this value unchanged. The transfer function of such an ideal low-pass filter would be

$$\Psi(e^{-\imath\lambda}) = \begin{cases} 1, & \text{for } \lambda \leq \lambda_c; \\ 0, & \text{for } \lambda > \lambda_c. \end{cases}$$

By expanding $\Psi(e^{-\imath\lambda})$ into a Fourier-series $\Psi(e^{-\imath\lambda}) = \sum_{j=-\infty}^{\infty} \psi_j e^{-\imath j\lambda}$, it is possible to determine the appropriate filter coefficients $\{\psi_j\}$. In the case of a low-pass filter, they are given by

$$\psi_j = \frac{1}{2\pi}\int_{-\lambda_c}^{\lambda_c} e^{-\imath j\omega} d\omega = \begin{cases} \frac{\lambda_c}{\pi}, & j = 0; \\ \frac{\sin(j\lambda_c)}{j\pi}, & j \neq 0. \end{cases}$$

The implementation of the filter in practice is not straightforward because only a finite number of coefficients can be used. Depending on the number of observations, the filter must be truncated at some integer q such that only those ψ_j with $|j| \leq q$ are actually employed. The two-sided nature of the filter makes the implementation problem even more severe for the recent observations because less future observations are available. For the most recent period, even no future observation is available. This problem is usually overcome by replacing the missing future values by their corresponding forecast. Despite this remedy, the filter works best in the middle of the sample and is more and more distorted as one approaches the beginning or the end of the sample.

Analogously to low-pass filters, it is possible to construct high-pass filters. Figure 6.7 compares the transfer function of an ideal high-pass filter with two filters truncated at $q = 8$ and $q = 32$, respectively. Obviously, the transfer function with

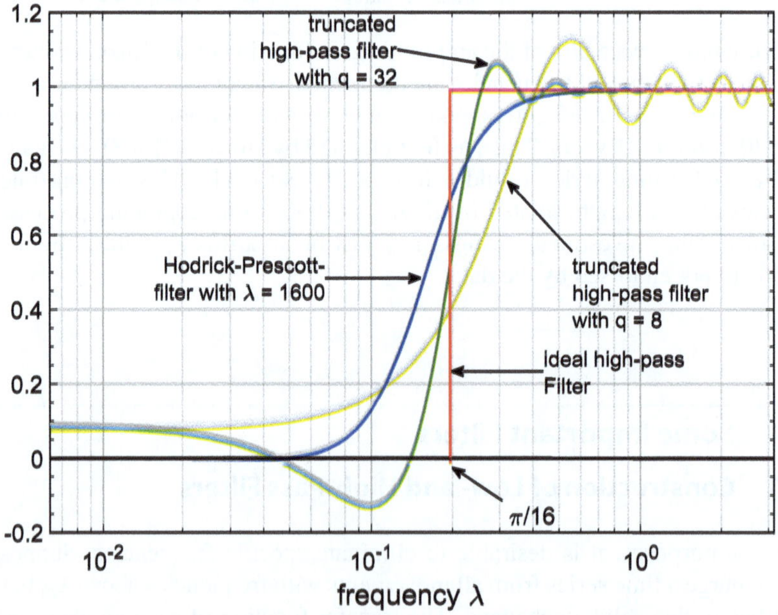

Fig. 6.7 Transfer function of the HP filter compared to alternative high-pass filters

the higher q approximates the ideal filter better. In the neighborhood of the critical frequency, in our case $\pi/16$, however, the approximation remains inaccurate. This is known as the Gibbs phenomenon.

6.5.2 The Hodrick-Prescott Filter

The Hodrick-Prescott filter (HP filter) has gained great popularity in the macroeconomic literature, particularly in the context of the real business cycle theory. This high-pass filter is designed to eliminate the trend and cycles of low frequency (high periodicity) and to bring out movements at business cycle frequencies (see Hodrick and Prescott 1980; King and Rebelo 1993; Brandner and Neusser 1992).[6]

One way to introduce the HP filter is to examine the problem of decomposing a time series $\{X_t\}$ additively into a growth component $\{G_t\}$ and a cyclical component $\{C_t\}$:

$$X_t = G_t + C_t.$$

This decomposition is, without further information, not unique. Following the suggestion of Whittaker (1923), the growth component should be approximated by a smooth curve. Based on this recommendation, Hodrick and Prescott suggest to solve the following *restricted least-squares problem* given a sample $X_1, \ldots, X_T$:

$$\underbrace{\sum_{t=1}^{T} (X_t - G_t)^2}_{\text{fit}} + \lambda \underbrace{\sum_{t=2}^{T-1} [(G_{t+1} - G_t) - (G_t - G_{t-1})]^2}_{\text{smoothness}} \longrightarrow \min_{\{G_t\}}$$

or in matrix notation

$$\underbrace{(X - G)'(X - G)}_{\text{fit}} + \lambda \underbrace{G' S_T' S_T G}_{\text{smoothness}} \quad \rightarrow \quad \min_{G}$$

where

$$S_T = \begin{pmatrix} 0 & 0 & 0 & 0 & \ldots & 0 & 0 & 0 \\ 1 & -2 & 1 & 0 & \ldots & 0 & 0 & 0 \\ 0 & 1 & -2 & 1 & \ldots & 0 & 0 & 0 \\ \vdots & \vdots & \vdots & \vdots & \ddots & \vdots & \vdots & \vdots \\ 0 & 0 & 0 & \ldots & 1 & -2 & 1 & 0 \\ 0 & 0 & 0 & \ldots & 0 & 1 & -2 & 1 \\ 0 & 0 & 0 & \ldots & 0 & 0 & 0 & 0 \end{pmatrix}.$$

[6] Alternatively, Baxter and King (1999) proposed a high-pass filters based on the approach outlined in Sect. 6.5.1.

and where $X = (X_1 \ldots, X_T)$ and $G = (G_1, \ldots, G_T)$. The above objective function has two terms. The first one measures the fit of $\{G_t\}$ to the data. The closer $\{G_t\}$ is to $\{X_t\}$, the smaller this term becomes. In the limit when $G_t = X_t$ for all t, the term is minimized and equal to zero. The second term measures the smoothness of the growth component by looking at the discrete analogue to the second derivative. This term is minimized if the changes of the growth component from one period to the next are constant. This, however, implies that G_t is a linear function (straight line). Thus, the above objective function represents a trade-off between fitting the data and smoothness of the approximating function. This trade-off is governed by the hyperparameter λ, which must be fixed a priori.[7]

The solution to this minimization problem is given by

$$\widehat{G}_T = (I_T + \lambda S_T' S_T)^{-1} X, \tag{6.13}$$

where $\widehat{G}_T = (\widehat{G}_{T1}, \widehat{G}_{T2}, \ldots, \widehat{G}_{TT})'$. This implies that the estimated growth component $\widehat{G}_{Tt}$ for period t is a weighted average of *all* observations:

$$\widehat{G}_{Tt} = \sum_{s=1}^{T} w_{Tts} X_s. \tag{6.14}$$

Hence, the HP filter is a two-sided filter. The computation of G_{Tt} uses both past and future values of X_t. The indexation by the sample size T emphasizes that the weights w_{Tts} are actually a function T. In addition, the weights also depend on the position of t within the sample. Thus, the weights have to be recomputed with every new observation. The difference $\widehat{C}_{Tt} = X_t - \widehat{G}_{Tt}$ gives the cyclical component and can be interpreted as an estimate of the output gap. This triple indexation makes it difficult to derive explicit formulas for the weights w_{Tts}.[8] Nevertheless, it is possible to derive several interesting properties:

(i) The cyclical component $\widehat{C}_{Tt} = X_t - \widehat{G}_{Tt}$ is in general not a stationary time series.
(ii) Because $S_T \iota = 0$ where $\iota = (1, 1, \ldots, 1)'$, $\sum_{s=1}^{T} w_{Tts} = 1$. This implies that the output gap is zero on average, i.e., $\sum_{t=1}^{T}(X_t - \widehat{G}_{Tt}) = 0$.
(iii) If the original series is a straight line, i.e., $X = (1, 2, \ldots, T)'$, $S_T X = 0$ and $\sum_{s=1}^{T} w_{Tts} s = t$. Hence, the HP filter transforms a straight line into a straight line.

The value of λ depends on the critical frequency and on the periodicity of the data (see Uhlig and Ravn 2002, for the latter). Hodrick and Prescott (1980) propose the following values for λ, which became standard in the literature:

---

[7] An alternative, but equivalent, interpretation of the HP filter can be given in terms of a state space model (see Sect. 17.2.6).

[8] For more insights, see de Jong and Sakarya (2016).

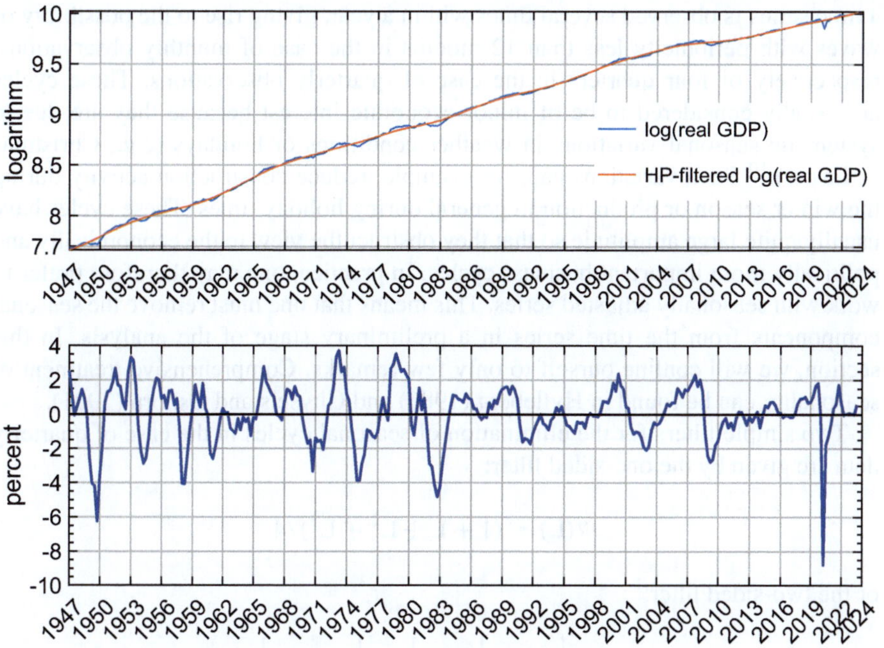

Fig. 6.8 HP-filtered USlogged GDP (upper panel) and its cyclical component (lower panel)

$$\lambda = \begin{cases} 6.25, & \text{yearly observations;} \\ 1600, & \text{quarterly observations;} \\ 14400, & \text{monthly observations.} \end{cases}$$

It can be shown that these choices for λ practically eliminate waves of periodicity longer than 8 years. The cyclical or business cycle component is therefore composed of waves with periodicity less than 8 years. Thus, the choice of λ implicitly defines the business cycle. Figure 6.7 compares the transfer function of the HP filter to the ideal high-pass filter and two approximate high-pass filters.[9]

As an example, Fig. 6.8 displays the HP-filtered US-logged GDP together with the original series in the upper panel and the implied business cycle component in the lower panel.

6.5.3 Seasonal Filters

Besides the elimination of trends, the removal of seasonal movements represents another important application in practice. Seasonal movements typically arise when

[9] As all filters, the HP filter systematically distorts the properties of the time series. Harvey and Jaeger (1993) show how the blind application of the HP filter can lead to the detection of spurious cyclical behavior. Hamilton (2018) provides another critical view of the HP filter.

a time series is observed several times within a year, giving rise to the possibility of waves with periodicity less than 12 months in the case of monthly observations, respectively of four quarters in the case of quarterly observations. These cycles are usually considered to be of minor economic interest because they are due to systematic seasonal variations in weather conditions or holidays (e.g., Christmas or Easter).[10] Such variations can, for example, reduce construction activity during the winter season or production in general during holiday times. These cycles have usually quite large amplitude so that they obstruct the view to the economically and politically more important business cycles. In practice, one may therefore prefer to work with seasonally adjusted series. This means that one must remove the seasonal components from the time series in a preliminary stage of the analysis. In this section, we will confine ourself to only few remarks. Comprehensive treatment of seasonality can be found in Hylleberg (1986) and Ghysels and Osborn (2001).

Two simple filters for the elimination of seasonal cycles in the case of quarterly data are given by the one-sided filter:

$$\Psi(L) = (1 + L + L^2 + L^3)/4$$

or the two-sided filter:

$$\Psi(L) = \frac{1}{8}L^2 + \frac{1}{4}L + \frac{1}{4} + \frac{1}{4}L^{-1} + \frac{1}{8}L^{-2}.$$

In practice, the so-called X-11 filter or its enhanced versions X-12 and X-13 filters developed by the US Census Bureau are often applied. This filter is a two-sided filter that makes, in contrast to the two examples above, use of all sample observations. As this filter not only adjusts for seasonality but also corrects for outliers, a blind mechanical use is not recommended. Gómez and Maravall (1996) developed an alternative method known under the name TRAMO-SEATS. More details on the implementation of both methods can be found in Eurostat (2024).

Figure 6.9 shows the effect of seasonal adjustment using TRAMO-SEATS by looking at the corresponding transfer functions of the growth rate of construction investment. One can clearly discern how the yearly and the half-yearly waves corresponding to the frequencies $\pi/2$ und π are dampened. On the other hand, the seasonal filter weakly amplifies a cycle of frequency 0.72 corresponding to a cycle of periodicity of 2 years.

6.5.4 Using Filtered Data

Whether or not to use filtered, especially seasonally adjusted, data is still an ongoing debate. Although the use of unadjusted data together with a correctly specified

[10] An exception to this view is provided by Miron (1996).

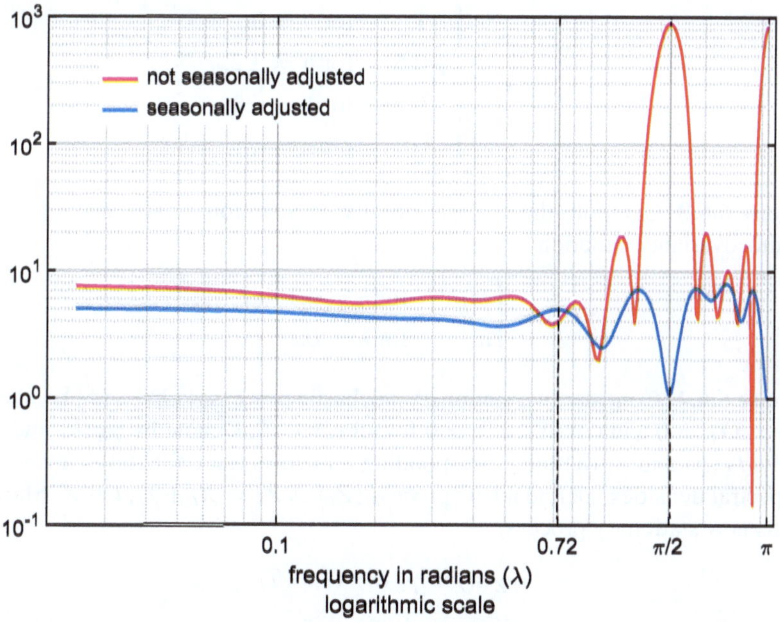

Fig. 6.9 Transfer function of growth rate of investment in the construction sector with and without seasonal adjustment

model is clearly the best choice, there is a nonnegligible uncertainty in modeling economic time series. Thus, in practice, one faces several trade-offs, which must be taken into account and which may depend on the particular context (Sims 1974, 1993; Hansen and Sargent 1993). On the one hand, the use of adjusted data may disregard important information on the dynamics of the time series and introduce some biases. On the other hand, the use of unadjusted data encounters the risk of misspecification, especially because usual measures of fit may put too large emphasis on fitting the seasonal frequencies, thereby neglecting other frequencies.

6.6 Exercises

Exercise 6.6.1 Consider a stationary stochastic process $\{X_t\}$ with autocovariance function $\gamma(h)$ and spectral density $f(\lambda)$. Compute $\gamma(h)$ if:

(i) $f(\lambda)$ is the density of the standard normal distribution
(ii) $f(\lambda) = \frac{1}{2}\exp(-|\lambda|)$

Exercise 6.6.2 Verify if the following function is the autocovariance function of some stationary stochastic process:

$$\gamma(h) = \begin{cases} 1 & \text{for } h = 0, \\ -0.5 & \text{for } h = \pm 2, \\ -0.25 & \text{for } h = \pm 3, \\ 0 & \text{otherwise.} \end{cases}$$

Exercise 6.6.3 Compute the spectral density of a stationary stochastic process if the autocovariance function is

$$\gamma(h) = \begin{cases} \frac{\sin ah}{h} & \text{for } h = \pm 1, \pm 2, \ldots, \\ a & \text{for } h = 0. \end{cases}$$

Exercise 6.6.4 Consider two stationary stochastic processes $\{X_t\}$ and $\{Y_t\}$ such that $\mathbb{E}X_t = \mathbb{E}Y_t = 0$ and $\operatorname{cov}(X_t, Y_s) = 0$ for all $t, s \in \mathbb{Z}$. Denote by $\gamma_X(h)$ and $\gamma_Y(h)$ and by $f_X(h)$ and $f_Y(h)$ the corresponding autocovariance functions, respectively the spectral densities. Define a new process $\{Z_t\}$ as $Z_t = X_t + Y_t, t \in \mathbb{Z}$. Show that for this new stationary process,

$$\gamma_Z(h) = \gamma_X(h) + \gamma_Y(h),$$
$$f_Z(\lambda) = f_X(\lambda) + f_Y(\lambda)$$

where $\gamma_Z(h)$ and $f_Z(\lambda)$ denote the autocovariance function and the spectral density of $\{Z_t\}$, respectively.

Exercise 6.6.5 Compute the autocovariance function of a stationary stochastic process with spectral density:

$$f(\lambda) = \frac{\pi - |\lambda|}{\pi^2}$$

Exercise 6.6.6 Compute the spectral density $f(\lambda)$ of a stationary stochastic process $\{X_t\}$ defined by the difference equation:

$$X_t = 0.99X_{t-3} + Z_t \qquad Z_t \sim \mathrm{WN}(0, 1).$$

(i) Do the trajectories of $\{X_t\}$ oscillate?
(ii) Evaluate the spectral density at $\lambda = \frac{2\pi}{3}$.
(iii) Compare this value with the spectral density of $\{Y_t\}$ where $Y_t = (X_{t-1} + X_t + X_{t+1})/3$ is evaluated at the same value.

Exercise 6.6.7 Compute the amplitude and phase gain functions for the following filters:

$$\Psi(\mathrm{L}) = \begin{cases} 1 - \mathrm{L} \\ 1 - \mathrm{L}^4 \\ (1 + \mathrm{L} + \mathrm{L}^2 + \mathrm{L}^3)/4 \\ \frac{1}{8}\mathrm{L}^2 + \frac{1}{4}\mathrm{L} + \frac{1}{4} + \frac{1}{4}\mathrm{L}^{-1} + \frac{1}{8}\mathrm{L}^{-2} \end{cases}$$

Integrated Processes 7

7.1 Definition, Properties, and Interpretation

Up to now the discussion concentrated on stationary, in particular stationary ARMA, processes. According to the Wold decomposition theorem (see Theorem 3.1), every regular stochastic process possesses a representation:

$$X_t = \mu + \Psi(\mathrm{L})U_t,$$

where $U_t = \Psi(\mathrm{L})Z_t$ with $\{Z_t\} \sim \mathrm{WN}(0, \sigma^2)$ and $\sum_{j=0}^{\infty} \psi_j^2 < \infty$. Typically, X_t is modeled as an ARMA process so that $\Psi(\mathrm{L}) = \frac{\Theta(\mathrm{L})}{\Phi(\mathrm{L})}$. This representation implies:

- $\mathbb{E}X_t = \mu$
- $\lim_{h\to\infty} \mathbb{P}_t X_{t+h} = \mu$

The above property is often referred to as *mean reverting* because the process moves around a constant mean. Deviations from this expected value μ are only temporary (transitory). Hence, the best long-run forecast is just the expected value of the process.

This property is often violated by economic time series, which typically have a tendency to grow. Classic examples are time series for GDP (see Fig. 1.3) or stock market indices (see Fig. 1.5). This trending property is not compatible with stationarity as the expected value is clearly not constant. In order to cope with this feature, two very different alternatives have been proposed. The first one consists in letting the expected value μ be a function of time $\mu(t)$. The most popular specification for $\mu(t)$ is a linear function, i.e., $\mu(t) = \alpha + \delta t$. Hence,

$$X_t = \underbrace{\alpha + \delta t}_{\text{linear trend}} + U_t = \underbrace{\alpha + \delta t}_{\text{linear trend}} + \Psi(\mathrm{L})Z_t.$$

K. Neusser, *Time Series Econometrics*, Springer Texts in Business and Economics,
https://doi.org/10.1007/978-3-031-88838-0_7

The process $\{X_t\}$ is then referred to as a *trend-stationary process*. In practice, one also encounters quadratic polynomials of t or piecewise linear functions. For example, $\mu(t) = \alpha_1 + \delta_1 t$ for $t \le t_0$ and $\mu(t) = \alpha_2 + \delta_2 t$ for $t > t_0$. The following exposition focuses on linear trend functions only.

The second alternative assumes that the time series becomes stationary after differentiation. The number of times one has to differentiate the process to achieve stationarity is called the order of integration. If d differentiations are necessary, the process is called integrated of order d and is denoted by $X_t \sim \mathrm{I}(d)$. If the resulting time series, $\Delta^d X_t = (1 - \mathrm{L})^d X_t$, is an ARMA(p,q) process, the original process is called an ARIMA(p,d,q) process. In economics, it is usually sufficient to differentiate the time series only once, i.e., $d = 1$.[1]

For expositional purposes, we restrict ourselves to the case of integrated processes of order one. Their formal definition is given below.

Definition 7.1 (Integrated Process) The stochastic process $\{X_t\}$ is called *integrated of order one* or *difference-stationary*, denoted as $X_t \sim \mathrm{I}(1)$, if and only if $\Delta X_t = X_t - X_{t-1}$ can be represented as

$$\Delta X_t = (1 - \mathrm{L})X_t = \delta + U_t$$

where $U_t = \Psi(\mathrm{L})Z_t$ with $\{Z_t\} \sim \mathrm{WN}(0, \sigma^2)$, $\Psi(1) \neq 0$, and $\sum_{j=0}^{\infty} j|\psi_j| < \infty$.

The qualification $\Psi(1) \neq 0$ is necessary to avoid trivial and uninteresting cases. If $\Psi(1) = 0$, it would be possible to write $\Psi(\mathrm{L})$ as $(1 - \mathrm{L})\widetilde{\Psi}(\mathrm{L})$ for some lag polynomial $\widetilde{\Psi}(\mathrm{L})$. This would, however, imply that the factor $1 - \mathrm{L}$ could be "canceled" in the above definition so that $\{X_t\}$ would already be stationary and the differentiation would be superfluous. The assumption $\Psi(1) \neq 0$ thus excludes the case where a trend-stationary process could be regarded as an integrated process. For each trend-stationary process $X_t = \alpha + \delta t + \widetilde{\Psi}(\mathrm{L})Z_t$, we have $\Delta X_t = \delta + \Psi(\mathrm{L})Z_t$ with $\Psi(\mathrm{L}) = (1 - \mathrm{L})\widetilde{\Psi}(\mathrm{L})$. This would violate the condition $\Psi(1) \neq 0$. Thus, a trend-stationary process cannot be a difference-stationary process.

The condition $\sum_{j=0}^{\infty} j|\psi_j| < \infty$ implies $\sum_{j=0}^{\infty} \psi_j^2 < \infty$ and is therefore stronger than necessary for the Wold representation to hold. In particular, it implies the Beveridge-Nelson decomposition of integrated processes into a linear trend, a random walk, and a stationary component (see Sect. 7.1.4). The condition is automatically fulfilled for all ARMA processes because $\{\psi_j\}$ decays exponentially fast to zero.

Integrated processes with $d > 0$ are also called unit root processes. This designation results from the fact that ARIMA(p,d,q) processes with $d > 0$ are ARMA processes with a d-fold root of one for the AR polynomial. Important prototypes of integrated processes are random walks with drift δ:

[1] Possible exceptions are time series for monetary aggregates or price levels.

$$X_t = \delta + X_{t-1} + Z_t, \qquad Z_t \sim \text{WN}(0, \sigma^2).$$

Trend-stationary and difference-stationary processes have quite different characteristics with respect to long-run forecasts, variances of the forecast error, and impulse response functions. In the next subsections, we will explore these properties in detail.

7.1.1 Long-Run Forecast

The optimal forecast h periods ahead in the least-squares sense given the infinite past of a trend-stationary process is

$$\widetilde{\mathbb{P}}_t X_{t+h} = \alpha + \delta(t+h) + \psi_h Z_t + \psi_{h+1} Z_{t-1} + \ldots$$

This implies

$$\lim_{h\to\infty} \mathbb{E}\left(\widetilde{\mathbb{P}}_t X_{t+h} - \alpha - \delta(t+h)\right)^2 = \sigma^2 \lim_{h\to\infty} \sum_{j=0}^{\infty} \psi_{h+j}^2 = 0$$

because $\sum_{j=0}^{\infty} \psi_j^2 < \infty$. Thus, the long-run forecast is given by the linear trend. Hence, even when X_t deviates from the trend line, it has a tendency to return to it. Deviations are therefore only of a temporary (transitory) nature. A trend-stationary process therefore behaves in the long-run like $\mu(t) = \alpha + \delta t$.

The forecast of an integrated process is

$$\widetilde{\mathbb{P}}_t \Delta X_{t+h} = \delta + \psi_h Z_t + \psi_{h+1} Z_{t-1} + \psi_{h+2} Z_{t-2} + \ldots$$

The level of X_{t+h} is by definition

$$X_{t+h} = (X_{t+h} - X_{t+h-1}) + (X_{t+h-1} - X_{t+h-2}) + \cdots + (X_{t+1} - X_t) + X_t$$

so that

$$\begin{aligned}
\widetilde{\mathbb{P}}_t X_{t+h} &= \widetilde{\mathbb{P}}_t \Delta X_{t+h} + \widetilde{\mathbb{P}}_t \Delta X_{t+h-1} + \ldots + \widetilde{\mathbb{P}}_t \Delta X_{t+1} + X_t \\
&= \delta + \psi_h Z_t + \psi_{h+1} Z_{t-1} + \psi_{h+2} Z_{t-2} + \ldots \\
&\quad + \delta + \psi_{h-1} Z_t + \psi_h Z_{t-1} + \psi_{h+1} Z_{t-2} + \ldots \\
&\quad + \delta + \psi_{h-2} Z_t + \psi_{h-1} Z_{t-1} + \psi_h Z_{t-2} + \ldots \\
&\quad + \cdots + X_t \\
&= X_t + \delta h \\
&\quad + (\psi_h + \psi_{h-1} + \ldots + \psi_1) Z_t
\end{aligned}$$

$$+ (\psi_{h+1} + \psi_h + \ldots + \psi_2)\, Z_{t-1}$$

$$\ldots$$

This shows that the long-run forecast of integrated processes also depends on a linear trend with slope δ. However, the intercept X_t is no longer a fixed number, but is stochastic. With each new realization of X_t, the intercept changes so that the trend line moves in parallel up and down. Due to this trending behavior of integrated processes, one also speaks in this context of stochastic trends. This issue can be well illustrated by the following two examples.

Example 1 If $\{X_t\}$ is a random walk with drift δ, the best forecast of X_{t+h} in period t based on the infinite remote past is

$$\widetilde{\mathbb{P}}_t X_{t+h} = \delta h + X_t.$$

The forecast thus increases at rate δ starting from the initial value of X_t. δ is therefore the slope of a linear trend. The intercept of this trend is stochastic and equal to X_t. Thus, the trend line moves in parallel up or down depending on the realization of X_t.

Example 2 If $\{X_t\}$ is an ARIMA(0,1,1) process with $\Delta X_t = \delta + Z_t + \theta Z_{t-1}$ and $|\theta| < 1$, the best forecast of X_{t+h} is

$$\widetilde{\mathbb{P}}_t X_{t+h} = \delta h + X_t + \theta Z_t.$$

As before the intercept changes randomly, but in contrast to the previous example, the intercept is given by $X_t + \theta Z_t$. If we consider the forecast given the infinite past, the invertibility of the process implies that Z_t can be expressed as a weighted sum of current and past realizations of ΔX_t (see Sects. 2.3 and 3.1).

7.1.2 Variance of Forecast Error

In the case of a trend-stationary process, the forecast error is

$$X_{t+h} - \widetilde{\mathbb{P}}_t X_{t+h} = Z_{t+h} + \psi_1 Z_{t+h-1} + \ldots + \psi_{h-1} Z_{t+1}.$$

As the mean of the forecast error is zero, its variance is

$$\mathbb{E}\left(X_{t+h} - \widetilde{\mathbb{P}}_t X_{t+h}\right)^2 = \left(1 + \psi_1^2 + \psi_2^2 + \ldots + \psi_{h-1}^2\right)\sigma^2.$$

For h going to infinity, this expression converges to $\sigma^2 \sum_{j=0}^{\infty} \psi_j^2 < \infty$. This is nothing but the unconditional variance of X_t. Thus, the variance of the forecast error increases with the length of the forecast horizon, but remains bounded for $h \to \infty$.

For the integrated process, the forecast error can be written as

$$X_{t+h} - \widetilde{\mathbb{P}}_t X_{t+h} = Z_{t+h} + (1 + \psi_1)\, Z_{t+h-1} + \ldots + (1 + \psi_1 + \psi_2 + \ldots + \psi_{h-1})\, Z_{t+1}.$$

The forecast error variance therefore is

$$\mathbb{E}\left(X_{t+h} - \widetilde{\mathbb{P}}_t X_{t+h}\right)^2 = \left[1 + (1 + \psi_1)^2 + \ldots + (1 + \psi_1 + \ldots + \psi_{h-1})^2\right]\sigma^2.$$

This expression also increases with the length of the forecast horizon h, but remains no longer bounded. It increases linearly in h to infinity.[2] The precision of the forecast therefore not only decreases with the forecasting horizon h as in the case of the trend-stationary model, but converges to zero. For the ARIMA(0,1,1) process in the example above, the forecasting error variance is

$$\mathbb{E}\,(X_{t+h} - \mathbb{P}_t X_{t+h})^2 = \left[1 + (h-1)\,(1 + \theta)^2\right]\sigma^2.$$

This expression clearly increases linearly with h.

7.1.3 Impulse Response Function

The impulse response function (dynamic multiplier) reports how a variable X_t responds to shocks over time. In the case of the trend-stationary process, the impulse response function is

$$\frac{\partial \widetilde{\mathbb{P}}_t X_{t+h}}{\partial Z_t} = \psi_h \longrightarrow 0 \quad \text{for}\, h \to \infty.$$

The effect of a shock thus declines with time and dies out eventually. Shocks have therefore only temporary (transitory) effects. In the case of an ARMA process, the effect even declines exponentially fast to zero (see the considerations in Sect. 2.3).[3]

For integrated processes, the impulse response function for ΔX_t implies :

$$\frac{\partial \widetilde{\mathbb{P}}_t X_{t+h}}{\partial Z_t} = 1 + \psi_1 + \psi_2 + \ldots + \psi_h.$$

---

[2] *Proof*: By assumption $\sum_{j=0}^{\infty} |\psi_j| < \sum_{j=0}^{\infty} j|\psi_j| < \infty$; hence, $\{\psi_j\}$ is absolutely summable so that $\Psi(1)$ converges. Moreover, as $\Psi(1) \neq 0$ by assumption, there exists $\varepsilon > 0$ and an integer m such that $\left|\sum_{j=0}^{h} \psi_j\right| > \varepsilon$ for all $h > m$. The squares are therefore bounded from below by $\varepsilon^2 > 0$ so that their infinite sum diverges.

[3] The use of the partial derivative notation is just a matter of convenience. It does not mean that X_{t+h} is differentiated in the literal sense.

For h going to infinity, this expression converges $\sum_{j=0}^{\infty} \psi_j = \Psi(1) \neq 0$. This implies that a shock experienced in period t will have a long-run or permanent effect. This long-run effect is called *persistence*. If $\{\Delta X_t\}$ is an ARMA process, the persistence is given by the expression

$$\Psi(1) = \frac{\Theta(1)}{\Phi(1)}.$$

Thus, for an ARIMA(0,1,1), the persistence is $\Psi(1) = \Theta(1) = 1 + \theta$. In the next section, we will discuss some examples. The long-run effect of a shock can thus be smaller or larger than one in this case.

7.1.4 The Beveridge-Nelson Decomposition

The Beveridge-Nelson decomposition represents an important analytical tool understanding the properties of integrated processes.[4] It shows how an integrated time series of order one can be represented as the sum of a linear trend, a random walk, and a stationary series. It may therefore be used to extract the cyclical component (business cycle component) of a time series and can thus be viewed as an alternative to the HP filter (see Sect. 6.5.2) or to more elaborated so-called structural time series models (see Sects. 17.1 and 17.5.2).

Before proceeding to the main theorem, notice the following simple, but useful, polynomial decomposition of $\Psi(\mathrm{L})$:

$$\begin{aligned}
\Psi(\mathrm{L}) - \Psi(1) &= 1 + \psi_1\mathrm{L} + \psi_2\mathrm{L}^2 + \psi_3\mathrm{L}^3 + \psi_4\mathrm{L}^4 + \ldots \\
&\quad - 1 - \psi_1 - \psi_2 - \psi_3 - \psi_4 - \ldots \\
&= \psi_1(\mathrm{L} - 1) + \psi_2(\mathrm{L}^2 - 1) + \psi_3(\mathrm{L}^3 - 1) + \psi_4(\mathrm{L}^4 - 1) + \ldots \\
&= (\mathrm{L} - 1)\left[\psi_1 + \psi_2(\mathrm{L} + 1) + \psi_3(\mathrm{L}^2 + \mathrm{L} + 1) + \ldots\right] \\
&= (\mathrm{L} - 1)\big[(\psi_1 + \psi_2 + \psi_3 + \ldots) + (\psi_2 + \psi_3 + \psi_4 + \ldots)\mathrm{L} \\
&\quad + (\psi_3 + \psi_4 + \psi_5 + \ldots)\mathrm{L}^2 + \ldots\big].
\end{aligned}$$

We state this results in the following lemma:

Lemma 7.1 *Let* $\Psi(\mathrm{L}) = \sum_{j=0} \psi_j \mathrm{L}^j$*; then*

$$\Psi(\mathrm{L}) = \Psi(1) + (\mathrm{L} - 1)\widetilde{\Psi}(\mathrm{L})$$

where $\widetilde{\Psi}(\mathrm{L}) = \sum_{j=0}^{\infty} \widetilde{\psi}_j \mathrm{L}^j$ *with* $\widetilde{\psi}_j = \sum_{i=j+1}^{\infty} \psi_i$.

[4] Neusser (2000) shows how a Beveridge-Nelson decomposition can also be derived for higher-order integrated processes.

As $\{X_t\}$ is integrated, we can decompose X_t additively as

$$\begin{aligned}
X_t &= X_0 + \sum_{j=1}^{t} \Delta X_j \\
&= X_0 + \sum_{j=1}^{t} \left\{\delta + \left[\Psi(1) + (\mathrm{L}-1)\widetilde{\Psi}(\mathrm{L})\right] Z_j\right\} \\
&= X_0 + \delta t + \Psi(1)\sum_{j=1}^{t} Z_j + \sum_{j=1}^{t} (\mathrm{L}-1)\widetilde{\Psi}(\mathrm{L}) Z_j \\
&= \underbrace{X_0 + \delta t}_{\text{linear trend}} + \underbrace{\Psi(1)\sum_{j=1}^{t} Z_j}_{\text{random walk}} + \underbrace{\widetilde{\Psi}(\mathrm{L})Z_0 - \widetilde{\Psi}(\mathrm{L})Z_t}_{\text{stationary component}}.
\end{aligned}$$

Note that the random walk component is always present because $\Psi(1) \neq 0$. The above decomposition leads to the following theorem.

Theorem 7.1 (Beveridge-Nelson Decomposition) *Every integrated process* $\{X_t\}$ *has a decomposition of the following form:*

$$X_t = \underbrace{X_0 + \delta t}_{\text{linear trend}} + \underbrace{\Psi(1)\sum_{j=1}^{t} Z_j}_{\text{random walk}} + \underbrace{\widetilde{\Psi}(\mathrm{L})Z_0 - \widetilde{\Psi}(\mathrm{L})Z_t}_{\text{stationary component}}.$$

The above representation is known as the Beveridge-Nelson decomposition.

Proof The only substantial issue is to show that $\widetilde{\Psi}(\mathrm{L})Z_0 - \widetilde{\Psi}(\mathrm{L})Z_t$ defines a stationary process. According to Theorem 6.5, it is sufficient to show that the coefficients of $\widetilde{\Psi}(\mathrm{L})$ are absolutely summable. It holds that

$$\sum_{j=0}^{\infty} |\widetilde{\psi}_j| = \sum_{j=0}^{\infty} \left| \sum_{i=j+1}^{\infty} \psi_i \right| \le \sum_{j=0}^{\infty} \sum_{i=j+1}^{\infty} |\psi_i| = \sum_{j=1}^{\infty} j|\psi_j| < \infty,$$

where the first inequality is a consequence of the triangular inequality and the second inequality follows from Definition 7.1 of an integrated process. □

Shocks to the random walk component have a permanent effect, which is measured by the coefficient $\Psi(1)$ of the random walk component. Hence, $\Psi(1)$ is also termed as the *persistence* of the integrated process. In macroeconomics, aggregate supply shocks are ascribed to have a long-run effect as they affect productivity. In contrast, monetary or demand shocks are viewed to have temporary effects only. Thus, the persistence $\Psi(1)$ can be interpreted as a measure for the importance of supply shocks (see Campbell & Mankiw, 1987, Cochrane, 1988, or Christiano & Eichenbaum, 1990). For a critical view from an econometric standpoint, see Hauser et al. (1999). A more sophisticated multivariate approach to identify supply and demand shocks and to disentangle their relative importance is provided in Sect. 15.4.

In business cycle analysis, it is often useful to decompose $\{X_t\}$ into a sum of a trend component T_t and a cyclical component C_t:

$$X_t = T_t + C_t.$$

In the case of a difference-stationary series, the cyclical component can be identified with the stationary component in the Beveridge-Nelson decomposition and the trend component with the random walk plus the linear trend. Suppose that $\{\Delta X_t\}$ follows an ARMA process $\Phi(\mathrm{L})\Delta X_t = c + \Theta(\mathrm{L})Z_t$; then $\Delta T_t = \delta + \Psi(1)Z_t$ can be identified as the trend component. This means that the trend component can be recursively determined from the observations by applying the following formula:

$$T_t = \frac{\Phi(\mathrm{L})}{\Theta(\mathrm{L})}\Psi(1)X_t.$$

The cyclical component is then simply the residual: $C_t = X_t - T_t$.

In the above decomposition, both the permanent (trend) component and the stationary (cyclical) component are driven by the same shock Z_t. A more sophisticated model would, however, allow that the two components are driven by different shocks. This idea is exploited in the so-called structural time series analysis where the different components (trend, cycle, season, and irregular) are modeled as being driven by separated shocks. As only the series $\{X_t\}$ is observed, not its components, this approach leads to serious identification problems. See the discussion in Harvey (1989), Hannan and Deistler (1988), or Mills (2003). In Sects. 17.1 and 17.5.2, we will provide an overall framework to deal with these issues.

Examples Let $\{\Delta X_t\}$ be a MA(q) process with $\Delta X_t = \delta + Z_t + \ldots + \theta_q Z_{t-q}$; then the persistence is given simply by the sum of the MA coefficients: $\Psi(1) = 1 + \theta_1 + \ldots + \theta_q$. Depending on the value of these coefficients, the persistence can be smaller or greater than one.

If $\{\Delta X_t\}$ is an AR(1) process with $\Delta X_t = \delta + \phi \Delta X_{t-1} + Z_t$ and assuming $|\phi| < 1$, $\Delta X_t = \frac{\delta}{1-\phi} + \sum_{j=0}^{\infty} \phi^j Z_{t-j}$. The persistence is given in this case as $\Psi(1) = \sum_{j=0}^{\infty} \phi^j = \frac{1}{1-\phi}$. For positive values of ϕ, the persistence is greater than one. Thus, a shock of one is amplified to have an effect larger than one in the long run.

If $\{\Delta X_t\}$ is assumed to follow an ARMA(1,1) process with $\Delta X_t = \delta + \phi \Delta X_{t-1} + Z_t + \theta Z_{t-1}$ and $|\phi| < 1$, then $\Delta X_t = \frac{\delta}{1-\phi} + Z_t + (\phi + \theta)\sum_{j=0}^{\infty} \phi^j Z_{t-j-1}$. The persistence is therefore given by $\Psi(1) = 1 + (\phi + \theta)\sum_{j=0}^{\infty} \phi^j = \frac{1+\theta}{1-\phi}$.

The computation of the persistence for the model estimated for Swiss GDP in Sect. 5.6 is more complicated because a fourth-order difference $1 - \mathrm{L}^4$ has been used instead of a first-order one. As $1-\mathrm{L}^4 = (1-\mathrm{L})(1+\mathrm{L}+\mathrm{L}^2+\mathrm{L}^3)$, it is possible to extend the above computations also to this case. For this purpose, we compute the persistence for $(1+\mathrm{L}+\mathrm{L}^2+\mathrm{L}^3)\ln \mathrm{BIP}_t$ in the usual way. The long-run effect on $\ln \mathrm{BIP}_t$ is therefore given by $\Psi(1)/4$ because $(1+\mathrm{L}+\mathrm{L}^2+\mathrm{L}^3)\ln \mathrm{BIP}_t$ is nothing but four times the moving average of the last four values. For the AR(2) model, we get a persistence of 1.42, whereas for the ARMA(1,3) model, the persistence is 1.34. Both values are definitely above one so that the permanent effect of a 1% shock to Swiss GDP is amplified to be larger than one in the long run. Campbell and Mankiw (1987) and Cochrane (1988) report similar values for the United States.

7.2 OLS Estimator with Integrated Variables

The estimation and testing of coefficients of models involving integrated variables is not without complications and traps because the usual asymptotic theory is typically invalid. The asymptotic distributions are in general no longer normal so that the usual critical values for the test statistics are no longer appropriate. A rigorous presentation of the issues involved requires a mathematical level beyond the scope of this monograph. The reader interested in technical details may consult Phillips (1987), Banerjee et al. (1993), or Stock (1994), among others.

We assume that $\{X_t\}$, $t = 0, 1, \ldots$, is generated by

$$X_t = \phi X_{t-1} + U_t, \qquad t = 1, , 2, \ldots, \qquad \text{with } X_0 = 0, \tag{7.1}$$

where $\{U_t\}$ is a stationary process with finite and positive long-run variance, i.e., $\omega_U = \sum_{h\in\mathbb{Z}} \gamma(h)$ exists and $\omega_U > 0$. In addition, U_t has to satisfy the moment condition $\sup_t \mathbb{E}|U_t|^\beta < \infty$ for some $\beta > 2$. Note, however, $\mathbb{V}u_t = \gamma(0) = \sigma^2$ is constant due to the stationarity of $\{U_t\}$. Furthermore, denote by S_t the partial sum $S_t = \sum_{j=1}^t U_j$. Processes $\{U_t\}$ that satisfy these requirements are Gaussian processes or stationary ARMA processes with appropriate moment conditions for the error term. Note that, if $\phi = 1$, this specification generalizes Definition 7.1 of integrated process.

For sample size T, the formula for the OLS estimator of ϕ is

$$\widehat{\phi}_T = \frac{\sum_{t=1}^T X_t X_{t-1}}{\sum_{t=1}^T X_{t-1}^2}.$$

Setting $\phi = 1$, this estimator can be written as

$$T(\widehat{\phi}_T - 1) = \frac{T^{-1}\sum_{t=1}^T X_{t-1}(X_t - X_{t-1})}{T^{-2}\sum_{t=1}^T X_{t-1}^2}. \tag{7.2}$$

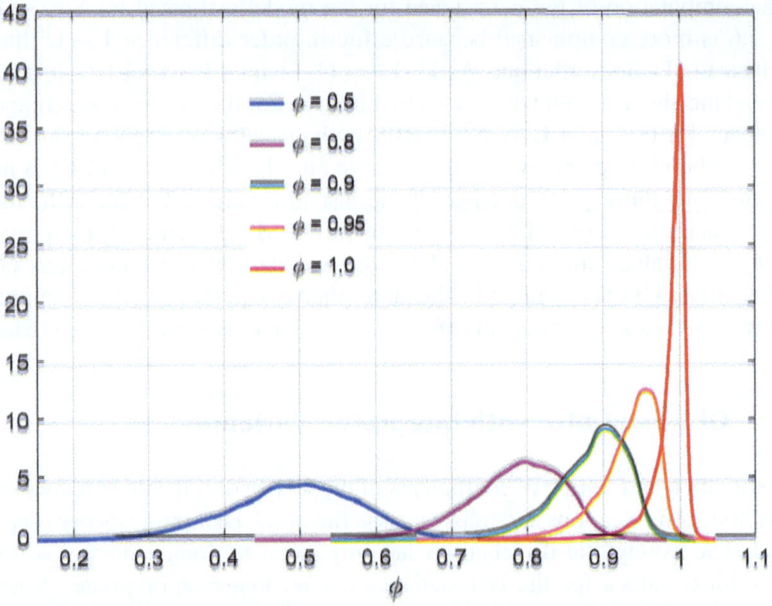

Fig. 7.1 Distribution of the OLS estimator of ϕ for $T = 100$ and 10,000 replications

The corresponding conventional t-statistic for the hypothesis $\phi = 1$ is

$$t_{\widehat{\phi}_T} = \left(\sum_{t=1}^{T} X_{t-1}^2\right)^{1/2} \frac{\widehat{\phi}_T - 1}{s_T} = \frac{\sum_{t=1}^{T} X_{t-1}(X_t - X_{t-1})}{\left(s_T^2 \sum_{t=1}^{T} X_{t-1}^2\right)^{1/2}} \tag{7.3}$$

where $s_T^2 = T^{-1} \sum_{t=1}^{T} (X_t - \widehat{\phi}_T X_{t-1})^2$.

Consider first the special, but instructive, case $U_t = Z_t \sim \text{IID}\, \text{N}(0, \sigma^2)$. If $|\phi| < 1$, the OLS estimator of ϕ, $\widehat{\phi}_T$, converges in distribution to a normal random variable (see Chap. 5 and in particular Sect. 5.2):

$$\sqrt{T}\left(\widehat{\phi}_T - \phi\right) \xrightarrow{d} \text{N}\left(0, 1 - \phi^2\right).$$

The estimated densities of the OLS estimator for alternative values of ϕ are plotted in Fig. 7.1. This figure was constructed using a Monte Carlo simulation of the above model for a sample size of $T = 100$ using 10,000 replications for each value of ϕ.[5] The figure shows that the distribution of $\widehat{\phi}_T$ becomes more and more concentrated if the true value of ϕ gets closer and closer to one. Moreover, the distribution gets also

[5] The densities were estimated using an adaptive kernel density estimator with Epanechnikov window (see Silverman, 1986).

more and more skewed to the left. This implies that the OLS estimator is downward biased and that this bias gets relatively more and more pronounced in small samples as ϕ approaches one. See the remarks at the end of Sect. 5.2.

The asymptotic distribution becomes degenerated for ϕ approaching one because the variance converges to zero in this case. The asymptotic distribution becomes useless for statistical inferences under this circumstance. This suggest that the estimator must be scaled by a larger factor than $\sqrt{T}$. It turns out that a scaling factor T is sufficient to obtain a nondegenerate asymptotic distribution. This result was first established by Dickey and Fuller (1976) and Dickey and Fuller (1981). However, the asymptotic distribution is no longer normal. It was first tabulated in Fuller (1976). The scaling with T instead of $\sqrt{T}$ implies that the OLS estimator converges at a higher rate to the true value $\phi = 1$. This property is known as *superconsistency* and is due to the fact that integrated processes exhibit larger variations and are therefore more informative than stationary processes.

Setting from now on $\phi = 1$, we first treat the simpler case with no serial autocorrelation in $\{U_t\}$ to get a deeper understanding of the issues involved and move to the general case later on. Specifically, we assume that $U_t = Z_t \sim \text{IID}\,\text{N}(0, \sigma^2)$. This specification implies that $\{X_t\}$ is a random walk because $X_t = S_t = Z_t + \ldots + Z_1$. In addition, $X_t \sim \text{N}(0, t\sigma^2)$ as X_t is the sum of independently, identically, normally distributed random variables. The OLS estimator in Eq. (7.2) then is

$$T\left(\widehat{\phi}_T - 1\right) = \frac{\sigma^{-2}T^{-1}\sum_{t=1}^{T} X_{t-1}Z_t}{\sigma^{-2}T^{-2}\sum_{t=1}^{T} X_{t-1}^2}.$$

The identity $X_t^2 = (X_{t-1} + Z_t)^2$ implies $X_{t-1}Z_t = \frac{1}{2}(X_t^2 - X_{t-1}^2 - Z_t^2)$. Hence, the numerator can be written as

$$\begin{aligned}
\frac{1}{\sigma^2 T}\sum_{t=1}^{T} X_{t-1}Z_t &= \frac{1}{2\sigma^2 T}\sum_{t=1}^{T}(X_t^2 - X_{t-1}^2 - Z_t^2) = \frac{1}{2\sigma^2 T}\left(X_T^2 - \sum_{t=1}^{T} Z_t^2\right) \\
&= \frac{1}{2}\left(\left(\frac{X_T}{\sigma\sqrt{T}}\right)^2 - \frac{1}{\sigma^2 T}\sum_{t=1}^{T} Z_t^2\right) \\
&\xrightarrow{\text{d}} \frac{1}{2}\left(\chi_1^2 - 1\right).
\end{aligned}$$

The standardized random variable $\frac{X_T}{\sigma\sqrt{T}}$ is distributed as N(0, 1). Hence, its square is χ_1^2 distributed. Kolmogorov's Law of Large Numbers (Theorem C.5) and the continuous mapping theorem (Theorem C.9) imply the converges of $T^{-1}\sum_{t=1}^{T} Z_t^2$ to σ^2. The numerator is therefore asymptotically distributed as a χ^2 distribution shifted by one and scaled by one-half.

The distribution of the denominator is more involved. It is, however, possible to compute its expected value and its variance:

$$\mathbb{E}\sum_{t=1}^{T} X_{t-1}^2 = \sigma^2 \frac{T(T-1)}{2}$$

$$\mathbb{V}\sum_{t=1}^{T} X_{t-1}^2 = \sigma^4 \frac{T(T-1)(T^2-T+1)}{3}.$$

The reader is invited to prove these assertions. From this expression, it becomes intuitively clear that the sum in the denominator must be scaled T^2 to obtain a nondegenerate distribution.

Using similar arguments, it can be shown that the t-statistic

$$t_{\widehat{\phi}_T} = \frac{\widehat{\phi}_T - 1}{\widehat{\sigma}_{\widehat{\phi}}} = \frac{\widehat{\phi}_T - 1}{\sqrt{\frac{s_T^2}{\sum_{t=1}^{T} X_{t-1}^2}}}$$

where $s_T^2 = \frac{1}{T-2}\sum_{t=2}^{T}\left(X_t - \widehat{\phi}_T X_{t-1}\right)^2$ is not asymptotically normal. Its distribution was also first tabulated by Fuller (1976). Figure 7.2 compares its density with the standard normal distribution in a Monte Carlo experiment using again a sample

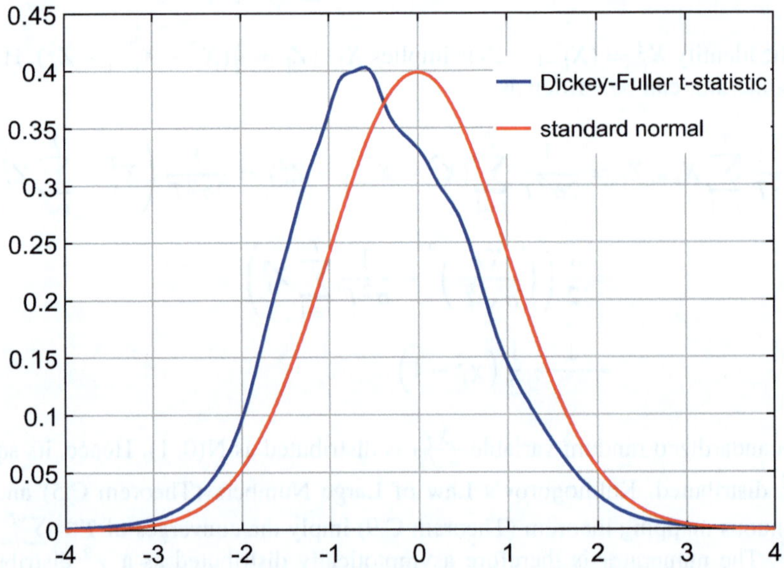

Fig. 7.2 Distribution of the Dickey-Fuller t-statistic for $T = 100$ and 10,000 replications and the standard normal distribution

of $T = 100$ and 10,000 replications. It is obvious that the t-distribution is shifted to the left. This implies that the critical values will be absolutely higher than for the standard case. In addition, one may observe a slight skewness.

To analyze the general case allowing with nontrivial autocorrelation in $\{U_t\}$, we need to go further and give a short introduction to the functional central limit theory (FCLT), which is a generalization of the conventional central limit theory (CLT) stated in Theorem C.13. To this end, we linearly interpolate between the sample points of the scaled partial sums to make it a continuous function on the interval $[0, 1]$:

$$\mathcal{S}_T(r) = \frac{1}{\sqrt{\omega_U T}} \sum_{t=1}^{T} \left[S_{t-1} + T\left(r - \tfrac{t-1}{T}\right) U_t \right] \mathbf{I}_{\left(\frac{t-1}{T}, \frac{t}{T}\right]}(r) \tag{7.4}$$

and $\mathcal{S}_T(0) = 0$. Note that $\mathcal{S}_T(1) = \frac{1}{\sqrt{\omega_U T}} S_T$. The serial autocorrelation of $\{U_t\}$ requires to scale by the long-run variance ω_U instead of unconditional variance σ^2. The transformation (7.4) maps the partial sum S_T into an element of $\mathbb{C}([0, 1])$, the space of continuous functions on $[0, 1]$. $\mathcal{S}_T(r)$ is therefore a random element in $\mathbb{C}([0, 1])$. As the sample size T increases, $\mathcal{S}_T(r)$ becomes increasingly dense on the interval $[0, 1]$. Donsker's theorem[6] then shows that $\mathcal{S}_T(r)$ converges weakly to a Brownian motion (See Durrett, 2019, Theorem 8.3.2):

$$\mathcal{S}_T(r) \Longrightarrow B_r. \tag{7.5}$$

The Brownian motion is the continuous analogue to the random walk and is defined precisely in Definition C.8. Weak converges, denoted by $\Longrightarrow$, mean that for all bounded, continuous functions $f : \mathbb{C}([0, 1]) \to \mathbb{R}$, $\lim_{T\to\infty} \mathbb{E} f(\mathcal{S}_T) - \mathbb{E} f(B)$. It is the analogue to convergence in distribution for function spaces like $\mathbb{C}([0, 1])$. A continuous mapping theorem also applies in this context:

$$\mathcal{S}_T(r) \Longrightarrow B_r \quad \text{implies} \quad f(\mathcal{S}_T(r)) \Longrightarrow f(B_r) \tag{7.6}$$

for any continuous function $f : \mathbb{C}([0, 1]) \to \mathbb{R}$. Setting $f(x) = x_1$, the standard CLT is recovered: $f(\mathcal{S}_T(r)) = \frac{1}{\sqrt{\omega_U T}} S_T \Longrightarrow f(B_r) = B_1 \sim \mathrm{N}(0, 1)$. In this sense, the FCLT is a generalization of the CLT.

Bearing this convergence to the Brownian motion in mind, it can be shown (Phillips, 1987) that

$$\frac{1}{T^{-1}} \sum_{t=1}^{T} X_{t-1}(X_t - X_{-1}) \Longrightarrow \omega \int_0^1 B_r \mathrm{d}B_r + \lambda,$$

[6] Donsker's theorem is also known as the functional central limit theorem or invariance principle. The latter name is due to the fact that the theorem applies to a wide range of stochastic processes.

$$\frac{1}{T^{-2}}\sum_{t=1}^{T} X_{t-1}^2 \Longrightarrow \omega \int_0^1 B_r^2 \mathrm{d}r$$

where $\lambda = \frac{1}{2}(\omega - \sigma^2) = \sum_{h=1}^{\infty} \gamma(h)$. The integral $\int_0^1 B_r \mathrm{d}B_r$ is a so-called Itô integral whose exact definition is beyond the scope of this monograph. For nice introduction to stochastic calculus, in particular to Itô integration, see Arguin (2022). The integral $\int_0^1 B_r^2 \mathrm{d}r$ is a standard Riemann integral. The main difference between the conventional CLT and the FCLT is that in the former case, the sample moments converge to constants, whereas in the latter, they converge to random variables. Applying the continuous mapping theorem, the OLS estimator given Eq. (7.2) converges weakly:

$$T(\widehat{\phi}_T - 1) \Longrightarrow \frac{\omega \int_0^1 B_r \mathrm{d}B_r + \lambda}{\omega \int_0^1 B_r^2 \mathrm{d}r} \tag{7.7}$$

When $\{U_t\}$ exhibits nontrivial autocorrelation, the regressor $X_{t-1} = \sum_{j=1}^{t-1} U_j$ becomes endogenous as it is correlated with U_t. Despite this fact, the result above shows that the OLS estimator with integrated variables is still consistent taking the correction factor λ into account. Similarly, the t-statistic (7.3) converges to

$$t_{\widehat{\phi}_T} \Longrightarrow \frac{\sqrt{\frac{\omega}{\sigma^2}} \int_0^1 B_r \mathrm{d}B_r + \frac{\lambda}{\sigma\sqrt{\omega}}}{\left(\int_0^1 B_r^2 \mathrm{d}r\right)^{1/2}} \tag{7.8}$$

If $U_t = Z_t \sim \mathrm{IID}\,\mathrm{N}(0, \sigma^2)$, $\omega_U = \sigma^2$ and $\lambda = 0$. The asymptotic distribution of the OLS estimator then simplifies to

$$T(\widehat{\phi}_T - 1) \Longrightarrow \frac{\int_0^1 B_r \mathrm{d}B_r}{\int_0^1 B_r^2 \mathrm{d}r} = \frac{\frac{1}{2}(B_1^2 - 1)}{\int_0^1 B_r^2 \mathrm{d}r}. \tag{7.9}$$

Similarly,

$$t_{\widehat{\phi}_T} \Longrightarrow \frac{\int_0^1 B_r \mathrm{d}B_r}{\left(\int_0^1 B_r^2 \mathrm{d}r\right)^{1/2}} = \frac{\frac{1}{2}(B_1^2 - 1)}{\left(\int_0^1 B_r^2 \mathrm{d}r\right)^{1/2}}. \tag{7.10}$$

The equality follows from Itô's formula (see Theorem C.16) setting $f(x) = x^2/2$ and noting that $B_0 = 0$. This effectively recovers the result derived previously because $B_1 \sim \mathrm{N}(0, 1)$ and hence $B_1^2 \sim \chi_1^2$. It also shows that behind the expressions involving Brownian motions are sometimes hidden common distribution functions. As mentioned previously, these are actually the distributions first tabulated by Fuller

(1976). Note that in contrast to the general asymptotic distributions in Eqs. (7.7) and (7.8), the distributions in Eqs. (7.9) and (7.10) are free from the nuisance parameters ω and σ^2.

Finally, we investigate the autocovariance function of a random walk. Using similar arguments as in Sect. 1.3, we get

$$\begin{aligned}\gamma(h) &= \mathbb{E}(X_T X_{T-h}) \\ &= \mathbb{E}\left[(Z_T + Z_{T-1} + \ldots + Z_1)(Z_{T-h} + Z_{T-h-1} + \ldots + Z_1)\right] \\ &= \mathbb{E}\left(Z_{T-h}^2 + Z_{T-h-1}^2 + \ldots + Z_1^2\right) = (T-h)\sigma^2.\end{aligned}$$

Thus, the correlation coefficient between X_T and X_{T-h} is

$$\rho(h) = \frac{\gamma(h)}{\sqrt{\mathbb{V}X_T}\sqrt{\mathbb{V}X_{T-h}}} = \frac{T-h}{\sqrt{T(T-h)}} = \sqrt{\frac{T-h}{T}}, \qquad h \leq T.$$

The autocorrelation coefficient $\rho(h)$ therefore monotonically decreases with h, holding the sample size T constant. The rate at which $\rho(h)$ falls is, however, smaller than for ARMA processes for which $\rho(h)$ declines exponentially fast to zero. Given h, the autocorrelation coefficient converges to one for $T \to \infty$. Figure 7.3 compares the theoretical and the estimated ACF of a simulated random walk with $T = 100$.

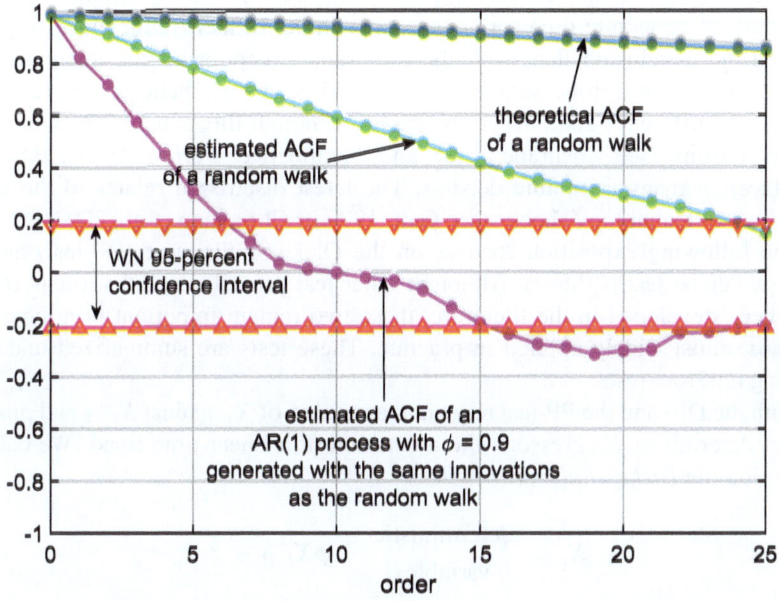

Fig. 7.3 ACF of a random walk with 100 observations

Typically, the estimated coefficients lie below the theoretical ones. In addition, we show the estimated ACF for an AR(1) process with $\phi = 0.9$ and using the same realizations of the white noise process as in the construction of the random walk. Despite the large differences between the ACF of an AR(1) process and a random walk, the ACF is only of limited use to discriminate between a stationary ARMA process and a random walk.

7.3 Unit-Root Tests

The previous Sects. 7.1 and 7.2 have shown that trend-stationary and integrated (difference-stationary) stochastic processes exhibit quite different algebraic (forecast, forecast error variance, persistence) and statistical (asymptotic distribution of OLS estimator) properties. It is therefore important to be able to discriminate among them. This also pertains to standard regression models for which the presence of integrated variables can lead to non-normal asymptotic distributions.

The ability to discriminate between trend-stationary and integrated (difference-stationary) processes is not only important from a statistical point of view, but pertains also to the economic interpretation. In macroeconomic theory, monetary and demand disturbances are alleged to have only temporary effects, whereas supply disturbances, in particular technology shocks, are supposed to have permanent effects. To put it in the language of time series analysis: monetary and demand shocks have a persistence of zero, whereas supply shocks have nonzero (positive) persistence. Nelson and Plosser (1982) were the first to investigate the trend properties of economic time series from this angle. In their influential study, they reached the conclusion that, with the important exception of the unemployment rate, most economic time series in the United States are better characterized as integrated (difference-stationary) processes. Although this conclusion came under severe scrutiny (see Cochrane, 1988 and Campbell & Perron, 1991), this issue resurfaces in many economic debates. The latest discussion relates to the nature and effect of technology shocks (see Galí, 1999 or Christiano et al., 2003).

The following exposition focuses on the Dickey-Fuller test (DF-test) and the Phillips-Perron test (PP-test). Although other test procedures and variants thereof have been developed in the literature, these two remain important prototypes and are those most widely applied in practice. These tests are summarized under the heading unit root tests.

Both the DF- and the PP-test rely on a regression of X_t against X_{t-1} and possibly further deterministic regressors like a constant or a linear time trend. We call this regression the *Dickey-Fuller regression*:

$$X_t = \begin{array}{c}\text{deterministic}\\ \text{variables}\end{array} + \phi X_{t-1} + Z_t. \tag{7.11}$$

Alternatively and numerically equivalent, one may run the Dickey-Fuller regression in difference form:

$$\Delta X_t = \begin{array}{c}\text{deterministic}\\ \text{variables}\end{array} + \beta X_{t-1} + Z_t$$

with $\beta = \phi - 1$. For both tests, the null hypothesis is that the process is integrated of order one, difference stationary, or has a unit root. Thus, we have

$$\mathbf{H}_0 : \phi = 1 \qquad \text{or} \qquad \beta = 0.$$

The alternative hypothesis $\mathbf{H}_1$ is that the process is trend-stationary or stationary with constant mean and is given by

$$\mathbf{H}_1 : -1 < \phi < 1 \qquad \text{or} \qquad -2 < \beta = \phi - 1 < 0.$$

Thus, the unit root test is a *one-sided test*. The advantage of the second formulation of the Dickey-Fuller regression is that the corresponding t-statistic can be readily read off from standard outputs of many computer packages, which makes additional computations unnecessary.

7.3.1 The Dickey-Fuller Test (DF-Test)

The Dickey-Fuller test comes in two forms. The first one, sometimes called the ρ-test, takes $T(\widehat{\phi} - 1)$ as the test statistic. As shown previously, this statistic is no longer asymptotically normally distributed. However, it was first tabulated by Fuller and can be found in textbooks like Fuller (1976) or Hamilton (1994a). The second and much more common form relies on the usual t-statistic for the hypothesis $\phi = 1$:

$$t_{\widehat{\phi}_T} = (\widehat{\phi}_T - 1)/\widehat{\sigma}_{\widehat{\phi}}.$$

If $Z_t \sim \text{IID}\,\text{N}(0, \sigma^2)$ and no deterministic component is included in the Dickey-Fuller regression, the asymptotic distribution is given in this case in Eq. (7.10).

The application of the Dickey-Fuller test as well as the Phillips-Perron test is obfuscated by the fact that the asymptotic distribution of the test statistic (ρ- or t-test) depends on the specification of the deterministic components and on the true data-generating process. This implies that depending on whether the Dickey-Fuller regression includes, for example, a constant and/or a time trend and on the nature of the true data-generating process, one has to use different tables and thus critical values. The asymptotic distributions for alternative specification of the deterministic part were first tabulated by Fuller (1976) and can be found, for example, in Hamilton (1994a). Later MacKinnon (1991) presented much more detailed tables where the critical values can be approximated for any sample size T by using interpolation

Table 7.1 The four most common cases for the unit root test

Data-generating process (null hypothesis)	Estimated regression (Dickey-Fuller regression)	ρ-test: $T(\widehat{\phi}-1)$	t-test
$X_t = X_{t-1} + Z_t$	$X_t = \phi X_{t-1} + Z_t$	Case 1	Case 1
$X_t = X_{t-1} + Z_t$	$X_t = \alpha + \phi X_{t-1} + Z_t$	Case 2	Case 2
$X_t = \alpha + X_{t-1} + Z_t, \alpha \neq 0$	$X_t = \alpha + \phi X_{t-1} + Z_t$		N(0,1)
$X_t = \alpha + X_{t-1} + Z_t$	$X_t = \alpha + \delta t + \phi X_{t-1} + Z_t$	Case 4	Case 4

formulas (see also Banerjee et al., 1993).[7] In the following, we will focus on the most common cases listed in Table 7.1.

In case 1, the Dickey-Fuller regression includes no deterministic component. Thus, a rejection of the null hypothesis implies that $\{X_t\}$ has to be a mean-zero stationary process. This specification is, therefore, only warranted if one can make sure that the data have indeed mean zero. As this is rarely the case, except, for example, when the data are the residuals from a previous regression,[8] case 1 is therefore more of theoretical than practical interest. Thus, if the data do not display a trend, which can be checked by a simple time plot, the Dickey-Fuller regression should include a constant. A rejection of the null hypothesis then implies that $\{X_t\}$ is a stationary process with mean $\mu = \frac{c}{1-\phi}$. If the data display a time trend, the Dickey-Fuller regression should also include a linear time trend as in case 4. A rejection of the null hypothesis then implies that the process is trend-stationary. In the case that the Dickey-Fuller regression contains no time trend and there is no time trend under the alternative hypothesis, asymptotic normality holds (West, 1988). This case is only of theoretical interest as it should a priori be clear whether the data are trending or not. In the instance where one is not confident about the trending nature of the time series, see the procedure outlined in Sect. 7.3.3.

In cases 2 and 4, it is of interest to investigate the joint hypothesis $\mathbf{H}_0 : \alpha = 0$ and $\phi = 1$, respectively $\mathbf{H}_0 : \delta = 0$ and $\phi = 1$. Again the corresponding F-statistic is no longer F-distributed, but has been tabulated (see Hamilton, 1994a, Table B7). The trade-off between t- and F-test in unit root testing is discussed in Sect. 7.3.3.

Most economic time series display a significant amount of autocorrelation. Hence, one cannot expect that Z_t in the Dickey-Fuller regression is independently, identically distributed. This implies that the asymptotic distributions for $T(\widehat{\phi}_T - 1)$ and $t_{\widehat{\phi}_t}$ involve the nuisance parameters ω and σ^2 (see, e.g., Eqs. (7.7) and (7.8) corresponding to case 1). One option to take this feature into account is the inclusion lagged differences $\Delta X_{t-1}, \ldots, \Delta X_{t-p+1}$ as additional regressors. The so modified Dickey-Fuller regression then becomes

[7] This interpolation formula is implemented in many software packages to compute the appropriate critical values.

[8] This fact may pose a problem by itself.

$$X_t = \begin{array}{c}\text{deterministic}\\ \text{variables}\end{array} + \phi X_{t-1} + \underbrace{\gamma_1 \Delta X_{t-1} + \ldots + \gamma_{p-1} \Delta X_{t-p+1}}_{\text{autoregressive correction}} + Z_t.$$

The number of additional regressors should be so chosen that the residual Z_t becomes white noise, hence free of autocorrelation. This modified test is called the augmented Dickey-Fuller test (ADF-test). Given this correction, the asymptotic distributions in case 1 are those in Eqs. (7.9) and (7.10). These distributions are effectively free from nuisance parameters and are the one tabulated by Fuller (1976) and others. For the coefficients of the autoregressive terms, asymptotic normality holds. This implies that the standard testing procedures (t-test, F-test) can be applied in the usual way with respect to these parameters. This remains true if instead of autoregressive correction terms, moving-average terms are used instead (see Said & Dickey, 1984).

For the ADF-test, the order p of the model should be chosen such that the residuals are close to being white noise. This can be checked, for example, by looking at the ACF of the residuals or by carrying out a Ljung-Box test (see Sect. 4.2). In case of doubt, it is better to choose a higher order. A consistent procedure to find the right order is to use Akaike's criterion (AIC). Another alternative strategy advocated by Ng and Perron (1995) is an iterative testing procedure that makes use of the asymptotic normality of the autoregressive correction terms. Starting from a maximal order $p - 1 = p_{max}$, the method amounts to the test whether the coefficient corresponding to the highest order is significantly different from zero. If the null hypothesis that the coefficient is zero is not rejected, the order of the model is reduced by one and the test is repeated. This is done as long as the null hypothesis is not rejected. If the null hypothesis is finally rejected, one sticks with the model and performs the ADF-test. The successive test are standard t-tests. It is advisable to use a rather high significance level, for example, a 10% level. The simulation results by Ng and Perron (1995) show that this procedure leads to a smaller bias compared to using the AIC criterion and that the reduction in power remains negligible.

7.3.2 The Phillips-Perron Test (PP-Test)

The Phillips-Perron test represents a valid alternative to the ADF-test. It is based on the simple Dickey-Fuller regression (without autoregressive correction terms) and corrects for autocorrelation by modifying the OLS estimate or the corresponding value of the t-statistic. The simple Dickey-Fuller regression with either constant or trend is

$$X_t = \begin{array}{c}\text{deterministic}\\ \text{variables}\end{array} + \phi X_{t-1} + U_t,$$

where $\{U_t\}$ need no longer be a white noise process, but can be any mean-zero stationary process fulfilling the assumptions in Eq. (7.1). $\{Z_t\}$ may, for example, be an ARMA process. In principle, the approach also allows for heteroskedasticity.[9]

The first step in the Phillips-Perron unit root test estimates the above appropriately specified Dickey-Fuller regression. The second step consists in the estimation of the unconditional variance $\sigma^2 = \gamma_U(0)$ and the long-run variance ω_U of the residuals $\widehat{U}_t$. This can be done using one of the methods prescribed in Sect. 4.4. These two estimates are then used in a third step to correct the ρ- and the t-test statistics. This correction would then take care of the autocorrelation present in the data. Finally, one can use the so modified test statistics to carry out the unit root test applying the same tables for the critical values as before.

When no deterministic component is taken into account (case 1 in Table 7.1), the modified test statistics according to Phillips (1987) are

$$\rho\text{-test}: \qquad T\left(\widehat{\phi}_T - 1\right) - \frac{1}{2}\left(\hat{\omega}_U - \hat{\sigma}^2\right)\left(\frac{1}{T^2}\sum_{t=1}^{T} X_{t-1}^2\right)^{-1};$$

$$\text{t-test}: \qquad \sqrt{\frac{\hat{\sigma}^2}{\hat{\omega}_U}}\, t_{\widehat{\phi}_T} - \frac{1}{2}\left(\hat{\omega}_U - \hat{\sigma}^2\right)\left(\frac{\hat{\omega}_U}{T^2}\sum_{t=1}^{T} X_{t-1}^2\right)^{-1/2}.$$

The ρ-test statistic is obtained from Eq. (7.7) by replacing ω_U, σ^2, and $\int_0^1 B_r^2 \mathrm{d}r$ by their estimates $\hat{\omega}_U$, $\hat{\sigma}^2$, and $T^{-2}\sum_{t=1}^{T} X_{t-1}^2$ and "solving" for the nuisance free Dickey-Fuller distribution $\int_0^1 B_r \mathrm{d}B_r / \int_0^1 B_r^2 \mathrm{d}r$. The statistic for the t-test can be obtained in the same way. If $\{U_t\}$ would be white noise, $\omega = \sigma^2 = \gamma(0)$, respectively $\hat{\sigma}^2 \approx \hat{\gamma}_U(0)$, the common Dickey-Fuller test statistic is obtained. Similar formulas can be derived for cases 2 and 4. As already mentioned, these modifications will not alter the asymptotic distributions, so the same critical values as for the ADF-test can be used.

The main advantage of the Phillips-Perron test is that the nonparametric correction allows for very general $\{U_t\}$ processes. The PP-test is particularly appropriate if $\{U_t\}$ has some MA components that can be only poorly approximated by low-order autoregressive terms. Another advantage is that one avoids the exact modeling of the process. It has been shown by Monte Carlo studies that the PP-test has more power compared to the DF-test, i.e., the PP-test rejects the null hypothesis more often when it is false, but that, on the other hand, it has also a higher size distortion, i.e., that it rejects the null hypothesis too often. Vogelsang and Wagner (2013) propose a modified PP-test that reflects the choice of the kernel function and the bank width in the estimation of the long-run variance.

[9] The exact assumptions can be found in Phillips (1987) and Phillips and Perron (1988).

7.3.3 Unit Root Test: Testing Strategy

Independently whether the Dickey-Fuller or the Phillips-Perron test is used, the specification of the deterministic component is important and can pose a problem in practice. On the one hand, if the deterministic part is underrepresented, for example, when only a constant, but no time trend is used, the test results are biased in favor of the null hypothesis, if the data do indeed have a trend. On the other hand, if too many deterministic components are used, the power of the test is reduced. It is therefore advisable to examine a plot of the time series in order to check whether a long-run trend is visible or not. In some circumstances, economic reasoning may help in this regard. Sometimes, however, it is difficult to make an appropriate choice a priori. We therefore propose the following testing strategy based on Elder and Kennedy (2001).

X_t **has a long-run trend**: As X_t grows in the long run, the Dickey-Fuller regression

$$X_t = \alpha + \delta t + \phi X_{t-1} + Z_t$$

should contain a linear trend.[10] In this case, either $\phi = 1$, $\delta = 0$ and $\alpha \neq 0$ (unit root case) or $\phi < 1$ with $\delta \neq 0$ (trend stationary case). We can then test the joint null hypothesis

$$\mathrm{H}_0 : \quad \phi = 1 \text{ and } \delta = 0$$

by a corresponding F-test. Note that the F-statistic, like the t-test, is not distributed according to the F-distribution. If the test does not reject the null, we conclude that $\{X_t\}$ is a unit root process with drift or equivalently a difference-stationary (integrated) process. If the F-test rejects the null hypothesis, there are three possible situations:

(i) The possibility $\phi < 1$ and $\delta = 0$ contradicts the primary observation that $\{X_t\}$ has a trend and can therefore be eliminated.
(ii) The possibility $\phi = 1$ and $\delta \neq 0$ can also be excluded because this would imply that $\{X_t\}$ has a quadratic trend, which is unrealistic.
(iii) The possibility $\phi < 1$ and $\delta \neq 0$ represents the only valid alternative. It implies that $\{X_t\}$ is stationary around a linear trend, i.e., that $\{X_t\}$ is trend-stationary.

Similar conclusions can be reached if, instead of the F-test, a t-test is used to test the null hypothesis $\mathrm{H}_0 : \phi = 1$ against the alternative $\mathrm{H}_1 : \phi < 1$. Thus, a non-rejection of H_0 is interpreted that $\delta = 0$. If, however, the null hypothesis H_0 is rejected, this implies that $\delta \neq 0$, because $\{X_t\}$ exhibits a long-run trend. The

[10] In case of autocorrelation of the residual, additional regressors, ΔX_{t-j}, $j > 0$, should be included leading to the ADF-test.

F-test is more powerful than the t-test. The t-test, however, is a one-sided test, which has the advantage that it actually corresponds to the primary objective of the test. In Monte Carlo simulations, the t-test has proven to be marginally superior to the F-test.

X_t **has no long-run trend**: In this case, $\delta = 0$ and the Dickey-Fuller regression should be run without a trend:[11]

$$X_t = \alpha + \phi X_{t-1} + Z_t.$$

Thus, we have either $\phi = 1$ and $\alpha = 0$ or $\phi < 1$ and $\alpha \neq 0$. The null hypothesis in this case therefore is

$$\mathrm{H}_0: \quad \phi = 1 \text{ and } \alpha = 0.$$

A rejection of the null hypothesis can be interpreted in three alternative ways:

(i) The case $\phi < 1$ and $\alpha = 0$ can be eliminated because it implies that $\{X_t\}$ would have a mean of zero, which is unrealistic for most economic time series.
(ii) The case $\phi = 1$ and $\alpha \neq 0$ can equally be eliminated because it implies that $\{X_t\}$ has a long-run trend, which contradicts our primary assumption.
(iii) The case $\phi < 1$ and $\alpha \neq 0$ is the only realistic alternative. It implies that the time series is stationary around a constant mean given by $\frac{\alpha}{1-\phi}$.

As before, one can use, instead of a F-test, a t-test of the null hypothesis $\mathrm{H}_0 : \phi = 1$ against the alternative hypothesis $\mathrm{H}_1 : \phi < 1$. If the null hypothesis is not rejected, we interpret this to imply that $\alpha = 0$. If, however, the null hypothesis H_0 is rejected, we conclude that $\alpha \neq 0$. Similarly, Monte Carlo simulations have proven that the t-test is marginally superior to the F-test.

The trend behavior of X_t is uncertain: This situation poses the following problem. Should the data exhibit a trend, but the Dickey-Fuller regression contains no trend, then the test is biased in favor of the null hypothesis. If the data have no trend, but the Dickey-Fuller regression contains a trend, the power of the test is reduced. In such a situation, one can adapt a two-stage strategy. Estimate the Dickey-Fuller regression with a linear trend:

$$X_t = \alpha + \delta t + \phi X_{t-1} + Z_t.$$

Use the t-test to test the null hypothesis $\mathrm{H}_0 : \phi = 1$ against the alternative hypothesis $\mathrm{H}_1 : \phi < 1$. If H_0 is not rejected, we conclude the process has a unit root with or without drift. The presence of a drift can then be investigated by

[11] In case of autocorrelation of the residual, additional regressors, ΔX_{t-j}, $j > 0$, should be included leading to the ADF-test.

a simple regression of ΔX_t against a constant followed by a simple t-test of the null hypothesis that the constant is zero against the alternative hypothesis that the constant is nonzero. As ΔX_t is stationary, the usual critical values can be used.[12] If the t-test rejects the null hypothesis H_0, we conclude that there is no unit root. The trend behavior can then be investigated by a simple t-test of the hypothesis $H_0 : \delta = 0$. In this test, the usual critical values can be used as $\{X_t\}$ is already viewed as being stationary.

7.3.4 Examples for Unit Root Tests

As our first example, we examine the logged real GDP for Switzerland, $\ln(\text{GDP}_t)$, where we have adjusted the series for seasonality by taking a moving average. The corresponding data are plotted in Fig. 1.3. As is evident from this plot, this variable exhibits a clear upward trend so that the Dickey-Fuller regression should include a constant and a linear time trend. Moreover, $\{\Delta \ln(\text{GDP}_t)\}$ is typically highly autocorrelated, which makes an autoregressive correction necessary. One way to make this correction is by augmenting the Dickey-Fuller regression by lagged $\{\Delta \ln(\text{GDP}_t)\}$ as additional regressors where the number of lags may be determined by AIC. The corresponding result is reported in the first column of Table 7.2. Despite our guess, AIC chooses no autoregressive correction term. The value of t-test statistic is -3.126, which is just above the 5% critical value $0-3.460$. Thus, the null hypothesis is not rejected. If the autoregressive correction is chosen according to the method proposed by Ng and Perron, three autoregressive lags have to be included. With this specification, the value of the t-test statistic is again just above the critical value, implying that the null hypothesis of the presence of a unit root can again not be rejected (see second column in Table 7.2).[13] The results of the ADF-tests is confirmed by the PP-test (column 3 in Table 7.2) where the computation of the long-run variance uses the quadratic spectral kernel function and a bandwidth of 1.32 according to Andrews' formula (see Sect. 4.4).

The second example examines the 3-month euro-interbank interest rate $\{R3m_t\}$. The series is plotted in Fig. 1.4. The issue whether this series has a linear trend or not is not easy to decide. On the one hand, the series clearly has a negative trend over the sample period considered. On the other hand, a negative time trend does not make sense from an economic point of view because interest rates are bounded from below by zero. Because of this uncertainty, it is advisable to include in the Dickey-Fuller regression both a constant and a trend to be on the safe side. Column 5 in Table 7.2 reports the corresponding results. The value of the t-statistic of the PP-test

[12] Eventually, one must correct the corresponding standard deviation by taking the autocorrelation in the residual into account. This can be done by using the long-run variance instead. In the literature, this correction is known as the Newey-West correction.

[13] The critical value changes slightly because the inclusion of additional autoregressive terms changes the sample size.

Table 7.2 Examples of unit root tests

	$\ln(\text{GDP}_t)$	$\ln(\text{GDP}_t)$	$\ln(\text{GDP}_t)$	R3m_t	R3m_t
Test	ADF	ADF	PP	PP	PP
Autoregressive correction	AIC	Ng and Perron	Quadratic spectral	Bartlett	Bartlett
Bandwidth			1.32	12	12
α	1.201	1.437	1.200	−0.088	0.008
δ	0.00047	0.00056	0.00046	0.00037	
ϕ	0.895	0.874	0.989	1.005	1.0098
γ_1		0.054			
γ_2		0.019			
γ_3		0.139			
$t_{\hat{\phi}}$	−3.126	−3.427	−3.170	−1.218	−2.161
Critical value (5%)	−3.460	−3.436	−3.436	−3.422	−2.869

Critical values based on MacKinnon (1996)

with the Bartlett kernel function and bandwidth of 5 according to the Newey-West rule of thumb is $-$ 1.218 and thus higher than the corresponding 5% critical of -3.422. Thus, we cannot reject the null hypothesis of the presence of a unit root. We therefore conclude that the process $\{\text{R3m}_t\}$ is integrated of order one, respectively difference-stationary. Based on this conclusion, the issue of the trend can now be decided by running a simple regression of ΔR3m_t against a constant. This leads to the following results:

$$\Delta\text{R3m}_t = \underset{(0.0148)}{\text{-0.0087}} \quad + \varepsilon_t .$$

where ε_t denotes the least-squares residual. The mean of ΔR3m_t is therefore $-$ 0.0087. This value is, however, statistically not significantly different from zero as indicated by the estimated standard error in parenthesis. Note that this estimate of the standard error has been corrected for autocorrelation (Newey-West correction). Thus, $\{\text{R3m}_t\}$ is not subject to a linear trend. One could have therefore run the Dickey-Fuller regression without the trend term. The result of corresponding to this specification is reported in the last column of Table 7.2. It confirms the presence of a unit root.

7.4 Generalizations of Unit Root Tests

7.4.1 Structural Breaks in the Trend Function

As we have seen, the unit root test depends heavily on the correct specification of the deterministic part. Most of the time, this amounts to decide whether a linear trend is present in the data or not. In the previous section, we presented a rule on how to proceed in case of uncertainty about the trend. Sometimes, however, the data exhibit a structural break in their deterministic component. If this structural break is ignored, the unit root test is biased in favor of the null hypothesis (i.e., in favor of a unit root) as demonstrated by Perron (1989). Unfortunately, the distribution of the test statistic under the null hypothesis, in our case the t-statistic, depends on the exact nature of the structural break and on its date of occurrence in the data. Following Perron (1989), we concentrate on three exemplary cases: a level shift, a change in the slope (change in the growth rate), and a combination of both possibilities. Figure 7.4 shows the three possibilities assuming that a break occurred in period T_B and where an AR(1) process with $\phi = 0.8$ was superimposed on the deterministic component.

The unit root test with the possibility of a structural break in period T_B is carried out using the Dickey-Fuller test. Thus, the date of the structural break is assumed to be known. This assumption, although restrictive, is justifiable in many applications. The first oil price shock in 1973 and the German reunification in 1989 are examples of structural breaks that can be dated exactly. Other examples would include changes in the way the data are constructed. These changes are usually documented by the data collecting agencies. Table 7.3 summarizes the three variants of the Dickey-Fuller regression allowing for structural breaks.[14]

Model A allows only for a level shift. Under the null hypothesis, the series undergoes a one-time shift at time T_B. This level shift is maintained under the null hypothesis that posits a random walk. Under the alternative, the process is viewed as being trend-stationary, whereby the trend line shifts parallel by $\alpha_B - \alpha$ at time T_B. Model B considers a change in the mean growth rate from α to α_B at time T_B. Under the alternative, the slope of time trend changes from δ to δ_B. Model C allows for both types of break to occur at the same time.

The unit root test with possible structural break for a time series X_t, $t = 0, 1, \ldots, T$, is implemented in two stages as follows. In the first stage, we regress X_t on the corresponding deterministic component using OLS. The residuals $\widetilde{X}_0, \widetilde{X}_1, \ldots, \widetilde{X}_T$ from this regression are then used to carry out a Dickey-Fuller test:

$$\widetilde{X}_t = \phi \widetilde{X}_{t-1} + Z_t, \qquad t = 1, \ldots, T.$$

The distribution of the corresponding t-statistic under the null hypothesis depends not only on the type of the structural break but also on the relative date of the break in the sample. Let this relative date be parameterized by $\lambda = T_B/T$. The asymptotic distribution of the t-statistic has been tabulated by Perron (1989). This table can be used to determine the critical values for the test. These critical values are smaller than those from the normal Dickey-Fuller table. Using a 5% significance level, the critical values range between -3.80 and -3.68 for model A, between -3.96 and -3.65 for model B, and between -4.24 and -3.75 for model C, depending on the value of λ. These values also show that the dependence on λ is only weak.

[14] See Eq. (7.11) and Table 7.1 for comparison.

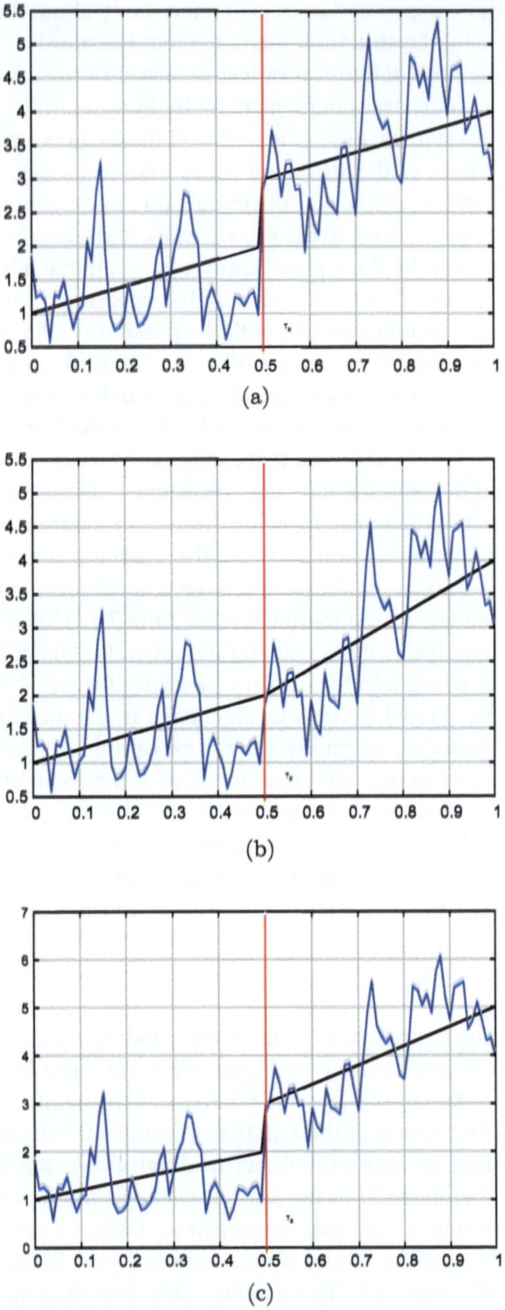

Fig. 7.4 Three types of structural breaks at T_B. (**a**) Level shift. (**b**) Change in slope. (**c**) Level shift and change in slope

Table 7.3 Dickey-Fuller regression allowing for structural breaks

	Model A: level shift
H_0 :	$X_t = \alpha + \mathbf{1}_{\{t=T_B+1\}}\delta_B + X_{t-1} + Z_t$
H_1 :	$X_t = \alpha + \delta t + \mathbf{1}_{\{t>T_B\}}(\alpha_B - \alpha) + \phi X_{t-1} + Z_t, \quad \phi < 1$
	Model B: change in slope (change in growth rate)
H_0 :	$X_t = \alpha + \mathbf{1}_{\{t>T_B\}}(\alpha_B - \alpha) + X_{t-1} + Z_t$
H_1 :	$X_t = \alpha + \delta t + \mathbf{1}_{\{t>T_B\}}(\delta_B - \delta)(t - T_B) + \phi X_{t-1} + Z_t, \quad \phi < 1$
	Modell C: level shift and change in slope
H_0 :	$X_t = \alpha + \mathbf{1}_{\{t=T_B+1\}}\delta_B + \mathbf{1}_{\{t>T_B\}}(\alpha_B - \alpha) + X_{t-1} + Z_t$
H_1 :	$X_t = \alpha + \delta t + \mathbf{1}_{\{t>T_B\}}(\alpha_B - \alpha) + \mathbf{1}_{\{t>T_B\}}(\delta_B - \delta)(t - T_B)$ $+ \phi X_{t-1} + Z_t, \quad \phi < 1$

$\mathbf{1}_{\{t=T_B+1\}}$ and $\mathbf{1}_{\{t>T_B\}}$ denote the indicator functions that take the value one if the condition is satisfied and the value zero otherwise

In the practical application of the test, one has to control for the autocorrelation in the data. This can be done by using the augmented Dickey-Fuller (ADF) test. This amounts to the introduction of $\Delta\widetilde{X}_{t-j}$, $t = 1, 2, \ldots, p-1$, as additional regressors in the above Dickey-Fuller regression. Thus, the order p can be determined by Akaike's information criterion (AIC) or by the iterative testing procedure of Ng and Perron (1995). Alternatively, one may use, instead of the ADF-test, the Phillips-Perron test. In this case, one computes the usual t-statistic for the null hypothesis $\phi = 1$ and corrects it using the formulas in Phillips and Perron (1988) as explained in Sect. 7.3.2. Which of the two methods is used is irrelevant for the determination of the critical values that can be extracted from Perron (1989).

Although it may be legitimate in some cases to assume that the time of the structural break is known (e.g., first oil price shock, financial market crisis, Covid-19 pandemic, Russia's aggression against Ukraine), we cannot take this for granted. It is therefore important to generalize the test allowing for an unknown date for the occurrence of a structural break. The work of Zivot and Andrews (1992) has shown that the procedure proposed by Perron can be easily expanded in this direction. We keep the three alternative models presented in Table 7.3, but change the null hypothesis to a random walk with drift with no exogenous structural break. Under the null hypothesis, $\{X_t\}$ is therefore assumed to be generated by

$$X_t = \alpha + X_{t-1} + Z_t, \qquad Z_t \sim \mathrm{WN}(0, \sigma^2).$$

The time of the structural T_B, respectively $\lambda = T_B/T$, is estimated in such a way that $\{X_t\}$ comes as close as possible to a trend-stationary process. Under the alternative hypothesis, $\{X_t\}$ is viewed as a trend-stationary process with unknown break point. The goal of the estimation strategy is to choose T_B, respectively λ, in such a way that the trend-stationary alternative receives the highest weight. Zivot and Andrews (1992) propose to estimate λ by minimizing the value of the t-statistic $t_{\hat{\phi}}(\lambda)$ under the hypothesis $\phi = 1$:

$$t_{\hat{\phi}}(\hat{\lambda}_{\inf}) = \inf_{\lambda \in \Lambda} t_{\hat{\phi}}(\lambda) \tag{7.12}$$

where Λ is a closed subinterval of (0, 1).[15] The distribution of the test statistic under the null hypothesis for the three cases is tabulated in Zivot and Andrews (1992). This table then allows to determine the appropriate critical values for the test. In practice, one has to take the autocorrelation of the time series into account by one of the methods discussed previously.

This testing strategy can be adapted to determine the time of a structural break in the linear trend irrespective of whether the process is trend-stationary or integrated of order one. The distributions of the corresponding test statistics have been tabulated by Vogelsang (1997). Perron (2006) surveys the corresponding literature.

7.4.2 Testing for Stationarity (KPSS Test)

The unit root tests we discussed so far tested the null hypothesis that the process is integrated of order one against the alternative hypothesis that the process is integrated of order zero (i.e., is stationary). However, one may be interested in reversing the null and the alternative hypothesis and test the hypothesis of stationarity against the alternative that the process is integrated of order one. Such a test has been proposed by Kwiatkowski et al. (1992), which is known as the KPSS-test. This test rests on the idea that according to the Beveridge-Nelson decomposition (see Sect. 7.1.4) each integrated process of order one can be seen as the sum of a linear time trend, a random walk, and a stationary process:

$$X_t = \alpha + \delta t + d \sum_{j=1}^{t} Z_j + U_t,$$

where $\{U_t\}$ denotes a stationary process. If $d = 0$, then the process becomes trend-stationary; otherwise it is integrated of order one.[16] Thus, one can state the null and the alternative hypothesis as follows:

$$\mathbf{H}_0 : d = 0 \qquad \text{against} \qquad \mathbf{H}_1 : d \neq 0.$$

Denote by $\{S_t\}$ the process of partial sums obtained from the residuals $\{e_t\}$ of a regression of X_t against a constant and a linear time trend, i.e., $S_t = \sum_{j=1}^{t} e_j$. Under the null hypothesis $d = 0$, $\{S_t\}$ is integrated of order one, whereas under the alternative, $\{S_t\}$ is integrated of order two. Based on this consideration, Kwiatkowski et al. (1992) propose the following test statistic for a time series with sample size T:

[15] Taking the infimum over Λ instead over (0, 1) is for theoretical reasons only. In practice, the choice of Λ plays no important role. For example, one may take $\Lambda = [0.01, 0.99]$.

[16] If the data exhibit no trend, one can set δ equal to zero.

Table 7.4 Critical values of the KPSS-test

	Regression without time trend		
Significance level	0.1	0.05	0.01
Critical value	0.347	0.463	0.739
	Regression with time trend		
Significance level	0.1	0.05	0.01
Critical value	0.119	0.146	0.216

See Kwiatkowski et al. (1992)

$$\text{KPSS-test statistic:} \qquad W_T = \frac{\sum_{t=1}^{T} S_t^2}{T^2 \widehat{\omega}_U} \tag{7.13}$$

where $\widehat{\omega}_U$ is an estimate of the long-run variance of $\{U_t\}$ (see Sect. 4.4). As $\{S_t\}$ is an integrated process under the null hypothesis, the variance of $\{S_t\}$ grows linearly in t (see Sect. 1.4.4 or 7.2) so that the sum of squared S_t diverges at rate T^2. Given its scaling, the test statistic is independent from further nuisance parameters. Under the alternative hypothesis, however, $\{S_t\}$ is integrated of order two. Thus, the null hypothesis will be rejected for large values of W_T. The corresponding asymptotic critical values of the test statistic are reported in Kwiatkowski et al. (1992) and reproduced in Table 7.4.

7.5 Regression with Integrated Variables

7.5.1 The Spurious Regression Problem

The discussion on the Dickey-Fuller and Phillips-Perron tests showed that in a regression of the integrated variables X_t on its past X_{t-1}, the standard $\sqrt{T}$-asymptotics no longer apply. A similar issue arises in a regression of one integrated variable X_t on another integrated variable Y_t. Suppose that both processes $\{X_t\}$ and $\{Y_t\}$ are generated as a random walk with no drift:

$$\begin{aligned} X_t &= X_{t-1} + U_t, & U_t &\sim \text{IID}(0, \sigma_U^2) \\ Y_t &= Y_{t-1} + V_t, & V_t &\sim \text{IID}(0, \sigma_V^2) \end{aligned}$$

where the processes $\{U_t\}$ and $\{V_t\}$ are independent from each other, i.e., $\mathbb{E}U_t V_s) = 0$ for all $s, t \in \mathbb{Z}$. Consider now the simple regression of Y_t on X_t and a constant:

$$Y_t = \alpha + \beta X_t + \varepsilon_t.$$

As the two random walks $\{X_t\}$ and $\{Y_t\}$ are independent, therefore uncorrelated, from each other by construction, one would expect that the OLS estimate $\hat{\beta}_T$ and the coefficient of determination R^2 should both tend to zero as the sample size T goes to infinity. This is, however, not true as has already been noted by Yule (1926) and, more recently, by Granger and Newbold (1974). The above regression will have a tendency to "discover" a relationship between Y_t and X_t despite the fact that there is none. This phenomenon is called *spurious correlation, nonsense correlation*, or *spurious regression*. Similarly, unreliable results would be obtained by using a simple t-test for the null hypothesis $\beta = 0$ against the alternative hypothesis $\beta \neq 0$. The reason for these treacherous findings is that the model is incorrect under the null as well as under the alternative hypothesis. Under the null hypothesis, $\{\varepsilon_t\}$ is an integrated process that violates the standard assumption for OLS. The alternative hypothesis is not true by construction.

To clarify this issue, examine the OLS estimate of β. The standard formula implies

$$\hat{\beta}_T = \frac{\sum_{t=1}^T (Y_t - \overline{X}_T)(X_t - \overline{Y}_T)}{\sum_{t=1}^T (X_t - \overline{X}_T)^2} = \frac{T^{-2}\sum_{t=1}^T Y_t X_t - (T^{-1/2}\overline{Y}_T)(T^{-1/2}\overline{X}_T)}{T^{-2}\sum_{t=1}^T X_t^2 - T^{-1}\overline{X}_T^2}$$

Going through the same arguments as in Sect. 7.2, the sample moments in the above expression converge weakly to their stochastic integral counterparts:

$$\hat{\beta}_T \quad \Rightarrow \quad \frac{\sigma_V}{\sigma_U} \frac{\int_0^1 B_r^U B_r^V \mathrm{d}r - \left(\int_0^1 B_r^U \mathrm{d}r\right)\left(\int_0^1 B_r^V \mathrm{d}r\right)}{\int_0^1 (B_r^U)^2 \mathrm{d}r - \left(\int_0^1 B_r^U \mathrm{d}r\right)^2} \tag{7.14}$$

where $\{B_t^U\}$ and $\{B_t^V\}$ are independent Brownian motions and where $T^{-1/2}\overline{X}_T$ and $T^{-1/2}\overline{Y}_T$ converge weakly to $\sigma_U \int_0^1 B_r^U \mathrm{d}r$ and $\sigma_V \int_0^1 B_r^V \mathrm{d}r$, respectively.[17] This shows that the estimated parameter $\hat{\beta}_T$ does not converge to zero. Corresponding results are obtained for the t-statistic and coefficient of determination R^2. The problem remains when $\{X_t\}$ and $\{Y_t\}$ are specified as random walks with drifts. A detailed analysis of the spurious regression problem is provided by Phillips (1986).

The spurious regression problem can be illustrated by a simple Monte Carlo study. Specifying $U_t \sim \mathrm{IID\,N}(0, 1)$ and $V_t \sim \mathrm{IID\,N}(0, 1)$, construct $N = 1000$ samples for $\{Y_t\}$ and $\{X_t\}$ of size $T = 1000$ according to the specification above. The sample size was chosen especially large to demonstrate that this is not a small sample phenomenon. As a contrast, construct two independent AR(1) processes with AR coefficients $\phi_X = 0.8$ and $\phi_Y = -0.5$. Figures 7.5a and b illustrate the drastic difference between a regression with stationary variables and a regression with integrated variables. Whereas the distribution of the OLS estimates of β is highly concentrated around the true value $\beta = 0$ in the stationary case, the distribution is very flat in the case of integrated variables. A similar conclusion holds for the corresponding t-value. The probability of obtaining a t-value greater than 1.96 is bigger than 0.95. This means that in more than 95% of the time, the t-statistic leads to a rejection of the null hypothesis and therefore suggests a

[17] Interestingly, when B_r is a Brownian motion, $\int_0^1 B_r \mathrm{d}r \sim \mathrm{N}(0, 1/3)$.

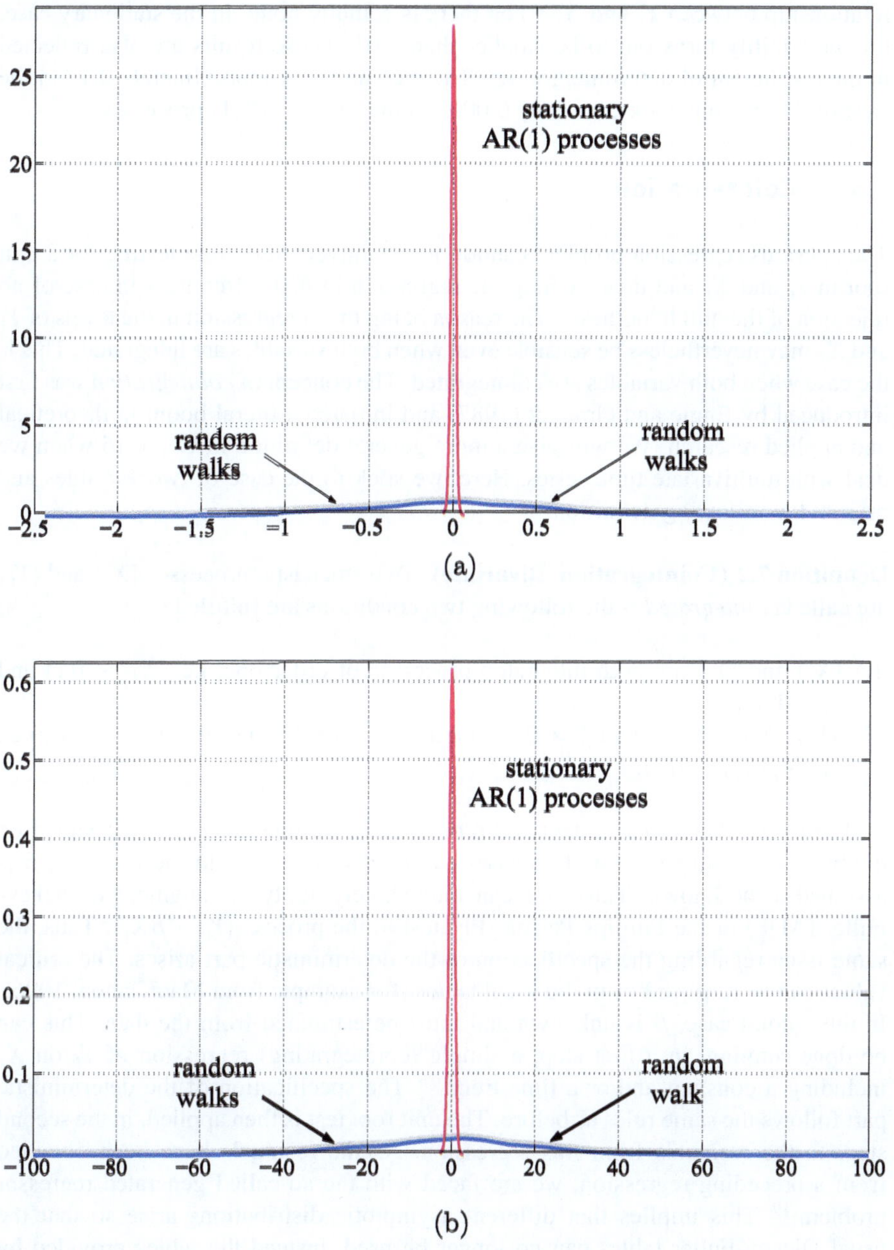

Fig. 7.5 Distribution of OLS estimate $\hat{\beta}$ and t-statistic $t_{\hat{\beta}}$ for two independent random walks and two independent AR(1) processes. **(a)** Distribution of $\hat{\beta}$. **(b)** Distribution of $t_{\hat{\beta}}$

relationship between Y_t and X_t when there is actually none. In the stationary case, this probability turns out to be smaller than 0.05. These results are also reflected in the coefficient of determination R^2. The median R^2 is approximately 0.17 in the case of the random walks, but only 0.0002 in the case of AR(1) processes.

7.5.2 Cointegration

The spurious regression problem cannot be circumvented by first testing for a unit root in Y_t and X_t and then running the regression in first differences in case of no rejection of the null hypothesis. The reason being that a regression in the levels of Y_t and X_t may nevertheless be sensible even when both variables are integrated. This is the case when both variables are cointegrated. The concept of *cointegration* was first introduced by Engle and Granger (1987) and initiated a literal boom in theoretical and applied research. We will give a more general definition in Chap. 16 when we deal with multivariate time series. Here, we stick to the case of two variables and present the following definition.

Definition 7.2 (Cointegration, Bivariate) Two stochastic processes $\{X_t\}$ and $\{Y_t\}$ are called *cointegrated* if the following two conditions are fulfilled:

(i) $\{X_t\}$ and $\{Y_t\}$ are both integrated processes of order one, i.e., $X_t \sim \mathrm{I}(1)$ and $Y_t \sim \mathrm{I}(1)$.
(ii) There exists a constant $\beta \neq 0$ such that $\{Y_t - \beta X_t\}$ is a stationary process, i.e., $\{Y_t - \beta X_t\} \sim \mathrm{I}(0)$.

The issue whether two integrated processes are cointegrated can be decided on the basis of a unit root test. Two cases can be distinguished. In the first one, β is assumed to be known. Thus, one can immediately apply the augmented Dickey-Fuller (ADF) or the Phillips-Perron (PP) test to the process $\{Y_t - \beta X_t\}$. Thus, the same issue regarding the specification of the deterministic part arises. The critical values can be retrieved from the usual tables (for example from MacKinnon, 1996). In the second case, β is unknown and must be estimated from the data. This can be done running, in a first step, a simple (cointegrating) regression of Y_t on X_t including a constant and/or a time trend.[18] The specification of the deterministic part follows the same rules as before. The unit root test is then applied, in the second step, to the residuals from this regression. As the residuals have been obtained from a preceding regression, we are faced with the so-called generated regressor problem.[19] This implies that different asymptotic distributions arise so that the usual Dickey-Fuller tables can no longer be used, instead the tables provided by

[18] In contrast to ordinary OLS regressions, it is irrelevant which variable is treated as the left-hand, respectively right-hand, variable.

[19] This problem was first analyzed by Nicholls and Pagan (1984) and Pagan (1984) in a stationary context.

Phillips and Ouliaris (1990) become the relevant ones. As before, the relevant asymptotic distribution depends on the specification of the deterministic part in the cointegrating regression. If this regression included a constant, the residuals have necessary a mean of zero so that the Dickey-Fuller regression should include no constant (case 1 in Table 7.1):

$$e_t = \phi e_{t-1} + \xi_t$$

where e_t and ξ_t denote the residuals from cointegrating and the residuals of the Dickey-Fuller regression, respectively. In most applications, it is necessary to correct for autocorrelation that can be done by including additional lagged differences $\Delta\hat{\varepsilon}_{t-1}, \ldots, \Delta\hat{\varepsilon}_{t-p+1}$ as in the ADF-test or by adjusting the t-statistic as in the PP-test. The test where β is estimated from a regression is called the *regression test for cointegration*.

All this shows that regressions with integration are not without pitfalls and that results from OLS regressions should be treated with care. At this point, we will no longer dwell on this subject, but refer to the papers by Stock and Watson (1988a), Sims et al. (1990), and Campbell and Perron (1991). They provide rules of thumb to deal with the issue involved. A thorough treatment of the topic of cointegration in a multivariate context is postponed to Chap. 16.

Example for Bivariate Cointegration

As an example, we consider the relation between the 3-month interbank interest rate (LIBOR: London Interbank Borrowed Rate), $\{\mathrm{R3m}_t\}$, and inflation rate, $\{\pi_t\}$, in Switzerland over the period from January 1989 to February 2012. Both time series are plotted in Fig. 7.6a. As they are integrated according to the unit root tests (not shown here), we can look for cointegration. The cointegrating regression delivers

$$\pi_t = -0.0088 + 0.5535\ \mathrm{R3m}_t + e_t, \qquad \mathrm{R}^2 = 0.7798. \tag{7.15}$$

The residuals e_t from this regression are plotted in Fig. 7.6b. The ADF unit root test of these residuals leads to a value of -3.617 for the t-statistic using an autoregressive correction of 13 lags according to the AIC criterion. The Dickey-Fuller regression includes no constant, because the cointegrating regression already included it. The corresponding value of the t-statistic resulting from the PP unit root test using a Bartlett window with bandwidth 7 is -4.294. Taking a significance level of 5%, the critical value according to Phillips and Ouliaris (1990, Table IIb) is -3.365.[20] Thus, the ADF- and the PP-test reject the null hypothesis of a unit root in the residuals. This implies that inflation and the short-term interest rate are cointegrated.

[20] For comparison, the corresponding critical value for the Dickey-Fuller statistic is -2.872 according to MacKinnon (1996).

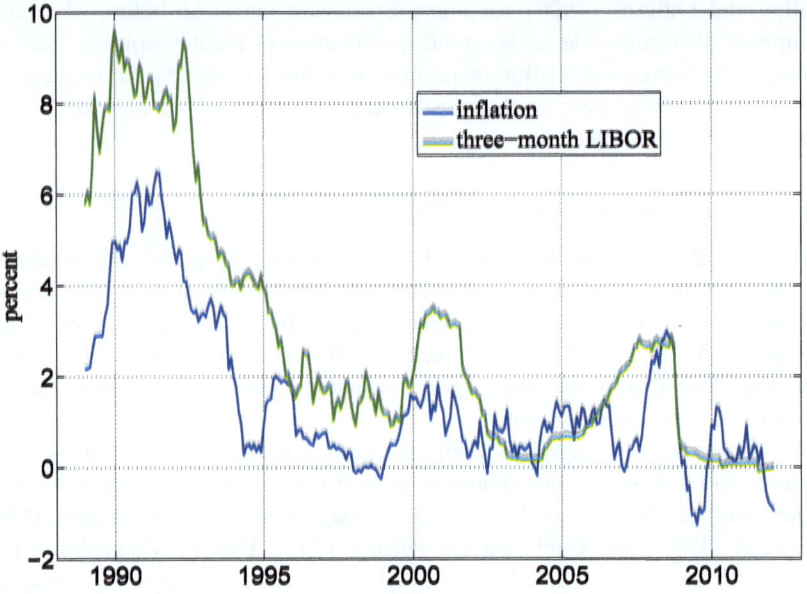

(a)

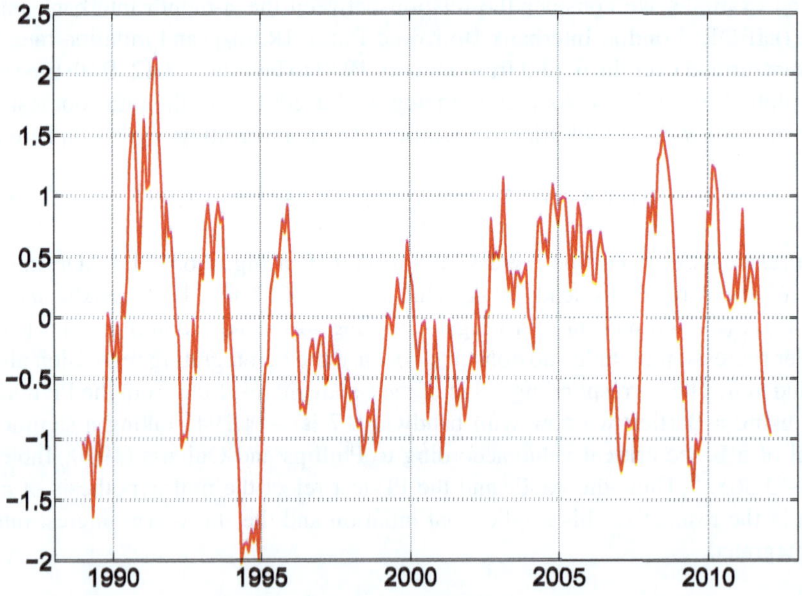

(b)

Fig. 7.6 Cointegration of inflation rate and 3-month interbank rate. (**a**) Inflation and 3-month interbank interest rate. (**b**) Residuals from cointegrating regression

7.6 Exercises

Exercise 7.1 Consider the random walk $\{X_t\}$, $t = 1, 2, \ldots$, defined as

$$X_t = X_{t-1} + Z_t, \qquad Z_t \sim \text{IID}\,\text{N}(0, \sigma^2), \text{ and } X_0 = 0.$$

Show that

$$\mathbb{E}\left(\sum_{t=1}^{T} X_{t-1}^2\right) = \sigma^2 \frac{T(T-1)}{2},$$

$$\mathbb{V}\left(\sum_{t=1}^{T} X_{t-1}^2\right) = \sigma^4 \frac{T(T-1)(T^2-T+1)}{3}.$$

Exercise 7.2 Show that $\int_0^1 B_t \mathrm{d}t \sim \text{N}(0, 1/3)$ where $\{B_t\}$, $t \in [0, \infty)$, is a Brownian motion.
Hint: Write the integral as the limit of a Riemann sum where the unit interval is partitioned into n intervals with $\left[\frac{j-1}{n}, \frac{j}{n}\right]$, $j = 1, 2, \ldots, n$

Exercise 7.3 Consider the random walk $\{X_t\}$, $t = 1, 2, \ldots$, defined as

$$X_t = X_{t-1} + Z_t,$$

where $X_0 = 0$ and where $\{Z_t\}$ is a mean-zero stationary process with autocovariance function $\gamma(h)$. Under the assumption $0 < \omega < \infty$ where $\omega = \sum_{h=-\infty}^{\infty} \gamma(h)$ denotes the long-run variance, compute $\mathbb{E}(\frac{1}{T} \sum_{t=1}^{T} X_{t-1} Z_t)$ and show that this expression converges $\lambda = \sum_{h=1}^{\infty} \gamma(h)$ for $T \to \infty$.
Hint: You may use the following result. If the infinite series $\sum_{j=1}^{\infty} a_j$ converges,

$$\lim_{T\to\infty} \sum_{j=1}^{\infty} \left(1 - \frac{j}{T}\right) a_j = \sum_{j=1}^{\infty} a_j.$$

Exercise 7.4 Download the corresponding time series for a country of your choice.[21] Test the following hypotheses by running appropriate Dickey-Fuller and/or cointegration tests:

(i) Are disposable income and consumption integrated processes? Are they cointegrated?

[21] A good resource for economic time series is FRED (Federal Reserve Economic Data) run by the St. Louis Federal Reserve Bank with homepage `https://fred.stlouisfed.org/`.

(ii) Test the purchasing power hypothesis. Is $\log(EP^*/P)$ stationary where P, P^*, and E denote the home country price level, the foreign country price level, and the exchange rate between the currencies of both countries. You may also try to test whether the relative purchasing power parity $\Delta E + \Delta P^* - \Delta P$ is stationary.

(iii) Test whether the interest rate parity $i^* + \Delta E - i$ is stationary where i and i^* are short-term interest rates in the home and the foreign country.

Exercise 7.5 You investigate the behavior of the monthly interest rate differential or spread in the United States (yield on US treasury securities with 10 years of maturity minus the 3-month treasury bill secondary market rate). Figure 7.7 displays a plot of this variable over the sample from January 1962 to August 2024. In addition, you conduct a unit root test by running the Dickey-Fuller regression with Δspread_t as the dependent variable. The results are reported in Table 7.5.

Which specification do you prefer for the augmented Dickey-Fuller test (ADF test)? State the null and alternative hypothesis and set a critical value. What is your conclusion? Are the long-run and the short-run interest rate cointegrated. If yes, what is the cointegrating vector?

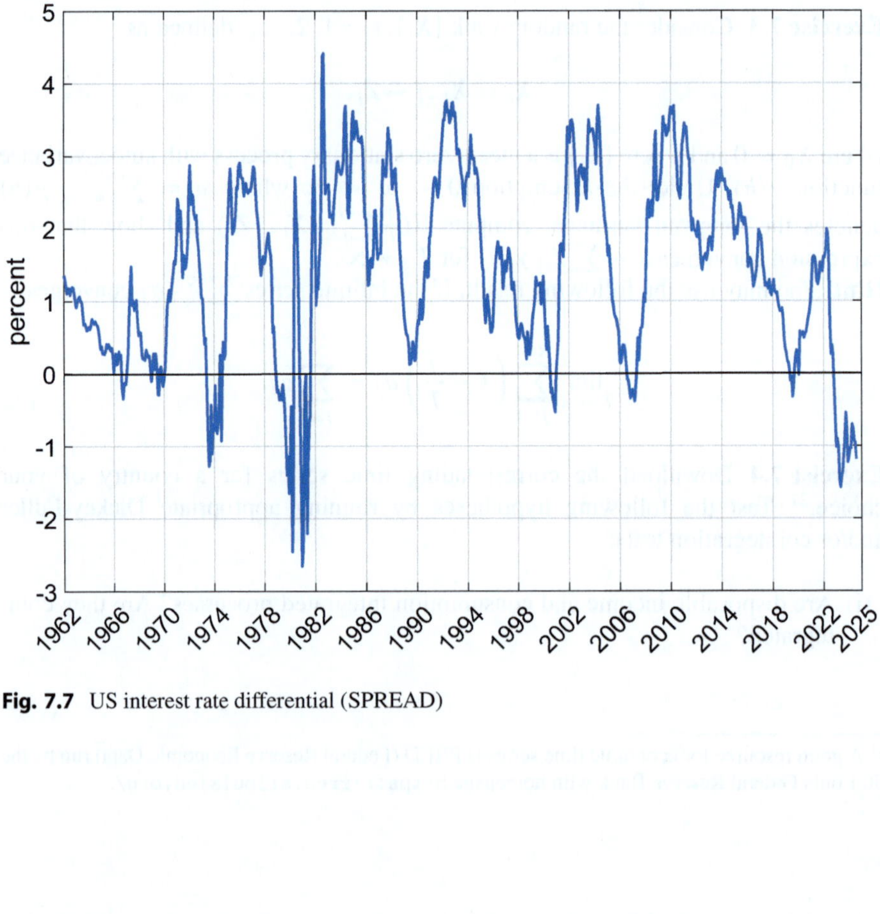

Fig. 7.7 US interest rate differential (SPREAD)

Table 7.5 Dickey-Fuller regressions with $\Delta spread_t$ as an dependent variable

Regressors	Specification 1	2	3
Constant	0.056	0.057	−0.0034
	(0.028)	(0.018)	[0.0135]
Trend	0.0000011		
	(0.0000050)		
spread(−1)	−0.042	−0.041	
	(0.010)	(0.010)	
Δspread(−1)	0.329	0.329	
	(0.036)	(0.036)	
Δspread(−2)	−0.194	−0.194	
	(0.037)	(0.037)	
Δspread(−3)	0.105	0.106	
	(0.037)	(0.037)	
$\mathbf{R}^2$	0.122	0.118	
AIC	0.596	0.594	0.710
BIC	0.633	0.624	0.716

Estimated standard errors in parenthesis
Newey-West adjusted (robust) standard errors in bracket

Models of Volatility

8

The prices of financial securities are often shaken by large and time-varying shocks. The amplitudes of these price movements are not constant over time. There are periods of high volatility and periods of low volatility. Within these periods, volatility seems to be positively autocorrelated: high amplitudes are likely to be followed by high amplitudes and low amplitudes by low amplitudes. This observation which is particularly relevant for high-frequency data, such as daily stock market returns, implies that the conditional variance of the one-period forecast error is no longer constant (homoskedastic), but time-varying (heteroskedastic) and autocorrelated. This insight motivated Engle (1982) and Bollerslev (1986) to model the variance of a stochastic process as time-varying. This effort triggered a huge and still growing literature.[1] The importance of volatility models stems, among other things, from the fact that the price of an option crucially depends on the variance of the underlying security price. Thus, with the surge of derivative markets in the last decades, the application of such models has seen a tremendous rise. Another use of volatility models is to assess the risk of an investment or portfolio. In the computation of the so-called value at risk (VaR), these models have become an indispensable tool. In the banking industry, due to the regulations of the Basel accords, such assessments are in particular relevant for the computation of the required equity capital backing-up assets of different risk categories.

The following exposition focuses on the class of autoregressive conditional heteroskedasticity models (ARCH models) and their generalization the generalized autoregressive conditional heteroskedasticity models (GARCH models). These models form the basis for even more generalized models (see Bollerslev et al., 1994 or Gouriéroux, 1997). Campbell et al. (1997) provide a broader economically motivated approach to the econometric analysis of financial market data.

[1] Robert F. Engle III was awarded the Nobel Prize in 2003 for his work on time-varying volatility. His Nobel lecture (Engle, 2004) is a nice and readable introduction to this literature.

K. Neusser, *Time Series Econometrics*, Springer Texts in Business and Economics,
https://doi.org/10.1007/978-3-031-88838-0_8

Before we embark on the exposition of volatility models, it seems useful to recapitulate the forecasting properties of stationary AR(1) models. Hence, let $\{X_t\}$ be defined as the solution of a first-order stochastic difference equation:

$$X_t = c + \phi X_{t-1} + Z_t, \qquad Z_t \sim \text{IID}(0, \sigma^2) \text{ and } |\phi| < 1.$$

Note that we made the stronger assumption that $\{Z_t\}$ is independently and identically distributed (IID) instead of being just white noise. The best linear forecast in the mean-squared-error sense of X_{t+1} conditional on $\{X_t, X_{t-1}, \ldots\}$, denoted by $\mathbb{P}_t X_{t+1}$, is given by (see Chap. 3)

$$\mathbb{P}_t X_{t+1} = c + \phi X_t.$$

In practice the parameters c and ϕ are replaced by their estimates. The *conditional* variance of the forecast error then becomes

$$\mathbb{E}_t \left(X_{t+1} - \mathbb{P}_t X_{t+1}\right)^2 = \mathbb{E}_t Z_{t+1}^2 = \sigma^2,$$

where $\mathbb{E}_t$ denotes the conditional expectation operator based on information $X_t, X_{t-1}, \ldots$. The conditional variance of the forecast error is therefore constant, irrespective of the current state.

The *unconditional* forecast is simply the expected value of $\mathbb{E}X_{t+1} = \mu = \frac{c}{1-\phi}$ with forecast error variance:

$$\mathbb{E}\left(X_{t+1} - \frac{c}{1-\phi}\right)^2 = \mathbb{E}\left(Z_{t+1} + \phi Z_t + \phi^2 Z_{t-1} + \ldots\right)^2 = \frac{\sigma^2}{1-\phi^2} > \sigma^2.$$

Thus the conditional as well as the unconditional variance of the forecast error are constant. In addition, the conditional variance is smaller and thus the conditional forecast more precise because it uses more information. Similar arguments can be made for ARMA models in general.

8.1 The GARCH(1,1) Model

Starting with the groundbreaking contributions of Engle (1982) and Bollerslev (1986), a myriad of volatility models have been proposed. Nevertheless the class of generalized autoregressive conditional heteroskedastic models, GARCH models, introduced by Bollerslev (1986) still serves as a reference in theoretical research as well as in empirical applications. We will analyze the GARCH(1,1) model in detail. This model exhibits all the interesting features required for a sensible volatility model. Generalizations and extensions are presented later on.

Definition 8.1 (GARCH(1,1) Process) A stochastic process $\{Z_t\}$ is called a generalized autoregressive conditional heteroskedastic process of order $(1, 1)$,

GARCH(1,1) process, if it is defined by the following recursion (stochastic difference equation) for $t \geq 1$:

$$Z_t = \nu_t \sigma_t, \qquad \nu_t \sim \text{IID}(0,1), \mathbf{P}[\nu_t = 0] = 0, \mathbb{E}|\nu_t| < \infty,$$
$$\sigma_t^2 = \alpha_0 + \alpha_1 Z_{t-1}^2 + \beta\sigma_{t-1}^2, \qquad \alpha_0 > 0, \alpha_1, \beta \geq 0, \alpha_1 + \beta > 0.$$

The process is initialized with ν_0 and σ_0^2 being strictly positive and finite (almost surely) independent random variables which are also independent from $\{\nu_t\}$, $t \geq 1$.

This definition requires several explanations:

(i) The randomness of $\{Z_t\}$ follows from the randomness of $\{\nu_t\}$. Hence, we may term ν_t as the innovation or input to the process. In contrast to ARMA models, this input enters in a multiplicative way
(ii) If $\beta = 0$, we obtain as a special case known as the ARCH(1) model originally introduced by Engle (1982).
(iii) The assumption $\alpha_0 > 0$ implies that $\sigma_t^2 > 0$ because $\alpha_1, \beta \geq 0$. Hence, the variance of Z_t, if it exists, is always strictly positive. Note, however, that this specification does not preclude an infinite variance.
(iv) The assumptions $\alpha_1, \beta \geq 0$ and $\alpha_1 + \beta > 0$ excludes the uninteresting case that both parameters are simultaneously equal to zero, implying a constant variance of Z_t.
(v) Because $\sigma_t^2 > 0$, the standardized process $\nu_t = Z_t/\sigma_t$ is well-defined.[2] As long as $\alpha_0 > 0$, the normalization $\mathbb{E}\nu_t^2 = 1$ is of no consequence.
(vi) It is possible to relax the assumption $\nu_t \sim \text{IID}(0,1)$ and just assume $\mathbb{E}_{t-1}\nu_t = 0$ and $\mathbb{E}_{t-1}\nu_t^2 = 1$. $\{\nu_t\}$ is then a martingale difference sequence (MDS). The memory requirement of such processes are weaker compared to IID processes, but stronger than for white noise processes. MDS have the property $\mathbb{E}(\mathbb{E}_{t-1}\nu_t) = \mathbb{E}\nu_t = 0$. Moreover, $\mathbb{E}(\mathbb{E}_{t-1}\nu_t^2) = \mathbb{E}\nu_t^2 = 1$ and $\gamma_\nu(h) = \mathbb{E}(\nu_t\nu_{t-h}) = \mathbb{E}(\mathbb{E}_{t-1}\nu_t\nu_{t-h}) = \mathbb{E}(\nu_{t-h}\mathbb{E}_{t-1}\nu_t) = 0$ for $|h| > 0$. Hence, $\nu_t \sim \text{WN}(0,1)$.
(vii) The conditions $\mathbf{P}[\nu_t = 0] = 0$ and $\mathbb{E}|\nu_t| < \infty$ ensure that ν_t is a non-degenerate random variable.
(viii) ν_t is not necessarily normally distributed. In fact, practice has shown that distributions with higher kurtosis (tailedness), e.g., t-distributions with low degrees of freedom, are better suited than the normal distribution to represent volatility in financial market data (see the example in Sect. 8.5).
(ix) The use of the conditional expectation induces a direction in time. Although the starting time is arbitrary, it is therefore not possible to run the process backward and define it for all integers $\mathbb{Z}$.

[2] σ_t always denotes the positive square root of σ_t^2.

Assuming that $\mathbb{E}\sigma_t^2$ exists and is finite, the definition of a GARCH(1,1) process immediately implies the following properties for $\{Z_t\}$:

(i) The expectation of Z_t is zero:

$$\mathbb{E}Z_t = \mathbb{E}\mathbb{E}_{t-1}(\nu_t\sigma_t) = \mathbb{E}(\sigma_t\mathbb{E}_{t-1}\nu_t) = 0.$$

(ii) The covariances between Z_t and Z_{t-h}, $|h| > 0$, are zero:

$$\mathbb{E}(Z_t Z_{t-h}) = \mathbb{E}\mathbb{E}_{t-1}(\nu_t\sigma_t\nu_{t-h}\sigma_{t-h}) = \mathbb{E}(\sigma_t\nu_{t-h}\sigma_{t-h}\mathbb{E}_{t-1}\nu_t) = 0.$$

(iii) The variance of Z_t is $\alpha_0/(\alpha_1 + \beta)$

$$\mathbb{E}(Z_t^2) = \mathbb{E}\mathbb{E}_{t-1}(\nu_t^2\sigma_t^2) = \mathbb{E}(\sigma_t^2\mathbb{E}_{t-1}\nu_t^2) = \frac{\alpha_0}{1-\alpha_1-\beta}$$

where the last equality is obtained by computing the stationary solution to the difference equation for σ_t^2. Theorem 8.1 derives conditions under which such a solution exists.

(iv) If ν_t has a symmetric distribution so does Z_t:

$$\mathbf{P}[Z_t \le -z] = \mathbf{P}[\nu_t \le -z/\sigma_t] = \mathbf{P}[\nu_t \ge z/\sigma_t] = \mathbf{P}[Z_t \ge z].$$

The first three properties show that $Z_t \sim \mathrm{WN}\left(0, \frac{\alpha_0}{1-\alpha_1-\beta}\right)$. Hence, Z_t and $Z_{t-|h|}$, $h = 1, 2, \ldots$, are uncorrelated, but they are not independent! In particular,

$$\mathbb{E}\left(Z_t|Z_{t-1}, Z_{t-2}, \ldots\right) = \mathbb{E}_t\nu_t\sqrt{\alpha_0 + \alpha_1 Z_{t-1}^2 + \beta\sigma_{t-1}^2} = 0$$

$$\begin{aligned}\mathbb{V}(Z_t|Z_{t-1}, Z_{t-2}, \ldots) &= \mathbb{E}\left(Z_t^2|Z_{t-1}, Z_{t-2}, \ldots\right) \\ &= \mathbb{E}_t\nu_t^2\left(\alpha_0 + \alpha_1 Z_{t-1}^2 + \beta\sigma_{t-1}^2\right) = \alpha_0 + \alpha_1 Z_{t-1}^2 + \beta\sigma_{t-1}^2.\end{aligned}$$

The conditional variance of Z_t therefore depends on Z_{t-h}, $h = 1, 2, \ldots$. Note that this dependence is positive because $\alpha_1, \beta \ge 0$ and $\alpha_1 + \beta > 0$. High (low) volatility is expected to be followed by high (low) volatility. The precision of the forecast, measured by the conditional variance of the forecast error, thus depends on the history of the process. This feature is not compatible with linear models and thus underlines the *nonlinear* character of the GARCH model and its generalizations.

Theorem 8.1 (Stationarity of GARCH(1,1) Processes) *The defining stochastic difference equation for the GARCH(1,1) model admits a stationary solution for* $\{Z_t\}$ *if*

$$\mathbb{E} \ln(\alpha_1 \nu_t^2 + \beta) < 0. \tag{8.1}$$

The solution is unique and strictly stationary. It is given by[3]

$$Z_t = \nu_t \sqrt{\alpha_0 \sum_{j=0}^{\infty} \prod_{i=1}^{j} (\alpha_1 \nu_{t-i}^2 + \beta)}. \tag{8.2}$$

Proof Define $Y_t = \sigma_t^2$ and rewrite the GARCH(1,1) model as

$$Y_t = \alpha_0 + \alpha_1 \nu_{t-1}^2 Y_{t-1} + \beta Y_{t-1} = \alpha_0 + (\alpha_1 \nu_{t-1}^2 + \beta) Y_{t-1}.$$

This defines a first-order difference equation with random time-varying coefficients $\xi_t = \alpha_1 \nu_t^2 + \beta > 0$. Iterate this equation backward k times to obtain

$$\begin{aligned} Y_t &= \alpha_0 + \alpha_0 \xi_{t=1} + \ldots + \alpha_0 \xi_{t-1} \ldots \xi_{t-k} + \xi_{t-1} \ldots \xi_{t-k} \xi_{t-k-1} Y_{t-k-1} \\ &= \alpha_0 \sum_{j=0}^{k} \prod_{i=1}^{j} \xi_{t-i} + \prod_{i=1}^{k+1} \xi_{t-i} Y_{t-k-1}. \end{aligned}$$

Taking the limit $k \to \infty$, we define the process $\{Y_t'\}$:

$$Y_t' = \alpha_0 (1 + \xi_{t-1} + \xi_{t-1}\xi_{t-2} + \xi_{t-1}\xi_{t-2}\xi_{t-3} + \ldots) = \alpha_0 \sum_{j=0}^{\infty} \prod_{i=1}^{j} \xi_{t-i}. \tag{8.3}$$

The right-hand side of this expression converges almost surely as can be seen from the following argument. Given that $\nu_t \sim \text{IID}(0, 1)$ and given the assumption $\mathbb{E} \log(\alpha_1 \nu_t^2 + \beta) < 0$, the Strong Law of Large Numbers (Theorem C.5) implies that

$$\limsup_{j \to \infty} \frac{1}{j} \left(\sum_{i=1}^{j} \log(\xi_{t-i}) \right) < 0 \quad \text{a.s.},$$

or equivalently

$$\limsup_{j \to \infty} \log \left(\prod_{i=1}^{j} \xi_{t-i} \right)^{1/j} < 0 \quad \text{a.s.}$$

[3] Thereby we use the convention $\prod_i^j = 1$ für $i > j$.

Thus,

$$\limsup_{j\to\infty}\left(\prod_{i=1}^{j}\xi_{t-i}\right)^{1/j} < 1 \quad \text{a.s.}$$

The application of the root test then shows that the infinite series (8.3) converges almost surely. Thus, $\{Y_t'\}$ is well-defined. It is easy to see that $\{Y_t'\}$ is strictly stationary and satisfies the difference equation. Moreover, if $\alpha_1 + \beta < 1$, we get

$$\mathbb{E}Y_t' = \alpha_0 \sum_{j=0}^{\infty} \mathbb{E}\prod_{i=1}^{j}\xi_{t-i} = \alpha_0 \sum_{j=0}^{\infty}(\alpha_1+\beta)^j = \frac{\alpha_0}{1-\alpha_1-\beta}.$$

Thus, $\sigma_Z^2 = \mathbb{E}Z_t^2 = \frac{\alpha_0}{1-\alpha_1-\beta} < \infty$.

To show uniqueness, we assume that there exists another strictly stationary process $\{Y_t\}$ which also satisfies the difference equation. This implies that

$$\begin{aligned}|Y_t - Y_t'| &= |\xi_{t-1}|\,|Y_{t-1} - Y_{t-1}'| = \left(\prod_{i=1}^{k}\xi_{t-i}\right)|Y_{t-k} - Y_{t-k}'| \\ &\le \left(\prod_{i=1}^{k}\xi_{t-i}\right)|Y_{t-k}| + \left(\prod_{i=1}^{k}\xi_{t-i}\right)|Y_{t-k}'|\end{aligned}$$

The assumption $\mathbb{E}\log\xi_t = \mathbb{E}\log(\alpha_1\nu_t^2+\beta) < 0$ together with the Strong Law of Large Numbers (Theorem C.5) imply

$$\prod_{i=1}^{k}\xi_{t-i} = \left(\exp\left(\frac{1}{k}\sum_{i=1}^{k}\log\xi_{t-i}\right)\right)^k \longrightarrow 0 \quad \text{a.s.}$$

As both solutions are strictly stationary so that the distribution of $|Y_{t-k}|$ and $|Y_{t-k}'|$ do not depend on t, this implies that both $\left(\prod_{i=1}^{k}\xi_{t-i}\right)|Y_{t-k}|$ and $\left(\prod_{i=1}^{k}\xi_{t-i}\right)|Y_{t-k}'|$ converge in probability to zero. Thus, $Y_t = Y_t'$ a.s. once the sequence ξ_t, respectively ν_t, is given. Because $Z_t = \nu_t\sqrt{Y_t'}$ this completes the proof. □

Jensen's inequality implies that

$$\mathbb{E}\log(\alpha_1\nu_t^2+\beta) \le \log\mathbb{E}(\alpha_1\nu_t^2+\beta) = \log(\alpha_1+\beta).$$

Hence, the condition $\alpha_1 + \beta < 1$ is sufficient, but not necessary, to ensure the existence of a strictly stationary solution. Thus even when $\alpha_1 + \beta = 1$, a strictly stationary solution exists, albeit one with infinite variance (see the IGARCH model discussed in Sect. 8.2). This can be exemplified using the specification $\alpha_1 = 1$, $\beta = 0$, and $\nu_t \sim \text{IID}\,\text{N}(0,1)$. In this case, the condition for a stationary solution is fulfilled, because $\mathbb{E}\ln(\alpha_1\nu_t^2+\beta) = \mathbb{E}\ln\nu_t^2 = -(\gamma+\ln 2) < 0$ where $\gamma = 0.577\ldots$ equals the Euler-Mascheroni constant. Hence according to Theorem 8.1, $Z_t = \nu_t\sigma_t$ and $\sigma_t^2 = \alpha_0 + Z_{t-1}^2$ define a strictly stationary process. However, the variance of this process is infinite as can be seen from the solution formula (8.2).

Often it is assumed that $\{\nu_t\}$ is Gaussian process, i.e., $\nu_t \sim \text{IID}\,\text{N}(0,1)$. Hence, the skewness $\mathbb{E}\nu_t^3$ is equal to zero. The independence assumption between ν_r and $Z_{t-|h|}$, $h = 1, 2, \ldots$, then implies that the skewness of Z_t is also zero, i.e. $\mathbb{E}Z_t^3 = 0$, implying that Z_t has a symmetric distribution. The distribution is, however, not normal as extreme realizations are more probable, a phenomenon known as the *heavy-tail property*. To see this, we compute the kurtosis κ of Z_t:[4]

$$\kappa = \frac{\mathbb{E}Z_t^4}{[\mathbb{E}Z_t^2]^2} = 3 \times \frac{1-(\alpha_1+\beta)^2}{1-(\alpha_1+\beta)^2-2\alpha_1^2} > 3 \tag{8.4}$$

if $\mathbb{E}Z_t^4$ exists. A necessary and sufficient condition for its existence is $(\alpha_1+\beta)^2 + 2\alpha_1^2 < 1$ (Zadrozny, 2005). A simpler, but only sufficient condition is

$$\sqrt{3}\frac{\alpha_1}{1-\beta} < 1. \tag{8.5}$$

The verification of these assertions is left to the reader as Exercise 8.6.1. Because the kurtosis of a normal distribution is 3, formula (8.4) shows that the distribution of Z_t has positive excess kurtosis and is therefore leptokurtic. This means that large positive or negative realizations have a higher probability than under a normal distribution.

Figure 8.1 summarizes the previous discussion and shows how the different assumptions and conditions divide up the parameter space in several regions. In region I, all conditions are fulfilled. The process has a strictly stationary solution with finite variance and kurtosis. In region II, the kurtosis no longer exists, but the variance still does as $\alpha_1+\beta < 1$ holds. In region III, the process has infinite variance, but a strictly stationary solution still exists. In region IV, no such solution exists.

To illustrate the difference between processes with parameters in region I and those in region II, Fig. 8.2 plots the realizations of two AR(1)-GARCH(1,0) processes. Both processes have been generated with the same realization of $\{\nu_t\}$ and the same parameters $\phi = 0.9$, $\alpha_0 = 1$, and $\beta = 0$. Whereas the first process

[4] As $\nu_t \sim \text{N}(0,1)$ its even moments, $m_{2k} = \mathbb{E}\nu_t^{2k}$, $k = 1, 2, \ldots$, are given by $m_{2k} = \prod_{j=1}^{k}(2j-1)$. Thus we get $m_4 = 3$, $m_6 = 15$, etc. As the normal distribution is symmetric, all odd moments are equal to zero.

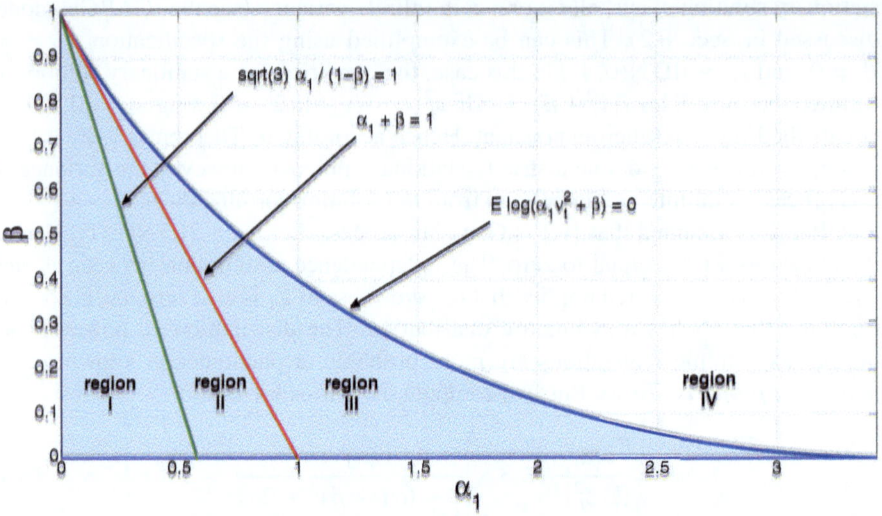

Fig. 8.1 Parameter region for which a strictly stationary solution to the GARCH(1,1) process exists assuming $\nu_t \sim \text{IID}\,\text{N}(0, 1)$

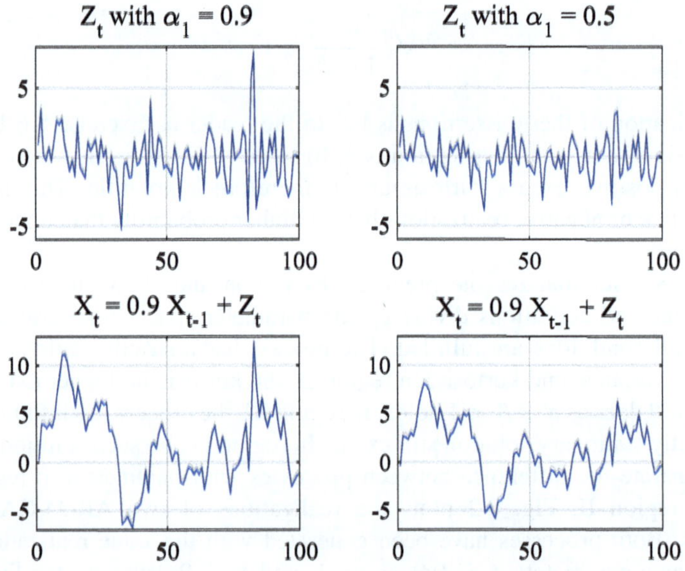

Fig. 8.2 Simulation of two GARCH(1,0) processes ($\alpha_1 = 0.9$ and $\alpha_1 = 0.5$)

(shown on the left panel of the figure) was generated with a value of $\alpha_1 = 0.9$, the second one had a value of $\alpha_1 = 0.5$. In both cases the stability condition, $\alpha_1 < 1$, is fulfilled, but for the first process $3\alpha_1^2 > 1$, so that the fourth moment does not exist. One can clearly discern the large fluctuations, in particular for the first process.

Forecasting

On many occasions it is necessary to obtain forecasts of the conditional variance σ_t^2. An example is given in Sect. 8.5 where the value at risk (VaR) of a portfolio several periods ahead must be evaluated. Denote by $\mathbb{P}_t\sigma_{t+h}^2$ the h period ahead forecast based on information available in period t. We assume that predictions are based on the infinite past. Then the one-period ahead forecast based on Z_t and σ_t^2, respectively, ν_t and σ_t^2, is

$$\mathbb{P}_t\sigma_{t+1}^2 = \alpha_0 + \alpha_1 Z_t^2 + \beta\sigma_t^2 = \alpha_0 + (\alpha_1\nu_t^2 + \beta)\sigma_t^2. \tag{8.6}$$

As $\nu_t \sim \text{IID}(0,1)$ and independent of Z_{t-j}, $j \geq 1$,

$$\mathbb{P}_t\sigma_{t+2}^2 = \alpha_0 + (\alpha_1 + \beta)\mathbb{P}_t\sigma_{t+1}^2.$$

Thus, forecast for $h \geqq 2$ can be obtained recursively as follows:

$$\begin{aligned}\mathbb{P}_t\sigma_{t+h}^2 &= \alpha_0 + (\alpha_1 + \beta)\mathbb{P}_t\sigma_{t+h-1}^2 \\ &= \alpha_0 \sum_{j=0}^{h-2}(\alpha_1 + \beta)^j + (\alpha_1 + \beta)^{h-1}\mathbb{P}_t\sigma_{t+1}^2.\end{aligned} \tag{8.7}$$

Assuming $\alpha_1 + \beta < 1$, the second term in the above expression vanishes as h goes to infinity. Thus, the contribution of the current conditional variance vanishes looking further and further into the future. The forecast of the conditional variance then approaches the unconditional one: $\lim_{h\to\infty}\mathbb{P}_t\sigma_{t+h}^2 = \frac{\alpha_0}{1-\alpha_1-\beta}$. If $\alpha_1 + \beta = 1$ as in the IGARCH model, the contribution of the current conditional variance is constant, but diminishes to zero relative to the first term. Finally, if $\alpha_1 + \beta > 1$, the two terms are of the same order, and we have a particularly persistent situation.

In practice, the parameters of the model are unknown and have therefore be replaced by an estimate. The method can be easily adapted for higher-order models. Instead of using the recursive approach outlined above, it is possible to use simulation methods by drawing repeatedly from the actual empirical distribution of the $\hat{\nu}_t = \hat{Z}_t/\hat{\sigma}_t$. This has the advantage to capture deviations from the underlying distributional assumptions (see Sect. 8.5 for a comparison of both methods). Such methods must be applied if nonlinear models for the conditional variance, like the TARCH model, are employed.

8.2 General Models of Volatility

The original work by Engle (1982) and Bollerslev (1986) triggered a huge amount of research in this field yielding a myriad of volatility models. Some of them are just straightforward generalizations; others set up new directions. In this section, we review some of the most popular ones.[5]

ARCH(p) Model

The simplest of such models is the ARCH(1) model originally introduced by Engle (1982). It is obtained as a special case of the GARCH(1,1) model by setting $\beta = 0$ in the defining difference equation (see Definition 8.1):

$$\text{ARCH(1)}: \qquad Z_t = \nu_t \sigma_t \quad \text{with } \sigma_t^2 = \alpha_0 + \alpha_1 Z_{t-1}^2. \tag{8.8}$$

A straightforward generalization proposed by Engle (1982) allows for additional lags in the ARCH Eq. (8.8). This leads to the ARCH(p) model

$$\text{ARCH(p)}: \qquad Z_t = \nu_t \sigma_t \quad \text{with } \sigma_t^2 = \alpha_0 + \sum_{j=1}^{p} \alpha_j Z_{t-j}^2 \tag{8.9}$$

where $\alpha_0 \geq 0$, $\alpha_j \geq 0$, $\sum_{j=1}^{p} \alpha_j > 0$, and $\nu_t \sim \text{IID}(0, 1)$ with ν_t independent from Z_{t-j}, $j = 1, \ldots, p$.

GARCH(p,q) Model

Similarly, a straightforward generalization of the GARCH(1,1) model is obtained by introducing additional lag in Z_{t-j}^2 and σ_{t-j}^2. These models are known as GARCH(p,q) models and were introduced by Bollerslev (1986):

$$\text{GARCH(p,q)}: \quad Z_t = \nu_t \sigma_t \quad \text{with } \sigma_t^2 = \alpha_0 + \sum_{j=1}^{p} \alpha_j Z_{t-j}^2 + \sum_{j=1}^{q} \beta_j \sigma_{t-j}^2 \tag{8.10}$$

where $\alpha_0 \geq 0$, $\alpha_j \geq 0$, $\beta_j \geq 0$, $\sum_{j=1}^{p} \alpha_j + \sum_{j=1}^{q} \beta_j > 0$, and $\nu_t \sim \text{IID}(0, 1)$ with ν_t independent from Z_{t-j}, $j \geq 1$.

This model is analogous to the ordinary ARMA model and allows for a parsimonious specification of the volatility process. All coefficients should be positive to guarantee that the variance is always positive. In addition it can be shown (see, e.g., Fan & Yao, 2003, 150 and the literature cited therein) that $\{Z_t\}$ is (strictly) stationary with finite variance if and only if

$$\sum_{j=1}^{p} \alpha_j + \sum_{j=1}^{q} \beta_j < 1. \tag{8.11}$$

[5] In the following presentation $\{\nu_t\}$ is always supposed to have the same properties as in the definition of the GARCH(1,1) model.

The proof is similar to the proof of Theorem 8.1. Many conclusions derived for the GARCH(1,1) model carry over to the GARCH(p,q) model (see Sect. 8.1). For simplicity, we omit a detailed exposition. Under this condition $\{Z_t\} \sim \text{WN}(0, \sigma_Z^2)$ with

$$\sigma_Z^2 = \mathbb{V}(Z_t) = \frac{\alpha_0}{1 - \sum_{j=1}^p \alpha_j - \sum_{j=1}^q \beta_j} > 0.$$

Assuming that $\{\nu_t\}$ is a Gaussian process, the distribution of Z_t is symmetric and its skewness therefore equal to zero. The fourth moment of Z_t, $\mathbb{E}Z_t^4$, exists if

$$\sqrt{3}\frac{\sum_{j=1}^p \alpha_j}{1 - \sum_{j=1}^q \beta_j} < 1.$$

This condition is sufficient, but not necessary. Compare this to condition (8.5) for the GARCH(1,1) model.[6] Furthermore, $\{Z_t\}$ is a white noise process with the heavy-tail property if $\{Z_t\}$ is strictly stationary with finite fourth moment.

The similarity to ARMA models can be extended further. $\{Z_t^2\}$ can be written as an ARMA$(\max\{p, q\}, q)$ process as it satisfies the difference equation

$$\begin{aligned} Z_t^2 &= \alpha_0 + \sum_{j=1}^p \alpha_j Z_{t-j}^2 + \sum_{j=1}^q \beta_j \sigma_{t-j}^2 + e_t \qquad (8.12) \\ &= \alpha_0 + \sum_{j=1}^{\max\{p,q\}} (\alpha_j + \beta_j) Z_{t-j}^2 + e_t - \sum_{j=1}^q \beta_j e_{t-j}, \end{aligned}$$

where $\alpha_{p+j} = \beta_{q+j} = 0$ for $j \geq 1$ and the "error term" e_t is defined as

$$e_t = Z_t^2 - \sigma_t^2 = (\nu_t^2 - 1)\left(\alpha_0 + \sum_{j=1}^p \alpha_j Z_{t-j}^2 + \sum_{j=1}^q \beta_j \sigma_{t-j}^2\right).$$

It is easy to see that $\mathbb{E}(e_t|Z_{t-1}, Z_{t-2}, \ldots) = 0$. Assuming that condition (8.11) holds, the "ARMA" model is causal and invertible with respect to $\{e_t\}$. Note, however, there is a circularity here because the noise process $\{e_t\}$ is defined in terms of Z_t^2 and is therefore not an exogenous process driving Z_t^2. Thus, one has to be cautious in the interpretation of $\{Z_t^2\}$ as an ARMA process.

[6] Zadrozny (2005) derives a necessary and sufficient condition for the existence of the fourth moment.

If $p = q = 1$, this defines an ARMA(1,1) process. Its autocorrelation function (ACF), $\rho_{Z^2}(h)$, can be computed using the methods in Sect. 2.4

$$\rho_{Z^2}(1) = \frac{(1-\beta^2-\alpha_1\beta)\alpha_1}{1-\beta^2-2\alpha_1\beta} = \frac{(1-\beta\varphi)(\varphi-\beta)}{1+\beta^2-2\varphi\beta},$$
$$\rho_{Z^2}(h) = (\alpha_1+\beta)\rho_{Z^2}(h-1) = \varphi\rho_{Z^2}(h-1), \qquad h = 2, 3, \ldots \tag{8.13}$$

with $\varphi = \alpha_1 + \beta$ (see also Bollerslev, 1988).

Further generalizations of the GARCH(p,q) model can be obtained by allowing deviations from the normal distribution for ν_t. In particular, distributions such as the t-distribution with low degrees of freedom which put more weight on extreme values have become popular. This seems warranted as prices on financial markets exhibit large and sudden fluctuations.[7]

Threshold GARCH Model

Assuming a symmetric distribution for ν_t and specifying a linear relationship between σ_t^2 and Z_{t-j}^2, respectively σ_{t-j}^2, $j > 0$, leads to a symmetric distribution for Z_t. It has, however, been observed that prices in many financial markets behave differently depending on whether the market moves up or down. This asymmetric behavior is accounted for by the asymmetric GARCH(1,1) model or threshold GARCH(1,1) model (TGARCH(1,1) model). This model was proposed by Glosten et al. (1993) and Zakoïan (1994):

$$\text{asymmetric GARCH(1,1)}: \; Z_t = \nu_t\sigma_t \quad \text{with}$$
$$\sigma_t^2 = \alpha_0 + \alpha_1 Z_{t-1}^2 + \beta\sigma_{t-1}^2 + \gamma \mathbf{1}_{\{Z_{t-1}<0\}} Z_{t-1}^2.$$

$\mathbf{1}_{\{Z_{t-1}<0\}}$ denotes the indicator function which takes on the value one if Z_{t-1} is negative and the value zero otherwise. Assuming, as before, that all parameters α_0, α_1, β, and γ are greater than zero, this specification postulates a leverage effect because negative realizations have a greater impact than positive ones. In order to obtain a stationary process with finite variance the condition $\alpha_1+\beta+\gamma/2 < 1$ must hold. This model can be generalized in an obvious way by allowing additional lags Z_{t-j}^2 and σ_{t-j}^2, $j > 1$ to enter the above specification.

IGARCH Model

Practice has shown that the sum $\alpha_1 + \beta$ in the GARCH(1,1) model is often close to one. Thus, it seems interesting to examine the limiting case where $\alpha_1 + \beta = 1$. This

[7] A thorough treatment of the probabilistic properties of GARCH processes can be found in Nelson (1990), Bougerol and Picard (1992a), Giraitis et al. (2000), and Klüppelberg et al. (2004, theorem 2.1).

model was proposed by Engle and Bollerslev (1986) and was termed the *integrated GARCH* (IGARCH) model in analogy to the notion of integrated processes (see Chap. 7). Equation (8.12) implies

$$Z_t^2 = \alpha_0 + Z_{t-1}^2 + e_t - \beta e_{t-1}$$

with $e_t = Z_t^2 - \sigma_t^2 = (\nu_t^2 - 1)(\alpha_0 + (1-\beta)Z_{t-1}^2 + \beta\sigma_{t-1}^2)$. Hence, the squared innovations Z_t^2 behave like a random walk with a MA(1) error term. Although the variance of Z_t becomes infinite, the difference equation still allows for a strictly stationary solution provided that $\mathbb{E}\log(\alpha_1\nu_t^2 + \beta) < 0$ (see Theorem 8.1 and the citations in footnote 7 for further details).[8] It has been shown by Lumsdaine (1986) and Lee and Hansen (1994) that standard inferences can still be applied even if $\alpha_1 + \beta = 1$. The model may easily generalized to higher lag orders.

Exponential GARCH Model

Another interesting and popular class of volatility models was introduced by Nelson (1991). The so-called exponential GARCH models or EGARCH models are defined as follows:

$$\begin{aligned}\log\sigma_t^2 &= \alpha_0 + \beta\log\sigma_{t-1}^2 + \gamma\left|\frac{Z_{t-1}}{\sigma_{t-1}}\right| + \delta\frac{Z_{t-1}}{\sigma_{t-1}} \\ &= \alpha_0 + \beta\log\sigma_{t-1}^2 + \gamma|\nu_{t-1}| + \delta\nu_{t-1}.\end{aligned}$$

Note that, in contrast to the previous specifications, the dependent variable is the logarithm of σ_t^2. This has the advantage that the variance is always positive irrespective of the values of the coefficients. Furthermore, the leverage effect is exponential rather than quadratic because $Z_t = \nu_t\exp(\sigma_t/2)$. The EGARCH model is also less recursive than the GARCH model as the volatility is specified directly in terms of the noise process $\{\nu_t\}$. Thus, the above EGARCH model can be treated as an AR(1) model in $\log\sigma_t^2$ with noise process $\gamma|\nu_{t-1}| + \delta\nu_{t-1}$. It is obvious that the model can be generalized to allow for additional lags both in σ_t^2 and ν_t. This results in an ARMA process for $\{\log\sigma_t^2\}$ for which the usual conditions for the existence of a causal and invertible solution can be applied (see Sect. 2.3). A detailed analysis and further properties of this model class can be found in Bollerslev et al. (1994), Gouriéroux (1997), and Fan and Yao (2003, 143-180).

ARCH-in-Mean Model

The ARCH-in-mean model or ARCH-M model was introduced by Engle et al. (1987) to allow for a feedback of volatility into the mean equation. More specifically, assume for the sake of simplicity that the variance equation is just represented

[8] As the variance becomes infinite, the IGARCH process is an example of a stochastic process which is strictly stationary, but not stationary.

by an ARCH(1) model:

$$Z_t = \nu_t \sigma_t \quad \text{with } \sigma_t^2 = \alpha_0 + \alpha_1 Z_{t-1}^2.$$

Then, the ARCH-M model is given

$$X_t = M_t \beta + g(\sigma_t^2) + Z_t \tag{8.14}$$

where g is a function of the volatility σ_t^2 and where M_t' consists of a vector of regressors, including lagged values of X_t. If $M_t = (1, X_{t-1})$ then we get the AR(1)-ARCH-M model. The most commonly used specification for g is a linear function: $g(\sigma_t^2) = \delta_0 + \delta_1 \sigma_t^2$. In the asset pricing literature, higher volatility would require a higher return to compensate the investor for the additional risk. Thus, if X_t denotes the return on some asset, we expect δ_1 to be positive. Note that any time variation in σ_t^2 translates into a serial correlation of $\{X_t\}$ (see Hong, 1991, for details). Of course, one could easily generalize the model to allow for more sophisticated mean and variance equations.

8.3 Tests for Heteroskedasticity

Before modeling the volatility of a time series, it is advisable to test whether heteroskedasticity is actually present in the data. For this purpose the literature proposed several tests of which we are going to examine two. For both tests the null hypothesis is that there is no heretoskedasticity, i.e., that there are no ARCH effects. These tests can also be useful in a conventional regression setting.

8.3.1 Autocorrelation of Quadratic Residuals

The first test is based on the autocorrelation function of squared residuals from a preliminary regression. This preliminary regression or mean regression produces a series $\widehat{Z}_t$ which should be approximately white noise if the equation is well specified. Then we can look at the ACF of the squared residuals $\widehat{Z}_t^2$ and apply the Ljung-Box test (see Eq. (4.5)).[9] Thus the test can be broken down into three steps.

(i) Estimate an ARMA model for $\{X_t\}$ and retrieve the residuals $\widehat{Z}_t$ from this model. Compute $\widehat{Z}_t^2$. These data can be used to estimate σ^2 as

$$\widehat{\sigma}^2 = \frac{1}{T} \sum_{t=1}^{T} \widehat{Z}_t^2$$

[9] Compare this with $\widehat{\rho}_{Z^2}(h)$ in Eq. (8.13), the ACF squared residuals in the case of GARCH(1,1) models.

Note that the ARMA model should be specified such that the residuals are approximately white noise.

(ii) Estimate the ACF for the squared residuals in the usual way:

$$\widehat{\rho}_{Z^2}(h) = \frac{\sum_{t=h+1}^{T}\left(\widehat{Z}_t^2 - \widehat{\sigma}^2\right)\left(\widehat{Z}_{t-h}^2 - \widehat{\sigma}^2\right)}{\sum_{t=1}^{T}\left(\widehat{Z}_t^2 - \widehat{\sigma}^2\right)^2}$$

(iii) Use one of the methods laid out in Chap. 4 to test the null hypothesis that $\{Z_t^2\}$ is white noise. It can be shown that under the null hypothesis $\sqrt{T}\widehat{\rho}_{Z^2}(h) \xrightarrow{\text{d}} \text{N}(0, 1)$. One can therefore construct confidence intervals for the ACF in the usual way. Alternatively, one may use the Ljung-Box test statistic (see Eq. (4.5)) to test the hypothesis that all correlation coefficients up to order N are simultaneously equal to zero:

$$Q' = T(T+2)\sum_{h=1}^{N}\frac{\hat{\rho}_{Z^2}^2(h)}{T-h}.$$

Under the null hypothesis this statistic is distributed as χ_N^2. To carry out the test, N should be chosen rather high, for example, equal to $T/4$.

8.3.2 Engle's Lagrange-Multiplier Test

Engle (1982) proposed a Lagrange-multiplier test. This test rests on an ancillary regression of the squared residuals $\widehat{Z}_t^2$ against a constant and lagged values $\widehat{Z}_{t-1}^2, \widehat{Z}_{t-2}^2, \ldots, \widehat{Z}_{t-p}^2$ where the $\{\widehat{Z}_t\}$ is again obtained from a preliminary regression. The auxiliary regression thus is

$$\widehat{Z}_t^2 = \alpha_0 + \alpha_1\widehat{Z}_{t-1}^2 + \alpha_2\widehat{Z}_{t-2}^2 + \ldots + \alpha_p\widehat{Z}_{t-p}^2 + \varepsilon_t,$$

where ε_t denotes the error term. The null hypothesis $\mathbf{H}_0 : \alpha_1 = \cdots = \alpha_p = 0$ is then tested against the alternative hypothesis $\mathbf{H}_1 : \alpha_j \neq 0$ for at least one j, $j = 1, \ldots, p$. As a test statistic, one can use the coefficient of determination times T, i.e., $T\text{R}^2$. This test statistic is distributed as a χ^2 with p degrees of freedom. Alternatively, one may use the conventional F-test.

8.4 Estimation of GARCH(p,q) Models

8.4.1 Maximum Likelihood Estimation

The literature proposed several methods to estimate models of volatility (see Fan & Yao, 2003, 156-162). The most popular one, however, is based on the maximum-likelihood method. We will describe this method using the GARCH(p,q) model. Related and more detailed accounts can be found in Weiss (1986), Bollerslev et al. (1994), and Hall and Yao (2003).

Specifically, we consider the following specification:

$$\text{mean equation} \qquad X_t = c + \phi_1 X_{t-1} + \ldots + \phi_r X_{t-r} + Z_t,$$

where

$$Z_t = \nu_t \sigma_t \qquad \text{with } \nu_t \sim \text{IID N}(0,1) \text{ and}$$

$$\text{variance equation} \qquad \sigma_t^2 = \alpha_0 + \sum_{j=1}^{p} \alpha_j Z_{t-j}^2 + \sum_{j=1}^{q} \beta_j \sigma_{t-j}^2.$$

For expository purposes, the mean equation represents a simple AR(r) process for which we assume that it is causal with respect to $\{Z_t\}$, i.e., that all roots of $\Phi(z)$ are outside the unit circle. As noted by Weiss (1986), the method outlined below can be easily adapted to other forms of the mean equation: simple or multiple regression models, ARMA processes, ARMA processes with additional exogenous variables (so-called ARMAX processes), and so forth. The method also incorporates the ARCH-in-mean model (see Eq. (8.14)) which allows for a feedback of the conditional variance σ_t on X_t. In addition, we assume that the coefficients of the variance equation are all positive, that $\sum_{j=1}^{p} \alpha_j + \sum_{j=1}^{q} \beta_j < 1$, and that $\mathbb{E}Z_t^4 < \infty$ exists.[10]

As ν_t is identically and independently standard normally distributed, the distribution of X_t conditional on $\mathcal{X}_{t-1} = \{X_{t-1}, X_{t-2}, \ldots\}$ is normal with mean $c + \phi_1 X_{t-1} + \ldots + \phi_r X_{t-r}$ and variance σ_t^2. The conditional density, $f(X_t|\mathcal{X}_{t-1})$, therefore is

$$f(X_t|\mathcal{X}_{t-1}) = \frac{1}{\sqrt{2\pi\sigma_t^2}} \exp\left(-\frac{Z_t^2}{2\sigma_t^2}\right)$$

where Z_t equals $X_t - c - \phi_1 X_{t-1} - \ldots - \phi_r X_{t-r}$ and σ_t^2 is given by the variance equation.[11] The joint density $f(X_1, X_2, \ldots, X_T)$ of a random sample $(X_1, X_2, \ldots, X_T)$ can therefore be factorized as

$$f(X_1, X_2, \ldots, X_T) = f(X_1, X_2, \ldots, X_{s-1}) \prod_{t=s}^{T} f(X_t|\mathcal{X}_{t-1})$$

[10] The existence of the fourth moment is necessary for the asymptotic normality of the maximum-likelihood estimator, but not for the consistence. It is possible to relax this assumption somewhat (see Hall & Yao, 2003).

[11] If ν_t is assumed to follow another distribution than the normal, one may use this distribution instead.

where s is an integer greater than p. The necessity, not to factorize the first $s - 1$ observations, relates to the fact that σ_t^2 can only be evaluated for $s > p$ in the ARCH(p) model. For the ARCH(p) model s can be set to $p + 1$. In the case of a GARCH model, σ_t^2 is given by weighted infinite sum of the $Z_{t-1}^2, Z_{t-2}^2, \ldots$ (see the expression (8.2) for σ_t^2 in the GARCH(1,1) model). For finite samples, this infinite sum must be approximated by a finite sum of s summands such that the numbers of summands s is increasing with the sample size (see Hall & Yao, 2003).

We then combine all parameters of the model in vectors $\phi = (c, \phi_1, \ldots, \phi_r)'$, $\alpha = (\alpha_0, \alpha_1, \ldots, \alpha_p)'$, and $\beta = (\beta_1, \ldots, \beta_q)'$. For a given realization $\mathbf{x}_T = (x_1, x_2, \ldots, x_T)$, the *likelihood function* conditional on $\mathbf{x}_T$, $\mathrm{L}(\phi, \alpha, \beta|\mathbf{x}_T)$, is defined as

$$\mathrm{L}(\phi, \alpha, \beta|\mathbf{x}_T) = f(x_1, x_2, \ldots, x_{s-1}) \prod_{t=s}^{T} f(x_t|\mathcal{X}_{t-1})$$

where in $\mathcal{X}_{t-1}$ the random variables are replaced by their realizations. The likelihood function can be seen as the probability of observing the data at hand given the values for the parameters. The method of maximum likelihood then consists in choosing the parameters (ϕ, α, β) such that the likelihood function is maximized. Thus we chose the parameter so that the probability of observing the data is maximized. In this way we obtain the maximum likelihood estimator. Taking the first s realizations as given deterministic starting values, we then get the *conditional likelihood function*.

In practice, we do not maximize the likelihood function but its logarithm taking $f(x_1, \ldots, x_{s-1})$ as a fixed constant which can be neglected asymptotically. Hence, we maximize

$$\begin{aligned}\log \mathrm{L}(\phi, \alpha, \beta|x) &= \sum_{t=s}^{T} \log f(x_t|\mathcal{X}_t) \\ &= -\frac{T}{2}\log 2\pi - \frac{1}{2}\sum_{t=s}^{T} \log \sigma_t^2 - \frac{1}{2}\sum_{t=s}^{T} \frac{z_t^2}{\sigma_t^2}\end{aligned}$$

where $z_t = x_t - c = \phi_1 x_{t-1} - \ldots - \phi_r x_{t-r}$ denotes the realization of Z_t. The maximum likelihood estimator is obtained by maximizing the likelihood function over the admissible parameter space. Usually, the implementation of the stationarity condition and the condition for the existence of the fourth moment turns out to be difficult and cumbersome to implement so that often these conditions are neglected and only checked in retrospect or some ad hoc solutions are envisaged. It can be shown that the (conditional) maximum likelihood estimator leads to consistent and asymptotically normally distributed estimates.[12] For reasons similar to the

[12] Jensen and Rahbek (2004) showed that, at least for the GARCH(1,1) case, the stationarity condition is not necessary.

maximum likelihood estimation of ARMA models (see Sect. 5.3), the maximum likelihood estimator remains meaningful even when $\{\nu_t\}$ is not normally distributed. In this case the quasi maximum likelihood estimator is obtained (see Hall & Yao, 2003 and Fan & Yao, 2003).

For numerical reasons, it is often convenient to treat the mean equation and the variance equation separately. As the mean equation is a simple AR(r) model, it can be estimated by ordinary least-squares (OLS) in a first step. This leads to consistent parameter estimates. However, due to the heteroskedasticity, this no longer true for the covariance matrix of the coefficients so that the usual t- and F-tests are not reliable. This problem can be circumvented by the use of the White correction (see White, 1980). In this way it is possible to find an appropriate specification for the mean equation without having to estimate the complete model. In the second step, one can then work with the residuals to find an appropriate ARMA model for the squared residuals. This leads to consistent estimates of the parameters of the variance equation. These estimates are under additional weakly assumptions asymptotically normally distributed (see Weiss, 1986). It should, however, be noted that this way of proceeding is, in contrast to the maximum likelihood estimator, not efficient because it neglect the nonlinear character of the GARCH model. The parameters found in this way can, however, serve as meaningful starting values for the numerical maximization procedure which underlies the maximum likelihood estimation.

A final remark concerns the choice of the parameter r, p, and q. Similarly to the ordinary ARMA models, one can use information criteria such as the Akaike or the Bayes criterion, to determine the order of the model (see Sect. 5.4).

8.4.2 Method of Moment Estimation

The maximization of the likelihood function requires the use of numerical optimization routines. Depending on the routine actually used and on the starting value, estimation results may turn out to be sensitive if the likelihood function is not well-behaved. It is therefore of interest to have alternative estimation methods at hand. The method of moments is such an alternative. It is similar to the Yule-Walker estimator (see Sect. 5.1) applied to the autocorrelation function of $\{Z_t^2\}$. This method not only leads to an analytic solution, but can also be easily implemented. Following Kristensen and Linton (2006), we will illustrate the method for the GARCH(1,1) model.

Equation (8.13) applied to $\rho_{Z^2}(1)$ and $\rho_{Z^2}(2)$ constitutes a nonlinear equation system in the unknown parameters β and α_1. This system can be reparameterized to yield an equation system in $\varphi = \alpha_1 + \beta$ and β which can be reduced to a single quadratic equation in β:

$$\beta^2 - b\beta - 1 = 0 \quad \text{where } b = \frac{\varphi^2 + 1 - 2\rho_{Z^2}(1)\varphi}{\varphi - \rho_{Z^2}(1)}.$$

The parameter b is well-defined because $\varphi = \alpha_1 + \beta \geq \rho_{Z^2}(1)$ with equality only if $\beta = 0$. In the following we will assume that $\beta > 0$. Under this assumption $b > 2$ so that the only solution with the property $0 < \beta < 1$ is given by

$$\beta = \frac{b - \sqrt{b^2 - 4}}{2}.$$

The moment estimator can therefore be constructed as follows:

(i) Estimate the correlations $\rho_{\widehat{Z}^2}(1)$ and $\rho_{\widehat{Z}^2}(2)$ and $\hat{\sigma}^2$ based on the formulas (8.13) in Sect. 8.3.
(ii) An estimate for $\varphi = \alpha_1 + \beta$ is then given by

$$\widehat{\varphi} = \widehat{(\alpha_1 + \beta)} = \frac{\hat{\rho}_{\widehat{Z}^2}(2)}{\hat{\rho}_{\widehat{Z}^2}(1)}.$$

(iii) Use the estimate $\widehat{\varphi}$ to compute an estimate for b:

$$\hat{b} = \frac{\widehat{\varphi}^2 + 1 - 2\hat{\rho}_{\widehat{Z}^2}(1)\widehat{\varphi}}{\widehat{\varphi} - \hat{\rho}_{\widehat{Z}^2}(1)}.$$

The estimate $\hat{\beta}$ for β is then

$$\hat{\beta} = \frac{\hat{b} - \sqrt{\hat{b}^2 - 4}}{2}.$$

(iv) The estimate for α_1 is $\hat{\alpha}_1 = \widehat{\varphi} - \hat{\beta}$. Because $\alpha_0 = \sigma^2(1 - (\alpha_1 + \beta))$, the estimate for α_0 is equal to $\hat{\alpha}_0 = \hat{\sigma}^2(1 - \widehat{\varphi})$.

Kristensen and Linton (2006) show that, given the existence of the fourth moment of Z_t, this method of moment leads to consistent and asymptotically normal distributed estimates. These estimates may then serve as starting values for the maximization of the likelihood function to improve efficiency.

8.5 Example: Swiss Market Index (SMI)

This section illustrates the methods discussed previously to analyze the volatility of the Swiss Market Index (SMI). The SMI is the most important stock market index for Swiss blue chip companies. It is constructed solely from stock market prices; dividends are not accounted for. The data consists of daily values of the index between January 1, 1989, and December 31, 2023. Figure 1.5 shows a plot of the data. Instead of analyzing the level of the SMI, we will investigate the daily return computed as logged difference. This gives rise to 8'593 observations accounting

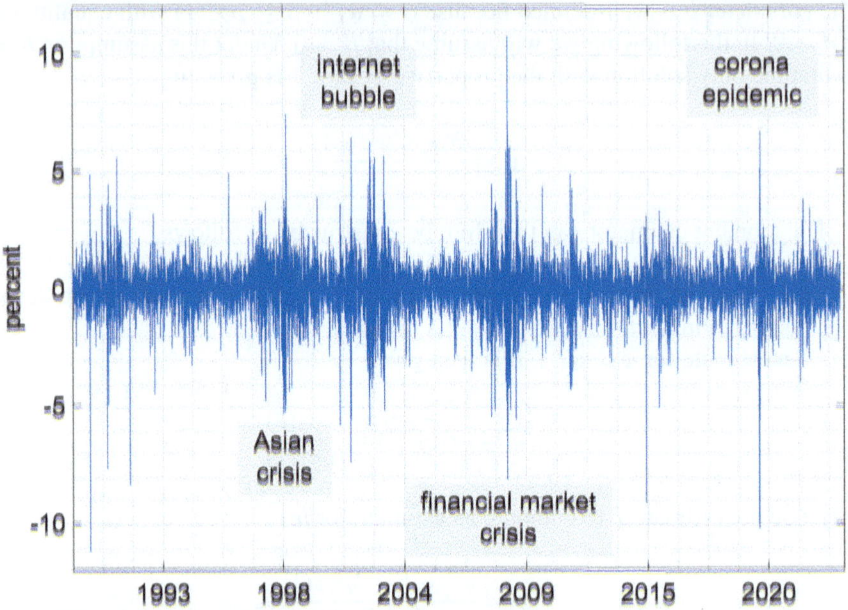

Fig. 8.3 Daily return of the SMI (Swiss Market Index) computed as $\Delta \log(\text{SMI}_t)$ between January 3, 1989, and November 15, 2023

for weekends and holidays. This time series is denoted by $X_t = \Delta \log(\text{SMI}_t)$ and plotted in Fig. 8.3. One can clearly discern phases of high volatility around the different crisis and low volatility between them. This represents a first sign of heteroskedasticity and positively correlated volatility.

Figure 8.4 shows a normal-quantile plot to compare the empirical distribution of the returns with those from a normal distribution. This plot clearly demonstrates that the probability of observing extreme values is bigger than warranted from a normal distribution. Thus, the distribution of returns is very likely to exhibit the heavy-tail property. A similar argument can be made by comparing the histogram of the returns and the density of a normal distribution with the same mean and the same variance shown in Fig. 8.5. Again one can see that absolutely large returns are more probable than expected from a normal distribution. Moreover, the histogram shows no obvious sign for an asymmetric distribution, but a higher peakedness.[13]

The next step in the analysis examines the estimated autocorrelation functions (ACF) of $\{X_t\}$ and $\{X_t^2\}$ plotted in Fig. 8.6. The estimated ACF of $\{X_t\}$ shows practically no significant autocorrelation so that we can consider $\{X_t\}$ be approximately white noise. A notable exception are the values for orders 1 and 5 which are outside the 95% confidence band given by ± 0.0205. The corresponding value of the Ljung-Box statistic with $L = 100$ is 179.02 which is just above the corresponding

[13] Part of this peak can be attributed to convention of putting zeros for the missing values.

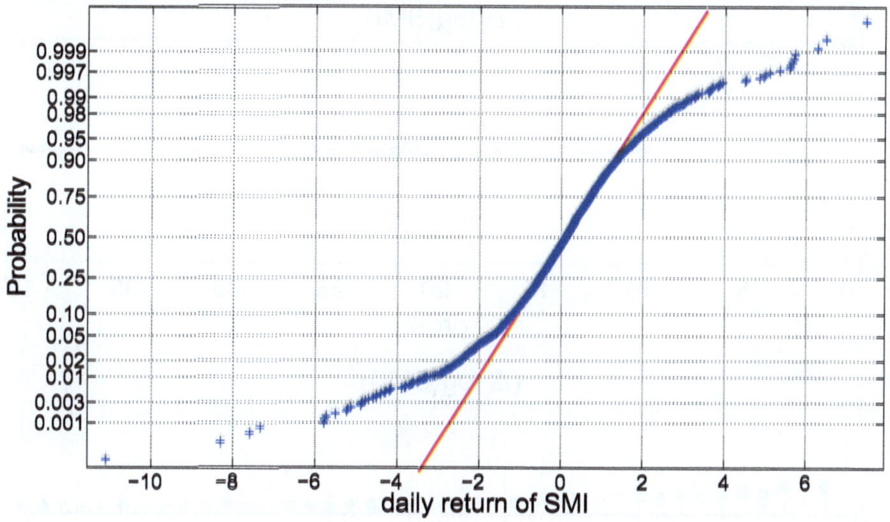

Fig. 8.4 Normal probability plot of the daily returns of the SMI (Swiss Market Index)

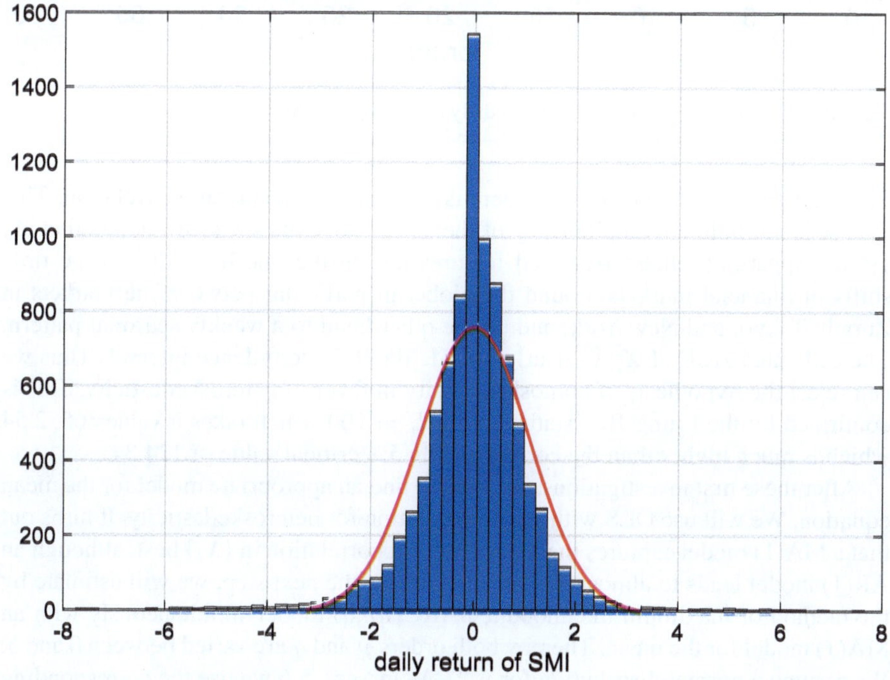

Fig. 8.5 Histogram of the daily returns of the SMI (Swiss Market Index) and the density of a fitted normal distribution (red line)

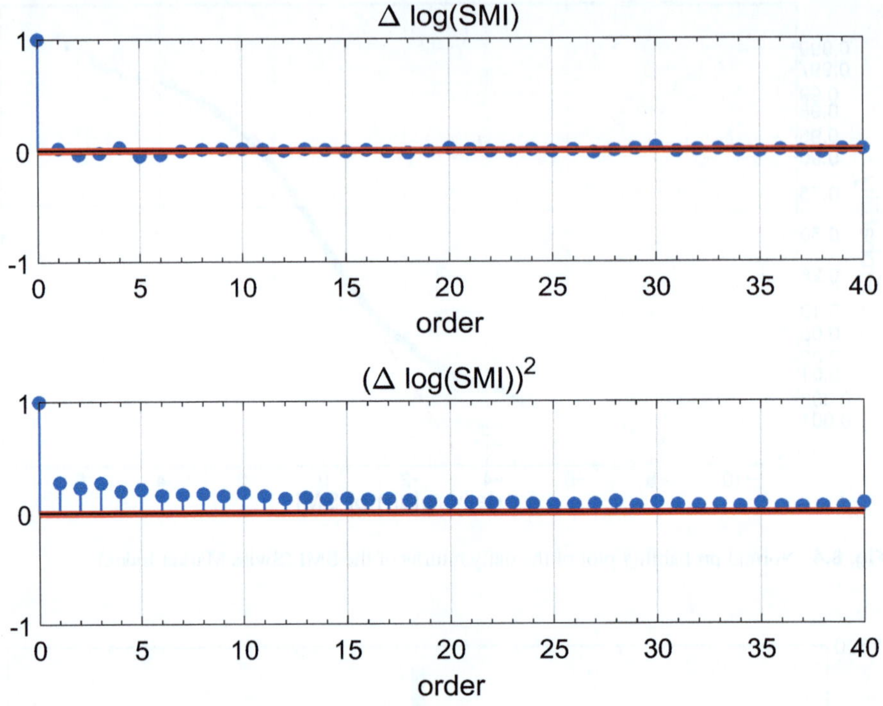

Fig. 8.6 ACF of daily returns and squared daily returns of the SMI

5% critical value of 124.34. Thus there is some sign of weak autocorrelation. This feature is not in line with efficiency of the Swiss stock market (see Campbell et al., 1997). Apparently, these observed features are on the one hand due to the time shifts of financial markets around the globe, in particular between the markets in Zurich, Tokyo, and New York, and on the other hand to a weekly seasonal pattern. The estimated ACF of X_t^2 is clearly outside the 95% confidence interval. Thus we can reject the hypothesis of homoskedasticity in favor of heteroskedasticity. This is confirmed by the Ljung-Box statistic with $L = 100$ which takes a values 6552.54 which is much higher than the corresponding 5% critical value of 124.34.

After these first investigations, we want to find an appropriate model for the mean equation. We will use OLS with White correction for heteroskedasticity. It turns out that a MA(1) model captures the first-order autocorrelation in $\{X_t\}$ best, although an AR(1) model leads to almost the same results. In the next step, we will estimate by the method of maximum likelihood a GARCH(p,q) model simultaneously with an MA(1) model for the mean. Thereby both orders p and q are varied between 0 and 5. We assume a normal distribution for ν_t.[14] As in Sect. 5.6 we use the corresponding

[14] All computations in this section are performed with MATLAB 2023b ©.

AIC and BIC values to select an appropriate model. As it turns out, AIC selects a GARCH(2,3) model whereas BIC favors a GARCH(1,1) model. We will continue working with the latter, the more parsimonious model

$$X_t = \underset{(0.0099)}{0.0521} + Z_t + \underset{(0.0116)}{0.0267} Z_{t-1}$$

with the corresponding variance equation

$$\sigma_t^2 = \underset{(0.0020)}{0.0454} + \underset{(0.0064)}{0.1387} Z_{t-1}^2 + \underset{(0.0064)}{0.8256} \sigma_{t-1}^2$$

where the estimated standard deviations are reported below the corresponding coefficient estimate. The small but significant value of 0.0267 for the MA(1) coefficient shows that there is a small but systematic correlation of the returns from one day to the next. This has to be expected given the ACF of $\Delta \log(\text{SMI})$ in upper panel of Fig. 8.6. The coefficients of the GARCH model are all positive, and their sum $\alpha_1 + \beta = 0.1387 + 0.8255 = 0.9643$ is statistically below one so that all conditions for the existence of stationary process are fulfilled.[15] Because $\sqrt{3}\frac{\alpha_1}{1-\beta} = \sqrt{3}\frac{0.1387}{1-0.8255} = 1.3771 > 1$, the condition for the existence of the fourth moment of Z_t is violated so that X_t is leptokurtic.

A significant improvement is obtained by using a t-distribution for ν_t and by introducing a threshold term:

$$X_t = \underset{(0.0088)}{0.0384} + Z_t + \underset{(0.0112)}{0.0209} Z_{t-1}$$

with the corresponding variance equation

$$\sigma_t^2 = \underset{(0.0035)}{0.0334} + \underset{(0.0084)}{0.0212} Z_{t-1}^2 + + \underset{(0.0140)}{0.1777} \mathbf{1}_{Z_{t-1}<0} Z_{t-1}^2 + \underset{(0.0096)}{0.8261} \sigma_{t-1}^2$$

The degrees of freedom for the t-distribution are estimated to be 7.9195 with estimated standard deviation 0.4464. The coefficient of the leverage term $\mathbf{1}_{Z_{t-1}<0} Z_{t-1}^2$ turns out to be significantly positive. Hence a downward movement of the SMI, i.e., $\mathbf{1}_{Z_{t-1}<0} = 1$, leads to an increase in volatility.

Value at Risk (VaR)

We are now in a position to use our ML estimates to compute the *value-at-risk* (VaR). The VaR is a popular measure to estimate the risk of an investment. In our case we consider the market portfolio represented by the stocks in the SMI. The VaR is defined as the maximal loss (in absolute value) of an investment which occurs

[15] The corresponding Wald test clearly rejects the null hypothesis $\alpha_1 + \beta = 1$ at a significance level of 1%.

with probability α over a time horizon h. Thus a 1% VaR for the return on the SMI for the next day is the threshold value of the return such that one can be confident with 99% that the loss will not exceed this value. Thus the α VaR at time t for h periods, $\text{VaR}^{\alpha}_{t,t+h}$, is nothing but the α-quantile of the distribution of the forecast of the return in h periods given information X_{t-k}, $k = 0, 1, 2, \ldots$. Formally, we have

$$\text{VaR}^{\alpha}_{t,t+h} = \inf\left\{x : \mathbf{P}\left[\widetilde{X}_{t+h} \leq x | X_t, X_{t-1}, \ldots\right] \geq \alpha\right\},$$

where $\widetilde{X}_{t+h}$ is the return of the portfolio over an investment horizon of h periods. This return is approximately equal to the sum of the daily returns: $\widetilde{X}_{t+h} = \sum_{j=1}^{h} X_{t+j}$.

The one period forecast error is given by $X_{t+1} - \widetilde{\mathbb{P}}_t X_{t+1}$ which is equal to $Z_{t+1} = \sigma_{t+1}\nu_{t+1}$. Thus the VaR for the next day is

$$\text{VaR}^{\alpha}_{t,t+1} = \inf\left\{x : \mathbf{P}\left[\nu_{t+1} \leq \frac{x - \widetilde{\mathbb{P}}_t X_{t+1}}{\sigma_{t+1}}\right] \geq \alpha\right\}.$$

This entity can be computed by replacing the forecast given the infinite past, $\widetilde{\mathbb{P}}_t X_{t+1}$, by a forecast given the finite sample information X_{t-k}, $k = 0, 1, 2, \ldots, t-1$, $\mathbb{P}_t X_{t+1}$, and by substituting σ_{t+1} by the corresponding forecast from variance equation, $\hat{\sigma}_{t,t+1}$. Thus we get

$$\widehat{\text{VaR}^{\alpha}_{t,t+1}} = \inf\left\{x : \mathbf{P}\left[\nu_{t+1} \leq \frac{x - \mathbb{P}_t X_{t+1}}{\hat{\sigma}_{t,t+1}}\right] \geq \alpha\right\}.$$

The computation of $\widehat{\text{VaR}^{\alpha}_{t,t+1}}$ requires to determine the α-quantile of the distribution of ν_t. This can be done in two ways. The first one uses the assumption about the distribution of ν_t explicitly. In the simplest case, ν_t is distributed as a standard normal so that the appropriate quantile can be easily retrieved. The 1% quantile for the standard normal distribution is -2.3263. The second approach is a non-parametric one and uses the empirical distribution function of $\hat{\nu}_t = \hat{Z}_t/\hat{\sigma}_t$ to determine the required quantile. This approach has the advantage that deviations from the standard normal distribution are accounted for. In our case, the 1% quantile is -2.6898 and thus considerably lower than the -2.3263 obtained from the normal distribution. Thus the VaR is under estimated by using the assumption of the normal distribution.

The corresponding computations for the SMI based on the estimated ARMA(0,1)-GARCH(1,1) model are reported in Table 8.1. A value of 2.53 for December 28, 2001, means that one can be 99% sure that the one period return of an investment in the stocks of the SMI will not be lower than -2.53%. The values for the non-parametric approach are typically considerably higher. The comparison of the VaR for different dates clearly shows how the risk evolves over time. It was particularly high at the time of the collapse of Lehman Brothers on September 15, 2008.

Table 8.1 One percent VaR for the next day of the return of the SMI according to the ARMA(0,1)-GARCH(1,1) model

Date	$\mathbb{P}_t X_{t+1}$	$\hat{\sigma}^2_{t,t+1}$	VaR ($\widehat{\text{VaR}^{0,01}_{t,t+1}}$) Parametric	Non-Parametric
28.12.2001	0.05	1.24	2.53	2.94
5.2.2003	0.07	2.37	3.51	4.07
15.9.2008	−0.06	3.93	5.67	5.39
17.2.2020	0.07	0.60	1.73	2.01
31.12.2023	0.07	0.40	1.41	1.64

8.6 Exercises

Exercise 8.6.1 *Let $\{Z_t\}$ be a GARCH(1,1) process.*

(i) *Show that the fourth moment of Z_t exists if $(\alpha_1 + \beta)^2 + 2\alpha_1^2 < 1$.*
(ii) *Show that the condition $\sqrt{3}\frac{\alpha_1}{1-\beta} < 1$ implies $(\alpha_1 + \beta)^2 + 2\alpha_1^2 < 1$.*
(iii) *Verify the formula (8.4) for the kurtosis κ of Z_t.*

Exercise 8.6.2 *Take a stock of your choice and perform a similar analysis for its price as in Sect. 8.5. Compare your results with a corresponding stock market index.*

Exercise 8.6.3 *Take an exchange rate of your choice and perform a similar analysis as in Sect. 8.5. Do exchange rates behave differently? Are they more volatile than typical stock market indices?*

Part II

Multivariate Time Series Analysis

9 Synopsis on Empirical Macroeconomic Research

Keynesian macroeconomic theory developed in the 1930s and 1940s, in particular its representation in terms of the IS- and LM-diagram, opened a new area in the application of statistical methods to economics, especially macroeconomics. Based on the path breaking work by Tinbergen (1939) and Klein (1950), this research gave rise to simultaneous equation systems which should capture all relevant aspect of an economy. The goal was to establish an empirically grounded tool which would enable the politicians to analyze the consequences of their policies and thereby fine-tune the economy to overcome or at least mitigate major business cycle fluctuations. This development was enhanced by the systematic compilation of national accounting data and by the advances in computer sciences.[1] These systems were typically built by putting together single equations such as consumption, investment, money demand, export and import, and Phillips-curve equations to an overall model. The Klein–Goldberger model for the United States was a first successful attempt in this direction (Klein and Goldberger 1955). Shocked by disturbances, Adelman and Adelman (1959) showed that these type of models exhibited cycles with properties similar to those found for the US economy.

As the model became more and detailed over time, they could, in the end, well include several hundreds or even thousands of equations. The climax of this development was the project LINK which linked the different national models to a world model by accounting for their interrelation through trade flows (Klein 1985). Although this research program brought many insights and spurred the development of econometrics as a separate field, by the mid-1970s, one had to admit that the idea to use large and very detailed models for forecasting and policy analysis was overly optimistic. In particular, the inability to forecast and cope with the oil crisis of the beginning 1970s raised doubts about the viability of this research strategy. In addition, more and more economist had concerns about the theoretical foundations of these models.

[1] See Epstein (1987) for an historical overview.

K. Neusser, *Time Series Econometrics*, Springer Texts in Business and Economics,
https://doi.org/10.1007/978-3-031-88838-0_9

The critique had several facets. First, it was argued that the bottom-up strategy of building a system from single equations is not compatible with general equilibrium theory which stresses the interdependence of economic activities. This insight was even reinforced by the advent of the theory of rational expectations. This theory postulated that expectations should be formed on the basis of all available information and not just by mechanically extrapolating from the past. This implies that developments in every part of the economy, in particular in the realm of economic policy making, should in principle be taken into account and shape the expectation formation. As expectations are omnipresent in almost every economic decision, all aspects of economic activities (consumption capital accumulation, investment, etc.) are inherently linked. Thus the strategy of using zero restrictions—which meant that certain variables were omitted from a particular equation—to identify the parameters in a simultaneous equation system was considered to be flawed. Second, the theory of rational expectations implied that the typical behavioral equations underlying these models are not invariant to changes in policies because economic agents would take into account systematic changes in the economic environment in their decision-making. This so-called Lucas-critique (Lucas 1976) undermined the basis for the existence of large simultaneous equation models. Third, simple univariate ARMA models proved to be as good in forecasting as the sophisticated large simultaneous models. Thus, it was argued that the effort or at least part of the effort devoted to these models was wasted.

In 1980, Sims (1980b) proposed an alternative modeling strategy. This strategy concentrates the modeling activity to only a few core variables, but places no restrictions whatsoever on the dynamic interrelation among them. Thus, every variable is considered to be endogenous and, in principle, dependent on all other variables of the model. In the linear context, the class of vector autoregressive (VAR) models has proven to be most convenient to capture this modeling strategy. They are easy to implement and to analyze. In contrast to the simultaneous equation approach, however, it is no longer possible to perform comparative static exercises and to analyze the effect of one variable on another one because every variable is endogenous a priori. Instead, one tries to identify and quantify the effect of shocks over time. These shocks are usually given some economic content, like demand or supply disturbances. However, these shocks are not directly observed, but are disguised behind the residuals from the VAR. Thus, the VAR approach also faces a fundamental identification problem. Since the seminal contribution by Sims, the literature has proposed several alternative identification schemes which will be discussed in Chap. 15 under the header of structural vector autoregressive (SVAR) models. The effects of these shocks are then further analyzed by computing impulse responses and forecast error variance decompositions.[2]

The reliance on shocks can be seen as a substitute for the lack of experiments in macroeconomics. The approach can be interpreted as a statistical analogue

[2] Watson (1994) and Kilian (2013) provide a general introduction. For an exhaustive treatment, see Kilian and Lütkepohl (2017).

to the identification of specific episodes where some unforseen event (shock) impinges on and propagates throughout the economy. Singling-out these episodes of quasi "natural experiments" as in Friedman and Schwartz (1963) convinced many economist of the role and effects of monetary policy.

Many concepts which have been introduced in the univariate context carry over in a straightforward manner to the multivariate context. However there are some new aspects. First, we will analyze the interaction among several variables. This can be done in a nonparametric way by examining the cross-correlations between time series or by building an explicit model. We will restrict ourselves to the class of VAR models as they are easy to handle and are overwhelmingly used in practice. Second, we will discuss several alternative approaches to identify the structural shocks from VAR models. After analyzing the identification problem in general, we describe short-run, long-run, and sign restrictions as possible remedies. Third, we will discuss the modeling of integrated variables in a more systematic way. In particular, we will extend the concept of cointegration to more than two variables. Finally, we will provide an introduction to the state space models as a general modeling approach. State space models are becoming increasingly popular in economics as they can be more directly linked to theoretical economic models.

Definitions and Stationarity

10

As in the univariate case, we start our exposition with the concept of stationarity which is also crucial in the multivariate setting. Before doing so, let us define the multivariate stochastic process.

Definition 10.1 (Stochastic process, multivariate) A multivariate stochastic process, $\{X_t\}$, is a family of random variables indexed by t, $t \in \mathbb{Z}$, defined on some given probability space. The random variables take values in $\mathbb{R}^n$, $n \geq 1$. n is called the dimension of the process.

Setting $n = 1$, the above definition includes as a special case univariate stochastic processes. This implies that the statements for multivariate processes carry over analogously to the univariate case. We view X_t as a column vector:

$$X_t = \begin{pmatrix} X_{1t} \\ \vdots \\ X_{nt} \end{pmatrix}.$$

Each element $\{X_{it}\}$ thereby represents a particular variable which may be treated as a univariate process. In example of Sect. 15.3.5, $\{X_t\}$ represents a multivariate process consisting of the growth rate of GDP Y_t, the unemployment rate U_t, the inflation rate P_t, the wage inflation rate W_t, and the growth rate of money M_t. Hence, in this example, $X_t = (Y_t, U_t, P_t, W_t, M_t)'$.

As in the univariate case, we characterize the joint distribution of the elements X_{it} and X_{jt} by the first two moments (if they exist), i.e., by the mean and the variance, respectively, covariance:

$$\begin{aligned} \mu_{it} &= \mathbb{E}X_{it}, \qquad i = 1, \ldots, n, \\ \gamma_{ij}(t,s) &= \mathbb{E}(X_{it} - \mu_{it})(X_{js} - \mu_{js}), \qquad i, j = 1, \ldots, n; \quad t, s \in \mathbb{Z}. \end{aligned} \tag{10.1}$$

K. Neusser, *Time Series Econometrics*, Springer Texts in Business and Economics,
https://doi.org/10.1007/978-3-031-88838-0_10

It is convenient to write these entities compactly as vectors and matrices:

$$\mu_t = \begin{pmatrix} \mu_{1t} \\ \vdots \\ \mu_{nt} \end{pmatrix} = \mathbb{E}X_t = \begin{pmatrix} \mathbb{E}X_{1t} \\ \vdots \\ \mathbb{E}X_{nt} \end{pmatrix}$$

$$\Gamma(t,s) = \begin{pmatrix} \gamma_{11}(t,s) & \dots & \gamma_{1n}(t,s) \\ \vdots & \ddots & \vdots \\ \gamma_{n1}(t,s) & \dots & \gamma_{nn}(t,s) \end{pmatrix} = \mathbb{E}(X_t - \mu_t)(X_s - \mu_s)'$$

Thus, we apply the expectations operator element-wise to vectors and matrices. The matrix-valued function $\Gamma(t,s)$ is called the *covariance function* of $\{X_t\}$.

In analogy to the univariate case, we define stationarity as the invariance of the first two moments to time shifts.

Definition 10.2 (Stationarity) A multivariate stochastic process $\{X_t\}$ is *stationary* if and only if for all integers r, s, and t we have:

(i) $\mu = \mu_t = \mathbb{E}X_t$ is constant (independent of t);
(ii) $\mathbb{E}X_t'X_t < \infty$;
(iii) $\Gamma(t,s) = \Gamma(t+r, s+r)$.

In the literature these properties are often called weak stationarity, covariance stationarity, or stationarity of second order. If $\{X_t\}$ is stationary, the covariance function only depends on the number of periods between t and s (i.e., on $t-s$) and not on t or s themselves. This implies that by setting $r = -s$ and $h = t - s$, the covariance function simplifies to

$$\begin{aligned}\Gamma(h) &= \Gamma(t-s) = \Gamma(t+r, s+r) = \Gamma(t+h, t) \\ &= \mathbb{E}(X_{t+h} - \mu)(X_t - \mu)' = \mathbb{E}(X_t - \mu)(X_{t-h} - \mu)'.\end{aligned}$$

For $h = 0$, $\Gamma(0)$ is the unconditional covariance matrix of X_t. Using the definition of the covariances in Eq. (10.1), we get

$$\Gamma(h) = \Gamma(-h)'.$$

Note that $\Gamma(h)$ is in general not symmetric for $h \neq 0$ because $\gamma_{ij}(h) \neq \gamma_{ji}(h)$ for $h \neq 0$.

Based on the covariance function of a stationary process, we define the *correlation function* $R(h)$ where $R(h) = (\rho_{ij}(h))_{i,j}$ with

$$\rho_{ij}(h) = \frac{\gamma_{ij}(h)}{\sqrt{\gamma_{ii}(0)\gamma_{jj}(0)}}.$$

In the case $i \neq j$, we refer to $\rho_{ij}(h)$ as the *cross-correlations* between two variables $\{X_{it}\}$ and $\{X_{jt}\}$. The correlation function can be written in matrix notation as

$$R(h) = V^{-1/2}\Gamma(h)V^{-1/2}$$

where V represents a diagonal matrix with diagonal elements equal to $\gamma_{ii}(0)$. Clearly, $\rho_{ii}(0) = 1$. As for the covariance matrix, we have that in general $\rho_{ij}(h) \neq \rho_{ji}(h)$ for $h \neq 0$. It is possible that $\rho_{ij}(h) > \rho_{ij}(0)$. We can summarize the properties of the covariance function by the following theorem.[1]

Theorem 10.1 *The covariance function of a stationary process $\{X_t\}$ has the following properties:*

(i) *For all $h \in \mathbb{Z}$, $\Gamma(h) = \Gamma(-h)'$;*
(ii) *for all $h \in \mathbb{Z}$, $|\gamma_{ij}(h)| \leq \sqrt{\gamma_{ii}(0) \times \gamma_{jj}(0)}$;*
(iii) *for each $i = 1, \ldots, n$, $\gamma_{ii}(h)$ is a univariate autocovariance function;*
(iv) *$\sum_{r,k=1}^{m} a_r'\Gamma(r-k)a_k \geq 0$ for all $m \in \mathbb{N}$ and all $a_1, \ldots, a_m \in \mathbb{R}^n$. This property is called non-negative definiteness (see Property 4 in Theorem 1.1 of Sect. 1.3 in the univariate case).*

Proof Property (i) follows immediately from the definition. Property (ii) is a consequence of the Cauchy-Bunyakovsky-Schwarz inequality (see theorem C.1). Property (iii) follows from the fact that $\gamma_{ii}(h)$ is the autocovariance function of the stationary process $\{X_{it}\}$. Property (iv) follows from $\mathbb{E}\left(\sum_{k=1}^{m} a_k'(X_{t-k} - \mu)\right)^2 \geq 0$. □

If not only the first two moments are invariant to time shifts, but the distribution as a whole, the process is said to be strictly stationarity.

Definition 10.3 (Strict stationarity) A multivariate process $\{X_t\}$ is called *strictly stationary* if and only if, for all $n \in \mathbb{N}$, $t_1, \ldots, t_n$, $h \in \mathbb{Z}$, the joint distributions of $(X_{t_1}, \ldots, X_{t_n})$ and $(X_{t_1+h}, \ldots, X_{t_n+h})$ are the same.

Example Consider the following example for $n = 2$:

$$X_{1t} = Z_t$$

$$X_{2t} = Z_t + 0.75Z_{t-2}$$

where $Z_t \sim \text{WN}(0, 1)$. We then have $\mu = \mathbb{E}X_t = 0$. The covariance function is given by

[1] We leave it to the reader to derive an analogous theorem for the correlation function.

$$\Gamma(h) = \begin{cases} \begin{pmatrix} 1 & 1 \\ 1 & 1.5625 \end{pmatrix}, & h = 0; \\ \begin{pmatrix} 0 & 0 \\ 0 & 0 \end{pmatrix}, & h = 1; \\ \begin{pmatrix} 0 & 0 \\ 0.75 & 0.75 \end{pmatrix}, & h = 2. \end{cases}$$

The covariance function is zero for $h > 2$. The values for $h < 0$ are obtained from property (i) in Theorem 10.1. The correlation function is

$$R(h) = \begin{cases} \begin{pmatrix} 1 & 0.8 \\ 0.8 & 1 \end{pmatrix}, & h = 0; \\ \begin{pmatrix} 0 & 0 \\ 0 & 0 \end{pmatrix}, & h = 1; \\ \begin{pmatrix} 0 & 0 \\ 0.60 & 0.48 \end{pmatrix}, & h = 2. \end{cases}$$

The correlation function is zero for $h > 2$. The values for $h < 0$ are obtained from property (i) in Theorem 10.1.

One idea in time series analysis is to construct more complicated process from simple ones, for example, by taking moving-averages. The simplest process is the white noise process which is uncorrelated with its own past. In the multivariate context, the white noise process is defined as follows.

Definition 10.4 (Multivariate white noise) A stochastic process $\{Z_t\}$ is called (multivariate) *white noise* with mean zero and covariance matrix $\Sigma > 0$, denoted by $Z_t \sim \text{WN}(0, \Sigma)$, if it is stationary and

$$\mathbb{E}Z_t = 0,$$

$$\Gamma(h) = \begin{cases} \Sigma, & h = 0; \\ 0, & h \neq 0. \end{cases}$$

If $\{Z_t\}$ is not only white noise, but independently and identically distributed, we write $Z_t \sim \text{IID}(0, \Sigma)$.

Remark 10.1 Even if each component of $\{Z_{it}\}$ is univariate white noise, this does not imply that $\{Z_t\} = \{(Z_{1t}, \ldots, Z_{nt})'\}$ is multivariate white noise. Take, for example, the process $Z_t = (u_t, u_{t-1})'$ where $u_t \sim \text{WN}(0, \sigma_u^2)$. Then $\Gamma(1) = \begin{pmatrix} 0 & 0 \\ \sigma_u^2 & 0 \end{pmatrix} \neq 0$.

Taking moving-averages of a white noise process, it is possible to generate new stationary processes. This leads to the definition of a linear process.

Definition 10.5 (Linear process) A stochastic process $\{X_t\}$ is called *linear* if there exists a representation

$$X_t = \sum_{j=-\infty}^{\infty} \Psi_j Z_{t-j}$$

where $Z_t \sim \text{IID}(0, \Sigma)$ and where the sequence $\{\Psi_j\}$ of the $n \times n$ matrices is absolutely summable, i.e., $\sum_{j=-\infty}^{\infty} \|\Psi_j\| < \infty$. If for all $j < 0$ $\Psi_j = 0$, the linear process is also called a MA(∞) process.

Theorem 10.2 *A linear process is stationary with mean of zero and covariance function*

$$\Gamma(h) = \sum_{j=-\infty}^{\infty} \Psi_{j+h} \Sigma \Psi_j' = \sum_{j=-\infty}^{\infty} \Psi_j \Sigma \Psi_{j-h}', \qquad h = 0, \pm 1, \pm 2, \ldots$$

Proof The required result is obtained by applying the properties of $\{Z_t\}$ to $\Gamma(h) = \mathbb{E} X_{t+h} X_t' = \lim_{m\to\infty} \mathbb{E}\left(\sum_{j=-m}^{m} \Psi_j Z_{t+h-j}\right)\left(\sum_{k=-m}^{m} \Psi_k Z_{t-k}\right)'$. □

Remark 10.2 The same conclusion is reached if $\{Z_t\}$ is a white noise process and not an IID process.

Insertion: Norm and Summability of Matrices
The definition of a linear process uses the convergence of a sequence of matrices $\{\Psi_j\}$, $j = 0, 1, 2, \ldots$. For this we need to define a norm for matrices. The literature considers different alternative definitions. For our purposes, the choice is not relevant as all norms are equivalent in finite dimensional vector spaces. We therefore choose the Frobenius, Hilbert–Schmidt, or Schur norm which is easy to compute.[2] This norm treats the elements of a $m \times n$ matrix $A = (a_{ij})$ as an element of the $\mathbb{R}^{m\times n}$ Euclidean space and defines the length of A, denoted by $\|A\|$, as $\|A\| = \sqrt{\sum_{i,j} a_{ij}^2}$. This leads to the formal definition below.

Definition 10.6 (Matrix norm) The Frobenius, Hilbert-Schmidt, or Schur norm of a $m \times n$ matrix A, denoted by $\|A\|$, is defined as

[2] For details see Meyer (2000, 279ff).

$$\|A\| = \sqrt{\sum_{i,j} a_{ij}^2} = \sqrt{\text{tr}(A'A)} = \sqrt{\sum_{i=1}^{n} \lambda_i}$$

where $\text{tr}(A'A)$ denotes the trace of $A'A$, i.e., the sum of the diagonal elements of $A'A$, and where λ_i are the n eigenvalues of $A'A$.

The matrix norm has the following properties:

$$\|A\| \geq 0 \quad \text{and} \quad \|A\| = 0 \text{ is equivalent to } A = 0,$$
$$\|\alpha A\| = |\alpha| \|A\| \text{ for all } \alpha \in \mathbb{R},$$
$$\|A\| = \|A'\|,$$
$$\|A + B\| \leq \|A\| + \|B\| \text{ for all matrices } A \text{ and } B \text{ of the same dimension},$$
$$\|AB\| \leq \|A\| \|B\| \text{ for all conformable matrices } A \text{ and } B.$$

The fourth and the last property are called *triangle inequality* and *submultiplicativity*, respectively.

A sequence of matrices $\{\Psi_j\}$, $j = 0, 1, \ldots$, is *absolutely summable* if and only if $\sum_{j=0}^{\infty} \|\Psi_j\| < \infty$ and *quadratic summable* if and only if $\sum_{j=0}^{\infty} \|\Psi_j\|^2 < \infty$. The absolute summability implies the quadratic summability, but not vice versa.

Corollary 10.1 *Absolute summability of $\{\Psi_j\}$ is equivalent to the absolute summability of each sequence $\{[\Psi_j]_{kl}\}$, $k, l = 1, \ldots, n$, i.e., to $\lim_{j\to\infty} |[\Psi_j]_{kl}|$ exists and is finite.*

Proof In particular, we have

$$|[\Psi_j]_{kl}| \leq \|\Psi_j\| = \sqrt{\sum_{k=1}^{n}\sum_{l=1}^{n} [\Psi_j]_{kl}^2} \leq \sum_{k=1}^{n}\sum_{l=1}^{n} |[\Psi_j]_{kl}|.$$

Summation over j gives

$$\sum_{j=0}^{\infty} |[\Psi_j]_{kl}| \leq \sum_{j=0}^{\infty} \|\Psi_j\| \leq \sum_{j=0}^{\infty}\sum_{k=1}^{n}\sum_{l=1}^{n} |[\Psi_j]_{kl}| = \sum_{k=1}^{n}\sum_{l=1}^{n}\sum_{j=0}^{\infty} |[\Psi_j]_{kl}|$$

The absolute convergence of each sequence $\{[\Psi_j]_{kl}\}$, $k, l = 1, \ldots, n$, follows from the absolute convergence of $\{\Psi_j\}$ by the first inequality. Conversely, the absolute convergence of $\{\Psi_j\}$ is implied by the absolute convergence of each sequence $\{[\Psi_j]_{kl}\}$, $k, l = 1, \ldots, n$, from the second inequality. □

Estimation of Mean and Covariance Function 11

11.1 Estimators and Their Asymptotic Distributions

As in the univariate case, stationary processes $\{X_t\}$ are described by their mean and (matrix) covariance functions. In the Gaussian case, this already characterizes the whole distribution. The estimation of these entities are therefore a crucial input in the empirical analysis. As it turns out, the results from the univariate process carry over analogously to the multivariate case. If the process is observed over the periods $t = 1, 2, \ldots, T$, then a natural estimator for the mean μ is the arithmetic mean or sample average

$$\widehat{\mu} = \overline{X}_T = \frac{1}{T}(X_1 + \ldots + X_T) = \begin{pmatrix} \overline{X}_1 \\ \vdots \\ \overline{X}_n \end{pmatrix}$$

and a theorem analogous to Theorem 4.1 in Sect. 4.1 applies.

Theorem 11.1 *Let $\{X_t\}$ be stationary process with mean μ and covariance function $\Gamma(h)$ then asymptotically, for $T \to \infty$,*

$$\mathbb{E}\left(\overline{X}_T - \mu\right)'\left(\overline{X}_T - \mu\right) \to 0, \text{ if } \gamma_{ii}(T) \to 0 \text{ for all } 1 \le i \le n;$$

$$T\mathbb{E}\left(\overline{X}_T - \mu\right)'\left(\overline{X}_T - \mu\right) \to \sum_{i=1}^{n}\sum_{h=-\infty}^{\infty} \gamma_{ii}(h),$$

$$\text{if } \sum_{h=-\infty}^{\infty} |\gamma_{ii}(h)| < \infty \text{ for all } 1 \le i \le n.$$

K. Neusser, *Time Series Econometrics*, Springer Texts in Business and Economics,
https://doi.org/10.1007/978-3-031-88838-0_11

Proof The Theorem can be established by applying Theorem 4.1 individually to each time series $\{X_{it}\}$, $i = 1, 2, \dots, n$. □

Thus, the sample average converges in mean square and therefore also in probability to the true mean. Thereby the second condition is more restrictive than the first one. They are, in particular, fulfilled for all VARMA processes (see Chap. 12). As in the univariate case analyzed in Sect. 4.1, it can be shown with some mild additional assumptions that $\overline{X}_T$ is also asymptotically normally distributed.

Theorem 11.2 *For any stationary process* $\{X_t\}$

$$X_t = \mu + \sum_{j=-\infty}^{\infty} \Psi_j Z_{t-j}$$

with $Z_t \sim \mathrm{IID}(0, \Sigma)$, $\sum_{j=-\infty}^{\infty} \|\Psi_j\| < \infty$, *and* $\sum_{-j=\infty}^{\infty} \Psi_j \neq 0$ *the arithmetic average* $\overline{X}_T$ *is asymptotically normal*

$$\sqrt{T}\left(\overline{X}_T - \mu\right) \xrightarrow{d} \mathrm{N}(0, \Omega)$$

where Ω *is known as the long-run variance given by*

$$\Omega = \sum_{h=-\infty}^{\infty} \Gamma(h) = \left(\sum_{j=-\infty}^{\infty} \Psi_j\right) \Sigma \left(\sum_{j=-\infty}^{\infty} \Psi_j'\right). \tag{11.1}$$

Proof The proof is a straightforward extension to the multivariate case of the one given for Theorem 4.2 of Sect. 4.1. □

The summability condition is quite general. It is, in particular, fulfilled by causal VARMA processes (see Chap. 12) as their coefficients matrices Ψ_j go exponentially fast to zero. The condition $\sum_{-j=\infty}^{\infty} \Psi_j \neq 0$ ensures that the long-run variance Ω is positive definite (regular). Remarks similar to those following Theorem 4.2 apply also in the multivariate case.

The above formula can be used to construct confidence regions for μ. This turns out, however, to be relatively complicated in practice so that often univariate approximations are used instead (Brockwell and Davis 1996, 228–229).

As in the univariate case, a natural estimator for the covariance matrix function $\Gamma(h)$ is given by the corresponding empirical moments $\widehat{\Gamma}(h)$:

$$\widehat{\Gamma}(h) = \begin{cases} T^{-1} \sum_{t=1}^{T-h} \left(X_{t+h} - \overline{X}_T\right)\left(X_t - \overline{X}_T\right)', & 0 \leq h \leq T-1; \\ \widehat{\Gamma}'(-h), & -T+1 \leq h < 0. \end{cases}$$

The estimator of the covariance function can then be applied to derive an estimator for the correlation function

$$\widehat{R}(h) = \hat{V}^{-1/2}\widehat{\Gamma}(h)\hat{V}^{-1/2}$$

where $\hat{V}^{1/2} = \operatorname{diag}\left(\sqrt{\hat{\gamma}_{11}(0)}, \ldots, \sqrt{\hat{\gamma}_{nn}(0)}\right)$. Under the conditions given in Theorem 11.2, the estimator of the covariance matrix of order h, $\widehat{\Gamma}(h)$, converges to the true covariance matrix $\Gamma(h)$. Moreover, $\sqrt{T}\left(\widehat{\Gamma}(h) - \Gamma(h)\right)$ is asymptotically normally distributed. In particular, we can state the following Theorem.

Theorem 11.3 *For any stationary process* $\{X_t\}$ *with*

$$X_t = \mu + \sum_{j=-\infty}^{\infty} \Psi_j Z_{t-j}$$

where $Z_t \sim \text{IID}(0, \Sigma)$, $\sum_{j=-\infty}^{\infty} \|\Psi_j\| < \infty$, *and* $\sum_{j=-\infty}^{\infty} \Psi_j \neq 0$ *the covariance matrix* $\widehat{\Gamma}(h)$ *converges for every fixed h in probability as* $T \to \infty$ *to* $\Gamma(h)$*:*

$$\widehat{\Gamma}(h) \xrightarrow{\;p\;} \Gamma(h)$$

Proof A proof can be given along the lines of Proposition 13.1. □

A non-parametric estimator of the long-run variance Ω defined in Eq. (11.1) is given by the following class of estimators:

$$\widehat{\Omega}_T = \sum_{h=-T+1}^{T-1} k\left(\frac{h}{\ell_T}\right)\widehat{\Gamma}(h)$$

where $k(x)$ is a kernel function and where $\widehat{\Gamma}(h)$ is the corresponding estimate of the covariance matrix at lag h. For the choice of the kernel function and the lag truncation parameter, the same principles apply as in the univariate case (see Sect. 4.4 and the corresponding references).

11.2 Testing Bivariate Cross-Correlations

The determination of the asymptotic distribution of $\widehat{\Gamma}(h)$ is complicated. We therefore restrict ourselves to the case of two time series.

Theorem 11.4 *Let $\{X_t\}$ be a bivariate stochastic process whose components can be described by*

$$X_{1t} = \sum_{j=-\infty}^{\infty} \alpha_j Z_{1,t-j} \quad \textit{with } Z_{1t} \sim \text{IID}(0, \sigma_1^2)$$

$$X_{2t} = \sum_{j=-\infty}^{\infty} \beta_j Z_{2,t-j} \quad \textit{with } Z_{2t} \sim \text{IID}(0, \sigma_2^2)$$

where $\{Z_{1t}\}$ and $\{Z_{2t}\}$ are independent from each other at all leads and lags and where $\sum_j |\alpha_j| < \infty$ and $\sum_j |\beta_j| < \infty$. Under these conditions the asymptotic distribution of the estimator of the cross-correlation function $\rho_{12}(h)$ between $\{X_{1t}\}$ and $\{X_{2t}\}$ is

$$\sqrt{T}\hat{\rho}_{12}(h) \xrightarrow{d} \text{N}\left(0, \sum_{j=-\infty}^{\infty} \rho_{11}(j)\rho_{22}(j)\right), \qquad h \geq 0. \tag{11.2}$$

For all h and k, $h \neq k$, $\left(\sqrt{T}\hat{\rho}_{12}(h), \sqrt{T}\hat{\rho}_{12}(k)\right)'$ converges in distribution to a bivariate normal distribution with mean zero, variances $\sum_{j=-\infty}^{\infty} \rho_{11}(j)\rho_{22}(j)$ and covariances $\sum_{j=-\infty}^{\infty} \rho_{11}(j)\rho_{22}(j+k-h)$.

This result can be used to construct a test of independence, or more precisely uncorrelatedness, between two time series. The above theorem, however, shows that the asymptotic distribution of $\sqrt{T}\hat{\rho}_{12}(h)$ depends on $\rho_{11}(h)$ and $\rho_{22}(h)$ and is therefore unknown. Thus, the test cannot be based on the estimated cross-correlation alone.[1]

This problem can, however, be overcome by implementing the following two-step procedure suggested by Haugh (1976).

First step: Estimate for each times series a univariate invertible ARMA model and compute the resulting residuals $\hat{Z}_{it} = \sum_{j=0}^{\infty} \hat{\pi}_j^{(i)} X_{i,t-j}$, $i = 1, 2$. If the ARMA models correspond to the true ones, these residuals should approximately be white noise. This first step is called pre-whitening.

Second step: Under the null hypothesis, the two time series $\{X_{1t}\}$ and $\{X_{2t}\}$ are uncorrelated with each other. This implies that the residuals $\{Z_{1t}\}$ and $\{Z_{2t}\}$ should also be uncorrelated with each other. The variance of the cross-correlations between $\{Z_{1t}\}$ and $\{Z_{2t}\}$ is therefore asymptotically equal to $1/T$ under the null hypothesis. Thus, one can apply the result of Theorem 11.4 to construct confidence intervals based on formula (11.2). A 95% confidence

[1] The theorem may also be used to conduct a causality test between two times series (see Sect. 14.5).

interval is therefore given by $\pm\, 1.96T^{-1/2}$. The Theorem may also be used to construct a test whether the two series are uncorrelated.

If one is not interested in modeling the two time series explicitly, the simplest way is to estimate a high-order AR model in the first step. Thereby, the order should be chosen high enough to obtain approximately white noise residuals in the first step. Instead of looking at each cross-correlation separately, one may also test the joint null hypothesis that all cross-correlations are simultaneously equal to zero. Such a test can be based on T times the sum of the squared cross-correlation coefficients. This statistic is distributed as a χ^2 with L degrees of freedom where L is the number of summands (see the Haugh-Pierce statistic (14.10) in Sect. 14.5).

11.3 Examples for Independence Tests

Two Independent AR Processes

Consider two AR(1) process $\{X_{1t}\}$ and $\{X_{2t}\}$ governed by the following stochastic difference equation $X_{it} = 0.8X_{i,t-1} + Z_{it}$, $i = 1, 2$. The two white noise processes $\{Z_{1t}\}$ and $\{Z_{2t}\}$ are such that they are independent from each other. $\{X_{1t}\}$ and $\{X_{2t}\}$ are therefore independent from each other too. We simulate realizations of these two processes over 400 periods. The estimated cross-correlation function of these so-generated processes are plotted in the upper panel of Fig. 11.1. From there one can see that many values are outside the 95% confidence interval given by $\pm$ $1.96T^{-1/2} = 0.098$, despite the fact that by construction both series are independent of each other. The reason is that the so computed confidence interval is not correct because it does not take the autocorrelation of each series into account. The application of Theorem 11.4 leads to the much larger 95% confidence interval of

$$\frac{\pm 1.96}{\sqrt{T}}\sqrt{\sum_{j=-\infty}^{\infty}\rho_{11}(j)\rho_{22}(j)} = \frac{\pm 1.96}{20}\sqrt{\sum_{j=-\infty}^{\infty} 0.8^j 0.8^j}$$

$$= \frac{\pm 1.96}{20}\sqrt{1+\frac{2\times 0.64}{1-0.64}} = \pm 0.209$$

which is more than twice as large. This confidence interval then encompasses most the cross-correlations computed with respect to the original series.

If one follows the testing procedure outline above instead and fits an AR(10) model for each process and then estimates the cross-correlation function of the corresponding residual series (filtered or pre-whitened time series), the plot in the lower panel of Fig. 11.1 is obtained.[2] This figure shows no significant cross-

[2] The order of the AR processes are set arbitrarily equal to 10 which is more than enough to obtain white noise residuals.

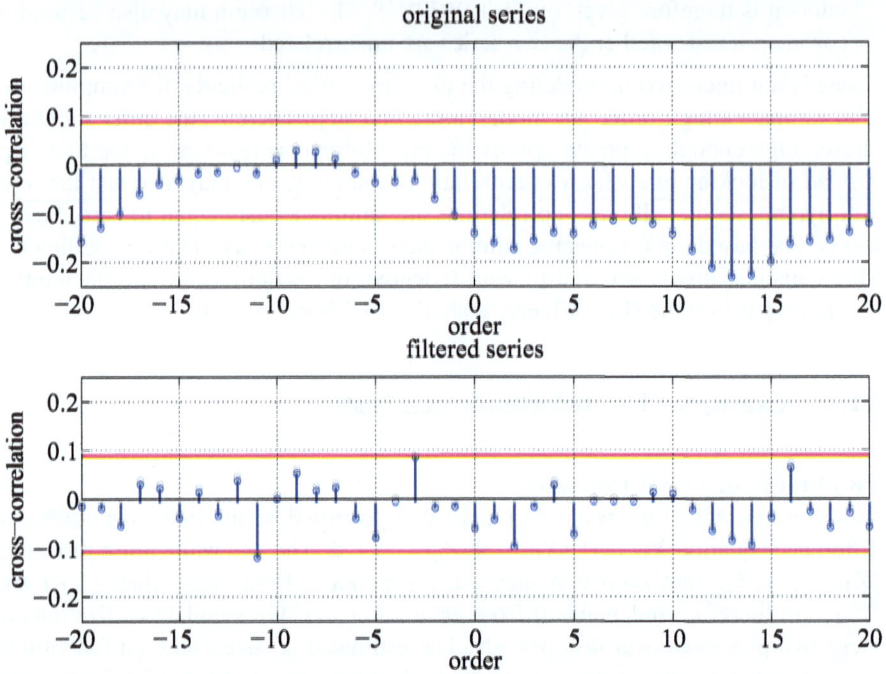

Fig. 11.1 Cross-correlations between two independent AR(1) processes with $\phi = 0.8$

correlation anymore so that one cannot reject the null hypothesis that both time series are independent from each other.

Consumption Expenditure and Advertisement

This application focuses on the interaction between nominal aggregate private consumption expenditure and nominal aggregate advertisement expenditures. Such an investigation was first conducted by Ashley et al. (1980) for the United States.[3] The upper panel of Fig. 11.2 shows the raw cross-correlations between the two time series where the order h runs from -20 to $+20$. Although almost all cross-correlations are positive and outside the conventional confidence interval, it would be misleading to infer a statistically significant positive cross-correlation. In order to test for independence, we filter both time series by an AR(10) model and estimate the cross-correlations for the residuals.[4] These are displayed in the lower panel of Fig. 11.2. In this figure, only the correlations of order 0 and 16 fall outside the confidence interval and can thus be considered as statistically significant. Thus, we can reject the null hypothesis of independence between the two series. However,

[3] The quarterly data are taken from Berndt (1991). They cover the period from the first quarter of 1956 to the fourth quarter of 1975. In order to achieve stationarity, we work with first differences.

[4] The order of the AR processes are set arbitrarily equal to 10 which is more than enough to obtain white noise residuals.

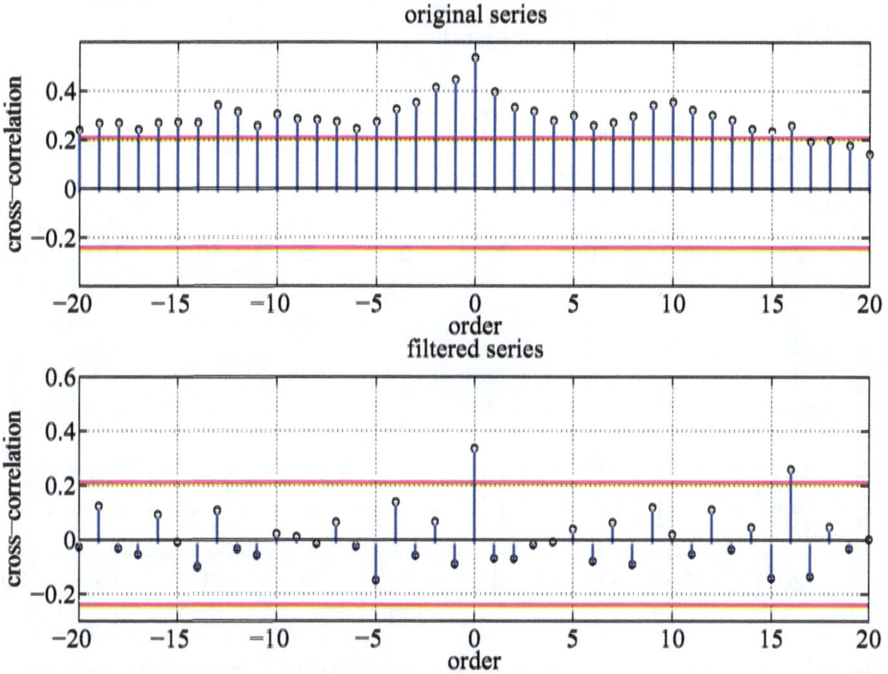

Fig. 11.2 Cross-correlations between aggregate nominal private consumption expenditures and aggregate nominal advertisement expenditures

most of the interdependence seems to come from the contemporaneous cross-correlation $\hat{\rho}_{12}(0)$. This is confirmed by a more detailed investigation in Berndt (1991) where no significant lead and/or lag relations are found.

Real Gross Domestic Product and Consumer Sentiment

The procedure outlined above can be used to examine whether one of the two time series is systematically leading, respectively lagging the other one. This is, for example, important in the judgment of the current state of the economy because first provisional national accounting data are usually published with a lag of at least one quarter. However, in the conduct of monetary policy more up-to-date knowledge is necessary. Such knowledge can be retrieved from leading indicator variables. These variables should be available earlier and be highly correlated with the variable of interest at a lead.

We investigate whether the Consumer Sentiment Index is a leading indicator for the percentage changes in real gross domestic product (GDP).[5] The raw cross-correlations are plotted in the upper panel of Fig. 11.3. It shows correlations at lags

[5] We use quarterly data from 1980:2 to 2023:4 for Switzerland as published by the State Secretariat for Economic Affairs SECO.

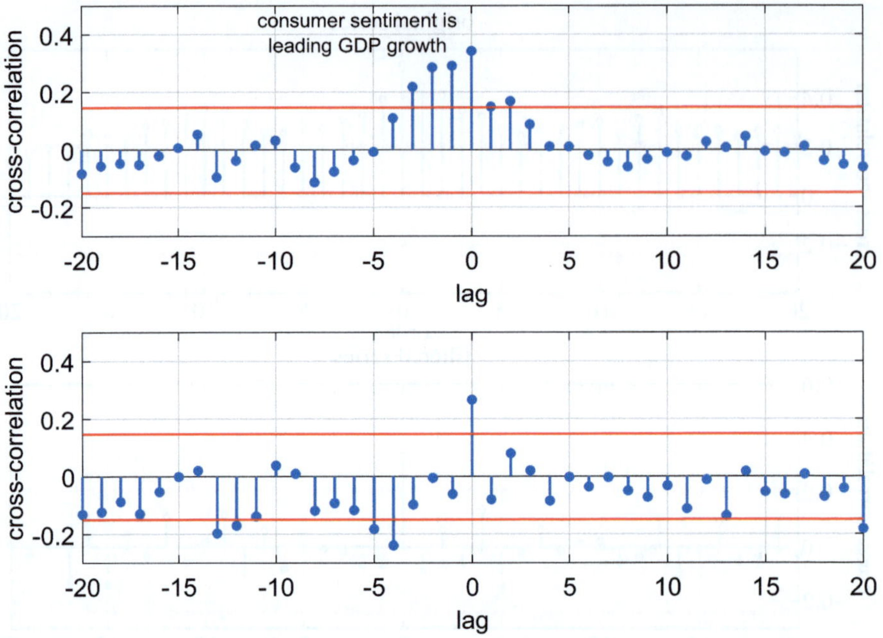

Fig. 11.3 Cross-correlations between real growth of GDP and the Consumer Sentiment Index

0, -1, -2, and -3 are outside the conventional confidence interval which would indicate that consumer sentiment is leading GDP growth.[6] However, the use of the conventional confidence intervals is misleading as the distribution of the raw cross-correlations depends on the autocorrelations of each series. Thus, instead we filter both time series by an AR(8) model and investigate the cross-correlations of the residuals.[7] The order of the AR model was chosen deliberately high to account for all autocorrelations. The cross-correlations of the filtered data are displayed in the lower panel of Fig. 11.3. As it turns out, that except for the positive contemporaneous correlation ($h = 0$), no other correlation is significantly different from zero. The Consumer Sentiment Index is therefore not a leading indicator for GDP growth. However, as national account data are published with a lag of more than one quarter, Consumer Sentiment data are still relevant in the assessment for the current economic situation.

[6] During the interpretation of the cross-correlations be aware of the ordering of the variables because $\rho_{12}(1) = \rho_{21}(-1) \neq \rho_{21}(1)$.

[7] With quarterly data it is wise to set to order as a multiple of four to account for possible seasonal movements. As it turns out $p = 8$ is more than enough to obtain white noise residuals.

11.4 Exercises

Exercise 11.4.1 Consider the following ARMA(1,1) process:

$$\begin{pmatrix} X_{1t} \\ X_{2t} \end{pmatrix} = \begin{pmatrix} 0.7 & 0 \\ 0 & 0.6 \end{pmatrix} \begin{pmatrix} X_{1,t-1} \\ X_{2,t-1} \end{pmatrix} + \begin{pmatrix} Z_{1t} \\ Z_{2t} \end{pmatrix} + \begin{pmatrix} 0.5 & 0.6 \\ -0.7 & 0.8 \end{pmatrix} \begin{pmatrix} Z_{1,t-1} \\ Z_{2,t-1} \end{pmatrix}$$

where $Z_t \sim \text{IID N}\left(\begin{pmatrix} 0 \\ 0 \end{pmatrix}, \begin{pmatrix} 1 & 0.71 \\ 0.71 & 1 \end{pmatrix} \right)$.

Compute the autocovariance function of $\{(X_{1t}, X_{2t})'\}$.

Exercise 11.4.2 You investigate the interdependence between real GDP growth, $\{Y_t\}$, and the growth rate in real fixed investment, $\{I_t\}$, over a period of 100 quarters. The estimated cross-correlations are listed in the Table 11.1.

(i) Construct a 95% confidence interval for the cross-correlations.
(ii) Is there a significant correlation between the two series?
(iii) Which series is leading? Which series is causal with respect to the other one in the sense of Granger (see the Pierce-Haugh statistic in Sect. 14.5)?
(iv) Is the use of the cross-correlations correct? How should the procedure be possibly modified?

Exercise 11.4.3 Investigate the lead/lag relationships between the following time series using actual data from a country of your choice:

(i) Manufacturing production and manufacturer's new orders;
(ii) Stock market return and economic performance as measured by real GDP growth or growth in manufacturing production;
(iii) Interest rate and residential construction;
(iv) Inflation and money stocks M1, M2, or M3.

Table 11.1 Estimated cross-correlations between $\{Y_t\}$ und $\{I_t\}$

h	$\rho(Y_t, I_{t-h})$	$\rho(Y_t, I_{t+h})$
0	0.29	0.29
1	0.16	0.30
2	−0.01	0.02
3	0.09	0.10
4	0.06	0.07

Vector Autoregressive Moving-Average Processes

12

As in the univariate case, vector autoregressive moving-average processes (VARMA processes or just ARMA processes) constitute by far the most important model class when it comes to empirical applications. These models arise as solutions to linear stochastic difference equations with constant coefficients.

Definition 12.1 (VARMA process) A stochastic process $\{X_t\}$ of dimension n is a *vector autoregressive moving-average process* of order (p, q), VARMA(p, q) process, if it fulfills the stochastic difference equation

$$X_t - \Phi_1 X_{t-1} - \ldots - \Phi_p X_{t-p} = Z_t + \Theta_1 Z_{t-1} + \ldots + \Theta_q Z_{t-q} \qquad (12.1)$$

where $\Phi_1, \ldots, \Phi_p, \Theta_1, \ldots, \Theta_q$ are $n \times n$ matrices such that $\Phi_p \neq 0$ and $\Theta_q \neq 0$ and where $Z_t \sim \text{WN}(0, \Sigma)$ with positiv definite covariance matrix Σ. $\{X_t\}$ is called a VARMA(p, q) process with mean μ if $\{X_t - \mu\}$ is a VARMA(p, q) process.

With the aid of the lag operator, we can write the difference equation compactly as

$$\Phi(\text{L})X_t = \Theta(\text{L})Z_t$$

where $\Phi(\text{L}) = \text{I}_n - \Phi_1\text{L} - \ldots - \Phi_p\text{L}^p$ and $\Theta(\text{L}) = \text{I}_n + \Theta_1\text{L} + \ldots + \Theta_q\text{L}^q$. $\Phi(\text{L})$ and $\Theta(\text{L})$ are $n \times n$ matrices whose elements are lag polynomials of order smaller or equal to p, respectively q. If $q = 0$, $\Theta(\text{L}) = \text{I}_n$ so that there is no moving-average part. The process is then a purely autoregressive one which is simply called a VAR(p) process. Similarly if $p = 0$, $\Phi(\text{L}) = \text{I}_n$, and there is no autoregressive part. The process is then a purely moving-average one and simply called a VMA(q) process. The theoretical importance of VARMA processes stems from the fact that every stationary process can be arbitrarily well approximated by a stationary VARMA, VAR, or VMA process.

K. Neusser, *Time Series Econometrics*, Springer Texts in Business and Economics,
https://doi.org/10.1007/978-3-031-88838-0_12

12.1 VAR(1) Processes

We start our discussion by analyzing the properties of the VAR(1) processes defined as solutions to the stochastic difference equations of the form

$$X_t = \Phi X_{t-1} + Z_t \quad \text{with } Z_t \sim \mathrm{WN}(0, \Sigma).$$

We assume that all eigenvalues $\lambda_1, \ldots, \lambda_n$ of Φ are absolutely strictly smaller than one. As the eigenvalues correspond to the inverses of the roots of the matrix polynomial $\det(\Phi(z)) = \det(I_n - \Phi z)$, this assumption implies that all roots must lie outside the unit circle:

$$\det(\mathrm{I}_n - \Phi z) \neq 0 \text{ for all } z \in \mathbb{C} \text{ with } |z| \leq 1.$$

For the sake of exposition, we will further assume that Φ is diagonalizable, i.e., there exists an invertible matrix P such that $J = P^{-1}\Phi P$ is a diagonal matrix with the eigenvalues of Φ on the diagonal.[1]

Consider the stochastic process

$$X_t = Z_t + \Phi Z_{t-1} + \Phi^2 Z_{t-2} + \ldots = \sum_{j=0}^{\infty} \Phi^j Z_{t-j}.$$

We will show that this process is stationary and fulfills the first-order difference equation above. For $\{X_t\}$ to be well-defined, we must show that $\sum_{j=0}^{\infty} \|\Phi^j\| < \infty$. Using the properties of the matrix norm leads to

$$\begin{aligned}\sum_{j=0}^{\infty} \|\Phi^j\| = \sum_{j=0}^{\infty} \|\mathrm{P} J^j \mathrm{P}^{-1}\| &\leq \sum_{j=0}^{\infty} \|\mathrm{P}\| \|J^j\| \|\mathrm{P}^{-1}\| \\ &\leq \sum_{j=0}^{\infty} \|\mathrm{P}\| \, \|\mathrm{P}^{-1}\| \sqrt{\sum_{i=1}^{n} |\lambda_i|^{2j}} \\ &\leq \|\mathrm{P}\| \, \|\mathrm{P}^{-1}\| \sqrt{n} \sum_{j=0}^{\infty} |\lambda_{\max}|^{2j} < \infty,\end{aligned}$$

where $\lambda_{\max}$ denotes the maximal eigenvalue of Φ in absolute terms. As all eigenvalues are required to be strictly smaller than one in absolute terms, this clearly

[1] The following exposition remains valid even if Φ is not diagonalizable. In this case one has to rely on the Jordan canonical form which requires somewhat more intricate computations (Meyer 2000).

also holds for $\lambda_{\max}$ so that infinite matrix sum converges. This implies that the process $\{X_t\}$ is stationary. In addition, we have that

$$X_t = \sum_{j=0}^{\infty} \Phi^j Z_{t-j} = Z_t + \Phi \sum_{j=0}^{\infty} \Phi^j Z_{t-1-j} = \Phi X_{t-1} + Z_t.$$

Thus, the process $\{X_t\}$ also fulfills the difference equation.

Next we demonstrate that this process is also the unique stationary solution to the difference equation. Suppose that there exists another stationary process $\{Y_t\}$ which also fulfills the difference equation. By successively iterating the difference equation

$$\begin{aligned} Y_t &= Z_t + \Phi Z_{t-1} + \Phi^2 Y_{t-2} \\ &\ldots \\ &= Z_t + \Phi Z_{t-1} + \Phi^2 Z_{t-2} + \ldots + \Phi^k Z_{t-k} + \Phi^{k+1} Y_{t-k-1}. \end{aligned}$$

Because $\{Y_t\}$ is assumed to be stationary, $\mathbb{V}Y_t = \mathbb{V}Y_{t-k-1} = \Gamma(0)$ so that

$$\mathbb{V}\left(Y_t - \sum_{j=0}^{k} \Phi^j Z_{t-j}\right) = \Phi^{k+1}\mathbb{V}(Y_{t-k-1})\Phi'^{k+1} = \Phi^{k+1}\Gamma(0)\Phi'^{k+1}.$$

The submultiplicativity of the norm then implies

$$\left\|\Phi^{k+1}\Gamma(0)\Phi'^{k+1}\right\| \leq \left\|\Phi^{k+1}\right\|^2 \|\Gamma(0)\| = \|P\|^2\|P^{-1}\|^2\|\Gamma(0)\| \left(\sum_{i=1}^{n} |\lambda_i|^{2(k+1)}\right).$$

As all eigenvalues of Φ are absolutely strictly smaller than one, the right hand side of the above expression converges to zero for k going to infinity. This implies that Y_t and $X_t = \sum_{j=0}^{\infty} \Phi^j Z_{t-j}$ are equal in the mean square sense and thus also in probability.

Based on Theorem 10.2, the mean and the covariance function of the VAR(1) process are

$$\mathbb{E}X_t = \sum_{j=0}^{\infty} \Phi^j \mathbb{E}Z_{t-j} = 0,$$

$$\Gamma(h) = \sum_{j=0}^{\infty} \Phi^{j+h}\Sigma\Phi'^j = \Phi^h \sum_{j=0}^{\infty} \Phi^j \Sigma \Phi'^j = \Phi^h \Gamma(0).$$

Analogously to the univariate case, it can be shown that there still exists a unique stationary solution if all eigenvalues of Φ are absolutely strictly greater than one.

This solution is, however, no longer causal with respect to $\{Z_t\}$. If some eigenvalues of Φ are on the unit circle, there exists no stationary solution.

12.2 Representation in Companion Form

A VAR(p) process of dimension n can be represented as a VAR(1) process of dimension $p \times n$. For this purpose we define the pn vector $Y_t = (X_t', X_{t-1}', \ldots, X_{t-p+1}')'$. This new process $\{Y_t\}$ is characterized by the following first-order stochastic difference equation:

$$Y_t = \begin{pmatrix} X_t \\ X_{t-1} \\ X_{t-2} \\ \vdots \\ X_{t-p+1} \end{pmatrix} = \begin{pmatrix} \Phi_1 & \Phi_2 & \ldots & \Phi_{p-1} & \Phi_p \\ I_n & 0 & \ldots & 0 & 0 \\ 0 & I_n & \ldots & 0 & 0 \\ \vdots & \vdots & \ddots & \vdots & \vdots \\ 0 & 0 & \ldots & I_n & 0 \end{pmatrix} \begin{pmatrix} X_{t-1} \\ X_{t-2} \\ X_{t-3} \\ \vdots \\ X_{t-p} \end{pmatrix} + \begin{pmatrix} Z_t \\ 0 \\ 0 \\ \vdots \\ 0 \end{pmatrix}$$

$$= \Phi Y_{t-1} + U_t$$

where $U_t = (Z_t, 0, 0, \ldots, 0)'$ with $U_t \sim \text{WN}\left(0, \begin{pmatrix} \Sigma & 0 \\ 0 & 0 \end{pmatrix}\right)$. This representation is also known as the *companion form* or *state space representation* (see also Chap. 17). In this representation the last $p(n-1)$ equations are simply identities so that there is no error term attached. This implies that the covariance matrix of U_t is positive semi-definite instead of positive definite. The latter name stems from the fact that Y_t encompasses all the information necessary to describe the state of the system. The matrix Φ is called the companion matrix of the VAR(p) process.[2]

The main advantage of the companion form is that by studying the properties of the VAR(1) model, one implicitly encompasses VAR models of higher order and also univariate AR(p) models which can be considered as special cases. The relation between the eigenvalues of the companion matrix and the roots of the polynomial matrix $\Phi(z)$ is given by the following formula (Gohberg et al. 1982):

$$\det\left(I_{np} - \Phi z\right) = \det\left(I_n - \Phi_1 z - \ldots - \Phi_p z^p\right). \tag{12.2}$$

In the case of the AR(p) process, the eigenvalues of Φ are just the inverses of the roots of the polynomial $\Phi(z)$. Further elaboration of state space models is given in Chap. 17.

[2] The representation of a VAR(p) process in companion form is not uniquely defined. Permutations of the elements in Y_t will lead to changes in the companion matrix.

12.3 Causal Representation

As will become clear in Chap. 15 and particularly in Sect. 15.1, the issue of the existence of a *causal representation* is even more important than in the univariate case. Before stating the main theorem, let us generalize the definition of a causal representation from the univariate case (see Definition 2.2 in Sect. 2.3) to the multivariate one.

Definition 12.2 (Causality, multivariate) A VARMA process $\{X_t\}$ with $\Phi(\mathrm{L})X_t = \Theta(\mathrm{L})Z_t$ is called *causal* with respect to $\{Z_t\}$ if and only if there exists a sequence of absolutely summable matrices $\{\Psi_j\}$, $j = 0, 1, 2, \ldots$, i.e. $\sum_{j=0}^{\infty} \|\Psi_j\| < \infty$, such that

$$X_t = \sum_{j=0}^{\infty} \Psi_j Z_{t-j}.$$

Theorem 12.1 *Let $\{X_t\}$ be a VARMA(p,q) process with $\Phi(\mathrm{L})X_t = \Theta(\mathrm{L})Z_t$ and assume that*

$$\det \Phi(z) \neq 0 \quad \text{for all } z \in \mathbb{C} \text{ with } |z| \leq 1,$$

then the stochastic difference equation $\Phi(\mathrm{L})X_t = \Theta(\mathrm{L})Z_t$ has exactly one stationary solution with causal representation

$$X_t = \sum_{j=0}^{\infty} \Psi_j Z_{t-j},$$

whereby the sequence of matrices $\{\Psi_j\}$ is absolutely summable and where the matrices are uniquely determined by the identity

$$\Phi(z)\Psi(z) = \Theta(z).$$

Proof The proof is a straightforward extension of the univariate case. □

Remark 12.1 Note that in contrast to the univariate case (see Theorem 2.1), the above Theorem 12.1 gives only sufficient conditions.

As in the univariate case, the coefficient matrices which make up the causal representation can be found by the method of undetermined coefficients, i.e., by equating $\Phi(z)\Psi(z) = \Theta(z)$. In the case of the VAR(1) process, the $\{\Psi_j\}$ has to obey the following recursion:

$$0: \quad \Psi_0 = I_n$$

$$
\begin{aligned}
z &: \quad \Psi_1 = \Phi\Psi_0 = \Phi \\
z^2 &: \quad \Psi_2 = \Phi\Psi_1 = \Phi^2 \\
&\quad \dots \\
z^j &: \quad \Psi_j = \Phi\Psi_{j-1} = \Phi^j
\end{aligned}
$$

The recursion in the VAR(2) case is

$$
\begin{aligned}
0 &: \quad \Psi_0 = I_n \\
z &: \quad -\Phi_1 + \Psi_1 = 0 && \Rightarrow \quad \Psi_1 = \Phi_1 \\
z^2 &: \quad -\Phi_2 - \Phi_1\Psi_1 + \Psi_2 = 0 && \Rightarrow \quad \Psi_2 = \Phi_2 + \Phi_1^2 \\
z^3 &: \quad -\Phi_1\Psi_2 - \Phi_2\Psi_1 + \Psi_3 = 0 && \Rightarrow \quad \Psi_3 = \Phi_1^3 + \Phi_1\Phi_2 + \Phi_2\Phi_1 \\
&\quad \dots
\end{aligned}
$$

Remark 12.2 Consider a VAR(1) process with $\Phi = \begin{pmatrix} 0 & \phi \\ 0 & 0 \end{pmatrix}$ with $\phi \neq 0$ then the matrices in the causal representation are $\Psi_j = \Phi^j = 0$ for $j > 1$. This means that $\{X_t\}$ has an alternative representation as a VMA(1) process because $X_t = Z_t + \Phi Z_{t-1}$. This simple example demonstrates that the representation of $\{X_t\}$ as a VARMA process is not unique. It is therefore impossible to always distinguish between VAR and VMA process of higher orders without imposing additional assumptions. These additional assumptions are much more complex in the multivariate case and are known as identifying assumptions. Thus, a general treatment of this identification problem is outside the scope of this book. See Hannan and Deistler (1988) for a general treatment of this issue. For this reason we will concentrate exclusively on VAR processes where identification is not an issue.

Example We illustrate the above concept by the following VAR(2) model:

$$
X_t = \begin{pmatrix} 0.8 & -0.5 \\ 0.1 & -0.5 \end{pmatrix} X_{t-1} + \begin{pmatrix} -0.3 & -0.3 \\ -0.2 & 0.3 \end{pmatrix} X_{t-2} + Z_t
$$

$$
\text{with} \quad Z_t \sim \text{WN}\left(\begin{pmatrix} 0 \\ 0 \end{pmatrix}, \begin{pmatrix} 1.0 & 0.4 \\ 0.4 & 2.0 \end{pmatrix} \right).
$$

In a first step, we check whether the VAR model admits a causal representation with respect to $\{Z_t\}$. For this purpose we have to compute the roots of the equation $\det(I_2 - \Phi_1 z - \Phi_2 z^2) = 0$:

$$\det\begin{pmatrix} 1-0.8z+0.3z^2 & 0.5z+0.3z^2 \\ -0.1z+0.2z^2 & 1+0.5z-0.3z^2 \end{pmatrix}$$
$$= 1-0.3z-0.35z^2+0.32z^3-0.15z^4 = 0.$$

The four roots are as follows: $-1.1973, 1.5650, 0.8828 \pm 1.6669\imath$. As they are all outside the unit circle, there exists a causal representation which can be found from the equation $\Phi(z)\Psi(z) = I_2$ by the method of undetermined coefficients. Multiplying the equation system out, we get:

$$\begin{aligned} I_2 - \Phi_1 z \quad & -\Phi_2 z^2 \\ +\Psi_1 z - \Phi_1\Psi_1 z^2 & -\Phi_2\Psi_1 z^3 \\ +\Psi_2 z^2 & - \Phi_1\Psi_2 z^3 - \Phi_2\Psi_2 z^4 \\ \ldots & \qquad\qquad = I_2. \end{aligned}$$

Equating the coefficients corresponding to z^j, $j = 1, 2, \ldots$

$$\begin{aligned} z: &\quad \Psi_1 = \Phi_1 \\ z^2: &\quad \Psi_2 = \Phi_1\Psi_1 + \Phi_2 = \Phi_1^2 + \Phi_2 \\ z^3: &\quad \Psi_3 = \Phi_1\Psi_2 + \Phi_2\Psi_1 = \Phi_1^3 + \Phi_1\Phi_2 + \Phi_2\Phi_1 \\ \ldots &\quad \ldots \\ z^j: &\quad \Psi_j = \Phi_1\Psi_{j-1} + \Phi_2\Psi_{j-2}. \end{aligned}$$

The last equation shows how to compute the sequence $\{\Psi_j\}$ recursively:

$$\Psi_1 = \begin{pmatrix} 0.8 & -0.5 \\ 0.1 & 0.5 \end{pmatrix}, \Psi_2 = \begin{pmatrix} 0.29 & -0.45 \\ -0.17 & 0.50 \end{pmatrix}, \Psi_3 = \begin{pmatrix} 0.047 & -0.310 \\ -0.016 & -0.345 \end{pmatrix}, \ldots$$

12.4 Computation of the Covariance Function of Causal VAR Processes

As in the univariate case, it is important to be able to compute the covariance and the correlation function of VARMA process (see Sect. 2.4). As explained in Remark 12.2, we will concentrate on VAR processes. Consider first the case of a causal VAR(1) process:

$$X_t = \Phi X_{t-1} + Z_t \qquad Z_t \sim \mathrm{WN}(0, \Sigma).$$

Multiplying the above equation first by X_t' and then successively by X_{t-h}' from the left, $h = 1, 2, \ldots$, and taking expectations, we obtain the Yule-Walker equations:

$$\mathbb{E}\left(X_t X_t'\right) = \Gamma(0) = \Phi\,\mathbb{E}\left(X_{t-1} X_t'\right) + \mathbb{E}\left(Z_t X_t'\right) = \Phi\Gamma(-1) + \Sigma,$$

$$\mathbb{E}\left(X_t X_{t-h}'\right) = \Gamma(h) = \Phi\,\mathbb{E}\left(X_{t-1} X_{t-h}'\right) + \mathbb{E}\left(Z_t X_{t-h}'\right) = \Phi\Gamma(h-1).$$

Knowing $\Gamma(0)$ and Φ, $\Gamma(h)$, $h > 0$, can be computed recursively from the second equation as

$$\Gamma(h) = \Phi^h \Gamma(0), \qquad h = 1, 2, \ldots \tag{12.3}$$

Given Φ and Σ, we can compute $\Gamma(0)$. For $h = 1$, the second equation above implies $\Gamma(1) = \Phi\Gamma(0)$. Inserting this expression in the first equation and using the fact that $\Gamma(-1) = \Gamma(1)'$, we get an equation in $\Gamma(0)$:

$$\Gamma(0) = \Phi\Gamma(0)\Phi' + \Sigma.$$

This equation can be solved for $\Gamma(0)$

$$\begin{aligned}\mathrm{vec}\Gamma(0) &= \mathrm{vec}(\Phi\Gamma(0)\Phi') + \mathrm{vec}\Sigma \\ &= (\Phi \otimes \Phi)\mathrm{vec}\Gamma(0) + \mathrm{vec}\Sigma,\end{aligned}$$

where $\otimes$ and "vec" denote the Kronecker-product and the vec-operator, respectively.[3] Thus,

$$\mathrm{vec}\Gamma(0) = (I_{n^2} - \Phi \otimes \Phi)^{-1}\mathrm{vec}\Sigma. \tag{12.4}$$

The assumption that $\{X_t\}$ is causal with respect to $\{Z_t\}$ guarantees that the eigenvalues of $\Phi \otimes \Phi$ are strictly smaller than one in absolute value, implying that $I_{n^2} - \Phi \otimes \Phi$ is invertible.[4]

If the process is a causal VAR(p) process, the covariance function can be found in two ways. The first one rewrites the process in companion form as a VAR(1) process and applies the procedure just outlined. The second way relies on the Yule-Walker equation. This equation is obtained by multiplying the stochastic difference equation from the left by X_t' and then successively by X_{t-h}', $h > 0$, and taking expectations:

$$\Gamma(0) = \Phi_1\Gamma(-1) + \ldots + \Phi_p\Gamma(-p) + \Sigma,$$

[3] The vec-operator stacks the column of a $n \times m$ matrix to a column vector of dimension nm. The properties of $\otimes$ and vec can be found, e.g., in Magnus and Neudecker (1988).

[4] If the eigenvalues of Φ are λ_i, $i = 1, \ldots, n$, then the eigenvalues of $\Phi \otimes \Phi$ are $\lambda_i\lambda_j$, $i, j = 1, \ldots, n$ (see Magnus and Neudecker 1988).

$$= \Phi_1\Gamma(1)' + \ldots + \Phi_p\Gamma(p)' + \Sigma,$$

$$\Gamma(h) = \Phi_1\Gamma(h-1) + \ldots + \Phi_p\Gamma(h-p). \tag{12.5}$$

The second equation can be used to compute $\Gamma(h)$, $h \geq p$, recursively taking $\Phi_1, \ldots, \Phi_p$ and the starting values $\Gamma(p-1), \ldots, \Gamma(0)$ as given. The starting value can be retrieved by transforming the VAR(p) model into the companion form and proceeding as explained above.

Example We illustrate the computation of the covariance function using the same example as in Sect. 12.3. First, we transform the model into the companion form:

$$Y_t = \begin{pmatrix} X_{1,t} \\ X_{2,t} \\ X_{1,t=1} \\ X_{2,t=1} \end{pmatrix} = \begin{pmatrix} 0.8 & -0.5 & -0.3 & -0.3 \\ 0.1 & -0.5 & -0.2 & 0.3 \\ 1 & 0 & 0 & 0 \\ 0 & 1 & 0 & 0 \end{pmatrix} \begin{pmatrix} X_{1,t-1} \\ X_{2,t-1} \\ X_{1,t-2} \\ X_{2,t-2} \end{pmatrix} + \begin{pmatrix} Z_{1,t} \\ Z_{2,t} \\ 0 \\ 0 \end{pmatrix}.$$

Equation (12.4) implies that $\Gamma_Y(0)$ is given by

$$\text{vec}\Gamma_Y(0) = \text{vec}\begin{pmatrix} \Gamma_X(0) & \Gamma_X(1) \\ \Gamma_X(1)' & \Gamma_X(0) \end{pmatrix} = (I_{16} - \Phi \otimes \Phi)^{-1}\text{vec}\begin{pmatrix} \Sigma & 0 \\ 0 & 0 \end{pmatrix}$$

so that $\Gamma_X(0)$ and $\Gamma_X(1)$ become

$$\Gamma_X(0) = \begin{pmatrix} 2.4201 & 0.5759 \\ 0.5759 & 3.8978 \end{pmatrix} \qquad \Gamma_X(1) = \begin{pmatrix} 1.3996 & -0.5711 \\ -0.4972 & -2.5599 \end{pmatrix}.$$

The other covariance matrices can then be computed recursively according to Eq. (12.5):

$$\Gamma_X(2) = \Phi_1\Gamma_X(1) + \Phi_2\Gamma_X(0) = \begin{pmatrix} 0.4695 & -05191 \\ 0.0773 & 2.2770 \end{pmatrix},$$

$$\Gamma_X(3) = \Phi_1\Gamma_X(2) + \Phi_2\Gamma_X(1) = \begin{pmatrix} 0.0662 & -0.6145 \\ -0.4208 & -1.8441 \end{pmatrix}.$$

Appendix: Autoregressive Final Form

Definition 12.1 defined the VARMA process $\{X_t\}$ as a solution to the corresponding multivariate stochastic difference equation (12.1). However, as pointed out by Zellner and Palm (1974), there is an equivalent representation in the form of n univariate ARMA processes, one for each X_{it}. Formally, these representations, also called *autoregressive final form* or *transfer function form* (Box and Jenkins 1976), can be written as

$$\det \Phi(\mathrm{L})X_{it} = \left[\Phi^*(\mathrm{L})\Theta(\mathrm{L})\right]_{i\bullet} Z_t$$

where the index $i\bullet$ indicates the i-th row of $\Phi^*(\mathrm{L})\Theta(\mathrm{L})$. Thereby $\Phi^*(\mathrm{L})$ denotes the adjugate matrix of $\Phi(\mathrm{L})$.[5] Thus each variable in X_t may be investigated separately as an univariate ARMA process. Thereby the autoregressive part will be the same for each variable. Note, however, that the moving-average processes are correlated across variables.

The disadvantage of this approach is that it involves rather long AR and MA lags as will become clear from the following example.[6] Take a simple two-dimensional VAR of order one, i.e., $X_t = \Phi X_{t-1} + Z_t$, $Z_t \sim \mathrm{WN}(0, \Sigma)$. Then the implied univariate processes will be an ARMA(2,1) process. After some straightforward manipulations, we obtain

$$(1 - (\phi_{11} + \phi_{22})\mathrm{L} + (\phi_{11}\phi_{22} - \phi_{12}\phi_{21})\mathrm{L}^2)X_{1t} = Z_{1t} - \phi_{22}Z_{1,t-1} + \phi_{12}Z_{2,t-1},$$

$$(1 - (\phi_{11} + \phi_{22})\mathrm{L} + (\phi_{11}\phi_{22} - \phi_{12}\phi_{21})\mathrm{L}^2)X_{2t} = \phi_{21}Z_{1,t-1} + Z_{2t} - \phi_{11}Z_{2,t-1}.$$

It can be shown by the means given in Sects. 1.4.3 and 1.5.2 that the right hand sides are observationally equivalent to MA(1) processes.

12.5 Exercises

Exercise 12.5.1 Consider a stationary stochastic process $\{Y_t\}$ with autocovariance function $\Gamma_Y(h)$. Let $\{U_t\}$ be a new process defined as

$$U_t = \sum_{j=-\infty}^{\infty} A_j Y_{t-j}, \tag{12.6}$$

where $\sum_{j=-\infty}^{\infty} ||A_j|| < \infty$. Show that the process $\{X_t\} = \{(Y_t', U_t')'\}$ is stationary. Compute the autocovariance function $\Gamma_X(h)$ of $\{Z_t\}$ using $\Gamma_Y(h)$.

Exercise 12.5.2 Consider a stationary process $\{Y_t\}$. Define a new process $\{X_t\} = \{Y_{kt}\}$ with $k \geq 2$. Show that the process $\{(X_t, Y_t)'\}$ is not stationary.

Exercise 12.5.3 Consider the three-dimensional stochastic process $X_t = (X_{1t}, X_{2t}, X_{3t})'$ defined by the difference equation

$$X_t = \begin{pmatrix} 0.7 & 0.1 & 0 \\ 0 & 0.4 & 0.1 \\ 0.9 & 0 & 0.8 \end{pmatrix} X_{t-1} + \begin{pmatrix} -0.2 & 0 & 0 \\ 0 & 0.1 & 0.1 \\ 0 & 0 & 0 \end{pmatrix} X_{t-2} + Z_t$$

---

[5] The elements of the adjugate matrix A^* of some matrix A are given by $[A^*]_{ij} = (-1)^{i+j}M_{ij}$ where M_{ij} is the minor (minor determinant) obtained by deleting the i-th column and the j-th row of A (Meyer 2000, p. 477).

[6] The degrees of the AR and the MA polynomial can be as large as np and $(n-1)p+q$, respectively.

where $Z_t \sim \text{WN}(0, \Sigma)$. The covariance matrix Σ is given by

$$\Sigma = \begin{pmatrix} 0.26 & 0.03 & 0 \\ 0.03 & 0.09 & 0 \\ 0 & 0 & 0.81 \end{pmatrix}.$$

(i) Is Σ a positive-definite matrix?
(ii) Is there a stationary solution to the difference equation?
(iii) When a stationary solution exits, is the solution for $\{X_t\}$ causal with respect to $\{Z_t\}$?

Exercise 12.5.4 Consider the bivariate VAR(2) model defined by the following stochastic difference equation:

$$X_t = \begin{pmatrix} 1.2 & -0.5 \\ 0.1 & -0.6 \end{pmatrix} X_{t-1} + \begin{pmatrix} -0.6 & -0.3 \\ -0.5 & -0.3 \end{pmatrix} X_{t-2} + Z_t$$

$$\text{where} \quad Z_t \sim \text{WN}\left(\begin{pmatrix} 0 \\ 0 \end{pmatrix}, \begin{pmatrix} 2.0 & 0.5 \\ 0.5 & 4.0 \end{pmatrix} \right).$$

(i) Does a stationary solution for $\{X_t\}$ exist which is causal with respect to $\{Z_t\}$?
(ii) If such a solution exists, compute Ψ_0, Ψ_1, Ψ_2, and Ψ_3 in the representation $X_t = \sum_{j=0}^{\infty} \Psi_j Z_{t-j}$.
(iii) Compute the covariance function $\Gamma_X(h)$ for $h = 0, \pm 1, \pm 2, \pm 3$.

Estimation of Vector Autoregressive Models 13

This chapter is concerned with the estimation of vector autoregressive (VAR) models. Given the order p of the VAR model, the asymptotic properties of several estimators (ordinary least squares (OLS), Yule-Walker estimator, and maximum likelihood estimation) are discussed. Detailed proofs are lengthy and cumbersome and therefore relegated to Sect. 13.4 which only treats the case of the OLS estimator. The interested reader is referred to the classic contribution by Mann and Wald (1943) and to Hannan and Deistler (1988, chapter 4), Reinsel (1993, chapters 4 and 5), and Lütkepohl (2005, chapter 3), among others.

Let $\{X_t\}$ a be stationary vector autoregressive process of order p which is causal with respect to a white noise process $\{Z_t\}$. Thereby, it is assumed that the order of the VAR is given a priori. Section 14.4 deals with the problem of order estimation by generalizing the information criteria presented in Sect. 5.4. Hence, $\{X_t\}$ is considered as the stationary solution of the following difference equation:

$$X_t - \Phi_1 X_{t-1} - \cdots = \Phi_p X_{t-p} = Z_t, \qquad Z_t \sim \text{IID}(0, \Sigma),\ \Sigma > 0,\ \Phi_p \neq 0,$$
$$\Phi(\mathrm{L}) X_t = Z_t. \tag{13.1}$$

The assumption of stationarity and causality are equivalent to the assumption that $\det \Phi(z) \neq 0$ for all $|z| \leq 1$. To derive the consistency and the asymptotic normality of the estimators considered we assume in addition that $\{Z_t\}$ is not only white noise but also IID (independently identically distributed) and that the fourth moments of the components Z_{it} of Z_t are finite, i.e., $\mathbb{E}Z_{it}^4 < c < \infty$ for some constant c. These assumptions turn out to be sufficient. In, for example, Hannan and Deistler (1988), weaker assumptions are discussed. In particular, it is possible to relax the IDD assumption with respect to the errors $\{Z_t\}$ and replace it by the weaker assumption that the error process is a martingale-difference sequence, an assumption which fits well into the VAR, respectively VARMA modeling strategy.

K. Neusser, *Time Series Econometrics*, Springer Texts in Business and Economics,
https://doi.org/10.1007/978-3-031-88838-0_13

13.1 Ordinary Least Squares Estimation

The starting point for our consideration is to translate the VAR(p) model into a multivariate regression model with n equations. Denoting by $\phi_{ij}^{(k)}$ the (i, j)-th element of the matrix Φ_k, $k = 1, 2, \ldots, p$, then the i-th equation is

$$X_{it} = \phi_{i1}^{(1)} X_{1,t-1} + \ldots + \phi_{in}^{(1)} X_{n,t-1} + \ldots + \phi_{i1}^{(p)} X_{1,t-p} + \ldots + \phi_{in}^{(p)} X_{n,t-p} + Z_{it}.$$

The i-th equation is therefore a regression equation with dependent variable X_{it}, regressors $X_{1,t-1}, \ldots, X_{n,t-1}, \ldots, X_{1,t-p}, \ldots, X_{n,t-p}$, and error term Z_{it}.

Two aspects are worth noting and important for the development of the theory. First, the errors terms of the different equations are correlated with each other as the covariances $\mathbb{E}(Z_{it} Z_{jt}) = \sigma_{ij}$ are in general different from zero. In the econometrics literature, this type of regression models is known as seemingly unrelated regressions (SUR) and was first analyzed by Zellner (1962). The name stems from the observation that even when the regressors in the different equations are independent from each other or different across equations, the correlation between the error terms makes the simultaneous estimation of all equations by generalized least squares (GLS) more efficient than using OLS equation by equation.[1] Second, each of the n equations has exactly the same regressors. In this special case, OLS estimation equation by equation and GLS estimation of all equations simultaneously turn out to coincide exactly (numerically). Note, however, that this equivalence fails if some coefficients in the VAR are restricted to be zero, e.g., in the case of testing for Wiener-Granger causality (see Sect. 14.5).

Given observations X_t, $t = -p + 1, \ldots, 0, 1, \ldots, T$, with sample size $T \geq 1$, the $T \times np$-regressor matrix $\mathbf{X}$ becomes[2]

$$\mathbf{X} = \begin{pmatrix} X_{1,0} & \ldots & X_{n,0} & \ldots & X_{1,-p+1} & \ldots & X_{n,-p+1} \\ X_{1,1} & \ldots & X_{n,1} & \ldots & X_{1,-p+2} & \ldots & X_{n,-p+2} \\ \vdots & \ddots & \vdots & \ddots & \vdots & \ddots & \vdots \\ X_{1,T-1} & \ldots & X_{n,T-1} & \ldots & X_{1,T-p} & \ldots & X_{n,T-p} \end{pmatrix} = \begin{pmatrix} X_0(p)' \\ X_1(p)' \\ \vdots \\ X_{T-2}(p)' \\ X_{T-1}(p)' \end{pmatrix},$$

where $X_t(p) = (X_t', X_{t-1}', \ldots, X_{t-p+2}', X_{t-p+1}')'$. The observations for $t = 1, \ldots, T$ can therefore be written as

[1] Strictly speaking, the argument is valid only for non-stochastic regressors (Zellner, 1962).

[2] Note that the observations $t = -p+1, \ldots, 0, 1, \ldots, T$ induce a sample size T due the lag order p. The first $t = -p + 1, \ldots, 0$ observations are treated as given and fixed. In Sect. 13.3 we will therefore analyze the conditional (conditional on the first p observations) likelihood function. This implies that the summations run from $1, \ldots, T$ instead of $p + 1, \ldots, T$ as in the univariate case (see Sect. 5.2). Clearly, it is only a matter of taste how the sample size is notated.

$$\underbrace{(X_1, X_2, \ldots, X_T)}_{=Y} = \underbrace{(\Phi_1, \Phi_2, \ldots, \Phi_p)}_{=\Phi} \underbrace{\begin{pmatrix} X_0 & X_1 & \ldots & X_{T-1} \\ X_{-1} & X_0 & \ldots & X_{T-2} \\ \vdots & \vdots & \ddots & \vdots \\ X_{-p+1} & X_{-p+2} & \ldots & X_{T-p} \end{pmatrix}}_{=\mathbf{X}'} + \underbrace{(Z_1, Z_2, \ldots, Z_T)}_{=Z},$$

or more compactly as

$$Y = \Phi\mathbf{X}' + Z.$$

There are two ways to rewrite the above model as a multivariate regression model with the observations of the dependent variable arranged as a vector. The data can be ordered either by observations or by equations. In the first case, we obtain

$$\text{vec}Y = \text{vec}(\Phi\mathbf{X}') + \text{vec}Z = (\mathbf{X} \otimes I_n)\text{vec}\Phi + \text{vec}Z, \tag{13.2}$$

with $\text{vec}Y = (X_{11}, X_{21}, \ldots, X_{n1}, X_{12}, X_{22}, \ldots, X_{n2}, \ldots, X_{1T}, X_{2T}, \ldots, X_{nT})'$.[3] An equivalent arrangement equation by equation then has $\text{vec}Y' = (X_{11}, X_{12}, \ldots, X_{1T}, X_{21}, X_{22}, \ldots, X_{2T}, \ldots, X_{n1}, X_{n2}, \ldots, X_{nT})'$ instead as the dependent variable. By permutation or commutation it is possible to move from one representation to the other. Let K_{nT} denote the $nT \times nT$ commutator matrix defined as $\text{vec}Y' = K_{nT}\text{vec}Y$. Using the calculation rules for the Kronecker product $\otimes$, the vec operator, and commutator matrices (Magnus & Neudecker, 1988), we obtain

$$\begin{aligned} \text{vec}Y' &= K_{nT}\text{vec}Y = K_{nT}\left(\text{vec}(\Phi\mathbf{X}') + \text{vec}Z\right) \\ &= K_{nT}(\mathbf{X} \otimes I_n)\text{vec}\Phi + K_{nT}\text{vec}Z \\ &= (I_n \otimes \mathbf{X})K_{n^2p}\text{vec}\Phi + K_{nT}\text{vec}Z \\ &= (I_n \otimes \mathbf{X})\text{vec}\Phi' + \text{vec}Z', \end{aligned} \tag{13.3}$$

where the $n^2 \times p$ commutator matrix K_{n^2p} rearranges $\text{vec}\Phi$ in $\text{vec}\Phi'$.[4]

[3] The vec operator stacks the column of a $m \times n$ matrix into a mn dimensional vector. If A and B are two matrices of dimensions $m \times n$ and $p \times q$, respectively, the Kronecker product $C = A \otimes B$ is a $mp \times nq$ block matrix such the ij-th block is $a_{ij}B$, $i = 1, \ldots, m$ and $j = 1, \ldots, n$.

[4] Alternatively, one can obtain the same result without the use of the commutator matrix by transposing the equation $Y = \Phi\mathbf{X}' + Z$ directly and then using the calculation rules for the vec operator and the Kronecker product as in Eq. (13.3).

The covariance matrix of the error term $\text{vec}Z$ in Eq. (13.2) is

$$\mathbb{V}(\text{vec}Z) = \mathbb{E}(\text{vec}Z)(\text{vec}Z)'$$
$$= \begin{pmatrix} \sigma_1^2 & \ldots & \sigma_{1n} & 0 & \ldots & 0 & \ldots & 0 & \ldots & 0 \\ \vdots & \ddots & \vdots & \vdots & \ddots & \vdots & \ldots & \vdots & \ddots & \vdots \\ \sigma_{n1} & \ldots & \sigma_n^2 & 0 & \ldots & 0 & \ldots & 0 & \ldots & 0 \\ 0 & 0 & 0 & \sigma_1^2 & \ldots & \sigma_{1n} & \ldots & 0 & \ldots & 0 \\ \vdots & \ddots & \vdots & \vdots & \ddots & \vdots & \ldots & \vdots & \ddots & \vdots \\ 0 & \ldots & 0 & \sigma_{n1} & \ldots & \sigma_n^2 & \ldots & 0 & \ldots & 0 \\ \vdots & \vdots & \vdots & \vdots & \vdots & \vdots & \ddots & \vdots & \vdots & \vdots \\ 0 & \ldots & 0 & 0 & \ldots & 0 & \ldots & \sigma_1^2 & \ldots & \sigma_{1n} \\ \vdots & \ddots & \vdots & \vdots & \ddots & \vdots & \ldots & \vdots & \ddots & \vdots \\ 0 & \ldots & 0 & 0 & \ldots & 0 & \ldots & \sigma_{n1} & \ldots & \sigma_n^2 \end{pmatrix} = I_T \otimes \Sigma.$$

This matrix is in general not proportional to the identity matrix.[5] Hence, the method of generalized least square (GLS) seems appropriate:

$$\begin{aligned} S(\Phi, \Sigma) &= (\text{vec}Z)'(I_T \otimes \Sigma)^{-1}(\text{vec}Z) \qquad (13.4) \\ &= (\text{vec}Y - (\mathbf{X} \otimes I_n)\text{vec}\Phi)'(I_T \otimes \Sigma)^{-1}(\text{vec}Y - (\mathbf{X} \otimes I_n)\text{vec}\Phi) \\ &\longrightarrow \min_{\Phi} \end{aligned}$$

The unique solution to this minimization problem is

$$\begin{aligned} \text{vec}\widehat{\Phi}_{\text{GLS}} &= \left((\mathbf{X} \otimes I_n)'(I_T \otimes \Sigma)^{-1}(\mathbf{X} \otimes I_n)\right)^{-1} (\mathbf{X} \otimes I_n)'(I_T \otimes \Sigma)^{-1}\text{vec}Y \\ &= \left((\mathbf{X}' \otimes I_n)(I_T \otimes \Sigma^{-1})(\mathbf{X} \otimes I_n)\right)^{-1} (\mathbf{X}' \otimes I_n)(I_T \otimes \Sigma^{-1})\text{vec}Y \\ &= \left((\mathbf{X}' \otimes \Sigma^{-1})(\mathbf{X} \otimes I_n)\right)^{-1} (\mathbf{X}' \otimes \Sigma^{-1})\text{vec}Y \\ &= \left((\mathbf{X}'\mathbf{X}) \otimes \Sigma^{-1}\right)^{-1} (\mathbf{X}' \otimes \Sigma^{-1})\text{vec}Y \\ &= \left((\mathbf{X}'\mathbf{X})^{-1} \otimes \Sigma\right)(\mathbf{X}' \otimes \Sigma^{-1})\text{vec}Y = \left(((\mathbf{X}'\mathbf{X})^{-1}\mathbf{X}') \otimes I_n\right)\text{vec}Y \\ &= \text{vec}\widehat{\Phi}_{\text{OLS}} = \text{vec}\widehat{\Phi}. \end{aligned}$$

[5] The covariance matrix of the error term $\text{vec}Z'$ can also be easily computed with the aid of the commutator matrix K_{nT}.

Because the covariance matrix Σ does not appear in the solution for $\mathrm{vec}\widehat{\Phi}_{\mathrm{GLS}}$, the GLS and the OLS estimator coincide. Hence, we have $\mathrm{vec}\widehat{\Phi}_{\mathrm{GLS}} = \mathrm{vec}\widehat{\Phi}_{\mathrm{OLS}}$ where the latter is defined as the solution of the minimizer of the function $S_{\mathrm{OLS}}(\Phi) = (\mathrm{vec}Z)'(\mathrm{vec}Z)$ with respect to Φ, respectively $\mathrm{vec}\Phi$. The solution is, of course, the one obtained previously:

$$\mathrm{vec}\widehat{\Phi} = \left(((\mathbf{X}'\mathbf{X})^{-1}\mathbf{X}') \otimes I_n\right) \mathrm{vec}Y. \tag{13.5}$$

Given these preliminaries, we can state the following theorem.

Theorem 13.1 (Asymptotic distribution of the OLS estimator). *Under the assumptions concerning $\{Z_t\}$ at the beginning of this chapter, the OLS estimator of the parameter matrix Φ in Eq.* (13.1) *is consistent and asymptotically normally distributed*

$$\operatorname{plim} \widehat{\Phi} = \Phi$$

$$\sqrt{T}\left(\mathrm{vec}\widehat{\Phi} - \mathrm{vec}\Phi\right) \xrightarrow{\ \mathrm{d}\ } \mathrm{N}\left(0, \mathbf{\Gamma}_p^{-1} \otimes \Sigma\right),$$

with

$$\mathbf{\Gamma}_p = \operatorname{plim} \frac{1}{T}(\mathbf{X}'\mathbf{X}) = \begin{pmatrix} \Gamma(0) & \Gamma(1) & \ldots & \Gamma(p-1) \\ \Gamma'(1) & \Gamma(0) & \ldots & \Gamma(p-2) \\ \vdots & \vdots & \ddots & \vdots \\ \Gamma'(p-1) & \Gamma'(p-2) & \ldots & \Gamma(0) \end{pmatrix},$$

and $\mathbf{\Gamma}_p$ positive definite.

Proof. See Sect. 13.4 □

Clearly, $\mathbf{\Gamma}_p$ equals the covariance matrix of the stacked process. This insight shows $\mathbf{\Gamma}_p$ is positive definite and therefore invertible provided that Σ is itself positive definite. If $\mathbf{\Gamma}_p$ would be singular, X_t could be perfectly forecasted from the finite past.[6]

To make the result of asymptotic normality valid for inferences, consistent estimators for $\mathbf{\Gamma}_p$ and Σ are needed. Such a "natural" consistent estimator for $\mathbf{\Gamma}_p$

[6] We even have a more general result (see Deistler & Scherrer, 2022, Kapitel V). If $\Gamma(h)$ denotes the autocovariance function of a stationary process $\{X_t\}$ with positive definite covariance matrix of the innovations, then the matrix $\mathbf{\Gamma}_p$, defined as above, then the correspondingly arranged block-covariance matrix $\mathbf{\Gamma}_s = \mathbb{V}(X_t(s)X_t(s)')$ is positive definite for all $s \geq 1$ where $X_t(s) = (X_t', X_{t-1}', \ldots, X_{t-s+1}')'$.

is according to Theorem 13.1 given by $\frac{1}{T}\mathbf{X}'\mathbf{X}$. A consistent estimator for Σ can be obtained from the residuals of the multivariate regression

$$\widehat{\Sigma} = \frac{1}{T}\sum_{t=1}^{T}\widehat{Z}_t\widehat{Z}_t' = \frac{1}{T}\widehat{Z}\widehat{Z}' = \frac{1}{T}(Y - \widehat{\Phi}\mathbf{X}')(Y - \widehat{\Phi}\mathbf{X}')' \tag{13.6}$$

where the sample size T corresponds to the number of residuals without degrees of freedom correction.

Theorem 13.2. *Under assumptions of Theorem 13.1*

$$\text{plim}\,\widehat{\Sigma} = \Sigma.$$

Proof. See Sect. 13.4 □

An asymptotically valid inference can therefore be obtained from the approximate normal distribution

$$\text{vec}\widehat{\Phi} \sim \text{N}\left(\text{vec}\Phi, (\mathbf{X}'\mathbf{X})^{-1} \otimes \widehat{\Sigma}\right).$$

The corresponding standard test statistics, like the t-, F- or χ^2 test statistics, can be computed and used in the usual way (see also the remarks at the end of Sect. 5.2).

Remark 13.1. The fact that the regressors in the VAR model are not strictly exogenous, but only predetermined, has important consequences for the properties of the OLS estimator and the corresponding test statistics. Predetermined regressors are regressors which are contemporaneously uncorrelated with the error term, but not with past error terms. This is obviously the case here because the regressors X_{t-j} are uncorrelated with Z_t, but not with past error terms $Z_{t-j}, \ldots, Z_1$. First, this implies that the OLS estimator is no longer unbiased. The application of the Gauss-Markov theorem in the OLS, respectively, the Gauss-Markov-Aitken theorem in the GLS case, is therefore not possible (see Schönfeld, 1969, Volume 1). Second, even if one is willing to assume normally distributed error terms $\{Z_t\}$, the OLS estimator is not normally distributed in finite samples. This implies that there are no exact tests available with respect to the parameters of VAR models. Instead, one must rely on asymptotic normality as an approximation.

Occasionally, an alternative estimator for Σ might be used:

$$\widetilde{\Sigma} = \frac{1}{T - np}\widehat{Z}\widehat{Z}' = \frac{T}{T - np}\widehat{\Sigma}. \tag{13.7}$$

This estimator corrects for the degrees of freedom in each of the n equations. Alternatively one may correct for the total number of estimated parameters $T - n^2p$.

Obviously, each of these variants also leads to consisted estimates, taking n and p as given. As the sample size T increases compared to n and p, the effect of the different normalizations vanishes. The above discussion concerning the bias of OLS the estimator, however, made it clear that none of the normalization lead to unbiased estimates for Σ.

13.2 Yule-Walker Estimator

As in the univariate case, it is possible to use the Yule-Walker equations for parameter estimation. They are obtained by multiplying the Eq. (13.1) from the right by X'_{t-j}, $j = 0, 1, \ldots, p$, and taking expectations:

$$\Gamma(0) - \Phi_1\Gamma(-1) - \cdots - \Phi_p\Gamma(-p) = \Sigma, \quad j = 0,$$
$$\Gamma(j) - \Phi_1\Gamma(j-1) - \cdots - \Phi_p\Gamma(j-p) = 0, \quad j = 1, \ldots, p.$$

Using the property $\Gamma(h) = \Gamma(-h)'$, the equations for $j = 1, \ldots, p$ can be written compactly as

$$\begin{pmatrix} \Gamma(-1) \\ \Gamma(-2) \\ \vdots \\ \Gamma(-p) \end{pmatrix} = \begin{pmatrix} \Gamma(0) & \Gamma(1) & \ldots & \Gamma(p-1) \\ \Gamma'(1) & \Gamma(0) & \ldots & \Gamma(p-2) \\ \vdots & \vdots & \ddots & \vdots \\ \Gamma'(p-1) & \Gamma'(p-2) & \ldots & \Gamma(0) \end{pmatrix} \begin{pmatrix} \Phi'_1 \\ \Phi'_2 \\ \vdots \\ \Phi'_p \end{pmatrix}. \tag{13.8}$$

This linear equation system (13.8) for Φ has a unique solution:

$$\Phi = (\Gamma(1)\,\Gamma(2)\,\ldots\,\Gamma(p))\,\mathbf{\Gamma}_p^{-1}.$$

The Yule-Walker estimator is then obtained by replacing the autocovariances by their estimates

$$\widehat{\Gamma}(h) = \frac{1}{T+p}\sum_{t=-p+1}^{T-h}(X_{t+h} - \overline{X}_T)(X_t - \overline{X}_T)', \quad 0 \le h \le p,$$
$$\widehat{\Gamma}(-h) = \widehat{\Gamma}(h)', \quad -p \le h < 0,$$

and $\overline{X}_T = \frac{1}{T+p}\sum_{t=-p+1}^{T} X_t$. Hence, the Yule-Walker estimator is defined as

$$\widehat{\Phi}_{YW} = \left(\widehat{\Gamma}(1)\,\widehat{\Gamma}(2)\,\ldots\,\widehat{\Gamma}(p)\right)\widehat{\mathbf{\Gamma}}_p^{-1}, \tag{13.9}$$

or in vectorized form

$$\text{vec}\widehat{\Phi}_{YW} = \left(\widehat{\mathbf{\Gamma}}_p^{-1} \otimes I_n\right) \text{vec}\left(\widehat{\Gamma}(1)\ \widehat{\Gamma}(2)\ \ldots\ \widehat{\Gamma}(p)\right).$$

The first Yule-Walker equation ($j = 0$) can be used to compute the Yule-Walker estimate for Σ:

$$\widehat{\Sigma}_{YW} = \widehat{\Gamma}(0) - \widehat{\Phi}_{1,YW}\widehat{\Gamma}(-1) - \cdots - \widehat{\Phi}_{p,YW}\widehat{\Gamma}(-p). \tag{13.10}$$

Theorem 13.3 (Yule-Walker Estimator). *Under the assumptions of Theorem 13.1, the Yule-Walker estimator has the following asymptotic properties:*

$$\text{plim}\,\widehat{\Phi}_{YW} = \Phi$$

$$\sqrt{T}\left(\text{vec}\widehat{\Phi}_{YW} - \text{vec}\Phi\right) \xrightarrow{d} \text{N}\left(0, \mathbf{\Gamma}_p^{-1} \otimes \Sigma\right)$$

$$\text{plim}\,\widehat{\Sigma}_{YW} = \Sigma.$$

Proof. The proof can be established using the results in Sect. 13.4. □

Theorems 13.1 and 13.3 show that the OLS and the Yule-Walker estimator are asymptotically equivalent. Even in small samples, both estimators often lead to similar results (Reinsel, 1993). However, notable differences can arise when the zeros of the VAR polynomial are near the unit circle. This has to do with the fact that Yule-Walker estimator always delivers parameter estimates such that the zeros of $\det(I_n - \widehat{\Phi}_{1,YW}z - \cdots - \widehat{\Phi}_{p,YW}z^p)$ are outside the closed unit circle so that the estimated VAR model is always causal with respect $\{\widehat{Z}_t\}$ (see Reinsel, 1993; Tjøstheim & Paulsen, 1983; Shaman & Stine, 1988).

Noting that $\mathbb{E}X_t = 0$, one might be tempted to replace the autocovariances in the definition of Yule-Walker estimator by their non-centered estimates $\frac{1}{T}\mathbf{X}'\mathbf{X}$ and $\frac{1}{T}Y\mathbf{X}$ instead of the usual centered ones $\widehat{\Gamma}(h)$. It then becomes immediately clear that both the OLS and the Yule-Walker estimator are equivalent. Thus, the differences in the treatment of the mean and the use of the observations $t = -p+1, \ldots, 0$ in the case of the Yule-Walker estimator are asymptotically negligible. Despite this, the incorporation of the first p observation in the estimation of $\Gamma(1), \ldots, \Gamma(p)$ is responsible for the causality implied by the Yule-Walker estimator (see Brockwell & Davis, 1991, section 8.1 and exercise 8.3 for the univariate case). Under the assumption $\mathbb{E}X_t = 0$, the difference can be interpreted as using the true mean or the arithmetic average for mean-correcting the data.[7]

[7] The difference actually vanishes if a VAR model with constant term is estimated (Lütkepohl, 2005).

13.3 Maximum Likelihood Estimation

As a third method, we consider the maximum likelihood estimator of the parameters of a VAR(p) model with normally distributed error terms, i.e., we assume that $Z_t \sim$ IID N. This assumption is sufficient for the consistency and the asymptotic normality of the Gaussian maximum likelihood estimator which is obtained from the maximization of the conditional (conditional on the observations $X_{-p+1}, \ldots, X_0$) likelihood function[8]

$$L(\Phi, \Sigma|Y) = \frac{1}{(2\pi)^{nT/2}}(\det\Sigma)^{-T/2}\exp\left(-\frac{1}{2}S(\Phi,\Sigma)\right),$$

where $S(\Phi, \Sigma)$ are defined as in Eq. (13.4).

In analogy to the classical linear regression model with a normally distributed error term, the maximization of the log-likelihood function leads to $\widehat{\Phi}_{ML} = \widehat{\Phi}$ and $\widehat{\Sigma}_{ML} = \widehat{\Sigma}$. In the current setting, the OLS, the Yule-Walker, and the ML estimator are therefore asymptotically equivalent.

13.4 Proof of the Asymptotic Normality of OLS Estimators

Before proceeding to the proofs of Theorems 13.1 and 13.2, it is necessary to establish some preliminary results.

Lemma 13.1. *The process* $\{\text{vec} Z_{t-j}Z'_{t-i}\}$, $i, j \in \mathbb{Z}$, $i \neq j$, *is white noise.*

Proof. Using the serial independence of $\{Z_t\}$, it immediately follows that

$$\begin{aligned}
\mathbb{E}\,\text{vec} Z_{t-j}Z'_{t-i} &= \mathbb{E}(Z_{t-i}\otimes Z_{t-j}) = 0,\\
\mathbb{V}(\text{vec} Z_{t-j}Z'_{t-i}) &= \mathbb{E}\left((Z_{t-i}\otimes Z_{t-j})(Z_{t-i}\otimes Z_{t-j})'\right)\\
&= \mathbb{E}\left((Z_{t-i}Z'_{t-i})\otimes(Z_{t-j}Z'_{t-j})\right) = \Sigma\otimes\Sigma,\\
\Gamma_{\text{vec} Z_{t-j}Z'_{t-i}}(h) &= \mathbb{E}\left((Z_{t-i}\otimes Z_{t-j})(Z_{t-i-h}\otimes Z_{t-j-h})'\right)\\
&= \mathbb{E}\left((Z_{t-i}Z'_{t-i-h})\otimes(Z_{t-j}Z'_{t-j-h})\right) = 0, \qquad h \neq 0.
\end{aligned}$$

□

Next, we prove that $\frac{1}{T}\mathbf{X}'\mathbf{X}$ is a consistent estimator of $\mathbf{\Gamma}_p$.

---

[8] Consistency and asymptotic normality with exactly the same asymptotic distribution also follows for the case of the quasi maximum likelihood estimator where the assumption of the normality of error terms is relaxed. In addition, there is asymptotically no loss of efficiency.

Proposition 13.1.

$$\frac{1}{T}\mathbf{X}'\mathbf{X} \xrightarrow{p} \mathbf{\Gamma}_p = \begin{pmatrix} \Gamma(0) & \Gamma(1) & \dots & \Gamma(p-1) \\ \Gamma'(1) & \Gamma(0) & \dots & \Gamma(p-2) \\ \vdots & \vdots & \ddots & \vdots \\ \Gamma'(p-1) & \Gamma'(p-2) & \dots & \Gamma(0) \end{pmatrix},$$

where $\mathbf{\Gamma}_p$ *is positive definite.*

Proof. Write $\frac{1}{T}(\mathbf{X}'\mathbf{X})$ as

$$\frac{1}{T}\mathbf{X}'\mathbf{X} = \begin{pmatrix} \widehat{G}(0) & \widehat{G}(1) & \dots & \widehat{G}(p-1) \\ \widehat{G}'(1) & \widehat{G}(0) & \dots & \widehat{G}(p-2) \\ \vdots & \vdots & \ddots & \vdots \\ \widehat{G}'(p-1) & \widehat{\Gamma}'(p-2) & \dots & \widehat{G}(0) \end{pmatrix}$$

where

$$\widehat{G}(h) = \frac{1}{T}\sum_{t=0}^{T-1} X_t X_{t-h}', \qquad h = 0, 1, \dots, p-1.$$

We show that each block $\widehat{G}(h)$ converges in probability to $\Gamma(h)$ which is equivalent to proof the consistency of the estimation of autocovariance function. Taking the causal representation $X_t = \sum_{j=0}^{\infty} \Psi_j Z_{t-j}$ into account,

$$\begin{aligned}
\widehat{G}(h) &= \frac{1}{T}\sum_{t=0}^{T-1} X_t X_{t-h}' = \frac{1}{T}\sum_{t=0}^{T-1}\sum_{j=0}^{\infty}\sum_{i=0}^{\infty} \Psi_j Z_{t-j} Z_{t-h-i}' \Psi_i' \\
&= \sum_{j=0}^{\infty}\sum_{i=0}^{\infty} \Psi_j \left(\frac{1}{T}\sum_{t=0}^{T-1} Z_{t-j} Z_{t-h-i}'\right) \Psi_i' \\
&= \sum_{j=0}^{\infty}\sum_{i=h}^{\infty} \Psi_j \left(\frac{1}{T}\sum_{t=0}^{T-1} Z_{t-j} Z_{t-i}'\right) \Psi_{i-h}' \\
&= \sum_{j=0}^{\infty}\sum_{\substack{i=h \\ i\neq j}}^{\infty} \Psi_j \left(\frac{1}{T}\sum_{t=0}^{T-1} Z_{t-j} Z_{t-i}'\right) \Psi_{i-h}' + \sum_{j=h}^{\infty} \Psi_j \left(\frac{1}{T}\sum_{t=0}^{T-1} Z_{t-j} Z_{t-j}'\right) \Psi_{j-h}' \\
&= G_\infty(h) + \sum_{j=h}^{\infty} \Psi_j \left(\frac{1}{T}\sum_{t=0}^{T-1} Z_{t-j} Z_{t-j}'\right) \Psi_{j-h}'.
\end{aligned}$$

According to Lemma 13.1, $\text{vec}\{Z_{t-j}Z'_{t-i}\}$, $i \neq j$, is white noise so that Theorem 11.1 implies

$$\frac{1}{T}\sum_{t=0}^{T-1} Z_{t-j}Z'_{t-i} \xrightarrow{\text{p}} 0, \qquad i \neq j.$$

Therefore all sample means in $G_\infty(h)$ converge to zero. This does, however, not imply that $G_\infty(h)$ also converges to zero. Consider a fixed, but arbitrary m, then

$$G_m(h) = \sum_{j=0}^{m}\sum_{\substack{i=h \\ i\neq j}}^{m+h} \Psi_j \left(\frac{1}{T}\sum_{t=0}^{T-1} Z_{t-j}Z'_{t-i}\right) \Psi'_{i-h} \xrightarrow{\text{p}} 0,$$

where $G_m(h)$ is defined similarly to $G_\infty(h)$ but with upper bound summations m, respectively $m+h$. From the Basic Approximation Theorem C.15 it follows that

$$G_\infty(h) \xrightarrow{\text{p}} 0.$$

because

$$\lim_{m\to\infty} \limsup_{T\to\infty} \mathbb{E}\|G_\infty(h) - G_m(h)\| = 0$$

where $\|\cdot\|$ denotes the matrix norm (see Definition 10.6).[9] Due to the absolute summability of Ψ_j and the boundedness of $\mathbb{E}\|Z_1 Z'_2\|$, the definitions of $G_\infty(h)$ and $G_m(h)$ imply that

$$\begin{aligned}
\mathbb{E}\|G_\infty(h) - G_m(h)\| &= \mathbb{E}\left\| \sum_{\substack{j>m \text{ or } i>m+h \\ i\neq j}} \Psi_j \left(\frac{1}{T}\sum_{t=0}^{T-1} Z_{t-j}Z'_{t-i}\right) \Psi'_{i-h} \right\| \\
&\leq \sum_{\substack{j>m \text{ or } i>m+h \\ i\neq j}} \|\Psi_j\| \left(\frac{1}{T}\sum_{t=0}^{T-1} \mathbb{E}\|Z_{t-j}Z'_{t-i}\|\right) \|\Psi_{i-h}\| \\
&\leq \sum_{\substack{j>m \text{ or } i>m+h \\ i\neq j}} \|\Psi_j\| \mathbb{E}\|Z_1 Z'_2\| \|\Psi_{i-h}\|
\end{aligned}$$

[9] Note that the convergence of the expectations of a sequence of integrable nonnegative random variables implies that the probability $\mathbf{P}(X_t > \varepsilon)$ converges to zero for every $\varepsilon > 0$. Moreover, convergence in distribution and convergence in probability are equivalent if the limit is a constant (see Theorem C.7 in Appendix C.)

$$\leq \sum_{\substack{j>m \text{ or } i>m \\ i\neq j}} \|\Psi_j\| \left(\mathbb{E}\|Z_1 Z_2'\|\right) \|\Psi_i\|$$

$$\leq \sum_{j>m} \|\Psi_j\| \left(\mathbb{E}\|Z_1 Z_2'\| \sum_{i} \|\Psi_i\|\right)$$

$$+ \left(\sum_{j} \|\Psi_j\| \, \mathbb{E}\|Z_1 Z_2'\|\right) \sum_{i>m} \|\Psi_i'\| \to 0,$$

for $m \to \infty$. Because these upper bounds hold independently of T, $G_\infty(h)$ converges to zero for every $h = 0, 1, \ldots, p-1$.

To derive the convergence (consistency) of $\widehat{G}(h)$ to $\Gamma(h)$, it remains to show that

$$\sum_{j=h}^{\infty} \Psi_j \left(\frac{1}{T}\sum_{t=0}^{T-1} Z_{t-j} Z_{t-j}'\right) \Psi_{j-h}'$$

$$= \sum_{j=h}^{\infty} \Psi_j \left(\frac{1}{T}\sum_{t=0}^{T-1} Z_t Z_t'\right) \Psi_{j-h}'$$

$$+ \sum_{j=h}^{\infty} \Psi_j \left(\frac{1}{T}\sum_{t=0}^{T-1} Z_{t-j} Z_{t-j}' - \frac{1}{T}\sum_{t=0}^{T-1} Z_t Z_t'\right) \Psi_{j-h}'$$

converges to $\Gamma(h)$. The term $\frac{1}{T}\sum_{t=1}^{T} Z_t Z_t'$ fulfills the requirements for the weak law of large numbers and converges to Σ (Brockwell & Davis, 1991, Proposition 7.3.4 or Theorem 11.1). To show that the second summand also converges to zero is left to the reader. Hence

$$\widehat{G}(h) \xrightarrow{\text{p}} \sum_{j=h}^{\infty} \Psi_j \Sigma \Psi_{j-h}' = \Gamma(h)$$

where the last equality follows from Theorem 10.2. □

Proposition 13.2. *Given the assumption in this chapter*

$$\frac{1}{\sqrt{T}} \sum_{t=1}^{T} \operatorname{vec}(Z_t X_{t-1}', Z_t X_{t-2}', \ldots, Z_t X_{t-p}')$$

$$= \frac{1}{\sqrt{T}}\text{vec}(\mathbf{ZX}) = \frac{1}{\sqrt{T}}(\mathbf{X}' \otimes I_n)\text{vec}Z$$

$$\xrightarrow{d} \text{N}(0, \mathbf{\Gamma}_p \otimes \Sigma).$$

Proof. The idea of the proof is to approximate $\{X_t\}$ by a simpler m-dependent process $\{X_t^{(m)}\}$ and to apply the Central Limit Theorem C.14 for m-dependent processes.[10] This leads to an asymptotic distribution which by the virtue of the basic approximation theorem C.15 converges to the asymptotic distribution of the original process.

Hence, define the m-dependent process $\{X_t^{(m)}\}$ as

$$X_t^{(m)} = Z_t + \Psi_1 Z_{t-1} + \ldots + \Psi_m Z_{t-m}, \qquad m = p, p+1, p+2, \ldots.$$

This allows to define the approximating process $\{Y_t^{(m)}\}$ by inserting $\{X_t^{(m)}\}$ and its lags:

$$Y_t^{(m)} = \text{vec}\left(Z_t X_{t-1}^{(m)\prime}, Z_t X_{t-2}^{(m)\prime}, \ldots, Z_t X_{t-p}^{(m)\prime}\right) = \begin{pmatrix} X_{t-1}^{(m)} \\ X_{t-2}^{(m)} \\ \vdots \\ X_{t-p}^{(m)} \end{pmatrix} \otimes Z_t.$$

Because Z_t is independent from all lagged $X_{t-j}^{(m)}$, $j = 1, \ldots, p$ for every t and because $\{X_t^{(m)}\}$ is a m-dependent process by construction, $\{Y_t^{(m)}\}$ is $(m+p)$-dependent. Clearly, $\{Y_t^{(m)}\}$ is also white noise, but not independent. In order to apply Theorem C.14, it remains to show that covariance matrix $\mathbf{V}_m = \mathbb{E}Y_t^{(m)} Y_t^{(m)\prime}$ is positive definite. Using the assumption that the fourth moments of the components of Z_t are finite,

$$\mathbf{V}_m = \mathbb{E}Y_t^{(m)} Y_t^{(m)\prime} = \mathbb{E}\left(\begin{pmatrix} X_{t-1}^{(m)} \\ X_{t-2}^{(m)} \\ \vdots \\ X_{t-p}^{(m)} \end{pmatrix} \otimes Z_t\right)\left(\begin{pmatrix} X_{t-1}^{(m)} \\ X_{t-2}^{(m)} \\ \vdots \\ X_{t-p}^{(m)} \end{pmatrix} \otimes Z_t\right)'$$

$$= \left(\mathbb{E}\begin{pmatrix} X_{t-1}^{(m)} \\ X_{t-2}^{(m)} \\ \cdots \\ X_{t-p}^{(m)} \end{pmatrix}\begin{pmatrix} X_{t-1}^{(m)} \\ X_{t-2}^{(m)} \\ \cdots \\ X_{t-p}^{(m)} \end{pmatrix}'\right) \otimes \mathbb{E}Z_t Z_t'$$

[10] The univariate version of this theorem carries over to multivariate processes.

$$
\begin{aligned}
&= \begin{pmatrix} \Gamma^{(m)}(0) & \Gamma^{(m)}(1) & \ldots & \Gamma^{(m)}(p-1) \\ \Gamma^{(m)}(1)' & \Gamma^{(m)}(0) & \ldots & \Gamma^{(m)}(p-2) \\ \vdots & \vdots & \ddots & \vdots \\ \Gamma^{(m)}(p-1)' & \Gamma^{(m)}(p-2)' & \ldots & \Gamma^{(m)}(0) \end{pmatrix} \otimes \Sigma \\
&= \mathbf{\Gamma}_p^{(m)} \otimes \Sigma
\end{aligned}
$$

where

$$
\begin{aligned}
\Gamma^{(m)}(h) &= \mathbb{E} X_{t-1}^{(m)} X_{t-1-h}^{(m)\prime} \\
&= \mathbb{E}\left(Z_{t-1} + \Psi_1 Z_{t-2} + \ldots + \Psi_m Z_{t-1-m}\right) \\
&\qquad \left(Z_{t-1-h} + \Psi_1 Z_{t-2-h} + \ldots + \Psi_m Z_{t-1-m-h}\right)' \\
&= \sum_{j=h}^{m} \Psi_j \Sigma \Psi_{j-h}', \qquad h = 0, 1, \ldots, p-1.
\end{aligned}
$$

Because Σ is by assumption positive definite, so is $\mathbf{\Gamma}_p^{(m)}$ positiv definite. Compare this with the discussion after the formulation of Theorem 13.1. The Kronecker product of two positive definite matrices is again positive definite. Hence, $\mathbf{V}_m$ is positive definite and the central limit theorem (C.14) for m-dependent processes can be applied:

$$
\frac{1}{\sqrt{T}} \sum_{t=1}^{T} \operatorname{vec}\left(Z_t X_{t-1}^{(m)\prime}, Z_t X_{t-2}^{(m)\prime}, \ldots, Z_t X_{t-p}^{(m)\prime}\right) \xrightarrow{\ \mathrm{d}\ } \mathrm{N}(0, \mathbf{\Gamma}_p^{(m)} \otimes \Sigma).
$$

Taking the limit $m \to \infty$, $\mathbf{V}_m$ converges to $V = \mathbf{\Gamma}_p \otimes \Sigma$, because $\mathbf{\Gamma}_p^{(m)} \to \mathbf{\Gamma}_p$. To apply Theorem C.15, it remains to show that $Y_t^{(m)}$ converges in the mean squared error sense uniformly in T (hence in probability) to $Y_t = \operatorname{vec}(Z_t X_{t-1}', Z_t X_{t-2}', \ldots, Z_t X_{t-p}')$. Consider for this purpose the covariance matrix of the approximation error:

$$
\begin{aligned}
&\mathbb{V}\left(\frac{1}{\sqrt{T}} \sum_{t=1}^{T} \left(\operatorname{vec}(Z_t X_{t-1}', \ldots, Z_t X_{t-p}') - W_t^{(m)}\right)\right) \\
&= \frac{1}{T} \mathbb{V}\left(\sum_{t=1}^{T} \operatorname{vec}\left(Z_t (X_{t-1} - X_{t-1}^{(m)})', \ldots, Z_t (X_{t-p} - X_{t-p}^{(m)})'\right)\right) \\
&= \frac{1}{T} \mathbb{V}\left(\sum_{t=1}^{T} \operatorname{vec}\left(Z_t \left(\sum_{j=m+1}^{\infty} \Psi_j Z_{t-1-j}\right)', \ldots, Z_t \left(\sum_{j=m+1}^{\infty} \Psi_j Z_{t-p-j}\right)'\right)\right)
\end{aligned}
$$

$$= \mathbb{V}\left(\text{vec}\left(Z_t\left(\sum_{j=m+1}^{\infty}\Psi_j Z_{t-1-j}\right)', \ldots, Z_t\left(\sum_{j=m+1}^{\infty}\Psi_j Z_{t-p-j}\right)'\right)\right)$$

$$= \mathbb{E}\left(\left(\begin{pmatrix}\sum_{j=m+1}^{\infty}\Psi_j Z_{t-1-j}\\ \vdots \\ \sum_{j=m+1}^{\infty}\Psi_j Z_{t-p-j}\end{pmatrix}\otimes Z_t\right)\left(\begin{pmatrix}\sum_{j=m+1}^{\infty}\Psi_j Z_{t-1-j}\\ \vdots \\ \sum_{j=m+1}^{\infty}\Psi_j Z_{t-p-j}\end{pmatrix}\otimes Z_t\right)'\right)$$

$$= \begin{pmatrix}\sum_{j=m+1}^{\infty}\Psi_j\Sigma\Psi_j' & \ldots & \ldots \\ \vdots & \ddots & \vdots \\ \ldots & \ldots & \sum_{j=m+1}^{\infty}\Psi_j\Sigma\Psi_j'\end{pmatrix}\otimes\Sigma.$$

The absolute summability of the matrices Ψ_j implies that this variance converges to zero independently from T and hence uniformly in T. Therefore

$$\frac{1}{\sqrt{T}}\sum_{t=1}^{T}\text{vec}(Z_t X_{t-1}', Z_t X_{t-2}', \ldots, Z_t X_{t-p}') \xrightarrow{\text{d}} \text{N}(0, \mathbf{\Gamma}_p\otimes\Sigma).$$

□

Proof of Theorem 13.1

Proof. We start by centering the OLS estimator:

$$\begin{aligned}\text{vec}\widehat{\Phi} &= (((\mathbf{X}'\mathbf{X})^{-1}\mathbf{X}')\otimes I_n)(\mathbf{X}\otimes I_n)\text{vec}\Phi + (((\mathbf{X}'\mathbf{X})^{-1}\mathbf{X}')\otimes I_n)\text{vec}Z\\ &= \text{vec}\Phi + (((\mathbf{X}'\mathbf{X})^{-1}\mathbf{X}')\otimes I_n)\text{vec}Z.\end{aligned}$$

Slutzky's Lemma C.10 implies for the convergence in probability

$$\begin{aligned}\text{plim}(\text{vec}\widehat{\Phi} - \text{vec}\Phi) &= \text{plim}\,\text{vec}\left(Z\mathbf{X}(\mathbf{X}'\mathbf{X})^{-1}\right)\\ &= \text{vec}\left(\text{plim}\frac{1}{T}Z\mathbf{X}\,\text{plim}\left(\frac{1}{T}\mathbf{X}'\mathbf{X}\right)^{-1}\right) = 0.\end{aligned}$$

The last result is an implication of Theorem 13.1 and the fact that $\text{plim}\,\frac{1}{T}ZX = 0$ which follows immediately from Theorem 13.2. Thus, we have proven the consistency of the OLS estimator.

The next step shows the asymptotic normality:

$$\begin{aligned}\sqrt{T}(\text{vec}\widehat{\Phi} - \text{vec}\Phi) &= \sqrt{T}\left(((\mathbf{X}'\mathbf{X})^{-1}\mathbf{X}')\otimes I_n\right)\text{vec}Z\\ &= \left(\left(\frac{1}{T}\mathbf{X}'\mathbf{X}^{-1}\right)\otimes I_n\right)\frac{1}{\sqrt{T}}(\mathbf{X}'\otimes I_n)\text{vec}Z.\end{aligned}$$

This follows again from Slutzky's Lemma C.10 and the central limit Theorem 13.2. The calculation rules for the Kronecker product show that the asymptotic covariance matrix equals

$$(\mathbf{\Gamma}_p^{-1} \otimes I_n)(\mathbf{\Gamma}_p \otimes \Sigma)(\mathbf{\Gamma}_p^{-1} \otimes I_n) = \mathbf{\Gamma}_p^{-1} \otimes \Sigma.$$

□

Proof of Theorem 13.2

Proof.

$$\begin{aligned}
\widehat{\Sigma} &= \frac{1}{T}(Y - \widehat{\Phi}\mathbf{X}')(Y - \widehat{\Phi}\mathbf{X}')' \\
&= \frac{1}{T}(Z + \Phi\mathbf{X}' - \widehat{\Phi}\mathbf{X}')(Z + \Phi\mathbf{X}' - \widehat{\Phi}\mathbf{X}')' \\
&= \frac{1}{T}(Z + (\Phi - \widehat{\Phi})\mathbf{X}')(Z + (\Phi - \widehat{\Phi})\mathbf{X}')' \\
&= \frac{1}{T}ZZ' + \frac{1}{T}Z\mathbf{X}(\Phi - \widehat{\Phi})' + (\Phi - \widehat{\Phi})\frac{1}{T}\mathbf{X}'Z' + (\Phi - \widehat{\Phi})\frac{1}{T}\mathbf{X}'\mathbf{X}(\Phi - \widehat{\Phi})'.
\end{aligned}$$

Theorems 13.1, 13.2, and C.10 immediately imply

$$\frac{Z\mathbf{X}(\Phi - \widehat{\Phi})'}{\sqrt{T}} \xrightarrow{\ p\ } 0$$

and

$$(\Phi - \widehat{\Phi})\frac{\mathbf{X}'\mathbf{X}}{T}\sqrt{T}(\Phi - \widehat{\Phi})' \xrightarrow{\ p\ } 0.$$

Therefore

$$\sqrt{T}\left(\frac{(Y - \widehat{\Phi}\mathbf{X}')(Y - \widehat{\Phi}\mathbf{X}')'}{T} - \frac{ZZ'}{T}\right) = \sqrt{T}\left(\widehat{\Sigma} - \frac{ZZ'}{T}\right) \xrightarrow{\ p\ } 0.$$

The triangular inequality for the matrix norm then implies

$$\|\hat{\Sigma} - \Sigma\| \leq \left\|\hat{\Sigma} - \frac{1}{T}ZZ'\right\| + \left\|\frac{1}{T}ZZ' - \Sigma\right\| \xrightarrow{\ p\ } 0.$$

Thereby, we used, as in the proof of Theorem 13.1, that, given our assumptions, $\frac{1}{T}ZZ' = \frac{1}{T}\sum_{t=1}^{T} Z_t Z_t'$ fulfills a law of large numbers and therefore converges to Σ. □

13.5 Exercises

Exercise 13.5.1. Show that vec$\widehat{\Phi}$ can also be obtained by minimizing the function $S_{\text{OLS}} = (\text{vec}Z)'(\text{vec}Z)$.

Exercise 13.5.2. Construct the commutator matrices K_{nT} und K_{n^2p} in Eq. (13.3) explicitly. Using these matrices compute the covariance matrix vecZ'.

Exercise 13.5.3. Show that the process $\{Y_t^{(m)}\}$ introduced in the proof of Proposition 13.2 is

(i) $(m + p)$ dependent;
(ii) white noise.

Exercise 13.5.4. Show the assertion

$$\sum_{j=h}^{\infty} \Psi_j \left(\frac{1}{T} \sum_{t=0}^{T-1} Z_{t-j} Z'_{t-j} - \frac{1}{T} \sum_{t=0}^{T-1} Z_t Z'_t \right) \Psi'_{j-h} \xrightarrow{\text{p}} 0,$$

used in the proof of Theorem 13.1.

Forecasting with VAR Models

14

14.1 Forecasting with Known Parameters

The discussion of forecasting with VAR models proceeds in two steps. First, we assume that the parameters of the model are known. Although this assumption is unrealistic, it will nevertheless allow us to introduce and analyze important concepts and ideas. The second step then investigates how the results established in the first step have to be amended if the unknown parameters are replaced by their estimates. The analysis will focus on stationary and causal VAR(1) processes. Processes of higher order can be accommodated by rewriting them in companion form. Thus,

$$X_t = \Phi X_{t-1} + Z_t, \qquad Z_t \sim \mathrm{WN}(0, \Sigma),$$

$$X_t = Z_t + \Psi_1 Z_{t-1} + \Psi_2 Z_{t-2} + \ldots = \sum_{j=0}^{\infty} \Psi_j Z_{t-j},$$

where $\Psi_j = \Phi^j$ and $\det(I_n - \Phi z) \neq 0, |z| \leq 1, z \in \mathbb{C}$. Consider the following forecasting problem: given observations $\{X_T, X_{T-1}, \ldots, X_1\}$, find a linear function, called predictor or forecast function, $\mathbb{P}_T X_{T+h}$, $h \geq 1$, which minimizes the expected quadratic forecast error

$$\mathbb{E}\,(X_{T+h} - \mathbb{P}_T X_{T+h})'\,(X_{T+h} - \mathbb{P}_T X_{T+h}) \\ = \mathbb{E}\,\mathrm{tr}(X_{T+h} - \mathbb{P}_T X_{T+h})(X_{T+h} - \mathbb{P}_T X_{T+h})'.$$

Thereby “tr” denotes the trace operator which takes the sum of the diagonal elements of a matrix. As we rely on linear forecasting functions, $\mathbb{P}_T X_{T+h}$ can be expressed as

K. Neusser, *Time Series Econometrics*, Springer Texts in Business and Economics,
https://doi.org/10.1007/978-3-031-88838-0_14

$$\mathbb{P}_T X_{T+h} = A_1 X_T + A_2 X_{T-1} + \ldots + A_T X_1 \tag{14.1}$$

with matrices $A_1, A_2, \ldots, A_T$ still to be determined. In order to simplify the exposition, we already accounted for the fact that the mean of $\{X_t\}$ is zero.[1] A justification for focusing on linear least-squares forecasts is given in Chap. 3. The first-order conditions for the least-squares minimization problem are given by the normal equations:

$$\begin{aligned}\mathbb{E}\left(X_{T+h} - \mathbb{P}_T X_{T+h}\right) X_s' &= \mathbb{E}\left(X_{T+h} - A_1 X_T - \ldots - A_T X_1\right) X_s' \\ &= \mathbb{E}X_{T+h}X_s' - A_1\mathbb{E}X_T X_s' - \ldots - A_T\mathbb{E}X_1 X_s' = 0, \quad 1 \leq s \leq T.\end{aligned}$$

These equations state that the forecast error $(X_{T+h} - \mathbb{P}_T X_{T+h})$ must be uncorrelated with the available information X_s, $s = 1, 2, \ldots, T$. The normal equations can be written as

$$\begin{aligned}(A_1, A_2, \ldots, A_T)&\begin{pmatrix} \Gamma(0) & \Gamma(1) & \ldots & \Gamma(T-1) \\ \Gamma'(1) & \Gamma(0) & \ldots & \Gamma(T-2) \\ \vdots & \vdots & \ddots & \vdots \\ \Gamma'(T-1) & \Gamma'(T-2) & \ldots & \Gamma(0) \end{pmatrix} \\ &= \left(\Gamma(h)\ \Gamma(h+1)\ \ldots\ \Gamma(T+h-1)\right).\end{aligned}$$

Denoting by $\mathbf{\Gamma}_T$ the matrix

$$\mathbf{\Gamma}_T = \begin{pmatrix} \Gamma(0) & \Gamma(1) & \ldots & \Gamma(T-1) \\ \Gamma'(1) & \Gamma(0) & \ldots & \Gamma(T-2) \\ \vdots & \vdots & \ddots & \vdots \\ \Gamma'(T-1) & \Gamma'(T-2) & \ldots & \Gamma(0) \end{pmatrix},$$

the normal equations can be written more compactly as

$$(A_1, A_2, \ldots, A_T)\,\mathbf{\Gamma}_T = \left(\Gamma(h)\ \Gamma(h+1)\ \ldots\ \Gamma(T+h-1)\right).$$

Using the assumption that $\{X_t\}$ is a VAR(1), $\Gamma(h)$ can be expressed as $\Gamma(h) = \Phi^h \Gamma(0)$ (see Eq. 12.3) so that the normal equations become

[1] If the mean is non-zero, a constant A_0 must be added to the forecast function.

$$(A_1, A_2, \ldots, A_T) \begin{pmatrix} \Gamma(0) & \Phi\Gamma(0) & \ldots & \Phi^{T-1}\Gamma(0) \\ \Gamma(0)\Phi' & \Gamma(0) & \ldots & \Phi^{T-2}\Gamma(0) \\ \vdots & \vdots & \ddots & \vdots \\ \Gamma(0)\Phi'^{T-1} & \Gamma(0)\Phi'^{T-2} & \ldots & \Gamma(0) \end{pmatrix}$$
$$= \left(\Phi^h\Gamma(0) \; \Phi^{h+1}\Gamma(0) \ldots \Phi^{T+h-1}\Gamma(0)\right).$$

The easily guessed solution is given by $A_1 = \Phi^h$ and $A_2 = \ldots = A_T = 0$. Thus, the sought-after forecasting function for the VAR(1) process is

$$\mathbb{P}_T X_{T+h} = \Phi^h X_T. \tag{14.2}$$

The forecast error $X_{T+h} - \mathbb{P}_T X_{T+h}$ has expectation zero. Thus, the linear least-squares predictor delivers unbiased forecasts. As

$$X_{T+h} = Z_{T+h} + \Phi Z_{T+h-1} + \ldots + \Phi^{h-1} Z_{T+1} + \Phi^h X_T,$$

the expected squared forecast error (mean squared error) MSE(h) is

$$\begin{aligned} \text{MSE}(h) &= \mathbb{E}\left(X_{T+h} - \Phi^h X_T\right)\left(X_{T+h} - \Phi^h X_T\right)' \\ &= \Sigma + \Phi\Sigma\Phi' + \ldots + \Phi^{h-1}\Sigma\Phi'^{h-1} = \sum_{j=0}^{h-1} \Phi^j \Sigma \Phi'^j. \end{aligned} \tag{14.3}$$

In order to analyze the case of a causal VAR(p) process with $T > p$, we transform the model into the companion form. For $h = 1$, we can apply the result above to get

$$\mathbb{P}_T Y_{T+1} = \Phi Y_T = \begin{pmatrix} \mathbb{P}_T X_{T+1} \\ X_T \\ X_{T-1} \\ \vdots \\ X_{T-p+2} \end{pmatrix} = \begin{pmatrix} \Phi_1 & \Phi_2 & \ldots & \Phi_{p-1} & \Phi_p \\ I_n & 0 & \ldots & 0 & 0 \\ 0 & I_n & \ldots & 0 & 0 \\ \vdots & \vdots & \ddots & \vdots & \vdots \\ 0 & 0 & \ldots & I_n & 0 \end{pmatrix} \begin{pmatrix} X_T \\ X_{T-1} \\ X_{T-2} \\ \vdots \\ X_{T-p+1} \end{pmatrix}.$$

This implies that

$$\mathbb{P}_T X_{T+1} = \Phi_1 X_T + \Phi_2 X_{T-1} + \ldots + \Phi_p X_{T-p+1}. \tag{14.4}$$

The forecast error is $X_{T+1} - \mathbb{P}_T X_{T+1} = Z_t$ which has mean zero and covariance variance matrix Σ. In general we have that $\mathbb{P}_T Y_{T+h} = \Phi^h Y_T$ so that $\mathbb{P}_T X_{T+h}$ is equal to

$$\mathbb{P}_T X_{T+h} = \Phi_1^{(h)} X_T + \Phi_2^{(h)} X_{T-1} + \ldots + \Phi_p^{(h)} X_{T-p+1}$$

where $\Phi_i^{(h)}$, $i = 1, \ldots, p$, denote the blocks in the first row of Φ^h. Alternatively, the forecast for $h > 1$ can be computed recursively. For $h = 2$ this leads to

$$\begin{aligned}\mathbb{P}_T X_{T+2} &= \mathbb{P}_T(\Phi_1 X_{T+1}) + \mathbb{P}_T(\Phi_2 X_T) + \ldots + \mathbb{P}_T\left(\Phi_p X_{T+2-p}\right) + \mathbb{P}_T(Z_{T+2}) \\ &= \Phi_1\left(\Phi_1 X_T + \Phi_2 X_{T-1} + \ldots + \Phi_p X_{T+1-p}\right) \\ &\quad + \Phi_2 X_T + \ldots + \Phi_p X_{T+2-p} \\ &= \left(\Phi_1^2 + \Phi_2\right) X_T + (\Phi_1\Phi_2 + \Phi_3) X_{T-1} \\ &\quad + \ldots + \left(\Phi_1\Phi_{p-1} + \Phi_p\right) X_{T+2-p} + \Phi_1\Phi_p X_{T+1-p}.\end{aligned}$$

For $h > 2$ we proceed analogously. This way of producing forecasts is sometimes called *iterated* forecasts.

In general, the forecast error of a causal VAR(p) process can be expressed as

$$\begin{aligned}X_{T+h} - \mathbb{P}_T X_{T+h} &= Z_{T+h} + \Psi_1 Z_{T+h-1} + \ldots + \Psi_{h-1} Z_{T+1} \\ &= \sum_{j=0}^{h-1} \Phi_j Z_{T+h-j}.\end{aligned}$$

The MSE(h) then is as before:

$$\text{MSE}(h) = \Sigma + \Psi_1 \Sigma \Psi_1' + \ldots + \Psi_{h-1}\Sigma\Psi_{h-1}' = \sum_{j=0}^{h-1} \Psi_j \Sigma \Psi_j'. \tag{14.5}$$

Example Consider again the VAR(2) model of Sect. 12.3. The forecast function in this case is then

$$\begin{aligned}\mathbb{P}_T X_{T+1} &= \Phi_1 X_t + \Phi_2 X_{t-1} \\ &= \begin{pmatrix} 0.8 & -0.5 \\ 0.1 & -0.5 \end{pmatrix} X_t + \begin{pmatrix} -0.3 & -0.3 \\ -0.2 & 0.3 \end{pmatrix} X_{t-1}, \\ \mathbb{P}_T X_{T+2} &= (\Phi_1^2 + \Phi_2) X_t + \Phi_1\Phi_2 X_{t-1} \\ &= \begin{pmatrix} 0.29 & -0.45 \\ -0.17 & 0.50 \end{pmatrix} X_t + \begin{pmatrix} -0.14 & -0.39 \\ 0.07 & -0.18 \end{pmatrix} X_{t-1}, \\ \mathbb{P}_T X_{T+3} &= (\Phi_1^3 + \Phi_1\Phi_2 + \Phi_2\Phi_1) X_t + (\Phi_1^2\Phi_2 + \Phi_2^2) X_{t-1} \\ &= \begin{pmatrix} 0.047 & -0.310 \\ -0.016 & -0.345 \end{pmatrix} X_t + \begin{pmatrix} 0.003 & -0.222 \\ -0.049 & 0.201 \end{pmatrix} X_{t-1}.\end{aligned}$$

Based on the results computed in Sect. 12.3, we can calculate the corresponding mean squared errors (MSE):

$$\text{MSE}(1) = \Sigma = \begin{pmatrix} 1.0 & 0.4 \\ 0.4 & 2.0 \end{pmatrix},$$

$$\text{MSE}(2) = \Sigma + \Psi_1 \Sigma \Psi_1' = \begin{pmatrix} 1.82 & 0.80 \\ 0.80 & 2.47 \end{pmatrix},$$

$$\text{MSE}(3) = \Sigma + \Psi_1 \Sigma \Psi_1' + \Psi_2 \Sigma \Psi_2' = \begin{pmatrix} 2.2047 & 0.3893 \\ 0.3893 & 2.9309 \end{pmatrix}.$$

A forecasting exercise with additional material is presented in Sect. 14.6.

14.2 Wold's Decomposition Theorem

At this stage we note that *Wold's theorem* or *Wold's decomposition* carries over to the multivariate case (see Sect. 3.2 for the univariate case). This Theorem asserts that every regular (non-singular) stationary process has a decomposition(representation) of the form[2]

$$X_t = \mu + \sum_{j=0}^{\infty} \Psi_j Z_{t-j},$$

where $\Psi_0 = I_n$, $Z_t \sim \text{WN}(0, \Sigma)$ with $\Sigma > 0$ and $\sum_{j=0}^{\infty} \|\Psi_j\|^2 < \infty$. As noted before, square summability of the $\|\Psi_j\|$ does not imply absolute summability. The innovations $\{Z_t\}$ have the property $Z_t = X_t - \widetilde{\mathbb{P}}_{t-1} X_t$ and consequently $Z_t = \widetilde{\mathbb{P}}_t Z_t$. Thereby $\widetilde{\mathbb{P}}_t$ denotes the linear least-squares predictor based on the infinite past $\{X_t, X_{t-1}, \ldots\}$. The interpretation of the multivariate case is analogous to the univariate one.

14.3 Forecasting with Estimated Parameters

In practice the parameters of the VAR model are usually unknown and have therefore to be estimated. In the previous section we have demonstrated that

$$\mathbb{P}_T X_{T+h} = \Phi_1 \mathbb{P}_T X_{T+h-1} + \ldots + \Phi_p \mathbb{P}_T X_{T+h-p}$$

[2] A stationary stochastic process is called singular if it can be perfectly forecasted from its infinite past. It is called regular or non-singular if there is no singular component (see Sect. 3.2).

where $\mathbb{P}_T X_{T+h-j} = Y_{T+h-j}$ if $j \geq h$. Replacing the true parameters by their estimates, we get the forecast function

$$\widehat{\mathbb{P}}_T X_{T+h} = \widehat{\Phi}_1 \widehat{\mathbb{P}}_T X_{T+h-1} + \ldots + \widehat{\Phi}_p \widehat{\mathbb{P}}_T X_{T+h-p}.$$

where a hat indicates the use of estimates. The forecast error can then be decomposed into two components:

$$\begin{aligned} X_{T+h} - \widehat{\mathbb{P}}_T X_{T+h} &= (X_{T+h} - \mathbb{P}_T X_{T+h}) + \left(\mathbb{P}_T X_{T+h} - \widehat{\mathbb{P}}_T X_{T+h}\right) \\ &= \sum_{j=0}^{h-1} \Phi_j Z_{T+h-j} + \left(\mathbb{P}_T X_{T+h} - \widehat{\mathbb{P}}_T X_{T+h}\right). \end{aligned} \tag{14.6}$$

Dufour (1985) has shown that, under the assumption of symmetrically distributed Z_t's (i.e., if Z_t and $-Z_t$ have the same distribution), the expectation of the forecast error is zero even when the parameters are replaced by their least-squares estimates. This result holds despite the fact that these estimates are biased in small samples. Moreover, the results do not assume that the model is correctly specified in terms of the order p. Thus, under quite general conditions, the forecast with estimated coefficients remains unbiased so that $\mathbb{E}\left(X_{T+h} - \widehat{\mathbb{P}}_T X_{T+h}\right) = 0$.

If the estimation is based on a different sample than the one used for forecasting, the two terms in the above expression are uncorrelated so that its mean squared error is by the sum of the two mean squared errors

$$\begin{aligned} \widehat{\text{MSE}}(h) = &\sum_{j=0}^{h-1} \Psi_j \Sigma \Psi_j' \\ &+ \mathbb{E}\left(\mathbb{P}_T X_{T+h} - \widehat{\mathbb{P}}_T X_{T+h}\right)\left(\mathbb{P}_T X_{T+h} - \widehat{\mathbb{P}}_T X_{T+h}\right)'. \end{aligned} \tag{14.7}$$

The last term can be evaluated by using the asymptotic distribution of the coefficients as an approximation. The corresponding formula turns out to be cumbersome. The technical details can be found in Lütkepohl (2005) and Reinsel (1993). The formula can, however, be simplified considerably if we consider a forecast horizon of only one period. We deduce the formula for a VAR of order one, i.e., taking $X_t = \Phi X_{t-1} + Z_t$, $Z_t \sim \text{WN}(0, \Sigma)$.

$$\mathbb{P}_T X_{T+h} - \widehat{\mathbb{P}}_T X_{T+h} = (\Phi - \widehat{\Phi}) X_T = \text{vec}\left((\Phi - \widehat{\Phi}) X_T\right) = (X_T' \otimes I_n)\,\text{vec}(\Phi - \widehat{\Phi}).$$

This implies that

$$\begin{aligned} &\mathbb{E}\left(\mathbb{P}_T X_{T+h} - \widehat{\mathbb{P}}_T X_{T+h}\right)\left(\mathbb{P}_T X_{T+h} - \widehat{\mathbb{P}}_T X_{T+h}\right)' \\ &= \mathbb{E}(X_T' \otimes I_n)\,\text{vec}(\Phi - \widehat{\Phi})(\text{vec}(\Phi - \widehat{\Phi}))'(X_T \otimes I_n) \end{aligned}$$

$$= \mathbb{E}(X_T' \otimes I_n)\frac{\Gamma_1^{-1} \otimes \Sigma}{T}(X_T \otimes I_n) = \frac{1}{T}\mathbb{E}(X_T'\Gamma_1^{-1}X_T) \otimes \Sigma$$
$$= \frac{1}{T}\mathbb{E}(\text{tr}X_T'\Gamma_1^{-1}X_T) \otimes \Sigma = \frac{1}{T}\text{tr}(\Gamma_1^{-1}\mathbb{E}(X_T X_T')) \otimes \Sigma$$
$$= \frac{1}{T}(\text{tr}(I_n) \otimes \Sigma) = \frac{n}{T}\Sigma.$$

Thereby, we have used the asymptotic normality of the least-squares estimator (see Theorem 13.1) and the assumption that forecasting and estimation uses different realizations of the stochastic process. Thus, for $h = 1$ and $p = 1$, we get

$$\widehat{\text{MSE}}(1) = \Sigma + \frac{n}{T}\Sigma = \frac{T+n}{T}\Sigma.$$

Higher-order models can be treated similarly using the companion form of VAR(p). In this case:

$$\widehat{\text{MSE}}(1) = \Sigma + \frac{np}{T}\Sigma = \frac{T+np}{T}\Sigma. \tag{14.8}$$

This is only an approximation as we applied asymptotic results to small sample entities. The expression shows that the effect of the substitution of the coefficients by their least-squares estimates vanishes as the sample becomes large. However, in small samples, the factor $\frac{T+np}{T}$ can be sizeable. In the example treated in Sect. 14.6, the covariance matrix Σ, taking the use of a constant into account and assuming 8 lags, has to be inflated by $\frac{T+np+1}{T} = \frac{196+4\times 8+1}{196} = 1.168$. Note also that the precision of the forecast, given Σ, diminishes with the number of parameters.

14.4 Modeling VAR Processes

The previous section treated the estimation of VAR models under the assumption that the order of the VAR, p, is known. In most cases, this assumption is unrealistic as the order p is unknown and must be retrieved from the data. We can proceed analogously as in the univariate case (see Sect. 5.1) and iteratively test the hypothesis that coefficients corresponding to the highest lag, i.e., $\Phi_p = 0$, are simultaneously equal to zero. Starting from a maximal order p_{max}, we test the null hypothesis that $\Phi_{p_{max}} = 0$ in the corresponding VAR(p_{max}) model. If the hypothesis is not rejected, we reduce the order by one to $p_{max} - 1$ and test anew the null hypothesis $\Phi_{p_{max}-1} = 0$ using the smaller VAR($p_{max} - 1$) model. One continues in this way until the null hypothesis is rejected. This gives, then, the appropriate order of the VAR. The different tests can be carried out either as Wald tests (F-tests) or as likelihood-ratio tests (χ^2-tests) with n^2 degrees of freedom. Although this successive testing procedure is not consistent when the significance level is kept constant, it nevertheless represents a practical and easy to implement strategy.

An alternative procedure to determine the order of the VAR relies on some information criteria. As in the univariate case, the most popular ones are the Akaike (AIC), the Schwarz or Bayesian (BIC) and the Hannan-Quinn criterion (HQC). The corresponding formula are

$$\begin{aligned}
\text{AIC(p):} &\quad \ln\det\widetilde{\Sigma}_p + \frac{2pn^2}{T}, \\
\text{BIC(p):} &\quad \ln\det\widetilde{\Sigma}_p + \frac{pn^2}{T}\ln T, \\
\text{HQC(p):} &\quad \ln\det\widetilde{\Sigma}_p + \frac{2pn^2}{T}\ln(\ln T),
\end{aligned}$$

where $\widetilde{\Sigma}_p$ denotes the degree of freedom adjusted estimate of the covariance matrix Σ for a model of order p (see Eq. 13.7). $n^2 p$ is the number of estimated coefficients. The estimated order is then given as the minimizer of one of these criteria. In practice, Akaike's criterion is the most popular one although it has a tendency to deliver orders which are too high. The BIC and the HQC criterion on the other hand deliver correct orders on average, but face the danger of omitted variable biases when the estimated order is too low. Examples are discussed in Sects. 14.6 and 15.3.5.

Following Lütkepohl (2005), Akaike's information criterion can be rationalized as follows. Take as a measure of fit the determinant of the one period approximate mean-squared errors $\widehat{\text{MSE}}(1)$ from Eq. (14.8) and take as an estimate of Σ the degrees of freedom corrected version in Eq. (13.7). The resulting criterion is called according to Akaike (1969) the *final prediction error* (FPE):

$$\text{FPE}(p) = \det\left(\frac{T+np}{T} \times \frac{T}{T-np}\widetilde{\Sigma}\right) = \left(\frac{T+np}{T-np}\right)^n \det\widetilde{\Sigma}. \tag{14.9}$$

Taking logs and using the approximations $\frac{T+np}{T-np} \approx 1+\frac{2np}{T}$ and $\log(1+\frac{2np}{T}) \approx \frac{2np}{T}$, we arrive at

$$\text{AIC}(p) \approx \log FPE(p).$$

14.5 Wiener-Granger Causality

The economic interpretation of VAR models often turn out to be difficult. As a first technique for understanding the dynamics of VAR processes, we analyze the concept of *causality* which was introduced by Granger (1969). The concept is also known as *Wiener-Granger causality* because Granger's idea goes back to the work of Wiener (1956). Take a multivariate time series $\{X_t\}$ and consider the forecast of $X_{1,T+h}$, $h \geq 1$, given $X_T, X_{T-1}, \ldots$ where $\{X_t\}$ has not only X_{1t} as a component but also another variables or group of variables X_{2t}. X_t may contain even further variables than $X_{1,t}$ and $X_{2,t}$. The mean-squared forecast error is denoted by $\text{MSE}_1(h)$. Compare this to an alternative forecast of $X_{1,T+h}$ given $\widetilde{X}_T, \widetilde{X}_{T-1}, \ldots$ where $\{\widetilde{X}_t\}$ is obtained from $\{X_t\}$ by eliminating the component $X_{2,t}$. The mean-squared error of this forecast is denoted by $\widetilde{\text{MSE}}_1(h)$. According to Granger, we can say that the second variable $X_{2,t}$ *causes* or *is causal for* $X_{1,t}$ if and only if

$$\text{MSE}(h)_1 < \widetilde{\text{MSE}}_1(h) \qquad \text{for some } h \geq 1.$$

This means that the information contained in $\{X_{2t}\}$ and its past improves the forecast of $\{X_{1t}\}$ in the sense of the mean-squared forecast error. Thus the concept of Wiener-Granger causality makes only sense for regular processes and rest on two principles:[3]

- The future cannot cause the past. Only the past can have a causal influence on the future.[4]
- A specific cause contains information not available otherwise.

The concept of Wiener-Granger causality played an important role in the debate between monetarists and Keynesians over the issue whether the money stock has an independent influence on real activity. It turned out that this question can only be resolved within a specific setting. Sims (1980a), for example, showed that the relationship between the growth rate of the money stock and changes in real activity depends on whether a short interest rate is accounted for in the empirical analysis or not. Another problem of the concept is that it is not unambiguously possible to infer a causal relationship just from the chronology of two variables as demonstrated by Tobin (1970). This and other conceptual issues (see Zellner, 1979 and the discussion in the next chapter) and econometric problems (Geweke, 1984) led to a decline in the practical importance of this concept.

We propose two econometric implementations of the causality concept. The first one is based on a VAR; the second one is nonparametric and uses cross-correlations. In addition, we propose an interpretation in terms of the causal representation, respectively the Wold decomposition theorem (see Sect. 14.2).

[3] Compare this to the concept of a causal representation developed in Sects. 12.3 and 2.3.

[4] Sometimes also the concept of *contemporaneous causality* is considered. This concept is, however, controversial and has therefore not gained much success in practice and will, therefore, not be pursued.

14.5.1 The VAR Approach

If one restricts oneself to linear least-squares forecasts, the above definition can be easily operationalized in the context of VAR models with only two variables (see also Sims, 1972). Consider first a VAR(1) model. Then according to the explanations in Sect. 14.1 the one-period forecast is

$$\mathbb{P}_T X_{T+1} = \begin{pmatrix} \mathbb{P}_T X_{1,T+1} \\ \mathbb{P}_T X_{2,T+1} \end{pmatrix} = \Phi X_T = \begin{pmatrix} \phi_{11} & \phi_{12} \\ \phi_{21} & \phi_{22} \end{pmatrix} \begin{pmatrix} X_{1,T} \\ X_{2,T} \end{pmatrix}$$

and therefore

$$\mathbb{P}_T X_{1,T+1} = \phi_{11} X_{1T} + \phi_{12} X_{2T}.$$

If $\phi_{12} = 0$ then the second variable does not contribute to the one-period forecast of the first variable and can therefore be omitted: $\text{MSE}_1(1) = \widetilde{\text{MSE}}_1(1)$ in this case. Note that

$$\Phi^h = \begin{pmatrix} \phi_{11}^h & 0 \\ * & \phi_{22}^h \end{pmatrix},$$

where $*$ is a placeholder for an arbitrary number. Thus the second variable is not only irrelevant for the one-period forecast but for any forecast horizon $h \geq 1$. Thus, the second variable is *not causal* for the first variable in the sense of Wiener-Granger causality.

These arguments can be easily extended to VAR(p) models. According to Eq. (14.4), we have that

$$\mathbb{P}_T X_{1,T+1} = \phi_{11}^{(1)} X_{1T} + \phi_{12}^{(1)} X_{2T} + \ldots + \phi_{11}^{(p)} X_{1,T-p+1} + \phi_{12}^{(p)} X_{2,T-p+1}$$

where $\phi_{ij}^{(k)}$ denotes (i, j)-th element, $i = 1, 2$, of the matrix Φ_k, $k = 1, \ldots, p$. In order for the second variable to have no influence on the forecast of the first one, we must have that $\phi_{12}^{(1)} = \phi_{12}^{(2)} = \ldots = \phi_{12}^{(p)} = 0$. This implies that all matrices Φ_k, $k = 1, \ldots, p$, must be lower triangular, i.e., they must be of the form $\begin{pmatrix} * & 0 \\ * & * \end{pmatrix}$. As the multiplication and addition of lower triangular matrices is again a lower triangular matrix, the second variable is irrelevant in forecasting the first one at any forecast horizon. This can be seen by computing the corresponding forecast function recursively as in Chap. 14.

Based on this insight, it is straightforward to test the null hypothesis that the second variable does not cause the first one within the VAR(p) context:

$$\mathbf{H}_0\text{: } \{X_{2t}\} \textit{ does not cause } \{X_{1t}\}.$$

In terms of the VAR model, this hypothesis can be stated as

$$\mathbf{H}_0 : \phi_{12}^{(1)} = \phi_{12}^{(2)} = \ldots = \phi_{12}^{(p)} = 0.$$

The alternative hypothesis is that the null hypothesis is violated. As the method of least-squares estimation leads to asymptotically normally distributed coefficient estimates under quite general assumptions, it is straightforward to test the above hypothesis by a Wald test (F-test). In the context of a VAR(1) model, a simple t-test is also possible.

If more than two variables are involved the concept of Wiener-Granger causality is no longer so easy to implement. Consider for expositional purposes a VAR(1) model in three variables with coefficient matrix:

$$\Phi = \begin{pmatrix} \phi_{11} & \phi_{12} & 0 \\ \phi_{21} & \phi_{22} & \phi_{23} \\ \phi_{31} & \phi_{32} & \phi_{33} \end{pmatrix}.$$

The one-period forecast function of the first variable then is

$$\mathbb{P}_T X_{1,T+1} = \phi_{11} X_{1T} + \phi_{12} X_{2T}.$$

Thus, the third variable X_{3T} is irrelevant for the one-period forecast of the first variable. However, as the third variable has an influence on the second variable, $\phi_{23} \neq 0$, and because the second variable has an influence on the first variable, $\phi_{12} \neq 0$, the third variable will provide indirectly useful information for the forecast of the first variable for forecasting horizons $h \geq 2$. Consequently, the concept of causality cannot immediately be extended from two to more than two variables.

It is, however, possible to merge variables one and two, or variables two and three, into groups and discuss the hypothesis that the third variable does not cause the first two variables, seen as a group; likewise that the second and third variable, seen as a group, does not cause the first variable. The corresponding null hypotheses then are

$$\mathbf{H}_0 : \phi_{23} = \phi_{13} = 0 \quad \text{or} \quad \mathbf{H}_0 : \phi_{12} = \phi_{13} = 0.$$

Under these null hypotheses, we get again lower (block-) triangular matrices:

$$\begin{pmatrix} \phi_{11} & \phi_{12} & \vdots & 0 \\ \phi_{21} & \phi_{22} & \vdots & 0 \\ \cdots & \cdots & \vdots & \cdots \\ \phi_{31} & \phi_{32} & \vdots & \phi_{33} \end{pmatrix} \quad \text{or} \quad \begin{pmatrix} \phi_{11} & \vdots & 0 & 0 \\ \cdots & \cdots & \cdots & \cdots \\ \phi_{21} & \vdots & \phi_{22} & \phi_{23} \\ \phi_{31} & \vdots & \phi_{32} & \phi_{33} \end{pmatrix}.$$

Each of these hypotheses can again be checked by a Wald test (F-test).

14.5.2 Wiener-Granger Causality and Causal Representation

We can get further insights into the concept of causality by considering a bivariate VAR, $\Phi(\mathrm{L})X_t = Z_t$, with causal representation $X_t = \Psi(\mathrm{L})Z_t$. Partitioning the matrices according to $\{X_{1t}\}$ and $\{X_{2t}\}$, Theorem 12.1 of Sect. 12.3 implies that

$$\begin{pmatrix} \Phi_{11}(z) & \Phi_{12}(z) \\ \Phi_{21}(z) & \Phi_{22}(z) \end{pmatrix} \begin{pmatrix} \Psi_{11}(z) & \Psi_{12}(z) \\ \Psi_{21}(z) & \Psi_{22}(z) \end{pmatrix} = \begin{pmatrix} 1 & 0 \\ 0 & 1 \end{pmatrix}$$

where the polynomials $\Phi_{12}(z)$ and $\Phi_{21}(z)$ have no constant terms. The hypothesis that the second variable does not cause the first one is equivalent in this framework to the hypothesis that $\Phi_{12}(z) = 0$. Multiplying out the above expression leads to the condition

$$\Phi_{11}(z)\Psi_{12}(z) = 0.$$

Because $\Phi_{11}(z)$ involves a constant term, the above equation implies that $\Psi_{12}(z) = 0$. Thus the causal representation is lower triangular. This means that the first variable is composed of the first shock, $\{Z_{1t}\}$ only, whereas the second variable involves both shocks $\{Z_{1t}\}$ and $\{Z_{2t}\}$. The univariate causal representation of $\{X_{1t}\}$ is therefore the same as the bivariate one.[5] Finally, note the similarity to the issue of the identification of shocks discussed in Chap. 15.

14.5.3 The Cross-Correlation Approach

In the case of two variables, the cross-correlations can be used to test for causality. This nonparametric test has the advantage that one does not have to rely on an explicit VAR model. This advantage becomes particularly relevant, if a VMA model must be approximated by a high-order AR model. Consider the cross-correlations

$$\rho_{12}(h) = \mathrm{corr}(X_{1t}, X_{2,t-h}).$$

If $\rho_{12}(h) \neq 0$ for $h > 0$, we can say that the past values of the second variable are useful for forecasting the first variable such that the second variable causes the first one in the sense of Wiener and Granger. Another terminology is that the second variable is a *leading indicator* for the first one. If in addition, $\rho_{12}(h) \neq 0$, for $h < 0$, so that the past values of the first variable help to forecast the second one, we have causality in both directions.

As the distribution of the cross-correlations of two independent variables depends on the autocorrelation of each variable, see Theorem 11.4, Haugh (1976) and Pierce

[5] As we are working with causal VARs, the above arguments also hold with respect to the Wold decomposition.

and Haugh (1977) propose a test based on the filtered time series. Analogously to the test for independence (see Sect. 11.2), we proceed in two steps:

Step 1: Estimate in the first step a univariate AR(p) model for each of the two time series $\{X_{1t}\}$ and $\{X_{2t}\}$. Thereby chose p such that the corresponding residuals $\{\hat{Z}_{1t}\}$ and $\{\hat{Z}_{2t}\}$ are white noise. This step is called prewhitening. Note that although $\{\hat{Z}_{1t}\}$ and $\{\hat{Z}_{2t}\}$ are both not autocorrelated, the cross-correlations $\rho_{Z_1,Z_2}(h)$ may still be non-zero for arbitrary orders h.

Step 2: As $\{\hat{Z}_{1t}\}$ and $\{\hat{Z}_{2t}\}$ are the forecast errors based on forecasts which rely only on the own past, the concept of causality carries over from the original variables to the residuals. The null hypothesis that the second variable does not cause the first variable in the sense of Wiener and Granger can then be checked by the *Haugh-Pierce statistic*:

$$\text{Haugh-Pierce statistic:} \quad T \sum_{h=1}^{L} \hat{\rho}^2_{Z_1,Z_2}(h) \sim \chi^2_L. \tag{14.10}$$

Thereby $\hat{\rho}^2_{Z_1,Z_2}(h)$, $h = 1, 2, \ldots$, denotes the squared estimated cross-correlation coefficients between $\{\hat{Z}_{1t}\}$ and $\{\hat{Z}_{2t}\}$. Under the null hypothesis that the second variable does not cause the first one, this test statistic is distributed as a χ^2 distribution with L degrees of freedom.

14.6 A VAR Model for the US Economy

This section illustrates the process of building a macroeconomic VAR forecasting model for the US economy. The model comprises the following four variables: GDP per capita ($\{Y_t\}$), price level in terms of the consumer price index (CPI) ($\{P_t\}$), real money stock M1 ($\{M_t\}$), and the 3 month treasury bill rate ($\{R_t\}$). All variables are, with the exception of the interest rate, in logged differences (growth rates). The components of X_t are with the exception of the interest rate stationary.[6] Thus, we aim at modeling $X_t = (\Delta \log Y_t, \Delta \log P_t, \Delta \log M_t, R_t)'$. The sample runs from the first quarter of 1959 to the first quarter of 2012. The estimation period, however, ends in the fourth quarter of 2008. The remaining 13 quarterly observations from the first quarter of 2009 to the first quarter of 2012 are reserved for an out-of-sample evaluation of the forecast performance. This forecast assessment has the advantage to account explicitly of the sampling variability in estimated parameter models.

[6] Although the unit root test indicate that R_t is integrated of order one, we do not difference this variable. This specification will not affect the consistency of the estimates nor the choice of the lag-length (Sims et al., 1990), but has the advantage that each component of X_t is expressed in percentage points which facilitates the interpretation.

Table 14.1 Information criteria for VAR models of different orders

Order	AIC	BIC	HQC
0	−14.498	−14.429	−14.470
1	−17.956	−17.611	−17.817
2	−18.638	**−18.016**	−18.386
3	−18.741	−17.843	−18.377
4	−18.943	−17.768	−18.467
5	−19.081	−17.630	**−18.493**
6	−19.077	−17.349	−18.377
7	−19.076	−17.072	−18.264
8	**−19.120**	−16.839	−18.195
9	−18.988	−16.431	−17.952
10	−18.995	−16.162	−17.847
11	−18.900	−15.789	−17.639
12	−18.884	−15.497	−17.512

Minimum in bold

The first step in the modeling process is the determination of the lag-length. Allowing for a maximum of twelve lags, the different information criteria produce the values reported in Table 14.1. Unfortunately, the three criteria deliver different orders: AIC suggests eight lags, HQC five lags, and BIC two lags. In such a situation, it is wise to keep all three models and to perform additional diagnostic tests.[7] One such test is to run a horse-race between the three models in terms of their forecasting performance.

Forecasts are evaluated according to the root-mean-squared-error (RMSE) and the mean-absolute-error (MAE)[8]

$$\text{RMSE}: \quad \sqrt{\frac{1}{h}\sum_{T+1}^{T+h}(\widehat{X}_{it} - X_{it})^2} \tag{14.11}$$

$$\text{MAE}: \quad \frac{1}{h}\sum_{T+1}^{T+h}|\widehat{X}_{it} - X_{it}| \tag{14.12}$$

where $\widehat{X}_{it}$ and X_{it} denote the forecast and the actual value of variable i in period t. Forecasts are computed for a horizon h starting in period T. We can gain further insights by decomposing the mean-squared-error additively into three components

[7] Such tests would include an analysis of the autocorrelation properties of the residuals and tests of structural breaks.

[8] Alternatively one could use the mean-absolute-percentage-error (MAPE). However, as all variables are already in percentages, the MAE is to be preferred.

$$\frac{1}{h}\sum_{T+1}^{T+h}(\widehat{X}_{lt} - X_{lt})^2 = \left(\left(\frac{1}{h}\sum_{T+1}^{T+h}\widehat{X}_{lt}\right) - \overline{X}_l\right)^2 + (\sigma_{\widehat{X}_l} - \sigma_{X_l})^2 + 2(1-\rho)\sigma_{\widehat{X}_l}\sigma_{X_l}.$$

The first component measures how far the mean of the forecasts $\frac{1}{h}\sum_{T+1}^{T+h}\widehat{X}_{lt}$ is away from the actual mean of the data $\overline{X}_l$. It therefore measures the *bias* of the forecasts. The second one compares the standard deviation of the forecast $\sigma_{\widehat{X}_l}$ to those of the data σ_{X_l}. Finally, the last component is a measure of the unsystematic forecast errors where ρ denotes the correlation between the forecast and the data. Ideally, each of the three components should be close to zero: there should be no bias, the variation of the forecasts should correspond to those of the data, and the forecasts and the data should be highly positively correlated. In order to avoid scaling problems, all three components are usually expressed as a proportion of $\frac{1}{h}\sum_{T+1}^{T+h}(\widehat{X}_{lt} - X_{lt})^2$:

$$\text{bias proportion:} \quad \frac{\left(\left(\frac{1}{h}\sum_{T+1}^{T+h}\widehat{X}_{lt}\right) - \overline{X}_l\right)^2}{\frac{1}{h}\sum_{T+1}^{T+h}(\widehat{X}_{lt} - X_{lt})^2} \tag{14.13}$$

$$\text{variance proportion:} \quad \frac{(\sigma_{\widehat{X}_l} - \sigma_{X_l})^2}{\frac{1}{h}\sum_{T+1}^{T+h}(\widehat{X}_{lt} - X_{lt})^2} \tag{14.14}$$

$$\text{covariance proportion:} \quad \frac{2(1-\rho)\sigma_{\widehat{X}_l}\sigma_{X_l}}{\frac{1}{h}\sum_{T+1}^{T+h}(\widehat{X}_{lt} - X_{lt})^2} \tag{14.15}$$

We use the three models to produce dynamic or iterated forecasts $\mathbb{P}_T X_{T+1}$, $\mathbb{P}_T X_{T+2}, \ldots, \mathbb{P}_T X_{T+h}$. Thus, forecasts for $h \geq 2$ are computed iteratively by inserting for the lagged variables the forecasts obtained in the previous steps. For details see Chap. 14. Alternatively, one may consider a recursive or rolling out-of-sample strategy where the model is reestimated each time a new observation becomes available. Thus, we would evaluate the one-period-ahead forecasts $\mathbb{P}_T X_{T+1}, \mathbb{P}_{T+1} X_{T+2}, \ldots, \mathbb{P}_{T+h-1} X_{T+h}$, the two-period-ahead forecasts $\mathbb{P}_T X_{T+2}, \mathbb{P}_{T+1} X_{T+3}, \ldots, \mathbb{P}_{T+h-2} X_{T+h}$, and so on. The difference between the recursive and the rolling strategy is that in the first case all observations are used for estimation, whereas in the second case, the sample is rolled over so that its size is kept fixed at T.

Figure 14.1 displays dynamic or iterated forecasts for the four variables expressed in log-levels, respectively in levels for the interest rate. Forecast are evaluated according to the performance measures explained above. The corresponding values are reported in Table 14.2. All models see a quick recovery after the 2008 recession in the wake of the financial crisis and are thus much too optimistic. The lowest RMSE for $\log Y_t$ is 5.678 for the VAR(8) model. Thus, GDP

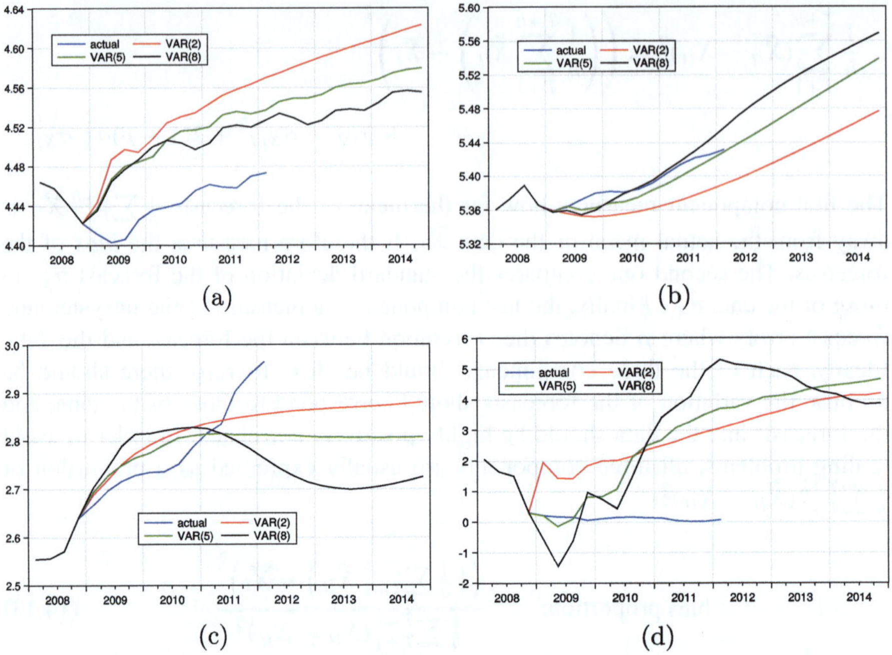

Fig. 14.1 Forecast comparison of alternative models. (**a**) $\log Y_t$. (**b**) $\log P_t$. (**c**) $\log M_t$. (**d**) R_t

per capita is predicted to be on average almost 6% too high over the forecast period. This overly optimistic forecast is reflected in a large bias proportion which amounts to more than 95%. The situation looks much better for the price level. All models see an increase in inflation starting in 2009. Especially, the two higher-order models fare much better. Their RMSE is just over 1%. The bias proportion is practically zero for the VAR(8) model. The forecast results of the real money stock are mixed. All models predict a quick recovery. This took indeed place, but at a more moderate pace. Starting in mid-2010 the unconventional monetary policy of quantitative easing, however, led to an unforeseen acceleration so that the forecasts turned out to be systematically too low for the later period. Interestingly, the smallest model fared significantly better than the other two. Finally, the results for the interest rates are very diverse. Whereas the VAR(2) model predicts a rise in the interest rate, the other models foresee a decline. The VAR(8) model even predicts a very drastic fall. However, all models miss the continuation of the low interest rate regime and forecasts an increase starting already in 2009. This error can again be attributed to the unforeseen low interest rate monetary policy which was implemented in conjunction with the quantitative easing. This misjudgment resulted in a relatively large bias proportion.

Up to now, we have just been concerned with *point forecasts*. Point forecasts, however, describe only one possible outcome and do not reflect the inherent uncertainty surrounding the prediction problem. It is, thus, a question of scientific

Table 14.2 Forecast evaluation of alternative VAR models

	VAR(2)	VAR(5)	VAR(8)
	$\log Y_t$		
RMSE	8.387	6.406	5.678
Bias proportion	0.960	0.961	0.951
Variance proportion	0.020	0.010	0.001
Covariance proportion	0.020	0.029	0.048
MAE	8.217	6.279	5.536
	$\log P_t$		
RMSE	3.126	1.064	1.234
Bias proportion	0.826	0.746	0.001
Variance proportion	0.121	0.001	0.722
Covariance proportion	0.053	0.253	0.278
MAE	2.853	0.934	0.928
	$\log M_t$		
RMSE	5.616	6.780	9.299
Bias proportion	0.036	0.011	0.002
Variance proportion	0.499	0.622	0.352
Covariance proportion	0.466	0.367	0.646
MAE	4.895	5.315	7.762
	R_t		
RMSE	2.195	2.204	2.845
Bias proportion	0.367	0.606	0.404
Variance proportion	0.042	0.337	0.539
Covariance proportion	0.022	0.057	0.057
MAE	2.125	1.772	2.299

RMSE and MAE for $\log Y_t$, $\log P_t$, and $\log M_t$ are multiplied by 100

integrity to present in addition to the point forecasts also confidence intervals. One straightforward way to construct such intervals is by computing the matrix of mean-squared-errors MSE using Eq. (14.5). The diagonal elements of this matrix can be interpreted as a measure of the forecast error variances for each variable. Under the assumption that the innovations $\{Z_t\}$ are Gaussian, such confidence intervals can be easily computed. However, in practice this assumption is likely to be violated. This problem can be circumvented by using the empirical distribution function of the residuals to implement a bootstrap method similar to the computation of the value-at-risk in Sect. 8.5. Figure 14.2 plots the forecasts of the VAR(8) model together with a 80% confidence interval computed from the bootstrap approach. It shows that, with the exception of the logged price level, the actual realizations fall out of the confidence interval despite the fact that the intervals are already relatively large. This documents the uniqueness of the financial crisis and gives a hard time for any forecasting model.

Instead of computing a confidence interval, one may estimate the probability distribution of possible future outcomes. This provides a complete description of the

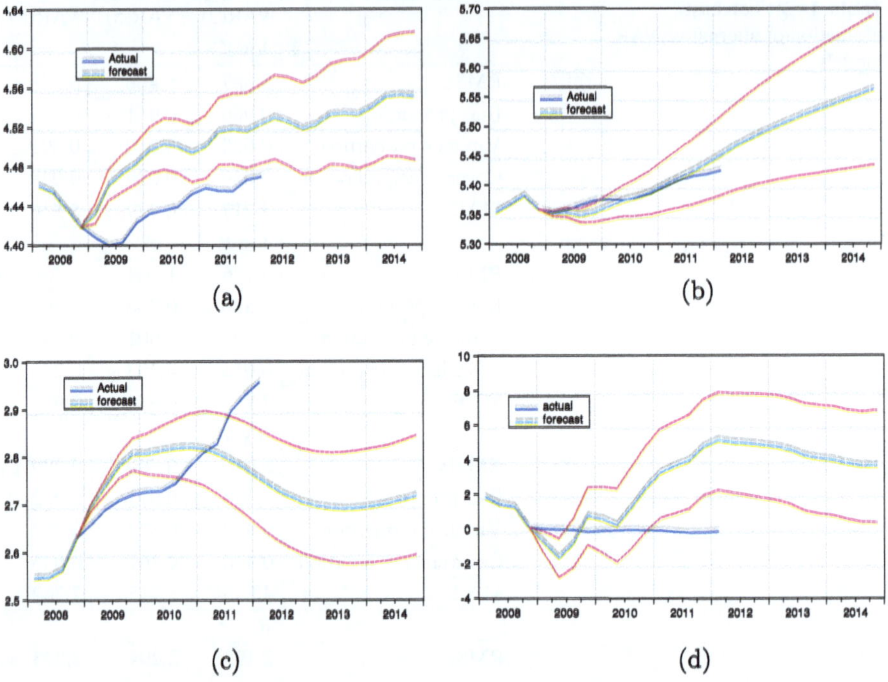

Fig. 14.2 Forecast of VAR(8) model with 80% confidence intervals (red dotted lines). (**a**) $\log Y_t$. (**b**) $\log P_t$. (**c**) $\log M_t$. (**d**) R_t

uncertainty related to the prediction problem (Christoffersen, 1998; Diebold et al., 1998; Tay & Wallis, 2000; Corradi & Swanson, 2006). Finally, one should be aware that the innovation uncertainty is not the only source of uncertainty. As the parameters of the model are themselves estimated, there is also a coefficient uncertainty. In addition, we have to face the possibility that the model is misspecified.

The forecasting performance of the VAR models may seem disappointing at first. However, this was only be a first attempt and further investigations are usually necessary. These may include the search for *structural breaks* (see Bai et al., 1998; Perron, 2006). Another reason for the poor forecasting may be due to the *over-parametrization* of VAR models. The VAR(8) model, for example, 32 lagged dependent variables plus a constant in each of the four equations which leads to a total 132 parameters. This problem can be dealt with by applying Bayesian shrinkage techniques. This approach, also known as Bayesian VAR (BVAR) models, was particularly successful when using the so-called Minnesota prior (see Doan et al., 1984; Litterman, 1986; Kunst & Neusser, 1986; Banbura et al., 2010). This technique is outlined in Sect. 18.1.

Besides these more fundamental issues, one may rely some technical remedies. One such remedy is the use of direct rather iterated forecasts. This difference is best explained in the context of the VAR(1) model $X_t = \Phi X_{t-1} + Z_t$, $Z_t \sim \mathrm{WN}(0, \Sigma)$.

The *iterated* forecast for X_{T+h} uses the OLS-estimate $\widehat{\Phi}$ to compute the forecast $\widehat{\Phi}^h X_T$ (see Chap. 14). Alternatively, one may estimate instead of the VAR(1), the model $X_t = \Upsilon X_{t-h} + Z_t$ and compute the *direct* forecast for X_{T+h} as $\widehat{\Upsilon} X_T$. Although $\widehat{\Upsilon}$ has larger variance than $\widehat{\Phi}$ if the VAR(1) is correctly specified, it is robust to misspecification (see Bhansali, 1999; Schorfheide, 2005; Marcellino et al., 2006).

Another interesting and common device is intercept correction or residual adjustment. Thereby the constant terms are adjusted in such a way that the residuals of the most recent observation become zero. The model is thereby set back on track. In this way the forecaster can guard himself against possible structural breaks. Residual adjustment can also serve as a device to incorporate anticipated events, like announced policies, which are not yet incorporated into the model. See Clements and Hendry (1996, 2006) for further details and additional forecasting devices.

Structural VAR (SVAR) Models 15

Although the estimation of VAR models poses no conceptual difficulties as outlined in the previous chapter, simple OLS estimation equation by equation is sufficient, the individual coefficients are almost impossible to interpret. On the one hand, there are usually many coefficients: A VAR(p) model with n variables, for example, has $p \times n$ coefficients per equation and thus $p \times n^2$ coefficients in total to interpret, disregarding intercept terms and the $(n+1)n/2$ parameters of the covariance matrix. On the other hand, there is in general no unambiguous relation between the VAR parameters and the coefficients of a particular (theoretical) model. The last problem is known as the *identification* problem. To overcome this problem, many techniques have been proposed to give an estimated VAR model an explicit economic interpretation. In this chapter we will present under the heading of structural vector autoregressive models (SVAR models) the most important techniques. An exhaustive treatment can be found in Kilian and Lütkepohl (2017).

15.1 Structural and Reduced Form

15.1.1 A Prototypical Example

The discussion in the previous section showed that the relation between VAR models and economic models is ambiguous. In order to better understand the quintessence of the problem, we first analyze a simple macroeconomic example. Let $\{y_t\}$ and $\{m_t\}$ denote the output and the money supply of an economy[1] and suppose that the relation between the two variables is represented by the following *simultaneous equation system*:

[1] If one is working with actual data, the variables are usually expressed in log-differences to achieve stationarity.

K. Neusser, *Time Series Econometrics*, Springer Texts in Business and Economics,
https://doi.org/10.1007/978-3-031-88838-0_15

$$\text{AD-curve:} \qquad X_{1t} = y_t = a_1 m_t + \gamma_{11} y_{t-1} + \gamma_{12} m_{t-1} + v_{yt}$$

$$\text{policy reaction curve:} \qquad X_{2t} = m_t = a_2 y_t + \gamma_{21} y_{t-1} + \gamma_{22} m_{t-1} + v_{mt}$$

Note the contemporaneous dependence of y_t on m_t in the aggregate demand curve (AD-curve) and a corresponding dependence of m_t on y_t in the policy reaction curve. These equations are typically derived from economic reasoning and may characterize a model explicitly derived from economic theory. In statistical terms, the simultaneous equation system is called the *structural form*. The error terms $\{v_{yt}\}$ and $\{v_{mt}\}$ are interpreted as demand shocks and money supply shocks, respectively. They are called *structural shocks* and are assumed to follow a multivariate white noise process:

$$V_t = \begin{pmatrix} v_{yt} \\ v_{mt} \end{pmatrix} \sim \text{WN}(0, \Omega) \qquad \text{with } \Omega = \begin{pmatrix} \omega_y^2 & 0 \\ 0 & \omega_m^2 \end{pmatrix}.$$

Note that the two structural shocks are assumed to be contemporaneously uncorrelated which is reflected in the assumption that Ω is a diagonal matrix. This assumption is uncontroversial. Otherwise, there would remain some unexplained relationship between them. The structural shocks can be interpreted as the statistical analog of an experiment in the natural sciences. The experiment corresponds in this case to a shift of the AD-curve due to, for example, a temporary non-anticipated change in government expenditures or money supply. The goal of the analysis is then to trace the reaction of the economy, in our case represented by the two variables $\{y_t\}$ and $\{m_t\}$, to these isolated and autonomous changes in aggregate demand and money supply. The structural equations imply that the reaction is not restricted to contemporaneous effects, but is spread out over time. We represent this reaction by the impulse response function.

We can write the system more compactly in matrix notation

$$\begin{pmatrix} 1 & -a_1 \\ -a_2 & 1 \end{pmatrix} \begin{pmatrix} y_t \\ m_t \end{pmatrix} = \begin{pmatrix} \gamma_{11} & \gamma_{12} \\ \gamma_{21} & \gamma_{22} \end{pmatrix} \begin{pmatrix} y_{t-1} \\ m_{t-1} \end{pmatrix} + \begin{pmatrix} 1 & 0 \\ 0 & 1 \end{pmatrix} \begin{pmatrix} v_{yt} \\ v_{mt} \end{pmatrix}$$

or

$$AX_t = \Gamma X_{t-1} + BV_t$$

where $A = \begin{pmatrix} 1 & -a_1 \\ -a_2 & 1 \end{pmatrix}$, $\Gamma = \begin{pmatrix} \gamma_{11} & \gamma_{12} \\ \gamma_{21} & \gamma_{22} \end{pmatrix}$ and $B = \begin{pmatrix} 1 & 0 \\ 0 & 1 \end{pmatrix}$.

Assuming that A is invertible (i.e., $a_1 a_2 \neq 1$), we can solve the above simultaneous equation system for the two endogenous variables y_t and m_t to get the *reduced form* of the model:

$$X_{1t} = y_t = \frac{\gamma_{11} + a_1\gamma_{21}}{1 - a_1 a_2} y_{t-1} + \frac{\gamma_{12} + a_1\gamma_{22}}{1 - a_1 a_2} m_{t-1} + \frac{v_{yt}}{1 - a_1 a_2} + \frac{a_1 v_{mt}}{1 - a_1 a_2}$$

$$= \phi_{11} y_{t=1} + \phi_{12} m_{t-1} + Z_{1t}$$

$$X_{2t} = m_t = \frac{\gamma_{21} + a_2\gamma_{11}}{1 = a_1 a_2} y_{t-1} + \frac{\gamma_{22} + a_2\gamma_{12}}{1 - a_1 a_2} m_{t-1} + \frac{a_2 v_{yt}}{1 - a_1 a_2} + \frac{v_{mt}}{1 - a_1 a_2}$$

$$= \phi_{21} y_{t=1} + \phi_{22} m_{t-1} + Z_{2t}.$$

Thus, the reduced form is a VAR(1) model with error term $\{Z_t\} = \{(Z_{1t}, Z_{2t})'\}$. The reduced form can be expressed in matrix notation:

$$X_t = A^{-1}\Gamma X_{t-1} + A^{-1} B V_t = \Phi X_{t-1} + Z_t$$

where

$$Z_t \sim \text{WN}(0, \Sigma) \quad \text{and} \quad \Sigma = A^{-1} B \Omega B' A'^{-1}.$$

Whereas the structural form represents the inner economic relations between the variables (economic model), the reduced form given by the VAR model summarizes their outer directly observable characteristics. As there is no unambiguous relation between the reduced and structural form, it is impossible to infer the inner economic relationships from the observations alone. This is known in statistics as the *identification problem*. Typically, a whole family of structural models is compatible with a particular reduced form. The models of the family are thus *observationally equivalent* to each other as they imply the same distribution for $\{X_t\}$. The identification problem can be overcome if one is willing to make additional *a priori assumptions*. The nature and the type of these assumption and their interpretation is subject of the rest of this chapter.

In our example, the parameters characterizing the structural and the reduced form are

$$\{a_1, a_2, \gamma_{11}, \gamma_{12}, \gamma_{21}, \gamma_{22}, \omega_y^2, \omega_m^2\}$$

and

$$\{\phi_{11}, \phi_{12}, \phi_{21}, \phi_{22}, \sigma_1^2, \sigma_{12}, \sigma_2^2\}.$$

As there are eight parameters in the structural form, but only seven parameters in the reduced form, there is no one-to-one relation between structural and reduced form. The VAR(1) model delivers estimates for the seven reduced form parameters, but there is no way to infer from these estimates the parameters of the structural form. Thus, there is a fundamental identification problem.

The simple counting of the number of parameters in each form tells us that we need at least one additional restriction on the parameters of the structural form. The simplest restriction is a zero restriction. Suppose that a_2 equals zero, i.e., that the central bank does not react immediately to current output. This seems reasonable because national accounting figures are usually released with some delay. With this assumption, we can infer the structural parameters from the reduced ones:

$$\gamma_{21} = \phi_{21}, \quad \gamma_{22} = \phi_{22},$$

$$v_{mt} = Z_{2t} \Rightarrow \omega_m^2 = \sigma_2^2, \quad \Rightarrow a_1 = \sigma_{12}/\sigma_2^2, \quad \Rightarrow \omega_y^2 = \sigma_1^2 - \sigma_{12}^2/\sigma_2^2$$

$$\gamma_{11} = \phi_{11} - (\sigma_{12}/\sigma_2^2)\phi_{21}, \quad \gamma_{12} = \phi_{12} - (\sigma_{12}/\sigma_2^2)\phi_{22}.$$

Remark 15.1 Note that, because $Z_t = A^{-1}BV_t$, the reduced form disturbances Z_t are a linear combination of the structural disturbances, in our case the demand disturbance v_{yt} and the money supply disturbance v_{mt}. In each period t, the endogenous variables output y_t and money supply m_t are therefore hit simultaneously by both shocks. It is thus not possible without further assumptions to assign the movements in Z_t and consequently in X_t to corresponding changes in the fundamental structural shocks v_{yt} and v_{mt}.

Remark 15.2 As Cooley and LeRoy (1985) already pointed out, the statement "money supply is not causal in the sense of Wiener and Granger for real economic activity," which, in our example, is equivalent to $\phi_{12} = 0$, is not equivalent to the statement "money supply does not influence real economic activity" because ϕ_{12} can be zero without a_1 being zero. Thus, the notion of causality is not very meaningful in inferring the inner (structural) relationships between variables.

15.1.2 Identification: The General Case

We now present the general identification problem in the context of VAR model.[2] The starting point of the analysis consists of a linear, respectively linearized model, derived ideally from economic theory, expressed in its *structural form*

$$AX_t = \Gamma_1 X_{t-1} + \cdots + \Gamma_p X_{t-p} + BV_t \tag{15.1}$$

where V_t comprises the structural disturbances. These disturbances usually have an economic interpretation, for example, as demand, supply, or monetary shocks. A is a $n \times n$ matrix which is normalized such that the diagonal consists of ones only. The matrix B is also normalized such that its diagonal contains only ones. The process of structural disturbances, $\{V_t\}$, is assumed to be a multivariate white noise process with diagonal covariance matrix Ω:

[2] A thorough treatment of the identification problem in econometrics can be found in Rothenberg (1971) and in the VAR context in Rubio-Ramírez et al. (2010) and Kilian and Lütkepohl (2017).

$$V_t \sim \mathrm{WN}(0, \Omega) \quad \text{with} \quad \Omega = \mathbb{E} V_t V_t' = \begin{pmatrix} \omega_1^2 & 0 & \dots & 0 \\ 0 & \omega_2^2 & \dots & 0 \\ \vdots & \vdots & \ddots & \vdots \\ 0 & 0 & \dots & \omega_n^2 \end{pmatrix}.$$

The assumption that the structural disturbance are uncorrelated with each other is not viewed as controversial as otherwise there would be unexplained relationships between the variables, meaning that the theoretical model is not fully specified. In the literature one encounters an alternative completely equivalent normalization which leaves the coefficients in B unrestricted but assumes the covariance matrix of V_t, Ω, to be equal to the identity matrix I_n.

The *reduced form* is obtained by solving the equation system with respect to X_t. Assuming that A is nonsingular, premultiplying equation (15.1) by A^{-1} leads to the reduced form which corresponds to a VAR(p) model:

$$\begin{aligned} X_t &= A^{-1}\Gamma_1 X_{t-1} + \cdots + A^{-1}\Gamma_p X_{t-p} + A^{-1} B V_t \qquad (15.2) \\ &= \Phi_1 X_{t-1} + \cdots + \Phi_p X_{t-p} + Z_t. \end{aligned}$$

The relation between the structural disturbances V_t and the reduced form disturbances Z_t is in the form of a simultaneous equation system:

$$A Z_t = B V_t. \qquad (15.3)$$

While the structural disturbances V_t are not directly observed, the reduced form disturbances Z_t are given as the residuals of the VAR moswl and can thus be estimated consistently (see Chap. 13). Hence, they can be considered as given. The relation between the coefficients of the lagged variables simply is

$$\Gamma_j = A\Phi_j, \qquad j = 1, 2, \dots, p.$$

Consequently, once A and B have been identified, not only the coefficients of the lagged variables in the structural form are identified but also the impulse response functions (see Sect. 15.3.1). We can therefore concentrate our analysis of the identification problem on represented by Eq. (15.3).

With these preliminaries, it is possible to state the identification problem more precisely. Equation (15.3) shows that the structural form is completely determined by the parameters (A, B, Ω). Taking the normalization of A and B into account, these parameters can be viewed as points in $\mathbb{R}^{n(2n-1)}$. These parameters determine the distribution of $Z_t = A^{-1} B V_t$ which is completely characterized by the covariance matrix of Z_t, Σ, as the mean is equal to zero.[3] Thus, the parameters

[3] As usual, we concentrate on the first two moments only.

of the reduced form, i.e., the independent elements of Σ taking the symmetry into account, are points in $\mathbb{R}^{n(n+1)/2}$. The relation between structural and reduced form can therefore be described by a function $g : \mathbb{R}^{n(2n-1)} \to \mathbb{R}^{n(n+1)/2}$:

$$\Sigma = g(A, B, \Omega) = A^{-1}B\Omega B'A'^{-1}. \tag{15.4}$$

Ideally, one would want to find the inverse of this function and retrieve, in this way, the structural parameters (A, B, Ω) from Σ. This is, however, in general not possible because the dimension of the domain space of g, $n(2n-1)$, is strictly greater, for $n \geq 2$, than the dimension of its range space, $n(n+1)/2$. This discrepancy between the dimensions of the domain and the range space of g is the source of the *identification problem*. To put it in another way, there are only $n(n+1)/2$ (nonlinear) equations for $n(2n-1)$ unknowns.[4]

To overcome the identification problem, we have to bring in additional information. A customary approach is to impose a priori assumptions on the structural parameters. The implicit function theorem tells us that we need

$$n(2n-1) - \frac{n(n+1)}{2} = \frac{3n(n-1)}{2} \tag{15.5}$$

such restrictions, so-called identifying restrictions, to be able to invert the function g. This is only a *necessary condition*. Note that the identification problem becomes increasingly severe with the dimension of the VAR because the number of necessary restrictions grows at a rate proportional to n^2.

This result can also be obtained by taking a geometrical viewpoint. The function g in Eq. (15.4) is invariant to the transformation

$$h : (A, B, \Omega) \longrightarrow (RA, RB\Omega^{1/2}Q\Omega^{-1/2}, D\Omega D^{-1})$$

where R, Q, and D are arbitrary invertible matrices such that R respects the normalization of A and B, Q is an orthogonal matrix, and D is a diagonal matrix.[5] It can be verified that

$$(g \circ h)(A, B, \Omega) = g(A, B, \Omega).$$

The dimensions of the matrices R, Q, and D are $n^2 - 2n$, $n(n-1)/2$, and n, respectively. Summing up gives $3n(n-1)/2 = n^2 - 2n + n(n-1)/2 + n$ degrees of freedom as before.

---

[4] Note also that our discussion of the identification problem focuses on local identification, i.e., the invertibility of g in an open neighborhood of Σ. See Rothenberg (1971) and Rubio-Ramírez et al. (2010) for details on the distinction between local and global identification.

[5] See the explanations following Lemma 15.1 in Sect. 15.5. There it is shown in a simplified, but generally valid, context how the alternative identification schemes are related (parameterized) by orthogonal matrices.

The applied time series literature proposed several identification schemes:

(i) Short-run restrictions place restrictions, usually zero restrictions, on the immediate impact of structural shocks (among many others, Sims, 1980b; Blanchard, 1989; Blanchard and Watson, 1986; Christiano et al., 1999). See Sect. 15.2 for details.
(ii) Long-run restrictions place restrictions, usually zero-restrictions, on the long-run impact of structural shocks (Blanchard and Quah, 1989; Galí, 1992). See Sect. 15.4 for details.
(iii) Sign restrictions restrict the set of possible impulse response functions (see Sect. 15.3.1) to follow a given sign pattern (Faust, 1998; Uhlig, 2005; Fry and Pagan, 2011; Kilian and Murphy, 2012; Rubio-Ramírez et al., 2010; Arias et al., 2014; Baumeister and Hamilton, 2015). This approach is complementary to the two previous identification schemes and will be discussed in Sect. 15.5.
(iv) Maximization of the contribution to the forecast error variance of some variable at some horizon with respect to a particular shock (Faust, 1998; Uhlig, 2004; Francis et al., 2014). This method has been seen as interesting application to the identification of news shocks (Barsky and Sims, 2011). See further details in Sect. 15.3.2.
(v) Identification through heteroskedasticity, e.g., by splitting the sample in two periods having different characteristics (Rigobon, 2003; Lanne et al., 2010; Lütkepohl et al., 2020a).
(vi) Using higher-order moments in the context of non-Gaussian error distributions (Lanne et al., 2017; Gouriéroux et al., 2017) is discussed in Sect. 15.6.
(vii) Restrictions derived from dynamic stochastic general equilibrium models (DSGE models). These restrictions often come as nonlinear cross-equation restrictions and are viewed as the hallmark of rational expectations models (Hansen and Sargent, 1980). Typically, the identification issue is overcome by imposing a priori restrictions via a Bayesian approach (Negro and Schorfheide (2004) among many others).
(viii) Identification using information on global versus idiosyncratic shocks in the context of multi-country or multi-region VAR models (Canova and Ciccarelli, 2009; Dees et al., 2007).
(ix) Instead of identifying all parameters, researchers may be interested in identifying only one equation or a subset of equations. This case is known as *partial identification*. The schemes presented above can be extended in a straightforward manner to the partial identification case.

These schemes are not mutually exclusive, but can be combined with each other. In the following, we will only cover the identification through short-run, long-run, sign restrictions, and npn-Gaussian error distributions, because these are by far the most popular ones. For further discussions, see Kilian and Lütkepohl (2017). The economic importance of these restrictions for the analysis of monetary policy has been emphasized by Christiano et al. (1999).

15.1.3 Identification in the Case $n = 2$

Before proceeding further, it is instructive to analyze the case $n = 2$ in more detail.[6] Assume for simplicity $A = I_2$, then the equation system (15.4) can be written explicitly as

$$\begin{aligned}
\sigma_1^2 &= \qquad\quad \omega_1^2 + (B)_{12}^2\omega_2^2, \\
\sigma_{12} &= (B)_{21}\omega_1^2 + (B)_{12}\omega_2^2, \\
\sigma_2^2 &= (B)_{21}^2\omega_1^2 + \qquad \omega_2^2
\end{aligned}$$

with unknowns $(B)_{12}, (B)_{21}, \omega_1^2$, and ω_2^2. Note that the assumption of Σ being positive definite implies that $(B)_{12}(B)_{21} \neq 1$. Thus, we can solve out ω_1^2 and ω_2^2 and reduce the three equations to only one

$$\left((B)_{12} - b_{21}^{-1}\right)\left((B)_{21} - b_{12}^{-1}\right) = r_{12}^{-2} - 1 \tag{15.6}$$

where b_{21} and b_{12} denote the least-squares regression coefficients of Z_{2t} on Z_{1t}, respectively of Z_{1t} on Z_{2t}, i.e., $b_{21} = \sigma_{12}/\sigma_1^2$ and $b_{12} = \sigma_{12}/\sigma_2^2$. r_{12} is the correlation coefficient between Z_{2t} and Z_{1t}, i.e., $r_{12} = \sigma_{12}/(\sigma_1\sigma_2)$. Note that imposing a zero restriction by setting $(B)_{12}$, for example, equal to zero, implies that $(B)_{21}$ equals b_{21}; and vice versa, setting $(B)_{21} = 0$, implies $(B)_{12} = b_{12}$. As a final remark, the right hand side of Eq. (15.6) is always positive as the inverse of the squared correlation coefficient is bigger than one. This implies both product terms must be of the same sign.

Equation (15.6) delineates all possible combinations of $(B)_{12}$ and $(B)_{21}$ which are compatible with a given covariance matrix Σ. Its graph represents a rectangular hyperbola in the parameter space $((B)_{12}, (B)_{21})$ with center $C = (b_{21}^{-1}, b_{12}^{-1})$ and asymptotes $(B)_{12} = b_{21}^{-1}$ and $(B)_{21} = b_{12}^{-1}$ and is plotted in Fig. 15.1.[7] The hyperbola consist of two disconnected branches with a pole at the center $C = (b_{21}^{-1}, b_{12}^{-1})$. At this point, the relation between the two parameters changes sign. The figure also indicates the two possible zero restrictions $(B)_{12} = 0$ and $(B)_{21} = 0$, called short-run restrictions. These two restrictions are connected and its path completely falls within one quadrant. Thus, along this path the sign of the parameters remain unchanged. Section 15.5 discusses sign restrictions in detail.

Suppose that instead of fixing a particular parameter, we only want to restrict its sign. Assuming that $(B)_{12} \geq 0$ implies that $(B)_{21}$ must lie in one of the two disconnected intervals $(-\infty, b_{21}]$ and $(b_{12}^{-1}, +\infty)$.[8] Although not very explicit, some economic consequences of this topological particularity are discussed in Fry and Pagan (2011). Alternatively, assuming $(B)_{12} \leq 0$ implies $(B)_{21} \in [b_{21}, b_{12}^{-1})$.

---

[6] The exposition is inspired by Leamer (1981).

[7] Granziera et al. (2013, section 2) provided an alternative geometric representation.

[8] That these two intervals are disconnected follows from the fact that Σ is positive definite.

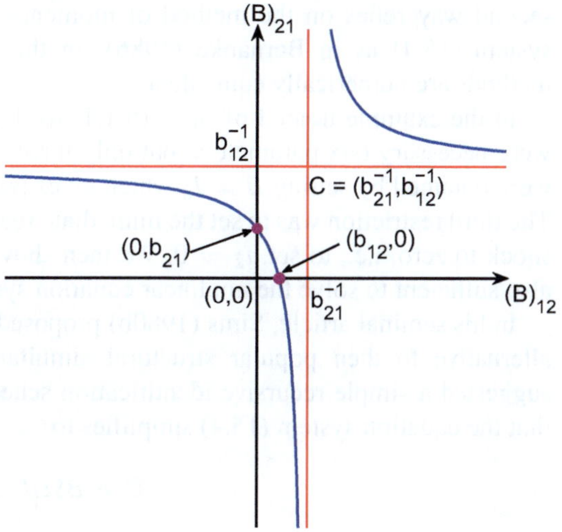

Fig. 15.1 Identification in a two-dimensional structural VAR with $\sigma_{12} > 0$

Thus, $(B)_{21}$ is unambiguously positive. Sign restrictions for $(B)_{21}$ can be discussed in the same way.

15.2 Identification via Short-Run Restrictions

Short-run restrictions represent the most common identification scheme encountered in practice. They impose direct linear restrictions on the structural parameters A and B and restrict in this way the contemporaneous effect of the structural shocks on the variables of the system. The most common type of such restrictions are *zero restrictions* which set certain coefficients a priori to zero. These zero restrictions are either derived from an explicit economic theory or are based on some ad hoc arguments. As explained above, it is necessary to have at least $3n(n-1)/2$ restrictions at hand. If there are more restrictions, we have an *overidentified* system. This is, however, rarely the case in practice because the number of necessary restrictions grows at a rate proportional to n^2. The case of overidentification is, thus, not often encountered and as such is not treated.[9] The way to find appropriate restrictions in a relatively large system is documented in Sect. 15.3.5. If the number of restrictions equals $3n(n-1)/2$, we say that the system is *exactly identified*.

Given the necessary number of a priori restrictions on the coefficients A and B, there are two ways to infer A, B, and Ω. The first one views the relation (15.3) as a simultaneous equation system in Z_t with error terms V_t and estimates the coefficients by instrumental variables as in Blanchard and Watson (1986).[10] The

[9] The case of overidentification is, for example, treated in Bernanke (1986).

[10] A version of the instrumental variable (IV) approach is discussed in Sect. 15.4.2.

second way relies on the method of moments and solves the nonlinear equation system (15.4) as in Bernanke (1986). In the case of exact identification, both methods are numerically equivalent.

In the example treated of Sect. 15.1.1, we had $n = 2$ so that three restrictions were necessary (six parameters, but only three equations). These three restrictions were obtained by setting $B = I_2$ which gives two restrictions (i.e., $b_{12} = b_{21} = 0$). The third restriction was to set the immediate reaction of money supply to a demand shock to zero, i.e., to set $a_2 = 0$. We then showed that these three restrictions are also sufficient to solve the nonlinear equation system (15.4).

In his seminal article, Sims (1980b) proposed the VAR approach as an adequate alternative to then popular structural simultaneous approach. In particular, he suggested a simple recursive identification scheme. This scheme takes $A = I_n$ so that the equation system (15.4) simplifies to

$$\Sigma = B\Omega B'.$$

He then assumes B to be a lower triangular matrix

$$B = \begin{pmatrix} 1 & 0 & \dots & 0 \\ * & 1 & \dots & 0 \\ \vdots & \vdots & \ddots & \vdots \\ * & * & \dots & 1 \end{pmatrix}$$

where $*$ is just a placeholder. The matrices B and Ω are uniquely determined by the *Cholesky decomposition* of the matrix Σ. The Cholesky decomposition factorizes a positive-definite matrix Σ uniquely into the product $B\Omega B'$ where B is a lower triangular matrix with ones on the diagonal and a diagonal matrix Ω with strictly positive diagonal entries (Meyer, 2000). As $Z_t = BV_t$, Sims' identification gives rise to the following interpretation. v_{1t} is the only structural shock which has an effect on X_{1t} in period t. All other shocks have no contemporaneous effect. Moreover, $Z_{1t} = v_{1t}$ so that the residual from the first equation is just equal to the first structural shock and that $\sigma_1^2 = \omega_1^2$. The second variable X_{2t} is contemporaneously affected only by v_{1t} and v_{2t}, and not by the remaining shocks $v_{3t}, \dots, v_{nt}$. In particular, $Z_{2t} = b_{21}v_{1t} + v_{2t}$ so that b_{21} can be retrieved from the equation $\sigma_{21} = b_{21}\omega_1^2$. This identifies the second structural shock v_{2t} and ω_2^2. Due to the triangular nature of B, the system is recursive, and all structural shocks and parameters can be computed successively. The application of the Cholesky decomposition as an identification scheme, however, rests crucially on the *ordering* of the variables $(X_{1t}, X_{2t}, \dots, X_{nt})'$ in the system.

Sims' elegant scheme, although easy to implement, becomes less plausible when the number of variables in the system increases. For this reason, more general schemes with $A \neq I_n$ and B not necessarily lower triangular have become more popular. However, even a for medium-sized systems with $n = 5$, 30 restrictions are necessary which stresses the imagination even of brilliant economists as the estimation of Blanchard's model in Sect. 15.3.5 shows.

Focusing on the identification of the matrices A and B brings also an advantage in terms of estimation. As shown in Chap. 13, the OLS-estimator of the VAR coefficient matrices $\Phi_1, \ldots, \Phi_p$ equals the GLS-estimator independently of Σ. Thus, the estimation of the structural parameters can be broken down into two steps. In the first step, the coefficient matrices $\Phi_1, \ldots, \Phi_p$ are estimated using OLS. The residuals are then used to estimate Σ which leads to an estimate of the covariance matrix (see Eq. (13.6)). In the second step, the coefficients of A, B, and Ω are estimated by solving the nonlinear equation system (15.4) using the advocated identification scheme, taking the estimate of Σ, $\widehat{\Sigma}$, as given. As $\sqrt{T}\left(\text{vech}(\widehat{\Sigma}) - \text{vech}(\Sigma)\right)$ converges in distribution to a normal distribution with mean zero, $\hat{A}$, $\hat{B}$, and $\widehat{\Omega}$ are also asymptotically normal because they are obtained by a one-to-one mapping from $\widehat{\Sigma}$.[11] The continuous mapping theorem further implies that $\hat{A}$, $\hat{B}$, and $\widehat{\Omega}$ converge to their true means and that their asymptotic covariance matrix can be obtained by an application of the delta-method (see Theorem E.1 in the Appendix E). Further details can be found in Bernanke (1986), Blanchard and Watson (1986), Giannini (1991), Hamilton (1994a), and Sims (1986).

15.3 Interpretation of VAR Models

15.3.1 Impulse Response Functions

The direct interpretation of VAR models is rather difficult because it is composed of many coefficients so that it becomes difficult to understand the dynamic interactions between the variables. It is therefore advantageous to simulate the dynamic effects of the different structural shocks by computing the *impulse response functions*. They show the effect over time of the structural shocks on the variables at issue. These effects can often be related to the underlying economic model and are thus at the heart of the VAR analysis. The examples in Sects. 15.3.4 and 15.3.5 provide some illustrations of this statement.

The impulse response functions are derived from the causal representation[12] of the stationary VAR process (see Sect. 12.3):

$$\begin{aligned} X_t &= Z_t + \Psi_1 Z_{t-1} + \Psi_2 Z_{t-2} + \ldots \\ &= A^{-1} B V_t + \Psi_1 A^{-1} B V_{t-1} + \Psi_2 A^{-1} B V_{t-2} + \ldots \end{aligned} \tag{15.7}$$

The effect of the j-th structural disturbance on the i-th variable after h periods is denoted (with a slight abuse of notation) as $\frac{\partial X_{i,t+h}}{\partial v_{jt}}$ and is thus given by the (i, j)-th

[11] The vech operator transforms a symmetric $n \times n$ matrix Σ into a $\frac{1}{2}n(n+1)$ vector by stacking the columns of Σ such that each element is listed only once.

[12] Sometimes the causal representation is called the MA(∞) representation.

element of the matrix $\Psi_h A^{-1} B$:

$$\frac{\partial X_{i,t+h}}{\partial v_{jt}} = \left[\Psi_h A^{-1} B\right]_{i,j}.$$

Clearly, the impulse response functions depends on the identification scheme chosen. There are n^2 impulse response functions if the system consists of n variables. Usually, the impulse response functions are represented graphically as a plot against h.

15.3.2 Forecast Error Variance Decomposition

Another instrument for the interpretation of VAR models is the *forecast error variance decomposition* ("FEVD") or variance decomposition for short which decomposes the total forecast error variance of a variable into the contribution of the variances of the structural shocks. It is again based on the causal representation of the VAR(p) model. According to Eq. (14.3) in Chap. 14, the variance of the forecast error or mean squared error (MSE) is given by

$$\begin{aligned}\text{MSE}(h) &= \mathbb{E}(X_{t+h} - \mathbb{P}_t X_{t+h})(X_{t+h} - \mathbb{P}_t X_{t+h})' \\ &= \sum_{j=0}^{h-1} \Psi_j \Sigma \Psi_j' = \sum_{j=0}^{h-1} \Psi_j A^{-1} B \Omega B' A'^{-1} \Psi_j'.\end{aligned}$$

Given a specific identification scheme and estimates of the structural parameters, it is possible to attribute the MSE to the variance of the structural disturbances. Thereby it is customary to write the contribution of each disturbance as a percentage of the total variance. For this purpose let us write the MSE(h) explicitly as

$$\text{MSE}(h) = \begin{pmatrix} m_{11}^{(h)} & * & \dots & * \\ * & m_{22}^{(h)} & \dots & * \\ \vdots & \vdots & \ddots & \vdots \\ * & * & \dots & m_{nn}^{(h)} \end{pmatrix}.$$

Our interest lies exclusively on the variances, $m_{ii}^{(h)}$, $i = 1, \dots, n$, so that we represent the uninteresting covariance terms by the placeholder $*$. These variances can be seen as a linear combination of the ω_i^2's because the covariance matrix of the structural disturbances $\Omega = \text{diag}\left(\omega_1^2, \dots, \omega_n^2\right)$ is a diagonal matrix

$$m_{ii}^{(h)} = d_{i1}^{(h)} \omega_1^2 + \dots + d_{in}^{(h)} \omega_n^2$$

or in matrix form

$$= e_i' \left(\sum_{j=0}^{h-1} \Psi_j \Sigma \Psi_j' \right) e_i = e_i' \left(\sum_{j=0}^{h-1} \Psi_j A^{-1} B \Omega B' A'^{-1} \Psi_j' \right) e_i$$

where the vector e_i has entries equal to zero, except for the i-th entry which is equal to one. Given the positive definiteness of Σ, the weights $d_{ij}^{(h)}$, $i, j = 1, \ldots, n$ and $h = 1, 2, \ldots$, are strictly positive. They can be computed as

$$d_{ij}^{(h)} = \left(\sum_{k=0}^{h-1} [\Psi_k A^{-1} B]_{ij}^2 \right)$$

In order to arrive at the percentage value of the contribution of the j-th disturbance to the MSE of the i-th variable at forecast horizon h, denoted by $f_{ij}^{(h)}$, we divide each summand in the above expression by the total sum:

$$f_{ij}^{(h)} = \frac{d_{ij}^{(h)} \omega_j^2}{m_{ii}^{(h)}}, \qquad i, j = 1, \ldots, n, \text{ for } h = 0, 1, 2, \ldots$$

The corresponding matrix expression is

$$= \frac{e_i' \left(\sum_{j=0}^{h-1} \Psi_j A^{-1} B \Omega^{1/2} e_j e_j' \Omega^{1/2} B' A'^{-1} \Psi_j' \right) e_i}{e_i' \left(\sum_{j=0}^{h-1} \Psi_j \Sigma \Psi_j' \right) e_i}.$$

Usually, these numbers are multiplied by 100 to give percentages and are either displayed graphically as a plot against h or in table form (see the example in Sect. 15.3.5). The forecast error variance $f_{ij}^{(h)}$ thus shows which percentage of the forecast variance of variable i at horizon h can be attributed to the j-th structural shock and thus measures the contribution of each of these shocks to the overall fluctuations of the variables in question.

The FEVD can be used as an alternative identification scheme, sometimes called *max share identification*. Assume for the ease of exposition that $A = I_n$. The VAR disturbances and the structural shocks are then simply related as $Z_t = BV_t$ (compare equation (15.3)). Moreover, take $\Omega = I_n$, but leave B unrestricted. This corresponds to a different, but equivalent normalization which economizes on the notation. Then the j-th structural disturbance can be identified by assuming that it maximizes the forecast error variance share with respect to variable i. Noting that, given Σ, B can be written as $B = RQ$ with R being the unique Cholesky factor of Σ and Q being an orthogonal matrix, this optimization problem can be casted as

$$\max_{q_j} e_i' \left(\sum_{j=0}^{h-1} \Psi_j R q_j q_j' R' \Psi_j' \right) e_i \qquad \text{s.t. } q_j' q_j = 1$$

where q_j is the j-th column of Q, i.e., $q_j = Qe_j$. The constraint $q_j'q_j = 1$ normalizes the vector to have length 1. From $Z_t = BV_t$ it then follows that corresponding structural disturbance is equal to $V_{jt} = q_j' R^{-1} Z_t$. Because $e_j' Q' R^{-1} \Sigma R'^{-1} Q e_k = 0$ for $j \neq k$, this shock is orthogonal to the other structural disturbances. For practical applications it is advisable for reasons of numerical stability to transform to optimization problem into an equivalent eigenvalue problem (see Faust, 1998, appendix).

15.3.3 Confidence Intervals

The impulse response functions and the variance decomposition are the most important tools for the analysis and interpretation of VAR models. It is therefore important not only to estimate these entities but also to provide corresponding confidence intervals to underpin the interpretation from a statistical perspective. In the literature, two approaches have been established: an analytic and a bootstrap approach. The analytic approach relies on the fact that the coefficient matrices Ψ_h, $h = 1, 2, \ldots$, are continuously differentiable functions of the estimated VAR coefficients: $\text{vec}(\Psi_h) = F_h(\beta)$ where β denotes as in Chap. 13 the vectorized form of the VAR coefficient matrices $\Phi_1, \ldots, \Phi_p$.[13] The relation between VAR coefficients and the causal representation (MA(∞) representation) was established in Sect. 12.3. This discussion shows that the functions $F_h : \mathbb{R}^{pn^2} \longrightarrow \mathbb{R}^{n^2}$ are highly nonlinear. In Chap. 13 it was shown that $\sqrt{T}\left(\widehat{\beta} - \beta\right) \xrightarrow{\text{d}} \text{N}\left(0, \Sigma \otimes \Gamma_p^{-1}\right)$ so that we can apply the continuous mapping theorem (see Theorem E.1 or Serfling (1980, 122-124)), sometimes also called the delta method to get

$$\sqrt{T}\left(F_h(\widehat{\beta}) - F_h(\beta)\right) \xrightarrow{\text{d}} \text{N}\left(0, \left(\frac{\partial F_h(\beta)}{\partial \beta'}\right)\left(\Sigma \otimes \Gamma_p^{-1}\right)\left(\frac{\partial F_h(\beta)}{\partial \beta'}\right)'\right)$$

where in practice the covariance matrix is estimated by replacing β and Σ by their estimate. The computation of the gradient matrices $\frac{\partial F_h(\beta)}{\partial \beta'}$ is rather involved, especially when h becomes large. Details can be found in Lütkepohl (1990, 2005) and Mittnik and Zadrozny (1993).

The use of this asymptotic approximation poses two problems. First, the complexity of the relationship between the Φ_i's and the Ψ_h's augments with h so that the quality of the approximation diminishes with h for any given sample size. This is true even when $\widehat{\beta}$ is exactly normally distributed. Second, the distribution of $\widehat{\beta}$ is approximated poorly by the normal distribution. This is particularly relevant when the roots of $\Phi(\text{L})$ are near the unit circle. In this case, the bias toward zero can become substantial (see the discussion in Sect. 7.2). These two problems become

[13] Recall that the vec operator stacks the columns of a $n \times m$ matrix to get one nm vector.

especially severe as h increases. For these reasons the analytic approach has seen only few applications.

The bootstrap approach (Monte Carlo or simulation approach), as advocated by Runkle (1987), Kilian (1998), and Sims and Zha (1999), has become the most favored approach. This is partly due to the development of powerful computer algorithms and the increased speed in computations. The so-called naive bootstrap approach consists of several steps.[14]

First step: Using a random number generator, new disturbances are created. This can be done in two ways. The first one assumes a particular distribution for V_t: $V_t \sim \text{N}(0, \widehat{\Omega})$, for example. The realizations $V_1, \ldots, V_T$ are then independent draws from this distribution. The second one takes random draws with replacement from the identified realizations $\hat{V}_1, \ldots, \hat{V}_T$.[15] The second way has the advantage that no explicit distributional assumption is made which results in a better approximation of the true distribution of $\hat{V}_t$.

Second step: Given the fixed starting values $X_{-p+1}, \ldots, X_0$, the estimated coefficients matrices $\widehat{\Phi}_1, \ldots, \widehat{\Phi}_p$ and the new disturbances drawn in step one, a new realization of the time series for $\{X_t\}$ is generated.

Third step: Estimate the VAR model, given the newly generated realizations for $\{X_t\}$, to obtain new estimates for the coefficient matrices.

Fourth step: Generate a new set of impulse response functions given the new estimates, taking the identification scheme as fixed.

The steps one to four are repeated several times to generate a whole family of impulse response functions which form the basis for the computation of the confidence bands. In many applications, these confidence bands are constructed in a naive fashion by connecting the confidence intervals for individual impulse responses at different horizons. This, however, ignores the fact that the impulse responses at different horizons are correlated which implies that the true coverage probability of the confidence band is different from the presumed one. Thus, the joint probability distribution of the impulse responses should serve as the basis of the computation of the confidence bands. Recently, several alternatives have been proposed which take this feature in account. Lütkepohl et al. (2020b) provide a comprehensive review of such methods.

The number of repetitions should be at least 500. The method can be refined somewhat if the bias toward zero of the estimates of the Φ's is taken into account. This bias can again be determined through simulation methods (Kilian, 1998). A critical appraisal of the bootstrap can be found in Sims and Zha (1999) where additional improvements are discussed. The bootstrap of the variance decomposition works in a similar way.

[14] The bootstrap is a resampling method. Efron and Tibshirani (1993) provide a general introduction to the bootstrap method.

[15] The draws can also be done blockwise. This has the advantage that possible remaining temporal dependences are taken in account.

15.3.4 Example: Advertisement and Sales

This example uses the VAR approach to analyze the dynamic relationship between advertisement expenditures and sales. For this purpose, we use the famous Lydia E. Pinkham Medicine Company data which cover yearly observations from 1907 to 1960. These data were among the first ones which have been used to quantify the effect of advertisement expenditures on sales. The data are taken from Berndt (1991, Chapter 8) where details on the specificities of the data and a summary of the literature can be found.

We denote the two-dimensional logged time series of advertisement expenditures and sales by $\{X_t\} = \{(\ln(\text{advertisement}_t), \ln(\text{sales}_t))'\}$. We consider VAR models of order one to six. For each VAR(p), $p = 1, 2, \ldots, 6$, we compute the corresponding information criteria AIC and BIC (see Sect. 14.4). Whereas AIC favors a model of order two, BIC proposes the more parsimonious model of order one. To be on the safe side, we work with a VAR model of order two whose estimates are reported below

$$X_t = \begin{pmatrix} 0.145 \\ (0.634) \\ 0.762 \\ (0.333) \end{pmatrix} + \begin{pmatrix} 0.451 & 0.642 \\ (0.174) & (0.302) \\ -0.068 & 1.245 \\ (0.091) & (0.159) \end{pmatrix} X_{t-1} + \begin{pmatrix} -0.189 & 0.009 \\ (0.180) & (0.333) \\ -0.176 & -0.125 \\ (0.095) & (0.175) \end{pmatrix} X_{t-2} + Z_t$$

where the estimated standard deviations of the coefficients are reported in parenthesis. The estimate $\widehat{\Sigma}$ of the covariance matrix Σ is

$$\widehat{\Sigma} = \begin{pmatrix} 0.038 & 0.011 \\ 0.011 & 0.010 \end{pmatrix}.$$

The estimated VAR(2) model is taken to be the reduced form model. The structural model contains two structural shocks: a shock to advertisement expenditures, V_{At}, and a shock to sales, V_{St}. The disturbance vector of the structural shock is thus $\{V_t\} = \{(V_{At}, V_{St})'\}$. It is related to Z_t via relation (15.3), i.e., $AZ_t = BV_t$. To identify the model, we thus need three restrictions.[16] We will first assume that $A = I_2$ which gives two restrictions. A plausible further assumption is that shocks to sales have no contemporaneous effects on advertisement expenditures. This zero restriction seems justified because advertisement campaigns have to be planned in advance. They cannot be produced and carried out immediately. This argument then delivers the third restriction as it implies that B is a lower triangular. This lower triangular matrix can be obtained from the Cholesky decomposition of $\widehat{\Sigma}$:

[16] Formula (15.5) for $n = 2$ gives 3 restrictions.

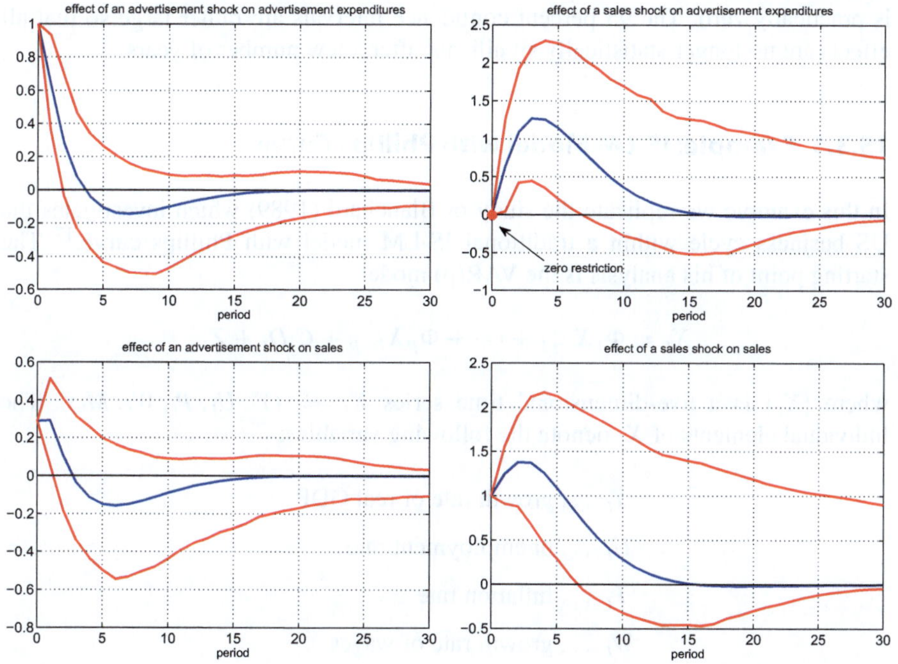

Fig. 15.2 Impulse response functions for advertisement expenditures and sales with 95 percent confidence intervals computed using the bootstrap procedure

$$\widehat{B} = \begin{pmatrix} 1 & 0 \\ 0.288 & 1 \end{pmatrix} \quad \text{and} \quad \widehat{\Omega} = \begin{pmatrix} 0.038 & 0 \\ 0 & 0.007 \end{pmatrix}.$$

The identifying assumptions then imply the impulse response functions plotted in Fig. 15.2.

The upper left figure shows the response of a sudden transitory increase in advertisement expenditures by one percent (i.e., of a one-percent increase of V_{At}) to itself. This shock is positively propagated to the future years, but is statistically zero after 4 years. After 4 years, the shock even changes to negative, but statistically insignificant, expenditures. The same shock produces an increase of sales by 0.3% in the current and next year as shown in the lower left figure. The effect then deteriorates and becomes even negative after 3 years. The right hand figures display the reaction of a sudden transitory increase of sales by one percent. Again, we see that the shock is positively propagated. Thereby the largest effect is reached after 2 years and then declines monotonically. The reaction of advertisement expenditures is initially equal to zero by construction as it corresponds to the identifying assumption with regard to B. Then, the effect starts to increase and reaches a maximum after 3 years and then declines monotonically. After 15 years the effect is practically zero. The 95 percent confidence intervals are rather large so that all effects are no longer statistically significant after a few number of years.

15.3.5 Example: IS-LM Model with Phillips Curve

In this example we replicate the study of Blanchard (1989) which investigates the US business cycle within a traditional IS-LM model with Phillips curve.[17] The starting point of his analysis is the VAR(p) model

$$X_t = \Phi_1 X_{t-1} + \cdots + \Phi_p X_{t-p} + C\, D_t + Z_t$$

where $\{X_t\}$ is a five-dimensional time series $X_t = (Y_t, U_t, P_t, W_t, M_t)'$. The individual elements of X_t denote the following variables:

Y_t ... growth rate of real GDP

U_t ... unemployment rate

P_t ... inflation rate

W_t ... growth rate of wages

M_t ... growth rate of money stock.

The VAR has attached to it a disturbance term $Z_t = (Z_{yt}, Z_{ut}, Z_{pt}, Z_{wt}, Z_{mt})'$. Finally, $\{D_t\}$ denotes the deterministic variables of the model such as a constant, time trend, or dummy variables. In the following, we assume that all variables are stationary.

The business cycle is seen as the result of five structural shocks which impinge on the economy:

V_{dt} ... aggregate demand shock

V_{st} ... aggregate supply shock

V_{pt} ... price shock

V_{wt} ... wage shock

V_{mt} ... money shock.

We will use the IS-LM model to rationalize the restrictions so that we will be able to identify the structural form from the estimated VAR model. The disturbance of the structural and the reduced form models are related by the simultaneous equation system

[17] The results do not match exactly those of Blanchard (1989), but are qualitatively similar.

$$AZ_t = BV_t$$

where $V_t = (V_{yt}, V_{st}, V_{pt}, V_{wt}, V_{mt})'$ and where A and B are 5×5 matrices with ones on the diagonal. Blanchard (1989) proposes the following specification:

$$\begin{aligned}
\text{(AD):} \quad & Z_{yt} = V_{dt} + b_{12}V_{st} \\
\text{(OL):} \quad & Z_{ut} = -a_{21}Z_{yt} + V_{st} \\
\text{(PS):} \quad & Z_{pt} = -a_{34}Z_{wt} - a_{31}Z_{yt} + b_{32}V_{st} + V_{pt} \\
\text{(WS):} \quad & Z_{wt} = -a_{43}Z_{pt} - a_{42}Z_{ut} + b_{42}V_{st} + V_{wt} \\
\text{(MR):} \quad & Z_{mt} = -a_{51}Z_{yt} - a_{52}Z_{ut} - a_{53}Z_{pt} - a_{54}Z_{wt} + V_{mt}.
\end{aligned}$$

In matrix notation, the above simultaneous equation system becomes

$$\begin{pmatrix} 1 & 0 & 0 & 0 & 0 \\ a_{21} & 1 & 0 & 0 & 0 \\ a_{31} & 0 & 1 & a_{34} & 0 \\ 0 & a_{42} & a_{43} & 1 & 0 \\ a_{51} & a_{52} & a_{53} & a_{54} & 1 \end{pmatrix} \begin{pmatrix} Z_{yt} \\ Z_{ut} \\ Z_{pt} \\ Z_{wt} \\ Z_{mt} \end{pmatrix} = \begin{pmatrix} 1 & b_{12} & 0 & 0 & 0 \\ 0 & 1 & 0 & 0 & 0 \\ 0 & b_{32} & 1 & 0 & 0 \\ 0 & b_{42} & 0 & 1 & 0 \\ 0 & 0 & 0 & 0 & 1 \end{pmatrix} \begin{pmatrix} V_{dt} \\ V_{st} \\ V_{pt} \\ V_{wt} \\ V_{mt} \end{pmatrix}.$$

The first equation is interpreted as an aggregate demand (AD) equation where the disturbance term related to GDP growth, Z_{yt}, depends on the demand shock V_{dt} and the supply shock V_{st}. The second equation is related to Okun's law (OL) which relates the unemployment disturbance Z_{ut} to the demand disturbance and the supply shock. Thereby an increase in GDP growth reduces unemployment in the same period by a_{21} whereas a supply shock increases it. The third and the fourth equation represent a price (PS) and wage setting (WS) system where wages and prices interact simultaneously. Finally, the fifth equation (MR) is supposed to determine the money shock (MR). No distinction is made between money supply and money demand shocks. A detailed interpretation of these equations is found in the original article by Blanchard (1989).

Given that the dimension of the system is five (i.e., $n = 5$), formula (15.5) instructs us that we need $3 \times (5 \times 4)/2 = 30$ restrictions. Counting the number of zero restrictions implemented above, we see that we have only 28 zeros. Thus we lack two additional restrictions. We can reach the same conclusion by counting the number of coefficients and the number of equations. The coefficients are $a_{21}, a_{31}, a_{34}, a_{42}, a_{43}, a_{51}, a_{52}, a_{53}, a_{54}, b_{12}, b_{32}, b_{42}$ and the diagonal elements of Ω, the covariance matrix of V_t. We therefore have to determine 17 unknown coefficients out of $(5 \times 6)/2 = 15$ equations. Thus we find again that we are short of two restrictions. Blanchard discusses several possibilities among which the restrictions $b_{12} = 1.0$ and $a_{34} = 0.1$ seem most plausible.

The sample period runs from the second quarter of 1959 to the second quarter of 2004 encompassing 181 observations. Following Blanchard, we include a constant in combination with a linear time trend in the model. Whereas BIC suggests a model of order one, AIC favors a model of order two. As a model of order one seems rather restrictive, we stick to the VAR(2) model whose estimated coefficients are reported below:[18]

$$\widehat{\Phi}_1 = \begin{pmatrix} 0.07 & -1.31 & 0.01 & 0.12 & 0.02 \\ -0.02 & 1.30 & 0.03 & -0.00 & -0.00 \\ -0.07 & -1.47 & 0.56 & 0.07 & 0.03 \\ 0.07 & 0.50 & 0.44 & 0.07 & 0.06 \\ -0.10 & 1.27 & -0.07 & 0.04 & 0.49 \end{pmatrix}$$

$$\widehat{\Phi}_2 = \begin{pmatrix} 0.05 & 1.79 & -0.41 & -0.13 & 0.05 \\ -0.02 & -0.35 & 0.00 & 0.01 & -0.00 \\ -0.04 & 1.38 & 0.28 & 0.05 & -0.00 \\ 0.07 & -0.85 & 0.19 & 0.10 & -0.04 \\ -0.02 & -0.77 & -0.07 & 0.11 & 0.17 \end{pmatrix}$$

$$\widehat{C} = \begin{pmatrix} 2.18 & -0.0101 \\ 0.29 & 0.0001 \\ 0.92 & -0.0015 \\ 4.06 & -0.0035 \\ -0.98 & -0.0025 \end{pmatrix}$$

$$\widehat{\Sigma} = \begin{pmatrix} 9.94 & -0.46 & -0.34 & 0.79 & 0.29 \\ -0.46 & 0.06 & -0.02 & -0.05 & -0.06 \\ -0.34 & -0.02 & 1.06 & 0.76 & 0.13 \\ 0.79 & -0.05 & 0.76 & 5.58 & 0.76 \\ 0.29 & -0.06 & 0.13 & 0.76 & 11.07 \end{pmatrix}.$$

The first column of $\widehat{C}$ relates to the constants, whereas the second column gives the coefficients of the time trend. From these estimates and given the identifying restrictions established above, the equation $\widehat{\Sigma} = A^{-1}B\Omega B'A'^{-1}$ uniquely determines the matrices A, B, and Ω:

$$\widehat{A} = \begin{pmatrix} 1 & 0 & 0 & 0 & 0 \\ 0.050 & 1 & 0 & 0 & 0 \\ 0.038 & 0 & 1 & 0.1 & 0 \\ 0 & 1.77 & -0.24 & 1 & 0 \\ 0.033 & 1.10 & 0.01 & -0.13 & 1 \end{pmatrix}, \quad \widehat{B} = \begin{pmatrix} 1 & 1 & 0 & 0 & 0 \\ 0 & 1 & 0 & 0 & 0 \\ 0 & -1.01 & 1 & 0 & 0 \\ 0 & 1.55 & 0 & 1 & 0 \\ 0 & 0 & 0 & 0 & 1 \end{pmatrix},$$

[18] To save space, the estimated standard errors of the coefficients are not reported.

$$\widehat{\Omega} = \begin{pmatrix} 9.838 & 0 & 0 & 0 & 0 \\ 0 & 0.037 & 0 & 0 & 0 \\ 0 & 0 & 0.899 & 0 & 0 \\ 0 & 0 & 0 & 5.162 & 0 \\ 0 & 0 & 0 & 0 & 10.849 \end{pmatrix}$$

In order to give better interpretation of the results, we have plotted the impulse response functions and their 95 percent confidence bands in Fig. 15.3. The results show that a positive demand shock has only a positive and statistically significant effect on GDP growth in the first three quarters, after that the effect becomes even slightly negative and vanishes after 16 quarters. The positive demand shock reduces unemployment significantly for almost 15 quarters. The maximal effect is achieved after three to four quarters. Although the initial effect is negative, the positive demand shock also drives inflation up which then pushes up wage growth. The supply shock also has a positive effect on GDP growth, but it takes more than four quarters before the effect reaches its peak. In the short run, the positive supply shock even reduces GDP growth. In contrast to the demand shock, the positive supply shock increases unemployment in the short run. The effect will only reduce unemployment in the medium to long run. The effect on price and wage inflation is negative.

Finally, we compute the forecast error variance decomposition according to Sect. 15.3.2. The results are reported in Table 15.1. In the short run, the identifying restrictions play an important role as reflected by the plain zeros. The demand shock accounts for almost all the variance of GDP growth in the short run. The value of 99.62% for forecast horizon of one quarter, however, diminishes as h increases to 40 quarters, but still remains with a value 86.13 very high. The supply shock on the contrary does not explain much of the variation in GDP growth. Even for a horizon of 40 quarters, it contributes only 6.11%. The supply shock is, however, important for the variation in the unemployment rate, especially in the short run. It explains more than 50% , whereas demand shocks account for only 42.22% . Its contribution diminishes with the increase of the forecast horizon giving room for price and wage shocks. The variance of the inflation rate is explained in the short run almost exclusively by price shocks. However, as the forecast horizon is increased, supply and wage shocks become relatively more important. The money growth rate does not interact much with the other variables. Its variation is almost exclusively explained by money shocks.

15.4 Identification via Long-Run Restrictions

15.4.1 A Prototypical Example

Besides short-run restrictions, essentially zero restrictions on the coefficients of A and/or B, Blanchard and Quah (1989) proposed *long-run restrictions* as an alternative. These long-run restrictions have to be seen as complementary to the

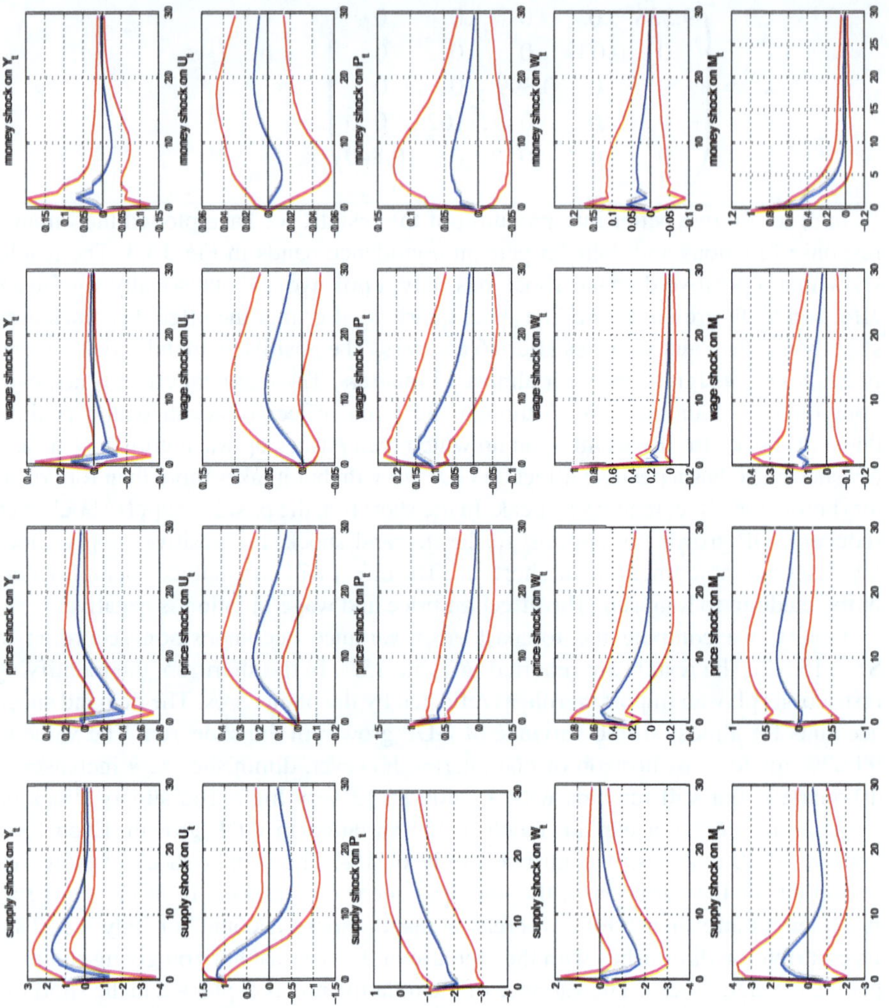

Fig. 15.3 Impulse response functions for the IS-LM model with Phillips curve with 95 percent confidence intervals computed using the bootstrap procedure (compare with Blanchard, 1989)

Table 15.1 Forecast error variance decomposition (FEVD) in terms of demand, supply, price, wage, and money shocks (percentages)

	Growth rate of real GDP				
Horizon	Demand	Supply	Price	Wage	Money
1	99.62	0.38	0	0	0
2	98.13	0.94	0.02	0.87	0.04
4	93.85	1.59	2.13	1.86	0.57
8	88.27	4.83	3.36	2.43	0.61
40	86.13	6.11	4.29	2.58	0.89
	Unemployment rate				
Horizon	Demand	Supply	Price	Wage	Money
1	42.22	57.78	0	0	0
2	52.03	47.57	0.04	0.01	0.00
4	64.74	33.17	1.80	0.13	0.16
8	66.05	21.32	10.01	1.99	0.63
40	39.09	16.81	31.92	10.73	0.89
	Inflation rate				
Horizon	Demand	Supply	Price	Wage	Money
1	0.86	4.18	89.80	5.15	0
2	0.63	13.12	77.24	8.56	0.45
4	0.72	16.79	68.15	13.36	0.97
8	1.79	19.34	60.69	16.07	2.11
40	2.83	20.48	55.84	17.12	3.74
	Growth rate of wages				
Horizon	Demand	Supply	Price	Wage	Money
1	1.18	0.10	0.97	97.75	0
2	1.40	0.10	4.30	93.50	0.69
4	2.18	2.75	9.78	84.49	0.80
8	3.80	6.74	13.40	74.72	1.33
40	5.11	8.44	14.19	70.14	2.13
	Growth rate of money stock				
Horizon	Demand	Supply	Price	Wage	Money
1	0.10	0.43	0.00	0.84	98.63
2	1.45	0.44	0.02	1.02	97.06
4	4.22	1.09	0.04	1.90	92.75
8	8.31	1.55	0.81	2.65	86.68
40	8.47	2.64	5.77	4.55	78.57

short-run ones as they can be combined. Long-run restrictions constrain the long-run effect of structural shocks. This technique makes only sense if some integrated variables are involved, because in the stationary case, the effects of all shocks vanish eventually. To explain this, we discuss the two-dimensional example given by Blanchard and Quah (1989).

They analyze a two-variable system consisting of logged real GDP denoted by $\{Y_t\}$ and the unemployment rate $\{U_t\}$. Logged GDP is typically integrated of order one (see Sect. 7.3.4 for an analysis for Swiss GDP) whereas U_t is considered to be stationary. Thus they apply the VAR approach to the stationary process $\{X_t\} = \{(\Delta Y_t, U_t)'\}$. Assuming that $\{X_t\}$ is already demeaned and follows a causal VAR process, we have the following representations:

$$X_t = \begin{pmatrix} \Delta Y_t \\ U_t \end{pmatrix} = \Phi_1 X_{t-1} + \cdots + \Phi_p X_{t-p} + Z_t$$

$$= \Psi(\mathrm{L}) Z_t = Z_t + \Psi_1 Z_{t-1} + \Psi_2 Z_{t-2} + \ldots.$$

For simplicity, we assume that $A = I_2$, so that

$$Z_t = BV_t = \begin{pmatrix} 1 & b_{12} \\ b_{21} & 1 \end{pmatrix} \begin{pmatrix} v_{dt} \\ v_{st} \end{pmatrix}$$

where $V_t = (v_{dt}, v_{st})' \sim \mathrm{WN}(0, \Omega)$ with $\Omega = \mathrm{diag}(\omega_d^2, \omega_s^2)$. Thereby $\{v_{dt}\}$ and $\{v_{st}\}$ denote demand and supply shocks, respectively. The causal representation of $\{X_t\}$ implies that the effect of a demand shock in period t on GDP growth in period $t + h$ is given by

$$\frac{\partial \Delta Y_{t+h}}{\partial v_{dt}} = [\Psi_h B]_{11}$$

where $[\Psi_h B]_{11}$ denotes the upper left hand element of the matrix $\Psi_h B$. Y_{t+h} can be written as $Y_{t+h} = \Delta Y_{t+h} + \Delta Y_{t+h-1} + \cdots + \Delta Y_{t+1} + Y_t$ so that the effect of the demand shock on the *level* of logged GDP is given by

$$\frac{\partial Y_{t+h}}{\partial v_{dt}} = \sum_{j=0}^{h} [\Psi_j B]_{11} = \left[\sum_{j=0}^{h} \Psi_j B \right]_{11}.$$

Blanchard and Quah (1989) propose, in accordance with conventional economic theory, to restrict the long-run effect of the demand shock on the level of logged GDP to zero:

$$\lim_{h \to \infty} \frac{\partial Y_{t+h}}{\partial v_{dt}} = \sum_{j=0}^{\infty} [\Psi_j B]_{11} = 0.$$

This implies that

$$\sum_{j=0}^{\infty} \Psi_j B = \left(\sum_{j=0}^{\infty} \Psi_j \right) B = \Psi(1) B = \begin{pmatrix} 0 & * \\ * & * \end{pmatrix}$$

where $*$ is a placeholder. This restriction is sufficient to infer b_{21} from the relation $[\Psi(1)]_{11}b_{11} + b_{21}[\Psi(1)]_{12} = 0$ and the normalization $b_{11} = 1$:

$$b_{21} = -\frac{[\Psi(1)]_{11}}{[\Psi(1)]_{12}} = -\frac{[\Phi(1)^{-1}]_{11}}{[\Phi(1)^{-1}]_{12}}.$$

The second part of the equation follows from the identity $\Phi(z)\Psi(z) = I_2$ which gives $\Psi(1) = \Phi(1)^{-1}$ for $z = 1$. The long-run effect of the supply shock on Y_t is left unrestricted and is therefore in general nonzero. Note that the implied value of b_{21} depends on $\Phi(1)$ and thus on $\Phi_1, \ldots, \Phi_p$. The results are therefore, in contrast to short-run restrictions, much more sensitive to the correct specification of the VAR.

The relation $Z_t = BV_t$ implies that

$$\Sigma = B \begin{pmatrix} \omega_d^2 & 0 \\ 0 & \omega_s^2 \end{pmatrix} B'$$

or more explicitely

$$\Sigma = \begin{pmatrix} \sigma_1^2 & \sigma_{12} \\ \sigma_{12} & \sigma_2^2 \end{pmatrix} = \begin{pmatrix} 1 & b_{12} \\ b_{21} & 1 \end{pmatrix} \begin{pmatrix} \omega_d^2 & 0 \\ 0 & \omega_s^2 \end{pmatrix} \begin{pmatrix} 1 & b_{21} \\ b_{12} & 1 \end{pmatrix}.$$

Taking b_{21} as already given from above, this equation system has three equations and three unknowns $b_{12}, \omega_d^2, \omega_s^2$ which is a necessary condition for a solution to exist.

Analytic Solution of the System

Because b_{21} is already determined from the long-run restriction, we rewrite the equation system[19] explicitly in terms of b_{21}:

$$\begin{aligned} \sigma_1^2 &= \omega_d^2 + b_{12}^2\omega_s^2 \\ \sigma_{12} &= b_{21}\omega_d^2 + b_{12}\omega_s^2 \\ \sigma_2^2 &= b_{21}^2\omega_d^2 + \omega_s^2. \end{aligned}$$

Using the last two equations, we can express ω_d^2 and ω_s^2 as functions of b_{12}:

$$\omega_d^2 = \frac{\sigma_{12} - b_{12}\sigma_2^2}{b_{21} - b_{12}b_{21}^2}$$

$$\omega_s^2 = \frac{\sigma_2^2 - b_{21}\sigma_{12}}{1 - b_{12}b_{21}}.$$

[19] This equation system is similar to the one analyzed in Sect. 15.1.3.

These expressions are only valid if $b_{21} \neq 0$ and $b_{12}b_{21} \neq 1$. The case $b_{21} = 0$ is not interesting given the subject of the analysis. It would simplify the original equation system strongly and would result in $b_{12} = \sigma_{12}/\sigma_2^2$, $\omega_d^2 = (\sigma_1^2\sigma_2^2 - \sigma_{12}^2)/\sigma_2^2 > 0$, and $\omega_s^2 = \sigma_2^2 > 0$. The case $b_{12}b_{21} = 1$ contradicts the assumption that Σ is a positive-definite matrix and can therefore be disregarded.[20]

Inserting the solutions of ω_d^2 and ω_s^2 into the first equation, we obtain a quadratic equation in b_{12}:

$$\left(b_{21}\sigma_2^2 - b_{21}^2\sigma_{12}\right) b_{12}^2 + \left(b_{21}^2\sigma_1^2 - \sigma_2^2\right) b_{12} + \left(\sigma_{12} - b_{21}\sigma_1^2\right) = 0.$$

The discriminant Δ of this equation is

$$\begin{aligned}
\Delta &= \left(b_{21}^2\sigma_1^2 - \sigma_2^2\right)^2 - 4\left(b_{21}\sigma_2^2 - b_{21}^2\sigma_{12}\right)\left(\sigma_{12} - b_{21}\sigma_1^2\right) \\
&= \left(b_{21}^2\sigma_1^2 + \sigma_2^2\right)^2 - 4b_{21}\sigma_{12}\left(b_{21}^2\sigma_1^2 + \sigma_2^2\right) + 4b_{21}^2\sigma_{12}^2 \\
&= \left(b_{21}^2\sigma_1^2 + \sigma_2^2 - 2b_{21}\sigma_{12}\right)^2 > 0.
\end{aligned}$$

The positivity of the discriminant implies that the quadratic equation has two real solutions $b_{12}^{(1)}$ and $b_{12}^{(2)}$:

$$\begin{aligned}
b_{12}^{(1)} &= \frac{\sigma_2^2 - b_{21}\sigma_{12}}{b_{21}\sigma_2^2 - b_{21}^2\sigma_{12}} = \frac{1}{b_{21}}, \\
b_{12}^{(2)} &= \frac{\sigma_{12} - b_{21}\sigma_1^2}{\sigma_2^2 - b_{21}\sigma_{12}}.
\end{aligned}$$

The first solution $b_{12}^{(1)}$ can be excluded because it violates the assumption $b_{12}b_{21} \neq 1$ which stands in contradiction to the positive-definiteness of the covariance matrix Σ. Inserting the second solution back into the solution for ω_d^2 and ω_s^2, we finally get

$$\begin{aligned}
\omega_d^2 &= \frac{\sigma_1^2\sigma_2^2 - \sigma_{12}^2}{b_{21}^2\sigma_1^2 - 2b_{21}\sigma_{12} + \sigma_2^2} > 0 \\
\omega_s^2 &= \frac{\left(\sigma_2^2 - b_{21}\sigma_{12}\right)^2}{b_{21}^2\sigma_1^2 - 2b_{21}\sigma_{12} + \sigma_2^2} > 0.
\end{aligned}$$

[20] If $b_{12}b_{21} = 1$, $\det\Sigma = \sigma_1^2\sigma_2^2 - \sigma_{12}^2 = 0$. This implies that Z_{1t} and Z_{2t} are perfectly correlated, i.e., $\rho_{Z_{1t},Z_{2t}}^2 = \sigma_{12}^2/(\sigma_1^2\sigma_2^2) = 1$.

Because Σ is a symmetric positive-definite matrix, $\sigma_1^2\sigma_2^2 - \sigma_{12}^2$ and the denominator $b_{21}^2\sigma_1^2 - 2b_{21}\sigma_{12} + \sigma_2^2$ are strictly positive. Thus, both solutions yield positive variances, and we have found the unique admissible solution.

15.4.2 The General Approach

The general case of long-run restrictions has a structure similar to the case of short-run restrictions. Take as a starting point again the structural VAR (15.1) from Sect. 15.1.2:

$$\begin{aligned} AX_t &= \Gamma_1 X_{t-1} + \cdots + \Gamma_p X_{t-p} + BV_t, \qquad V_t \sim \mathrm{WN}(0, \Omega), \\ A(\mathrm{L})X_t &= BV_t \end{aligned}$$

where $\{X_t\}$ is stationary and causal with respect to $\{V_t\}$. As before the matrix A is normalized to have ones on its diagonal and is assumed to be invertible, Ω is a diagonal matrix with $\Omega = \mathrm{diag}(\omega_1^2, \ldots, \omega_n^2)$, and B is a matrix with ones on the diagonal. The matrix polynomial $A(\mathrm{L})$ is defined as $A(\mathrm{L}) = A - \Gamma_1\mathrm{L} - \cdots - \Gamma_p\mathrm{L}^p$. The reduced form is given by

$$\Phi(\mathrm{L})X_t = Z_t, \qquad Z_t \sim \mathrm{WN}(0, \Sigma)$$

where $AZ_t = BV_t$ and $A\Phi_j = \Gamma_j$, $j = 1, \ldots, p$, respectively, $A\Phi(\mathrm{L}) = A(\mathrm{L})$.

The long-run variance of $\{X_t\}$, J, (see Eq. (11.1) in Chap. 11) can be derived from the reduced as well as from the structural form, which gives the following expressions:

$$\begin{aligned} J &= \Phi(1)^{-1}\Sigma\, \Phi(1)^{-1\prime} = \Phi(1)^{-1}A^{-1}B\Omega B'A'^{-1}\Phi(1)^{-1\prime} \\ &= A(1)^{-1}B\Omega B'A(1)^{-1\prime} \\ &= \Psi(1)\Sigma\, \Psi(1)' = \Psi(1)A^{-1}B\Omega B'A'^{-1}\Psi(1)' \end{aligned}$$

where $X_t = \Psi(\mathrm{L})Z_t$ denotes the causal representation of $\{X_t\}$ with respect to $\{Z_t\}$. The long-run variance J can be estimated by adapting the methods in Sect. 4.4 to the multivariate case. Thus, the above equation system has a similar structure as the system (15.4) which underlies the case of short-run restrictions. As before, we get $n(n+1)/2$ equations with $2n^2 - n$ unknowns. The nonlinear equation system is therefore undetermined for $n \geq 2$. Therefore, $3n(n-1)/2$ additional equations or restrictions are necessary to achieve identification. Hence, conceptually we are in a similar situation as in the case of short-run restrictions.[21]

[21] See Rubio-Ramírez et al. (2010) for a unified treatment of both types of restrictions.

In practice, it is customary to achieve identification through zero restrictions where some elements of $\Psi(1)A^{-1}B$, respectively $\Phi(1)^{-1}A^{-1}B$, are set a priori to zero. Setting the ij-th element $[\Psi(1)A^{-1}B]_{ij} = [\Phi(1)^{-1}A^{-1}B]_{ij}$ equal to zero amounts to set the *cumulative* effect of the j-th structural disturbance V_{jt} on the i-th variable equal to zero. If the i-th variable enters X_t in first differences, as was the case for Y_t in the previous example, this zero restriction restrains the long-run effect on the level of that variable.

An interesting simplification arises if one assumes that $A = I_n$ and that $\Psi(1)B = \Phi(1)^{-1}B$ is a lower triangular matrix. In this case, B and Ω can be estimated from the Cholesky decomposition of the estimated long-run variance $\hat{J}$. Let $\hat{J} = \hat{L}\hat{D}\hat{L}'$ be the Cholesky decomposition where $\hat{L}$ is lower triangular matrix with ones on the diagonal and $\hat{D}$ is a diagonal matrix with strictly positive diagonal entries. As $\hat{J} = \hat{\Phi}(1)^{-1}B\hat{\Omega}B'\hat{\Phi}(1)^{-1\prime}$, the matrix of structural coefficients can then be estimated as $\hat{B} = \hat{\Phi}(1)\hat{L}\hat{U}^{-1}$. The multiplication by the inverse of the diagonal matrix $U = \operatorname{diag}(\hat{\Phi}(1)\hat{L})$ is necessary to guarantee that the normalization of $\hat{B}$ (diagonal elements equal to one) is respected. Ω is then estimated as $\hat{\Omega} = \hat{U}\hat{D}\hat{U}$.

Instead of using a method of moments approach, it is possible to use an instrumental variable (IV) approach. For this purpose, we rewrite the reduced form of X_t in the Dickey-Fuller form (see Eqs. (7.11) and (16.4))

$$\Delta X_t = -\Phi(1)X_{t-1} + \widetilde{\Phi}_1 \Delta X_{t-1} + \cdots + \widetilde{\Phi}_{p-1}\Delta X_{t-p+1} + Z_t,$$

where $\widetilde{\Phi}_j = -\sum_{i=j+1}^{p} \Phi_i$, $j = 1, 2, \ldots, p-1$. For the ease of exposition, we assume $B = I_n$ so that $AZ_t = V_t$. Multiplying this equation by A yields

$$A\Delta X_t = -A\Phi(1)X_{t-1} + A\widetilde{\Phi}_1 \Delta X_{t-1} + \cdots + A\widetilde{\Phi}_{p-1}\Delta X_{t-p+1} + V_t. \tag{15.8}$$

Consider for simplicity the case that $A\Phi(1)$ is a lower triangular matrix. This implies that the structural shocks $V_{2t}, V_{3t}, \ldots, V_{nt}$ have no long-run impact on the first variable X_{1t}. It is, therefore, possible to estimate the coefficients $A_{12}, A_{13}, \ldots, A_{1n}$ by instrumental variables taking $X_{2,t-1}, X_{3,t-1}, \ldots, X_{n,t-1}$ as instruments.

For $n = 2$ the Dickey-Fuller form of the equation system (15.8) is

$$\begin{pmatrix} 1 & A_{12} \\ A_{21} & 1 \end{pmatrix} \begin{pmatrix} \Delta\tilde{X}_{1t} \\ \Delta\tilde{X}_{2t} \end{pmatrix} = -\begin{pmatrix} [A\Phi(1)]_{11} & 0 \\ [A\Phi(1)]_{21} & [A\Phi(1)]_{22} \end{pmatrix} \begin{pmatrix} \tilde{X}_{1,t-1} \\ \tilde{X}_{2,t-1} \end{pmatrix} + \begin{pmatrix} V_{1t} \\ V_{2t} \end{pmatrix},$$

respectively

$$\begin{aligned} \Delta\tilde{X}_{1t} &= -A_{12}\Delta\tilde{X}_{2t} - [A\Phi(1)]_{11}\tilde{X}_{1,t-1} + V_{1t} \\ \Delta\tilde{X}_{2t} &= -A_{21}\Delta\tilde{X}_{1t} - [A\Phi(1)]_{21}\tilde{X}_{1,t-1} - [A\Phi(1)]_{22}\tilde{X}_{2,t-1} + V_{2t}. \end{aligned}$$

Thereby $\Delta\tilde{X}_{1t}$ and $\Delta\tilde{X}_{2t}$ denote the OLS residuals from a regression of ΔX_{1t}, respectively ΔX_{2t} on $(\Delta X_{1,t-1}, \Delta X_{2,t-1}, \ldots, \Delta X_{1,t-p+1}, \Delta X_{2,t-p+1})$. $\tilde{X}_{2,t-1}$ is a valid instrument for $\Delta\tilde{X}_{2t}$ because this variable does not appear in the first equation. Thus, A_{12} can be consistently estimated by the IV approach. For the estimation of A_{21}, we can use the residuals from the first equation as instruments because V_{1t} and V_{2t} are assumed to be uncorrelated. From this example, it is easy to see how this recursive method can be generalized to more than two variables. Note also that the IV approach can also be used in the context of short-run restrictions.

The issue whether a technology shock leads to a reduction of hours worked in the short run led to a vivid discussion on the usefulness of long-run restrictions for structural models (Galí, 1999; Christiano et al., 2003, 2006; Chari et al., 2008). From an econometric point of view, it turned out, on the one hand, that the estimation of $\Phi(1)$ is critical for the method of moments approach. The IV approach, on the other hand, depends on the strength or weakness of the instrument used (Pagan and Robertson, 1998; Gospodinov, 2008).

It is, of course, possible to combine both short- and long-run restrictions. An interesting application of both techniques was presented by Galí (1992). In doing so, one must be aware that both types of restrictions are consistent with each other and that counting the number of restrictions gives only a necessary condition.

15.4.3 Example: Identifying Aggregate Demand and Supply Shocks

In this example, we follow Blanchard and Quah (1989) and investigate the behavior of the growth rate of real GDP and the unemployment rate for the United States over the period from the first quarter 1979 to the second quarter of 2004 (102 observations). The AIC and the BIC suggest models of order two and one, respectively. Because some coefficients of $\widehat{\Phi}_2$ are significant at the 10% level, we prefer to use the VAR(2) model which results in the following estimates:[22]

$$\widehat{\Phi}_1 = \begin{pmatrix} 0.070 & -3.376 \\ -0.026 & 1.284 \end{pmatrix}, \quad \widehat{\Phi}_2 = \begin{pmatrix} 0.029 & 3.697 \\ -0.022 & -0.320 \end{pmatrix},$$

$$\widehat{\Sigma} = \begin{pmatrix} 7.074 & -0.382 \\ -0.382 & 0.053 \end{pmatrix}.$$

These results can be used to estimate $\Phi(1) = I_2 - \Phi_1 - \Phi_2$ and consequently also $\Psi(1) = \Phi(1)^{-1}$:

$$\widehat{\Phi}(1) = \begin{pmatrix} 0.901 & -0.321 \\ 0.048 & 0.036 \end{pmatrix}$$

$$\widehat{\Psi}(1) = \widehat{\Phi}(1)^{-1} = \begin{pmatrix} 0.755 & 6.718 \\ -1.003 & 18.832 \end{pmatrix}.$$

[22] The results for the constants are suppressed to save space.

Assuming that $Z_t = BV_t$ and following the argument in Sect. 15.4.1 that the demand shock has no long-run impact on the level of real GDP, the estimate of b_{21} is

$$\hat{b}_{21} = -[\widehat{\Psi}(1)]_{11}/[\widehat{\Psi}(1)]_{12} = -0.112.$$

The two solutions of the quadratic equation for b_{12} are -8.894 and 43.285. As the first solution results in a negative variance for ω_2^2, we can disregard this solution and stick to the second one. The second solution makes also sense economically, because a positive supply shock leads to positive effects on GDP. Setting $b_{12} = 43.285$ gives the following estimates for covariance matrix of the structural shocks Ω:

$$\widehat{\Omega} = \begin{pmatrix} \widehat{\omega}_d^2 & 0 \\ 0 & \widehat{\omega}_s^2 \end{pmatrix} = \begin{pmatrix} 4.023 & 0 \\ 0 & 0.0016 \end{pmatrix}.$$

The big difference in the variance of both shocks clearly shows the greater importance of demand shocks for business cycle movements.

Figure 15.4 shows the impulse response functions of the VAR(2) identified by the long-run restriction. Each figure displays the dynamic effect of a demand and a supply shock on real GDP and the unemployment rate, respectively, where the size of the initial shock corresponds to one standard deviation. The result conforms well with standard economic reasoning. A positive demand shock increases real GDP and lowers the unemployment rate in the short run. The effect is even amplified

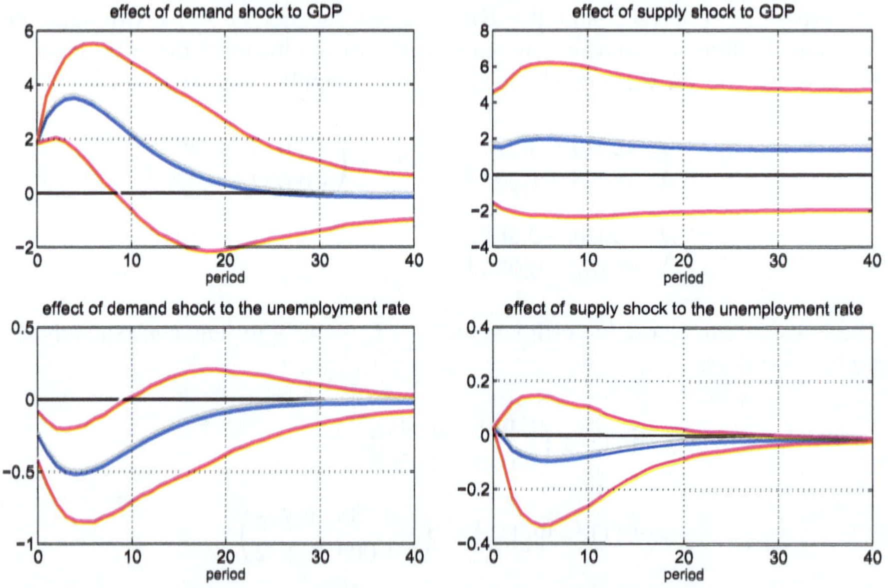

Fig. 15.4 Impulse response functions of the Blanchard-Quah model (Blanchard and Quah, 1989) with 95 percent confidence intervals computed using the bootstrap procedure

for some quarters before it declines monotonically. After 30 quarters, the effect of the demand has practically vanished so that its long-run effect becomes zero as imposed by the restriction. The supply shock has a similar short-run effect on real GDP, but initially increases the unemployment rate. Only when the effect on GDP becomes stronger after some quarters will the unemployment rate start to decline. In the long-run, the supply shock has a positive effect on real GDP but no effect on unemployment. Interestingly, only the short-run effects of the demand shock are statistically significant at the 95 percent level.

15.5 Sign Restrictions

In recent years the use of sign restrictions has attracted a lot of attention. Pioneering contributions have been provided by Faust (1998), Canova and Nicoló (2002), and Uhlig (2005). Since then the literature has abounded by many applications in many contexts. Sign restrictions try to identify the impact of the structural shocks by requiring that the signs of the impulse response coefficients have to follow a given pattern. The motivation behind this development is that economists are often more confident about the sign of an economic relationship than about its exact magnitude. This seems to be true also for zero restrictions, whether they are viewed as short- or long-run restrictions. This insight already led Samuelson (1947) to advocate a calculus of qualitative relations in economics. Unfortunately, this approach has been forgotten in the progression of economic analysis.[23] With the rise in popularity of sign restrictions his ideas may see a revival.

To make the notion of sign restrictions precise, we introduce a language based on the following notation and definitions. Sign restrictions will be specified as *sign pattern matrices*. These matrices make use of the sign function of a real number x, $\text{sgn}(x)$, defined as

$$\text{sgn}(x) = \begin{cases} 1, & \text{if } x > 0; \\ -1, & \text{if } x < 0; \\ 0, & \text{if } x = 0. \end{cases}$$

Definition 15.1 A *sign pattern matrix* or *pattern* for short is a matrix whose elements are solely from the set $\{1, -1, 0\}$. Given a sign pattern matrix S, the *sign pattern class of* S is defined by

$$\mathcal{S}(S) = \{M \in \mathrm{M}(n) \mid \text{sgn}(M) = S\}$$

where $M(n)$ is the set of all $n \times n$ matrices and where sgn is applied element-wise to M. Clearly, $\mathcal{S}(S) \equiv \mathcal{S}(\text{sgn}(S))$.

[23] It is interesting to note that Samuelson's ideas have fallen on fruitful grounds in areas like computer science or combinatorics (see Brualdi and Shader, 1995; Hall and Li, 2014).

Remark 15.1 Often the set $\{+, -, 0\}$ is used instead of $\{+1, -1, 0\}$ to denote the sign patterns.

Remark 15.2 In some instances we do not want to restrict all signs but only a subset of it. In this case, the elements of the sign pattern matrix S may come from the larger set $\{-1, 0, 1, \#\}$ where # stands for an unspecified sign. S is then called a *generalized sign pattern matrix* or a *generalized pattern*. The addition + and the multiplication × of (generalized) sign pattern matrices are defined in a natural way.

In order not to overload the discussion, we set $A = I_n$ and focus on the case where $Z_t = BV_t$.[24] Moreover, we use a different, but completely equivalent normalization. In particular, we relax, on the one hand, the assumption that B has only ones on its diagonal, but assume on the other hand that $\Omega = I_n$. Note that $\Sigma = \mathbb{E}Z_t Z_t' = BB'$ is a strictly positive definite matrix. Assuming that a causal representation of $\{X_t\}$ in terms of $\{Z_t\}$ and thus also in terms of $\{V_t\}$ exists, we can represent X_t as

$$X_t = BV_t + \Psi_1 BV_{t-1} + \Psi_2 BV_{t-2} + \ldots = \sum_{h=0}^{\infty} \Psi_h BV_{t-h} = \Psi(\mathrm{L})BV_t.$$

Denote by $\mathcal{B}(\Sigma)$ the set of invertible matrices B such that $\Sigma = BB'$, i.e., $\mathcal{B}(\Sigma) = \{B \in \mathrm{GL}(n) \mid BB' = \Sigma\}$.[25] Thus, $\mathcal{B}(\Sigma)$ is the set of all feasible structural factorizations (models).

Sign restrictions on the impulse responses $[\Psi_h B]_{i,j}$ can then be defined in terms of a sequence of (generalized) sign pattern matrices $\{S_h\}$, $h = 0, 1, 2, \ldots$

Definition 15.2 (Sign Restrictions) A causal VAR *allows* a sequence of (generalized) sign pattern matrices $\{S_h\}$ if and only if there exists $B \in \mathcal{B}(\Sigma)$ such that

$$\Psi_h B \in \mathcal{S}(S_h), \quad \text{for all } h = 0, 1, 2, \ldots \tag{15.9}$$

Remark 15.3 As $\|\Psi_j B\|$ converges to zero for $j \to \infty$, it seems reasonable to impose sign restrictions only up to some horizon $h^{\max} < \infty$. In this case, S_h, $h > h^{\max}$, is equal to the generalized sign pattern matrix whose elements consist exclusively of #'s. A case of particular interest is given by $h^{\max} = 0$. In this case, we drop the index 0 and say that the VAR allows (generalized) sign pattern matrix S.

Remark 15.4 With this notation we can also represent (short-run) zero restrictions if the sign patterns are restricted to 0 and #.

---

[24] The case with general A matrices can be treated analogously.

[25] $\mathrm{GL}(n)$ is known as the general linear group. It is the set of all invertible $n \times n$ matrices.

A natural question to ask is how restrictive a prescribed sign pattern is. This amounts to the question whether a given VAR can be compatible with any sign pattern. As is already clear from the discussion of the two-dimensional case in Sect. 15.1.3, this is not the case. As the set of feasible parameters can be represented by a rectangular hyperbola, there will always be one quadrant with no intersection with the branches of the hyperbola. In the example plotted in Fig. 15.1, this is quadrant III. Thus, configurations with $(B)_{21} < 0$ and $(B)_{12} < 0$ are not feasible given $(\Sigma)_{12} > 0$. This argument can be easily extended to models of higher dimensions. Thus, there always exist sign patterns which are incompatible with a given Σ.

As pointed out in Sect. 15.2, there always exists a unique upper triangular matrix R, called the Cholesky factor of Σ, such that $\Sigma = R'R$. Thus, $\mathcal{B}(\Sigma) \neq \emptyset$ because $R \in \mathcal{B}(\Sigma)$.

Lemma 15.1 *Let the Cholesky factor of* Σ *be* R, *then*

$$\mathcal{B}(\Sigma) = \{B \in \mathrm{GL}(n) \mid \exists Q \in \mathcal{O}(n) : B = QR\}.$$

Proof Suppose $B = R'Q$ with $Q \in \mathcal{O}(n)$, then $BB' = R'QQ'R = \Sigma$. Thus, $B \in \mathcal{B}(\Sigma)$. If $B \in \mathcal{B}(\Sigma)$, define $Q = (BB')^{-1/2}B$. Then, $QQ' = (BB')^{-1/2}BB'(BB')^{-1/2} = I_n$. Thus, $Q \in \mathcal{O}(n)$. □

This lemma establishes that there is a one-to-one function φ_Σ from the group of orthogonal matrices $\mathcal{O}(n)$ onto the set of feasible structural factorizations $\mathcal{B}(\Sigma)$. From the proof, we see that $\varphi_\Sigma(Q) = R'Q$ and $\varphi_\Sigma^{-1}(B) = (BB')^{-1/2}B$. As φ_Σ and φ_Σ^{-1} are clearly continuous, φ_Σ is a homeomorphism.

To make the presentation more transparent, we focus on sign restrictions only and disregard zero restrictions. Arias et al. (2014) show how sign and zero restrictions can be treated simultaneously. Thus, the entries of $\{S_h\}$ are elements of $\{-1, +1, \#\}$ only. Assume that a VAR allows sign patterns $\{S_h\}$, $h = 0, 1, \ldots, h^{\max}$. Then according to Definition 15.2, there exists $B \in \mathcal{B}(\Sigma)$ such that $\Psi_h B \in \mathcal{S}(S_h)$ for all $h = 0, 1, \ldots, h^{\max}$. As the (strict) inequality restrictions delineate an open subset of $B \in \mathcal{B}(\Sigma)$, there exist other nearby matrices which also fulfill the sign restrictions. Sign restrictions therefore do not identify one impulse response sequence, but a whole set. Thus, the impulse responses are called *set identified*.

This set is usually difficult to characterize algebraically so that one has to rely on computer simulations. Conditional on the estimated VAR, thus conditional on $\{\widehat{\Psi}_j\}$ and $\widehat{\Sigma}$, Lemma 15.1 suggests a simple and straightforward algorithm (see Rubio-Ramírez et al., 2010; Arias et al., 2014, for further details):

step 1: Draw at random an element Q from the uniform distribution on the set of orthogonal matrices $\mathcal{O}(n)$.

step 2: Convert Q into a random element of $\mathcal{B}(\widehat{\Sigma})$ by applying $\varphi_{\widehat{\Sigma}}$ to Q. As $\varphi_{\widehat{\Sigma}}$ is a homeomorphism, this imposes a uniform distribution on $\mathcal{B}(\Sigma)$.

step 3: Compute the impulse responses with respect to $\varphi_{\widehat{\Sigma}}(Q)$, i.e., compute $\widehat{\Psi}_h \varphi_{\widehat{\Sigma}}(Q)$.

step 4: Keep those models with impulse response functions which satisfy the prescribed sign restrictions $\widehat{\Psi}_h \varphi_{\widehat{\Sigma}}(Q) \in \mathcal{S}(S_h)$, $h = 0, 1, \ldots, h^{\max}$.

step 5: Repeat steps 1–4 until a satisfactory number of feasible structural models with impulse responses obeying the sign restrictions have been obtained.

The implementation of this algorithm requires a way to generate random draws Q from the uniform distribution on $\mathcal{O}(n)$.[26] This is not a straightforward task because the elements of Q are interdependent as they must ensure the orthonormality of the columns of Q. Edelman and Rao (2005) propose the following efficient two-step procedure. First, draw $n \times n$ matrices X such that $X \sim \mathrm{N}(0, I_n \otimes I_n)$, i.e., each element of X is drawn independently from a standard normal distribution. Second, perform the QR-decomposition which factorizes each matrix X into the product of an orthogonal matrix Q and an upper triangular matrix R normalized to have positive diagonal entries.[27]

As the impulse responses are only set identified, the way to report the results and how to conduct inference becomes a matter of discussion. Several methods have been proposed in the literature:

(i) One straightforward possibility consists in reporting, for each horizon h, the median of the impulse responses. Although simple to compute, this method presents some disadvantages. The median responses will not correspond to any of the structural models. Moreover, the orthogonality of the structural shocks will be lost. Fry and Pagan (2011) propose the *median–target method* as an ad hoc remedy to this shortage. They advocate to search for the admissible structural model whose impulse responses come closest to the median ones.

(ii) Another possibility is to search for the admissible structural model which maximizes the share of the *forecast error variance* at some horizon of a given variable after a particular shock.[28] An early application of this method can be found in Faust (1998). This method remains, however, uninformative about the relative explanatory power of alternative admissible structural models.

(iii) The *penalty function approach* by Mountford and Uhlig (2009) does not accept or reject particular impulse responses depending on whether it is in accordance with the sign restrictions (see step 4 in the above algorithm). Instead, it asso-

---

[26] It can be shown that this probability measure is the unique measure μ on $\mathcal{O}(n)$ which satisfies the normalization $\mu(\mathcal{O}(n)) = 1$ and the (left)-invariance property $\mu(Q\mathfrak{Q}) = \mu(\mathfrak{Q})$ for every $\mathfrak{Q} \subseteq \mathcal{O}(n)$ and $Q \in \mathcal{O}(n)$. In economics, this probability measure is often wrongly referred to as the Haar measure. The Haar measure is not normalized and is, thus, unique only up to a proportionality factor.

[27] Given a value of n, the corresponding MATLAB commands are `[Q,R]=qr(randn(n)); Q = Q*diag(sign(diag(R)));` (see Edelman and Rao, 2005).

[28] The minimization of the forecast error variance share have also been applied as an identification device outside the realm of sign restrictions.

ciates for each possible impulse response function and every sign restriction a value which rewards a "correct" sign and penalizes a "wrong" sign. Mountford and Uhlig (2009) propose the following ad hoc penalty function: $f(x) = 100x$ if $\text{sgn}(x)$ is wrong and $f(x) = x$ if $\text{sgn}(x)$ is correct. The impulse response function which minimizes the total (standardized) penalty is then reported.

(iv) The exposition becomes more coherent if viewed from a Bayesian perspective. From this perspective, the uniform distribution on $\mathcal{O}(n)$, respectively on $\mathcal{B}(\widehat{\Sigma})$, is interpreted as diffuse or uninformative prior distribution.[29] The admissible structural models which have been retained in step 5 of the algorithm are then seen as draws from the corresponding posterior distribution. The most likely model is then given by the model which corresponds to the mode of the posterior distribution. This model is associated with an impulse response function which can then be reported. This method also allows the construction of $100(1-\alpha)$ percent highest posterior density credible sets (see Inoue and Kilian, 2013, for details). As shown by Moon and Schorfheide (2012), these sets cannot, even in a large sample context, be interpreted as approximate frequentist confidence intervals. Recently, however, Granziera et al. (2018) proposed a frequentist approach to the construction of error bands for sign identified impulse responses. The breakdown of the asymptotic equivalence of Bayesian and frequentist set-identified models, in particular structural VAR models, was analyzed in depth by Giacomini and Kitagawa (2021).

15.6 Non-Gaussian Identification

In the previous sections, the identification of structural VAR models was based on second moments only.[30] As the normal (Gaussian) distribution is completely characterized by the first two moments, the attempt to make use of higher-order moments will not provide additional information. This situation will thoroughly change if we leave the realm of the normal distribution. It this case the identification problem is completely dissolved. Systematic deviation from the normal distribution are typically observed in time series related to financial markets (stock price, exchange rates, etc.). In Chap. 8 we showed that these time series have a kurtosis (if it exists) which is typically much larger compared to a normal distribution. See in particular the analysis of the properties of the GARCH(1,1) model in Sect. 8.1.

Many ideas and methods in this context have been developed in engineering. The book by Hyvärinen et al. (2001) provides an easily accessible introduction to the subject. The independent components analysis (ICA) proposes procedures and statistical techniques to extract structural components from non-normally distributed measurements and signals. In the presentation of this identification

[29] Whether this distribution is always the "natural" choice in economics has recently been disputed by Baumeister and Hamilton (2015).

[30] First moments are not informative because the expectations of Z_t and V_t are zero.

method, we follow the standard practice to set $A = I_n$ and to replace the weaker assumption of uncorrelatedness by the stronger assumption of independence (Lanne et al., 2017).

Assumption 15.1 (Independence of Structural Disturbances) *The process of structural disturbances* $\{V_t\}$ *has the following properties:*

(i) $V_t \sim \text{IID}(0, \Omega)$ *where* $\Omega = I_n$*;*
(ii) the elements of B *are unrestricted;*
(iii) at most one component of V_t *is normally distributed.*

The normalization for Ω and B adopted in Assumption 15.1 is completely equivalent to the assumption that Ω is a diagonal matrix and B a matrix with ones on the diagonal. In addition, we assume that $\mathbb{E}Z_t Z_t' = \Sigma = BB'$ is positive definite. Hence, B is invertible.

Theorem 15.2 shows that the identification problem dissipates under the assumptions made above. The proof of this theorem rests on the Skitovich-Darmois theorem (for a proof see Kagan et al., 1973, Chapter 3).

Theorem 15.1 (Skitovich-Darmois Theorem) *Let* $X_1, \ldots, X_n$ *be independent random variables and* L_1 *and* L_2 *two linear combinations of the* X_i*'s independent of each other, i.e.,*

$$L_1 = \sum_{i=1}^{n} a_i X_i \quad \textit{und} \quad L_2 = \sum_{i=1}^{n} b_i X_i.$$

Then all random variables X_k *such that* $a_k b_k \neq 0$ *are normally distributed.*

Theorem 15.2 (Identification with Non-Gaussian Disturbances) *Under the assumptions made above, the matrix* B *is uniquely determined up to permutation of its components and up to the signs of the structural disturbances. Hence, given two structural disturbance processes* V_t *and* $\widetilde{V}_t$ *with* $Z_t = BV_t$ *and* $Z_t = \widetilde{B}\widetilde{V}_t$ *there exists a signed permutation matrix* P *such that* $B = \widetilde{B}P$*.*[31]

Proof The proof of the statement is by contradiction.[32] Suppose there are two structural models with the same reduced form. Hence, there exist two invertible matrices B and $\widetilde{B}$ and disturbance vectors V_t and $\widetilde{V}_t$ such that

$$Z_t = BV_t \quad \text{and} \quad Z_t = \widetilde{B}\widetilde{V}_t$$

[31] A signed permutation matrix is a permutation matrix whose nonzero entries are ± 1.

[32] Similar proofs are provided by Comon (1994), Gouriéroux et al. (2017), and Lanne et al. (2017).

where both structural models fulfill Assumptions 15.1 outlined above. Then

$$V_t = Q\widetilde{V}_t \quad \text{where} \quad Q = B^{-1}\widetilde{B}.$$

Because As $QQ' = B^{-1}\widetilde{B}\widetilde{B}'B'^{-1} = B^{-1}\Sigma B'^{-1} = I_n$ and $\Sigma = BB'$, Q is an orthonormal matrix.

Assumptions 15.1 imply that $\widetilde{V}_{1t}, \ldots, \widetilde{V}_{nt}$ are independent from each other and that there is at most one normally distributed marginal distribution. Because $V_{1t}, \ldots, V_{nt}$ are by assumption also independent, the Skitovich-Darmois theorem (see Theorem 15.1) implies that there is at most one column k of Q with at least two nonzero entries q_{ik} and q_{jk}, $i \neq j$. Hence

$$V_{it} = q_{ik}\widetilde{V}_{kt} + \sum_{\ell=1,\ldots,n;\ell\neq k} q_{i\ell}\widetilde{V}_{\ell t},$$

$$V_{jt} = q_{jk}\widetilde{V}_{kt} + \sum_{\ell=1,\ldots,n;\ell\neq k} q_{j\ell}\widetilde{V}_{\ell t}$$

where $\widetilde{V}_{kt}$ is normally distributed with positive variance. As there can only be at most one normally distributed random variable, $q_{i\ell}q_{j\ell} = 0$, $\ell = 1, \ldots, n$, $\ell \neq k$. Hence, $\mathbb{E}V_{it}V_{jt} = q_{ik}q_{jk}\mathbb{E}\widetilde{V}_{kt}^2 \neq 0$. This stands, however, in contradiction with the assumption that V_{it} and V_{jt} are independent. Therefore only one entry in each column of Q can be nonzero. This entry can only be $+1$ or -1 because Q is an orthonormal matrix. Hence, each column of Q has exactly one entry equal to ± 1, and all other entries are zero.

The same argument obviously also holds for $\widetilde{V}_t = Q'V_t$. Hence, each row of Q has exactly one entry equal ± 1 and all other entries equal to zero. Thus, Q is a signed permutation matrix. □

That the identification problem is only solved up to a signed permutation matrix is irrelevant, because the arrangement of the structural disturbances their labeling is in any case arbitrary and therefore inconsequential for the interpretation of the impulse response functions.

The preferred estimation strategy is the method of maximum likelihood.[33] As the Gaussian likelihood is obviously out of consideration, the question arises which distribution to use instead. Depending on whether or not the kurtosis is larger or smaller compared to the normal distribution (or equivalently whether the excess kurtosis is positive or negative), different distributions can be considered for the construction of the likelihood function. For example, in the case of positive excess

[33] In the literature also, the method of moments is proposed. Thereby the kurtosis serves as a measure of the deviation for the normal distribution. This methods relies on the estimation of fourth moments which is, however, heavily driven by outliers in the data. A comparison of alternative estimation methods is provided in Hyvärinen et al. (2001).

kurtosis one may consider Student t distributions with low degrees of freedom. It can be shown that, under not too restrictive technical assumptions, the maximum likelihood estimator is consistent and asymptotically normally distributed. Based on this result, it is possible to make inferences and tests concerning the parameters of the model. See Gouriéroux et al. (2017) and Lanne et al. (2017) for details. In particular, it would be possible to test the relevance of the alternative identification schemes discussed previously (e.g., short-run zero restrictions).

Remark 15.3 Because orthonormal transformations of normally distributed random variables are again normally distributed, it is clear that the above statement depends crucially on the assumption that at most one component of V_t can be normally distributed. How restrictive this assumption is in practice remains an open issue.

Cointegration

16

As already mentioned in Chap. 7, many raw economic time series are nonstationary and become stationary only after some transformation. The most common of these transformations is the formation of differences, perhaps after having taken logs. In most cases, first differences are sufficient to achieve stationarity. The so-transformed time series can then be analyzed in the context of VAR models as explained in previous chapters. However, many economic theories are formalized in terms of the original series so that we may want to use the VAR methodology to infer also the behavior of the original (untransformed) series. Yet by taking first differences, we lose probably important information on the levels. Thus, it seems worthwhile to develop an approach that allows us to take the information on the levels into account and at the same time take care of the nonstationary character of the variables. The concept of *cointegration* tries to achieve this double requirement.

The following exposition focuses on stochastic processes, which are integrated of order one, i.e., on time series that become stationary after having taking first differences. However, as we have already mentioned in Sect. 7.5.1, a regression between integrated variables may lead to spurious correlations, which make statistical inferences and interpretations of the estimated coefficients a delicate issue (see, e.g., Stock & Watson, 1988a). A way out of this dilemma is presented by the theory of *cointegrated processes*. Loosely speaking, a multivariate process is cointegrated if there exists a linear combination of the process that is stationary although each process taken individually may be integrated. In many cases, this linear combination can be directly related to economic theory, which has made the analysis of cointegrated processes an important research topic. A first flavor of this theory was already given in Sect. 7.5.1 for the bivariate case. In this chapter, the concept of cointegration is analyzed in more detail.

The concept of cointegration goes back to the work of Engle and Granger (1987), which is itself based on the precursor study of Davidson et al. (1978). In the meantime, the literature has grown tremendously. Good introductions can be

K. Neusser, *Time Series Econometrics*, Springer Texts in Business and Economics,
https://doi.org/10.1007/978-3-031-88838-0_16

found in Banerjee et al. (1993), Watson (1994), or Lütkepohl (2005). For the more statistically inclined reader, Johansen (1995) is a good reference.

16.1 A Theoretical Example

Before we present the general theory of cointegration within the realm of VAR processes, it is instructive to introduce the concept in the well-known class of present discounted value models. These models relate some variable X_t to present discounted value of another variable Y_t:

$$X_t = \gamma(1-\beta)\sum_{j=0}^{\infty}\beta^j \mathbb{P}_t Y_{t+j} + u_t, \qquad 0 < \beta < 1,$$

where $u_t \sim \mathrm{WN}(0, \sigma_u^2)$ designates a preference shock. Thereby, β denotes the subjective discount factor and γ is some unspecified parameter. The present discounted value model states that the variable X_t is proportional to the sum of expected future Y_{t+j}, $j = 0, 1, 2, \ldots$, discounted by the factor β. We can interpret X_t and Y_t as the price and the dividend of a share, as the interest rate on long- and short-term bonds, or as consumption and income. In order to operationalize this model, we will assume that forecasts are computed as linear mean-squared error forecasts. The corresponding forecast operator is denoted by $\mathbb{P}_t$. Furthermore, we will assume that the forecaster observes Y_t and its past $Y_{t-1}, Y_{t-2}, \ldots$ The goal of the analysis is the investigation of the properties of the bivariate process $\{(X_t, Y_t)'\}$. The analysis of this important class models presented below is based on Campbell and Shiller (1987).[1]

The model is closed by assuming some specific time series model for $\{Y_t\}$. In this example, we will assume that $\{Y_t\}$ is an integrated process of order one (see Definition 7.1 in Sect. 7.1) such that $\{\Delta Y_t\}$ follows an AR(1) process:

$$\Delta Y_t = \mu(1-\phi) + \phi\Delta Y_{t-1} + v_t, \qquad |\phi| < 1 \text{ and } v_t \sim \mathrm{WN}(0, \sigma_v^2).$$

This specification of the $\{Y_t\}$ process implies that $\mathbb{P}_t \Delta Y_{t+h} = \mu(1-\phi^h) + \phi^h \Delta Y_t$. Because $\mathbb{P}_t Y_{t+h} = \mathbb{P}_t \Delta Y_{t+h} + \cdots + \mathbb{P}_t \Delta Y_{t+1} + Y_t$, $h = 0, 1, 2, \ldots$, the present discounted value model can be manipulated to give:

[1] A more recent interesting application of this model is given by the work of Beaudry and Portier (2006).

$$
\begin{aligned}
X_t &= \gamma(1-\beta)\left[Y_t + \beta \mathbb{P}_t Y_{t+1} + \beta^2 \mathbb{P}_t Y_{t+2} + \ldots\right] + u_t \\
&= \gamma(1-\beta)[\ Y_t \\
&\quad + \beta\, Y_t + \beta\, \mathbb{P}_t \Delta Y_{t+1} \\
&\quad + \beta^2 Y_t + \beta^2 \mathbb{P}_t \Delta Y_{t+1} + \beta^2 \mathbb{P}_t \Delta Y_{t+2} \\
&\quad + \beta^3 Y_t + \beta^3 \mathbb{P}_t \Delta Y_{t+1} + \beta^3 \mathbb{P}_t \Delta Y_{t+2} + \beta^3 \mathbb{P}_t \Delta Y_{t+3} \\
&\quad + \ldots] + u_t \\
&= \gamma(1-\beta)\left[\frac{1}{1-\beta} Y_t + \frac{\beta}{1-\beta} \mathbb{P}_t \Delta Y_{t+1} + \frac{\beta^2}{1-\beta} \mathbb{P}_t \Delta Y_{t+2} + \ldots\right] + u_t
\end{aligned}
$$

This expression shows that the integratedness of $\{Y_t\}$ is transferred to $\{X_t\}$. Bringing Y_t to the left, we get the following expression:

$$
S_t = X_t - \gamma Y_t = \gamma \sum_{j=1}^{\infty} \beta^j \mathbb{P}_t \Delta Y_{t+j} + u_t .
$$

The variable S_t is occasionally referred to as the spread. If γ is greater than zero, expected increases in ΔY_{t+j}, $j \geq 1$, have a positive impact on the spread today. For $\gamma = 1$, S_t can denote the log of the price-dividend ratio of a share or minus the logged savings ratio as in the permanent income model of Campbell (1987). If investors expect positive (negative) change in the dividends tomorrow, they want to buy (sell) the share thereby increasing (decreasing) its price already today. In the context of the permanent income hypothesis expected positive income changes lead to a reduction in today's saving rate. If, on the contrary, households expect negative income changes to occur in the future, they will save already today ("saving for the rainy days").

Inserting for $\mathbb{P}_t \Delta Y_{t+j}$, $j = 0, 1, \ldots$, the corresponding forecast equation $\mathbb{P}_t \Delta Y_{t+h} = \mu(1-\phi^h) + \phi^h \Delta Y_t$ leads to

$$
S_t = \frac{\beta\gamma\mu(1-\phi)}{(1-\beta)(1-\beta\phi)} + \frac{\beta\gamma\phi}{1-\beta\phi} \Delta Y_t + u_t .
$$

The remarkable feature about this relation is that $\{S_t\}$ is a stationary process because both $\{\Delta Y_t\}$ and $\{u_t\}$ are stationary, despite the fact that $\{Y_t\}$ and $\{X_t\}$ are both integrated processes of order one. This phenomenon is termed *cointegration*. The mean of S_t is:

$$
\mathbb{E} S_t = \frac{\beta\gamma\mu}{1-\beta} .
$$

From the relation between S_t and ΔY_t and the AR(1) representation of $\{\Delta Y_t\}$, we can deduce a VAR representation of the joint process $\{(S_t, \Delta Y_t)'\}$:

$$\begin{pmatrix} S_t \\ \Delta Y_t \end{pmatrix} = \mu(1-\phi)\begin{pmatrix} \frac{\beta\gamma}{(1-\beta)(1-\beta\phi)} + \frac{\beta\gamma\phi}{1-\beta\phi} \\ 1 \end{pmatrix} + \begin{pmatrix} 0 & \frac{\beta\gamma\phi^2}{1-\beta\phi} \\ 0 & \phi \end{pmatrix}\begin{pmatrix} S_{t-1} \\ \Delta Y_{t-1} \end{pmatrix}$$
$$+ \begin{pmatrix} u_t + \frac{\beta\gamma\phi}{1-\beta\phi} v_t \\ v_t \end{pmatrix}.$$

Further algebraic transformations lead to a VAR representation of order two for the level variables $\{(X_t, Y_t)'\}$:

$$\begin{pmatrix} X_t \\ Y_t \end{pmatrix} = c + \Phi_1 \begin{pmatrix} X_{t-1} \\ Y_{t-1} \end{pmatrix} + \Phi_2 \begin{pmatrix} X_{t-2} \\ Y_{t-2} \end{pmatrix} + Z_t$$
$$= \mu(1-\phi)\begin{pmatrix} \frac{\gamma}{(1-\beta)(1-\beta\phi)} \\ 1 \end{pmatrix} + \begin{pmatrix} 0 & \gamma + \frac{\gamma\phi}{1-\beta\phi} \\ 0 & 1+\phi \end{pmatrix}\begin{pmatrix} X_{t-1} \\ Y_{t-1} \end{pmatrix}$$
$$+ \begin{pmatrix} 0 & \frac{-\gamma\phi}{1-\beta\phi} \\ 0 & -\phi \end{pmatrix}\begin{pmatrix} X_{t-2} \\ Y_{t-2} \end{pmatrix} + \begin{pmatrix} 1 & \frac{\gamma}{1-\beta\phi} \\ 0 & 1 \end{pmatrix}\begin{pmatrix} u_t \\ v_t \end{pmatrix}$$

In order to check whether the stochastic difference equation possesses a stationary solution, we must locate the roots of the matrix polynomial $\det \Phi(z) = \det(I_2 - \Phi_1 z - \Phi_2 z^2) = 0$ (see Theorem 12.1). As

$$\det \Phi(z) = \det \begin{pmatrix} 1 & \left(-\gamma - \frac{\gamma\phi}{1-\beta\phi}\right) z + \frac{\gamma\phi}{1-\beta\phi} z^2 \\ 0 & 1-(1+\phi)z + \phi z^2 \end{pmatrix} = 1 - (1+\phi)z + \phi z^2,$$

the roots are $z_1 = 1/\phi$ and $z_2 = 1$. Thus, only the root z_1 lies outside the unit circle, whereas the root z_2 lies on the unit circle. The existence of a *unit root* precludes the existence of a stationary solution. Note that we have just one unit root, although each of the two processes taken individually is integrated of order one.

The above VAR representation can be further transformed to yield a representation of the differenced process $\{(\Delta X_t, \Delta Y_t)'\}$:

$$\begin{pmatrix} \Delta X_t \\ \Delta Y_t \end{pmatrix} = \mu(1-\phi)\begin{pmatrix} \frac{\gamma}{(1-\beta)(1-\beta\phi)} \\ 1 \end{pmatrix} - \begin{pmatrix} 1 & -\gamma \\ 0 & 0 \end{pmatrix}\begin{pmatrix} X_{t-1} \\ Y_{t-1} \end{pmatrix}$$
$$+ \begin{pmatrix} 0 & \frac{\gamma\phi}{1-\beta\phi} \\ 0 & \phi \end{pmatrix}\begin{pmatrix} \Delta X_{t-1} \\ \Delta Y_{t-1} \end{pmatrix} + \begin{pmatrix} 1 & \frac{\gamma}{1-\beta\phi} \\ 0 & 1 \end{pmatrix}\begin{pmatrix} u_t \\ v_t \end{pmatrix}.$$

This representation can be considered as a generalization of the Dickey-Fuller regression in first difference form (see Eq. (7.11)). In the multivariate case, it is known as the vector error correction model (VECM) or vector error correction representation. In this representation, the matrix

$$\Pi = -\Phi(1) = \begin{pmatrix} -1 & \gamma \\ 0 & 0 \end{pmatrix}$$

is of special importance. This matrix is singular and of rank one. This is not an implication that is special to this specification of the present discounted value model but arises generally as shown in Campbell (1987) and Campbell and Shiller (1987). In the VECM representation, all variables except $(X_{t-1}, Y_{t-1})'$ are stationary by construction. This implies that $-\Pi(X_{t-1}, Y_{t-1})'$ must be stationary too, despite the fact that $\{(X_t, Y_t)'\}$ is not stationary as shown above. Multiplying $-\Pi(X_{t-1}, Y_{t-1})'$ out, one obtains two linear combinations that define stationary processes. However, as Π has only rank one, there is just one linearly independent combination. The first one is $X_{t-1} - \gamma Y_{t=1}$ and equals S_{t-1}, which was already shown to be stationary. The second one is degenerate because it yields zero. This property is another consequence of the phenomenon *cointegration*.

Because Π has rank one, it can be written as the product of two vectors α and β:

$$\Pi = \alpha\beta' = \begin{pmatrix} -1 \\ 0 \end{pmatrix} \begin{pmatrix} 1 \\ -\gamma \end{pmatrix}'.$$

Clearly, this decomposition of Π is not unique because $\tilde{\alpha} = a\alpha$ and $\tilde{\beta} = a^{-1}\beta$, $a \neq 0$, would also qualify for such a decomposition as $\Pi = \tilde{\alpha}\tilde{\beta}'$. The vector β is called a *cointegration vector*. It has the property that $\{\beta'(X_t, Y_t)'\}$ defines a stationary process despite the fact that $\{(X_t, Y_t)'\}$ is non-stationary. The cointegration vector thus defines a linear combination of X_t and Y_t, which is stationary. The matrix α, here only a vector, is called the *loading matrix* and its elements the *loading coefficients*.

The VAR and the VECM representations are both well suited for estimation. However, if we want to compute the impulse responses, we need a causal representation. Such a causal representation does not exist due to the unit root in the VAR process for $\{(X_t, Y_t)'\}$ (see Theorem 12.1). To circumvent this problem, we split the matrix $\Phi(z)$ into the product of two matrices $M(z)$ and $V(z)$. $M(z)$ is a diagonal matrix that encompasses all unit roots on its diagonal. $V(z)$ has all its roots outside the unit circle so that $V^{-1}(z)$ exists for $|z| < 1$. In our example, we get:

$$\Phi(z) = M(z)V(z) = \begin{pmatrix} 1 & 0 \\ 0 & 1-z \end{pmatrix} \begin{pmatrix} 1 & \left(-\gamma - \frac{\gamma\phi}{1-\beta\phi}\right)z + \frac{\gamma\phi}{1-\beta\phi}z^2 \\ 0 & 1-\phi z \end{pmatrix}.$$

Multiplying $\Phi(z)$ with $\widetilde{M}(z) = \begin{pmatrix} 1-z & 0 \\ 0 & 1 \end{pmatrix}$ from the left, we find:

$$\widetilde{M}(z)\Phi(z) = \widetilde{M}(z)M(z)V(z) = (1-z)I_2V(z) = (1-z)V(z).$$

The application of this result to the VAR representation of $\{(X_t, Y_t)\}$ leads to a causal representation of $\{(\Delta X_t, \Delta Y_t)\}$:

$$\Phi(\mathrm{L})\begin{pmatrix} X_t \\ Y_t \end{pmatrix} = M(\mathrm{L})V(\mathrm{L})\begin{pmatrix} X_t \\ Y_t \end{pmatrix} = c + Z_t$$

$$\widetilde{M}(\mathrm{L})\Phi(\mathrm{L})\begin{pmatrix} X_t \\ Y_t \end{pmatrix} = (1-\mathrm{L})V(\mathrm{L})\begin{pmatrix} X_t \\ Y_t \end{pmatrix}$$

$$= \mu(1-\phi)\begin{pmatrix} 1-\mathrm{L} & 0 \\ 0 & 1 \end{pmatrix}\begin{pmatrix} \frac{\gamma}{(1-\beta)(1-\beta\phi)} \\ 1 \end{pmatrix} + \begin{pmatrix} 1-\mathrm{L} & 0 \\ 0 & 1 \end{pmatrix} Z_t$$

$$V(\mathrm{L})\begin{pmatrix} \Delta X_t \\ \Delta Y_t \end{pmatrix} = \begin{pmatrix} 0 \\ \mu(1-\phi) \end{pmatrix} + \begin{pmatrix} 1-\mathrm{L} & 0 \\ 0 & 1 \end{pmatrix} Z_t$$

$$\begin{pmatrix} \Delta X_t \\ \Delta Y_t \end{pmatrix} = \mu\begin{pmatrix} \gamma \\ 1 \end{pmatrix} + V^{-1}(\mathrm{L})\begin{pmatrix} 1-\mathrm{L} & 0 \\ 0 & 1 \end{pmatrix} Z_t$$

$$\begin{pmatrix} \Delta X_t \\ \Delta Y_t \end{pmatrix} = \mu\begin{pmatrix} \gamma \\ 1 \end{pmatrix} + \Psi(\mathrm{L})Z_t.$$

The polynomial matrix $\Psi(\mathrm{L})$ can be recovered by the method of undetermined coefficients from the relation between $V(z)$ and $\Psi(z)$:

$$V(z)\Psi(z) = \begin{pmatrix} 1-z & 0 \\ 0 & 1 \end{pmatrix}$$

In this exposition, we abstain from the explicit computation of $V^{-1}(\mathrm{L})$ and $\Psi(\mathrm{L})$. However, the following relation holds:

$$V(1) = \begin{pmatrix} 1 & -\gamma \\ 0 & 1-\phi \end{pmatrix} \Longrightarrow V^{-1}(1) = \begin{pmatrix} 1 & \frac{\gamma}{1-\phi} \\ 0 & \frac{1}{1-\phi} \end{pmatrix}.$$

Implying that

$$\Psi(1) = V^{-1}(1)\begin{pmatrix} 0 & 0 \\ 0 & 1 \end{pmatrix} = (1-\phi)^{-1}\begin{pmatrix} 0 & \gamma \\ 0 & 1 \end{pmatrix}.$$

The cointegration vector $\beta = (1, -\gamma)'$ and the loading matrix $\alpha = (-1, 0)'$ therefore have the following properties:

$$\beta'\Psi(1) = \begin{pmatrix} 0 & 0 \end{pmatrix} \quad \text{and} \quad \Psi(1)\alpha = \begin{pmatrix} 0 \\ 0 \end{pmatrix}.$$

Like in the univariate case (see Theorem 7.1 in Sect. 7.1.4), we can also construct the Beveridge-Nelson decomposition in the multivariate case. For this purpose, we decompose $\Psi(\mathrm{L})$ as follows:

$$\Psi(\mathrm{L}) = \Psi(1) + (\mathrm{L}-1)\widetilde{\Psi}(\mathrm{L})$$

with $\widetilde{\Psi}_j = \sum_{i=j+1}^{\infty} \Psi_i$. This result can be used to derive the multivariate Beveridge-Nelson decomposition (see Theorem 16.1 in Sect. 16.2.3):

$$\begin{aligned}
\begin{pmatrix} X_t \\ Y_t \end{pmatrix} &= \begin{pmatrix} X_0 \\ Y_0 \end{pmatrix} + \mu \begin{pmatrix} \gamma \\ 1 \end{pmatrix} t + \Psi(1) \sum_{j=1}^{t} Z_j + \text{stationary process} \\
&= \begin{pmatrix} X_0 \\ Y_0 \end{pmatrix} + \mu \begin{pmatrix} \gamma \\ 1 \end{pmatrix} t + \frac{1}{1-\phi} \begin{pmatrix} 0 & \gamma \\ 0 & 1 \end{pmatrix} \begin{pmatrix} 1 & \frac{\gamma}{1-\beta\phi} \\ 0 & 1 \end{pmatrix} \sum_{j=1}^{t} \begin{pmatrix} u_j \\ v_j \end{pmatrix} \\
&\quad + \text{stationary process} \\
&= \begin{pmatrix} X_0 \\ Y_0 \end{pmatrix} + \mu \begin{pmatrix} \gamma \\ 1 \end{pmatrix} t + \frac{1}{1-\phi} \begin{pmatrix} 0 & \gamma \\ 0 & 1 \end{pmatrix} \sum_{j=1}^{t} \begin{pmatrix} u_j \\ v_j \end{pmatrix} \\
&\quad + \text{stationary process.}
\end{aligned} \tag{16.1}$$

The Beveridge-Nelson decomposition represents the process $\{(X_t, Y_t)'\}$ as a sum of three components: a linear trend, a multivariate random walk, and a stationary process. Multiplying the Beveridge-Nelson decomposition from the left by the cointegration vector $\beta = (1, -\gamma)'$, we see that both the trend and the random walk component are eliminated and that only a stationary component remains.

Because the first column of $\Psi(1)$ consists of zeros, only the second structural shock, namely, $\{v_t\}$, will have a long-run (permanent) effect. The long-run effect is $\gamma/(1-\phi)$ for the first variable, X_t, and $1/(1-\phi)$ for the second variable, Y_t. The first structural shock (preference shock) $\{u_t\}$ has no long-run effect, and its impact is of a transitory nature only. This decomposition into permanent and transitory shocks is not typical for this model but can be done in general as part of the so-called common trend representation (see Sect. 16.2.4).

Finally, we simulate the reaction of the system to a unit valued shock in v_t. Although this shock only has a temporary influence on ΔY_t, it will have a permanent effect on the level Y_t. Taking $\phi = 0.8$, we get long-run effect (persistence) of $1/(1-\phi) = 5$ as explained in Sect. 7.1.3. The present discounted value model then implies that this shock will also have a permanent effect on X_t too. Setting $\gamma = 1$, this long-run effect is given by $\gamma(1-\beta)\sum_{j=0}^{\infty} \beta^j (1-\phi)^{-1} = \gamma/(1-\phi) = 5$. Because this long-run effect is anticipated in period t, the period of the occurrence of the shock, X_t, will increase by more than one. The spread turns, therefore, into positive. The error correction mechanism will then dampen the effect on future

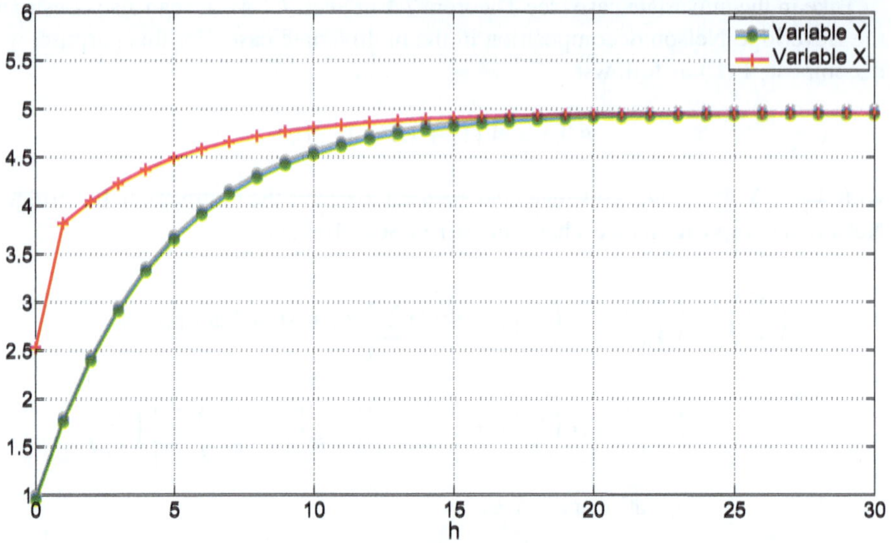

Fig. 16.1 Impulse response functions of the present discounted value model after a unit shock to Y_t ($\gamma = 1, \beta = 0.9, \phi = 0.8$)

changes of X_t so that the spread will return steadily to zero. The corresponding impulse responses of both variables are displayed in Fig. 16.1.

Figure 16.2 displays the trajectories of both variables after a stochastic simulation where both shocks $\{u_t\}$ and $\{v_t\}$ are drawn from a standard normal distribution. One can clearly discern the non-stationary character of both series. However, as it is typically for cointegrated series, they move more or less in parallel to each other. This parallel movement is ensured by the error correction mechanism. The difference between both series, which is equal to the spread under this parameter constellation, is mean reverting around zero.

16.2 Cointegrated Processes

16.2.1 Definition

After this intuitive introduction, we give a precise and general definition of cointegrated processes and derive the different representations we have seen in the previous section. Given an arbitrary regular (purely non-deterministic) stationary process $\{U_t\}_{t\in\mathbb{Z}}$ of dimension n, $n \geq 1$, with mean zero and some distribution for the starting random variable X_0, we can define recursively a process $\{X_t\}$, $t = 0, 1, 2, \ldots$, as

$$X_t = \mu + X_{t-1} + U_t, \qquad t = 1, 2, \ldots$$

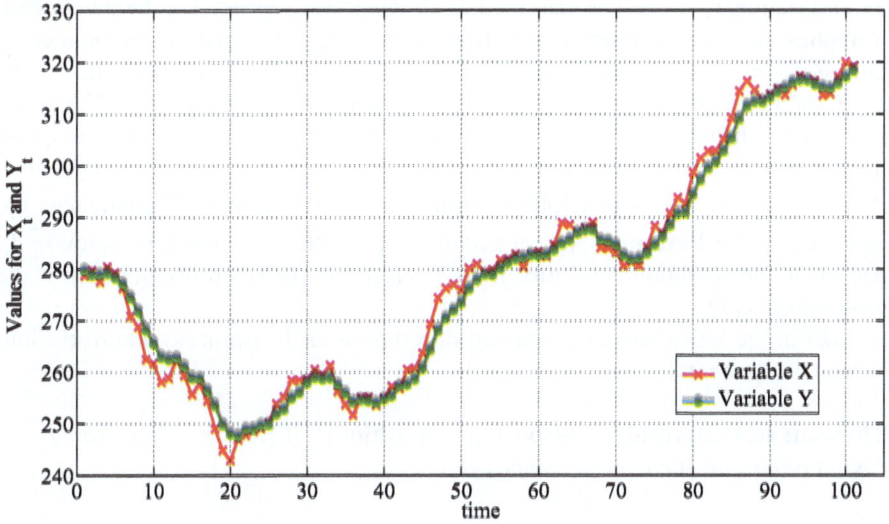

Fig. 16.2 Stochastic simulation of the present discounted value model under standard normally distributed shocks ($\gamma = 1, \beta = 0.9, \phi = 0.8$)

Thereby, μ denotes an arbitrary constant vector of dimension n. If $U_t \sim \mathrm{WN}(0, \Sigma)$, then $\{X_t\}$ is a multivariate random walk with drift μ. In general, however, $\{U_t\}$ is autocorrelated and possesses a Wold representation $U_t = \Psi(L)Z_t$ (see Sect. 14.2) such that

$$\Delta X_t = \mu + U_t = \mu + \Psi(\mathrm{L})Z_t = \mu + Z_t + \Psi_1 Z_{t-1} + \Psi_2 Z_{t-2} + \ldots, \quad (16.2)$$

where $Z_t \sim \mathrm{WN}(0, \Sigma)$ and $\sum_{j=0}^{\infty} \|\Psi_j\|^2 < \infty$ with $\Psi_0 = I_n$. Given these preliminaries, we introduce the following definitions.

Definition 16.1 A regular stationary process $\{U_t\}$ with mean zero is integrated of order zero, $I(0)$, if and only if it can be represented as

$$U_t = \Psi(\mathrm{L})Z_t = Z_t + \Psi_1 Z_{t-1} + \Psi_2 Z_{t-2} + \ldots$$

such that $Z_t \sim \mathrm{WN}(0, \Sigma)$, $\sum_{j=0}^{\infty} j\|\Psi_j\| < \infty$, and $\Psi(1) = \sum_{j=0}^{\infty} \Psi_j \neq 0$.

Definition 16.2 A stochastic process $\{X_t\}$ is integrated of order d, $I(d)$, $d = 0, 1, 2, \ldots$, if and only if $\Delta^d(X_t - \mathbb{E}(X_t))$ is integrated of order zero.

In the following we concentrate on I(1) processes. The definition of an I(1) process implies that $\{X_t\}$ equals $X_t = X_0 + \mu t + \sum_{j=1}^{t} U_j$ and is thus non-stationary even if $\mu = 0$. The condition $\Psi(1) \neq 0$ corresponds to the one in the univariate case (compare Definition 7.1 in Sect. 7.1). On the one hand, it precludes the case that a trend-stationary process is classified as an integrated process. On the other hand, it implies that $\{X_t\}$ is in fact non-stationary. Indeed, if the condition is violated so that $\Psi(1) = 0$, we could express $\Psi(\mathrm{L})$ as $(1 - \mathrm{L})\widetilde{\Psi}(\mathrm{L})$. Thus we could cancel $1-\mathrm{L}$ on both sides of Eq. (16.2) to obtain a stationary representation of $\{X_t\}$, given some initial distribution for X_0. This would then contradict our primal assumption that $\{X_t\}$ is non-stationary. The condition $\sum_{j=0}^{\infty} j\|\Psi_j\| < \infty$ is stronger than $\sum_{j=0}^{\infty} \|\Psi_j\|^2 < \infty$, which follows from the Wold's theorem. It guarantees the existence of the Beveridge-Nelson decomposition (see Theorem 16.1 below).[2] In particular, the condition is fulfilled if $\{U_t\}$ is a causal ARMA process, which is the prototypical case.

Like in the univariate case, we can decompose an I(1) process additively into several components.

Theorem 16.1 (Beveridge-Nelson Decomposition) *If $\{X_t\}$ is an integrated process of order one, it can be decomposed as*

$$X_t = X_0 + \mu t + \Psi(1)\sum_{j=1}^{t} Z_j + V_t,$$

where $V_t = \widetilde{\Psi}(\mathrm{L})Z_0 - \widetilde{\Psi}(\mathrm{L})Z_t$ with $\widetilde{\Psi}_j = \sum_{i=j+1}^{\infty} \Psi_i$, $j = 0, 1, 2, \ldots$, and $\{V_t\}$ stationary.

Proof Following the proof of the univariate case (see Sect. 7.1.4):

$$\Psi(\mathrm{L}) = \Psi(1) + (\mathrm{L} - 1)\widetilde{\Psi}(\mathrm{L})$$

with $\widetilde{\Psi}_j = \sum_{i=j+1}^{\infty} \Psi_i$. Thus,

$$\begin{aligned}
X_t &= X_0 + \mu t + \sum_{j=1}^{t} U_j = X_0 + \mu t + \sum_{j=1}^{t} \Psi(\mathrm{L})Z_j \\
&= X_0 + \mu t + \sum_{j=1}^{t} \left(\Psi(1) + (\mathrm{L} - 1)\widetilde{\Psi}(\mathrm{L})\right) Z_j \\
&= X_0 + \mu t + \Psi(1)\sum_{j=1}^{t} Z_j + \sum_{j=1}^{t}(\mathrm{L} - 1)\widetilde{\Psi}(\mathrm{L})Z_j
\end{aligned}$$

[2] This condition could be relaxed and replaced by the condition $\sum_{j=0}^{\infty} j^2\|\Psi_j\|^2 < \infty$. In addition, this condition is an important assumption for the application of the law of large numbers and for the derivation of the asymptotic distribution (Phillips & Solo, 1992).

$$= X_0 + \mu t + \Psi(1)\sum_{j=1}^{t} Z_j + \widetilde{\Psi}(\mathrm{L})Z_0 - \widetilde{\Psi}(\mathrm{L})Z_t.$$

The only point left is to show that $\widetilde{\Psi}(\mathrm{L})Z_0 - \widetilde{\Psi}(\mathrm{L})Z_t$ is stationary. Based on Theorem 10.2, it is sufficient to show that the coefficient matrices are absolutely summable. This can be derived by applying the triangular inequality and the condition for integrated processes:

$$\sum_{j=0}^{\infty}\|\widetilde{\Psi}_j\| = \sum_{j=0}^{\infty}\left\|\sum_{i=j+1}^{\infty}\Psi_i\right\| \le \sum_{j=0}^{\infty}\sum_{i=j+1}^{\infty}\|\Psi_i\| = \sum_{j=1}^{\infty} j\|\Psi_j\| < \infty.$$

□

The process $\{X_t\}$ can therefore be viewed as the sum of a linear trend, $X_0 + \mu t$, with stochastic intercept, a multivariate random walk, $\Psi(1)\sum_{j=0}^{t} Z_t$, and a stationary process $\{V_t\}$. Based on this representation, we define the notion of cointegration (Engle & Granger, 1987).

Definition 16.3 (Cointegration) A multivariate stochastic process $\{X_t\}$ is called *cointegrated* if $\{X_t\}$ is integrated of order one and if there exists a vector $\beta \in \mathbb{R}^n$, $\beta \neq 0$, such that $\{\beta' X_t\}$ is integrated of order zero, given a corresponding distribution for the initial random variable X_0. β is called the *cointegrating* or *cointegration vector*. The *cointegrating rank* is the maximal number, r, of linearly independent cointegrating vectors $\beta_1, \ldots, \beta_r$. These vectors span a linear space called the *cointegration space*.

The Beveridge-Nelson decomposition implies that β is a cointegrating vector if and only if $\beta'\Psi(1) = 0$. In this case, the random walk component $\sum_{j=1}^{t} Z_j$ is annihilated, and only the deterministic and the stationary component remain.[3] For some issues, it is of interest whether the cointegration vector β also eliminates the trend component. This would be the case if $\beta'\mu = 0$. See Sect. 16.3 for details.

The cointegration vectors are determined only up to some basis transformations. If $\beta_1, \ldots, \beta_r$ is a basis for the cointegration space, then $(\beta_1, \ldots, \beta_r)R$ is also a basis for the cointegration space for any nonsingular $r \times r$ matrix R because $((\beta_1, \ldots, \beta_r)R)'\Psi(1) = 0$.

[3] The distribution of X_0 is thereby chosen such that $\beta' X_0 = \beta'\widetilde{\Psi}(\mathrm{L})Z_0$.

16.2.2 Vector Autoregressive (VAR) and Vector Error Correction Models (VECM)

Although the Beveridge-Nelson decomposition is very useful from a theoretical point of view, in practice, it is often more convenient to work with alternative representations. Most empirical investigations of integrated processes start from a VAR(p) model, which has the big advantage that it can be easily estimated:

$$X_t = c + \Phi_1 X_{t-1} + \cdots + \Phi_p X_{t-p} + Z_t, \qquad Z_t \sim \text{WN}(0, \Sigma) \tag{16.3}$$

where $\Phi(\text{L}) = I_n - \Phi_1\text{L} - \cdots - \Phi_p\text{L}^p$ and c is an arbitrary constant. Subtracting X_{t-1} on both sides of the difference equation, the VAR model becomes:

$$\Delta X_t = c + \Pi X_{t-1} + \Gamma_1 \Delta X_{t-1} + \cdots + \Gamma_{p-1}\Delta X_{t-p+1} + Z_t \tag{16.4}$$

where $\Pi = -\Phi(1) = -I_n + \Phi_1 + \cdots \Phi_p$ and $\Gamma_i = -\sum_{j=i+1}^{p} \Phi_j$. We will make the following assumptions:

(i) All roots of the polynomial $\det \Phi(z)$ are outside the unit circle or equal to one, i.e.,

$$\det \Phi(z) = 0 \Longrightarrow \begin{cases} |z| > 1 \text{ or} \\ z = 1, \end{cases}$$

(ii) The matrix Π is singular with rank r, $1 \leq r < n$.
(iii) $\text{Rank}(\Pi) = \text{Rank}(\Pi^2)$.

Assumption (i) ensures that $\{X_t\}$ is an integrated process with order of integration $d \geq 1$. Moreover, it precludes other roots on the unit circles than one. The case of seasonal unit roots is treated in Hylleberg et al. (1990) and Johansen and Schaumburg (1998).[4] Assumption (ii) implies that there exists at least $n - r$ unit roots and two $n \times r$ matrices α and β with full column rank r such that

$$\Pi = \alpha\beta'.$$

The columns of β thereby represent the cointegration vectors, whereas α denotes the so-called loading matrix. The decomposition of Π in the product of α and β' is not unique. For every non-singular $r \times r$ matrix R, we can generate an alternative decomposition $\Pi = \alpha\beta' = (\alpha R'^{-1})(\beta R)'$. Finally, assumption (iii) implies that the order of integration is exactly one and not greater. The number of unit roots is

[4] The seasonal unit roots are the roots of $z^s - 1 = 0$ where s denotes the number of seasons. These roots can be expressed as $\cos(2k\pi/s) + \iota \sin(2k\pi/s)$, $k = 0, 1, \ldots, s-1$.

therefore exactly $n = r$.[5] This has the implication that $\Phi(z)$ can be written as

$$\Phi(z) = U(z)M(z)V(z)$$

where the roots of the matrix polynomials $U(z)$ and $V(z)$ are all outside the unit circle and where $M(z)$ equals

$$M(z) = \begin{pmatrix} (1-z)I_{n-r} & 0 \\ 0 & I_r \end{pmatrix}.$$

This representation of $\Phi(z)$ is a special form of the Smith-McMillan factorization of polynomial matrices (see Kailath, 1980 and Yoo, 1987). This factorization isolates the unit roots in one simple matrix so that the system can be analyzed more easily.

These assumptions will allow us to derive from the VAR(p) model several representations where each of them brings with it a particular interpretation. Replacing Π by $\alpha\beta'$ in Eq. (16.4), we obtain the *vector error correction representation* or *vector error correction model* (VECM):

$$\Delta X_t = c + \alpha\beta' X_{t-1} + \Gamma_1 \Delta X_{t-1} + \cdots + \Gamma_{p-1}\Delta X_{t-p+1} + Z_t. \qquad (16.5)$$

Multiplying both sides of the equation by $(\alpha'\alpha)^{-1}\alpha'$ and solving for $\beta' X_{t-1}$, we get:

$$\beta' X_{t-1} = (\alpha'\alpha)^{-1}\alpha' \left(\Delta X_t - c - \sum_{j=1}^{p-1} \Gamma_j \Delta X_{t-j} - Z_t \right).$$

α has full column rank r so that $\alpha'\alpha$ is a non-singular $r \times r$ matrix. As the right-hand side of the equation represents a stationary process, also the left-hand side must be stationary. This means that the r-dimensional process $\{\beta' X_{t-1}\}$ is stationary despite the fact that $\{X_t\}$ is integrated and has potentially a unit root with multiplicity n.

The term error correction was coined by Davidson et al. (1978). They interpret the mean of $\beta' X_t$, $\mu^* = \mathbb{E}\beta' X_t$, as the long-run equilibrium or steady state around which the system fluctuates. The deviation from equilibrium (error) is therefore given by $\beta' X_{t-1} - \mu^*$. The coefficients of the loading matrix α should then guarantee that deviations from the equilibrium are corrected over time by appropriate changes (corrections) in X_t.

An Illustration

To illustrate the concept of the error correction model, we consider the following simple system with $\alpha = (\alpha_1, \alpha_2)'$, $\alpha_1 \neq \alpha_2$, and $\beta = (1, -1)'$. For simplicity,

[5] For details, see Johansen (1995), Neusser (2000), and Bauer and Wagner (2012).

we assume that the long-run equilibrium μ^* is zero. Ignoring higher-order lags, we consider the system:

$$\begin{aligned} \Delta X_{1t} &= \alpha_1(X_{1,t-1} - X_{2,t-1}) + Z_{1t} \\ \Delta X_{2t} &= \alpha_2(X_{1,t-1} - X_{2,t-1}) + Z_{2t}. \end{aligned}$$

The autoregressive polynomial of this system is:

$$\Phi(z) = \begin{pmatrix} 1-(1+\alpha_1)z & \alpha_1 z \\ -\alpha_2 z & 1-(1-\alpha_2)z \end{pmatrix}.$$

The determinant of this polynomial is $\det\Phi(z) = 1-(2+\alpha_1-\alpha_2)z + (1+\alpha_1-\alpha_2)z^2$ with roots equal to $z = 1$ and $z = 1/(1+\alpha_1-\alpha_2)$. This shows that assumption (i) is fulfilled. As $\Pi = \begin{pmatrix} \alpha_1 & -\alpha_1 \\ \alpha_2 & -\alpha_2 \end{pmatrix}$, the rank of Π equals one, which implies assumption (ii). Finally,

$$\Pi^2 = \begin{pmatrix} \alpha_1^2 - \alpha_1\alpha_2 & -\alpha_1^2 + \alpha_1\alpha_2 \\ -\alpha_2^2 + \alpha_1\alpha_2 & \alpha_2^2 - \alpha_1\alpha_2 \end{pmatrix}.$$

Thus, the rank of Π^2 is also one because $\alpha_1 \neq \alpha_2$. Hence, assumption (iii) is also fulfilled.

We can gain an additional insight into the system by subtracting the second equation from the first one to obtain:

$$X_{1t} - X_{2t} = (1+\alpha_1-\alpha_2)(X_{1,t-1} - X_{2,t-1}) + Z_{1t} - Z_{2t}.$$

The process $\beta' X_t = X_{1t} - X_{2t}$ is stationary and causal with respect to $Z_{1t} - Z_{2t}$ if and only if $|1+\alpha_1-\alpha_2| < 1$, or equivalently if and only if $-2 < \alpha_1 - \alpha_2 < 0$. Note the importance of the assumption that $\alpha_1 \neq \alpha_2$. It prevents that $X_{1t} - X_{2t}$ becomes a random walk and thus a non-stationary (integrated) process. A sufficient condition is that $-1 < \alpha_1 < 0$ and $0 < \alpha_2 < 1$, which imply that a positive (negative) error, i.e., $X_{1,t-1} - X_{2,t-1} > 0 (< 0)$, is corrected by a negative (positive) change in X_{1t} and a positive (negative) change in X_{2t}. Although the shocks Z_{1t} and Z_{2t} push $X_{1t} - X_{2t}$ time and again away from its long-run equilibrium, the error correction mechanism ensures that the variables are adjusted in such a way that the system moves back to its long-run equilibrium.

16.2.3 The Beveridge-Nelson Decomposition

From the VAR representation, we aim at a causal representation or MA(∞) representation for $\{\Delta X_t\}$. In contrast to a normal causal stationary VAR model, the presence of unit roots precludes the simple application of the method of undetermined coefficients but requires an additional effort. Starting with the VAR representation in Eq. (16.3), multiply $\Phi(\mathrm{L})X_t = U(\mathrm{L})M(\mathrm{L})V(\mathrm{L})X_t = c + Z_t$ from the left by $U^{-1}(\mathrm{L})$ to obtain:

$$M(\mathrm{L})V(\mathrm{L})X_t = U^{-1}(1)c + U^{-1}(\mathrm{L})Z_t.$$

Multiplying this equation by $\widetilde{M}(\mathrm{L}) = \begin{pmatrix} I_{n-r} & 0 \\ 0 & (1-\mathrm{L})I_r \end{pmatrix}$ leads to

$$V(\mathrm{L})\Delta X_t = \widetilde{M}(1)U^{-1}(1)c + \widetilde{M}(\mathrm{L})U^{-1}(\mathrm{L})Z_t,$$

which finally implies

$$\begin{aligned} \Delta X_t &= V^{-1}(1)\widetilde{M}(1)U^{-1}(1)c + V^{-1}(\mathrm{L})\widetilde{M}(\mathrm{L})U^{-1}(\mathrm{L})Z_t \\ &= \mu + \Psi(\mathrm{L})Z_t. \end{aligned}$$

This is the MA(∞) representation of $\{\Delta X_t\}$ and corresponds to Eq. (16.2).

Because $\Pi = -\Phi(1) = -U(1)M(1)V(1)$, the following relation holds for the appropriately partitioned matrices:

$$\begin{aligned} \Phi(1) &= \begin{pmatrix} U_{11}(1) & U_{12}(1) \\ U_{21}(1) & U_{22}(1) \end{pmatrix} \begin{pmatrix} 0 & 0 \\ 0 & I_r \end{pmatrix} \begin{pmatrix} V_{11}(1) & V_{12}(1) \\ V_{21}(1) & V_{22}(1) \end{pmatrix} \\ &= \begin{pmatrix} U_{12}(1) \\ U_{22}(1) \end{pmatrix} \begin{pmatrix} V_{21}(1) & V_{22}(1) \end{pmatrix}. \end{aligned}$$

This implies that we can define α and β as

$$\alpha = -\begin{pmatrix} U_{12}(1) \\ U_{22}(1) \end{pmatrix} \quad \text{and} \quad \beta = \begin{pmatrix} V_{21}(1)' \\ V_{22}(1)' \end{pmatrix}.$$

$U(1)$ and $V(1)$ are non-singular so that α and β have full column rank r. Based on this derivation, the following lemma holds.

Lemma 16.1 *The columns of the so-defined matrix β are the cointegration vectors for the process $\{X_t\}$. The corresponding matrix of loading coefficients is α, which fulfills $\Psi(1)\alpha = 0$.*

Proof We must show that $\beta'\Psi(1) = 0$, which is the defining property of cointegration vectors. Denoting by $(V^{(ij)}(1))_{i,j=1,2}$ the appropriately partitioned matrix of $V(1)^{-1}$, we obtain:

$$\beta'\Psi(1) = \beta' \begin{pmatrix} V^{(11)}(1) & V^{(12)}(1) \\ V^{(21)}(1) & V^{(22)}(1) \end{pmatrix} \begin{pmatrix} I_{n-r} & 0 \\ 0 & 0 \end{pmatrix} U^{-1}(1)$$

$$= \left(V_{21}(1)\ V_{22}(1)\right)\begin{pmatrix} V^{(11)}(1) & 0 \\ V^{(21)}(1) & 0 \end{pmatrix} U^{-1}(1)$$

$$= \left(V_{21}(1)V^{(11)}(1) + V_{22}(1)V^{(21)}(1) \vdots 0\right) U^{-1}(1) = 0_n$$

where the last equality is a consequence of the property of the inverse matrix.

With the same arguments, we can show that $\Psi(1)\alpha = 0$. □

The equivalence between the VEC and the MA representation is known in the literature as Granger's representation theorem. Granger's representation theorem immediately implies the Beveridge-Nelson decomposition:

$$X_t = X_0 + \Psi(1)c\,t + \Psi(1)\sum_{j=1}^{t} Z_j + V_t \tag{16.6}$$

$$= X_0 + V^{-1}(1)\widetilde{M}(1)U^{-1}(1)c\,t + V^{-1}(1)\widetilde{M}(1)U^{-1}(1)\sum_{j=1}^{t} Z_j + V_t \tag{16.7}$$

where the stochastic process $\{V_t\}$ is stationary and defined as $V_t = \widetilde{\Psi}(\mathrm{L})Z_0 - \widetilde{\Psi}(\mathrm{L})Z_t$ with $\widetilde{\Psi}_j = \sum_{i=j+1}^{\infty} \Psi_i$ and $\Psi(\mathrm{L}) = V^{-1}(\mathrm{L})\widetilde{M}(\mathrm{L})U^{-1}(\mathrm{L})$. As $\beta'\Psi(1) = \beta' V^{-1}(1)\widetilde{M}(1)U^{-1}(1) = 0$, β eliminates the stochastic trend (random walk), $\sum_{j=1}^{t} Z_t$, as well as the deterministic linear trend $\mu t = V^{-1}(1)\widetilde{M}(1)U^{-1}(1)c\,t$.

An interesting special case is obtained when the constant c is a linear combination of the columns of α, i.e., if there exists a vector g such that $c = \alpha g$. Under this circumstance, $\Psi(1)c = \Psi(1)\alpha g = 0$, and the linear trend vanishes, and we have $\mathbb{E}\Delta X_t = 0$. In this case, the data will exhibit no trend although the VAR model contains a constant. A similar consideration can be made if the VAR model is specified to contain a constant and a linear time trend $d\,t$. The Beveridge-Nelson decomposition would then imply that the data should follow a quadratic trend. However, in the special case that d is a linear combination of the columns of α, the quadratic trend disappears, and only the linear remains because of the constant.

16.2.4 Common Trend and Triangular Representation

The matrix $\Psi(1)$ in the Beveridge-Nelson decomposition is singular. This implies that the multivariate random walk $\Psi(1)\sum_{j=1}^{\infty} Z_j$ does not consist of n independent univariate random walks. Instead only $n - r$ independent random walks make up the stochastic trend so that $\{X_t\}$ is driven by $n - r$ stochastic trends. In order to emphasize this fact, we derive from the Beveridge-Nelson decomposition the so-called common trend representation (Stock & Watson, 1988b).

As $\Psi(1)$ has rank $n-r$, there exists a $n \times r$ matrix γ such that $\Psi(1)\gamma = 0$. Denote by $\gamma^{\perp}$ the $n \times (n-r)$ matrix whose columns are orthogonal to γ, i.e., $\gamma'\gamma^{\perp} = 0$. The Beveridge-Nelson decomposition can then be rewritten as:

$$\begin{aligned} X_t &= X_0 + \Psi(1)\left(\gamma^{\perp} \vdots \gamma\right)\left(\gamma^{\perp} \vdots \gamma\right)^{-1} c\, t \\ &\quad + \Psi(1)\left(\gamma^{\perp} \vdots \gamma\right)\left(\gamma^{\perp} \vdots \gamma\right)^{-1} \sum_{j=1}^{t} Z_j + V_t \\ &= X_0 + \left(\Psi(1)\gamma^{\perp} \vdots 0\right)\left(\gamma^{\perp} \vdots \gamma\right)^{-1} c\, t \\ &\quad + \left(\Psi(1)\gamma^{\perp} \vdots 0\right)\left(\gamma^{\perp} \vdots \gamma\right)^{-1} \sum_{j=1}^{t} Z_j + V_t \\ &= X_0 + \left(\Psi(1)\gamma^{\perp} \vdots 0\right)\tilde{c}\, t + \left(\Psi(1)\gamma^{\perp} \vdots 0\right)\sum_{j=1}^{t} \widetilde{Z}_j + V_t \end{aligned}$$

where $\tilde{c} = \left(\gamma^{\perp} \vdots \gamma\right)^{=1} c$ and $\widetilde{Z}_j = \left(\gamma^{\perp} \vdots \gamma\right)^{-1} Z_j$. Therefore, only the first $n-r$ elements of the vector $\tilde{c}$ are relevant for the deterministic linear trend. The remaining elements are multiplied by zero and are thus irrelevant. Similarly, for the multivariate random walk, only the first $n-r$ elements of the process $\{\widetilde{Z}_t\}$ are responsible for the stochastic trend. The remaining elements of $\widetilde{Z}_t$ are multiplied by zero and thus have no permanent but only a transitory influence. The above representation decomposes the shocks orthogonally into *permanent* and *transitory* ones (Gonzalo & Ng, 2001). The previous lemma shows that one can choose for γ the matrix of loading coefficients α.

Summarizing the first $n-r$ elements of $\tilde{c}$ and $\widetilde{Z}_t$ to $\tilde{c}_1$ and $\widetilde{Z}_{1t}$, respectively, we arrive at the *common trend representation*:

$$X_t = X_0 + B\tilde{c}_1\, t + B\sum_{j=1}^{t} \widetilde{Z}_{1j} + V_t$$

where the $n \times (n-r)$ matrix B is equal to $\Psi(1)\gamma^{\perp}$.

Applying these results to our introductory example, we arrive at

$$B = \frac{1}{1-\phi}\begin{pmatrix} \gamma \\ 1 \end{pmatrix}, \quad \tilde{c} = \mu(1-\phi), \quad \text{and} \quad \widetilde{Z}_{1t} = u_t.$$

This again demonstrates that the trend, the linear, and the stochastic trend are exclusively stemming from the nonstationary variables. In the example analyzed in Sect. 16.1, this is $\{Y_t\}$ as can be seen from Eq. (16.1).

Finally, we want to present a triangular representation that is well suited to deal with the nonparametric estimation approach advocated by Phillips (1991) and Phillips and Hansen (1990). In this representation, we normalize the cointegration vector such that $\beta = (I_r, -b')'$. In addition, we partition the vector X_t into X_{1t} and X_{2t} such that X_{1t} contains the first r and X_{2t} the last $n - r$ elements. $X_t = (X'_{1t}, X_{2t})'$ can then be expressed as:

$$X_{1t} = b'X_{2t} + \pi_1 D_t + u_{1t}$$
$$\Delta X_{2t} = \pi_2 \Delta D_t + u_{2t}$$

where D_t summarizes the deterministic components such as constant and linear time trend. $\{u_{1t}\}$ and $\{u_{2t}\}$ denote potentially autocorrelated stationary time series.

16.3 Johansen's Test for Cointegration

In Sect. 7.5.1, we have already discussed a regression-based test for cointegration among two variables. It was based on a unit root test of the residuals from a bivariate regression of one variable against the other. In this regression, it turned out to be irrelevant which of the two variables was chosen as the regressor and which one as the regressand. This method can, in principle, be extended to more than two variables. However, with more than two variables, the choice of the regressand becomes more crucial as not all variables may be part of the cointegrating relation. Moreover, more than one independent cointegrating relation may exist. For these reasons, it is advantageous to use a method that treats all variables symmetrically. The *cointegration test* developed by Johansen fulfills this criterion because it is based on a VAR, which does not single out a particular variable. This test has received wide recognition and is most often used in practice. The test serves two purposes. First, we want to determine the number r of cointegrating relationships. Second, we want to test properties of the cointegration vector β and the loading matrix α.

The exposition of the Johansen test follows closely the work of Johansen where the derivations and additional details can be found (Johansen, 1988, 1991, 1995). Starting point of the analysis is a VAR(p) model with constant c in VEC form as in Eq. (16.4):

$$\Delta X_t = c + \Pi X_{t-1} + \Gamma_1 \Delta X_{t-1} + \cdots + \Gamma_{p-1} \Delta X_{t-p+1} + Z_t,$$
$$t = 1, 2, \ldots, T, \tag{16.8}$$

where $Z_t \sim$ IID N$(0, \Sigma)$ and given starting values $X_0 = x_0, \ldots, X_{-p+1} = x_{-p+1}$. T denotes the sample size. The problem can be simplified by regressing ΔX_t as well as X_{t-1} against $c, \Delta X_{t-1}, \ldots, \Delta X_{t-p+1}$ and working with the residuals from these regressions.[6] This simplification results in a VAR model of order one. Hence, without loss of generality, we base the analysis on a VAR(1) process without constant term:

$$\Delta X_t = \Pi X_{t-1} + Z_t$$

where $Z_t \sim \text{IID N}(0, \Sigma)$.[7]

The phenomenon of cointegration manifests itself in the singularity of the matrix Π. In particular, the rank of Π gives the number of linearly independent cointegrating relationships. Denoting the rank of Π by r, $0 \leq r \leq n$, we can formulate a sequence of hypotheses:

$$\mathbf{H}(r) : \text{rank}(\Pi) \leq r, \qquad r = 0, 1, \ldots, n.$$

Hypothesis $\mathbf{H}(r)$, thus, implies that there exists *at most* r linearly independent cointegrating vectors. The sequence of hypotheses is nested in the sense that $\mathbf{H}(r)$ implies $\mathbf{H}(r+1)$:

$$\mathbf{H}(0) \subseteq \mathbf{H}(1) \subseteq \ldots \subseteq \mathbf{H}(n).$$

The hypothesis $\mathbf{H}(0)$ means that $\text{rank}(\Pi) = 0$. In this case, $\Pi = 0$, and there exists no cointegration vector. $\{X_t\}$ is driven in this case by n independent random walks, and the VAR process becomes a VAR process in $\{\Delta X_t\}$, which in our simplified version just means that $\Delta X_t = Z_t \sim \text{IID N}(0, \Sigma)$. The hypothesis $\mathbf{H}(n)$ places no restriction on Π and includes in this way the case that the level of $\{X_t\}$ is already stationary. Of particular interest are the hypotheses between these two extreme ones where non-degenerate cointegrating vectors are possible. Usually, not just the number of linearly independent cointegrating vectors r is of interest but also their shape. Hence, hypotheses tests about the structure of the cointegrating vectors β are to be developed.

Johansen's test is conceived as a likelihood-ratio test. This means that we must determine the likelihood function for a sample $X_1, X_2, \ldots, X_T$, where T denotes the sample size. As we assumed that $\{Z_t\} \sim \text{IID N}(0, \Sigma)$, the logged likelihood function for the parameters α, β, and Σ conditional on the starting values is

$$\begin{aligned}\ell(\alpha, \beta, \Sigma) = & -\frac{Tn}{2}\ln(2\pi) + \frac{T}{2}\ln\det(\Sigma^{-1}) \\ & -\frac{1}{2}\sum_{t=1}^{T}(\Delta X_t - \alpha\beta' X_{t-1})'\Sigma^{-1}(\Delta X_t - \alpha\beta' X_{t-1})\end{aligned}$$

[6] If the VAR model (16.8) contains further deterministic components besides the constant, these components have to be accounted for in these regressions.

[7] This two-stage least-squares procedure is also known as partial regression and is part of the Frisch-Waugh-Lowell Theorem (Davidson & MacKinnon, 1993, 19-24).

where $\Pi = \alpha\beta'$. For fixed given β, α can be estimated by a regression of ΔX_t on $\beta' X_{t-1}$:

$$\hat{\alpha} = \hat{\alpha}(\beta) = S_{01}\beta(\beta' S_{11}\beta)^{-1}$$

where the moment matrices S_{00}, S_{11}, S_{01} and S_{10} are defined as:

$$\begin{aligned}
S_{00} &= \frac{1}{T}\sum_{t=1}^{T}(\Delta X_t)(\Delta X_t)' \\
S_{11} &= \frac{1}{T}\sum_{t=1}^{T} X_{t-1}X_{t-1}' \\
S_{01} &= \frac{1}{T}\sum_{t=1}^{T}(\Delta X_t)X_{t-1}' \\
S_{10} &= S_{01}'.
\end{aligned}$$

The covariance matrix of the residuals then becomes:

$$\widehat{\Sigma} = \widehat{\Sigma}(\beta) = S_{00} - S_{01}\beta(\beta' S_{11}\beta)^{-1}\beta' S_{10}.$$

Using these results, the concentrated log-likelihood function is obtained:

$$\begin{aligned}
\ell(\beta) = \ell(\hat{\alpha}(\beta), \beta, \widehat{\Sigma}(\beta)) &= -\frac{Tn}{2}\ln(2\pi) - \frac{T}{2}\ln\det(\widehat{\Sigma}(\beta)) - \frac{Tn}{2} \\
&= -\frac{Tn}{2}\ln(2\pi) - \frac{Tn}{2} - \frac{T}{2}\ln\det\left(S_{00} - S_{01}\beta(\beta' S_{11}\beta)^{-1}\beta' S_{10}\right). \qquad (16.9)
\end{aligned}$$

The expression $\frac{Tn}{2}$ in the above equation is derived as follows:

$$\begin{aligned}
&\frac{1}{2}\sum_{t=1}^{T}(\Delta X_t - \hat{\alpha}\beta' X_{t-1})'\widehat{\Sigma}^{-1}(\Delta X_t - \hat{\alpha}\beta' X_{t-1}) \\
&= \frac{1}{2}\operatorname{tr}\left(\sum_{t=1}^{T}(\Delta X_t - \hat{\alpha}\beta' X_{t-1})(\Delta X_t - \hat{\alpha}\beta' X_{t-1})'\widehat{\Sigma}^{-1}\right) \\
&= \frac{1}{2}\operatorname{tr}\left((T S_{00} - T\hat{\alpha}\beta' S_{10} - T S_{01}\beta\hat{\alpha}' + T\hat{\alpha}\beta' S_{11}\beta\hat{\alpha}')\widehat{\Sigma}^{-1}\right) \\
&= \frac{T}{2}\operatorname{tr}\left(\underbrace{(S_{00} - \hat{\alpha}\beta' S_{10})}_{=\widehat{\Sigma}}\widehat{\Sigma}^{-1}\right) = \frac{Tn}{2}.
\end{aligned}$$

The log-likelihood function is thus maximized if

$$\det(\widehat{\Sigma}(\beta)) = \det\left(S_{00} - S_{01}\beta(\beta' S_{11}\beta)^{-1}\beta' S_{10}\right)$$
$$= \det S_{00} \frac{\det\left(\beta'(S_{11} - S_{10}S_{00}^{-1}S_{01})\beta\right)}{\det(\beta' S_{11}\beta)}$$

is minimized over β.[8] The minimum is obtained by solving the following generalized eigenvalue problem (Johansen, 1995):

$$\det\left(\lambda S_{11} - S_{10}S_{00}^{-1}S_{01}\right) = 0.$$

This eigenvalue problem delivers n eigenvalues

$$1 \geq \hat{\lambda}_1 \geq \hat{\lambda}_2 \geq \ldots \geq \hat{\lambda}_n \geq 0$$

with corresponding n eigenvectors $\hat{\beta}_1, \ldots, \hat{\beta}_n$. These eigenvectors are normalized such that $\hat{\beta}' S_{11}\hat{\beta} = I_n$. Therefore, we have that

$$\operatorname{argmin}_\beta \det(\widehat{\Sigma}(\beta)) = (\det S_{00}) \prod_{i=1}^{n} \hat{\lambda}_i.$$

Remark 16.1 In the case of cointegration, Π is singular with rank $\widehat{\Pi} = r$. To estimate r, it seems natural to investigate the number of nonzero eigenvalues of $\widehat{\Pi} = S_{01}S_{11}^{-1}$. However, because eigenvalues may be complex, it is advantageous not to investigate the eigenvalues of $\widehat{\Pi}$ but those of $\widehat{\Pi}'\widehat{\Pi}$, which are all real and positive due to the symmetry of $\widehat{\Pi}'\widehat{\Pi}$. These eigenvalues are called the *singular values* of $\widehat{\Pi}$.[9] Noting that

$$0 = \det\left(\lambda S_{11} - S_{10}S_{00}^{-1}S_{01}\right) = \det S_{11} \det\left(\lambda I_n - S_{11}^{-1/2}S_{10}S_{00}^{-1}S_{01}S_{11}^{-1/2}\right)$$
$$= \det S_{11} \det\left(\lambda I_n - (S_{00}^{-1/2}S_{01}S_{11}^{-1/2})'(S_{00}^{-1/2}S_{01}S_{11}^{-1/2})\right),$$

[8] Thereby we make use of the following equality for partitioned matrices:

$$\det\begin{pmatrix} A_{11} & A_{12} \\ A_{21} & A_{22} \end{pmatrix} = \det A_{11} \det(A_{22} - A_{21}A_{11}^{-1}A_{12}) = \det A_{22} \det(A_{11} - A_{12}A_{22}^{-1}A_{21})$$

where A_{11} and A_{22} are invertible matrices (see, e.g., Meyer, 2000, p. 475).

[9] An appraisal of singular values can be found in Strang (1988) or Meyer (2000).

the generalized eigenvalue problem above therefore just determines the singular values of $S_{00}^{-1/2} S_{01} S_{11}^{-1/2} = S_{00}^{-1/2} \widehat{\Pi} S_{11}^{1/2}$.

Remark 16.2 Based on the observation that, for $n = 1$, $\lambda = \frac{S_{01} S_{10}}{S_{11} S_{00}}$ equals the squared empirical correlation coefficient between ΔX_t and X_{t-1}, we find that the eigenvalues λ_j and $j = 1, \ldots, n$ are nothing but the squared canonical correlation coefficients (see Johansen, 1995; Reinsel, 1993). Thereby, the largest eigenvalue, $\hat{\lambda}_1$, corresponds to the largest squared correlation coefficient that can be achieved between linear combinations of ΔX_1 and X_{t-1}. Thus β_1 gives the linear combination of the integrated variable X_{t-1}, which comes closest in the sense of correlation to the stationary variable $\{\Delta X_t\}$. The second eigenvalue λ_2 corresponds to the maximal squared correlation coefficient between linear combinations of ΔX_t and X_{t-1}, which are orthogonal to the linear combination corresponding to λ_1. The remaining squared canonical correlation coefficients are obtained by iterating this procedure n times.

If the dimension of the cointegrating space is r, then $\hat{\beta}$ consists of those eigenvectors that correspond to the r largest eigenvalues $\hat{\lambda}_1, \ldots, \hat{\lambda}_r$. The remaining eigenvalues $\lambda_{r+1}, \ldots, \lambda_n$ should be zero. Under the null hypothesis $\mathbf{H}(r)$, the log-likelihood function (16.9) can be finally expressed as

$$\ell(\hat{\beta}_r) = -\frac{Tn}{2} \ln \pi - \frac{Tn}{2} - \frac{T}{2} \ln \det S_{00} - \frac{T}{2} \sum_{i=1}^{r} \ln(1 - \lambda_i).$$

The expression for the optimized likelihood function is used to construct the Johansen's likelihood-ratio test. There are two versions of the test depending on the alternative hypothesis:

$$\begin{aligned} \text{trace test:} \quad & \mathbf{H}(r) \text{ against } \mathbf{H}(n), \\ \text{max test:} \quad & \mathbf{H}(r) \text{ against } \mathbf{H}(r+1). \end{aligned}$$

The corresponding likelihood ratio test statistics are therefore:

$$\text{trace test:} \quad 2(\ell(\hat{\beta}_n) - \ell(\hat{\beta}_r)) = -T \sum_{j=r+1}^{n} \ln(1 - \hat{\lambda}_j) \approx T \sum_{j=r+1}^{n} \hat{\lambda}_j,$$

$$\text{max test:} \quad 2(\ell(\hat{\beta}_{r+1}) - \ell(\hat{\beta}_r)) = -T \ln(1 - \hat{\lambda}_{r+1}) \approx T \hat{\lambda}_{r+1}.$$

In practice, it is useful to adopt a sequential test strategy based on the trace test. Given some significance level, we test in a first step the null hypothesis $\mathbf{H}(0)$ against $\mathbf{H}(n)$. If the test does not reject the null hypothesis, we conclude that $r = 0$ and that there is no cointegrating relation. If the test rejects the null hypothesis, we conclude that there is at least one cointegrating relation. We then test in a second step the null hypothesis $\mathbf{H}(1)$ against $\mathbf{H}(n)$. If the test does not reject the null hypothesis, we conclude that there exists one cointegrating relation, i.e., that $r = 1$. If the test rejects the null hypothesis, we examine the next hypothesis $\mathbf{H}(2)$ and so on. In this way, we obtain a test sequence. If in this sequence, the null hypothesis $\mathbf{H}(r)$ is not rejected but $\mathbf{H}(r+1)$ is, we conclude that r linearly independent cointegrating relations exist as explained in the diagram below.

$$\begin{array}{ccccc}
\mathbf{H}(0) \text{ against } \mathbf{H}(n) & \xrightarrow{\text{rejection}} & \mathbf{H}(1) \text{ against } \mathbf{H}(n) & \xrightarrow{\text{rejection}} & \mathbf{H}(2) \text{ against } \mathbf{H}(n) \ldots \\
\downarrow & & \downarrow & & \downarrow \\
r = 0 & & r = 1 & & r = 2
\end{array}$$

If in this sequence we do not reject $\mathbf{H}(r)$ for some r, it is useful to perform the max test $\mathbf{H}(r)$ against $\mathbf{H}(r+1)$ as a robustness check. The asymptotic distributions of the test statistics are, like in the Dickey-Fuller unit root test, nonstandard and depend on the specification of the deterministic components.

16.3.1 Specification of Deterministic Components

As mentioned previously, the asymptotic distribution of Johansen's test depends on the specification of the deterministic components. Thus, some care must be devoted to this issue. We illustrate this point by decomposing the model additively into a linear deterministic and a stochastic component in vector error correction form (see Johansen, 1995, 80–84 and Lütkepohl, 2005, section 6.4):

$$X_t = \mu_0 + \mu_1 t + Y_t \tag{16.10}$$

$$\Delta Y_t = \Pi Y_{t-1} + Z_t = \alpha\beta' Y_{t-1} + Z_t. \tag{16.11}$$

For the ease of exposition, we have omitted the autoregressive corrections. Eliminating Y_t using $Y_t = X_t - \mu_0 - \mu_1 t$ and $\Delta Y_t = \Delta X_t - \mu_1$ leads to

$$\Delta X_t - \mu_1 = \alpha\beta' \left(X_{t-1} - \mu_0 - \mu_1(t-1)\right) + Z_t.$$

This equation can be rewritten as

$$\Delta X_t = c_0 + c_1(t-1) + \alpha\beta' X_{t-1} + Z_t \tag{16.12}$$

with $c_0 = \mu_1 - \alpha\beta'\mu_0$ and $c_1 = -\alpha\beta'\mu_1$

$$= c_0 + \alpha(\beta', -\beta'\mu_1)X_{t-1}^0 + Z_t \tag{16.13}$$

where $X_t^0 = (X_t', t)'$. Equation (16.12) is just the vector error correction model (16.4) augmented by the linear trend term $c_1 t$. If the term c_1 would be left

Table 16.1 Trend specifications in vector error correction models

Case	Deterministic term in VECM or VAR	Restriction	Trend in X_t	$\mathbb{E}\Delta X_t$	$\mathbb{E}(\beta' X_t)$
I	None	—	Zero	Zero	Zero
II	c_0	$c_0 = \alpha\gamma_0$	Constant	Zero	Constant
III	c_0	None	Linear	Constant	Constant
IV	$c_0 + c_1 t$	$c_1 = \alpha\gamma_1$	Linear	Constant	Linear
V	$c_0 + c_1 t$	None	Quadratic	Linear	Linear

Table inspired by Johansen (2007)

unrestricted, arguments similar to those in Sect. 16.2.3 would show that X_t exhibits a deterministic quadratic trend with coefficient vector $\Psi(1)c_1$. This, however, contradicts the specification in Eq. (16.10). However, if we recognize that c_1 in Eq. (16.12) is actually restricted to lie in the span of α, i.e., that $c_1 = \alpha\gamma_1$ with $\gamma_1 = -\beta'\mu_1$, no quadratic trend would emerge in the levels because $\Psi(1)\alpha = 0$ by Granger's representation Theorem 16.1. Alternatively, one may view the time trend as showing up in the error correction term, respectively being part of the cointegrating relation, as in Eq. (16.13).

Similarly, one may consider the case that X_t has a constant mean μ_0, i.e., that $\mu_1 = 0$ in Eq. (16.10). This leads to the same error correction specification (16.12), but without the term $c_1 t$. Leaving the constant c_0 unrestricted, this will generate a linear trend $\Psi(1)c_0 t$ as shown in Sect. 16.2.3. In order to reconcile this with the assumption of a constant mean, we must recognize that $c_0 = \alpha\gamma_0$ with $\gamma_0 = -\beta'\mu_0$.

Based on these arguments, we can summarize the discussion by distinguishing five different cases displayed in Table 16.1.[10] This table also shows the implications for $\mathbb{E}\Delta X_t$ and $\mathbb{E}(\beta' X_t)$. They can be read off from Eqs. (16.12) and (16.13).

The corresponding asymptotic distributions of the trace as well as the max test statistic in these five cases are tabulated in Johansen (1995), MacKinnon et al. (1999), and Osterwald-Lenum (1992).[11] The finite sample properties of these tests can be quite poor. Thus, more recently, bootstrap methods have proven to provide a successful alternative in practice (Cavaliere et al., 2012).

16.3.2 Testing Hypotheses on Cointegrating Vectors

As mentioned previously, the cointegrating vectors are not unique, only the cointegrating space is. This makes the cointegrating vectors often difficult to interpret economically, despite some basis transformation. It is therefore of interest to see whether the space spanned by the cointegrating vectors summarized in the columns of $\hat{\beta}$ can be viewed as a subspace spanned by some hypothetical vectors $H =$

[10] Compare these cases to those for the unit root test (see Sect. 7.3.1).

[11] The tables by MacKinnon et al. (1999) allow for exogenous integrated variables.

$(h_1, \ldots, h_s)$, $r \leq s < n$. If this hypothesis is true, the cointegrating vectors should be linear combinations of the columns of H so that the null hypothesis can be formulated as

$$\mathbf{H}_0 : \beta = H\varphi \tag{16.14}$$

for some $s \times r$ matrix φ. Under this null hypothesis, this amounts to solve an analogous general eigenvalue problem:

$$\det\left(\varphi H' S_{11} H - H' S_{10} S_{00}^{-1} S_{01} H\right) = 0.$$

The solution of this problem is given by the eigenvalues $1 > \tilde{\lambda}_1 \geq \tilde{\lambda}_2 \geq \ldots \tilde{\lambda}_s > 0$ with corresponding normalized eigenvectors. The likelihood ratio test statistic for this hypothesis is then

$$T \sum_{j=1}^{r} \ln \frac{1 - \tilde{\lambda}_j}{1 - \hat{\lambda}_j}.$$

This test statistic is asymptotically distributed as a χ^2 distribution with $r(n - s)$ degrees of freedom.

With similar arguments it is possible to construct a test of the null hypothesis that the cointegrating space spanned by the columns of $\hat{\beta}$ contains some hypothetical vectors $K = (h_1, \ldots, h_s)$, $1 \leq s \leq r$. The null hypothesis can then be formulated as

$$\mathbf{H}_0 : K\varphi = \beta \tag{16.15}$$

for some $s \times r$ matrix φ. Like in the previous case, this hypothesis can also be tested by the corresponding likelihood ratio test statistic, which is asymptotically distributed as a χ^2 distribution with $s(n - r)$ degrees of freedom. Similarly, it is possible to test hypotheses on α and joint hypotheses on α and β (see Johansen, 1995; Kunst & Neusser, 1990; Lütkepohl, 2005).

16.4 An Example

This example reproduces the study by Neusser (1991) with data for the United States over the period first quarter of 1950 to fourth quarter of 2005. The starting point is a VAR model, which consists of four variables: real gross domestic product (Y), real private consumption (C), real gross investment (I), and the ex-post real interest rate (R). All variables, except the real interest rate, are in logs. First, we identify a VAR model for these variables where the order is determined by Akaike's (AIC), Schwarz' (BIC), or Hannan-Quinn' (HQ) information criteria. The AIC suggests seven lags, whereas the other criteria propose a VAR of order two. As the VAR(7) consists of many statistically insignificant coefficients, we prefer the more parsimonious VAR(2) model, which produces the following estimates:

$$X_t = \begin{pmatrix} Y_t \\ C_t \\ I_t \\ R_t \end{pmatrix} = \begin{pmatrix} 0.185 \\ (0.047) \\ 0.069 \\ (0.043) \\ 0.041 \\ (0.117) \\ -0.329 \\ (0.097) \end{pmatrix} + \begin{pmatrix} 0.951 & 0.254 & 0.088 & 0.042 \\ (0.086) & (0.091) & (0.033) & (0.032) \\ 0.157 & 0.746 & 0.065 & -0.013 \\ (0.079) & (0.084) & (0.031) & (0.030) \\ 0.283 & 0.250 & 1.304 & 0.026 \\ (0.216) & (0.229) & (0.084) & (0.081) \\ 0.324 & -0.536 & -0.024 & 0.551 \\ (0.178) & (0.189) & (0.069) & (0.067) \end{pmatrix} X_{t-1}$$

$$+ \begin{pmatrix} -0.132 & -0.085 & -0.089 & -0.016 \\ (0.085) & (0.093) & (0.033) & (0.031) \\ -0.213 & 0.305 & -0.066 & 0.112 \\ (0.078) & (0.085) & (0.031) & (0.029) \\ -0.517 & 0.040 & -0.364 & 0.098 \\ (0.214) & (0.233) & (0.084) & (0.079) \\ -0.042 & 0.296 & 0.005 & 0.163 \\ (0.176) & (0.192) & (0.069) & (0.065) \end{pmatrix} X_{t-2} + Z_t$$

where the estimated standard errors of the corresponding coefficients are reported in parenthesis. The estimate covariance matrix Σ, $\widehat{\Sigma}$, is

$$\widehat{\Sigma} = 10^{-4} \times \begin{pmatrix} 0.722 & 0.428 & 1.140 & 0.002 \\ 0.428 & 0.610 & 1.026 & -0.092 \\ 1.140 & 1.026 & 4.473 & -0.328 \\ 0.002 & -0.092 & -0.328 & 3.098 \end{pmatrix}.$$

The sequence of the hypotheses starts with $\mathbf{H}(0)$, which states that there exists no cointegrating relation. The alternative hypothesis is always $\mathbf{H}(n)$, which says that there are n cointegrating relations. According to Table 16.2, the value of the trace test statistic is 111.772, which is clearly larger than the 5% critical value of 47.856. Thus, the null hypothesis $\mathbf{H}(0)$ is rejected, and we consider next the hypothesis

Table 16.2 Evaluation of the results of Johansen's cointegration test

		Trace statistic		Max statistic	
Null hypothesis	Eigenvalue	Test statistic	Critical value	Test statistic	Critical value
$\mathbf{H}(0): r = 0$	0.190	111.772	47.856	47.194	27.584
$\mathbf{H}(1): r \leq 1$	0.179	64.578	29.797	44.075	21.132
$\mathbf{H}(2): r \leq 2$	0.081	20.503	15.495	18.983	14.265
$\mathbf{H}(3): r \leq 3$	0.007	1.520	3.841	1.520	3.841

Critical 5% values are taken from MacKinnon et al. (1999)

H(1). This hypothesis is again clearly rejected so that we move on to hypothesis **H**(2). Because **H**(3) is not rejected, we conclude that there exists three cointegrating relations. To check this result, we test the hypothesis **H**(2) against **H**(3) using the max test. As this test also rejects **H**(2), we can be pretty confident that there are three cointegrating relations given as:

$$\hat{\beta} = \begin{pmatrix} 1.000 & 0.000 & 0.000 \\ 0.000 & 1.000 & 0.000 \\ 0.000 & 0.000 & 1.000 \\ -258.948 & -277.869 & -337.481 \end{pmatrix}.$$

In this form, the cointegrating vectors are economically difficult to interpret. We therefore ask whether they are compatible with the following hypotheses:

$$\beta_C = \begin{pmatrix} 1.0 \\ -1.0 \\ 0.0 \\ 0.0 \end{pmatrix}, \qquad \beta_I = \begin{pmatrix} 1.0 \\ 0.0 \\ -1.0 \\ 0.0 \end{pmatrix}, \qquad \beta_R = \begin{pmatrix} 0.0 \\ 0.0 \\ 0.0 \\ 1.0 \end{pmatrix}.$$

These hypotheses state that the log-difference (ratio) between consumption and GDP, the log-difference (ratio) between investment and GDP, and the real interest rate are stationary. They can be rationalized in the context of the neoclassical growth model (see King et al., 1991; Neusser, 1991). Each of them can be brought into the form of Eq. (16.15), where β is replaced by its estimate $\hat{\beta}$. The corresponding test statistics for each of the three cointegrating relations is distributed as a χ^2 distribution with one degree of freedom,[12] which gives a critical value of 3.84 at the 5% significance level. The corresponding values for the test statistic are 12.69, 15.05, and 0.45, respectively. This implies that we must reject the first two hypotheses β_C and β_I. However, the conjecture that the real interest is stationary cannot be rejected. Finally, we can investigate the joint hypothesis $\beta_0 = (\beta_C, \beta_I, \beta_R)$, which can be represented in the form (16.14). In this case, the value of the test statistic is 41.20, which is clearly above the critical value of 7.81 inferred from the χ_3^2 distribution.[13] Thus, we must reject this joint hypothesis.

[12] The degrees of freedom are computed according to the formula: $s(n - r) = 1(4 - 3) = 1$.

[13] The degrees of freedom are computed according to the formula: $r(n - s) = 3(4 - 3) = 3$.

State-Space Models and the Kalman Filter 17

The state space representation is a flexible technique originally developed in automatic control engineering to represent, model, and control dynamic systems. Thereby, the unobserved or partially observed state of a system in period t is summarized by an m-dimensional vector X_t. The evolution of the state is then described by a VAR model of order one usually called the state equation. A second equation describes the connection between the state and the observations given by a n-dimensional vector Y_t. Despite its simple structure, state space models encompass a large variety of model classes: VARMA, respectively, VARIMA models;[1] unobserved-component models; factor models; structural time series models that decompose a given time series into a trend, a seasonal, and a cyclical component; models with measurement errors; VAR models with time-varying parameters, etc. See the examples given in Sect. 17.2.

From a technical point of view, the main advantage of state space modeling is the unified treatment of estimation, forecasting, and smoothing. At the center of the analysis stands the Kalman filter named after its inventor Rudolf Emil Kálmán (Kalman, 1960, 1963). He developed a projection-based algorithm that recursively produces a statistically optimal estimate of the state. The versatility and the ease of implementation have made the Kalman filter an increasingly popular tool also in the economically oriented times series literature. In this chapter, we present just an introduction to the subject and refer to Anderson and Moore (1979), Brockwell and Davis (1991, Chapter 12), Brockwell and Davis (1996, Chapter 8), Hamilton (1994a, Chapter 13), Hamilton (1994b), Hannan and Deistler (1988), or Harvey (1989) and in particular to Durbin and Koopman (2011) and Kim and Nelson (1999) for further details.

[1] VARIMA models stand for vector autoregressive integrated moving-average models.

K. Neusser, *Time Series Econometrics*, Springer Texts in Business and Economics,
https://doi.org/10.1007/978-3-031-88838-0_17

17.1 The State Space Model

We consider a dynamical system whose state at each point in time t is determined by a vector X_t. The evolution of the system over time is then described by a *state equation*. The state is, however, unobserved or only partly observed to the outside observer. Thus, a second equation, called the *observation equation*, is needed to describe the connection of the state and the observations. This relation may be subject to measurement errors. The equation system consisting of state and observation equation is called a state space model, which is visualized in Fig. 17.1. The state equation typically consists of a VAR model of order one, whereas the observation equation has the structure of multivariate linear regression model.[2] Despite the simple structure of each of these two components taken separately, their combination is very versatile and able to represent a great variety of models.

In the case of time invariant coefficients,[3] we can set up these two equations as follows:

$$\text{state equation:} \qquad X_{t+1} = FX_t + V_{t+1}, \qquad t = 1, 2, \ldots \tag{17.1}$$

$$\text{observation equation:} \qquad Y_t = A + GX_t + W_t, \qquad t = 1, 2, \ldots \tag{17.2}$$

Thereby X_t denotes an m-dimensional vector, which describes the state of the system in period t. The evolution of the state is represented as a vector autoregressive

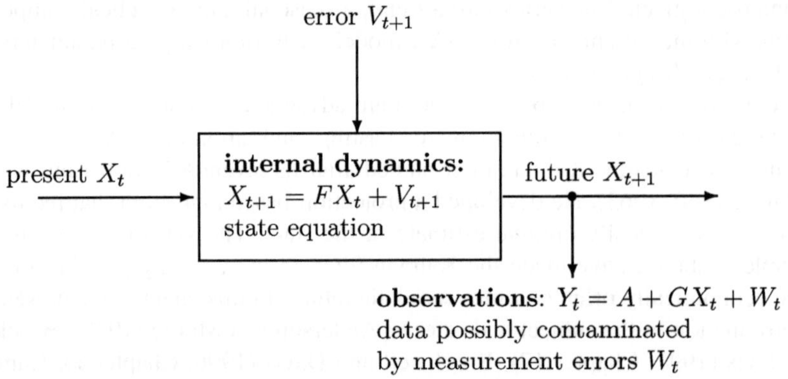

Fig. 17.1 State space model

[2] We will focus on linear dynamic models only. With the availability of fast and cheap computing facilities, non-linear approaches have gained some popularity. See Durbin and Koopman (2011) for an exposition.

[3] For the ease of exposition, we will present first the time-invariant case and analyze the case of time-varying coefficients later.

model of order one with coefficient matrix F and disturbances V_{t+1}.[4] As we assume that the state X_t is unobservable or at least partly unobservable, we need a second equation that relates the state to the observations. In particular, we assume that there is a linear time-invariant relation given by A and G of the n-dimensional vector of observations, Y_t, to the state X_t. This relation may be contaminated by measurement errors W_t. The system is initialized in period $t = 1$.

We make the following simplifying assumption of the state space model represented by Eqs. (17.1) and (17.2).

(i) $\{V_t\} \sim \text{WN}(0, Q)$, where Q is a constant nonnegative definite $m \times m$ matrix.
(ii) $\{W_t\} \sim \text{WN}(0, R)$, where R is a constant nonnegative definite $n \times n$ matrix.
(iii) The two disturbances are uncorrelated with each other at all leads and lags, i.e.:

$$\mathbb{E}(W_s V_t') = 0, \qquad \text{for all } t \text{ and } s.$$

(iv) V_t and W_t are multivariate normally distributed.
(v) X_1 is uncorrelated with V_t as well as with W_t, $t = 1, 2, \ldots$

Remark 17.1 In a more general context, we can make both covariance matrices Q and R time-varying and allow for contemporaneous correlations between V_t and W_t (see Example 17.5.1).

Remark 17.2 As both the state and the observation equation may include identities, the covariance matrices are not necessarily positive definite, but only nonnegative definite.

Remark 17.3 Neither $\{X_t\}$ nor $\{Y_t\}$ is assumed to be stationary.

Remark 17.4 The specification of the state equation and the normality assumption imply that the sequence $\{X_1, V_1, V_2, \ldots\}$ is independent so that the conditional distribution X_{t+1} given $X_t, X_{t-1}, \ldots, X_1$ equals the conditional distribution of X_{t+1} given X_t. Thus, the process $\{X_t\}$ satisfies the *Markov property*. As the dimension of the state vector X_t is arbitrary, it can be expanded in such a way as to encompass every component X_{t-1} for any t (see, e.g., the state space representation of a VAR(p) model with $p > 1$). However, there remains the problem of the smallest dimension of the state vector (see Sect. 17.4.2).

Remark 17.5 The state space representation is not unique. Defining, for example, a new state vector $\tilde{X}_t$ by multiplying X_t with an invertible matrix P, i.e., $\tilde{X}_t = PX_t$, all properties of the system remain unchanged. Naturally, we must redefine all the system matrices accordingly: $\tilde{F} = PFP^{-1}$, $\tilde{Q} = PQP'$, $\tilde{G} = GP^{-1}$.

[4] In control theory, the state equation (17.1) is amended by an additional term HU_t, which represents the effect of control variables U_t. These exogenous controls are used to regulate the system.

Given X_1, we can iterate the state equation forward in time:

$$X_t = F^{t-1}X_1 + \sum_{j=1}^{t-1} F^{j-1}V_{t+1-j}, \qquad t = 1, 2, \ldots$$

$$Y_t = A + GF^{t-1}X_1 + \sum_{j=1}^{t-1} GF^{j-1}V_{t+1-j} + W_t, \qquad t = 1, 2, \ldots$$

The state equation is called stable or causal if all eigenvalues of F are inside the unit circle, which is equivalent when all roots of $\det(\mathrm{I}_m - Fz) = 0$ are outside the unit circle (see Sect. 12.3). In this case, the state equation has a unique stationary solution:

$$X_t = \sum_{j=0}^{\infty} F^{j-1}V_{t+1-j}. \tag{17.3}$$

The process $\{Y_t\}$ is therefore also stationary, and we have:

$$Y_t = A + \sum_{j=0}^{\infty} GF^{j-1}V_{t+1-j} + W_t. \tag{17.4}$$

In the case of a stationary state space model, we may do without an initialization period and take $t \in \mathbb{Z}$.

In the case of a stable state equation, we can easily deduce the covariance function for $\{X_t\}$, $\Gamma_X(h)$, $h = 0, 1, 2, \ldots$ According to Sect. 12.4

$$\Gamma_X(0) = F\Gamma_X(0)F' + Q,$$

$$\Gamma_X(h) = F^h\Gamma_X(0), \qquad h = 1, 2, \ldots$$

where $\Gamma_X(0)$ is uniquely determined given the stability assumption. Similarly, we can derive the covariance function for the observation process, $\Gamma_Y(h)$, $h = 0, 1, 2, \ldots$:

$$\Gamma_Y(0) = G\Gamma_X(0)G' + R,$$

$$\Gamma_Y(h) = GF^h\Gamma_X(0)G', \qquad h = 1, 2, \ldots$$

17.2 Examples of State Space Models

The following examples should illustrate the versatility of the state space model and demonstrate how many economically relevant models can be represented in this form.

17.2.1 VAR(p) Process

Suppose that $\{Y_t\}$ follows a n-dimensional VAR(p) process given by $\Phi(L)Y_t = Z_t$, respectively, by $Y_t = \Phi_1 Y_{t-1} + \dots + \Phi_p Y_{t-p} + Z_t$, with $Z_t \sim \text{WN}(0, \Sigma)$. Then the companion form of the VAR(p) process (see Sect. 12.2) just represents the state equation (17.1):

$$X_{t+1} = \begin{pmatrix} Y_{t+1} \\ Y_t \\ Y_{t-1} \\ \vdots \\ Y_{t-p+1} \end{pmatrix} = \begin{pmatrix} \Phi_1 & \Phi_2 & \dots & \Phi_{p-1} & \Phi_p \\ I_n & 0 & \dots & 0 & 0 \\ 0 & I_n & \dots & 0 & 0 \\ \vdots & \vdots & \ddots & \vdots & \vdots \\ 0 & 0 & \dots & I_n & 0 \end{pmatrix} \begin{pmatrix} Y_t \\ Y_{t-1} \\ Y_{t-2} \\ \vdots \\ Y_{t-p} \end{pmatrix} + \begin{pmatrix} Z_{t+1} \\ 0 \\ 0 \\ \vdots \\ 0 \end{pmatrix}$$

$$= FX_t + V_{t+1},$$

with $V_{t+1} = (Z'_{t+1}, 0, 0, \dots, 0)'$ and $Q = \begin{pmatrix} \Sigma & 0 \\ 0 & 0 \end{pmatrix}$. The observation equation is just an identity because all components of X_t are observable:

$$Y_t = (\mathrm{I}_n, 0, 0, \dots, 0)X_t = GX_t.$$

Thus, $G = (I_n, 0, 0, \dots, 0)$ and $R = 0$. Assuming that X_t is already mean adjusted, $A = 0$.

17.2.2 ARMA(1,1) Process

The representation of ARMA processes as a state space model is more involved when moving-average terms are present. Suppose that $\{Y_t\}$ is an ARMA(1,1) process defined by the stochastic difference equation $Y_t = \phi Y_{t-1} + Z_t + \theta Z_{t-1}$ with $Z_t \sim \text{WN}(0, \sigma^2)$ and $\phi\theta \neq 0$.

Let $\{X_t\}$ be the AR(1) process defined by the stochastic difference equation $X_t - \phi X_{t-1} = Z_t$, and define the state vector $\mathbf{X}_t$ by $\mathbf{X}_t = (X_t, X_{t-1})'$; then, we can write the observation equation as:

$$Y_t = (1, \theta)\mathbf{X}_t = G\mathbf{X}_t$$

with $R = 0$. The state equation is then

$$\mathbf{X}_{t+1} = \begin{pmatrix} X_{t+1} \\ X_t \end{pmatrix} = \begin{pmatrix} \phi & 0 \\ 1 & 0 \end{pmatrix} \begin{pmatrix} X_t \\ X_{t-1} \end{pmatrix} + \begin{pmatrix} Z_{t+1} \\ 0 \end{pmatrix} = F\mathbf{X}_t + V_{t+1},$$

where $Q = \begin{pmatrix} \sigma^2 & 0 \\ 0 & 0 \end{pmatrix}$. It is easy to verify that the so defined process $\{Y_t\}$ satisfies the stochastic difference equation $Y_t = \phi Y_{t-1} + Z_t + \theta Z_{t-1}$. Indeed $Y_t - \phi Y_{t-1} = (1, \theta)\mathbf{X}_t - \phi(1, \theta)\mathbf{X}_{t-1} = X_t + \theta X_{t-1} - \phi X_{t-1} - \theta\phi X_{t-2} = (X_t - \phi X_{t-1}) + \theta(X_{t-1} - \phi X_{t-2}) = Z_t + \theta Z_{t-1}$.

If $|\phi| < 1$, the state equation defines a causal process $\{X_t\}$ so that the unique stationary solution is given by Eq. (17.3). This implies a stationary solution for $\{Y_t\}$ too. It is thus easy to verify whether this solution equals the unique solution of the ARMA stochastic difference equation.

The state space representation of an ARMA model is not unique. An alternative representation in the case of a causal system is given by:

$$X_{t+1} = \phi X_t + (\phi + \theta)Z_t = FX_t + V_{t+1}$$
$$Y_t = X_t + Z_t = X_t + W_t.$$

Note that in this representation the dimension of the state vector is reduced from two to one. Moreover, the two disturbances $V_{t+1} = (\phi + \theta)Z_t$ and $W_t = Z_t$ are perfectly correlated.

17.2.3 ARMA(p,q) Process

It is straightforward to extend the above representation to ARMA(p,q) models.[5] Let $\{Y_t\}$ be defined by the following stochastic difference equation:

$$\Phi(\mathrm{L})Y_t = \Theta(\mathrm{L})Z_t \qquad \text{with } Z_t \sim \mathrm{WN}(0, \sigma^2) \text{ and } \phi_p\theta_q \neq 0.$$

Define r as $r = \max\{p, q + 1\}$ and set $\phi_j = 0$ for $j > p$ and $\theta_j = 0$ for $j > q$. Then, we can set up the following state space representation with state vector $\mathbf{X}_t$ and observation equation

$$Y_t = (1, \theta_1, \ldots, \theta_{r-1})\mathbf{X}_t$$

where the state vector equals $\mathbf{X}_t = (X_t, \ldots, X_{t-r+2}, X_{t-r+1})'$ and where $\{X_t\}$ follows an AR(p) process $\Phi(\mathrm{L})X_t = Z_t$. The AR(p) process can be transformed into companion form to arrive at the state equation:

$$\mathbf{X}_{t+1} = \begin{pmatrix} \phi_1 & \phi_2 & \ldots & \phi_{r-1} & \phi_r \\ 1 & 0 & \ldots & 0 & 0 \\ 0 & 1 & \ldots & 0 & 0 \\ \vdots & \vdots & \ddots & \vdots & \vdots \\ 0 & 0 & \ldots & 1 & 0 \end{pmatrix} \mathbf{X}_t + \begin{pmatrix} Z_t \\ 0 \\ 0 \\ \vdots \\ 0 \end{pmatrix}.$$

[5] See also Exercise 17.2.

17.2.4 Missing Observations

The state space approach is best suited to deal with missing observations. However, in this situation, the coefficient matrices are no longer constant but time-varying. Consider the following simple example of an AR(1) process for which we have only observations for the periods $t = 1, \ldots, 100$ and $t = 102, \ldots, 200$, but not for period $t = 101$, which is missing. This situation can be represented in state space form as follows:

$$X_{t+1} = \phi X_t + Z_t$$
$$Y_t = G_t X_t + W_t$$
$$G_t = \begin{cases} 1, & t = 1, \ldots, 100, 102, \ldots, 200; \\ 0, & t = 101. \end{cases}$$
$$R_t = \begin{cases} 0, & t = 1, \ldots, 100, 102, \ldots, 200; \\ c > 0, & t = 101. \end{cases}$$

This means that $W_t = 0$ and that $Y_t = X_t$ for all t except for $t = 101$. For the missing observation, we have $G_{101} = Y_{101} = 0$. The variance for this observation is set arbitrarily to $R_{101} = c > 0$.

The same idea can be used to obtain quarterly data when only yearly data are available. This problem typically arises in statistical offices that have to produce, for example, quarterly GDP data from yearly observations incorporating quarterly information from indicator variables (see Sect. 17.5.1). More detailed analysis for the case of missing data can be found in Harvey and Pierse (1984) and Brockwell and Davis (1991, Chapter 12.3).

17.2.5 Time-Varying Coefficients

Consider a regression model with time-varying parameter vector β_t:

$$Y_t = x_t' \beta_t + W_t \tag{17.5}$$

where Y_t is an observed dependent variable, x_t is a K-vector of exogenous regressors, and W_t is a white noise error term. Depending on the specification of the evolution of β_t, several models have been proposed in the literature:

Hildreth-Houck : $\beta_t = \bar{\beta} + v_t$

Harvey-Phillips: $\beta_t - \bar{\beta} = F(\beta_t - \bar{\beta}) + v_t$

Cooley-Prescott: $\beta_t = \beta_t^p + v_{1t}$

$$\beta_t^p = \beta_{t-1}^p + v_{2t}$$

where v_t, v_{1t}, and v_{2t} are white noise error terms. In the first specification, proposed originally proposed by Hildreth and Houck (1968), the parameter vector is in each period just a random variable with mean $\bar{\beta}$ and variance given by the variance of v_t. Departures from the mean are seen as being only of a transitory nature. In the specification by Harvey and Phillips (1982), assuming that all eigenvalues of F are strictly smaller than one in absolute value, the parameter vector is a mean reverting stationary VAR process of order one. In this case, the departures from the mean can have a longer duration depending on the eigenvalues of F. The last specification due to Cooley and Prescott (1973, 1976) views the parameter vector as being subject to transitory and permanent shifts. Whereas shifts in v_{1t} have only a transitory effect on β_t, movements in v_{2t} result in permanent effects.

In the Cooley-Prescott specification, for example, the state is given by $X_t = (\beta_t', \beta_t^{p\prime})'$, and the state equation can be written as:

$$X_{t+1} = \begin{pmatrix} \beta_{t+1} \\ \beta_{t+1}^p \end{pmatrix} = \underbrace{\begin{pmatrix} 0 & 1 \\ 0 & 1 \end{pmatrix}}_{=F} \begin{pmatrix} \beta_t \\ \beta_t^p \end{pmatrix} + \begin{pmatrix} 1 & 1 \\ 0 & 1 \end{pmatrix} \begin{pmatrix} v_{1t} \\ v_{2t} \end{pmatrix}$$

The observation equation then becomes:

$$Y_t = y_t = \begin{pmatrix} x_t \\ 0 \end{pmatrix}' X_t + W_t$$

Thus, $A = 0$ and $G_t = (x_t', 0)$. Note that this an example of a state space model with time-varying coefficients. In Sect. 18.3, we will discuss time-varying coefficient models in the context of VAR models.

17.2.6 Structural Time Series Analysis

An important application of the state space representation in economics is the decomposition of a given time series into a trend, cyclical, seasonal, and irregular component. This type of analysis is usually coined structural time series analysis (see Harvey, 1989; Mills, 2003) and is part of the classical Wiener-Kolmogorov filter theory. Consider, for example, the additive decomposition of a time series $\{Y_t\}$ into a trend T_t, a seasonal component S_t, a cyclical component $\{C_t\}$, and an irregular or cyclical component W_t:

$$Y_t = T_t + S_t + C_t + W_t.$$

The above equation relates the observed time series to its unobserved components and is called the *basic structural model* (BSM) (Harvey, 1989).

The state space representation is derived in several steps. Consider first the case with no seasonal and no cyclical component. In this approach, the trend is typically viewed as a random walk with time-varying drift δ_{t-1}:

$$T_t = \delta_{t-1} + T_{t-1} + \varepsilon_t, \qquad \varepsilon_t \sim \mathrm{WN}(0, \sigma_\varepsilon^2)$$

$$\delta_t = \delta_{t-1} + \xi_t, \qquad \xi_t \sim \mathrm{WN}(0, \sigma_\xi^2).$$

The second equation models the drift as a random walk. The two disturbances $\{\varepsilon_t\}$ and $\{\xi_t\}$ are assumed to be uncorrelated with each other and with $\{W_t\}$. Defining the state vector $X_t^{(T)}$ as $X_t^{(T)} = (T_t, \delta_t)'$, the state and the observation equations become:

$$X_{t+1}^{(T)} = \begin{pmatrix} T_{t+1} \\ \delta_{t+1} \end{pmatrix} = \begin{pmatrix} 1 & 1 \\ 0 & 1 \end{pmatrix} \begin{pmatrix} T_t \\ \delta_t \end{pmatrix} + \begin{pmatrix} \varepsilon_{t+1} \\ \xi_{t+1} \end{pmatrix} = F^{(T)} X_t^{(T)} + V_{t+1}^{(T)}$$

$$Y_t = (1, 0) X_t^{(T)} + W_t$$

with $W_t \sim \mathrm{WN}(0, \sigma_W^2)$. This representation is called the local linear trend (LLT) model and implies that $\{Y_t\}$ follows an ARIMA(0,2,2) process (see Exercise 17.6.1).

In the special case of a constant drift equal to δ, $\sigma_\xi^2 = 0$, and we have $\Delta Y_t = \delta + \varepsilon_t + W_t - W_{t-1}$. $\{\Delta Y_t\}$ therefore follows a MA(1) process with $\rho(1) = -\sigma_W^2/(\sigma_\varepsilon^2 + 2\sigma_W^2) = -(2+\kappa)^{-1}$, where $\kappa = \sigma_\varepsilon^2/\sigma_W^2$ is called the signal-to-noise ratio. Note that the first-order autocorrelation is necessarily negative. Thus, this model is not suited for time series with positive first-order autocorrelation in its first differences.

The seasonal component is characterized by two conditions $S_t = S_{t-d}$ and $\sum_{t=1}^{d} S_t = 0$, where d denotes the frequency of the data.[6] Given starting values $S_1, S_0, S_{-1}, \ldots, S_{-d+3}$, the subsequent values can be computed recursively as:

$$S_{t+1} = -S_t - \cdots - S_{t-d+2} + \eta_{t+1}, \qquad t = 1, 2, \ldots$$

where a noise $\eta_t \sim \mathrm{WN}(0, \sigma_\eta^2)$ is taken into account.[7] The state vector related to the seasonal component, $X_t^{(S)}$, is defined as $X_t^{(S)} = (S_t, S_{t-1}, \ldots, S_{t-d+2})'$, which gives the state equation

$$X_{t+1}^{(S)} = \begin{pmatrix} -1 & -1 & \ldots & -1 & -1 \\ 1 & 0 & \ldots & 0 & 0 \\ 0 & 1 & \ldots & 0 & 0 \\ \vdots & \vdots & \ddots & \vdots & \vdots \\ 0 & 0 & \ldots & 1 & 0 \end{pmatrix} X_t^{(S)} + \begin{pmatrix} \eta_{t+1} \\ 0 \\ \vdots \\ 0 \\ 0 \end{pmatrix} = F^{(S)} X_t^{(S)} + V_{t+1}^{(S)}$$

with $Q^{(S)} = \mathrm{diag}(\sigma_\eta^2, 0, \ldots, 0)$.

[6] Four in the case of quarterly and twelve in the case of monthly observations.

[7] Alternative seasonal models can be found in Harvey (1989) and Hylleberg (1986).

Combining the trend and the seasonal model to an overall model with state vector X_t given by $X_t = \left(X_t^{(T)\prime}, X_t^{(S)\prime}\right)'$, we arrive at the state equation:

$$X_{t+1} = \begin{pmatrix} F^{(T)} & 0 \\ 0 & F^{(S)} \end{pmatrix} X_t + \begin{pmatrix} V_{t+1}^{(T)} \\ V_{t+1}^{(S)} \end{pmatrix} = FX_t + V_{t+1}$$

with $Q = \text{diag}(\sigma_\varepsilon^2, \sigma_\delta^2, \sigma_\eta^2, 0, \ldots, 0)$. The observation equation then becomes:

$$Y_t = \begin{pmatrix} 1 & 0 & 1 & 0 & \ldots & 0 \end{pmatrix} X_t + W_t$$

with $R = \sigma_W^2$.

Finally, we can add a cyclical component $\{C_t\}$, which is modeled as a harmonic process (see Sect. 6.2) with frequency λ_C, respectively, periodicity $2\pi/\lambda_C$:

$$C_t = A\cos(\lambda_C t) + B\sin(\lambda_C t)$$

Following Harvey (1989, p.39), we let the parameters A and B evolve over time by introducing the recursion

$$\begin{pmatrix} C_{t+1} \\ C_{t+1}^* \end{pmatrix} = \rho \begin{pmatrix} \cos\lambda_C & \sin\lambda_C \\ -\sin\lambda_C & \cos\lambda_C \end{pmatrix} \begin{pmatrix} C_t \\ C_t^* \end{pmatrix} + \begin{pmatrix} V_{1,t+1}^{(C)} \\ V_{2,t+1}^{(C)} \end{pmatrix}$$

where $C_0 = A$ and $C_0^* = B$ and where $\{C_t^*\}$ is an auxiliary process. The dampening factor ρ allows for additional flexibility in the specification. $\{V_{1,t}^{(C)}\}$ and $\{V_{2,t}^{(C)}\}$ are two mutually uncorrelated white-noise processes. It is instructive to examine the spectral density (see Sect. 6.1) of the cyclical component in Fig. 17.2. It can be shown (see Exercise 17.6.2) that $\{C_t\}$ follows an ARMA(2,1) process.

The cyclical component can be incorporated into the state space model above by augmenting the state vector X_{t+1} by the cyclical components C_{t+1} and C_{t+1}^* and the error term V_{t+1} by $\{V_{1,t+1}^{(C)}\}$ and $\{V_{2,t+1}^{(C)}\}$. The observations equation has to be amended accordingly. Section 17.5.2 presents an empirical application of this approach.

17.2.7 Dynamic Factor models

Dynamic factor models are an interesting approach when it comes to modeling simultaneously a large cross-section of times series. The concept was introduced into macroeconomics by Sargent and Sims (1977) and was then developed further and popularized by Quah and Sargent (1993), Reichlin (2003) and Breitung and Eickmeier (2006), among others. The idea is to view each time series Y_{it}, $i = 1, \ldots, n$, as the sum of a linear combination of some joint unobserved factors

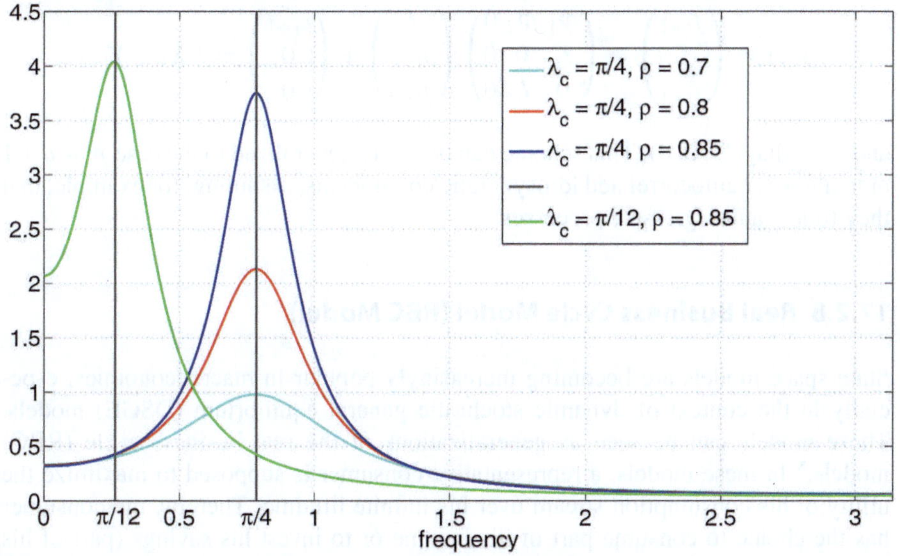

Fig. 17.2 Spectral density of the cyclical component for different values of λ_C and ρ

$f_t = (f_{1t}, \dots, f_{rt})'$ and an idiosyncratic component $\{W_{it}\}$, $i = 1, \dots n$. Dynamic factor models are particularly effective when the number of factors r is small compared to the number of time series n. In practice, several hundred time series are related to a handful factors. In matrix notation, we can write the observation equation for the dynamic factor model as follows:

$$Y_t = \Lambda_0 f_t + \Lambda_1 f_{t-1} + \cdots + \Lambda_q f_{t-q} + W_t$$

where Λ_i and $i = 0, 1, \dots, q$ are $n \times r$ matrices. The state vector X_t equals $(f_t', \dots, f_{t-q}')'$ if we assume that the idiosyncratic component is white noise, i.e., $W_t = (W_{1t}, \dots, W_{nt})' \sim \text{WN}(0, R)$. The observation equation can then be written compactly as:

$$Y_t = GX_t + W_t$$

where $G = (\Lambda_0, \Lambda_1, \dots, \Lambda_q)$. Usually, we assume that R is a diagonal matrix. The correlation between the different time series is captured exclusively by the joint factors.

The state equation depends on the assumed dynamics of the factors. One possibility is to model $\{f_t\}$ as a VAR(p) process with $\Phi(\text{L}) f_t = e_t$, $e_t \sim \text{WN}(0, \Sigma)$, and $p \le q + 1$, so we can use the state space representation of the VAR(p) process from above. For the case $p = 2$ and $q = 2$, we get:

$$X_{t+1} = \begin{pmatrix} f_{t+1} \\ f_t \\ f_{t-1} \end{pmatrix} = \begin{pmatrix} \Phi_1 & \Phi_2 & 0 \\ I_r & 0 & 0 \\ 0 & I_r & 0 \end{pmatrix} \begin{pmatrix} f_t \\ f_{t-1} \\ f_{t-2} \end{pmatrix} + \begin{pmatrix} e_{t+1} \\ 0 \\ 0 \end{pmatrix} = FX_t + V_{t+1}$$

and $Q = \text{diag}(\Sigma, 0, 0)$. This scheme can be easily generalized to the case $p > q+1$ or to allow for autocorrelated idiosyncratic components, assuming, for example, that they follow autoregressive processes.

17.2.8 Real Business Cycle Model (RBC Model)

State space models are becoming increasingly popular in macroeconomics, especially in the context of dynamic stochastic general equilibrium (DSGE) models. These models can be seen as generalizations of the real business cycle (RBC) models.[8] In these models, a representative consumer is supposed to maximize the utility of his consumption stream over his infinite lifetime. Thereby, the consumer has the choice to consume part of his income or to invest his savings (part of his income that is not consumed) at the market rate of interest. These savings can be used as a mean to finance investment projects, which increase the economy-wide capital stock. The increased capital stock then allows for increased production in the future. The production process itself is subject to a random shocks called technology shocks.

The solution of this optimization problem is a nonlinear dynamic system, which determines the capital stock and consumption in every period. Its local behavior can be investigated by linearizing the system around its steady state. This equation can then be interpreted as the state equation of the system. The parameters of this equation F and Q are related, typically in a nonlinear way, to the parameters describing the utility and the production function as well as the process of technology shocks. Thus, the state equation summarizes the behavior of the theoretical model.

The parameters of the state equation can then be estimated by relating the state vector, given by the capital stock and the state of the technology, via the observation equation to some observable variables, like real GDP, consumption, investment, or the interest rate. This then completes the state space representation of the model, which can be analyzed and estimated using the tools presented in Sect. 17.4.[9]

[8] Prototypical models can be found in King et al. (1988) or Woodford (2003). Canova (2007) and DeJong and Dave (2007) present a good introduction to the analysis of DSGE models.

[9] See Sargent (2004) or Fernández-Villaverde et al. (2007) for systematic treatment of state space models in the context of macroeconomic models. In this literature, the use of Bayesian methods is widespread (see An & Schorfheide, 2007; DeJong & Dave, 2007).

17.3 Filtering and Smoothing

As we have seen, the state space model provides a very flexible framework for a wide array of applications. We therefore want to develop a set of tools to handle this kind of models in terms of interpretation and estimation. In this section, we will analyze the problem of inferring the unobserved state from the data given the parameters of the model. In Sect. 17.4, we will then investigate the estimation of the parameters by maximum likelihood.

In many cases, the state of the system is not or only partially observable. It is therefore of interest to infer from the data $Y_1, Y_2, \ldots, Y_T$ the state vector X_t. Three types of problems can be distinguished depending on the information used:

(i) *Prediction* problem: estimation of X_t from $Y_1, \ldots, Y_{t-1}$
(ii) *Filtering* problem: estimation of X_t from $Y_1, \ldots, Y_{t-1}, Y_t$
(iii) *Smoothing* problem: estimation of X_t from $Y_1, \ldots, Y_T$

For the ease of exposition, we will assume that the disturbances V_t and W_t are normally distributed. The recursive nature of the state equation implies that $X_t = F^{t-1}X_1 + \sum_{j=0}^{t-2} F^j V_{t-j}$. Therefore, X_t is also normally distributed for all t, if X_1 is normally distributed. From the observation equation, we can infer also that Y_t is normally distributed, because it is the sum of two normally distributed random variables $A + GX_t$ and W_t. Thus, under these assumptions, the vector $(X_1', \ldots, X_T', Y_1', \ldots, Y_T')'$ is jointly normally distributed:

$$\begin{pmatrix} X_1 \\ \vdots \\ X_T \\ Y_1 \\ \vdots \\ Y_T \end{pmatrix} \sim \mathrm{N}\left(\begin{pmatrix} 0 \\ \mu_Y \end{pmatrix}, \begin{pmatrix} \Gamma_X & \Gamma_{YX} \\ \Gamma_{XY} & \Gamma_Y \end{pmatrix}\right)$$

where the covariance matrices $\Gamma_X, \Gamma_{YX}, \Gamma_{XY}$ and Γ_Y can be retrieved from the model given the parameters.

For the understanding of the rest of this section, the following theorem is essential (see standard textbooks, like Amemiya, 1994; Greene, 2008; Anderson, 2003).

Theorem 17.1 *Let Z be a n-dimensional normally distributed random variable with $Z \sim \mathrm{N}(\mu, \Sigma)$. Consider the partitioned vector $Z = (Z_1', Z_2')'$, where Z_1 and Z_2 are of dimensions $n_1 \geq 1$ and $n_2 \geq 1$, $n = n_1 + n_2$, respectively. The corresponding partitioning of the covariance matrix Σ is*

$$\Sigma = \begin{pmatrix} \Sigma_{11} & \Sigma_{12} \\ \Sigma_{21} & \Sigma_{22} \end{pmatrix}$$

where $\Sigma_{11} = \mathbb{V}Z_1$, $\Sigma_{22} = \mathbb{V}Z_2$, *and* $\Sigma_{12} = \Sigma_{21}' = \text{cov}(Z_1, Z_2) = \mathbb{E}(Z_1 - \mathbb{E}Z_1)'(Z_2 - \mathbb{E}Z_2)$. *Then the partitioned vectors* Z_1 *and* Z_2 *are normally distributed. Moreover, the conditional distribution of* Z_1 *given* Z_2 *is also normal with mean and variance*

$$\mathbb{E}(Z_1|Z_2) = \mathbb{E}Z_1 + \Sigma_{12}\Sigma_{22}^{-1}(Z_2 - \mathbb{E}Z_2),$$
$$\mathbb{V}(Z_1|Z_2) = \Sigma_{11} - \Sigma_{12}\Sigma_{22}^{-1}\Sigma_{21}.$$

This formula can be directly applied to figure out the mean and the variance of the state vector given the observations. Setting $Z_1 = (X_1', \ldots, X_t')'$, the predicted values are obtained if $Z_2 = (Y_1', \ldots, Y_{t-1}')'$; the filtered values are obtained if $Z_2 = (Y_1', \ldots, Y_t')'$; the smoothed values are obtained if $Z_2 = (Y_1', \ldots, Y_T')'$.

AR(1) Process with Measurement Errors

We illustrate the above ideas by analyzing a univariate AR(1) process with measurement errors:[10]

$$X_{t+1} = \phi X_t + v_{t+1}, \qquad v_t \sim \text{IID}\,\text{N}(0, \sigma_v^2)$$
$$Y_t = X_t + w_t, \qquad w_t \sim \text{IID}\,\text{N}(0, \sigma_w^2).$$

For simplicity, we assume $|\phi| < 1$. Suppose that we only have observations Y_1 and Y_2 at our disposal. The joint distribution of $(X_1, X_2, Y_1, Y_2)'$ is normal. The covariances can be computed by applying the methods discussed in Chap. 2:

$$\begin{pmatrix} X_1 \\ X_2 \\ Y_1 \\ Y_2 \end{pmatrix} \sim \text{N}\left(\begin{pmatrix} 0 \\ 0 \\ 0 \\ 0 \end{pmatrix}, \frac{\sigma_v^2}{1-\phi^2}\begin{pmatrix} 1 & \phi & 1 & \phi \\ \phi & 1 & \phi & 1 \\ 1 & \phi & 1 + \frac{\sigma_w^2(1-\phi^2)}{\sigma_v^2} & \phi \\ \phi & 1 & \phi & 1 + \frac{\sigma_w^2(1-\phi^2)}{\sigma_v^2} \end{pmatrix}\right)$$

The smoothed values are obtained by applying the formula from Theorem 17.1:

$$\mathbb{E}\left(\begin{pmatrix} X_1 \\ X_2 \end{pmatrix} \middle| Y_1, Y_2\right) =$$
$$\frac{1}{\left(1 + \frac{\sigma_w^2(1-\phi^2)}{\sigma_v^2}\right)^2 - \phi^2}\begin{pmatrix} 1 & \phi \\ \phi & 1 \end{pmatrix}\begin{pmatrix} 1 + \frac{\sigma_w^2(1-\phi^2)}{\sigma_v^2} & -\phi \\ -\phi & 1 + \frac{\sigma_w^2(1-\phi^2)}{\sigma_v^2} \end{pmatrix}\begin{pmatrix} Y_1 \\ Y_2 \end{pmatrix}$$

---

[10] Sargent (1989) provides an interesting application showing the implications of measurement errors in macroeconomic models.

Note that for the last observation, Y_2 in our case, the filtered and the smoothed values are the same. For X_1, the filtered value is

$$\mathbb{E}(X_1|Y_1) = \frac{1}{1 + \frac{\sigma_w^2(1-\phi^2)}{\sigma_v^2}} Y_1.$$

An intuition for this result can be obtained by considering some special cases. For $\phi = 0$, the observations are not correlated over time. The filtered value for X_1 therefore corresponds to the smoothed one. This value lies between zero, the unconditional mean of X_1, and Y_1 with the variance ratio σ_w^2/σ_v^2 delivering the weights: the smaller the variance of the measurement error, the closer the filtered value is to Y_1. This conclusion holds also in general. If the variance of the measurement error is relatively large, the observations do not deliver much information so that the filtered and the smoothed values are close to the unconditional mean.

For large systems, the method suggested by Theorem 17.1 may run into numerical problems due to the inversion of the covariance matrix of Y, Σ_{22}. This matrix can become rather large as it is of dimension $nT \times nT$. Fortunately, there exist recursive solutions to this problem known as the Kalman filter, respectively, the Kalman smoother.

17.3.1 The Kalman Filter

The Kalman filter circumvents the problem of inverting a large $nT \times nT$ matrix by making use of the Markov property of the system (see Remark 17.4). The distribution of X_t given the observations up to period t can thereby be computed recursively from the distribution of the state in period $t-1$ given the information available up to period $t-1$. Starting from some initial distribution in period 0, we can in this way obtain in T steps the distribution of the state variable for all time periods t. In each step, only an $n \times n$ matrix must be inverted. To describe the procedure in detail, we introduce the following notation customary in the literature:

$$\mathbb{E}(X_t|Y_1, \ldots, Y_h) = X_{t|h}$$
$$\mathbb{V}(X_t|Y_1, \ldots, Y_h) = P_{t|h}.$$

Suppose, we have already determined the distribution of X_t conditional on the observations $Y_1, \ldots, Y_t$. Because we are operating in a framework of normally distributed random variables, the distribution is completely characterized by its conditional mean $X_{t|t}$ and variance $P_{t|t}$. The goal is to carry forward these entities to obtain $X_{t+1|t+1}$ and $P_{t+1|t+1}$ having observed an additional data point Y_{t+1}. This problem can be decomposed into a *forecasting* and an *updating* step.

Step 1: Forecasting Step The state equation and the assumption about the disturbance term V_{t+1} imply:

$$X_{t+1|t} = FX_{t|t} \qquad (17.6)$$

$$P_{t+1|t} = FP_{t|t}F' + Q$$

The observation equation then allows to compute a forecast of Y_{t+1}, where we assume for simplicity that $A = 0$:

$$Y_{t+1|t} = GX_{t+1|t} \qquad (17.7)$$

Step 2: Updating Step In this step, the additional information coming from the observation Y_{t+1} is processed to update the conditional distribution of the state vector. The joint conditional distribution of $(X'_{t+1}, Y'_{t+1})'$ given $Y_1, \ldots, Y_t$ is

$$\begin{pmatrix} X_{t+1} \\ Y_{t+1} \end{pmatrix} \Bigg| Y_1, \ldots, Y_t \sim \mathrm{N}\left(\begin{pmatrix} X_{t+1|t} \\ Y_{t+1|t} \end{pmatrix}, \begin{pmatrix} P_{t+1|t} & P_{t+1|t}G' \\ GP_{t+1|t} & GP_{t+1|t}G' + R \end{pmatrix} \right)$$

As all elements of the distribution are available from the forecasting step, we can again apply Theorem 17.1 to get the distribution of the filtered state vector at time $t+1$:

$$X_{t+1|t+1} = X_{t+1|t} + P_{t+1|t}G'(GP_{t+1|t}G' + R)^{-1}(Y_{t+1} - Y_{t+1|t}) \qquad (17.8)$$

$$P_{t+1|t+1} = P_{t+1|t} - P_{t+1|t}G'(GP_{t+1|t}G' + R)^{-1}GP_{t+1|t} \qquad (17.9)$$

where we replace $X_{t+1|t}$, $P_{t+1|t}$, and $Y_{t+1|t}$ by $FX_{t|t}$, $FP_{t|t}F' + Q$, and $GFX_{t|t}$, respectively, which have been obtained from the forecasting step.

Starting from given values for $X_{0|0}$ and $P_{0|0}$, we can therefore iteratively compute $X_{t|t}$ and $P_{t|t}$ for all $t = 1, 2, \ldots, T$. Only the information from the last period is necessary at each step. Inserting Eq. (17.8) into Eq. (17.6), we obtain the forecasting equation:

$$X_{t+1|t} = FX_{t|t-1} + FP_{t|t-1}G'(GP_{t|t-1}G' + R)^{-1}(Y_t - GX_{t|t-1})$$

where the matrix

$$K_t = FP_{t|t-1}G'(GP_{t|t-1}G' + R)^{-1}$$

is known as the *(Kalman) gain matrix*. It prescribes how the innovation $Y_t - Y_{t|t-1} = Y_t - GX_{t|t-1}$ leads to an update of the predicted state.

Initializing the Algorithm It remains to determine how to initialize the recursion, in particular, how to set the starting values for $X_{0|0}$ and $P_{0|0}$. If X_t is stationary and causal with respect to V_t, the state equation has the solution $X_0 = \sum_{j=0}^{\infty} F^j V_{t-j}$. Thus,

$$X_{0|0} = \mathbb{E}(X_0) = 0$$
$$P_{0|0} = \mathbb{V}(X_0)$$

where $P_{0|0}$ solves the equation (see Sect. 12.4)

$$P_{0|0} = FP_{0|0}F' + Q.$$

According to Eq. (12.4), the solution of the above matrix equation is:

$$\text{vec}(P_{0|0}) = [I - F \otimes F]^{-1}\text{vec}(Q).$$

If the process is not stationary, we can set $X_{0|0}$ to zero and $P_{0|0}$ to infinity. In practice, a very large number is sufficient.

17.3.2 The Kalman Smoother

The Kalman filter determines the distribution of the state at time t given the information available up to this time. In many instances, we want, however, to make an optimal forecast of the state given all the information available, i.e., the whole sample. Thus, we want to determine $X_{t|T}$ and $P_{t|T}$. The Kalman filter determines the smoothed distribution for $t = T$, i.e., $X_{T|T}$ and $P_{T|T}$. The idea of the Kalman smoother is again to determine the smoothed distribution in a recursive manner. For this purpose, we let the recursion run backward. Starting with the last observation in period $t = T$, we proceed back in time by letting t take successively the values $t = T - 1, T - 2, \ldots$ until the first observation in period $t = 1$.

Using again the linearity of the equations and the normality assumption,

$$\begin{pmatrix} X_t \\ X_{t+1} \end{pmatrix} \Bigg| Y_1, Y_2, \ldots, Y_t \sim \text{N}\left(\begin{pmatrix} X_{t|t} \\ FX_{t|t} \end{pmatrix}, \begin{pmatrix} P_{t|t} & P_{t|t}F' \\ FP_{t|t} & P_{t+1|t} \end{pmatrix}\right)$$

This implies that

$$\mathbb{E}(X_t|Y_1, \ldots, Y_t, X_{t+1}) = X_{t|t} + P_{t|t}F'P_{t+1|t}^{-1}(X_{t+1} - X_{t+1|t}).$$

The above mean is only conditional on all information available up to time t and on the information at time $t + 1$. The Markov property implies that this mean also incorporates the information from the observations $Y_{t+1}, \ldots, Y_T$. Thus, we have:

$$\begin{aligned}\mathbb{E}(X_t|Y_1, \ldots, Y_T, X_{t+1}) &= \mathbb{E}(X_t|Y_1, \ldots, Y_t, X_{t+1}) \\ &= X_{t|t} + P_{t|t}F'P_{t+1|t}^{-1}(X_{t+1} - X_{t+1|t})\end{aligned}$$

Applying the law of iterated expectations or means (see, e.g., Amemiya, 1994, p. 78), we can derive $X_{t|T}$:

$$\begin{aligned} X_{t|T} &= \mathbb{E}(X_t|Y_1,\ldots,Y_T) = \mathbb{E}(\mathbb{E}(X_t|Y_1,\ldots,Y_T,X_{t+1})|Y_1,\ldots,Y_T) \\ &= \mathbb{E}(X_{t|t} + P_{t|t}F'P_{t+1|t}^{-1}(X_{t+1} - X_{t+1|t})|Y_1,\ldots,Y_T) \\ &= X_{t|t} + P_{t|t}F'P_{t+1|t}^{-1}(X_{t+1|T} - X_{t+1|t}). \end{aligned} \tag{17.10}$$

The algorithm can now be implemented as follows. In the first step, compute $X_{T-1|T}$ according to Eq. (17.10) as

$$X_{T-1|T} = X_{T-1|T-1} + P_{T-1|T-1}F'P_{T|T-1}^{-1}(X_{T|T} - X_{T|T-1}).$$

All entities on the right-hand side can readily be computed by applying the Kalman filter. Having found $X_{T-1|T}$, we can again use Eq. (17.10) for $t = T-2$ to evaluate $X_{T-2|T}$:

$$X_{T-2|T} = X_{T-2|T-2} + P_{T-2|T-2}F'P_{T-1|T-2}^{-1}(X_{T-1|T} - X_{T-1|T-2}).$$

Proceeding backward through the sample, we can derive a complete sequence of smoothed states $X_{T|T}, X_{T-1|T}, X_{T-2|T}, \ldots, X_{1|T}$. These calculations are based on the computations of $X_{t|t}$, $X_{t+1|t}$, $P_{t|t}$, and $P_{t+1|t}$, which have already been obtained from the Kalman filter. The smoothed covariance matrix $P_{t|T}$ is given as (see Hamilton, 1994a, Section 13.6):

$$P_{t|T} = P_{t|t} + P_{t|t}FP_{t+1|t}^{-1}(P_{t+1|T} - P_{t+1|t})P_{t+1|t}^{-1}F'P_{t|t}.$$

Thus, we can compute also the smoothed variance with the aid of the values already determined by the Kalman filter.

AR(1) Process with Measurement Errors (Continued)

We continue our illustrative example of an AR(1) process with measurement errors and just two observations. First, we determine the filtered values for the state vector with the aid of the Kalman filter. To initialize the process, we have to assign a distribution to X_0. For simplicity, we assume that $|\phi| < 1$ so that it makes sense to assign the stationary distribution of the process as the distribution for X_0:

$$X_0 \sim \mathrm{N}\left(0, \frac{\sigma_V^2}{1-\phi^2}\right)$$

Then, we compute the forecasting step as the first step of the filter (see Eq. (17.6)):

$$X_{1|0} = \phi X_{0|0} = 0$$

$$P_{1|0} = \phi^2 \frac{\sigma_v^2}{1-\phi^2} + \sigma_v^2 = \frac{\sigma_v^2}{1-\phi^2}$$

$$Y_{1|0} = 0.$$

$P_{1|0}$ was computed by the recursive formula from the previous section but is, of course, equal to the unconditional variance. For the updating step, we get from Eqs. (17.8) and (17.9):

$$X_{1|1} = \left(\frac{\sigma_v^2}{1-\phi^2}\right)\left(\frac{\sigma_v^2}{1-\phi^2} + \sigma_w^2\right)^{-1} Y_1 = \frac{1}{1 + \frac{\sigma_w^2(1-\phi^2)}{\sigma_v^2}} Y_1$$

$$P_{1|1} = \left(\frac{\sigma_v^2}{1-\phi^2}\right) - \left(\frac{\sigma_v^2}{1-\phi^2}\right)^2 \left(\frac{\sigma_v^2}{1-\phi^2} + \sigma_w^2\right)^{-1}$$

$$= \frac{\sigma_v^2}{1-\phi^2}\left(1 - \frac{1}{1 + \frac{\sigma_w^2(1-\phi^2)}{\sigma_v^2}}\right)$$

These two results are then used to calculate the next iteration of the algorithm. This will give the filtered values for $t = 2$, which would correspond to the smoothed values because we just have two observations. The forecasting step is:

$$X_{2|1} = \frac{\phi}{1 + \frac{\sigma_w^2(1-\phi^2)}{\sigma_v^2}} Y_1$$

$$P_{2|1} = \frac{\phi^2\sigma_v^2}{1-\phi^2}\left(1 - \frac{1}{1 + \frac{\sigma_w^2(1-\phi^2)}{\sigma_v^2}}\right) + \sigma_v^2$$

Next we perform the updating step to calculate $X_{2|2}$ and $P_{2|2}$. It is easy to verify that this leads to the same results as in the first part of this example.

An interesting special case is obtained when $\phi = 1$ so that the state variable is a simple random walk. In this case, the unconditional variance of X_t and consequently also of Y_t are no longer finite. As mentioned previously, we can initialize the Kalman filter by $X_{0|0} = 0$ and $P_{0|0} = \infty$. This implies:

$$Y_{1|0} = X_{1|0} = X_{0|0} = 0$$

$$P_{1|0} = P_{0|0} + \sigma_V^2 = \infty.$$

Inserting this result in the updating equations (17.8) and (17.9), we arrive at:

$$X_{1|1} = \frac{P_{1|0}}{P_{1|0} + \sigma_W^2}(Y_1 - Y_{1|0}) = \frac{P_{0|0} + \sigma_V^2}{P_{0|0} + \sigma_V^2 + \sigma_W^2} Y_1$$

$$P_{1|1} = P_{1|0} - \frac{P_{1|0}^2}{P_{1|0} + \sigma_W^2} = (P_{0|0} + \sigma_V^2)\left(1 - \frac{P_{1|0}}{P_{1|0} + \sigma_W^2}\right) = \frac{(P_{0|0} + \sigma_V^2)\sigma_W^2}{P_{0|0} + \sigma_V^2 + \sigma_W^2}.$$

Letting $P_{0|0}$ go to infinity leads to:

$$X_{1|1} = Y_1$$
$$P_{1|1} = \sigma_W^2.$$

Thus, the filtered variance is finite for $t = 1$ although $P_{1|0}$ was infinite.

17.4 Estimation of State Space Models

Up to now, we have assumed that the parameters of the system are known and that only the state is unknown. In most economic applications, however, also the parameters are unknown and have therefore to be estimated from the data. One big advantage of the state space models is that they provide an integrated approach to forecasting, smoothing, and estimation. In particular, the Kalman filter turns out to be an efficient and quick way to compute the likelihood function. Thus, it seems natural to estimate the parameters of state space models by the method of maximum likelihood.

17.4.1 The Likelihood Function

The joint unconditional density of the observations $(Y_1', \ldots, Y_T')'$ can be factorized into the product of conditional densities as follows:

$$\begin{aligned} f(Y_1, \ldots, Y_T) &= f(Y_T | Y_1, \ldots, Y_{T-1}) f(Y_1, \ldots, Y_{T-1}) \\ &= \vdots \\ &= f(Y_T | Y_1, \ldots, Y_{T-1}) f(Y_{T-1} | Y_1, \ldots, Y_{T-2}) \ldots f(Y_2 | Y_1) f(Y_1) \end{aligned}$$

Each conditional density is the density of a normal distribution and is therefore given by:

$$f(Y_t | Y_1, \ldots, Y_{t-1}) = (2\pi)^{-n/2} (\det \Delta_t)^{-1/2} \exp\left[-\frac{1}{2}(Y_t - Y_{t|t-1})' \Delta_t^{-1} (Y_t - Y_{t|t-1})\right]$$

where $\Delta_t = GP_{t|t-1}G' + R$. The Gaussian likelihood function L is therefore equal to

$$L = (2\pi)^{-(Tn)/2} \left(\prod_{t=1}^{T} \det(\Delta_t) \right)^{-1/2}$$
$$\exp\left[-\frac{1}{2} \sum_{t=1}^{T} (Y_t - Y_{t|t-1})' \Delta_t^{-1} (Y_t - Y_{t|t-1}) \right].$$

Note that all the entities necessary to evaluate the likelihood function are provided by the Kalman filter. Thus, the evaluation of the likelihood function is a by-product of the Kalman filter. The maximum likelihood estimator (MLE) is then given by the maximizer of the likelihood function or, more conveniently, the log-likelihood function. Usually, there is no analytic solution available, so one must resort to numerical methods. An estimation of the asymptotic covariance matrix can be obtained by evaluating the Hessian matrix at the optimum. Under the usual assumptions, the MLE is consistent and delivers asymptotically normally distributed estimates (Greene, 2008; Amemiya, 1994).

The direct maximization of the likelihood function is often not easy in practice, especially for large systems with many parameters. The expectation-maximization algorithm, EM algorithm for short, represents a valid, though slower, alternative. As the name indicates, it consists of two steps, which have to be carried out iteratively. Based on some starting values for the parameters, the first step (expectation step) computes estimates, $X_{t|T}$, of the unobserved state vector X_t using the Kalman smoother. In the second step (maximization step), the likelihood function is maximized taking the estimates of X_t, $X_{t|T}$, as additional observations. The treatment of $X_{t|T}$ as additional observations allows to reduce the maximization step to a simple multivariate regression. Indeed, by treating $X_{t|T}$ as if they were known, the state equation becomes a simple VAR(1), which can be readily estimated by linear least squares to obtain the parameters F and Q. The parameters A, G, and R are also easily retrieved from a regression of Y_t on $X_{t|T}$. Based on these new parameter estimates, we go back to step one and derive new estimates for $X_{t|T}$, which are then used in the maximization step. One can show that this procedure maximizes the original likelihood function (see Dempster et al., 1977; Wu, 1983). A more detailed analysis of the EM algorithm in the time series context is provided by Brockwell and Davis (1996).[11]

[11] The analogue to the EM algorithm in the Bayesian context is given by the Gibbs sampler. In contrast to the EM algorithm, we compute in the first step not the expected value of the states, but we draw a state vector from the distribution of state vectors given the parameters. In the second step, we do not maximize the likelihood function but draw a parameter from the distribution of parameters given the state vector drawn previously. Going back and forth between these two steps, we get a Markov chain in the parameters and the states whose stationary distribution is exactly the distribution of parameters and states given the data. A detailed description of Bayesian methods

Sometimes, it is of interest not only to compute parameter estimates and to derive from them estimates for the state vector via the Kalman filter or smoother but also to find confidence intervals for the estimated state vector to take the uncertainty into account. If the parameters are known, the methods outlined previously showed how to obtain these confidence intervals. If, however, the parameters have to be estimated, there is a double uncertainty: the uncertainty from the filter and the uncertainty arising from the parameter estimates. One way to account for this additional uncertainty is by the use of simulations. Thereby, we draw a given number of parameter vectors from the asymptotic distribution and compute for each of these draws the corresponding estimates for the state vector. The variation in these estimates is then a measure of the uncertainty arising from the estimation of the parameters (see Hamilton, 1994a, Section 13.7).

17.4.2 Identification

As emphasized in Remark 17.5 of Sect. 17.1, the state space representations are not unique. See, for example, the two alternative representations of the ARMA(1,1) model in Sect. 17.1. This non-uniqueness of state space models poses an identification problem because different specifications give rise to observationally equivalent models.[12] This problem is especially serious if all states are unobservable. In practice, the identification problem results in difficulties in the numerical maximization of the likelihood function. For example, one may obtain large differences for small variations in the starting values; or one may encounter difficulties in the inversion of the matrix of second derivatives.

The identification of state space models can be checked by transforming them into VARMA models and by investigating the issue in this reparameterized setting (Hannan & Deistler, 1988; Deistler & Scherrer, 2022). Exercise 17.6.6 invites the reader to apply this method to the AR(1) model with measurement errors. System identification is a special field in systems theory and will not be pursued further here. A systematic treatment can be found in the textbook by Ljung (1999).

17.5 Examples

17.5.1 Computing Quarterly GDP from Yearly Data

The official data for quarterly GDP are released in Switzerland by the State Secretariat for Economic Affairs (SECO). They estimate these data, taking the

and the Gibbs sampler can be found in Geweke (2005). Kim and Nelson (1999) discuss this method in the context of state space models.

[12] Remember that, in our context, two representations are equivalent if they generate the same mean and covariance function for $\{Y_t\}$.

yearly values provided by the Federal Statistical Office (FSO) as given. This division of tasks is not uncommon in many countries. Many statistical office use some form of disaggregation to produce quarterly national account data. One of the most popular methods for disaggregation of yearly data into quarterly ones was proposed by Chow and Lin (1971).[13] It is a regression-based method that can take additional information in the form of indicator variables (i.e., variables that are measured at the higher frequency and correlated at the lower frequency with the variable of interest) into account. This procedure is, however, rather rigid. The state space framework is much more flexible and ideally suited to deal with missing observations. Applications of this framework to the problem of disaggregation were provided by Bernanke et al. (1997) and Cuche and Hess (2000), among others. We will illustrate this approach below.

Starting point of the analysis are the yearly growth rates of GDP and indicator variables, which are recorded at the quarterly frequency and which are correlated with GDP growth. In our application, we will consider the growth of industrial production (IP) and the index on consumer sentiment (C) as indicators. Both variables are available on a quarterly basis from 1990 onward. For simplicity, we assume that the annualized quarterly growth rate of GDP, $\{Q_t\}$, follows an AR(1) process with mean μ:

$$Q_t - \mu = \phi(Q_{t-1} - \mu) + w_t, \qquad w_t \sim \mathrm{WN}(0, \sigma_w^2)$$

In addition, we assume that GDP is related to industrial production and consumer sentiment by the following two equations:

$$\begin{aligned} IP_t &= \alpha_{IP} + \beta_{IP} Q_t + v_{IP,t} \\ C_t &= \alpha_C + \beta_C Q_t + v_{C,t} \end{aligned}$$

where the residuals $v_{IP,t}$ and $v_{C,t}$ are uncorrelated. Finally, we define the relation between quarterly and yearly GDP growth as:

$$J_t = \frac{1}{4}Q_t + \frac{1}{4}Q_{t-1} + \frac{1}{4}Q_{t-2} + \frac{1}{4}Q_{t-3}, \qquad t = 4, 8, 12 \ldots$$

We can now bring these equations into state space form. Thereby, the observation equation is given by

$$Y_t = A_t + G_t X_t + W_t$$

with state and observations vectors

[13] Similarly, one may envisage the disaggregation of yearly data into monthly ones or other forms of disaggregation.

$$X_t = \begin{pmatrix} Q_t - \mu \\ Q_{t-1} - \mu \\ Q_{t-2} - \mu \\ Q_{t-3} - \mu \end{pmatrix}, \qquad Y_t = \begin{cases} \begin{pmatrix} J_t \\ IP_t \\ C_t \end{pmatrix}, t = 4, 8, 12, \ldots; \\ \begin{pmatrix} 0 \\ IP_t \\ C_t \end{pmatrix}, t \neq 4, 8, 12, \ldots \end{cases}$$

and time-varying coefficient matrices

$$A_t = \begin{cases} \begin{pmatrix} \mu \\ \alpha_{IP} \\ \alpha_C \end{pmatrix}, t = 4, 8, 12, \ldots; \\ \begin{pmatrix} 0 \\ \alpha_{IP} \\ \alpha_C \end{pmatrix}, t \neq 4, 8, 12, \ldots \end{cases}$$

$$G_t = \begin{cases} \begin{pmatrix} \frac{1}{4} & \frac{1}{4} & \frac{1}{4} & \frac{1}{4} \\ \beta_{IP} & 0 & 0 & 0 \\ \beta_C & 0 & 0 & 0 \end{pmatrix}, t = 4, 8, 12, \ldots; \\ \begin{pmatrix} 0 & 0 & 0 & 0 \\ \beta_{IP} & 0 & 0 & 0 \\ \beta_C & 0 & 0 & 0 \end{pmatrix}, \quad t \neq 4, 8, 12, \ldots \end{cases}$$

$$R_t = \begin{cases} \begin{pmatrix} 0 & 0 & 0 \\ 0 & \sigma_{IP}^2 & 0 \\ 0 & 0 & \sigma_C^2 \end{pmatrix}, t = 4, 8, 12, \ldots; \\ \begin{pmatrix} 1 & 0 & 0 \\ 0 & \sigma_{IP}^2 & 0 \\ 0 & 0 & \sigma_C^2 \end{pmatrix}, t \neq 4, 8, 12, \ldots \end{cases}$$

The state equation becomes:

$$X_{t+1} = FX_t + V_{t+1}$$

where

$$F = \begin{pmatrix} \phi & 0 & 0 & 0 \\ 1 & 0 & 0 & 0 \\ 0 & 1 & 0 & 0 \\ 0 & 0 & 1 & 0 \end{pmatrix}, \quad Q = \begin{pmatrix} \sigma_w^2 & 0 & 0 & 0 \\ 0 & 0 & 0 & 0 \\ 0 & 0 & 0 & 0 \\ 0 & 0 & 0 & 0 \end{pmatrix}$$

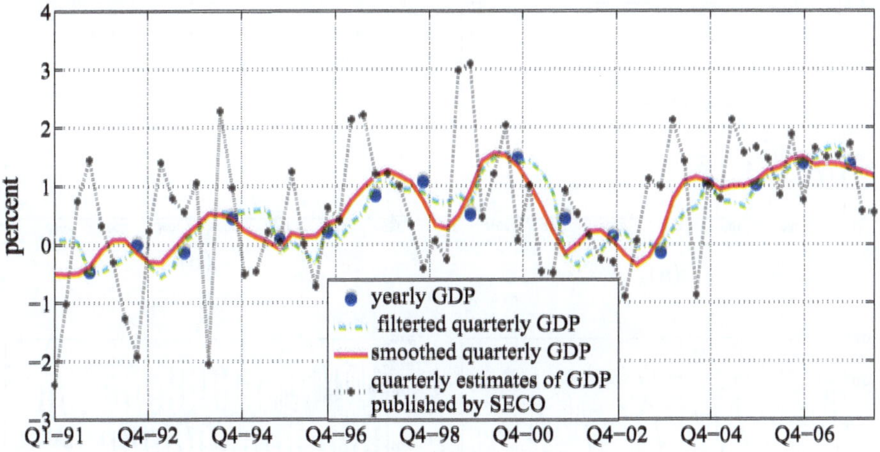

Fig. 17.3 Estimates of quarterly GDP growth rates for Switzerland

Figure 17.3 plots the different estimates of GDP growth and compares them with the data released by State Secretariat for Economic Affairs (SECO).

17.5.2 Structural Time Series Analysis

A customary practice in business cycle analysis is to decompose a time series into several components. As an example, we estimate a structural time series model, which decomposes a times series additively into a local linear trend, a business cycle component, a seasonal component, and an irregular component. This is the specification studied under the heading of basic structural model (BSM) in Sect. 17.2.6. We carry over the specification explained there to apply it to quarterly real GDP of Switzerland. Figure 17.4 shows the smoothed estimates of the various components. In the upper-left panel, the demeaned logged original series (see Fig. 17.4a) is plotted. One clearly discerns the trend and the seasonal variations. The upper-right panel shows the local linear trend (LLT). As one can see, the trend is not a straight line but exhibits pronounced waves at low frequency. The business cycle component showed in Fig. 17.4c is much more volatile. The large drop of about 2.5% in 2008/2009 corresponds to the financial markets crisis in the aftermath of the collapse of Lehman Brothers. The lower-right panel plots the seasonal component (see Fig. 17.4d). From a visual inspections, one can infer that the volatility of the seasonal component is much larger than the cyclical component (compare the scale of the two components) so that movements in GDP are dominated by seasonal fluctuations. Moreover, the seasonal component changes its character over time. The irregular component, which is not shown, has only very small variance.

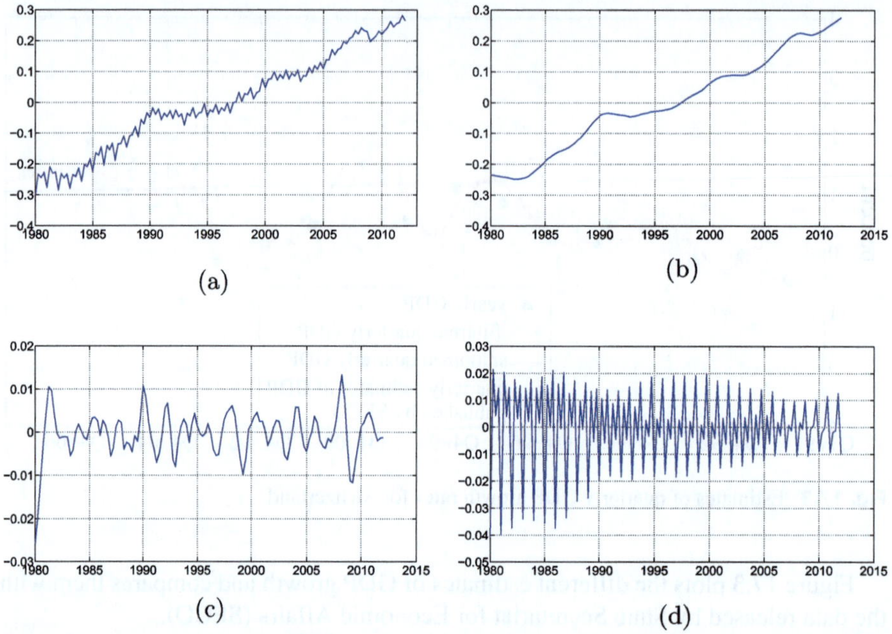

Fig. 17.4 Components of the basic structural model (BSM) for real GDP of Switzerland. (**a**) Logged Swiss GDP (demeaned). (**b**) Local linear trend (LLT). (**c**) Business cycle component. (**d**) Seasonal component

17.6 Exercises

Exercise 17.6.1 *Consider the basic structural time series model for* $\{Y_t\}$:

$$Y_t = T_t + W_t, \qquad W_t \sim \mathrm{WN}(0, \sigma_W^2),$$

$$T_t = \delta_{t-1} + T_{t-1} + \varepsilon_t, \qquad \varepsilon_t \sim \mathrm{WN}(0, \sigma_\varepsilon^2),$$

$$\delta_t = \delta_{t-1} + \xi_t, \qquad \xi_t \sim \mathrm{WN}(0, \sigma_\xi^2),$$

where the error terms W_t, ε_t, *and* ξ_t *are uncorrelated with each other at all leads and lags.*

(i) *Show that* $\{Y_t\}$ *follows an ARIMA(0,2,2) process.*
(ii) *Compute the autocorrelation function of* $\{\Delta^2 Y_t\}$.

Exercise 17.6.2 *If the cyclical component of the basic structural model for* $\{Y_t\}$ *is:*

$$\begin{pmatrix} C_t \\ C_t^* \end{pmatrix} = \rho \begin{pmatrix} \cos\lambda_C & \sin\lambda_C \\ -\sin\lambda_C & \cos\lambda_C \end{pmatrix} \begin{pmatrix} C_{t-1} \\ C_{t-1}^* \end{pmatrix} + \begin{pmatrix} V_{1,t}^{(C)} \\ V_{2,t}^{(C)} \end{pmatrix}$$

where $\{V_{1,t}^{(C)}\}$ *and* $\{V_{2,t}^{(C)}\}$ *are mutually uncorrelated white noise processes.*

(i) *Show that* $\{C_t\}$ *follows an ARMA(2,1) process with* $\gamma_h(h) = \rho^h \cos\lambda_C h$.

Exercise 17.6.3 *Write the ARMA(p,q) process* $Y_t = \phi_1 X_{t-1} + \cdots + \phi_p X_{t-p} + Z_t + \theta_1 Z_{t-1} + \cdots + \theta_q Z_{t-q}$ *as a state space model such that the state vector* X_t *is given by:*

$$X_t = \begin{pmatrix} Y_t \\ Y_{t-1} \\ \vdots \\ Y_{t-p} \\ Z_{t-1} \\ Z_{t-2} \\ \vdots \\ Z_{t-q} \end{pmatrix}.$$

Exercise 17.6.4 *Show that* X_t *and* Y_t *have a unique stationary and causal solution if all eigenvalues of* F *are absolutely strictly smaller than one. Use the results from Sect. 12.3.*

Exercise 17.6.5 *Find the Kalman filter equations for the following system:*

$$X_t = \phi X_{t-1} + w_t$$
$$Y_t = \lambda X_t + v_t$$

where λ *and* ϕ *are scalars and where*

$$\begin{pmatrix} v_t \\ w_t \end{pmatrix} \sim \mathrm{N}\left(\begin{pmatrix} 0 \\ 0 \end{pmatrix}, \begin{pmatrix} \sigma_v^2 & \sigma_{vw} \\ \sigma_{vw} & \sigma_w^2 \end{pmatrix} \right).$$

Exercise 17.6.6 *Consider the state space model of an AR(1) process with measurement error analyzed in Sect. 17.3 :*

$$X_{t+1} = \phi X_t + v_{t+1}, \qquad v_t \sim \mathrm{IIDN}(0, \sigma_v^2)$$
$$Y_t = X_t + w_t, \qquad w_t \sim \mathrm{IIDN}(0, \sigma_w^2).$$

For simplicity, assume that $|\phi| < 1$.

(i) *Show that* $\{Y_t\}$ *is an ARMA(1,1) process given by* $Y_t - \phi Y_{t-1} = Z_t + \theta Z_{t-1}$ *with* $Z_t \sim \mathrm{WN}(0, \sigma_Z^2)$.

(ii) *Show that the parameters of the state space,* $\phi, \sigma_v^2, \sigma_w^2$, *and those of the ARMA(1,1) model are related by the equation*

$$\theta \sigma_Z^2 = -\phi \sigma_w^2,$$

$$\frac{1}{1+\theta^2} = \frac{-\phi \sigma_w^2}{\sigma_v^2 + (1+\phi^2)\sigma_w^2},$$

(iii) *Why is there an identification problem?*

Advanced Time Series Models 18

18.1 Bayesian Time Series Models

The approach to time series analysis presented so far relied on a frequentist notion of probability. The aim thereby is to estimate the "true" parameters θ of a model from the data (sample). While the data are treated as stochastic, the parameters are considered to be fixed non-stochastic quantities. While probability statements bear on the estimator of θ for repeated samples, the Bayesian approach models the uncertainty over the unobserved parameters via an prior distribution. This allows to model explicitly the information, respectively, the perception the researcher has on the parameter. Thereby the concept of a probability is a subjective one, which does not rely on the idea of a repeated sample. The emphasis in the analysis is then how the observed data modify the prior subjective perception of the researcher. Berger (1985), Cox (2006), Gorroochurn (2012, Kapitel 14), or Diaconis and Skyrms (2018, Kapitel 6) provide good intelligible introductions to both views, which go beyond its pure statistical significance.

Besides these fundamental issues, practical considerations also play a role in the context of VAR modelling. Even medium-sized VAR models already contain (too) many parameters. For example, a five dimensional VAR model with six lags has 170 parameters, including constant terms and the covariance matrix. Given typical sample sizes in the order 100–200 results in parameter estimates with small precision. This manifests itself in many non-zero but statistically insignificant estimates, which impair on the forecasting performance of VAR models (e.g., Kunst & Neusser, 1986). The Bayesian approach allows a tighter connection between economic theory and empirical analysis as the prior perception of the researcher should ideally be motivated by economic reasoning (see, e.g., An and Schorfheide (2007) and Del Negro and Schorfheide (2004)). These considerations and the development of efficient algorithms in connection with greater computational power led to increased applications of Bayesian methods in econometric analysis. In the

K. Neusser, *Time Series Econometrics*, Springer Texts in Business and Economics,
https://doi.org/10.1007/978-3-031-88838-0_18

context of time series analysis, this led to the Bayesian vector autoregressive (BVAR) models. The exposition in this section follows Kilian and Lütkepohl (2017, chapter 5).

18.1.1 Preliminaries

The presentation of Bayesian models requires the introduction of new concepts and notations. As explained above, the Bayesian approach treats the observations $\mathbf{x} = (x_1', \ldots, x_T')'$, $x_t \in \mathbb{R}^n$, as given, whereas the prior subjective information of the researcher about the stochastic parameter vector θ is represented by a so-called prior distribution with *prior density function* $g(\theta)$. The joint density function of the parameters and the observations $f(\theta, \mathbf{x})$ can be factorized into a product:

$$f(\theta, \mathbf{x}) = g(\theta|\mathbf{x}) f(\mathbf{x})$$

where the density of the parameters conditional on the observations $g(\theta|\mathbf{x})$ is called the *posterior density function* and $f(x)$ is just the unconditional density function of the data. The application of Bayes theorem then leads to

$$g(\theta|\mathbf{x}) = \frac{f(\mathbf{x}|\theta)g(\theta)}{f(\mathbf{x})} = \frac{\mathrm{L}(\theta|\mathbf{x})g(\theta)}{f(\mathbf{x})}, \tag{18.1}$$

where $f(\mathbf{x}|\theta)$ is nothing but the likelihood function $\mathrm{L}(\theta|\mathbf{x})$. Because the Bayesian approach treats the data as given, the unconditional density of the observations $f(\mathbf{x})$ can be regarded as a fixed normalizing factor, which ensures that the posterior density integrates to one. Hence, $f(\mathbf{x})$ is often neglected:

$$g(\theta|\mathbf{x}) \propto f(\mathbf{x}|\theta)g(\theta) = \mathrm{L}(\theta|\mathbf{x})g(\theta) \tag{18.2}$$

where $\propto$ denotes proportionality. The conditional density function given the observations or posterior density function is therefore proportional to the product of the likelihood function and the prior density function of the parameters. The data enter the posterior density therefore only via the likelihood function.

In contrast to the frequentist approach where hypothesis testing plays a central role, the Bayesian approach aims at the evaluation of the empirical validity of different models. Suppose we want to evaluate two models $M_1 = M(\theta_1)$ and $M_2 = M(\theta_2)$, $\theta_1 \neq \theta_2$. Define for this purpose the *posterior odds ratio* as

$$\frac{g(M_1|\mathbf{x})}{g(M_2|\mathbf{x})} = \frac{g(M_1)}{g(M_2)} \times \frac{f(\mathbf{x}|M_1)}{f(\mathbf{x}|M_2)} = \frac{g(M_1)}{g(M_2)} \times \frac{L(M_1|\mathbf{x})}{L(M_2|\mathbf{x})}.$$

Thereby, $g(M_1)/g(M_2)$ is known as the *prior odds ratio* and $f(\mathbf{x}|M_1)/f(\mathbf{x}|M_2)$, respectively, $L(M_1|\mathbf{x})/L(M_2|\mathbf{x})$, as the ratio of marginal likelihoods or Bayes factor.

The marginal likelihood functions are obtained by integrating out the parameters in the likelihood function:

$$f(\mathbf{x}|M(\theta_i)) = \int f(x|M(\theta_i))g(\theta_i)d\theta_i, \qquad i = 1, 2.$$

This essentially averages parameter uncertainty within each model. If the posterior odds ratio is greater than one, model M_1 is to be preferred, whereas a ratio smaller than one favors model M_2. If both models have the same prior density, then the Bayes factor decides.

Despite the fact that the Bayesian approach presents an intuitive, clear, and coherent methodology, its practical implementation is not without technical and conceptual difficulties. One such difficulty centers on the reporting of the results, which are present only in the form of the posterior distribution $g(\theta|\mathbf{x})$. A second difficulty arises in the specification of the prior distribution $g(\theta)$. It is not an easy task to cast the subjection perception of the researcher into a valid prior distribution. Both problems are treated here only cursory. The interested reader should consult the corresponding literature (e.g., Berger, 1985, Cox, 2006, Canova, 2007, or Koop & Korobilis, 2010).

Reporting the Posterior Distribution

In many applications, one may not care about the whole posterior distribution but only about some properties of it, like its mean or mode. Hence, suppose we are interested in some function $h(\theta)$ whose expectation is given by

$$\mathbb{E}h(\theta|\mathbf{x}) = \int h(\theta)g(\theta|\mathbf{x})d\theta.$$

If $h(\theta) = \theta$, this amounts to the expected value of the posterior distribution of θ. The elements of the vector $\mathbb{E}h(\theta|\mathbf{x})$, or some subset of it, are typically reported in a table.

The evaluation of the integral is not a trivial task. On the one hand, the functional relationships between the elements of θ, respectively, $h(\theta)$, may be very complex; on the other hand, the dimension of the parameter vector may be very large, for example, in medium-sized VAR models (see the discussion in the Introduction). One may therefore very quickly reach the limits of computational power. This is aggravated by the fact that the posterior distribution is typically not available in analytical form and does not belong to some known distribution family. To overcome these problems, simulation methods are used. Suppose it is possible to sample the posterior distribution $g(\theta|\mathbf{x})$ and to generate a sample $\theta^{(i)}$, $i = 1, 2, \ldots, M$, of size M. Then the law of large numbers (LLN) tells us that $\mathbb{E}h(\theta|\mathbf{x})$ can be approximated for large enough M by the arithmetic average:

$$\frac{1}{M}\sum_{i=1}^{M} h(\theta^{(i)}) \xrightarrow{\text{a.s.}} \mathbb{E}h(\theta \mid \mathbf{x}) = \int h(\theta)g(\theta \mid \mathbf{x})d\theta.$$

Markov Chain Monte Carlo (MCMC) methods have proven to be powerful tools to generate samples from a target distribution with density $g(\theta|\mathbf{x})$. Its purpose is to generate a Markov chain whose unique stationary distribution (limit distribution) corresponds exactly to the posterior distribution of θ. One customary algorithm in this respect is the *Metropolis Hastings algorithm*. This iterative scheme works as follows. First, one choses a so-called proposal density function $q(x \mid y)$. This density is typically taken to be symmetric, i.e., $q(x \mid y) = q(y \mid x)$, and often equal to the normal distribution centered around y. This implies that values near y are more likely. Given some $\theta^{(i)}$ from iteration step i, draw a random realization $\tilde{\theta}$ from the proposal density $q(\tilde{\theta} \mid \theta^{(i)})$. The next value $\theta^{(i+1)}$ in the iteration is obtained according to the rule:

$$\theta^{(i+1)} = \begin{cases} \tilde{\theta}, & \text{if } u \leq \alpha; \\ \theta^{(i)}, & \text{if } u > \alpha. \end{cases}$$

Thereby, α denotes the ratio $g(\tilde{\theta}|\mathbf{x})/g(\theta^{(i)}|\mathbf{x})$, and u is a random draw from the uniform distribution on the unit interval $[0, 1]$. The proposal $\tilde{\theta}$ will therefore be accepted if it has a higher probability than the old one. If the probability of the proposal is lower, then the algorithm rejects it with some probability and stays with the old value. The algorithm therefore generates a sequence $\theta^{(i)}$, whose values fall more often into regions of high probability and less often into regions of low probability. Under quite general assumptions, it can be shown that this sequence resembles more and more a sample taken from the target distribution $g(\theta \mid \mathbf{x})$.

Despite its efficiency, the Metropolis Hastings algorithm faces two problems, which have to be overcome in practice. First, the algorithm generates sequences whose values are not independent but autocorrelated. One solution is to take only each k-th value where k is known as the *jump wide*. This number may have to be rather high, thereby increasing the number of required iterations substantially. Second, depending on the starting value, the distribution of the first draws may eventually be very far from the target distribution. For this reason, first draws are usually disregarded. This practice is known as burn-in phase. If the dimension of θ is very high, one can resort to the Gibbs sampler, which considers in each iteration step only some elements of θ and leaves the rest unchanged. In this way, one may adapt the jump wide k to each element of θ individually.

18.1.2 Bayesian Parameter Estimation

Specification of the Prior Distribution

The pivotal point in Bayesian analysis is the specification of the prior distribution. In the context of VAR modelling, we will subsequently only deal with the specification of the prior distribution for the parameter matrices $\Phi_1, \ldots, \Phi_p$ and not for the covariance matrix Σ. Despite this simplification, this is not an easy task because the joint distribution of all parameters must be specified. One way to proceed is to take as a prior distribution the normal distribution and take the covariance matrix

Σ as given. In practice, it will be replaced by the covariance matrix estimated from the OLS residuals. As in Chap. 13, Eq. (13.2) we will adopt the vectorized version of the VAR model and view it as a regression equation:

$$\text{vec}Y = \text{vec}(\Phi \mathbf{X}') + \text{vec}Z = (\mathbf{X} \otimes I_n)\text{vec}\Phi + \text{vec}Z,$$

where $\text{vec}Y = (X_{11}, X_{21}, \ldots, X_{n1}, X_{12}, X_{22}, \ldots, X_{n2}, \ldots, X_{1T}, X_{2T}, \ldots, X_{nT})'$ and similarly for the residuals Z_t. The regressor matrix then is $(\mathbf{X} \otimes I_n)$.

In the following, we will denote $\text{vec}Y$ and $\text{vec}\Phi$ by y, respectively, ϕ. The prior distribution of ϕ is specified as a normal distribution with mean ϕ_0 and covariance matrix V_ϕ:

$$\phi \sim \text{N}(\phi_0, V_\phi).$$

The density function of the prior distribution $g(\phi)$ there is

$$\begin{aligned} g(\phi) &= \frac{1}{(2\pi)^{n^2p/2}} (\det V_\phi)^{-1/2} \exp\left\{-\tfrac{1}{2}(\phi - \phi_0)' V_\phi^{-1} (\phi - \phi_0)\right\} \\ &= \frac{1}{(2\pi)^{n^2p/2}} (\det V_\phi)^{-1/2} \exp\left\{-\tfrac{1}{2}\left(V_\phi^{-1/2}(\phi - \phi_0)\right)' \left(V_\phi^{-1/2}(\phi - \phi_0)\right)\right\}. \end{aligned}$$

As in Sect. 13.3, the Gaussian likelihood function then becomes:

$$\begin{aligned} L(\phi|y) &= \frac{1}{(2\pi)^{nT/2}} (\det(I_T \otimes \Sigma))^{-1/2} \\ &\quad \times \exp\left\{-\frac{1}{2}(y - (\mathbf{X} \otimes I_n)\phi)'(I_T \otimes \Sigma)^{-1}(y - (\mathbf{X} \otimes I_n)\phi)\right\} \\ &= \frac{1}{(2\pi)^{nT/2}} (\det(I_T \otimes \Sigma))^{-1/2} \\ &\quad \times \exp\left\{-\tfrac{1}{2}\left((I_T \otimes \Sigma^{-1/2})y - (\mathbf{X} \otimes \Sigma^{-1/2})\phi)\right)' \right. \\ &\quad \left. \times \left((I_T \otimes \Sigma^{-1/2})y - (\mathbf{X} \otimes \Sigma^{-1/2})\phi)\right) \right\} \end{aligned}$$

The posterior density $g(\phi|y) = g(\phi)L(\phi|y)$ is therefore proportional to

$$\begin{aligned} g(\phi|y) \propto \exp&\left\{-\tfrac{1}{2}\left(V_\phi^{-1/2}(\phi - \phi_0)\right)' \left(V_\phi^{-1/2}(\phi - \phi_0)\right)\right. \\ -\frac{1}{2}&\left.\left((I_T \otimes \Sigma^{-1/2})y - (\mathbf{X} \otimes \Sigma^{-1/2})\phi\right)' \left((I_T \otimes \Sigma^{-1/2})y - (\mathbf{X} \otimes \Sigma^{-1/2})\phi\right)\right\}. \end{aligned}$$

In order to simplify the presentation of the posterior density, define

$$w = \begin{pmatrix} V_\phi^{-1/2}\phi_0 \\ (I_T \otimes \Sigma^{-1/2})y \end{pmatrix} \quad \text{and} \quad W = \begin{pmatrix} V_\phi^{-1/2} \\ (\mathbf{X} \otimes \Sigma^{-1/2}) \end{pmatrix}.$$

The posterior density then can be written as

$$\begin{aligned} g(\phi|y) &\propto \exp\left\{-\tfrac{1}{2}(w - W\phi)'(w - W\phi)\right\} \\ &\propto \exp\left\{-\tfrac{1}{2}\left[(\phi - \phi_\mathrm{p})'W'W(\phi - \phi_\mathrm{p}) + (w - W\phi_\mathrm{p})'(w - W\phi_\mathrm{p})\right]\right\} \end{aligned}$$

where ϕ_p is defined as

$$\begin{aligned} \phi_\mathrm{p} &= (W'W)^{-1}W'w \\ &= \left(V_\phi^{-1} + (\mathbf{X}'\mathbf{X} \otimes \Sigma^{-1})\right)^{-1}\left(V_\phi^{-1}\phi_0 + (\mathbf{X}' \otimes \Sigma^{-1})y\right). \end{aligned} \tag{18.3}$$

Because the second term in the equation for $g(\phi|y)$ does not depend ϕ, the posterior density finally is proportional to

$$g(\phi|y) \propto \exp\left\{-\tfrac{1}{2}(\phi - \phi_\mathrm{p})'\Sigma_\mathrm{p}^{-1}(\phi - \phi_\mathrm{p})\right\}$$

where $\Sigma_\mathrm{p} = (W'W)^{-1} = \left(V_\phi^{-1} + (\mathbf{X}'\mathbf{X} \otimes \Sigma^{-1})\right)$. Hence, the posterior distribution is also a normal distribution with mean ϕ_p and covariance matrix Σ_p. Inference on the parameters can therefore be made in the usual way.

Note that in this setting, the prior distribution, the likelihood function, and therefore the posterior distribution are all normal distributions. This is an example of conjugate distributions. Choosing a prior distribution that is conjugate to the likelihood function is an important element in Bayesian analysis because it brings with it substantial simplifications in the calculation of many statistics and makes computationally costly simulation techniques superfluous. The exponential distribution family is an important example in this context. Their density is of the form $m(y)\exp\{s(y)'\psi(\phi) - k(\psi(\phi))\}$ where $m(y)$ is a non-negative function of the data y and $s(y)$ a sufficient statistic. Both functions depend only on the data and not on the parameters. The function $\psi(\phi)$ denotes a one-to-one transformation (parametrization) of ϕ. Finally, the function $k(\psi)$ is a normalization factor, which ensures that the density integrates to one. Besides the normal distribution, the binomial, Poisson, and gamma distribution are further important examples that fall in the family of exponential distributions.

An equivalent parametrization of the prior distribution is given by

$$C_\phi\phi_0 = c_\phi + e \quad \text{with} \quad e \sim \mathrm{N}(0, I_{n^2p}),$$

where $C_\phi \in \mathbb{R}^{n^2p \times n^2p}$ denotes a given invertible matrix and $c_\phi \in \mathbb{R}^{n^2p}$ a vector. Hence, $\phi_0 \sim \mathrm{N}(C_\phi^{-1}c, C_\phi^{-1}C_\phi^{-1\prime})$. Inserting this parametrization into the posterior density derived above leads to

$$\phi_{\mathrm{p}} = \left(C_\phi^{-1}C_\phi^{-1\prime} + (\mathbf{X}'\mathbf{X} \otimes \Sigma^{-1})\right)^{-1}\left(C_\phi' c_\phi + (\mathbf{X}' \otimes \Sigma^{-1})y\right).$$

The advantage in this parametrization is that it avoids the inversion of the matrix V_ϕ, which can be computational burdensome, especially for large matrices. Thus, computations become numerically more stable.

This representation of ϕ_{p} can also be interpreted as a generalized least-squares (GLS) estimator of ϕ in the regression model:

$$\begin{pmatrix} y \\ c_\phi \end{pmatrix} = \begin{pmatrix} (\mathbf{X} \otimes I_n) \\ C_\phi \end{pmatrix}\phi + \varepsilon \quad \text{mit} \quad \varepsilon \sim \left(0, \begin{pmatrix} \Sigma \otimes I_T & 0 \\ 0 & I_{n^2p} \end{pmatrix}\right)$$

The specification of a prior distribution thus amounts algebraically to the availability of additional observations.

The matrices V_ϕ, respectively, C_ϕ, in the alternative parametrization, play a crucial role in the specification of the prior distribution as they are central in the determination of the posterior distribution. The inverse V_ϕ^{-1} is known as the *precision matrix*. In the limit, as V_ϕ^{-1} tends to the zero matrix, Eq. (18.3) shows that the expected value of the posterior distribution converges to the OLS estimator $\hat{\phi} = ((\mathbf{X}'\mathbf{X})^{-1}\mathbf{X}' \otimes I_n)y$. Hence, the matrix V_ϕ^{-1} describes how informative the prior distribution is. Large values of V_ϕ^{-1} mean that the prior is very informative, whereas small values mean that the prior has little information. Note, however, that the prior distribution may be informative with respect to some parameters, but non-informative with respect to others. In the Bayesian literature, there is a discussion about the correct specification of *noninformative prior* (*diffuse prior*) distributions. A natural candidate would be the uniform distribution. This distribution is, however, not defined over the whole region $\mathbb{R}^{n^2p}$.

The Minnesota Prior Distribution

A basic difficulty in Bayesian analysis is that research may have diverse opinions about the a priori information. It has therefore become customary to choose the prior distribution from a given family. Thereby, the members differ only by a small number of parameters called hyperparameters. In this way, it is possible to compare the different priors across researchers and at the same time to simplify its specification. This is especially relevant when the number of parameters is large. In the context of VAR models, the Minnesota prior distribution introduced by Doan et al. (1984), Litterman (1986), and Sims and Zha (1998) in the analysis of macroeconomic time series is a primary example.[1]

[1] In the literature, there exists different variants, which differ only in details.

The Minnesota prior of VAR models relies on the normal distribution and rests on the belief that most macroeconomic time series are very persistent at least taken in levels or log-levels and are therefore close to random walks. Accordingly, the expectation of θ_0 is equal to zero with the exception of the diagonal elements of Φ_1, whose expectations are equal to one. Hence, this prior distribution implies that $\{X_t\}$ behaves as a random walk with no drift. The covariance matrix V is specified as a diagonal matrix. The complete Minnesota prior distribution thus consists of the following building blocks:

$$\phi_{ii}^{(1)} \sim \mathrm{N}(1, \gamma^2), \qquad i = 1, \ldots, n;$$

$$\phi_{ii}^{(h)} \sim \mathrm{N}\left(0, \frac{\gamma^2}{h^2}\right), \qquad i = 1, \ldots, n \text{ and } h = 2, \ldots, p;$$

$$\phi_{ij}^{(h)} \sim \mathrm{N}\left(0, \frac{\omega^2 \gamma^2 \tau_i^2}{h^2 \tau_j^2}\right), \qquad i, j = 1, \ldots, n, i \neq j, \text{ und } h = 1, \ldots, p;$$

where γ^2 and ω^2 are the hyperparameters of the prior distribution. Thereby, γ^2 is shrinkage parameter, which controls the researcher's strength in his belief. The smaller this value, the stronger is the belief. This belief increases harmonically with the lag length h. The hyperparameter ω^2 stands for the importance of the interrelationships between the different variables. A value ω^2 smaller than one means $X_{j,t-h}$ is seen as less important for the explanation of the i-th variable than its own lag $X_{i,t-h}$. The ratio τ_i^2/τ_j^2 finally control for the relative magnitude of variables X_{it} and X_{jt}. For example, τ_i^2 may be set equal to the variance of the residuals from a simple univariate AR(1) model. The VAR model usually includes a constant whose prior distribution has mean zero and a very large variance. Hence, the prior for the constant becomes close to being noninformative.

Having accepted the Minnesota prior as the prior distribution, the researcher has to stipulate the values for the hyperparameters γ^2 and ω^2. According to Litterman (1986), $\gamma = 0.2$ and $\omega = 0.3$ have proven to be reliable values in macroeconomic applications. Instead of using this rule of thumb, it is possible to choose the hyperparameters to minimize the forecasting precision or to maximize the marginal likelihood function (Giannone et al., 2015).[2]

As an example, consider a bivariate VAR(2) model with constant term:

$$X_t = c + \Phi_1 X_{t-1} + \Phi_2 X_{t-2} + Z_t$$

where $\phi = (c, [\Phi_1]_{11}, [\Phi_1]_{21}, [\Phi_1]_{12}, [\Phi_1]_{22}, [\Phi_2]_{11}, [\Phi_2 1]_{21}, [\Phi_2]_{12}, [\Phi_2]_{22})'$. The prior distribution is completely determined by $\phi_0 = (0, 1, 0, 0, 1, 0, 0, 0, 0)'$ and its covariance matrix V_ϕ where

[2] Strictly speaking, this violates the Bayesian spirit because the prior distribution should not depend on the observations. However, if these observations do not enter the likelihood function, this approach may be legitimate.

$$V_\phi = \begin{pmatrix} V_\phi^{(c)} & 0 & 0 \\ 0 & V_\phi^{(1)} & 0 \\ 0 & 0 & V_\phi^{(2)} \end{pmatrix}.$$

According to the Minnesota prior, the diagonal blocks are given by

$$V_\phi^{(c)} = \kappa \begin{pmatrix} \hat{\tau}_1^2 & 0 \\ 0 & \hat{\tau}_2^2 \end{pmatrix},$$

$$V_\phi^{(1)} = \gamma^2 \begin{pmatrix} 1 & 0 & 0 & 0 \\ 0 & w^2\hat{\tau}_2^2/\hat{\tau}_1^2 & 0 & 0 \\ 0 & 0 & w^2\hat{\tau}_1^2/\hat{\tau}_2^2 & 0 \\ 0 & 0 & 0 & 1 \end{pmatrix}$$

and

$$V_\phi^{(2)} = \frac{\gamma^2}{4} \begin{pmatrix} 1 & 0 & 0 & 0 \\ 0 & w^2\hat{\tau}_2^2/\hat{\tau}_1^2 & 0 & 0 \\ 0 & 0 & w^2\hat{\tau}_1^2/\hat{\tau}_2^2 & 0 \\ 0 & 0 & 0 & 1 \end{pmatrix}.$$

Thereby, the parameter κ takes on a large value to account for the fact that the prior put on the constant is rather loose.

18.2 Structural Breaks

Time series analysis has been presented up to now under the tacit assumption that the coefficients (parameters) remain unchanged over time. This presumption is, however, hard to justify in economics, especially when the sample spans a long period of time. Reasons for time-varying coefficients are diverse. First, the economy is subject to structural changes. Second, systematic or random policy changes result in corresponding changes of the reduced form coefficients as emphasized by Lucas (1976). Third if VAR models are interpreted as nonlinear models linearized along its solution paths. Fourth, macroeconomic relations are often the result of aggregating microeconomic decision rules. Hence, if the composition of the decision-makers varies, the macroeconomic relationship changes. For at least these reasons, it is advisable to recognize time-varying coefficients as a possibility. A test for structural breaks is presented in this section. Models for time-varying coefficients are then discussed in subsequent Sects. 18.3 and 18.4.

There is an extensive literature dealing with the detection and dating of structural breaks in the context of time series analysis. This literature is comprehensively summarized by Perron (2006), among others. A compact account can also be found in Aue and Horváth (2011), where additional testing procedures, like the CUSUM test, are presented. In this short exposition, we follow Bai et al. (1998) and focus on the Chow-type testing procedure. For technical details, the reader is referred to these papers.

18.2.1 Test Methodology

For simplicity, we consider a VAR(1) process that allows for exactly one structural break at some known date t_b:[3]

$$X_t = d_t(t_b)\left(c^{(1)} + \Phi^{(1)} X_{t-1}\right) + (1 - d_t(t_b))\left(c^{(2)} + \Phi^{(2)} X_{t-1}\right) + Z_t \qquad (18.4)$$

where $d_t(t_b)$ denotes a dummy variable

$$d_t(t_b) = \begin{cases} 1, & t \leq t_b; \\ 0, & t > t_b. \end{cases}$$

Thus, before time t_b, the coefficients of the VAR process are given by $c^{(1)}$ and $\Phi^{(1)}$, whereas after t_b, they are given by $c^{(2)}$ and $\Phi^{(2)}$. The error process $\{Z_t\}$ is assumed to be IID(0, Σ), with Σ positive definite.[4] Suppose further that the roots of $\Phi^{(1)}(z)$ as well as those of $\Phi^{(2)}(z)$ are outside the unit circle. Thus, the process admits a stationary and causal with respect to $\{Z_t\}$ before and after date t_b.

The assumption of a structural break at some known date t_b can then be investigated by testing the hypothesis

$$\mathbf{H}_0 : c^{(1)} = c^{(2)} \text{ and } \Phi^{(1)} = \Phi^{(2)} \quad \text{against} \quad \mathbf{H}_1 : c^{(1)} \neq c^{(2)} \text{ or } \Phi^{(1)} \neq \Phi^{(2)}.$$

Similarly, one may consider tests where only the constant, the autoregressive coefficients, or, if present, the time trend change. The standard way to test such a hypothesis is via the F-statistic. Given a sample ranging from period 0 to period T, the strategy is to partition all variables and matrices along the break date t_b. Following the notation and the spirit in Chap. 13, define $Y = \text{vec}(Y^{(1)}, Y^{(2)})$, where $Y^{(1)} = (X_1, X_2, \ldots, X_{t_b})$ and $Y^{(2)} = (X_{t_b+1}, X_{t_b+2}, \ldots, X_T)$, $Z = (Z_1, Z_2, \ldots, Z_T)$, and

$$\mathbf{X}^{(1)} = \begin{pmatrix} 1 & X_{1,0} & \ldots & X_{n,0} \\ 1 & X_{1,1} & \ldots & X_{n,1} \\ \vdots & \vdots & \ddots & \vdots \\ 1 & X_{1,t_b-1} & \ldots & X_{n,t_b-1} \end{pmatrix} \quad \mathbf{X}^{(2)} = \begin{pmatrix} 1 & X_{1,t_b} & \ldots & X_{n,t_b} \\ 1 & X_{1,t_b+1} & \ldots & X_{n,t_b+1} \\ \vdots & \vdots & \ddots & \vdots \\ 1 & X_{1,T-1} & \ldots & X_{n,T-1} \end{pmatrix},$$

[3] Generalizations to higher-order processes is straightforward.

[4] We omit, for the ease of exposition, to state in a rigorous way the technical assumptions necessary to proof the assertions made later.

then the model (18.4) can be written as

$$\operatorname{vec} Y = \operatorname{vec}(Y^{(1)}, Y^{(2)}) = \underbrace{\begin{pmatrix} \mathbf{X}^{(1)} \otimes I_n & 0 \\ 0 & \mathbf{X}^{(2)} \otimes I_n \end{pmatrix}}_{\mathbf{X}} \underbrace{\operatorname{vec}(c^{(1)}, \Phi^{(1)}, c^{(2)}, \Phi^{(2)})}_{\beta} + \operatorname{vec} Z.$$

The least-squares estimator becomes

$$\hat{\beta} = \operatorname{vec}(\hat{c}^{(1)}, \widehat{\Phi}^{(1)}, \hat{c}^{(2)}, \widehat{\Phi}^{(2)}) = (\mathbf{X}'\mathbf{X})^{-1}\mathbf{X}' \operatorname{vec} Y$$
$$= \begin{pmatrix} ((\mathbf{X}^{(1)'}\mathbf{X}^{(1)})^{-1}\mathbf{X}^{(1)'}) \otimes I_n & 0 \\ 0 & ((\mathbf{X}^{(2)'}\mathbf{X}^{(2)})^{-1}\mathbf{X}^{(2)'}) \otimes I_n \end{pmatrix} \operatorname{vec}(Y^{(1)}, Y^{(2)}).$$

This amounts to estimate the model separately over the two sample periods. The corresponding Wald test can be implemented by defining $R = (I_{n^2+n}, -I_{n^2+n})$ and computing the F-statistic

$$\mathrm{F}(t_b) = (R\hat{\beta})'[R(\mathbf{X}'\widehat{\Sigma}_{t_b}^{-1}\mathbf{X})R']^{-1}(R\hat{\beta}) \tag{18.5}$$

where $\hat{\beta} = \operatorname{vec}(\hat{c}^{(1)}, \widehat{\Phi}^{(1)}, \hat{c}^{(2)}, \widehat{\Phi}^{(2)})$ and where $\widehat{\Sigma}_{t_b}$ is computed from the least-squares residuals $\widehat{Z}_t$ as $\widehat{\Sigma}_{t_b} = \frac{1}{T}\sum_{t=1}^{T} \widehat{Z}_t\widehat{Z}_t'$ given break date t_b. Under the standard assumptions made in Chap. 13, this test statistic converges for $T \to \infty$ to a chi-square distribution with $n^2 + n$ degrees of freedom.[5] This test is known in the literature as the Chow test.

The previous analysis assumed that the potential break date t_b is known. This assumption often turns out to be unrealistic in practice. The question then arises how to determine a potential break date. Quandt (1960) proposed a simple procedure: compute the Chow test for all possible break dates and take as the break date the date where the F-statistic reaches its maximal value. Despite its simplicity, Quandt's procedure could not be implemented coherently because it was not clear which distribution to use for the construction of the critical values. This problem remained open for more than 30 years until the contribution of Andrews (1993).[6] Denote by $\lfloor x \rfloor$ the value of x rounded to the nearest integer toward minus infinity, and then the maximum Wald statistic and the logarithm of the Andrews and Ploberger (1994) exponential Wald statistic can be written as follows:

---

[5] As the asymptotic theory requires that t_b/T does not go to zero, one has to assume that both the number of periods before and after the break go to infinity.

[6] A textbook version of the test can be found in Stock and Watson (2011).

$$\text{sup F}: \quad \sup_{\tau \in (\tau^*, 1-\tau^*)} \text{F}(\lfloor T\tau \rfloor)$$

$$\text{exp F}: \quad \log \int_{\tau^*}^{1-\tau^*} \exp(\tfrac{1}{2} F(\lfloor T\tau \rfloor)) d\tau$$

where τ^* denotes the percentage of the sample that is trimmed. Usually, τ^* takes the value of 0.15 or 0.10. Critical values for low degrees of freedom are tabulated in Andrews (1993, 2003) and Stock and Watson (2011). It is possible to construct an asymptotic confidence interval for the break date. The corresponding formula can be found in Bai et al. (1998, p.401-402).

18.2.2 An Example

The use of the structural break test is demonstrated using historical data for the United Kingdom. The data consist of logged per capita real GDP, logged per capita real government expenditures, logged per capita real government revenues, the inflation based on the consumer price index, and a long-term interest rate over a sample period from 1830 to 2003. The basis for the analysis consists of a five variable VAR(2) model including a constant term and a linear trend. Three alternative structural break modes are investigated: break in the intercept, break in the intercept and the time trend, and break in all coefficients, including the VAR coefficients. The corresponding F-statistics are plotted in Fig. 18.1 against all possible break dates, allowing for a trimming value of 10%. The horizontal lines show for all three alternative break modes the corresponding critical values for the supF test given 5% significance levels. These critical values have been obtained

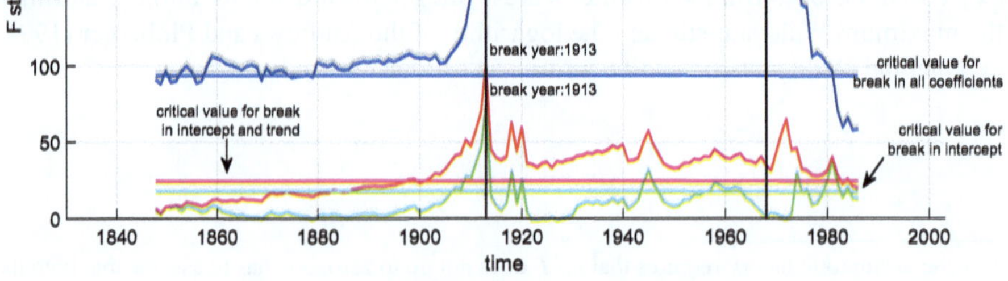

Fig. 18.1 Analysis of breaks dates with the sup F test statistic for historical UK time series

from Monte Carlo simulations as in Andrews (1993, 2003) and are given as 18.87, 28.09, and 97.39.[7]

Figure 18.1 shows that for all three modes, a significant structural break occurs. The corresponding values of the supF statistics are 78.06, 104.75, and 285.22. If only the deterministic parts are allowed to change, the break date is located in 1913. If all coefficients are allowed to change, the break is dated in 1968. However, all three F-statistics show a steep increase in 1913. Thus, if only one break is allowed, 1913 seems to be the most likely one.[8] The breaks are quite precisely dated. The corresponding standard errors are estimated to be 2 years for the break in the intercept only and 1 year for the other two break modes.

18.3 Time-Varying Parameters

This section discusses time-varying coefficient vector autoregressive models (TVC-VAR models). This model class retains the flavor of VAR models but assumes that they are only valid locally. Consider for this purpose a VAR(1) model with time-varying autoregressive coefficients Φ_t:

$$X_{t+1} = \Phi_t X_t + Z_{t+1}, \qquad Z_t \sim \text{IID}(0, \Sigma) \text{ with } \Sigma > 0, \quad t \in \mathbb{Z}. \tag{18.6}$$

This model can be easily generalized to higher-order VARs (see below), or, alternatively, one may think of Eq. (18.6) as a higher-order VAR in companion form. The autoregressive coefficient matrix is assumed to be stochastic. Thus, Φ_t is a random $n \times n$ matrix. Models of this type have been widely discussed in the probabilistic literature because they arise in many diverse contexts. In economics, Eq. (18.6) can be interpreted as the probabilistic version describing the value of a perpetuity, i.e., the present discounted value of a permanent commitment to pay a certain sum each period. Thereby, Z_t denotes the random periodic payments and Φ_t the random cumulative discount factors. The model also plays an important role in the characterization of the properties of volatility models as we have seen in Sect. 8.1 (see in particular the proof of Theorems 8.1). In this presentation, the above model is interpreted as a locally valid VAR process.

A natural question to ask is under which conditions Eq. (18.6) admits a stationary solution. An answer to this question can be found by iterating the equation backward in time:

$$\begin{aligned} X_t &= \Phi_{t-1} X_{t-1} + Z_t = \Phi_{t-1}(\Phi_{t-2} X_{t-2} + Z_{t-1}) + Z_t \\ &= Z_t + \Phi_{t-1} Z_{t-1} + \Phi_{t-1}\Phi_{t-2} X_{t-2} \end{aligned}$$

[7] Assuming a trimming value of 0.10, Andrews (2003, table I) reports critical values of 18.86 for $p = 5$, which corresponds to changes in the intercept only, and 27.27 for $p = 10$, which corresponds to changes in intercept and time trend.

[8] See Perron (2006) for a discussion of multiple breaks.

$$= Z_t + \Phi_{t-1}Z_{t-1} + \Phi_{t-1}\Phi_{t-2}Z_{t-2} + \Phi_{t-1}\Phi_{t-2}\Phi_{t-3}X_{t-3}$$

$$\ldots$$

$$= \sum_{j=0}^{k}\left(\prod_{i=1}^{j}\Phi_{t-i}\right)Z_{t-j} + \left(\prod_{i=1}^{k+1}\Phi_{t-i}\right)X_{t-k-1}, \quad k = 0, 1, 2, \ldots$$

where it is understood that $\prod_{i=1}^{0} = I_n$. This suggests as a solution candidate

$$X_t = \lim_{k\to\infty}\sum_{j=0}^{k}\left(\prod_{i=1}^{j}\Phi_{t-i}\right)Z_{t-j}$$

$$= Z_t + \Phi_{t-1}Z_{t-1} + \Phi_{t-1}\Phi_{t-2}Z_{t-2} + \Phi_{t-1}\Phi_{t-2}\Phi_{t-3}Z_{t-3} + \ldots \tag{18.7}$$

Based on results obtained by Brandt (1986) and extended by Bougerol and Picard (1992b), the following theorem holds.

Theorem 18.1 (Solution TVC-VAR(1)) *Let* $\{(\Phi_t, Z_t)\}$ *be a strictly stationary ergodic process such that:*

(i) $\mathbb{E}(\log^+ \|\Phi_t\|) < \infty$ *and* $\mathbb{E}(\log^+ \|Z_t\|) < \infty$ *where* x^+ *denotes* $\max\{x, 0\}$*;*
(ii) the top Lyapounov exponent γ *defined as*

$$\gamma = \inf_{t\in\mathbb{N}}\left\{\mathbb{E}\left(\frac{1}{t+1}\log\|\Phi_0\Phi_{-1}\ldots\Phi_{-t}\|\right)\right\}$$

is strictly negative.

Then X_t *as defined in Eq.* (18.7) *converges a.s. and* $\{X_t\}$ *is the unique strictly stationary solution of Eq.* (18.6).

Remark 18.1 The condition on the top Lyapunov exponent can be interpreted by saying that the autoregressive matrices $\{\Phi_t\}$ must have their eigenvalues absolutely strictly smaller than one "on average." However, it is not sufficient that $\rho(\Phi_t)$, the spectral radius of Φ_t, is strictly smaller than one for every t as shown by the following example:[9]

$$\Phi_t = \begin{pmatrix} 0 & 1 + \frac{(-1)^t}{2} \\ 1 - \frac{(-1)^t}{2} & 0 \end{pmatrix}.$$

[9] The spectral radius of an $n \times n$ matrix is the maximum of its absolute eigenvalues.

The eigenvalues for this matrix are $\pm\sqrt{3}/2$. Hence, $\rho(\Phi_t) < 1$ for every t, but $\rho(\Phi_{t+1}\Phi_t) = 9/4 > 1$. See also Francq and Zakoïan (2001) for more details.

Remark 18.2 Although Theorem 18.1 states only sufficient conditions, these assumptions can hardly be relaxed.

The solution (18.7), if it exists, is similar to a causal representation. The matrix sequence $\{\prod_{i=1}^{h} \Phi_{t+h-i}\}_{h=0,1,2,\ldots} = \{I_n, \Phi_t, \Phi_{t+1}\Phi_t, \Phi_{t+2}\Phi_{t+1}\Phi_t, \ldots\}$ represents the effect of an impulse in period t to X_{t+h}, $h = 0, 1, 2, \ldots$ and can therefore be interpreted as impulse response functions. In contrast to the impulse response functions studied so far, they are clearly random and time dependent because the effect of Z_t depends on future coefficients. In particular, the effect of Z_t on X_{t+h}, $h \geq 1$, is not the same as the effect of Z_{t-h} on X_t. Nevertheless, it is possible to construct meaningful impulse response functions by Monte Carlo simulations. One may then report the mean of the impulse responses or some quantiles for different time periods.[10] Alternatively, one may ignore the randomness and time dependency and define "local" impulse responses as Φ_t^h, $h = 0, 1, 2, \ldots$. Note, however, that the impulse responses so defined still vary with time. Irrespective to how the impulse responses are constructed, they can be interpreted in the same way as in the case of constant coefficients. In particular, we may use some of the identification schemes discussed in Chap. 15 and compute the impulse responses with respect to structural shocks. Similar arguments apply to the forecast error variance decomposition (FEVD).

The model is closed by fixing a law of motion for Φ_t. As already mentioned in Sect. 17.2.5, there are several possibilities. In this presentation, we adopt the following flexible autoregressive specification:

$$\beta_{t+1} - \bar{\beta} = F(\beta_t - \bar{\beta}) + V_{t+1} \qquad V_t \sim \text{WN}(0, Q) \tag{18.8}$$

where $\beta_t = \operatorname{vec} \Phi_t$ denotes the n^2 vector of stacked coefficients. Q is assumed to be fixed and is, usually, specified as a diagonal matrix. If the eigenvalues of F are inside the unit circle, the autoregressive model is mean-reverting and $\bar{\beta}$ can be interpreted as the average coefficient vector. The formulation in Eq. (18.8) is, however, not restricted to this case and allows explicitly the possibility that $\{\beta_t\}$ follows a random walk. This specification has become very popular in the empirical macroeconomic literature and was initially adopted by Cogley and Sargent (2001) to analyze the dynamics of inflation across different policy regimes.[11]

The model consisting of Eqs. (18.6) and (18.8) can be easily reformulated as a state space model by defining $\xi_t = \beta_t - \bar{\beta}$ as the state vector. The state and the measurement equation can then be written as:

[10] Potter (2000) discusses the primal problems of defining impulse responses in a nonlinear context.

[11] They allow for a correlation between V_t and Z_t.

$$\text{state equation:} \qquad \xi_{t+1} = F\xi_t + V_{t+1} \tag{18.9}$$

$$\text{measurement equation:} \qquad X_t = (X_{t-1}' \otimes I_n)\bar{\beta} + (X_{t-1}' \otimes I_n)\xi_t + Z_t. \tag{18.10}$$

Conditional on initial values for the coefficients and their covariances, the state space model can be estimated by maximum likelihood by applying the Kalman filter (see Sect. 17.4 and Kim and Nelson, 1999). One possibility to initialize the Kalman filter is to estimate the model for some initial sample period assuming fixed coefficients and extract from these estimates the corresponding starting values.

As it turns out, allowing time variation only in the coefficients of the VAR model overstates the role attributed to structural changes. We therefore generalize the model to allow for time-varying volatility. More specifically, we also allow Σ in Eq. (18.6) to vary with time. The modeling of the time variation in Σ is, however, not a straightforward task because we must ensure that in each period, Σ_t is a symmetric positive definite matrix. One approach is to specify a process especially designed for modeling the dynamics of covariance matrices. This so-called Wishart autoregressive process was first introduced to economics by Gouriéroux et al. (2009) and successfully applied by Burren and Neusser (2013). It leads to a nonlinear state space system, which can be estimated with the particle filter, a generalization of the Kalman filter.

Another more popular approach was initiated by Cogley and Sargent (2005) and Primiceri (2005). It is based on the Cholesky factorization of the time-varying covariance matrix Σ_t. Using the same notation as in Sect. 15.2, Σ_t is decomposed as

$$\Sigma_t = B_t \Omega_t B_t' \tag{18.11}$$

where B_t is a time-varying lower triangular matrix with ones on the diagonal and Ω_t a time-varying diagonal matrix with strictly positive diagonal elements.[12] The logged diagonal elements of Ω_t are then assumed to evolve as independent univariate random walks. This specification can be written in matrix terms as

$$\Omega_t = \Omega_{t-1} \exp(D_t) \tag{18.12}$$

where D_t is a diagonal matrix with $\text{diag}(D_t) \sim \text{WN}(0, \Omega_D)$. In the above formulation, exp denotes the matrix exponential.[13] Taking the matrix logarithm, we get exactly the formulation of Cogley and Sargent (2005) and Primiceri (2005). For the time evolution of B_t, we propose a similar specification:

---

[12] It is possible to consider other short-run-type identification schemes (see Sect. 15.2) than the Cholesky factorization.

[13] The matrix exponential of a matrix A is defined as $\exp(A) = \sum_{k=0}^{\infty} \frac{1}{k!} A^k$, where A is any matrix. Its inverse $\log(A)$ is defined only for $\|A\| < 1$ and is given by $\log(A) = \sum_{k=1}^{\infty} \frac{(-1)^{k-1}}{l} A^k$.

$$B_t = B_{t-1} \exp(C_t) \tag{18.13}$$

where C_t is a strictly lower triangular matrix, i.e., C_t is a lower triangular matrix with zeros on the diagonal. The non-zero entries of C_t, denoted by $[C_t]_{i>j}$, are assumed to follow a multivariate white noise process with diagonal covariance matrix Σ_B, i.e., $[C_t]_{i>j} \sim \text{WN}(0, \Sigma_B)$. It can be shown that the matrix exponential of strictly lower triangular matrices are triangular matrices with ones on the diagonal. As the set of triangular matrices with ones on the diagonal form a group, called the *unipotent group* and denoted by SLT_n, the above specification is well-defined. Moreover, this formulation is a very natural one as the set of strictly lower triangular matrices is the tangent space of SLT_n at the identity (see Baker, 2002, for details). Thus, Eq. (18.13) can be interpreted as a log-linearized version of B_t. The technique proposed for the evolution of B_t in Eq. (18.13) departs from Primiceri (2005), who models each element of the inverse of B_t and therefore misses a coherent system theoretic approach.

Although this TVC-VAR model with time-varying volatility can in principle also be estimated by maximum likelihood, this technique can hardly be implemented successfully in practice. The main reason is that the likelihood function of such a model, even when the dimension and the order of the VAR is low, is a very high-dimensional nonlinear object with probably many local maxima. Moreover, as the variances governing the time variation are small, at least for some of the coefficients, the likelihood function is flat in some regions of the parameter space. These features make maximization of the likelihood function difficult, if not impossible, in practice. For these reasons, Bayesian techniques have been used almost exclusively. There is, however, also a conceptional issue involved. As the Bayesian approach does not strictly distinguish between fixed "true" parameters and random samples, it is better suited to handle TVC-VAR models that treat the parameters as random. The prior beliefs are then incorporated in the Kalman filter by specifying as starting values $\xi_{0|0}$ and $P_{0|0}$ the mean and the variance of the prior distribution (see Sect. 17.3.1). Primiceri (2005), Del Negro and Primiceri (2015), Cogley and Sargent (2005), Canova (2007), and Koop and Korobilis (2010), among others, are prime applications for these techniques.

18.4 Regime Switching Models

The regime switching models are similar to the time-varying models discussed in the previous section. The difference is that the time variation is governed by a hidden Markov chain with a finite state space $\mathcal{S} = \{1, 2, \ldots, k\}$. Usually, the number of states k is small and is equal in practice to two or maximal three. The states have usually an economic connotation. For example, if k equals two, state 1 might correspond to a boom phase whereas state 2 to a recession. Such models have a long tradition in economics and have therefore been used extensively. Seminal references include Goldfeld and Quandt (1973, 1976), Hamilton (1994a), Kim and Nelson (1999), Krolzig (1997), Maddala (1986), Rubio-Ramírez et al. (2006), and Hubrich and Waggoner (2022). Frühwirth-Schnatter (2006) presents a detailed statistical analysis of regime switching models.

Consider, as before, the TVC-VAR(1) model given in Eq. (18.6) as a starting point. We associate to each state $j \in \mathcal{S}$ a coefficient matrix $\Phi^{(j)}$. Thus, in the regime switching model, the coefficients Φ_t can only assume a finite number values $\Phi^{(1)}, \ldots, \Phi^{(k)}$ depending on the state of the Markov chain. The actual value assigned to Φ_t is governed by a Markov chain defined by a fixed but unknown transition probability matrix P where

$$[P]_{ij} = \mathbf{P}\left(\Phi_t = \Phi^{(j)} | \Phi_{t-1} = \Phi^{(i)}\right) \qquad i, j = 1, \ldots, k. \tag{18.14}$$

Thus, $[P]_{ij}$ is the probability that Φ_t takes the value $\Phi^{(j)}$, given that it assumed the value $\Phi^{(i)}$ in the previous period. The probability that Φ_{t+h} is in state j given that Φ_t was in state i is therefore $[P^h]_{ij}$. The definition of the transition matrix in Eq. (18.14) implies that P is a stochastic matrix, i.e., that $[P]_{ij} \geq 0$ and $\sum_{j=1}^{k} [P]_{ij} = 1$. Moreover, it is assumed that the chain is regular, meaning that it is ergodic (irreducible) and aperiodic.[14] This is equivalent to the existence of a fixed-integer $m > 0$ such that P^m has only strictly positive entries (see Berman & Plemmons, 1994, Chapter 8). Regular Markov chains have a unique ergodic (stationary) distribution vector π with strictly positive entries determined by $\pi' P = \pi'$. This distribution is approached from any initial distribution vector π_0, i.e., $\lim_{t\to\infty} \pi_0' P^t = \pi'$. Moreover, $\lim_{t\to\infty} P^t = P^\infty$, where P^∞ is a transition matrix with all rows equal to π'. Given this setup, we can again invoke Theorem 18.1 and verify whether a (strictly) stationary solution of the form of Eq. (18.7) exists.

Given observations $x_0, x_1, \ldots, x_{T-1}1, x_T$ for $X_0, X_1, \ldots, X_{T-1}, X_T$, a maximum likelihood approach can be set up to estimate the unknown parameters $\Phi^{(1)}, \ldots, \Phi^{(k)}, \Sigma, P$.[15] Collect these parameters into a vector θ, and denote by $s_t \in \mathcal{S}$ the state of the Markov chain in period t and by $\mathcal{X}_t = (x_0, x_1, \ldots, x_{t-1}, x_t)$ the information available up to period t. Write the conditional density of x_t given $s_t = j$ and observations $\mathcal{X}_{t-1}$ as

$$f(x_t | s_t = j, \mathcal{X}_{t-1}; \theta).$$

The joint density of $(x_t, s_t = j)$ is

$$f(x_t, s_t = j | \mathcal{X}_{t-1}; \theta) = f(x_t | s_t = j, \mathcal{X}_{t-1}; \theta) \times P(s_t = j | \mathcal{X}_{t-1}; \theta)$$

---

[14] A chain is called ergodic or irreducible if for all states i and j, there is a strictly positive probability that the chain moves from state i to state j in finitely many steps. A chain is called aperiodic if it can return to any state i at irregular times. See, among others, Norris (1998) and Berman and Plemmons (1994) for an introduction to Markov chains and its terminology.

[15] The presentation of the maximum likelihood approach follows closely the exposition by Hamilton (1994a, chapter 22), where more details can be found.

where in analogy to the Kalman filter, the expressions $P(s_t = j|\mathcal{X}_{t-1};\theta)$ and $j = 1,\dots,k$ are called the predicted transition probabilities. The conditional marginal density of x_t then becomes

$$f(x_t|\mathcal{X}_{t-1};\theta) = \sum_{j=1}^{k} f(x_t|s_t = j, \mathcal{X}_{t-1};\theta) \times P(s_t = j|\mathcal{X}_{t-1};\theta).$$

In the case of $Z_t \sim \text{IID}\,\text{N}(0,\Sigma)$, the above density is a finite mixture of Gaussian distributions (see Frühwirth-Schnatter, 2006, for details). The (conditional) log likelihood function is therefore given by

$$\ell(\theta) = \sum_{t=1}^{T} \log f(x_t|\mathcal{X}_{t-1};\theta).$$

In order to evaluate the likelihood function, note that the joint density of $(x_t, s_t = j)$ may also be factored as

$$f(x_t, s_t = j|\mathcal{X}_{t-1};\theta) = P(s_t = j|\mathcal{X}_t;\theta) \times f(x_t|\mathcal{X}_{t-1};\theta).$$

Combining these expressions, one obtains an expression for the filtered transition probabilities $P(s_t = j|\mathcal{X}_t;\theta)$:

$$\begin{aligned} P(s_t = j|\mathcal{X}_t;\theta) &= \frac{f(x_t|s_t = j, \mathcal{X}_{t-1};\theta) \times P(s_t = j|\mathcal{X}_{t-1};\theta)}{f(x_t|\mathcal{X}_{t-1};\theta)} \\ &= \frac{f(x_t|s_t = j, \mathcal{X}_{t-1};\theta) \times P(s_t = j|\mathcal{X}_{t-1};\theta)}{\sum_{j=1}^{k} f(x_t|s_t = j, \mathcal{X}_{t-1};\theta) \times P(s_t = j|\mathcal{X}_{t-1};\theta)}. \end{aligned} \tag{18.15}$$

Next period's predicted transition probabilities are then obtained by multiplication with the transition matrix:

$$\begin{pmatrix} P(s_{t+1} = 1|\mathcal{X}_t;\theta) \\ \vdots \\ P(s_{t+1} = k|\mathcal{X}_t;\theta) \end{pmatrix} = P' \times \begin{pmatrix} P(s_t = 1|\mathcal{X}_t;\theta) \\ \vdots \\ P(s_t = k|\mathcal{X}_t;\theta) \end{pmatrix} \tag{18.16}$$

Given initial probabilities $P(s_1 = j|\mathcal{X}_0;\theta)$ and $j = 1,\dots,k$ and a fixed value for θ, Eqs. (18.15) and (18.16) can be iterated forward to produce a sequence of predicted transition probabilities $(P(s_t = 1|\mathcal{X}_{t-1};\theta),\dots,P(s_t = k|\mathcal{X}_{t-1};\theta))'$, $t = 1,2,\dots,T$, which can be used to evaluate the Gaussian likelihood function. Numerical procedures must then be used for the maximization of the likelihood function. This task is not without challenge because the likelihood function of Gaussian mixture models typically has singularities and many local maxima.

Kiefer (1978) showed that there exists a bounded local maximum, which yields a consistent and asymptotically normal estimate for θ for which standard errors can be constructed in the usual way. In practice, problems encountered during the maximization can be alleviated by experimentation with alternative starting values. Thereby, the initial probability $(P(s_1 = 1|\mathcal{X}_0; \theta), \ldots, P(s_1 = k|\mathcal{X}_0; \theta)$ could either be treated as additional parameters as in Goldfeld and Quandt (1973) or set to the uniform distribution. For technical details and alternative estimation strategies, like the EM algorithm, see Hamilton (1994a, chapter 22) and in particular (Frühwirth-Schnatter, 2006).

By reversing the above recursion, it is possible to compute smoothed transition probabilities $P(s_t = j|\mathcal{X}_T; \theta)$ (see Kim, 1994):

$$P(s_t = j|\mathcal{X}_T; \theta) = P(s_t = j|\mathcal{X}_t; \theta) \sum_{i=1}^{k} [P]_{ij} \frac{P(s_{t+1} = i|\mathcal{X}_T; \theta)}{P(s_{t+1} = i|\mathcal{X}_t; \theta)}$$

The iteration is initialized with $P(s_T = j|\mathcal{X}_T; \theta)$, which has been computed in the forward recursion.

The basic model can and has been generalized in several dimensions. The most obvious one is the inclusion of additional lags beyond the first one. The second one concerns the possibility of a regime switching covariance matrix Σ. These modifications can be accommodated using the methods outlined above. Third, one may envision time-varying transition probabilities to account for duration dependence. In business cycle analysis, for example, the probability of moving out of a recession may depend on how long the economy has already been in the recession regime. This idea can be implemented by modeling the transition probabilities via a logit specification:

$$[P]_{ij} = \frac{\exp(z_t'\alpha_i)}{1 + \exp(z_t'\alpha_i)}, \qquad i \neq j,$$

where z_t includes a constant and a set of additional variables. These additional variables can be some exogenous variables but, more interestingly, may include some lagged variables x_{t-d} (Krolzig, 1997). Note that the transition probabilities do not only depend on z_t but also on the state. The resulting model has some features shared with the smooth transition autoregressive model of Granger and Teräsvirta (1993). Early economic applications of regime switching models with time-varying transition probabilities can be found in Diebold et al. (1994), Filardo (1994), and Filardo and Gordon (1998).

An important aspect in practice is the determination of the number of regimes. Unfortunately, there is no direct test available for the null hypothesis $k = m$ against the alternative $k = m + 1$. The reason is that the likelihood contains parameters that are only present under the alternative. The parameters describing the $m + 1$-th state are unidentified under the null hypothesis. The problem has been analyzed by Andrews and Ploberger (1994) in a general theoretical context. Alternatively, one may estimate the model under the null hypothesis and conduct a series of specification tests as proposed by Hamilton (1996). It has also been suggested to use the information criteria like AIC and BIC to determine the number of regimes (Frühwirth-Schnatter, 2006, p. 346–347):

$$\text{AIC} = -2\ell(\theta) + 2k(k-1)$$
$$\text{BIC} = -2\ell(\theta) + \log(T)k(k-1)$$

where $k(k-1)$ are the free parameters in the transition matrix P.

18.5 Smooth Transition and Threshold VAR Models

A further class of nonlinear models often encountered in practice are *threshold and smooth transition models*. These models have the form

$$X_t = c + \sum_{j=1}^{p} \Phi_j X_{t-j} + g(Y_t; \alpha)\left(\tilde{c} + \sum_{j=1}^{p} \widetilde{\Phi}_j X_{t-j}\right) + Z_t \tag{18.17}$$

where the transition function $g(Y_t; \alpha)$ is a $n \times n$ matrix function, which determines when and to which extent there is a change in the coefficient matrices. If $g(Y_t; \alpha) = 0$, the standard linear VAR model prevails. The function $g(Y_t; \alpha)$ depends on some variable Y_t, which may consist of exogenous variables (i.e., variables not included in X_t) or of X_t delayed by some period d (i.e., X_{t-d}). Estimation may again be conducted by the maximum likelihood method. Granger and Teräsvirta (1993) and Hubrich and Teräsvirta (2013) provide a survey of this class of models with more details and further references.

One common specification for the transition function is

$$g(Y_t; \alpha) = (1 - \exp(-\gamma(Y_t - \nu)^2))I_n.$$

This results in the exponential smooth transition VAR (EST-VAR) model. When Y_t is close to ν, $g(Y_t; \alpha)$ is close to zero, and we are back in the standard linear case. If Y_t gets further and further away from ν, the VAR with coefficients $c, \Phi_1, \ldots, \Phi_p$ transforms smoothly to a VAR with coefficients $\tilde{c}, \widetilde{\Phi}_1, \ldots, \widetilde{\Phi}_p$.

Another common specification of the transition function is

$$g(Y_t; \alpha) = \mathrm{I}_{\{Y_t > \nu\}}$$

where $\mathrm{I}_{\{Y_t > \nu\}}$ denotes the indicator function. In this case, we obtain the threshold VAR (TVAR) model. With this specification, the parameters jump if $Y_t > \nu$. Thereby, the threshold value ν may be known or unknown. An interesting application is Galvao and Marcellino (2014).

Complex Numbers

A

The simple quadratic equation $x^2 + 1 = 0$ has no solution in the field of real numbers, $\mathbb{R}$. Thus, it is necessary to envisage the larger field of complex numbers $\mathbb{C}$. A complex number z is an ordered pair (a, b) of real numbers where ordered means that we regard (a, b) and (b, a) as distinct if $a \neq b$. Let $x = (a, b)$ and $y = (c, d)$ be two complex numbers. Then we endow the set of complex numbers with an addition and a multiplication in the following way:

$$\text{addition:} \qquad x + y = (a, b) + (c, d) = (a + c, b + d)$$

$$\text{multiplication:} \qquad xy = (a, b)(c, d) = (ac - bd, ad + bc).$$

These two operations will turn $\mathbb{C}$ into a field where $(0, 0)$ and $(1, 0)$ play the role of 0 and 1.[1] The real numbers $\mathbb{R}$ are embedded into $\mathbb{C}$ because we identify any $a \in \mathbb{R}$ with $(a, 0) \in \mathbb{C}$.

The number $\imath = (0, 1)$ is of special interest. It solves the equation $x^2 + 1 = 0$, i.e., $\imath^2 = -1$, the other solution being $-\imath = (0, -1)$. Thus any complex number (a, b) may be written as $(a, b) = a + \imath b$ where a, b are arbitrary real numbers.[2]

An element z in this field can be represented in two ways:

$$z = a + \imath b \qquad \text{Cartesian coordinates}$$

---

[1] Subtraction and division can be defined accordingly:

$$\text{subtraction:} \qquad (a, b) - (c, d) = (a - c, b - d)$$

$$\text{division:} \qquad (a, b)/(c, d) = \frac{(ac + bd, bc - ad)}{(c^2 + d^2)}, \quad c^2 + d^2 \neq 0.$$

[2] A more detailed introduction of complex numbers can be found in Rudin (1976, 1987) or any other mathematics textbook.

K. Neusser, *Time Series Econometrics*, Springer Texts in Business and Economics,
https://doi.org/10.1007/978-3-031-88838-0

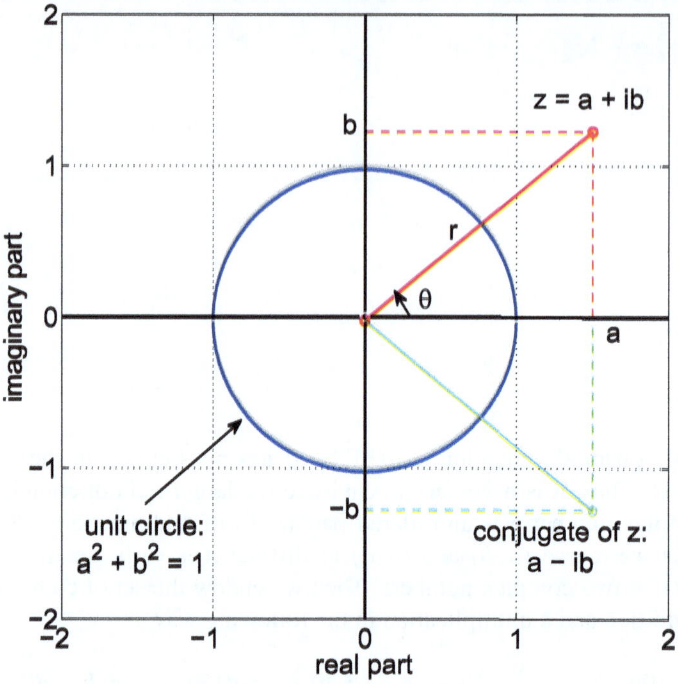

Fig. A.1 Representation of a complex number

$$= re^{\imath\theta} = r(\cos\theta + \imath\sin\theta) \qquad \text{polar coordinates.}$$

In the representation in Cartesian coordinates, $a = \mathrm{Re}(z) = \Re(z)$ is called the *real part*, whereas $b = \mathrm{Im}(z) = \Im(z)$ is called the *imaginary part* of z.

A complex number z can be viewed as a point in the two-dimensional Cartesian coordinate system with coordinates (a, b). This geometric interpretation is represented in Fig. A.1.

The *absolute value* or *modulus* of z, denoted by $|z|$, is given by $r = \sqrt{a^2 + b^2}$. Thus, the absolute value is nothing but the distance of z viewed as a point in the complex plane (the two-dimensional Cartesian coordinate system) to the origin (see Fig. A.1). θ denotes the angle to the positive real axis (x-axis) measured in radians. It is denoted by $\theta = \arg z$. It holds that $\tan\theta = \frac{b}{a}$. Finally, the conjugate of z, denoted by $\bar{z}$, is defined by $\bar{z} = a - \imath b$.

From the definition of complex numbers in polar coordinates, we immediately derive the following implications:

$$\cos\theta = \frac{e^{\imath\theta} + e^{-\imath\theta}}{2} = \frac{a}{r},$$

$$\sin\theta = \frac{e^{\imath\theta} - e^{-\imath\theta}}{2\imath} = \frac{b}{r}.$$

Further implications are De Moivre's formula and Pythagoras' theorem (see Fig. A.1):

$$\text{de Moivre's formula} \qquad \left(re^{\imath\theta}\right)^n = r^n e^{\imath n\theta} = r^n(\cos n\theta + \imath \sin n\theta)$$

$$\text{Pythagoras' theorem} \qquad 1 = e^{\imath\theta}e^{-\imath\theta} = (\cos\theta + \imath\sin\theta)(\cos\theta - \imath\sin\theta)$$
$$= \cos^2\theta + \sin^2\theta$$

From Pythagoras' theorem, it follows that $r^2 = a^2 + b^2$. The representation in polar coordinates allows to derive many trigonometric formulas.

Consider the polynomial $\Phi(z) = \phi_0 - \phi_1 z - \phi_2 z^2 - \cdots - \phi_p z^p$ of order $p \geq 1$ with $\phi_0 = 1$.[3] The *fundamental theorem of algebra* then states that every polynomial of order $p \geq 1$ has exactly p roots in the field of complex numbers. Thus, the field of complex numbers is algebraically complete. Denote these roots by $\lambda_1, \ldots, \lambda_p$, allowing that some roots may appear several times. The polynomial can then be factorized as

$$\Phi(z) = \left(1 - \lambda_1^{-1}z\right)\left(1 - \lambda_2^{-1}z\right)\cdots\left(1 - \lambda_p^{-1}z\right).$$

This expression is well-defined because the assumption of a nonzero constant $(\phi_0 = 1 \neq 0)$ excludes the possibility of roots equal to zero. If we assume that the coefficients ϕ_j, $j = 0, \ldots, p$, are real numbers, the complex roots appear in conjugate pairs. Thus, if $z = a + \imath b$, $b \neq 0$, is a root, then $\bar{z} = a - \imath b$ is also a root.

[3] The notation with "$-\phi_j z^j$" instead of "$\phi_j z^j$" was chosen to conform to the notation of AR-models.

Linear Difference Equations

B

Linear difference equations play an important role in time series analysis. We therefore summarize the most important results.[1] Consider the following linear difference equation of order p with constant coefficients. This equation is defined by the recursion:

$$X_t = \phi_1 X_{t-1} + \cdots + \phi_p X_{t-p}, \qquad \phi_p \neq 0, t \in \mathbb{Z}.$$

Thereby $\{X_t\}$ represents a sequence of real numbers, and $\phi_1, \ldots, \phi_p$ are p constant coefficients. The above difference equation is called *homogeneous* because it involves no other variable than X_t. A solution to this equation is a function $F : \mathbb{Z} \to \mathbb{R}$ such that its values $F(t)$ or F_t reduce the difference equation to an identity.

It is easy to see that if $\{X_t^{(1)}\}$ and $\{X_t^{(2)}\}$ are two solutions than $\{c_1 X_t^{(1)} + c_2 X_t^{(2)}\}$, for any $c_1, c_2 \in \mathbb{R}$ is also a solution. The set of solutions forms therefore a linear space (vector space).

Definition B.1 A set of solutions $\{\{X_t^{(1)}\}, \ldots, \{X_t^{(m)}\}\}$, $m \leq p$, is called *linearly independent* if

$$c_1 X_t^{(1)} + \cdots + c_m X_t^{(m)} = 0, \qquad \text{for } t = 0, 1, \ldots, p-1$$

implies that $c_1 = \cdots = c_m = 0$. Otherwise we call the set *linearly dependent.*

Given arbitrary starting values $x_0, \ldots, x_{p-1}$ for $X_0, \ldots, X_{p-1}$, the difference equation determines all further through the recursion:

$$X_t = \phi_1 X_{t-1} + \cdots + \phi_p X_{t-p} \qquad t = p, p+1, \ldots.$$

[1] For more detailed presentations, see Agarwal (2000), Elaydi (2005), or Neusser (2021).

K. Neusser, *Time Series Econometrics*, Springer Texts in Business and Economics,
https://doi.org/10.1007/978-3-031-88838-0

Similarly for X_t mit $t = -1, -2, \ldots$. Suppose we have p linearly independent solutions $\{\{X_t^{(1)}\}, \ldots, \{X_t^{(p)}\}\}$, then there exists exactly p numbers $c_1, \ldots, c_p$ such that the solution

$$X_t = c_1 X_t^{(1)} + c_2 X_t^{(2)} + \cdots + c_p X_t^{(p)}$$

is compatible with arbitrary starting values $x_0, \ldots, x_{p-1}$. These starting values then determine uniquely all values of the sequence $\{X_t\}$. Thus, $\{X_t\}$ is the only solution compatible with starting values. The goal therefore consists in finding p linearly independent solutions.

We guess that the solutions are of the form $X_t = z^{-t}$ where z may be a complex number. If this guess is right, then we must have for $t = 0$:

$$1 - \phi_1 z - \cdots - \phi_p z^p = 0.$$

This equation is called the *characteristic equation*.[2] Thus, z must be a root of the polynomial $\Phi(z) = 1 - \phi_1 z - \cdots - \phi_p z^p$. From the fundamental theorem of algebra, we know that there are exactly p roots in the field of complex numbers. Denote these roots by $z_1, \ldots, z_p$.

Suppose that these roots are different from each other. In this case, $\{\{z_1^{-t}\}, \ldots, \{z_p^{-t}\}\}$ constitutes a set of p linearly independent solutions. To show this, it is sufficient to verify that the determinant of the matrix

$$W = \begin{pmatrix} 1 & 1 & \ldots & 1 \\ z_1^{-1} & z_2^{-1} & \ldots & z_p^{-1} \\ z_1^{-2} & z_2^{-2} & \ldots & z_p^{-2} \\ \vdots & \vdots & & \vdots \\ z_1^{-p+1} & z_2^{-p+1} & \ldots & z_p^{-p+1} \end{pmatrix}$$

is different from zero. This determinant is known as Vandermonde's determinant and is equal to $\det W = \prod_{1 \le i < j \le p} (z_i - z_j)$. This determinant is clearly different from zero because the roots are different from each other. The general solution to the difference equation therefore is

$$X_t = c_1 z_1^{-t} + \cdots + c_p z_p^{-t} \tag{B.1}$$

where the constants $c_1, \ldots, c_p$ are determined from initial conditions.

In the case where some roots of the characteristic polynomial are equal, the general solution becomes more involved. Let $z_1, \ldots, z_r$, $r < p$, be the roots that are different from each other, and denote their corresponding multiplicities by

---

[2] Sometimes, one can find $z^p - \phi_1 z^{p-1} - \cdots - \phi_p = 0$ as the characteristic equation. The roots are of the two characteristic equations that are then reciprocal to each other.

$m_1, \ldots, m_r$. It holds that $\sum_{j=1}^{r} = p$. The general solution is then given by

$$X_t = \sum_{j=1}^{r} \left(c_{j0} + c_{j1} t + \cdots + c_{jm_j-1} t^{m_j-1} \right) z_j^{-t} \tag{B.2}$$

where the constants c_{ji} are again determined from initial conditions.

Stochastic Convergence

C

This appendix presents the relevant concepts and theorems from probability theory. The reader interested in more details should consult corresponding textbooks, for example, Billingsley (1986), Brockwell and Davis (1991), Durrett (2019), Grimmett and Stirzaker (2001), Hogg and Craig (1995), or Kallenberg (2002) among many others.

In the following, all real random variables or random vectors X are defined with respect to some probability space $(\Omega, \mathfrak{A}, \mathbf{P})$. Thereby, Ω denotes an arbitrary space with σ-field $\mathfrak{A}$ and probability measure $\mathbf{P}$. A random variable, respectively, random vector, X is then defined as a measurable function from Ω to $\mathbb{R}$, respectively, $\mathbb{R}^n$. The probability space Ω plays no role as it is introduced just for the sake of mathematical rigor. The interest rather focuses on the distributions induced by $\mathbf{P} \circ X^{-1}$.

We will make use of the following important inequalities.

Theorem C.1 (Cauchy-Bunyakovsky-Schwarz Inequality) *For arbitrary random variables X and Y,*

$$|\mathbb{E}(XY)| \leq \sqrt{\mathbb{E}X^2}\sqrt{\mathbb{E}Y^2}.$$

The equality holds if and only if $X = \frac{\mathbb{E}(XY)}{\mathbb{E}(Y^2)} Y$.

Theorem C.2 (Minkowski's Inequality) *Let X and Y be two random variables with $\mathbb{E}|X|^2 < \infty$ and $\mathbb{E}|Y|^2 < \infty$; then,*

$$\left(\mathbb{E}|X+Y|^2\right)^{1/2} \leq \left(\mathbb{E}|X|^2\right)^{1/2} + \left(\mathbb{E}|Y|^2\right)^{1/2}.$$

K. Neusser, *Time Series Econometrics*, Springer Texts in Business and Economics,
https://doi.org/10.1007/978-3-031-88838-0

Theorem C.3 (Chebyshev's Inequality) *If* $\mathbb{E}|X|^r < \infty$ *for* $r \geq 0$*, then for every* $r \geq 0$ *and any* $\varepsilon > 0$*,*

$$\mathbf{P}[|X| \geq \varepsilon] \leq \varepsilon^{-r}\mathbb{E}|X|^r.$$

Theorem C.4 (Borel-Cantelli Lemma) *Let* $A_1, A_2, \ldots \in \mathfrak{A}$ *be an infinite sequence of events in some probability space* $(\Omega, \mathfrak{A}, \mathbf{P})$ *such that* $\sum_{k=1}^{\infty} \mathbf{P}(A_k) < \infty$*. Then,* $\mathbf{P}\{A_k \text{ i.o.}\} = 0$*. The event* $\{A_k \text{ i.o.}\}$ *is defined by* $\{A_k \text{ i.o.}\} = \limsup_k\{A_k\} = \bigcap_{k=1}^{\infty}\bigcup_{j=k}^{\infty} A_j$*, where i.o. stands for infinitely often.*

On several occasions, it is necessary to evaluate the limit of a sequence of random variables. In probability theory, several concepts of convergence are discussed: *almost sure convergence*, *convergence in probability*, *convergence in r-th mean* (*convergence in quadratic mean*), and *convergence in distribution*. We only give definitions and the most important theorems, leaving an in-depth discussion to the relevant literature. Although not explicitly mentioned, many of the theorem below also hold in an analogous way in a multidimensional context.

Definition C.1 (Almost Sure Convergence) For random variables X and $\{X_t\}$ defined on the same probability space $(\Omega, \mathfrak{A}, \mathbf{P})$, we say that $\{X_t\}$ *converges almost surely* or *with probability one* to X if

$$\mathbf{P}\left\{\omega \in \Omega : \lim_{t\to\infty} X_t(\omega) = X(\omega)\right\} = 1.$$

This fact is denoted by $X_t \xrightarrow{a.s.} X$ or $\lim X_t = X$ a.s.

Theorem C.5 (Kolmogorov's Strong Law of Large Numbers) *Let* $X, X_1, X_2, \ldots$ *be identically and independently distributed random variables. Then, the arithmetic average* $\overline{X}_T = \frac{1}{T}\sum_{t=1}^{T} X_t$ *converges almost surely to* $\mathbb{E}X$ *if and only if* $\mathbb{E}|X| < \infty$*.*

Definition C.2 (Convergence in Probability) For random variables X and $\{X_t\}$ defined on the same probability space, we say that $\{X_t\}$ converges in *probability* to X if

$$\lim_{t\to\infty} \mathbf{P}[|X_t - X| > \varepsilon] = 0 \qquad \text{for all } \varepsilon > 0.$$

This fact is denoted by $X_t \xrightarrow{p} X$ or $\operatorname{plim} X_t = X$.

Remark C.1 If X and $\{X_t\}$ are real valued random vectors, we replace the absolute value in the definition above by the Euclidean norm $\|.\|$. This is, however, equivalent to saying that every component X_{it} converges in probability to X_i, the i-th component of X.

Definition C.3 (Convergence in r-th Mean) A sequence $\{X_t\}$ of random variables converges in *r-th mean* to a random variable X if

$$\lim_{t\to\infty} \mathbb{E}(|X_t - X|^r) = 0 \qquad \text{for } r > 0.$$

We denote this fact by $X_t \xrightarrow{r} X$. If $r = 1$, we say that the sequence converges absolutely, and if $r = 2$, we say that the sequence converges in mean square, which is denoted by $X_t \xrightarrow{m.s.} X$.

Remark C.2 In the case $r = 2$, the corresponding definition for random vectors is

$$\lim_{t\to\infty} \mathbb{E}(\|X_t - X\|^2) = \lim_{t\to\infty} \mathbb{E}(X_t - X)'(X_t - X) = 0.$$

Theorem C.6 (Riesz-Fisher Theorem) *Let $\{X_t\}$ be a sequence of random variables such that $\sup_t \mathbb{E}|X_t|^2 < \infty$. Then there exists a random variable X with $\mathbb{E}|X|^2 < \infty$ such that*

$$X_t \xrightarrow{m.s.} X \quad \textit{if and only if} \quad \mathbb{E}|X_t - X_s|^2 \to 0 \quad \textit{for } t, s \to \infty.$$

This version of the Riesz-Fisher theorem provides a condition, known as the Cauchy criterion, which is often easier to verify when the limit is unknown.

Definition C.4 (Convergence in Distribution) A sequence $\{X_t\}$ of random vectors with corresponding distribution functions $\{F_{X_t}\}$ converges in *distribution*, if there exists an random vector X with distribution function F_X such that

$$\lim_{t\to\infty} F_{X_t}(x) = F_X(x) \qquad \text{for all } x \in C$$

where C denotes the set of points for which $F_X(x)$ is continuous. We denote this fact by $X_t \xrightarrow{d} X$.

Note that, in contrast to the previously mentioned modes of convergence, convergence in distribution does not require that all random vectors be defined on the same probability space. The convergence in distribution states that, for large enough t, the distribution of X_t can be approximated by the distribution of X.

The following theorem relates the four convergence concepts.

Theorem C.7 (Relation Between Convergence Definitions)

(i) *If $X_t \xrightarrow{a.s.} X$, then $X_t \xrightarrow{p} X$.*
(ii) *If $X_t \xrightarrow{p} X$, then there exists a subsequence $\{X_{t_n}\}$ such that $X_{t_n} \xrightarrow{a.s.} X$.*
(iii) *If $X_t \xrightarrow{r} X$, then $X_t \xrightarrow{p} X$ by Chebyschev's inequality (Theorem C.3).*

(iv) *If* $X_t \xrightarrow{p} X$, *then* $X_t \xrightarrow{d} X$.

(v) *If* X *is a fixed constant, then* $X_t \xrightarrow{d} X$ *implies* $X_t \xrightarrow{p} X$. *Thus, the two concepts are equivalent under this assumption.*

These facts can be summarized graphically:

$$\begin{array}{ccccc} & & X_{t_n} \xrightarrow{a.s.} X & & \\ & & \Uparrow & & \\ X_t \xrightarrow{a.s.} X & \Longrightarrow & X_t \xrightarrow{p} X & \Longrightarrow & X_t \xrightarrow{d} X \\ & & \Uparrow & & \\ & & X_t \xrightarrow{r} X & & \end{array}$$

A further useful theorem is:

Theorem C.8 *If* $\mathbb{E}X_t \longrightarrow \mu$ *and* $\mathbb{V}X_t \longrightarrow 0$, *then* $X_t \xrightarrow{m.s.} \mu$ *and consequently* $X_t \xrightarrow{p} \mu$.

Theorem C.9 (Continuous Mapping Theorem) *For any continuous function* $f : \mathbb{R}^n \longrightarrow \mathbb{R}^m$ *and random vectors* $\{X_t\}$ *and* X *defined on some probability space, the following implications hold:*

(i) $X_t \xrightarrow{a.s.} X$ *implies* $f(X_t) \xrightarrow{a.s.} f(X)$.

(ii) $X_t \xrightarrow{p} X$ *implies* $f(X_t) \xrightarrow{p} f(X)$.

(iii) $X_t \xrightarrow{d} X$ *implies* $f(X_t) \xrightarrow{d} f(X)$.

An important application of the Continuous Mapping Theorem is the so-called Delta method which can be used to approximate the distribution of $f(X_t)$ (see Appendix E).

A further useful result is given by:

Theorem C.10 (Slutzky's Lemma) *Let* $\{X_t\}$ *and* $\{Y_t\}$ *be two sequences of random vectors such that* $X_t \xrightarrow{d} X$ *and* $Y_t \xrightarrow{d} c$, *c constant, then*

(i) $X_t + Y_t \xrightarrow{d} X + c$,

(ii) $Y_t' X_t \xrightarrow{d} c'X$.

(iii) $X_t / Y_t \xrightarrow{d} X/c$ *if* c *is a nonzero scalar.*

Theorem C.11 *Let X_t be a sequence of random variables that converge in distribution to X. If Y_t is a sequence of random variables such that*

$$\text{plim}(X_t - Y_t) = 0,$$

then Y_t converges also in distribution to X.

Like the (cumulative) distribution function, the characteristic function provides an alternative way to describe a random variable.

Definition C.5 (Characteristic Function) The *characteristic function* of a real random vector X, denoted by φ_X, is defined by

$$\varphi_X(s) = \mathbb{E}e^{\imath\lambda' X}, \qquad \lambda \in \mathbb{R}^n,$$

where $\imath$ is the imaginary unit.

If, for example, $X \sim \mathrm{N}(\mu, \sigma^2)$, then $\varphi_X(s) = \exp(\imath s\mu - \frac{1}{2}\sigma^2 s^2)$. The characteristic function uniquely determines the distribution of X. Thus, if two random variables have the same characteristic function, they have the same distribution. Moreover, convergence in distribution is equivalent to convergence of the corresponding characteristic functions.

Theorem C.12 (Convergence of Characteristic Functions, Lévy) *Let $\{X_t\}$ be a sequence of real random variables with corresponding characteristic functions φ_{X_t}; then*

$$X_t \xrightarrow{d} X \quad \textit{if and only if} \quad \lim_{t\to\infty} \varphi_{X_t}(\lambda) = \varphi_X(\lambda), \quad \textit{for all } \lambda \in \mathbb{R}^n.$$

In many cases, the limiting distribution is a normal distribution. In which case, one refers to the asymptotic normality.

Definition C.6 (Asymptotic Normality) A sequence of random variables $\{X_t\}$ with "means" μ_t and "variances" $\sigma_t^2 > 0$ is said to be *asymptotically normally* distributed if

$$\sigma_t^{-1}(X_t - \mu_t) \xrightarrow{\mathrm{d}} X \sim \mathrm{N}(0, 1).$$

Note that the definition does not require that $\mu_t = \mathbb{E}X_t$ nor that $\sigma_t^2 = \mathbb{V}(X_t)$. Asymptotic normality is obtained if the X_t's are identically and independently distributed with constant mean and variance. In this case, the central limit theorem (CLT) holds.

Theorem C.13 (Central Limit Theorem (CLT)) *Let $\{X_t\}$ be a sequence of identically and independently distributed random variables with constant mean μ and constant variance σ^2; then*

$$\sqrt{T}\,\frac{\overline{X}_T - \mu}{\sigma} \xrightarrow{d} \mathrm{N}(0, 1),$$

where $\overline{X}_T = T^{-1}\sum_{t=1}^{T} X_t$ is the arithmetic average.

It is possible to relax the assumption of identically distributed variables in various ways so that there exists a variety of CLTs in the literature. For our purpose, it is especially important to relax the independence assumption. A natural way to do this is by the notion of m-*dependence*.

Definition C.7 (m-Dependence) A strictly stationary random process $\{X_t\}$ is called *m-dependent* for some nonnegative integer m if and only if the two sets of random variables $\{X_\tau, \tau \leq t\}$ and $\{X_\tau, \tau \geq t + m + 1\}$ are independent.

Note that for such processes $\Gamma(j) = 0$ for $j > m$. This type of dependence allows to prove the following generalized central limit theorem (see Brockwell & Davis, 1991).

Theorem C.14 (CLT for m-Dependent Processes) *Let $\{X_t\}$ be a strictly stationary mean zero m-dependent process with autocovariance function $\Gamma(h)$ such that $\mathbf{V}_m = \sum_{h=-m}^{m} \Gamma(h) \neq 0$; then*

(i) $\lim_{T\to\infty} T\mathbb{V}(\overline{X}_T) = \mathbf{V}_m$ *and*
(ii) $\sqrt{T}\,\overline{X}_T$ *is asymptotically normal* $\mathrm{N}(0, \mathbf{V}_m)$.

Often it is difficult to derive the asymptotic distribution of $\{X_t\}$ directly. This situation can be handled by approximating the original process $\{X_t\}$ by a process $\{X_t^{(m)}\}$, which is easier to handle in terms of its asymptotic distribution and where the precision of the approximation can be "tuned" by the parameter m.

Theorem C.15 (Basic Approximation Theorem) *Let $\{X_t\}$ and $\{X_t^{(m)}\}$ be two random vector processes such that:*

(i) $X_t^{(m)} \xrightarrow{d} X^{(m)}$ *as* $t \to \infty$ *for each* $m = 1, 2, \ldots$
(ii) $X^{(m)} \xrightarrow{d} X$ *as* $m \to \infty$
(iii) $\lim_{m\to\infty} \limsup_{t\to\infty} \mathbf{P}[|X_t - X_t^{(m)}| > \epsilon] = 0$ *for every* $\epsilon > 0$

Then

$$X_t \xrightarrow{d} X \qquad \text{as } t \to \infty.$$

Definition C.8 (Brownian Motion) A stochastic process $\{B_t\}$ on $t \in [0, T]$ is called a (standard) *Brownian motion* if the following properties hold:

(i) $B_0 = 0$.
(ii) For any $s < t$, the increment $B_t - B_s \sim \mathrm{N}(0, t - s)$.
(iii) The increments $B_{t_2} - B_{t_1}, \ldots, B_{t_n} - B_{t_{n-1}}$ are independently distributed for any $n \in \mathbb{N}$ and any choice $0 \leq t_1 < t_2 < \cdots < t_n$.
(iv) The paths $t \rightarrow B_t$ are continuous functions with probability one.

Note that this definition implies $B_1 \sim \mathrm{N}(0, 1)$. Arguin (2022) provides a nice introduction to the properties of the Brownian motion and to the Itô integral. A stochastic equivalent to the fundamental theorem of calculus is Itô's formula.

Theorem C.16 (Itô's Formula) *If $\{B_t\}$ is a Brownian motion and f a twice continuously differentiable function,*

$$f(B_t) = f(B_0) = \int_0^t f'(B_r)\mathrm{d}B_r + \frac{1}{2}\int_0^t f''(B_r)\mathrm{d}r, \qquad t \leq T. \tag{C.1}$$

Beveridge-Nelson Decomposition

D

The Beveridge-Nelson decomposition proves to be an indispensable tool in this book. Based on the seminal paper by Phillips and Solo (1992), we prove the following Theorem for matrix polynomials where $\|.\|$ denotes the matrix norm (see Definition 10.6 in Chap. 10). The univariate version is then a special case with the absolute value replacing the norm.

Theorem D.1 *Any a lag polynomial* $\Psi(\mathrm{L}) = \sum_{j=0}^{\infty} \Psi_j \mathrm{L}^j$ *where* Ψ_j *are* $n \times n$ *matrices with* $\Psi_0 = I_n$ *can be represented by*

$$\Psi(\mathrm{L}) = \Psi(1) - (I_n - \mathrm{L})\widetilde{\Psi}(\mathrm{L}) \tag{D.1}$$

where $\widetilde{\Psi}(\mathrm{L}) = \sum_{j=0}^{\infty} \widetilde{\Psi}_j \mathrm{L}$ *with* $\widetilde{\Psi}_j = \sum_{i=j+1}^{\infty} \Psi_i$. *Moreover,*

$$\sum_{j=1}^{\infty} j^2 \|\Psi_j\|^2 < \infty \quad \textit{implies} \quad \sum_{j=0}^{\infty} \|\widetilde{\Psi}_j\|^2 < \infty \textit{ and } \|\Psi(1)\| < \infty.$$

Proof The first part of the Theorem is obtained by the algebraic manipulations below:

$$\begin{aligned}
\Psi(\mathrm{L}) - \Psi(1) &= (I_n + \Psi_1 \mathrm{L} + \Psi_2 \mathrm{L}^2 + \ldots) - (I_n + \Psi_1 + \Psi_2 + \ldots) \\
&= \Psi_1(\mathrm{L} - I_n) + \Psi_2(\mathrm{L}^2 - I_n) + \Psi_3(\mathrm{L}^3 - I_n) + \ldots \\
&= (\mathrm{L} - I_n)[\Psi_1 + \Psi_2(\mathrm{L} + I_n) + \Psi_3(\mathrm{L}^2 + \mathrm{L} + I_n) + \ldots] \\
&= -(I_n - \mathrm{L}) \Bigg[\underbrace{(\Psi_1 + \Psi_2 + \Psi_3 + \ldots)}_{\widetilde{\Psi}_0} +
\end{aligned}$$

K. Neusser, *Time Series Econometrics*, Springer Texts in Business and Economics,
https://doi.org/10.1007/978-3-031-88838-0

$$\left. \underbrace{(\Psi_2 + \Psi_3 + \ldots)}_{\widetilde{\Psi}_1} \mathrm{L} + \underbrace{(\Psi_3 + \ldots)}_{\widetilde{\Psi}_2} \mathrm{L}^2 + \ldots \right]$$

Taking any $\delta \in (1/2, 1)$, the second part of the Theorem follows from

$$\begin{aligned}
\sum_{j=0}^{\infty} \|\widetilde{\Psi}_j\|^2 &= \sum_{j=0}^{\infty} \left\| \sum_{i=j+1}^{\infty} \Psi_j \right\|^2 \leq \sum_{j=0}^{\infty} \left(\sum_{i=j+1}^{\infty} \|\Psi_j\| \right)^2 \\
&= \sum_{j=0}^{\infty} \left(\sum_{i=j+1} i^{\delta} \|\Psi_j\| i^{-\delta} \right)^2 \\
&\leq \sum_{j=0}^{\infty} \left(\sum_{i=j+1}^{\infty} i^{2\delta} \|\Psi_j\|^2 \right) \left(\sum_{i=j+1}^{\infty} i^{-2\delta} \right) \\
&\leq (2\delta - 1)^{-1} \sum_{j=0}^{\infty} \left(\sum_{i=j+1}^{\infty} i^{2\delta} \|\Psi_i\|^2 \right) j^{1-2\delta} \\
&= (2\delta - 1)^{-1} \sum_{i=0}^{\infty} \left(\sum_{j=0}^{i-1} j^{1-2\delta} \right) i^{2\delta} \|\Psi_i\|^2 \\
&\leq [(2\delta - 1)(2 - 2\delta)]^{-1} \sum_{j=0}^{\infty} j^{2\delta} \|\Psi_i\|^2 j^{2-2\delta} \\
&= [(2\delta - 1)(2 - 2\delta)]^{-1} \sum_{j=0}^{\infty} j^2 \|\Psi_i\|^2 < \infty.
\end{aligned}$$

The first inequality follows from the triangular inequality for the norm. The second inequality is Hölder's inequality (see, e.g., Naylor & Sell, 1982, p. 548) with $p = q = 2$. The third and the fourth inequality follow from the Lemma below. The last inequality, finally, follows from the assumption.
The last assertion follows from

$$\begin{aligned}
\|\Psi(1)\| \leq \sum_{j=0}^{\infty} \|\Psi_j\| &= \|I_n\| + \sum_{j=1}^{\infty} j \|\Psi_j\| j^{-1} \\
&\leq \|I_n\| + \left(\sum_{j=1}^{\infty} j^2 \|\Psi_j\|^2 \right)^2 \left(\sum_{j=1}^{\infty} j^{-2} \right)^2 < \infty.
\end{aligned}$$

The last inequality is again a consequence of Hölder's inequality. The summability assumption then guarantees the convergence of the first term in the product. Cauchy's condensation test finally establishes the convergence of the last term. □

Lemma D.1 *The following results are useful:*

(i) For any $b > 0$, $\sum_{i=j+1}^{\infty} i^{-1-b} \leq b^{-1} j^{-b}$.
(ii) For any $c \in (0, 1)$, $\sum_{j=1}^{i} j^{c-1} \leq c^{-1} i^{c}$.

Proof Let k be a number greater than j; then $k^{-1-b} \leq j^{-1-b}$, and

$$k^{-1-b} \leq \int_{k-1}^{k} j^{-1-b} \mathrm{d}j = b^{-1}(k-1)^{-b} - b^{-1} k^{-b}.$$

This implies that $\sum_{k=j+1}^{\infty} k^{-1-b} \leq b^{-1} j^{-b}$. This proves part (i) by changing the summation index back from k to j. Similarly, $k^{c-1} \leq j^{c-1}$, and

$$k^{c-1} \leq \int_{k-1}^{k} j^{c-1} \mathrm{d}j = c^{-1} k^{c} - c^{-1}(k-1)^{c}.$$

Therefore, $\sum_{k=1}^{i} k^{c-1} \leq c^{-1} i^{c}$, which proves part (ii) by changing the summation index back from k to j. □

Remark D.1 An alternative common assumption is $\sum_{j=1}^{\infty} j \|\Psi_j\| < \infty$. It is, however, easy to see that this assumption is more restrictive as it implies the one assumed in the Theorem, but not vice versa. See Phillips and Solo (1992) for more details.

The Delta Method

E

It is often the case that it is possible to obtain an estimate $\hat{\beta}_T$ of some parameter β, but that one is really interested in a function f of β. The continuous mapping theorem then suggests to estimate $f(\beta)$ by $f(\hat{\beta}_T)$. But then the question arises how the distribution of $\hat{\beta}_T$ is related to the distribution of $f(\hat{\beta}_T)$.

Expanding the function into a first-order Taylor approximation allows to derive the following theorem.

Theorem E.1 *Let $\{\hat{\beta}_T\}$ be a K-dimensional sequence of random variables with the property $\sqrt{T}(\hat{\beta}_T - \beta) \xrightarrow{\text{d}} N(0, \Sigma)$; then*

$$\sqrt{T}\left(f(\hat{\beta}_T) - f(\beta)\right) \xrightarrow{\text{d}} \mathrm{N}\left(0, \nabla f(\beta)\, \Sigma\, \nabla f(\beta)'\right),$$

where $f : \mathbb{R}^K \longrightarrow \mathbb{R}^J$ is a continuously differentiable function with Jacobian matrix (matrix of first-order partial derivatives) $\nabla f(\beta) = \partial f(\beta)/\partial \beta'$.

Proof See Serfling (Serfling, 1980, 122-124). □

Remark E.1 In the one-dimensional case where $\sqrt{T}(\hat{\beta}_T - \beta) \xrightarrow{\text{d}} \mathrm{N}(0, \sigma^2)$ and $f : \mathbb{R} \longrightarrow \mathbb{R}$, the above theorem becomes:

$$\sqrt{T}\left(f(\hat{\beta}_T) - f(\beta)\right) \xrightarrow{\text{d}} \mathrm{N}\left(0, [f'(\beta)]^2\sigma^2\right)$$

where $f'(\beta)$ is the first derivative evaluated at β.

K. Neusser, *Time Series Econometrics*, Springer Texts in Business and Economics,
https://doi.org/10.1007/978-3-031-88838-0

Remark E.2 The $J \times K$ Jacobian matrix of first-order partial derivatives is defined as

$$\nabla f(\beta) = \partial f(\beta)/\partial\beta' = \begin{pmatrix} \frac{\partial f_1(\beta)}{\partial\beta_1} & \dots & \frac{\partial f_1(\beta)}{\partial\beta_K} \\ \vdots & \ddots & \vdots \\ \frac{\partial f_J(\beta)}{\partial\beta_1} & \dots & \frac{\partial f_J(\beta)}{\partial\beta_K} \end{pmatrix}.$$

Remark E.3 In most applications β is not known so that one evaluates the Jacobian matrix at $\hat{\beta}_T$.

Example (Univariate) Suppose we have obtained an estimate of β equal to $\hat{\beta} = 0.6$ together with an estimate for its variance $\hat{\sigma}^2_{\hat{\beta}} = 0.2$. We can then approximate the variance of $f(\hat{\beta}) = 1/\hat{\beta} = 1.667$ by

$$\hat{\mathbb{V}}(f(\hat{\beta})) = \left[\frac{-1}{\hat{\beta}^2}\right]^2 \hat{\sigma}^2_{\hat{\beta}} = 1.543.$$

Example (Multivariate) In the process of computing the impulse response function of a VAR(1) model with $\Phi = \begin{pmatrix} \phi_{11} & \phi_{12} \\ \phi_{21} & \phi_{22} \end{pmatrix}$ one has to calculate $\Psi_2 = \Phi^2$. If we stack all coefficients of Φ into a vector $\beta = \text{vec}(\Phi) = (\phi_{11}, \phi_{21}, \phi_{12}, \phi_{22})'$ then we get:

$$f(\beta) = \text{vec}\,\Psi_2 = \text{vec}\,\Phi^2 = \begin{pmatrix} \psi_{11}^{(2)} \\ \psi_{21}^{(2)} \\ \psi_{12}^{(2)} \\ \psi_{22}^{(2)} \end{pmatrix} = \begin{pmatrix} \phi_{11}^2 + \phi_{12}\phi_{21} \\ \phi_{11}\phi_{21} + \phi_{21}\phi_{22} \\ \phi_{11}\phi_{12} + \phi_{12}\phi_{22} \\ \phi_{12}\phi_{21} + \phi_{22}^2 \end{pmatrix},$$

where $\Psi_2 = \left[\psi_{ij}^{(2)}\right]$. The Jacobian matrix then becomes:

$$\nabla f(\beta) = \begin{pmatrix} \frac{\partial\psi_{11}^{(2)}}{\partial\phi_{11}} & \frac{\partial\psi_{11}^{(2)}}{\partial\phi_{21}} & \frac{\partial\psi_{11}^{(2)}}{\partial\phi_{12}} & \frac{\partial\psi_{11}^{(2)}}{\partial\phi_{22}} \\ \frac{\partial\psi_{21}^{(2)}}{\partial\phi_{11}} & \frac{\partial\psi_{21}^{(2)}}{\partial\phi_{21}} & \frac{\partial\psi_{21}^{(2)}}{\partial\phi_{12}} & \frac{\partial\psi_{21}^{(2)}}{\partial\phi_{22}} \\ \frac{\partial\psi_{12}^{(2)}}{\partial\phi_{11}} & \frac{\partial\psi_{12}^{(2)}}{\partial\phi_{21}} & \frac{\partial\psi_{12}^{(2)}}{\partial\phi_{12}} & \frac{\partial\psi_{12}^{(2)}}{\partial\phi_{22}} \\ \frac{\partial\psi_{22}^{(2)}}{\partial\phi_{11}} & \frac{\partial\psi_{22}^{(2)}}{\partial\phi_{21}} & \frac{\partial\psi_{22}^{(2)}}{\partial\phi_{12}} & \frac{\partial\psi_{22}^{(2)}}{\partial\phi_{22}} \end{pmatrix}$$

$$= \begin{pmatrix} 2\phi_{11} & \phi_{12} & \phi_{21} & 0 \\ \phi_{21} & \phi_{11} + \phi_{22} & 0 & \phi_{21} \\ \phi_{12} & 0 & \phi_{11} + \phi_{22} & \phi_{12} \\ 0 & \phi_{12} & \phi_{21} & 2\phi_{22} \end{pmatrix}.$$

In Sect. 15.3.4, we obtained the following estimate for a VAR(1) model for $\{X_t\} = \{(\ln(\mathrm{A}_t), \ln(\mathrm{S}_t))'\}$:

$$X_t = \hat{c} + \hat{\Phi} X_{t-1} + \hat{Z}_t = \begin{pmatrix} -0.141 \\ 0.499 \end{pmatrix} + \begin{pmatrix} 0.316 & 0.640 \\ -0.202 & 1.117 \end{pmatrix} X_{t-1} + \hat{Z}_t.$$

The estimated covariance matrix of $\operatorname{vec} \hat{\Phi}$, $\hat{\mathrm{V}}(\operatorname{vec} \hat{\Phi})$, was:

$$\hat{\mathrm{V}}(\hat{\beta}) = \hat{\mathrm{V}}(\operatorname{vec} \hat{\Phi}) = \begin{pmatrix} 0.0206 & 0.0069 & -0.0201 & -0.0067 \\ 0.0069 & 0.0068 & -0.0067 & -0.0066 \\ -0.0201 & -0.0067 & 0.0257 & 0.0086 \\ -0.0067 & -0.0066 & 0.0086 & 0.0085 \end{pmatrix}.$$

We can then approximate the variance of $f(\hat{\beta}) = \operatorname{vec}(\Phi^2)$ by

$$\hat{\mathrm{V}}(f(\operatorname{vec} \hat{\Phi})) = \hat{\mathrm{V}}(\operatorname{vec} \hat{\Phi}^2) = \nabla f(\operatorname{vec} \Phi)|_{\Phi=\hat{\Phi}} \, \hat{\mathrm{V}}(\operatorname{vec} \hat{\Phi}) \, \nabla f(\operatorname{vec} \Phi)|'_{\Phi=\hat{\Phi}}.$$

This leads to:

$$\hat{\mathrm{V}}(f(\operatorname{vec} \hat{\Phi})) = \begin{pmatrix} 0.0245 & 0.0121 & -0.0245 & -0.0119 \\ 0.0121 & 0.0145 & -0.0122 & -0.0144 \\ -0.0245 & -0.0122 & 0.0382 & 0.0181 \\ -0.0119 & -0.0144 & 0.0181 & 0.0213 \end{pmatrix}.$$

Bibliography

Abraham, B., & Ledolter, J. (1983). *Statistical methods for forecasting*. Wiley.

Adelman, I., & Adelman, F. L. (1959). The dynamic properties of the Klein-Goldberger model. *Econometrica, 27,* 596–625.

Agarwal, R. P. (2000). *Difference equations and inequalities* (2nd ed.). Dekker.

Akaike, H. (1969). Fitting autoregressive models for prediction. *Annals of the Institute for Statistical Mathematics, 21,* 243–247.

Amemiya, T. (1994). *Introduction to statistics and econometrics*. Harvard University Press.

An, S., & Schorfheide, F. (2007). Bayesian analysis of DSGE models. *Econometric Reviews, 26,* 113–172.

Anderson, B. D. O., & Moore, J. B. (1979). *Optimal filtering*. Electrical Engeneering Series. Prentice-Hall.

Anderson, T. W. (2003). *An introduction to multivariate statistical analysis* (3rd ed.). Wiley.

Andrews, D. W. K. (1991). Heteroskedasticity and autocorrelation consistent covariance matrix estimation. *Econometrica, 59,* 817–858.

Andrews, D. W. K. (1993). Tests for parameter instability and structural change with unknown change point. *Econometrica, 61,* 821–856.

Andrews, D. W. K. (2003). Tests for parameter instability and structural change with unknown change point: A corrigendum. *Econometrica, 71,* 395–397.

Andrews, D. W. K., & Monahan, J. C. (1992). An improved heteroskedasticity and autocorrelation consistent covariance matrix estimator. *Econometrica, 60,* 953–966.

Andrews, D. W. K., & Ploberger, W. (1994). Optimal tests when a nuisance parameter is present only under the alternative. *Econometrica, 62,* 1383–1414.

Arguin, L.-P. (2022). *A first course in stochastic calculus*. Number 53 in Pure and Applied Undergraduate Texts. American Matematical Society.

Arias, J. E. , Rubio-Ramírez, J., & Waggoner, D. F. (2014). *Inference based on SVARs identified with sign and zero restrictions: Theory and applications*. FRB Atlanta Working Paper 2014–1, Federal Reserve Bank of Atlanta.

Ashley, R., Granger, C. W. J., & Schmalensee, R. (1980). Advertising and aggregate consumption: An analysis of causality. *Econometrica, 48,* 1149–1168.

Aue, A., & Horváth, L. (2011). Structural breaks in time series. *Journal of Time Series Analysis, 34,* 1–16.

Bai, J., Lumsdaine, R. L., & Stock, J. H. (1998). Testing for and dating common breaks in multivariate time series. *Review of Economic Studies, 65,* 395–432.

Baker, A. (2002). *Matrix groups - An introduction to lie group theory*. Springer.

Banbura, M., Giannone, D., & Reichlin, L. (2010). Large Bayesian vector autoregressions. *Journal of Applied Econometrics, 25,* 71–92.

Banerjee, A., Dolado, J. J., Galbraith, J. W., & Hendry, D. F. (1993). *Co-integration, error-correction, and the econometric analysis of non-stationary data*. Oxford University Press.

K. Neusser, *Time Series Econometrics*, Springer Texts in Business and Economics,
https://doi.org/10.1007/978-3-031-88838-0

Barsky, R. B., & Sims, E. R. (2011). News shocks and business cycles. *Journal of Monetary Economics, 58*(3), 273–289.

Bauer, D., & Wagner, M. (2012). A state space canonical form for unit root processes. *Econometric Theory, 28,* 1313–1349.

Baumeister, C., & Hamilton, J. D. (2015). Sign restrictions, structural vector autoregressions, and useful prior information. *Econometrica, 83,* 1963–1999.

Baxter, M., & King, R. G. (1999). Measuring business cycles: Approximate band-pass filters for economic time series. *Review of Economics and Statistics, 81,* 575–593.

Beaudry, P., & Portier, F. (2006). Stock prices, news and economic fluctuations. *American Economic Review, 96,* 1293–1307.

Berger, J. O. (1985). *Statistical decision theory and Bayesian analysis*. Springer Series in Statistics (2nd ed.). Springer Science+Business Media.

Berman, A., & Plemmons, R. J. (1994). *Nonnegative matrices in the mathematical sciences.* Number 9 in Classics in Applied Mathematics. Society of Industrial and Applied Mathematics.

Bernanke, B. S. (1986). Alternative explanations of money-income correlation. *Carnegie-Rochester Conference Series on Public Policy, 25,* 49–99.

Bernanke, B. S., Gertler, M., & Watson, M. W. (1997). Systematic monetary policy and the effects of oil price shocks. *Brookings Papers on Economic Activity, 28,* 91–142.

Berndt, E. R. (1991). *The Practice of econometrics*. Addison Wesley.

Bhansali, R. J. (1999). Parameter estimation and model selection for multistep prediction of a time series: A review. In S. Gosh (Ed.), *Asymptotics, nonparametrics, and time series* (pp. 201–225). Dekker.

Billingsley, P. (1986). *Probability and measure*. Wiley Series in Probability and Statistics (2nd ed.). Wiley.

Blanchard, O. J. (1989). A traditional interpretation of macroeconomic fluctuations. *American Economic Review, 79,* 1146–1164.

Blanchard, O. J., & Quah, D. (1989). The dynamic effects of aggregate demand and supply disturbances. *American Economic Review, 79,* 655–673.

Blanchard, O. J., & Watson, M. W. (1986). Are business cycles all alike? In R. Gordon (Ed.), *The American business cycle: Continuity and change* (pp. 123–179). University of Chicago Press.

Bollerslev, T. (1986). Generalized autoregressive conditional heteroskedasticity. *Journal of Econometrics, 31,* 307–327.

Bollerslev, T. (1988). On the correlation structure for the generalized autoregressive conditional heteroskedastic process. *Journal of Time Series Analysis, 9,* 121–131.

Bollerslev, T., Engle, R. F. , & Nelson, D. B. (1994). ARCH models. In R. F. Engle & D. L. McFadden, (Eds.), *Handbook of econometrics* (Vol. 4, Chap. 49, pp. 2959–3038). Elsevier.

Bougerol, P., & Picard, N. (1992). Stationarity of GARCH processes and of some nonnegative time series. *Journal of Econometrics, 52,* 115–127.

Bougerol, P., & Picard, N. (1992). Strict stationarity of generalized autoregressive processes. *Annals of Probability, 20,* 1714–1730.

Box, G. E. P., & Jenkins, G. M. (1976). *Time series analysis: Forecasting and control* (Rev. ed.).

Brandner, P., & Neusser, K. (1992). Business cycles in open economies: Stylized facts for Austria and Germany. *Weltwirtschaftliches Archiv, 128,* 67–87.

Brandt, A. (1986). The stochastic equation $y_{n+1} = a_n y_n + b_n$ with stationary coefficients. *Advances in Applied Probability, 18,* 211–220.

Breitung, J., & Eickmeier, S. (2006). Dynamic factor models. In O. Hübler & J. Frohn (Eds.), *Modern econometric analysis* (Chap. 3, pp. 25–40). Springer.

Brockwell, P. J., & Davis, R. A. (1991). *Time series: Theory and methods* (2nd ed.). Springer.

Brockwell, P. J., & Davis, R. A. (1996). *Introduction to time series and forecasting*. Springer.

Brualdi, R. A., & Shader, B. L. (1995). *Matrices of sign-solvable linear systems*. Number 116 in Cambridge Tracts in Mathematics. Cambridge University Press.

Burren, D., & Neusser, K. (2013). The role of sectoral shifts in the decline of real GDP volatility. *Macroeconomic Dynamics, 17,* 477–500.

Campbell, J. Y. (1987). Does saving anticipate declining labor income? An alternative test of the permanent income hypothesis. *Econometrica, 55*, 1249–1273.

Campbell, J. Y., Lo, A. W., & MacKinlay, A. C. (1997). *The econometrics of financial markets*. Princeton University Press.

Campbell, J. Y., & Mankiw, N. G. (1987). Are output fluctuations transitory? *Quarterly Journal of Economics, 102*, 857–880.

Campbell, J. Y., & Perron, P. (1991). Pitfalls and opportunities: What macroeconomists should know about unit roots. In O. J. Blanchard & S. Fischer (Eds.), *NBER Macroeconomics Annual 1991* (Vol. 6, pp. 141–201). MIT Press.

Campbell, J. Y., & Shiller, R. J. (1987). Cointegration and tests of present value models. *Journal of Political Economy, 95*, 1062–1088.

Canova, F. (2007). *Methods for applied macroeconomic research*. Princeton University Press.

Canova, F., & Ciccarelli, M. (2009). Estimating multi-country VAR models. *International Economic Review, 50*, 929–959.

Canova, F., & Nicoló, G. D. (2002). Monetary disturbances matter for business fluctuations in the G-7. *Journal of Monetary Economics, 49*, 1131–1159.

Cavaliere, G., Rahbek, A., & Taylor, A. M. R. (2012). Bootstrap determination of the co-integration rank in vector autoregressive models. *Econometrica, 80*, 1721–1740.

Chari, V. V., Kehoe, P. J., & McGrattan, E. R. (2008). Are structural VARs with long-run restrictions useful in developing business cycle theory? *Journal of Monetary Economics, 55*, 1337–1352.

Chow, G., & Lin, A. (1971). Best linear unbiased interpolation, distribution, and extrapolation of time series by related series. *Review of Economics and Statistics, 53*, 372–375.

Christiano, L. J., & Eichenbaum, M. (1990). Unit roots in real GNP: Do we know and do we care? *Carnegie-Rochester Conference Series on Public Policy, 32*, 7–62.

Christiano, L. J., Eichenbaum, M., & Evans, C. L. (1999). Monetary policy shocks: What have we learned and to what end? In J. B. Taylor & M. Woodford (Eds.), *Handbook of macroeconomics* (Vol. 1A, Chap. 2, pp. 65–148). North-Holland.

Christiano, L. J., Eichenbaum, M., & Vigfusson, R. J. (2003). *What happens after a technology shock?* NBER Working Paper 9819, NBER.

Christiano, L. J., Eichenbaum, M., Vigfusson, R. J., Kehoe, P. J., & Watson, M. W. (2006). Assessing structural VARs [with comments and discussion]. In D. Acemoglu, K. Rogoff, & M. Woodford (Eds.), *NBER Macroeconomics Annual 2006* (Vol. 21, pp. 1–105). MIT Press.

Christoffersen, P. F. (1998). Evaluating interval forecasts. *International Economic Review, 39*, 841–862.

Clements, M. P., & Hendry, D. F. (1996). Intercept corrections and structural change. *Journal of Applied Econometrics, 11*, 475–494.

Clements, M. P., & Hendry, D. F. (2006). Forecasting with breaks. In *Handbook of economic forecasting* (Vol. 1, pp. 605–657). Elsevier.

Cochrane, J. H. (1988). How big is the random walk in GNP? *Journal of Political Economy, 96*, 893–920.

Cogley, T., & Sargent, T. J. (2001). Evolving post-world war II U.S. inflation dynamics. In B. S. Bernanke & K. Rogoff (Eds.), *NBER macroeconomics annual 2001* (Vol. 16, pp. 331–373). MIT Press.

Cogley, T., & Sargent, T. J. (2005). Drift and volatilities: Monetary policies and outcomes in the post WWII US. *Review of Economic Dynamics, 8*, 262–302.

Comon, P. (1994). Independent component analaysis: A new concept? *Signal Processing, 36*, 287–314.

Cooley, T. F., & LeRoy, S. F. (1985). Atheoretical macroeconometrics: A critique. *Journal of Monetary Economics, 16*, 283–308.

Cooley, T. F., & Prescott, E. C. (1973). Varying parameter regression. A theory and some applications. *Annals of Economic and Social Measurement, 2*, 463–474.

Cooley, T. F., & Prescott, E. C. (1976). Estimation in the presence of stochastic parameter variation. *Econometrica, 44*, 167–184.

Corradi, V., & Swanson, N. R. (2006). Predictive density evaluation. *Handbook of economic forecasting* (Vol. 1, pp. 197–284). Elsevier.

Cox, D. R. (2006). *Principles of statistical inference*. Cambridge University Press.

Cuche, N. A., & Hess, M. A. (2000). Estimating monthly GDP in a general Kalman filter framework: Evidence from Switzerland. *Economic and Financial Modelling, 7,* 153–194.

Davidson, J. E. H., Hendry, D. F., Srba, F., & Yeo, S. (1978). Econometric modelling of the aggregate time-series relationship between consumers' expenditure and income in the United Kingdom. *Economic Journal, 88,* 661–692.

Davidson, R., & MacKinnon, J. G. (1993). *Estimation and inference in econometrics*. Oxford University Press.

de Jong, R. M., & Sakarya, N. (2016). The econometrics of the Hodrick-Prescott filter. *Review of Economics and Statistics, 98,* 310–317.

Dees, S., Mauro, F. D., Pesaran, M. H., & Smith, V. (2007). Exploring the international linkages of the euro area: A global VAR analysis. *Journal of Applied Econometrics, 22,* 1–38.

Deistler, M., & Neusser, K. (1994). Prognosen uni- und multivariater Zeitreihen. In P. Mertens (ed.), *Prognoserechnung* (5th ed., pp. 259–277). Physica-Verlag.

Deistler, M., & Scherrer, W. (2022). *Time series models*. Springer Nature Switzerland AG.

DeJong, D. N., & Dave, C. (2007). *Structural macroeconomics*. Princeton University Press.

Del Negro, M., & Primiceri, G. E. (2015). Time varying structural vector autoregressions and monetary policy: A corrigendum. *Review of Economic Studies, 82,* 1342–1345.

Del Negro, M., & Schorfheide, F. (2004). Priors from general equilibrium models for VARs. *International Economic Review, 45,* 643–673.

Dempster, A. P., Laird, N. M., & Rubin, D. B. (1977). Maximum likelihood estimation from incomplete data via the EM algorithm. *Journal of the Royal Statistical Society, Series B, 39,* 1–38.

Diaconis, P., & Skyrms, B. (2018). *Ten great ideas about chance*. Princeton University Press.

Dickey, D. A., & Fuller, W. A. (1976). Distribution of the estimators for autoregressive time series with a unit root. *Journal of the American Statistical Association, 74,* 427–431.

Dickey, D. A., & Fuller, W. A. (1981). Likelihood ratio statistics for autoregressive time series with a unit root. *Econometrica, 49,* 1057–1072.

Diebold, F. X., Gunther, T. A., & Tay, A. S. (1998). Evaluating density forecasts, with applications to financial risk management. *International Economic Review, 39,* 863–883.

Diebold, F. X., Lee, J.-H., & Weinbach, G. C. (1994). Regime switching with time-varying transition probabilities. In C. P. Hargreaves (Ed.), *Nonstationary time series analysis and cointegration* (pp. 283–302). Oxford University Press.

Doan, T., Litterman, R. B., & Sims, C. A. (1984). Forecasting and conditional projection using realistic prior distributions. *Econometric Reviews, 3,* 1–100.

Dufour, J.-M. (1985). Unbiasedness of predictions from estimated autoregressions. *Econometric Theory, 1,* 387–402.

Durbin, J. (1960). The fitting of time series models. *Revue de l'Institut International de Statistique, 28,* 233–244.

Durbin, J., & Koopman, S. J. (2011). *Time series analysis by state space methods* (2nd ed.). Oxford University Press.

Durrett, R. (2019). *Probability: Theory and Examples* (5th ed.). Cambridge University Press.

Edelman, A., & Rao, N. R. (2005). Random matrix theory. *Acta Numerica, 14,* 1–65.

Efron, B., & Tibshirani, R. J. (1993). *An introduction to the bootstrap*. Monographs on Statistics and Applied Probability (Vol. 57). Chapman & Hall/CRC.

Elaydi, S. (2005). *An introduction to difference equations* (3rd ed.). Springer Science+Business Media.

Elder, J., & Kennedy, P. E. (2001). Testing for unit roots: What should students be taught? *Journal of Economic Education, 32,* 137–146.

Elliott, G., & Timmermann, A. (2008). Economic forecasting. *Journal of Economic Literature, 46,* 3–56.

Engle, R. F. (1982). Autoregressive conditional heteroskedasticity with estimates of the variance of the United Kingdom inflation. *Econometrica, 50,* 987–1007.
Engle, R. F. (2004). Risk and volatility: Econometric models and financial practice. *American Economic Review, 94,* 405–420.
Engle, R. F., & Bollerslev, T. (1986). Modelling the persistence of conditional variances. *Econometric Review, 5,* 1–50.
Engle, R. F., & Granger, C. W. J. (1987). Co-integration and error correction: Representation, estimation and testing. *Econometrica, 55,* 251–276.
Engle, R. F., Lilien, D., & Robins, R. (1987). Estimating time varying risk premia in the term structure: The ARCH-M model. *Econometrica, 55,* 391–407.
Epstein, R. J. (1987). *A history of econometrics*. North-Holland.
Eurostat. (2024). *ESS Guidelines on seasonal adjustment* (2024 edition). Luxembourg: EUROSTAT.
Fan, J., & Yao, Q. (2003). *Nonlinear time series*. Springer.
Faust, J. (1998). The robustness of identified VAR conclusions about money. *Carnegie-Rochester Conference Series in Public Policy, 49,* 207–244.
Fernández-Villaverde, J., Rubio-Ramírez, J. F., Sargent, T. J., & Watson, M. W. (2007). ABCs and (Ds) of understanding VARs. *American Economic Review, 97,* 1021–1026.
Filardo, A. J. (1994). Business-cycle phases and their transitional dynamics. *Journal of Business & Economic Analysis, 12,* 299–308.
Filardo, A. J., & Gordon, S. F. (1998). Business cycle duration. *Journal of Econometrics, 85,* 99–123.
Francis, N., Owyang, M., Roush, J., & DiCecio, R. (2014). A flexible finite-horizon alternative to long-run restrictions with an application to technology shocks. *Review of Economics and Statistics, 96,* 638–647.
Francq, C., & Zakoïan, J.-M. (2001). Stationarity of multivariate Markov-switching ARMA models. *Journal of Econometrics, 102,* 339–364.
Friedman, M., & Schwartz, A. J. (1963). *A monetary history of the United States, 1867–1960*. Priceton University Press.
Frisch, R. (1933). Propagation problems and impulse problems in dynamic economics. In *Economic essays in honour of Gustav Cassel* (pp. 171–205). Frank Cass.
Frühwirth-Schnatter, S. (2006). *Finite mixture and Markov switching models*. Springer Science + Business Media LLC.
Fry, R. A., & Pagan, A. R. (2011). Sign restrictions in structural vector autoregressions: A critical review. *Journal of Economic Literature, 49,* 938–960.
Fuller, W. A. (1976). *Introduction to statistical time series*. Wiley.
Galí, J. (1992). How well does the IS-LM model fit postwar U.S. data? *Quarterly Journal of Economics, 107,* 709–738.
Galí, J. (1999). Technology, employment, and the business cycle: Do technology shocks explain aggregate fluctuations? *American Economic Review, 89,* 249–271.
Galvao, A. B., & Marcellino, M. (2014). The effects of the monetary policy stance on the transmission mechanism. *Studies in Nonlinear Dynamics & Econometrics, 18,* 217–236.
Geweke, J. F. (1984). Inference and causality in economic time series models. In Z. Griliches & M. D. Intriligator (Eds.), *Handbook of econometrics* (Vol. 2, Chap. 19, pp. 1101–1144). Elsevier.
Geweke, J. F. (2005). *Contemporary Bayesian econometrics and statistics*. Wiley Series in Probability and Statistics. Wiley.
Ghysels, E., & Osborn, D. R. (2001). *The econometric analysis of seasonal time series*. Themes in Modern Econometrics. Cambridge University Press.
Giacomini, R., & Kitagawa, T. (2021). Robust Bayesian inference for set-identified models. *Econometrica, 89,* 1519–1556.
Giannini, C. (1991). *Topics in structural VAR econometrics*. Quaderni di Ricerca 21, Università degli Studi di Anacona, Dipartimento di Economia.
Giannone, D., Lenza, M., & Primiceri, G. E. (2015). Prior selection for vector autoregressions. *Review of Economics and Statistics, 97,* 436–451.

Giraitis, L., Kokoszka, P., & Leipus, R. (2000). Stationary ARCH models: Dependence structure and central limit theorem. *Econometric Theory, 16*, 3–22.

Glosten, L. R., Jagannathan, R., & Runkle, D. E. (1993). On the relation between expected value and the volatility of the nominal excess returns on stocks. *Journal of Finance, 48*, 1779–1801.

Gohberg, I., Lancaster, P., & Rodman, L. (1982). *Matrix polynomials*. Academic.

Goldfeld, S. M., & Quandt, R. E. (1973). A Markov model for switching regressions. *Journal of Econometrics, 1*, 3–15.

Goldfeld, S. M., & Quandt, R. E. (1976). *Studies in nonlinear estimation*. Ballinger Publishing Company.

Gómez, V., & Maravall, A. (1996). *Programs TRAMO and SEATS*. Instructions for the user (with some updates). Working Paper 9628, Servicio de Estudios, Banco de España.

Gonzalo, J., & Ng, S. (2001). A systematic framework for analyzing the dynamic effects of permanent and transitory schocks. *Journal of Economic Dynamics and Control, 25*, 1527–1546.

Gorroochurn, P. (2012). *Classic problems in probability*. Wiley.

Gospodinov, N. (2008). Inference in nearly nonstationary SVAR models with long-run identifying restrictions. *Journal of Business and Economic Statistics, 28*, 1–12.

Gouriéroux, C. (1997). *ARCH models and financial applications*. Springer.

Gouriéroux, C., Jasiak, J., & Sufana, R. (2009). The Wishart autoregressive process of multivariate stochastic volatility. *Journal of Econometrics, 150*, 167–181.

Gouriéroux, C., Monfort, A., & Renne, J.-P. (2017). Statistical inference for independent component analysis: Application to structural VAR models. *Journal of Econometrics, 196*, 111–126.

Granger, C. W. J. (1964). *Spectral analysis of economic time series*. Princeton University Press.

Granger, C. W. J. (1966). The typical spectral shape of an economic variable. *Econometrica, 34*, 150–161.

Granger, C. W. J. (1969). Investigating causal relations by econometric models and cross-spectral methods. *Econometrica, 37*, 424–438.

Granger, C. W. J., & Newbold, P. (1974). Spurious regression in econometrics. *Journal of Econometrics, 2*, 111–120.

Granger, C. W. J., & Teräsvirta, T. (1993). *Modelling nonlinear economic relationships*. Oxford University Press.

Granziera, E., Moon, H. R., & Schorfheide, F. (2013). Inference for VARs identified with sign restrictions. *Quantitative Economics, 9*, 1087–1121.

Granziera, E., Moon, H. R., & Schorfheide, F. (2018). Inference for VARs identified with sign restrictions. *Quantitative Economics, 9*(3), 1087–1121.

Greene, W. H. (2008). *Econometric anlysis* (7th ed.). Prentice Hall.

Grimmett, G., & Stirzaker, D. (2001). *Probability and random processes* (3rd ed.). Oxford University Press.

Haan, W. J., & Levin, A. T. (1997). A practitioner's guide to robust covariance matrix estimation. In G. S. Maddala & C. R. Rao (Eds.), *Handbook of statistics: Robust inference* (Vol. 15, pp. 299–342). Elsevier.

Hall, F. J., & Li, Z. (2014). Sign pattern matrices. In L. Hogben (Ed.), *Handbook of linear algebra* (Chap. 42, 2nd ed., pp. 1–32). Chapman & Hall/CRC.

Hall, P., & Yao, Q. (2003). Inference in ARCH and GARCH models with heavy-tailed errors. *Econometrica, 71*, 285–317.

Hall, R. E. (1978). Stochastic implications of the life cycle-permanent income hypothesis: Theory and evidence. *Journal of Political Economy, 86*, 971–987.

Hamilton, J. D. (1994a). *Time series analysis*. Princeton University Press.

Hamilton, J. D. (1994b). State-space models. In R. F. Engle & D. L. McFadden (Eds.), *Handbook of econometrics* (Vol. 4, Chap. 50, pp. 3039–3080). Elsevier.

Hamilton, J. D. (1996). Specification testing in Markov-switching time-series models. *Journal of Econometrics, 70*, 127–157.

Hamilton, J. D. (2018). Why you should never use the Hodrick-Prescott filter. *Review of Economics and Statistics, 100*, 831–843.

Hannan, E. J., & Deistler, M. (1988). *The statistical theory of linear systems*. Wiley.

Hansen, L. P., & Sargent, T. J. (1980). Formulating and estimating dynamic linear rational expectations models. *Journal of Economic Dynamics and Control, 2*, 7–46.

Hansen, L. P., & Sargent, T. J. (1991). Two difficulties in interpreting vector autoregressions. In L. P. Hansen & T. J. Sargent (Eds.), *Rational expectations econometrics*. Underground Classics in Economics (pp. 77–119). Westview.

Hansen, L. P., & Sargent, T. J. (1993). Seasonality and approximation errors in rational expectations models. *Journal of Econometrics, 55*, 21–55.

Harvey, A. C. (1989). *Forecasting, structural time series models and the Kalman filter*. Cambridge University Press.

Harvey, A. C., & Jaeger, A. (1993). Detrending, stylized facts and the business cycle. *Journal of Applied Econometrics, 8*, 231–247.

Harvey, A. C., & Phillips, G. D. (1982). Estimation of regression models with time varying parameters. . In M. Deistler, E. Fürst, & G. Schödiauer (Eds.), *Economic dynamics and time series analysis games* (pp. 306–321). Physica-Verlag.

Harvey, A. C., & Pierse, R. G. (1984). Estimating missing observations in economic time series. *Journal of the American Statistical Association, 79*, 125–131.

Haugh, L. D. (1976). Checking the independence of two covariance stationary time series: A univariate residual cross-correlation approach. *Journal of the American Statistical Association, 71*, 378–385.

Hauser, M. A., Pötscher, B. M., & Reschenhofer, E. (1999). Measuring persistence in aggregate output: ARMA models, fractionally integrated ARMA models and nonparametric procedures. *Empirical Economics, 24*, 243–269.

Hildreth, C., & Houck, J. P. (1968). Some estimators for a linear model with random coefficients. *Journal of American Statistical Association, 63*, 584–595.

Hodrick, R. J., & Prescott, E. C. (1980). *Post-war U.S. business cycles: An empirical investigation*. Discussion Paper 451, Carnegie-Mellon University, Pittsburgh.

Hogg, R. V., & Craig, A. T. (1995). *Introduction to mathematical statistics* (5th ed.). Prentice-Hall.

Hong, E. P. (1991). The autocorrelation structure for the GARCH-M process. *Economics Letters, 37*, 129–132.

Howrey, E. P. (1968). A spectrum analysis of the long swing hypothesis. *International Economic Review, 9*, 228–252.

Hubrich, K., & Teräsvirta, T. (2013). *Thresholds and smooth transitions in vector autoregressive models*. Advances in Econometrics (Vol. 32, pp. 273–326).

Hubrich, K., & Waggoner, D. (2022). *The transmission of financial shocks and leverage of financial institutions: An endogenous regime switching framework*. Finance and Economics Discussion Series 2022-034, Board of Governors of the Federal Reserve System, Washington.

Hylleberg, S. (1986). *Seasonality in regression*. Academic.

Hylleberg, S., Engle, R. F., Granger, C. W. J., & Yoo, B. (1990). Seasonal integration and cointegration. *Journal of Econometrics, 44*, 215–238.

Hyvärinen, A., Karhunen, J., & Oja, E. (2001). *Independent component analysis*. Wiley.

Inoue, A., & Kilian, L. (2013). Inference on impulse response functions in structural VAR models. *Journal of Econometrics, 177*, 1–13.

Jansson, M. (2002). Consistent covariance matrix estimation for linear processes. *Econometric Theory, 18*, 1449–1459.

Jensen, S. T., & Rahbek, A. (2004). Asymptotic normality for non-stationary, explosive GARCH. *Econometric Theory, 20*, 1203–1226.

Johansen, S. (1988). Statistical analysis of cointegration vectors. *Journal of Economic Dynamics and Control, 12*, 231–254.

Johansen, S. (1991). Estimation and hypothesis testing of cointegration vectors in Gaussian vector autoregressive models. *Econometrica, 59*, 1551–1580.

Johansen, S. (1995). *Likelihood-based inference in cointegrated vector autoregressive models*. Oxford University Press.

Johansen, S. (2007). Cointegration: A survey. In T. C. Mills & K. Patterson (Eds.), *Econometric Theory*. Palgrave Handbook of Econometrics (Vol. 1, pp. 540–577). Palgrave MacMillan.

Johansen, S., & Schaumburg, E. (1998). Likelihood analysis of seasonal cointegration. *Journal of Econometrics, 88,* 301–339.

Kagan, A. M., Linnik, Y. V., & Rao, C. R. (1973). *Characterization problems in mathematical statistics*. Wiley.

Kailath, T. (1980). *Linear systems*. Prentice Hall.

Kallenberg, O. (2002). *Foundations of modern probability*. Probability and its Applications (2nd ed.). Springer.

Kalman, R. E. (1960). A new approach to linear filtering and prediction problems. *Journal of Basic Engeneering, Transactions of the ASME Series D, 82,* 35–45.

Kalman, R. E. (1963). New methods in Wiener filtering theory. In J. L. Bogdanoff & F. Kozin (Eds.), *Proceedings of the First Symposium of Engeneering Applications of Random Function Theory and Probability* (pp. 270–388). Wiley.

Kendall, M. G. (1954). Note on the bias in the estimation of autocorelation. *Biometrika, 41,* 403–404.

Kiefer, N. M. (1978). Discrete parameter variation: Efficient estimation of a switching regression model. *Econometrica, 46,* 427–434.

Kilian, L. (1998). Small-sample confidence intervals for impulse response functions. *Review of Economics and Statistics, 80,* 186–201.

Kilian, L. (2013). Structural vector autoregressions. In N. Hashimzade & M. Thornton (Eds.), *Handbook of research methods and applications in empirical macroeconomics* (pp. 515–554). Edward Elgar.

Kilian, L., & Lütkepohl, H. (2017). *Structural vector autoregressive analysis*. Cambridge University Press.

Kilian, L., & Murphy, D. P. (2012). Why agnostic sign restrictions are not enough: Understanding the dynamics of oil market VAR models. *Journal of the European Economic Association, 10,* 1166–1188.

Kim, C.-J. (1994). Dynamic linear models with Markov-switching. *Journal of Econometrics, 60,* 1–22.

Kim, C.-J., & Nelson, C. R. (1999). *State-space models with regime-switching: Classical and gibbs-sampling approaches with applications*. MIT Press.

King, R. G., Plosser, C. I., & Rebelo, S. (1988). Production, growth, and business cycles: I. The basic neoclassical model. *Journal of Monetary Economics, 21,* 195–232.

King, R. G., Plosser, C. I., Stock, J. H., & Watson, M. W. (1991). Stochastic trends and economic fluctuations. *American Economic Review, 81,* 819–840.

King, R. G., & Rebelo, S. T. (1993). Low frequency filtering and real business cycles. *Journal of Economic Dynamics and Control, 17,* 201–237.

Klein, L. (1950). *Economic fluctuations in the United States 1921–1941*. Wiley.

Klein, L. R. (1985). New developments in project LINK. *American Economic Review, 75,* 223–227.

Klein, L. R., & Goldberger, A. S. (1955). *An econometric model of the United States, 1929–1952*. North Holland.

Klüppelberg, C., Lindner, A., & Maller, R. (2004). A continuous time GARCH process driven by a Lévy process: Stationarity and second order behaviour. *Journal of Applied Probability, 41,* 601–622.

Kolmogorov, A. N. (1939). Sur l'interpolation et extrapolation des suites stationaires. *Comptes rendus hebdomadaires des scéances de l'Académie des Sciences, 208,* 2043–2045.

Koop, G., & Korobilis, D. (2010). Bayesian multivariate time series methods for empirical macroeconomics. *Foundations and Trends in Econometrics, 3,* 267–358.

Kristensen, D., & Linton, O. (2006). A closed-form estimator for the GARCH(1,1)-model. *Econometric Theory, 22,* 323–337.

Krolzig, H.-M. (1997). *Markov-switching vector autoregressions. Modelling, statistical inference, and application to business cycle analysis*. Springer.

Kunst, R., & Neusser, K. (1986). A forecasting comparison of some VAR techniques. *International Journal of Forecasting, 2,* 447–456.

Kunst, R., & Neusser, K. (1990). Cointegration in a macroeconomic system. *Journal of Applied Econometrics, 5,* 351–365.

Kuznets, S. (1930). *Secular movements in production and prices. Their nature and their bearing upon cyclical fluctuations*. Houghton Mifflin.

Kwiatkowski, D., Phillips, P. C. B., Schmidt, P., & Shin, Y. (1992). Testing the null hypothesis of stationarity against the alternative of a unit root: How sure are we that economic time series have a unit root? *Journal of Econometrics, 54,* 159–178.

Lanne, M., Lütkepohl, H., & Maciejowska, K. (2010). Structural autoregressions with Markov switching. *Journal of Economics Dynamics and Control, 34,* 121–131.

Lanne, M., Meitz, M., & Saikkonen, P. (2017). Identification and estimation of non-Gaussian structural vector autoregressions. *Journal of Econometrics, 196,* 288–304.

Leamer, E. E. (1981). Is it a demand curve, or is it a supply curve? Partial identification through inequality constraints. *Review of Economics and Statistics, 63,* 319–327.

Lee, S.-W., & Hansen, B. E. (1994). Asymptotic theory for the GARCH(1,1) quasi-maximum likelihood estimator. *Econometric Theory, 10,* 29–52.

Lippi, M., & Reichlin, L. (1993). The dynamic effects of aggregate demand and supply disturbances: Comment. *American Economic Review, 83,* 644–652.

Litterman, R. B. (1986). Forecasting with Bayesian vector autoregressions: Five years of experience. *Journal of Business and Economic Statistics, 4,* 25–38.

Ljung, L. (1999). *System identification: Theory for the user* (2nd ed.). Prentice Hall.

Lucas, R. E. (1976). Econometric policy evaluation: A critique. *Carnegie-Rochester Conference Series on Public Policy, 1,* 19–46.

Lumsdaine, R. L. (1986). Consistency and asymptotic normality of the quasi-maximum likelihood estimator in IGARCH(1,1) and covariance stationary GARCH(1,1) models. *Econometrica, 64,* 575–596.

Lütkepohl, H. (1990). Asymptotic distributions of impulse response functions and forecast error variance decomposition. *Review of Economics and Statistics, 72,* 116–125.

Lütkepohl, H. (2005). *New introduction to multiple time series analysis*. Springer.

Lütkepohl, H., Meitz, M., Netšunajev, A., & Saikkonen, P. (2020a). Testing identification via heteroskedasticity in structural vector autoregressive models. *Econometrics Journal, 24,* 1–22. ISSN 1368-4221.

Lütkepohl, H., Staszewska-Bystrova, A., & Winker, P. (2020). Constructing joint confidence bands for impulse response functions of VAR models: A review. *Econometrics and Statistics, 13,* 69–83.

MacKinnon, J. G. (1991). Critical values for co-integration tests. In R. F. Engle & C. W. J. Granger (Eds.), *Long-run economic relationships* (pp. 267–276). Oxford University Press.

MacKinnon, J. G. (1996). Numerical distribution functions for unit root and cointegration tests. *Journal of Applied Econometrics, 11,* 601–618.

MacKinnon, J. G., Haug, A., & Michelis, L. (1999). Numerical distribution functions of the likelihood ratio test for cointegration. *Journal of Applied Econometrics, 14,* 563–577.

MacKinnon, J. G., & Smith, A. A., Jr. (1998). Approximate bias correction in econometrics. *Journal of Econometrics, 85,* 205–230.

Maddala, G. S. (1986). Disequilibrium, self-selection, and switching models. In Z. Griliches & M. D. Intriligator (Eds.), *Handbook of econometrics* (Vol. 3, Chap. 28, pp. 1633–1688). North-Holland.

Magnus, J. R., & Neudecker, H. (1988). *Matrix differential calculus with applications in statistics and econometrics*. Wiley.

Mann, H. B., & Wald, A. (1943). On the statistical treatment of linear stochastic difference equations. *Econometrica, 11,* 173–220.

Marcellino, M., Stock, J. H., & Watson, M. W. (2006). A comparison of direct and iterated multistep AR methods for forecasting macroeconomic time series. *Journal of Econometric, 135,* 499–526.

Marriott, F. H. C., & Pope, J. A. (1954). Bias in the estimation of autocorrelation. *Biometrika, 41,* 393–402.

Mertens, P., & Rässler, S. (2005). Prognoserechnung - Einführung und Überblick. In P. Mertens & S. Rässler (Eds.), *Prognoserechnung* (pp. 1–37). Physica-Verlag.
Meyer, C. D. (2000). *Matrix analysis and applied linear algebra.* Society for Industrial and Applied Mathematics.
Mills, T. C. (2003). *Modelling trends and cycles in economic time series.* Palgrave Texts in Econometrics. Palgrave Macmillan.
Miron, J. A. (1996). *The economics of seasonal cycles.* MIT Press.
Mittnik, S., & Zadrozny, P. A. (1993). Asymptotic distributions of impulse responses, step responses and variance decompositions of estimated linear dynamic models. *Econometrica, 61,* 857–870.
Moon, H. R., & Schorfheide, F. (2012). Bayesian and frequentist inference in partially identified models. *Econometrica, 80,* 755–782.
Mountford, A., & Uhlig, H. (2009). What are the effects of fiscal policy shocks? *Journal of Applied Econometrics, 24,* 960–992.
Muth, J. (1960). Optimal properties of exponentially weighted forecasts. *Journal of the American Statistical Association, 55,* 299–306.
Naylor, A. W., & Sell, G. R. (1982). *Linear operator theory in engeneering and science.* Applied Mathematical Sciences (Vol. 40). Springer.
Negro, M. D., & Schorfheide, F. (2004). Priors from general equilibrium models for VARs. *International Economic Review, 45,* 643–673.
Nelson, C. R., & Plosser, C. I. (1982). Trends and random walks in macro-economic time series: Some evidence and implications. *Journal of Monetary Economics, 10,* 139–162.
Nelson, D. B. (1990). Stationarity and persistence in the GARCH(1,1) model. *Econometric Theory, 6,* 318–334.
Nelson, D. B. (1991). Conditional heteroskedasticity in asset returns: A new approach. *Econometrica, 59,* 347–370.
Neusser, K. (1991). Testing the long-run implications of the neoclassical growth model. *Journal of Monetary Economics, 27,* 3–37.
Neusser, K. (2000). An algebraic interpretation of cointegration. *Economics Letters, 67,* 273–281.
Neusser, K. (2012). The role of sectoral shifts in the decline of real GDP volatility. *Macroeoconomic Dynamics, 17,* 477–500.
Neusser, K. (2021). Difference equations for economists. http://www.neusser.ch/downloads/DifferenceEquations.pdf
Newey, W. K., & West, K. D. (1994). Automatic lag selection in covariance matrix estimation. *Review of Economic Studies, 61,* 631–653.
Ng, S., & Perron, P. (1995). Unit root tests in ARMA models with data dependent methods for the selection of the truncation lag. *Journal of the American Statistical Association, 90,* 268–281.
Nicholls, D. F., & Pagan, A. R. (1984). Estimating predictions, prediction errors and their standard deviations using constructed variables. *Journal of Econometrics, 24,* 293–310.
Norris, J. R. (1998). *Markov chains.* Cambridge Series in Statistical and Probabilistic Mathematics. Cambridge University Press.
Ogaki, M. (1992). *An introduction to the generalized method of moments.* RCER Working Paper 314, University of Rochester.
Orcutt, G. H., & Winokur, H. S., Jr. (1969). First order autoregression inference, estimation, and prediction. *Econometrica, 37,* 1–14.
Osterwald-Lenum, M. (1992). A note with quantiles of the asymptotic distribution of the maximum likelihood cointegration rank test statistics. *Oxford Bulletin of Economics and Statistics, 54,* 461–471.
Pagan, A. R. (1984). Econometric issues in the analysis of regressions with generated regressors. *International Economic Review, 25,* 183–209.
Pagan, A. R., & Robertson, O. C. (1998). Structural models of the liquidity effect. *Review of Economics and Statistics, 80,* 202–217.
Perron, P. (1989). The Great Crash, the oil price shock, and the unit root hypothesis. *Econometrica, 57,* 1361–1401.

Perron, P. (2006). Dealing with structural breaks. In K. Patterson & T. C. Mills (Eds.), *Palgrave Handbooks of Econometrics* (Vol. 1, pp. 278–352). Palgrave MacMillan.

Phillips, P. C. B. (1986). Understanding spurious regressions in econometrics. *Journal of Econometrics, 33,* 311–340.

Phillips, P. C. B. (1987). Time series regression with a unit root. *Econometrica, 55,* 277–301.

Phillips, P. C. B. (1991). Optimal inference in cointegrating systems. *Econometrica, 59,* 283–306.

Phillips, P. C. B. (2005). HAC estimation by automated regression. *Econometric Theory, 21*(1), 116–142.

Phillips, P. C. B., & Hansen, B. E. (1990). Statistical inference in instrumental variables regresssion with I(1) processes. *Review of Economic Studies, 57,* 99–125.

Phillips, P. C. B., & Ouliaris, S. (1990). Asymptotic properties of residual based tests of cointegration. *Econometrica, 58,* 165–193.

Phillips, P. C. B., & Perron, P. (1988). Testing for a unit root in time series regression. *Biometrika, 75,* 335–346.

Phillips, P. C. B., & Solo, V. (1992). Asymptotics for linear processes. *Annals of Statistics, 20,* 971–1001.

Pierce, D. A., & Haugh, L. D. (1977). Causality in temporal systems - Characterization and survey. *Journal of Econometrics, 5,* 265–293.

Potter, S. M. (2000). Nonlinear impulse response functions. *Journal of Economic Dynamics and Control, 24,* 1425–1446.

Press, H., & Tukey, J. W. (1956). Power spetral methods of analysis and their application to problems in airplane dynamics. In *Flight Test Manual* (pp. 1–41). NATO Advisory Group for Aeronautical Research and Development.

Priestley, M. B. (1981). *Spectral analysis and time series* (Vol. 1&2). Academic.

Primiceri, G. E. (2005). Time varying structural vector autoregressions and monetary policy. *Review of Economic Studies, 72,* 821–852.

Quah, D. (1990). Permanent and transitory movements in labor income: An explanation for "excess smoothness" in consumption. *Journal of Political Economy, 98,* 449–475.

Quah, D., Sargent, T. J. (1993). A dynamic index model for large cross sections. In J. H. Stock & M. W. Watson (Eds.), *Business cycles, indicators, and forecasting* (Chap. 7, pp. 285–310). University of Chicago Press.

Quandt, R. E. (1960). Tests of the hypothesis that a linear regression system obeys two separate regimes. *Journal of the American Statistical Association, 55,* 324–330.

Reichlin, L. (2003). Factor models in large cross sections of time series. In *Advances in econometrics, theory and applications*. Econometric Society Monographs (Vol. III, pp. 47–86). Cambridge University Press.

Reinsel, G. C. (1993). *Elements of multivariate time series analysis*. Springer Series in Statistics. Springer.

Rigobon, R. (2003). Identification through heteroskedasticity. *Review of Economics and Statistics, 85,* 777–792.

Robinson, E. A. (1982). A historical perspective of spectrum estimation. *Proceedings of the IEEE, 70,* 885–907.

Rosenblatt, M. (2000). *Gaussian and non-Gaussian linear time series and random fields*. Springer.

Rothenberg, T. J. (1971). Identification of parametric models. *Econometrica, 39,* 577–591.

Rubio-Ramírez, J. F., Waggoner, D. F., & Zha, T. (2006). *Markov-switching structural vector autoregressions: Theory and application*. Computing in Economics and Finance 2006 69, Society for Computational Economics.

Rubio-Ramírez, J. F., Waggoner, D. F., & Zha, T. (2010). Structural vector autoregresions: Theory of identification and algorithms for inference. *Review of Economic Studies, 77,* 665–696.

Rudin, W. (1976). *Principles of mathematical analysis* (3rd ed.). McGraw-Hill.

Rudin, W. (1987). *Real and complex analysis* (3rd ed.). McGraw-Hill.

Runkle, D. E. (1987). Vector autoregressions and reality. *Journal of Business and Economic Statistics, 5,* 437–442.

Said, S. E., & Dickey, D. A. (1984). Testing for unit roots in autoregressive-moving average models of unknown order. *Biometrika, 71,* 599–607.

Samuelson, P. A. (1947). *Foundations of economic analysis*. Harvard University Press.

Samuelson, P. A. (1965). Proof that properly anticipated prices fluctuate randomly. *Industrial Management Review, 6,* 41–49.

Sargent, T. J. (1987). *Macroeconomic theory* (2nd ed.). Academic.

Sargent, T. J. (1989). Two models of measurements and the investment accelerator. *Journal of Political Economy, 97,* 251–87.

Sargent, T. J. (2004). *Recursive macroeconomic theory* (2nd ed.). MIT Press.

Sargent, T. J., & Sims, C. A. (1977). Business cycle modelling without pretending to have too much a priori economic theory. In C. A. Sims (Ed.), *New methods in business cycle research* (pp. 45–109). Federal Reserve Bank of Minneapolis.

Schönfeld, P. (1969). *Methoden der Ökonometrie. Band 1: Lineare Regressionsmodelle*. Vahlen, Berlin and Frankfurt.

Schorfheide, F. (2005). VAR forecasting under misspecification. *Journal of Econometrics, 128,* 99–136.

Serfling, R. J. (1980). *Approximation theorems of mathematical statistics*. Wiley Series in Probability and Statistics. Wiley.

Shaman, P., & Stine, R. A. (1988). The bias of autoregressive coefficient estimators. *Journal of the American Statistical Association, 83,* 842–848.

Silverman, B. W. (1986). *Density estimation*. Chapman and Hall.

Sims, C. A. (1972). Money, income, and causality. *American Economic Review, 62,* 540–552.

Sims, C. A. (1974). Seasonality in regression. *Journal of the American Statistical Association, 69,* 618–626.

Sims, C. A. (1980). Comparison of interwar and postwar business cycles: Monetarism reconsidered. *American Economic Review, 70,* 250–257.

Sims, C. A. (1980). Macroeconomics and reality. *Econometrica, 48,* 1–45.

Sims, C. A. (1986). Are forecasting models usable for policy analysis. *Federal Reserve Bank of Minneapolis Quarterly Review, 10,* 2–16.

Sims, C. A. (1993). Rational expectations modeling with seasonally adjusted data. *Journal of Econometrics, 55,* 9–19.

Sims, C. A., Stock, J. H., & Watson, M. W. (1990). Inference in linear time series with some unit roots. *Econometrica, 58,* 113–144.

Sims, C. A., & Zha, T. (1998). Bayesian methods for dynamic multivariate models. *International Economic Review, 39,* 949–968.

Sims, C. A., & Zha, T. (1999). Error bands for impulse responses. *Econometrica, 67,* 1113–1155.

Slutzky, E. (1937). The summation of random causes as the source of cyclic processes. *Econometrica, 5,* 105–146.

Stock, J. H. (1994). Unit roots, structural breaks and trends. In R. F. Engle & D. L. McFadden (Eds.), *Handbook of econometrics* (Vol. 4, Chap. 46, pp. 2739–2841). Elsevier.

Stock, J. H., & Watson, M. W. (1988a). Variable trends in economic time series. *Journal of Economic Perspectives, 2,* 147–174.

Stock, J. H., & Watson, M. W. (1988b). Testing for common trends. *Journal of American Statistical Association, 83,* 1097–1107.

Stock, J. H., & Watson, M. W. (2011). *Introduction to econometrics* (3rd ed.). Addison-Wesley Longman.

Stoica, P., & Selén, Y. (2004). Model-Order selection: A review of information criterion rules. *IEEE Signal Processing Magazine, 21,* 36–47.

Strang, G. (1988). *Linear algebra and its applications* (3rd ed.). Harcourt Brace Jovanovich.

Sul, D., Phillips, P. C. B., & Choi, C.-Y. (2005). Prewhitening bias in HAC estimation. *Oxford Bulletin of Economics and Statistics, 67,* 517–546.

Tay, A. S., & Wallis, K. F. (2000). Density forecasting: A survey. *Journal of Forecasting, 19,* 235–254.

Tinbergen, J. (1939). *Statistical testing of business cycle theories*. League of Nations.

Tjøstheim, D., & Paulsen, J. (1983). Bias of some commonly-used time series estimates. *Biometrika, 70*, 389–399; Corrigendum: 71 (1984), 656 (1983).

Tobin, J. (1970). Money and income: Post hoc ergo propter hoc? *Quarterly Journal of Economics, 84,* 310–317.

Uhlig, H. (2004). Do technology shocks lead to a fall in total hours worked? *Journal of the European Economic Association, 2,* 361–371.

Uhlig, H. (2005). What are the effects of monetary policy on output? Results from an agnostic identification procedure. *Journal of Monetary Economics, 52,* 381–419.

Uhlig, H., & Ravn, M. (2002). On adjusting the HP-filter for the frequency of observations. *Review of Economics and Statistics, 84,* 371–376.

Vogelsang, T. J. (1997). Wald-type tests for detecting breaks in the trend function of a dynamic time series. *Econometric Theory, 13,* 818–849.

Vogelsang, T. J., & Wagner, M. (2013). A fixed-b perspective on the Phillips-Perron tests. *Econometric Theory, 29,* 609–628.

Watson, M. W. (1994). Vector autoregressions and cointegration. In R. F. Engle & D. L. McFadden (Eds.), *Handbook of econometrics* (Vol. 4, Chap. 47, pp. 2843–2915). Elsevier.

Weiss, A. A. (1986). Asymptotic theory for ARCH models: Estimation and testing. *Econometric Theory, 2,* 107–131.

West, K. D. (1988). Asymptotic normality, when regressors have a unit root. *Econometrica, 56,* 1397–1417.

White, H. (1980). A heteroskedasticity consistent covariance matrix estimator and a direct test for heteroskedasticity. *Econometrica, 48,* 817–838.

Whittaker, E. T. (1923). On a new method of graduation. *Proceedings of the Edinburgh Mathematical Society, 41,* 63–75.

Wiener, N. (1956). The theory of prediction. In E. F. Beckenbach (Ed.), *Modern mathematics for engineers* (Ser. 1. pp. 165–1987). McGraw-Hill.

Woodford, M. (2003). *Interest and prices: Foundations of a theory of monetary policy*. Princeton University Press.

Wu, C. F. J. (1983). On the convergence of the EM algorithm. *Annals of Statistics, 11,* 95–103.

Yoo, B. (1987). *Multi-Cointegrated Time Series and a Generalized Error Correction Model*. Ph.D. Thesis, University of California, San Diego, CA.

Yule, G. U. (1926). Why do we sometimes get nonsense correlations between time series? A study in sampling and the nature of time series. *Journal of the Royal Statistical Society, 89,* 1–63.

Yule, G. U. (1927). On a method of investigating periodicities in disturbed series, with special reference to Wolfer' sunspot numbers. *Philosophical Transactions of the Royal Society, A, 226,* 267–298.

Zadrozny, P. A. (2005). *Necessary and sufficient restrictions for existence of a unique fourth moment of a univariate GARCH(p,q) process*. CESifo Working Paper 1505, CESifo, 2005.

Zakoïan, J.-M. (1994). Threshold heteroskedastic models. *Journal of Economic Dynamics and Control, 18,* 931–955.

Zellner, A. (1962). An efficient method of estimating seemingly unrelated regressions and tests for aggregation bias. *Journal of the American Statistical Association, 57,* 348–368.

Zellner, A. (1979). Causality and econometrics. *Carnegie-Rochester Conference Series on Public Policy, 10,* 9–54.

Zellner, A., & Palm, F. (1974). Time series analysis and simultaneous equation econometric models. *Journal of Econometrics, 2,* 17–54.

Zivot, E., & Andrews, D. W. K. (1992). Further evidence on the Great Crash, the oil-price shock, and the unit-root hypothesis. *Journal of Business and Economic Statistics, 10,* 251–270.

Index

K. Neusser, *Time Series Econometrics*, Springer Texts in Business and Economics, https://doi.org/10.1007/978-3-031-88838-0